A CONSUMERS' REPUBLIC

A Consumers' Republic

THE POLITICS OF MASS CONSUMPTION
IN POSTWAR AMERICA

Lizabeth Cohen

Alfred A. Knopf

NEW YORK / 2003

THIS IS A BORZOI BOOK
PUBLISHED BY ALFRED A. KNOPF

A portion was previously published in the *Chronicle of
Higher Education.*

Library of Congress Cataloging-in-Publication Data
Cohen, Lizabeth.
    A consumers' republic : the politics of mass consumption in
postwar America / by Lizabeth Cohen.
        p. cm.
    Includes index.
    ISBN 0-375-40750-2 (hc.)
    1. Consumption (Economics)—United States.   2. Consumer
behavior—United States.   3. United States—Social conditions—
1980–   I. Title.

HC110.C6   C537   2003
339.4'7'0973—dc21   2002141599

Manufactured in the United States of America
First Edition

For Julia and Natalie

Contents

A CONSUMERS' REPUBLIC

Prologue

The author (right) and her sister in front of their ranch-style house in suburban Paramus, New Jersey, 1956. (Collection of Lizabeth Cohen)

I was born in February 1952, and after what was then a standard five-day stay at the hospital, I moved into my first home in Paramus, New Jersey, a brand-new ranch-style house in one of the many subdivisions being carved out of Paramus's woods and farms. My parents had recently bought this 960-square-foot house for $11,990, thanks to $2000 in savings crucially supplemented by a 4.5 percent GI mortgage for which my father qualified as a World War II vet. The GI Bill had already subsidized his business school education. Dorothy Rodbell and Paul Cohen had married two years earlier, when they were twenty-two and twenty-nine, respectively. For a long four months they had lived with my mother's parents in Manhattan as they navigated what was still a severe housing shortage following the war. In April 1950 they moved into a newly built garden apartment right across the George Washington Bridge in Fort Lee, New Jersey. Less than two years later, they became new suburban homeowners

My family's suburban voyage did not end in Paramus. Four years later, my sister now in tow, we moved three miles away to a larger, more expensive house in a more established, solidly middle-class town. Whereas our neighborhood of young families in Paramus had been socially and economically diverse—Protestants, Catholics, and Jews, professionals living next door to factory foremen, people employed locally as well as Manhattan commuters—our new town was more of a conventional bedroom community. Four years later, when I was eight, we were on the move again, this time to an upper-middle-class suburb in New York's Westchester County. Beyond my parents' upward mobility, measured through their serial acquisition of more expensive homes in communities of ever higher socioeconomic profiles, New Jersey's inadequate and overly property tax–dependent system of school funding had driven them away. Our new town had nationally touted public schools and a population willing and able to pay for them with steep property taxes, necessary despite New York's greater state support for its local schools.

During those first eight years of my life in New Jersey, I watched postwar mass suburbia develop, what in this book I call "the landscape of mass consumption." New limited-access highways bypassed slower, established commercial routes. Along their path, suburban settlements sprouted on what had been fields of corn, celery, spinach, and cabbage. Shopping centers—in my case, Paramus's Bergen Mall and Garden State Plaza—became the new centers of community life, providing a place to spend a Saturday, to attend an evening concert, to take the children to visit Santa Claus, to see candidates campaign. Like many in my baby boomer generation, I grew up in a world of kids—on the block, in overflowing schools, and on television, where so many programs and advertisements seemed to have been made just for us, from *Captain Kangaroo, Romper Room,* and the *Howdy Doody Show* when we were young to *Rin Tin Tin, Lassie,* and *American Bandstand* as we grew older.

But my world was not only defined by class and age; race mattered as well. In both of these New Jersey towns, I remember few people who were not white: a handful of highly educated immigrants from Taiwan, no African Americans. The most prominent social division we lived with was between public and parochial school kids. In the more privileged community in Westchester, our recently built subdivision was very near to the substantial homes of two African-American families, one that of a doctor, the other of a dentist. Significantly, these families had built their beautiful custom houses on large plots of land on the edge of town. When new homes went up and expanded the town to its geographical borders in the early 1960s, these two black families found themselves suddenly surrounded by neighbors, but still on the social margins of the community.

As my world grew beyond my town, and I grew into adulthood, I became increasingly active in electoral politics, working on Eugene McCarthy's and then Robert Kennedy's presidential campaigns in 1968, for John Lindsay's reelection as mayor of New York in 1969, and as one of only a handful of paid staff on Congresswoman Shirley Chisholm's presidential campaign in 1972. Looking back on those campaigns, I now can identify political trends analyzed in this book—more reliance on television, more orientation toward professional expertise in polling and advertising, more targeted campaigning to segments of the electorate. In the Chisholm campaign in particular, one of our toughest challenges was balancing the conflicting agendas of our two main voter segments: white feminists and African Americans. Although civil rights and anti–Vietnam War activism preoccupied me, as it did many in my generation, I was nonetheless quite aware of the rising consumer movement of the 1960s and 1970s chronicled toward the end of this book. I admired Ralph Nader, for years considered grapes food for boycotting not eating, and welcomed increased government regulation of manufactured goods and the environment. I was vaguely aware that my father's cousin Arnold Elkind was appointed chairman of the National Commission on Product Safety by President Lyndon Johnson, taking some pride in my family's own small contribution to making modern America a safer place to live. Was I ever conscious during these years from 1952 to the mid-1970s of living in what this book calls a *Consumers' Republic,* an economy, culture, and politics built around the promises of mass consumption, both in terms of material life and the more idealistic goals of greater freedom, democracy, and equality? Probably not, but I did grow up cognizant of the privilege of living in such a prosperous United States, whose bounty I expected to be available to all Americans. Where it was not—in the trouble spots we called the Deep South, Appalachia, and Harlem—action needed to be taken. It is doubtful that I undertook any deeper analysis of the more complex underpinnings of the affluent society in which I grew up.

I tell my own story at length here not because it is unusual, but, quite the opposite, because it is not. The outlines of my life will prove to be common patterns lived by many Americans in the decades following World War II. I, along with many others, was a child of the Consumers' Republic, even if unaware of it at the time. Though that is my birthright, it is only through writing this book that I have come to terms with the benefits and costs of having grown up during the prosperous decades following World War II, in a society where the pursuit of that prosperity defined many more dimensions of life than most of us recognized at the time.

Although there are many ways that historians might conceptualize the second half of the twentieth century, which in our lifetimes has moved from the front pages of daily newspapers to the annals of history, I have put Americans' encounter with mass consumption at the center of my analysis. I am convinced that Americans after World War II saw their nation as the model for the world of a society committed to mass consumption and what were assumed to be its far-reaching benefits. Mass consumption did not only deliver wonderful things for purchase—the televisions, air conditioners, and computers that have transformed American life over the last half century. It also dictated the most central dimensions of postwar society, including the political economy (the way public policy and the mass consumption economy mutually reinforced each other), as well as the political culture (how political practice and American values, attitudes, and behaviors tied to mass consumption became intertwined). I am arguing that in the aftermath of World War II a fundamental shift in America's economy, politics, and culture took place, with major consequences for how Americans made a living, where they dwelled, how they interacted with others, what and how they consumed, what they expected of government, and much else. Other historians have stressed the Cold War as the fundamental shaper of postwar America. The Consumers' Republic had close ties to the Cold War, not least of which was its powerful symbolism as the prosperous American alternative to the material deprivations of communism. But I want to suggest as well that much of importance in America's postwar history happened outside of the Cold War frame, and applying it too exclusively can obscure other crucial developments.

Americans' identities as citizens and consumers are often presented as opposites. Citizens, individuals in a political relationship with government, are assumed to embrace a larger public interest, as they must fulfill duties and obligations in the larger society to earn basic rights and privileges. Consumers, concerned with satisfying private material desires, are often denigrated for their personal indulgence, perhaps stemming from the word's original meaning: "to devour, waste, and spend."[1] But it quickly became apparent to me that no simple distinction between these roles held true over the course of the twentieth century, particularly by the 1930s. Rather than isolated ideal types, citizen and consumer were ever-shifting categories that sometimes overlapped, often were in tension, but always reflected the permeability of the political and economic spheres. Hence, this book will describe several different citizen-consumer ideal types that prevailed at particular moments in time. *Citizen consumers* of the New Deal and World War II eras put the market power of the consumer to work politically, not only to save a capitalist America in the midst of the Great Depression, but also to safeguard the rights of individual consumers and the larger "general good." In this effort, they often sought the government as ally. The competing ideal of the *purchaser consumer* during the late 1930s and World War II championed pursuit of self-interest in the marketplace out of confidence in the ameliorative effects of aggregate purchasing power; in wartime, however, such behavior would undermine homefront needs. In the postwar Consumers' Republic, a new ideal emerged—the *purchaser as citizen*—as an alluring compromise. Now the consumer satisfying personal material wants actually served the national interest, since economic recovery after a decade and a half of depression and war depended on a dynamic mass consumption economy. Most recently, during the last two decades, a new combined *consumer/citizen/taxpayer/voter* has gained influence in a *Consumerized Republic,* where self-interested citizens increasingly view government policies like other market transactions, judging them by how well served they feel personally.

Analyzing the Consumers' Republic's integration of citizenship and consumership has engaged me in many other aspects of postwar American life: its class structure, race relations, and gender dynamics; the evolution of residential communities and commercial centers; the reshaping of mass markets; the changing role of government; and the many political efforts to promote new kinds of corporate and governmental policies toward consumers. This book explores all these issues.

One set of questions in particular, about the shifting boundaries of class in the postwar era, grew directly out of my previous work. When I finished an earlier book, *Making a New Deal: Industrial Workers in Chicago, 1919–1939,* over a decade ago, I found myself eager to probe what the industrial workers of the interwar era had experienced after World War II. Surely, at last, they had secured a foothold in the mass consumer society whose inclusiveness in the 1920s was limited and whose reach in the 1930s was foreshortened by the Great Depression. As I began to follow their story through World War II into the postwar era, I also investigated the experiences of more middle-class Americans to learn to what extent the lives of blue- and white-collar Americans converged in an era known as the heyday of "mass" consumption. How much, I wanted to know, did the supposedly cohesive (some contemporary critics went so far as to claim conformist) "mass" culture of the Eisenhower and Kennedy years erase the class as well as racial and ethnic distinctions that clearly had shaped the prewar era? If workers in the 1930s had effectively used their toehold in mass culture and mass consumption to transcend ethnic and racial divisions and mobilize as a working class, how might working- and middle-class Americans in the postwar period have exploited mass culture's integrative potential to eliminate their class differences?

I make no claims to be the first to recognize the centrality of mass consumption to twentieth-century American society. In fact, the increased attention paid it after the Second World War only supports my argument for its ubiquitousness in the postwar era. Awareness of the far-reaching impact of mass consumption began much earlier. At the turn of the century, economist Thorstein Veblen developed the concept of "conspicuous consumption" in his *Theory of the Leisure Class* (1899) to argue that social emulation expressed through extravagant personal display—not the purely rational economic motive to enrich oneself—motivated all social classes within the capitalist society of the Gilded Age to aspire to the standards set by the elite. Over the next decade, economist Simon Patten further extended the explanatory importance of mass consumption, though he found more to praise than Veblen did. Patten argued that as the American economy advanced from scarcity to abundance, the realm of consumption and leisure offered workers, many of them new immigrants, more satisfaction and pleasure than degrading industrial work and provided the nation with the chance to build a more cohesive society free of class and ethnic divisions.

It was in the post–World War II period, however, when mass consumption was extensively reshaping the nation, that theorists and critics most consistently identified it as a key influence in defining American society. Historian David Potter, in *People of Plenty* (1954), claimed that all of American history and Americans' "national character" derived from an economy of inexhaustible abundance. In the twentieth century that abundance took the form of a "consumer's culture," and advertising "joined the charmed circle of institutions which fix the values and standards of society." In 1957, in a controversial exposé of the new black middle class that he claimed had emerged over the previous two decades, *Black Bourgeoisie,* sociologist E. Franklin Frazier argued that this self-appointed African-American elite depended on "conspicuous consumption" in their own black world, social and material emulation of whites, and an overconfidence in the health of "Negro business" to compensate for deep-seated inferiority rooted in America's destructive history of racial segregation. A year later, in his best-seller *The Affluent Society* (1958), economist John Kenneth Galbraith blamed the voracious American pursuit of private consumption and the engines of corporate advertising that fed it for neglecting "social consumption"—the roads, schools, hospitals, and other infrastructure needed for a humane society. "Private opulence amid public squalor" was how Galbraith condemned what he saw around him.

David Riesman, in two collections of essays—*The Lonely Crowd: A Study of the Changing American Character* (1950) and *Abundance for What?* (1964, but including many essays written during the 1950s)—probed the numerous ways that affluence was changing American society. He focused particularly on the new "social character" of "other-directedness," marked by a greater orientation to peer groups which, he argued, had come, with the new frontier of consumption, to replace the "inner-directedness" connected to an earlier economy and culture of production. With the publication of *One-Dimensional Man* (1964), Herbert Marcuse brought the cultural criticism of the Frankfurt School of Hegelian Marxism to an emerging New Left in America, deploring the extent to which mass consumption and mass culture bought complacency from the masses, dulling their capacity for intellectual, spiritual, and political resistance. And Daniel Bell, in *The Cultural Contradictions of Capitalism* (1976), despaired that late capitalist consumerism fueled personal gratification over the needs of what he called the "public household," dangerously undermining social solidarity and shared, previously religion-based moral values.[2] Each of these trenchant observers of society and many others I have not mentioned, though advancing diverse and in many cases conflicting views of modern capitalism, recognized that mass consumption had become a central defining engine, not simply of the American economy but of its politics and culture as well.

The critique of mass consumption, of course, went far beyond the biting commentary and far-ranging analyses of intellectuals. The Beats in the 1950s, the hippies in the 1960s, the "Small Is Beautiful" and environmentally sensitive Greens of the 1970s, and some strands of the religious right of the 1980s all developed identities based on a rejection of a mainstream culture built around mass consumption. Cultural rebels shared intellectuals' obsession with mass consumption, even as they defined themselves as countercultural by denouncing its values and practices, confirming just how much mass consumption stood at the core of how Americans regarded their society in the second half of the twentieth century.

At the heart of my analysis of postwar America is the concept of the Consumers' Republic. This was not a term that Americans used at the time to refer to the world in which they were living. It is my shorthand for what I document in Chapter 3 was a strategy that emerged after the Second World War for reconstructing the nation's economy and reaffirming its democratic values through promoting the expansion of mass consumption. Inevitably, the Consumers' Republic becomes an abstraction in this book that may at times seem to obscure from view the agency of individual actors and social groups. That is never my intention, but I realize that this ambiguity may be the cost of putting a name to what was in reality a complex shared commitment on the part of policymakers, business and labor leaders, and civic groups to put mass consumption at the center of their plans for a prosperous postwar America. To discuss the repeated articulation and implementation of this consensus view every time I make reference to its common priorities would be tiresome indeed. Where and when these shapers of postwar society disagreed, I have made every effort to reveal their differences.

As for my use of "republic," I employ it because it invokes the language that was used so often after the Second World War to describe America's national mission in the Cold War world. In the hands of the "consensus historians" of the 1950s, the American Revolution and the subsequent United States Constitution became moments of careful republic building, not the more democratic struggle of "the people" against "the interests" that the preceding generation of "Progressive historians" like Charles Beard and Carl Becker had emphasized. Clinton Rossiter's *Seedtime of the Republic* (1953) and Edmund Morgan's *The Birth of the Republic* (1956) were only two of many volumes to appear that stressed the more conservative commitments of the nation's founders to political stability, economic development, and international security—not so unlike the goals of the United States in the Cold War era, it might be noted. Likewise, the Pledge of Allegiance to the American flag "and to the republic for which it stands," originally written in 1892 but not officially given congressional sanction until 1942, took on new popularity in the 1950s, prompting Congress to add the phrase "under God" in 1954 to make it more censorious of a "godless" communist enemy.[3] Although the label the Consumers' Republic never crossed the lips or flowed from the pens of those writing in the 1950s, its insights and language would have felt familiar to many of them.

I turn to New Jersey at a number of crucial moments in this book, such as when I seek to probe closely the World War II home front, civil rights activism after the war, booming postwar suburbs and shopping centers in the shadow of declining cities, and battlegrounds for the consumer movement of the 1960s and 1970s. After spending the first eight years of my life in New Jersey, I returned there to live with my own family from 1994 to 1997 in the midst of researching the book (ironically to find myself thrown into the same school funding wars that had discouraged my parents more than thirty years earlier). This book moves back and forth between exploring national trends and rooting them in the localities of New Jersey. Both views, a bird's-eye capturing Washington, D.C., and the fifty states and a closer-up picture where more subtle patterns and interactions can be gleaned, are crucial to my analysis.

To some extent, I could have situated this local investigation anywhere; the trends I explore occurred nationally. But in some critical ways, New Jersey proved the ideal setting. It was the quintessential postwar suburban state. Despite a population growth of almost two million between 1940 and 1960—a 50 percent increase in two decades—every major city except Paterson lost population, and Paterson barely offset the out-migration of higher-income residents to the suburbs with a large in-migration of low-income people with a high birthrate. As the postwar era progressed, as much as 70 percent of the state would qualify as suburban.[4] And perhaps even more significant, New Jersey had an activist state supreme court over the postwar period that made decisions, often historic ones, arising out of the critical social, economic, and cultural changes under way in the era. The suburbanization of residences and commerce and the new inequalities that resulted from them—through restrictive zoning, increasingly unaffordable privatized housing, growing differentials in school spending, and disputes over free speech and assembly in privately owned shopping centers, the new "town centers" of the suburbs—all engaged the New Jersey Supreme Court's attention. Historians, like journalists, policymakers, and citizens more generally, tend to pay most attention to the decisions of the United States Supreme Court, but in the second half of the twentieth century crucial debates around rights deemed to be protected by state constitutions were reserved for state courts to adjudicate. To look only at the federal courts is to lose sight of pivotal battles that took place over the consequences of creating a landscape of mass consumption during the era of the Consumers' Republic.

Part I of this book, "The Origins of the Postwar Consumers' Republic," begins by rooting the new postwar order in a longer history of the place of consumption in the American economy and politics, including what I call the "first-wave consumer movement" of the Progressive Era at the beginning of the twentieth century. I then focus on the 1930s, when, I argue, the critical foundations of the postwar Consumers' Republic were laid. Statemakers at the top and women and African Americans at the grass roots, many denied access to traditional avenues of power, seized upon the citizen consumer role as a new way of upholding the public interest. They thereby built a "second-wave consumer movement." How and why did attention to mass consumption and the influence of mass consumers grow in an era of horrifying depression, I ask, and what kinds of expectations did politically engaged citizen consumers harbor for their society? Chapter 2 moves into the era of World War II, when the link between consumption and citizenship was reinforced by government agencies like the Office of Price Administration, by women who essentially managed the home front through their domestic and civic activities, and by African Americans who experienced their denial of full citizenship regularly through their exclusion from sites of consumption, such as at theaters, restaurants, hotels, and commissaries on military bases. I probe how different groups imagined postwar America as a result of their wartime experiences, promoting competing visions for what "the return to normalcy" would mean.

Part II, "The Birth of the Consumers' Republic," introduces the vision that won out, the notion of a Consumers' Republic that entrusted the private mass consumption marketplace, supported by government resources, with delivering not only economic prosperity but also loftier social and political ambitions for a more equal, free, and democratic nation. In Chapter 3, I investigate how key postwar policies, such as the GI Bill, revisions in the wartime income tax, and the restructuring of collective bargaining, were designed to promote the goals of the Consumers' Republic, and I assess their actual impact, particularly on the fate of women and the working class. Chapter 4 undertakes the same kind of analysis of how the infrastructure supporting the Consumers' Republic played out for a third social group, African Americans. I explore the benefits and costs to black Americans of a postwar society built around the promises of a mass consumer market.

Part III, "The Landscape of Mass Consumption," consists of a pair of chapters: Chapter 5, devoted to the transformation in residential patterns resulting from the suburbanization of metropolitan areas; and Chapter 6, concerned with the new commercial marketplace structures that accompanied the decentralization of urban living. The expansion of mass suburbia—a plan to solve the horrendous postwar housing shortage through the extensive construction of privately owned, single-family homes—promised to create a more egalitarian and democratic society as more Americans than ever before would own a stake in their communities. But the outcome—measured by how many enjoyed a fair share of property and prime public services—fell far short of these aspirations. Likewise, regional shopping centers promoted themselves as the new civic centers of booming suburban towns. But their dominance over commercial life crippled existing market centers, and their legal status as privately owned property raised new challenges to free speech and assembly. Through the restructuring of both residential communities and commercial centers, the Consumers' Republic introduced new kinds of divisions in postwar society while it aimed, with its democratic ambitions, to overcome old ones.

Part IV, "The Political Culture of Mass Consumption," consists of another pair of chapters, the first on culture, the second on politics. In Chapter 7, I investigate the shifting strategies employed by marketers and advertisers to promote the mass consumption at the base of the Consumers' Republic. As the initial assumption that mass consumption was best supported through mass marketing retreated in the face of saturated markets and declining profits, a new approach—market segmentation—gained ground by the late 1950s, bringing with it implications that transcended who sold what to whom. I particularly look at how political campaigners and politicians applied the formulas of market segmentation to the political arena and assess their impact on the practice of campaigning, on the way candidates and voters related to each other, and on the viability of our political system itself. Finally, Chapter 8 examines the political movement that challenged many of the directions the Consumers' Republic had taken by the mid-1960s. I argue that the "third-wave consumer movement" of the 1960s and 1970s grew out of unfulfilled promises of the Consumers' Republic. Mobilized purchasers as citizens were both propelled by their expectations as participants in the Consumers' Republic and constrained by the limitations of that vision. When the nation went into severe economic crisis in the mid-1970s, the critical underpinnings of the Consumers' Republic and its associated consumer movement collapsed, though the assumption that consumer well-being was central to the well-being of America persisted. My story closes by following how presidents from Ford through Clinton transformed the Consumers' Republic into what I call the *Consumerization of the Republic,* justifying the new order by claiming it served the interests of consumers. In a concluding Epilogue, I briefly bring this history into the present day and suggest some of the implications to be drawn from this analysis of postwar America.

I hope that readers, aware of how my life has conformed to the larger patterns set out in this book, will begin to contemplate how their own lives may also have been shaped by these economic, political, social, and cultural structures that reigned over the second half of the twentieth century and still are with us in many ways today. But in urging that consideration, I mean in no way to imply that individuals do not still make critically important choices about where they live and shop, what they consume, and how they relate to government as citizens, nor that societies like ours should not monitor and redress the unacceptable outcomes, such as discrimination and inequality, that may result from their seemingly inflexible infrastructures. Recognizing the societal pressures toward certain kinds of thinking and behaving ultimately makes independent action not less significant but more so. If we all are citizens and we all are consumers, how we choose to mix the two reveals a great deal about who we are as individual Americans as well as about the virtue of the America we live in at any particular moment in time.

PART ONE

The Origins of the Postwar Consumers' Republic

CHAPTER 1

Depression: Rise of the Citizen Consumer

A paradox arose in the midst of the Great Depression of the 1930s. Hard times forced many Americans to struggle to find and keep work, to feed their families, and to hold on to their homes or pay their rent. Yet increasingly they were being viewed by policymakers—and were thinking of themselves—as consumers, as purchasers of goods in the marketplace. Even as many people were barely making ends meet in the thirties, two images of the consumer came to prevail and, in fact, competed for dominance. On the one hand, what I will call citizen consumers were regarded as responsible for safeguarding the general good of the nation, in particular for prodding government to protect the rights, safety, and fair treatment of individual consumers in the private marketplace. On the other hand, purchaser consumers were

---

Overleaf: From the Great Depression to the end of the Second World War, the foundations of the Consumers' Republic began to be laid, as consumers figured ever more centrally in efforts to achieve a more prosperous economy and democratic polity. During World War II, for example, the home construction industry organized traveling "Post-War Home" shows to entice Americans with models of the kind of houses they could expect to buy at war's end. Consumers across the economic spectrum were encouraged to imagine "home" as a newly built, single-family detached house for purchase in the suburbs, not a rented residence in a multiple dwelling in the city. (Courtesy of Northwest Museum of Arts & Culture/Eastern Washington State Historical Society, Spokane)

viewed as contributing to the larger society more by exercising purchasing power than through asserting themselves politically.

Consider these two contrasting depictions of the consumer from the 1930s. When in 1933, Congress passed the National Industrial Recovery Act, it authorized this keystone program of the first New Deal to include representatives of the "consuming public" alongside business and labor. In practice this meant that the National Recovery Administration (NRA) made consumers members of some code authorities as well as established a Consumer Advisory Board (CAB), which, despite a constant struggle to get equitable recognition from NRA officials, gave consumers a legitimate voice in the federal government's efforts to foster recovery. After angry consumer advocates descended upon Washington to complain about the inadequacy of the CAB, a Consumers' Counsel was added as well.

The comments of one of CAB's members, the prominent Columbia University sociologist Robert S. Lynd, document well the citizen consumer perspective that prevailed among New Dealers at the time. Again and again Lynd articulated the importance of empowering consumers—whom he labeled "forgotten men"—to a viable democracy. The consumer "stands there alone—a man barehanded, against the accumulated momentum of 43,000,000 horse power and their army of salesmen, advertising men, and other jockeys. He knows he buys wastefully . . . that his desires and insecurities are exploited continually, that even his Government withholds from him vitally important information by which both it and industry save millions of dollars annually." As a remedy, Lynd and other New Dealers repeatedly called for permanent representation of the consumer point of view in government, most fully through the creation of a federal consumer agency to complement those already devoted to commerce, agriculture, and labor. They also sought protections for consumers against exploitation by business or government, such as requiring quality and labeling standards for all products. Nothing less than the viability of American democracy was at stake, Lynd insisted. "The only way that democracy can survive . . . is through the quality of living it can help the rank-and-file of its citizens to achieve," not simply an adequate standard of living.[1]

The competing vision of Americans as purchaser consumers came through powerfully in a twenty-six-minute public relations film that the Chevrolet Motor Company produced in 1937, entitled *From Dawn to Sunset*. Released only months after General Motors, Chevrolet's parent company, signed an historic union contract with the United Auto Workers (UAW), it depicted employees in twelve plant cities serving the corporation and the nation more as purchasers of goods, including but by no means limited to cars, than as workers in factories. The film followed the typical day of an "army of interdependent automotive workers and salaried personnel" in these twelve cities, showing repeated scenes of workers receiving pay packets and then, often accompanied by wives and children, spending them in downtown stores on everything from new living-room furniture to children's bicycles and stylish clothing. To triumphal music, the narrator proclaimed that "tens of thousands of men on one single payroll have money for themselves and their families to spend," making possible "the pleasure of buying, the spreading of money, and the enjoyment of all the things that paychecks can buy."

Chevrolet obviously had a vested interest in depicting new UAW members as well-paid and job-secure customers rather than as tenacious rank-and-file unionists. But much more was at stake. That Chevrolet sought to improve its public image by boasting that "the purchasing power of pay packets fuels the local economies of twelve plant cities" revealed the company's confidence in consumers as the savior of the nation's economy. Because "America has a ready purse and gives eager acceptance to what the men of motors have built," the United States will enjoy "a prosperity greater than history has ever known," the film proclaimed. It was the buying power of consumers in the aggregate, not the protection of individual consumers in the marketplace, that manufacturers like General Motors, along with a growing number of economists and government officials by the late 1930s, thought would bring the United States out of depression and ensure its survival as a democratic nation.[2]

Why in the thirties did a wide range of Americans, from ordinary citizens to policymakers, begin to recognize that consumer interests and behavior had profound economic and political consequences for the nation? And what did it mean that they endorsed two very different prescriptions—the citizen consumer and the purchaser consumer—for the proper role of consumers? Answering these questions matters not only for understanding the 1930s, but the decades that followed as well. The new expectations that Americans developed during the Great Depression for how consumers should contribute to a healthy economy and polity would leave a legacy for World War II and the postwar era.

DISCOVERING THE CONSUMER INTEREST

The 1930s, of course, were not the first time that Americans took note of the importance of consumption and consumers. Almost from its initial European settlement, America participated in an economy of commercial exchange, and gradually over the centuries a market revolution increased the amount of goods that Americans purchased rather than made at home (or did without). Not only did people consume more ready-made products as time passed, but the accumulation of luxury goods—at first, imported china and textiles, later fineries manufactured domestically—marked distinctions among Americans, such as between urban and rural dwellers and among social classes. Moreover, at crucial moments of political conflict, Americans exercised their clout as consumers, withdrawing their purchasing power to put economic pressure on their opponents. On the eve of the American Revolution of the late eighteenth century, colonists shirked imported British tea and fabrics. Likewise, nineteenth-century workers organized boycotts of their employers' goods as part of their campaigns for shorter hours, higher wages, and better working conditions. But despite the longstanding significance of consumption in their lives, when Americans before the twentieth century contemplated what made for the most robust national economy, the most stable American polity, and the most independent citizenry, they overwhelmingly pointed to the vitality of production and the power of producers.[3]

The Progressive Era of the late nineteenth and early twentieth centuries marked a significant shift toward recognizing the centrality of consumers to the nation's economy and polity, so much so that I will refer to it as the "first-wave consumer movement." Aspects of the Progressive program could qualify as proto–citizen consumer, anticipating as they did concerns and responses that would emerge more fully in the "second-wave consumer movement" of the 1930s and 1940s. The Progressives identified consumers as a new category of the American citizenry, an ideal broad-based constituency desirous and deserving of political and social reforms to limit the dangers of an industrializing, urbanizing, and politically corruptible twentieth-century America. Because all men and women were thought to suffer as consumers from unfairly jacked-up prices, defective manufactured goods, and unresponsive if not deceitful politicians, reform was easily pursued in their name. Progressives sought more direct democracy—primaries, initiatives, referenda, recalls, and female suffrage—as well as specific remedies to protect consumers and taxpayers from exploitation, such as municipal and consumer ownership of utilities and fairer tax policies. The Pure Food and Drug Act and the Meat Inspection Act (1906), although weak, were passed to set some minimum standards for the safety and quality of goods increasingly being produced for national markets. And Progressives promoted anti-trust legislation, culminating in the Federal Trade Commission Act (FTC, 1914), to protect against monopolies that violated an idealized America where consumers were best served by local, independent, and competitive businesses.[4]

Consumers at the grass roots complemented Progressive reformers' efforts by asserting their power in the marketplace. Housewives in some local communities successfully boycotted merchants to bring down prices when they climbed too high. Particularly well documented are the protests of New York's immigrant Jewish housewives in kosher meat boycotts in 1902, rent strikes in 1904 and 1907–08, and cost-of-living protests in 1917.[5]

Likewise, organized workers who long had rejected wage labor as slavery depriving workers of their freedom as citizen producers now accepted the reality of industrialized labor and began to agitate for "a living wage" adequate to provide an "American standard of living" for working-class consumers. A fair shake at consumption—achievable through the eight-hour day, government-regulated minimum wages, and union labels—seemed to promise workers both a better quality of life and full rights as citizens. In the tradition of their nineteenth-century antecedents, workers also expanded their use of consumer boycotts to punish uncooperative employers, as during the Seattle labor movement's impressive organizing drive after World War I.[6]

Most visible nationally were the efforts of middle-class women's reform organizations, such as the National Consumers' League (NCL) and its state chapters, to convince female consumers to practice "ethical consumption," selective buying to pressure employers and the state to improve wages and working conditions for employed women and children. Through its symbolic "Consumers' White Label" campaign, for example, the league urged consumers to purchase only white muslin underwear bearing a label testifying to its manufacture under morally acceptable and sanitary conditions, both to protect their own families from injurious goods and to lobby for protective labor legislation, child labor laws, and improvements in retail and factory work environments. The NCL viewed consumer organization instrumentally as a strategy to better the working conditions of producers; only tangentially did it concern itself with the exploitation of the consumer.[7]

During the 1920s mass consumption—the production, distribution, and purchase of standardized, brand-name goods aimed at the broadest possible buying public—grew more prevalent. By the end of the decade, most Americans, regardless of how much money they had to spend, recognized the growing dominance of mass consumption in the nation's purchasing. Not all Americans participated equally in mass consumer markets; many more lacked a car, washing machine, vacuum cleaner, and radio in 1930 than had one. Yet the expansion of a middle class with more time and money to spend, the extension of consumer credit and installment buying, and the burgeoning of advertising ensured that more and more Americans would consider themselves mass consumers by the 1930s.[8]

At the same time that mass consumption boomed in the 1920s, however, governments only acted minimally to protect consumers from the growing dangers of substandard and sometimes dangerous products, unfair pricing, and misleading advertising. Manufacturers, distributors, and advertisers essentially enjoyed free rein in the increasingly national mass marketplace. During this business-dominated decade, consumers' political consciousness was not high. Much of the fervor had gone out of Progressive Era reform movements. But so long as exciting new products like automobiles, radios, and household appliances kept coming on the market, and affluence seemed to be growing—at least for the middle and upper classes who could afford these consumer durables—few challenged the status quo by calling for stronger regulation.[9] General acceptance of a doctrine of "voluntary compliance" even weakened the authority of the existing regulatory agencies established during the Progressive Era, the FTC and the Federal Drug Administration (FDA). Rather, those in power in a Republican-dominated Washington argued that the consumers' and manufacturers' joint interests were best served by allowing business to pursue unfettered technological innovations and economic efficiencies. The free market would do the rest to deliver to consumers the best-quality goods at the cheapest prices.

As most Americans concentrated on getting ever greater access to the fruits of mass consumption, some persistent Consumers' Leaguers and unionists still sought to enlist consumers in the battle to improve the conditions under which these goods were made. But few Americans during these years considered consumers a self-conscious, identifiable interest group on a par with labor and business whose well-being required attention for American capitalism and democracy to prosper. That shift in mind-set would await the economic collapse of the Great Depression and the second-wave consumer movement it inspired.

The depression and the Democratic administration's eclectic efforts to overcome it, collectively known as the New Deal, remade the American political economy. A national welfare state emerged, industrial relations were restructured around state-sanctioned collective bargaining, and the federal government assumed a more active role in the economy. Less often mentioned but equally noteworthy was a growing recognition by those in and out of government of the importance of considering the consumer interest in reconstructing a viable economy and polity. By the end of the depression decade, invoking "the consumer" would become an acceptable way of promoting the public good, of defending the economic rights and needs of ordinary citizens.

Economist John Kenneth Galbraith argued in his *American Capitalism* of 1952, and historian Ellis Hawley elaborated a decade later, that a lasting impact of the New Deal lay in the way it implemented the concept of "countervailing power" or "counterorganization." By this Galbraith and Hawley meant the New Deal government's efforts to organize economically weak groups to balance more powerful interests. This approach to restoring the economic equilibrium upset by the Great Depression avoided more direct confrontation with existing bastions of power such as big business.[10]

Well known is the New Deal's "counterorganization" of farmers, laborers, and small businessmen. Less appreciated is its growing attentiveness to consumers as a way of institutionalizing, and protecting, the public interest. As the federal government vastly expanded in authority, it became imperative politically that the general good somehow be represented. Making "consumers" a residual category and empowering them to speak for the public became a way of mitigating the excessive power of other political blocs, including the state itself. Attending to the consumer also conformed to another prevailing tendency of the New Deal, the commitment to resuscitate a severely damaged economy without jettisoning the basic tenets of capitalism. Empowering the consumer seemed to many New Dealers a way of enhancing the public's stake in society and the economy while still preserving the free enterprise system.

The concrete achievements of what I have termed the second-wave consumer movement could be considered meager.[11] But that assessment misses how the Great Depression spawned a larger reconceptualization of the role of the consumer among state policymakers and in civil society that World War II and the postwar period would extend. "I believe we are at the threshold of a fundamental change in our popular economic thought," Franklin Roosevelt forecast in his presidential campaign of 1932, "[and] that in the future we are going to think less about the producer and more about the consumer."[12] Although FDR's administration would only gradually break with the classical economic thinking that had dominated during the 1920s and early depression, by the end of his presidency in 1945 he had presided over a recalibration of the balance between consumer and producer interests thought necessary to keep a democratic society and capitalist economy viable. Longtime consumer activist Esther Peterson, who served in the administrations of Presidents Kennedy, Johnson, and Carter, would unequivocally assert years later: "The idea of consumer representation came during the F.D.R. period."[13]

Roosevelt's perception as early as 1932 that the consumer was becoming more central likely grew out of a rumbling of consumer discontent that had begun in the mid-1920s and intensified as the depression worsened in the early 1930s. In best-selling books such as Stuart Chase's *The Tragedy of Waste* (1925), Chase and Frederick J. Schlink's *Your Money's Worth* (1927), and Schlink and Arthur Kallet's *100,000,000 Guinea Pigs: Dangers in Everyday*

Foods, Drugs, and Cosmetics (1933), a small coterie of economists, engineers, and social activists began to call for impartial product testing and enforced commodity standards to protect consumers from the deceptions of merchandisers. Consumers, they argued, were paying too high a price for the success of mass production. Soon after *Your Money's Worth* appeared, Schlink transformed his small, local consumer club and testing lab in White Plains, New York, into a more substantial national organization, Consumers' Research, with its own bimonthly publication and a membership of 40,000 by 1932 that was growing fast. Other independent product-testing organizations, Intermountain Consumers' Service and Consumers Union, followed. Although highly critical of the abuse of consumers, particularly by advertisers, these consumer advocates did not call for any major structural changes in the economy or government. Rather, they hoped that scientific research into product quality would allow the free market to work better, by creating more knowledgeable consumers capable of keeping exploitative merchandisers in check. As Americans faced steadily declining incomes with the deterioration of the economy in the 1930s, they increasingly looked to the burgeoning consumer movement's books and publications for help in getting the most from their dollars.[14]

Consumer cooperatives, retail outlets owned and operated by their customers, were another aspect of the consumer movement to which Roosevelt paid increasing attention during his presidency, ultimately establishing a special commission in 1936 to study their success abroad. Although the cooperative movement predated the 1930s and was never as influential in the United States as in Europe—involving only 1.5 percent of all retail sales nationally—a new wave of interest in consumer cooperatives accompanied the Great Depression. Estimates indicate that co-op associations and membership more than doubled between 1933 and 1936, and again by 1940, enjoying "mushroom growth," in the words of the New Jersey Federation of Consumer Cooperatives. Before the 1930s, cooperativism was mostly the project of utopians devoted to bringing the Rochdale ideal of worker-owned stores and housing from England to America or of ethnic groups like Finns, with their tradition of cooperatives, and Italians, eager to buy their native foods. During the depression decade, however, cooperative ventures attracted more diverse consumers—middle-class suburbanites, labor union members, African-American community groups, and others.

The depression also saw an expansion of the goods and services offered cooperatively to include electricity, petroleum, telephones, appliances, restaurants, insurance, credit unions, milk, medical care, laundry, and housing. The cooperative system broadened beyond retail sales as well to encompass whole-

The Consumers' Club of Jersey Homesteads in Hightstown, New Jersey (later renamed Roosevelt), organized a cooperative grocery store and kosher butcher shop, thereby participating in the trend toward cooperative buying that flourished during the Great Depression. (Courtesy of Library of Congress)

sale distribution and even, in a few cases, production in cooperatively owned factories. While cooperative leaders were ideologically committed to building an alternative social order around the elimination of the profit motive, a vision that most cooperative buyers did not fully embrace, by participating in cooperative ventures members nonetheless became more aware of their interests as consumers and of possible alternatives to the traditional capitalist marketplace. When the Newark Consumers' Cooperative League, for example, decided to launch its operation with a cooperative laundry, it hoped to save its members money not through the "false economy [of striving] for lower prices by beating down the wages of labor," but by expanding its membership base. The league extended "a special invitation to trade unionists and workers of all kinds to recognize their position as consumers and as such to ally themselves to their fellows."[15]

FDR's interest in the consumer was also undoubtedly fed by liberal reformers both within and outside his circle of advisers as they grappled with ways to pull the United States out of the Great Depression. Rexford Tugwell, Gardiner Means, Raymond Moley, and Adolf Berle, Jr., were all Columbia University professors (two economists, a political scientist, and a lawyer, respectively) who became part of Roosevelt's "brains trust," advising him through the 1932 campaign and into office. In advocating a planned economy to balance the narrow self-interest of business, these advisers considered consumers a crucial part of the larger community whose interests needed to be taken better into account.[16] A political challenge to the Democratic Party and Roosevelt from the left, moreover, put the consumer at the center of a critique of the mainstream political parties. In the fall of 1929, democratic and educational theorist John Dewey and progressive economist Paul Douglas founded a new third party, the League for Independent Political Action, around the interests of consumers, because "the needs and troubles of the people are connected with problems of consumption, with problems of the maintenance of a reasonably decent and secure standard of living." The existing parties, they argued, grew out of "that stage of American life when the American people as a whole felt that society was to advance by means of industrial inventions and their application," and Americans still clung to protecting the interests of producers at the expense of consumers, even when that era had long passed.

Although the league was loosely modeled on the British Labour Party, it saw its primary political base not in the working class but in the middle class—teachers, small merchants, and white-collar workers—which, in Dewey's words, "represents most adequately the interests of the consumer." The league never gained much popular political support, and in targeting the middle classes even managed to alienate otherwise sympathetic Socialists. But Dewey's and Douglas's prominence in progressive circles and their writings, such as Dewey's three-part series "The Need for a New Party" in *The New Republic* (March–April 1931) and Douglas's *The Coming of a New Party* (1932), drew attention to the converging interests of consumers in the economy and voting citizens in a democracy.[17] Even before the New Deal had come into being, then, the consumer was being clothed in the mantle of the public interest. Over the course of the 1930s, New Deal policymakers would experiment with different ways of recognizing consumers, and consumers themselves would increasingly mobilize around that identity to make economic and political demands of those in power.

While many different conceptions of the proper role for consumers circulated in the experimental air of the New Deal era, the two conceptions mentioned earlier—what I have called the citizen consumer and the purchaser consumer—predominated. The citizen consumer ideal was embraced by New Deal policymakers in Washington and consumer activists at the grass roots, both of whom sought consumer representation in government and new legislation and regulation to protect consumers better in the marketplace. In contrast, the purchaser consumer perspective saw consumers as the potential source of expanded demand that could pull the United States out of severe depression. Although advocates of these two viewpoints usually favored one over the other, it was possible for policymakers to embrace both. Given that the citizen consumer ideal emerged alongside the first New Deal during President Roosevelt's first term, and the purchaser consumer more systematically later in the decade with the acceptance of a Keynesian approach to managing the economy, some New Dealers moved from the first concept to the second, and others found it possible to endorse both simultaneously.

PROMOTING THE CITIZEN CONSUMER FROM WASHINGTON

Roosevelt's New Deal institutionalized the consumer viewpoint in many of its agencies, although concrete achievements in protecting consumers' rights and needs remained limited. The NRA provided the prototype. Its basic premise was that industrialists within particular economic sectors should agree upon codes of fair competition setting minimum prices and maximum wages and working hours, free of any anti-trust prosecution, to expand consumption and thereby draw the nation out of depression. In recognition of consumers' key role in recovery, the NRA placed consumers alongside labor and business on some NRA code authorities and on a Consumer Advisory Board.

Members of the CAB often expressed frustration with the business orientation of the code authorities and NRA administrators, who too often seemed to forsake consumer protection to invoke the old mutuality of interests between business and consumers through patriotic campaigns, such as those featuring display cards with the NRA's blue eagle that urged, "When you buy cigars you help provide incomes for farmers, labor, salesmen, dealers and yourself. Buy now."[18] The truth was that NRA administrators under the leadership of director General Hugh Johnson still functioned within a classical economic paradigm where attention focused on achieving recovery through more efficient production, with the assumption that increased consumption would follow automatically. The reigning "Say's Laws of Markets" assured classical economists that in a competitive market system the supply of goods and the demand for them would always reach equilibrium, a perfect system with self-correcting feedback mechanisms. Administration officials may have viewed underconsumption as a major cause of depression, but they still believed that the route to improving consumer fortunes—and hence the economy—lay with assisting business, not its customers.[19]

Nonetheless, CAB members managed "to make consumers' wants known" in the corridors of power. Staffed with liberal, consumer-minded economists, sociologists, and reformers like Robert S. Lynd, Gardiner Means, and Paul Douglas, the CAB battled the code authorities and NRA administrators to protect consumers from prices fixed too high, to implement quality standards and informational labeling of goods to ensure that consumers got their money's worth, and to sponsor county-level consumer councils to make consumers' voices heard at the local level. When the NRA went defunct in 1935, after the United States Supreme Court ruled it unconstitutional, the CAB was dismissed by many as a failure, along with the rest of the NRA. But that rejection overlooks the mark it left on national consciousness. As sociologist and CAB member Lynd noted, "It was no secret around Washington as the N.R.A. episode wore on that the consumer representatives in Washington embodied this 'public interest' in their proposals day in and day out far more nearly than did either of the far bigger and better supported advisory boards representing industry and labor." Whereas once business was assumed by definition to serve the general welfare as it prospered, by the end of the NRA it was generally understood among policymakers that the public interest needed independent representation to balance producers and labor. Empowering "consumers" as a distinct constituency offered a viable strategy for protecting the general good.[20]

The Agricultural Adjustment Administration's (AAA) Office of the Consumer Counsel proved the most effective model for incorporating the consumer interest, both because of its official status within the agency and the strong leadership of its successive counsels, liberal reformers Frederick C. Howe and Donald E. Montgomery. While the AAA devoted itself to increasing farm prices by controlling supply to restore the livelihoods and purchasing power of farmers, the counsel's office watched out for the consumer, lobbying to ensure that farm produce was plentiful enough and price increases fair. Although the counsel did not always succeed in protecting consumers' best interests, he and his department managed to keep the public informed about how agricultural policy affected them through press conferences, radio broadcasts, and the regular publication of the *Consumers' Guide,* which by the mid-1930s had become almost a service organ of the consumer movement.[21]

Another effective effort at involving consumers in New Deal programs revolved around delivering reasonably priced electricity to American farmers. The Tennessee Valley Authority (TVA, established in 1933) and particularly the Rural Electrification Administration (REA, established in 1936) organized and financed cooperative associations to bring electricity to rural America, so poorly served by private power companies that as late as 1935, nine out of ten rural homes were not electrified. In mobilizing people at the grass roots, these government-sanctioned and -supported cooperatives became long-lasting strongholds of consumer activism.[22] Furthermore, a number of other successful New Deal agencies not commonly associated with consumer advocacy aimed to protect consumers while also propping up the institutional foundations of capitalism: the Federal Housing Administration (FHA) and Home Owners' Loan Corporation (HOLC) offered consumers dependable, low-cost home financing, the Federal Deposit Insurance Corporation (FDIC) guaranteed bank deposits, and the Securities and Exchange Commission (SEC) regulated public offerings of corporate securities.[23]

Other efforts to defend consumers' interests proved less successful. The Consumers' Counsel of the National Bituminous Coal Commission, empowered by Congress to represent the consumer point of view on a commission established to revitalize the bituminous coal industry, faced tremendous hostility from the commission during its short life from 1937 to 1940.[24] Nor did anything come of the concerted effort of New Dealers like Leon Henderson, Jacob Baker, and Thomas Blaisdell to establish a cabinet-level department of the consumer to balance the Departments of Commerce, Labor, and Agriculture and coordinate government initiatives related to consumers.[25]

But even though the New Deal frequently fell short in delivering on its commitment to the consumer, often favoring traditionally powerful constituencies like business and farming, New Dealers from FDR on down persisted in trumpeting the consumer interest as a way of making more palatable the state expansion in which they were engaged. Roosevelt justified the new consumer offices in his New Deal agencies as representing "a new principle in government"—that consumers have the right "to have their interests represented in the formulation of government policy. . . . Never before had the particular problems of consumers been so thoroughly and unequivocally accepted as the direct responsibility of government. The willingness to fulfill that responsibility was, in essence, an extension and amplification of the meaning and content of democratic government." Gardiner Means, on leave from Columbia to serve on the NRA's CAB and as economic adviser on finance to the secretary of agriculture, elaborated that consumer representation in government "may well be the key that will open the way to a truly American solution of the problem which is leading other countries in the direction of either fascism or communism." If consumers were empowered as watchdogs, these state builders seemed to be reassuring themselves as well as others, a strong central government could become a vehicle for greater democracy rather than an agent of totalitarianism, as many critics feared.[26]

The New Deal's recognition of consumers went beyond giving their representatives seats at agency negotiating tables. In 1938 the first substantial regulatory legislation since the Progressive Era passed Congress: the Food, Drug, and Cosmetic Act and the Wheeler-Lea Amendment to the Clayton Anti-Trust Act of 1914. These were not easy laws to push through. Five years of debate, delays, and revisions plagued the visionary consumer protection legislation originally proposed in 1933, and the end results reflected compromises with food, drug, cosmetics, and advertising industries determined to stave off further regulation. But while consumer advocates then and after rightfully despaired of the difficulties encountered in strengthening basic consumer protections, particularly in legislating quality standards and grade labels for commodities, the events of the 1930s nonetheless reversed trends of the 1920s, when the state's role in mediating between producers and consumers had been minimal. The passage of these two new laws extended the FDA's jurisdiction to include cosmetics and medical devices, and expanded its ability to require new labeling and prevent adulteration and misbranding. The new legislation empowered the agency to require drug manufacturers to prove that products were safe before they could put them on the market, and it strengthened enforcement procedures against hazardous substances. Although consumer advocates lost the battle to give control over advertising to the more stringent FDA rather than to the FTC, the FTC nonetheless gained new powers over harmful business practices, including the right to take action against advertising that threatened the public interest, regardless of whether competition was jeopardized. These 1938 laws hardly provided models of consumer protection legislation, yet they marked another way that the state moved beyond the level of concern for consumer interests it had demonstrated in the Progressive Era.[27]

WOMEN AS CITIZEN CONSUMERS

Policymakers and economists in Washington were not the only ones embracing the ideal of citizen consumers during the 1930s. Many ordinary Americans became much more self-conscious about their identities and interests as consumers. In fact, the story of Washington's increased investment in consumers is incomplete if not put in the context of a grassroots upsurge of consumer activism over the decade, often overlooked by scholars more attentive to the mobilization of producers through the labor movement of the 1930s. In some cases, as with consumer lobbying for protective legislation, the impact of grassroots organizing on governmental action is easily discernible. In other cases, the influence of consumer assertiveness in shaping policy is harder to track.

Regardless, the New Deal's sudden attention to consumers as a voice of the public interest offered otherwise underrepresented groups an opportunity to become another "countervailing power" worthy of official recognition. Farmers had found that their agricultural difficulties were of central concern to the New Deal's AAA. Industrialists' struggles to revive their mills and factories had become the project of the NRA. Working people's success in unionizing partially resulted from New Deal legislation that recognized workers' right to organize and bargain collectively, such as Section 7A of the National Industrial Recovery Act, and later the National Labor Relations Act. Ethnic groups throughout the country had seized the opportunity offered through the building of a national, broad-based Democratic Party to institutionalize themselves in organizations like Polish Democratic Clubs or Italian-American Democratic Leagues.[28] For social groups not otherwise well represented, in particular women and African Americans, identification as consumers offered a new opportunity to make claims on those wielding public and private power in American society.

When Kenneth Dameron offered a scholarly analysis of "The Consumer Movement" in the *Harvard Business Review* in 1939, he defined it as a "series of efforts having in common the feeling of dissatisfaction with goods and services and the marketing practices involved in their distribution, coupled with . . . a demand for information and for protection in the market." To attain these ends, he noted, consumers "are turning to government protection . . . and are . . . substituting collective action for individual action," which, although common among labor and capital groups, "has never before had any sustained use by consumers." In probing the reasons for this recent consumer upsurge, Dameron returned again and again to the initiative of women. He suggested that they had become more price- and quality-conscious buyers for their families in a depression economy, the prime beneficiaries of a recent explosion of consumer education classes offered by high schools and colleges, and a growing presence in the paid labor force, all of which had changed their "economic viewpoint." "They want their money's worth. They have acquired more of a purchasing-agent viewpoint."[29]

Indeed, with the exception of the consumer cooperative and product-testing wings of the movement, women made up much of the leadership and rank and file of the consumer movement during the 1930s. Through existing and newly founded organizations, they lobbied New Deal agencies and Congress demanding that the federal government provide greater consumer representation and stronger legal protections. They expanded consumer education programs in schools and communities, so by the end of the decade the subject had become an integral part of curricula at all levels, the Consumer Education Association had been established, and annual conferences at the newly founded Institute for Consumer Education at Stephens College in Columbia, Missouri (funded by a quarter-million-dollar grant from the Alfred P. Sloan Foundation), cultivated a national leadership and showcased research and programs in the field.[30] And women orchestrated boycotts and other buyers' actions to protest high prices to retailers, distributors, manufacturers, and government policymakers. In a report briefing executives on the consumer movement, *Business Week* concluded that "it is these organized women's groups that constitute the real strength of the consumer movement." An early chronicler of the movement concurred: "Not since the demand for suffrage have women been drawn so closely together on a common issue."[31]

Women's consumer activism in the 1930s was built upon a base of existing female organizations with middle-class memberships. At the heart of the consumer offensive was the 15,000-member American Home Economics Association, long committed to improving standards in home living but now joined by groups taking new interest in consumer issues as they moved into center stage with the New Deal. The American Association of University Women (AAUW), the General Federation of Women's Clubs (GFWC), the National League of Women Voters, the National Federation of Business and Professional Women's Clubs, the National Congress of Parents and Teachers, as well as groups with narrower constituencies such as the National Council of Jewish Women, the National Council of Catholic Women, and the YWCA, became influential advocates for consumer demands, such as stricter food and drug legislation, the setting of quality and performance standards for commodities, a new federal department of the consumer, and protection of consumers from unfair trade practices. *Business Week*'s reporter expressed a surprise felt by many at the sudden seriousness with which many of these established middle-class women's organizations embraced a new political agenda. "Until recent years the consumer movement was supposed to be nothing but a lot of ladies' bridge clubs meeting every Thursday and setting up committees between rubbers to heckle the local advertisers and merchants. The depression, however, . . . brought the consumer interest to the fore in the already organized women's organizations," the largest and most established of which was the GFWC, with over two million members.

Once assumed to be "conservative, easily diverted, not particularly interested in the theory of consumer economics," according to *Business Week,* the GFWC under the leadership of its new president, Sadie Orr Dunbar, transformed itself into a pressure group for the consumer cause. The GFWC and other national women's organizations proved themselves particularly influential in the long struggle for the Food, Drug, and Cosmetic Act of 1938, working through their cooperatively supported lobbying arm, the Women's Joint Congressional Committee. Known affectionately as the "Women's Joint," it was described by veteran consumer activist Caroline Ware as "that sturdy group of women's organizations in the 1930s that met monthly to plan strategy."[32]

Women's organizations embraced consumer issues with remarkable energy during the 1930s. They orchestrated committees, conferences, exhibits, fact-finding missions, lobbying efforts, and more, establishing themselves as the new protectors of the consumer interest in civil society as well as within the expanding sphere of the state. The following are but a few examples: A citywide Consumer Conference of Cincinnati, made up of over forty organizations, sponsored radio broadcasts, public lectures, and classes advocating informative labeling, meat grading, and other consumer protections. The major women's organizations in New Jersey jointly sponsored a consumer institute at Rutgers University in 1937, followed by a test project on informative product labeling. A "baby carriage parade" in New York City co-sponsored by the Milk Consumers Protective Committee and the Henry Street Settlement House pressured New York's governor and Department of Agriculture to grant a license to a Consumer-Farmer Milk Cooperative. An exhibit, "Today's Consumers Live in Blunderland," mounted by the AAUW in Washington in 1940, attracted national attention.

In these and a multitude of other venues, women used their existing organizational strength to advocate for consumers, in the process establishing new authority for themselves as guardians of the public welfare. Dr. Kathryn McHale, general director of the AAUW, told President Roosevelt, "There is no interest which is more fundamental than that of consumers. All residents of our nation are consumers in large or limited way. No matter what our other interests, we have in common one function—that of consumption." Because women do most of the nation's buying, McHale told the AAUW's members at the association's annual convention in 1935, we women have the responsibility and potential to influence the nation's standards for production, purchase, and consumption. A few years later, after the new Food, Drug, and Cosmetic Act had been won, a speaker at a meeting of the American Home Economics Association gave it and similar organizations the credit: "It was the women—I don't think there is any doubt about that—who put it over."[33]

Women's involvement in consumer issues led to the establishment of new organizations, not just the reorientation of existing ones. In some places, the NRA's county consumer councils developed into permanent consumer organizations; the Department of Agriculture counted twenty-two still active in 1939. Elsewhere in the country, including all major cities, new groups emerged to educate and agitate, taking such names as the previously mentioned Consumer Conference of Cincinnati, the City Action Committee Against the High Cost of Living in New York, and the Women's League Against the High Cost of Living in Detroit. Although rising prices provided the initial rationale for these organizations, many of them quickly broadened their concerns to other forms of consumer exploitation.

One organization was unique enough to warrant special mention. The League of Women Shoppers of New York was founded in 1935 by upper- and middle-class progressive women—many well known in art, business, and society circles—to support the burgeoning labor movement, particularly among women workers. Appealing to other female consumers to "Use Your Buying Power for Justice," they picketed and boycotted employers whose workers were on strike, in many cases lending crucial prestige and purchasing power to the strikers' cause. Formed during a strike at Ohrbach's Department Store in New York, they brought their social connections and legitimation to many labor struggles in that city, often picketing in evening gowns and furs to attract publicity. By 1938, they had formed a National League of Women Shoppers, Inc., headquartered in New York, and fifteen active chapters in large cities all over the country, bringing the national membership to somewhere between 15,000 and 25,000. Although their primary commitment was to support striking workers, by the late 1930s the outbreak of war in Europe reoriented them toward the consumer's plight, as living costs rose and goods became scarce. Soon they took on many of the issues that concerned the consumer movement.[34] The National Consumers' League, which had been similarly committed to using purchasing power to improve working conditions since early in the century, likewise began to pay more attention to consumer issues by the end of the thirties.[35]

With eruptions of consumer activities occurring all over the country, activists sought some national coordination. They founded two umbrella organizations to represent consumer groups in Washington, provide information and educational materials to local organizations, and sponsor conferences: the Emergency Conference of Consumer Organizations, founded in 1933 specifically to lobby the NRA in behalf of consumers, and its direct descendant, the Consumers' National Federation, established in the spring of 1937 with Helen Hall of the Henry Street Settlement as its chair. Although historians have paid more heed to the emergence of new male-dominated labor unions representing producers than to the rise of women's organizations committed to improving the lives of consumers during the 1930s, the depression inspired tens of thousands of American women to join together not only to protect their families from a declining standard of living and other forms of exploitation in the marketplace, but also to safeguard society more broadly.[36]

After the achievement of suffrage in 1920, energetic political organizing by women receded and their voting patterns became indistinguishable from men's, with voting rates even lagging behind at times. The consumer movement of the 1930s revived women's political activism, differentiating it from men's. While men, particularly immigrants and African Americans, were reawakening to political parties, female consumer activists were turning consumption into a new realm of politics, and its policing into a new kind of political mission for themselves. When "leaders of consumer organizations with several million members throughout the nation" met with First Lady Eleanor Roosevelt in January 1940 to discuss with her the need for still greater government attention to the consumer, all seventeen representatives were women. The only men in the room were officials from government agencies invited to attend, according to a press release from the Consumers' National Federation.[37]

The work of women's organizations was complemented by impressive mobilization of female consumers at the grass roots. More diverse in class, race, ethnicity, and political orientation than the women generally attracted to the established consumer groups, this rank and file often galvanized around high prices, but went beyond them in their demands. At a high point during the meat boycotts of 1935, women in cities throughout the country succeeded in effectively shutting down the retail butcher trade as well as implicating the wholesale meatpackers whose profiteering they held greatly responsible for recent price hikes. In Los Angeles in March 1935, more than 10,000 women joined a "housewives strike against meat prices" organized by two local groups, the Housewives League of Los Angeles and Southern California and the United Conference Against the High Cost of Living. Taking to the streets, radio airwaves, and telephone lines, boycotters spread the message widely not to buy meat that had increased in price 2 percent in one month. In May a coalition of neighborhood groups in New York City with strong roots in Jewish areas of Brooklyn and the Bronx and in the black community of Harlem, and with close ties to the Communist Party, closed down thousands of butcher shops and organized mass demonstrations at the meatpacking plants of Manhattan. By June 1935 the *Wall Street Journal* was alarmed enough at the contagion of protest to devote a front-page story to how "consumer resistance to advancing food prices has continued to gather momentum until currently it is being reported from practically every important center of the country. . . . The stop buying movement has been especially distressing to the large grocery and meat chains and is having an unfavorable effect on their earnings."

The protests continued to spread as the summer progressed. In Detroit in late July, a group of women in the white working-class district of Ham-tramck so successfully organized a meat boycott to secure a 20 percent price reduction that all butchers closed down "because there's no one to sell to," according to the president of the Hamtramck Butchers and Grocers Associa-tion. In no time, women's action committees involving thousands of women sprang up all over Wayne County and a permanent organization, the Women's League Against the High Cost of Living, was founded, with dynamic boycott organizer Mary Zuk as chair. The league's platform went beyond the meat issue to demand reductions in the price of other food and rent, improvements in housing conditions, the lowering of taxes on small homes, and the abolish-ment of the sales tax. The league's activities soon expanded to include mass marches through Detroit's streets and the storming of meatpacking plants, where kerosene was poured on thousands of pounds of warehoused meat. In the middle of August, Detroit protesters traveled to Chicago to join allies there in a march on the symbolic heart of the meatpacking industry, the Union Stockyards. They arrived in a city that was already highly organized by its own broad-based United Conference Against the High Cost of Living and in neigh-borhood consumer clubs dedicated to educating members on a wide range of issues ranging from compulsory meat grading to cheaper and purer milk. Throughout the infamous "meatless" spring, summer, and fall of 1935, reports of women's political activism came in from all over the country—from Philadelphia to Seattle, from Boston to Miami, and from places large and small in between.[38]

This was not the first time, of course, that American women had mounted buyers' strikes against high prices: recall the cost-of-living protests of Jewish women in New York before and during World War I. But women's consumer actions during the 1930s were distinguishable in several ways. While women still rallied their neighbors and targeted local shops, as they had earlier in the century, they had become much more interested and success-ful in coordinating their protests on a citywide, metropolitan, and even national level. Influential alliances that crossed locale, ethnicity, race, and, most noticeably, class resulted. As a consumer economist of the time noted, the organized consumer boycott was used more frequently during the depres-sion than ever before: "It is only within the past several years that the people of the so-called middle class have participated in such strikes on even a city-wide basis."[39] For example, in Los Angeles, boycott leaders ranged from Sadie

Goldstein, a working-class, Jewish Communist Party member, to Margaret Matteson, a real estate agent who claimed to be the aunt of heiress Doris Duke Cromwell. While Polish and African-American working-class women in Hamtramck aggressively picketed butcher shops and taunted violators of the boycott, middle-class native-born women set up card tables on street corners in their own neighborhoods to solicit no-meat pledges from passing housewives. The organizing style may have been different, but the goal was shared. In Chicago, officeholders of the United Conference Against the High Cost of Living included in 1937 representatives from such disparate groups as the Women High School Teachers, Fur Workers Local #45, Postal Clerks Union #1, the American Lithuanian Literary Society, and the Parent-Teacher Association.

Much as in Los Angeles, Detroit, and Chicago, consumer protest elsewhere brought together middle- and working-class women, the latter of whom, though often led by Communist Party or labor movement activists, reached far beyond those ranks to include women of diverse political persuasions, ethnicity, and race. New forms of communication such as the telephone and the national media helped women make connections beyond their homogeneous neighborhoods and hometowns. Whether middle-class club members or working-class housewives, these women felt empowered as consumers to criticize the workings of the market. And their protests over the price of meat often expanded to include other products and services, such as rents, utility rates, and taxes, and calls for more government regulation of the marketplace, making them champions of a broad-based public interest.[40]

The new cosmopolitanism of the meat boycotters not only affected their organizing strategies, it also helped them recognize that government, and the federal government in particular, both played a crucial role in creating the conditions against which they were protesting and offered a solution to them. In many places, boycotters tried to get city councils and state legislatures to set ceilings on prices, and leaders in New York, Washington State, Michigan, and elsewhere followed up buyers' strikes with campaigns for city and state office built on consumer-oriented platforms.

Most common was a new orientation toward Washington. Although female meat boycotters organized to shut down neighborhood butcher shops for charging excessive prices, they understood that those prices resulted from national distribution networks of the meatpackers, and even more importantly, the increasing role being played by the federal government in setting prices. Repeatedly they organized letter-writing campaigns and pilgrimages to the President, Congress, and particularly the Department of Agriculture and its secretary, Henry Wallace. Organizers like Mary Zuk of Detroit communicated to supporters that the AAA's withdrawal of livestock from the market to raise farm prices and the federal government's new meat-processing tax were as responsible as the packers' profiteering for the rising cost of living. On many occasions, she and her allies around the country traveled to Washington to confront Secretary Wallace in person. (He preferred to blame the western drought for the price hikes!) As consumption increasingly became a concern of New Deal Washington, protest by female consumers against "unfair prices and practices"—whether picketing against high prices outside neighborhood butcher shops or lobbying in Congress for stricter regulation of products— made women political players not only in local communities, but in the nation at large.[41]

Women's claim on the politics of consumption was sustained not only by their own actions, but by the general disinterest toward matters of consumption conveyed by the most politically mobilized social group of the era, labor, as it made tremendous strides of its own during the 1930s. A newly militant labor movement fought for union recognition, workplace improvements like seniority and grievance procedures, and better wages. The demand for higher wages carried the potential for workers to view themselves as consumers as much as producers, given the impact of prices on standard of living, and at other times in the history of unions workers had defined a "living wage" in consumption terms. But in the fervor of industrial organizing during the New Deal, explicit consumer concerns took a back seat. A labor columnist for *The New Republic* complained that "apathy on the part of labor" toward consumer issues even discouraged the collection of data relevant to "the position of workers as consumers." Robert Lynd voiced similar frustration that labor's representatives in Washington exhibited "little concern for the possibility of maximizing real earnings through bolstering their role as consumers."[42] Despite the fact that many women workers were joining organized labor's ranks, the new Congress of Industrial Organizations (CIO) and rejuvenated American Federation of Labor (AFL) became male identified, as labor militancy became cloaked in masculine language and imagery, and unions promoted a "culture of unity" that not only crossed racial and ethnic lines, but also unified family members around the familial authority of the male breadwinner.[43] This identification of unionism with men and with productionist workplace issues made politicization in the realm of consumption appear all the more female.

Within the labor movement, however, women in the rank and file and union auxiliaries more enthusiastically clamored to the consumer cause, replicating within unions the larger society's sexual division of labor between the politics of consumption and production. Many of these women could be found on the streets of working-class neighborhoods like Detroit's Hamtramck boycotting meat and picketing utility companies. And when female unionists fought their own battles against employers, they often developed organizing strategies that recognized the efficacy of consumer power. The Hotel and Restaurant Employees Union, for example, relied on "sip-ins," where "customers" would mob a fancy restaurant and sit for hours sipping one cup of coffee. Department store campaigns used the "button, button" tactic in which union supporters would fill up shopping carts with goods and then refuse to purchase anything unless served by a worker wearing a union button.[44] The labor movement may have officially relegated consumption to a secondary place, but that did not prevent female unionists from bringing a consumer orientation to their political activism within it.

By the end of the decade, however, there were hints that the mainstream of organized labor was becoming more aware of the importance of consumption to workers' well-being. For example, a Pontiac local of the United Auto Workers Union threatened that its three thousand members would start a rent strike if rents were not lowered, as rent increases had absorbed wage gains made through striking. Consumer education programs sponsored by labor unions began to expand, typified in the publication of a pamphlet entitled "The Worker as a Consumer" by the International Ladies' Garment Workers' Union (ILGWU) intended for use in labor study groups. Union commitment to consumer cooperatives, particularly credit unions, grew beyond labor's longstanding—but generally unfulfilled—official endorsement of cooperativism. And when twenty-five leaders of the Consumers' National Federation went to Washington to lobby President Roosevelt for a consumer agency in the federal government, a delegation sent to visit leaders of the CIO and the AFL delighted in reporting a sympathetic hearing to its arguments that "high money wages alone cannot secure to American working men an abundant living if as individual consumers they lose as poor buyers across the counter the gains made by collective bargaining with industry."[45] All these actions indicated that the New Deal's new union recruits were starting to realize that the pay packet could not be separated from the amount and quality of what could be bought in the marketplace. Wartime inflation would only make that message clearer.

But as Mark Starr, education director of the ILGWU, concluded in 1940, consumer-oriented activity at that point was still a "small drop in a large bucket." The labor movement could do much more than it was doing. Not until the postwar period would unions commit themselves to developing "consumer" along with "wage" consciousness among their rank and file, although Consumers Union (CU), which split off from Schlink's Consumers'

Research (CR) in 1936 over a labor dispute, distinguished itself from CR by taking labor standards into account in its recommendations about product quality, thus setting out a welcome mat to unions.[46] But unions largely ignored the invitation. For most of the 1930s, the labor movement's mobilization around producer rather than consumer issues left women, outside as well as inside unions, toting the shopping bag alone.

Women who organized, lobbied, and boycotted were giving the cultural and economic role assigned them in the household as consumer a new political significance. Seeing an emerging political space for the consumer in the way state structure and economic policy were reconfigured with the New Deal, they moved to fill it. Sometimes government initiative prepared the ground and women cultivated it, as when they kept viable the county consumer organizations created under the NRA long after the NRA had ended. Other times, women goaded the state to action, as when they pressured Congress to pass more stringent protective legislation. While mobilizing as wives and mothers to protect the economic viability of their families, as women had done for generations, they were making further claims to be citizen protectors of the general good of the nation.

BLACK POWER OF THE PURSE

African Americans in the urban North also mobilized politically as consumers during the 1930s, and in ways unique to their racial situation. By boycotting some merchants while favoring others, organizing cooperatives, and undertaking other kinds of consumer activism, African Americans asserted themselves in the retail marketplace on an unprecedented scale. Faced with devastating economic hardship from the Great Depression, northern blacks—most of whom were relative newcomers to the region's cities—had little recourse. They were already enthusiastically exercising the franchise, an important attraction of northern residence, and by 1936 shifted the majority of their votes from the Republicans to the Democrats, helping to ensure the survival of New Deal relief programs upon which many depended. As they were disproportionately losing jobs in the private sector, giving them the highest rates of unemployment in many cities, organizing at the workplace made little sense, until later in the 1930s when they could join the CIO's larger offensive.[47] The Communist Party offered some immediate help against tenant evictions and relief discrimination, but full-fledged membership in this Moscow-oriented political organization appealed to only a small number of northern blacks.[48]

A remaining, and promising, resource was African-American spending power. If properly channeled, it could be a powerful club for demanding jobs and fairer treatment from white store owners and a way of favoring black-owned businesses and cooperatives, whose greater profits would then circulate in black communities. Black residents of every major northern city and racial leaders of diverse political persuasions, ranging from the "conservative" spokesmen of the National Negro Business League to the more "radical" National Negro Congress and the well-known Socialist and founder of the National Association for the Advancement of Colored People (NAACP) W.E.B. Du Bois, recognized over the course of the thirties the benefits of politicizing African-American consumers on a mass scale.

If African-American consumer activism reached a new height during the 1930s, it grew from deep roots. Several historical efforts to improve black circumstances through consumer action prepared the ground. The consumer boycott was the major strategy with which blacks had protested on a mass scale the imposition of Jim Crow laws in the South in the late nineteenth and early twentieth centuries, particularly those mandating the segregation of trolley cars in all major southern cities. Although the streetcar boycotts failed, the fact that the determination of thousands of black riders had managed to deprive urban transit companies of profits for periods ranging from a few weeks to a couple years, and even to drive a few into bankruptcy, remained an important memory of resistance passed on from generation to generation. When black leaders in Lynchburg, Virginia, condemned a new segregation law relegating blacks to the back of trolley cars as "a gratuitous insult . . . to every one with a drop of Negro blood," and urged a boycott to "touch to the quick the white man's pocket. 'Tis there his conscience lies," they helped create a model for retaliating against discrimination in the purchase of goods and services through withdrawing consumer patronage.[49]

Even where boycotts were not feasible because African Americans depended on the monopoly or credit a local merchant controlled, relations with southern white merchants proved fraught with tension, making retail exchange a moment when blacks expected, and resented, economic exploitation and racial discrimination. As farmers they were caught in merchants' claws of credit and debt. Even beyond that, as the national consumer market extended its reach into the South by the turn of the century, blacks fell victim to southern whites' elaborate Jim Crowism in settings of consumption and leisure such as stores, restaurants, and movie theaters, as whites came to fear that the growing availability, and inherent democracy, of commodities could undermine their own superior social status. Although after the Civil War African Americans throughout the nation legally had full economic rights in a free market, black consumption of material goods and services soon became limited by the same white anxiety about blacks' proper place in racial and class hierarchies that constrained their working and voting.[50]

The institutionalization of segregation in the late-nineteenth-century South fueled another response among African Americans that ultimately contributed to the consumer activism of the 1930s: the drive for separate black-owned businesses. As Booker T. Washington conceptualized it when he brought together leading clergy and businessmen of the era to found the National Negro Business League in 1900, black business enterprise promised economic as well as racial progress. Washington said in his opening address, "Whenever I have seen a black man who was succeeding in his business, who was a taxpayer, and who possessed intelligence and high character, that individual was treated with the highest respect by the members of the white race. In proportion as we can multiply these examples, North and South, will our problem be solved."[51] "Negro captains of industry," Washington and his followers thought, would bring blacks their fair share of the fruits of American capitalism: profits, jobs, and social prestige. By the 1920s the need for "Negro businessmen" had evolved into a broader call for a "separate black economy," whose success depended as much on committed black consumers as ambitious black entrepreneurs. With the Great Migration of southern blacks to northern cities creating a vast "Negro market" of thousands of people solidly massed in compact communities, black purchasing power could hold the key to the race's prosperity. Advocates of a black economy had also widened beyond conservative businessmen to include black nationalists and socialist-leaning "New Negroes," all of whom believed that racial solidarity in the marketplace would buy black economic and social power along with material comforts.[52]

Ironically, the heir to political accommodationist Washington as champion of black capitalism during the 1920s was Jamaican-born black nationalist Marcus Garvey. Only a few years before the onset of the Great Depression, Garvey's Universal Negro Improvement Association sponsored numerous black-run commercial enterprises—a Black Star Line of steamships to transport African-American settlers to Garvey's proposed African nation and then to carry on trade with the motherland; chains of restaurants, groceries, hotels, and laundries; and a printing plant, a black doll factory, and other industrial ventures. Although these enterprises collapsed with Garvey's conviction and deportation from the United States for mail fraud, his movement's several million supporters were nonetheless exposed to a message perhaps more lasting than "back to Africa": African-American salvation through selling and buying black.[53]

African Americans thus met the crisis of the Great Depression familiar with the potential use of their purchasing power for political ends. But their mobilization as consumers during the 1930s reached an entirely new level of intensity. Despite the extended discourse about consumer boycotting and black capitalism over the previous three decades, success had been limited. Jim Crow continued to preside over the purchase of goods and services in the South and was surprisingly present in the North as well. Except for a few large insurance companies, "race businesses" mostly consisted of small groceries and proprietorships in trades where whites had little interest in competing, such as barbershops and funeral homes. In fact, compared to most ethnic groups, African Americans were substantially underrepresented in business ownership for their presence in the population. Severe shortages of capital and credit plagued businessmen's entrepreneurial efforts, making it difficult for them to offer customers the merchandise selection, low prices, and credit terms that white shopkeepers in black neighborhoods could. A lack of business experience likewise limited their competitiveness. Hence, an unusually high failure rate among African-American-owned businesses made Garvey's short-lived enterprises typical. Not surprisingly, only a fraction of black consumers' dollars ever found their way into black merchants' pockets.[54]

Consumer activism among African Americans during the Great Depression took a number of forms. Most dramatic was a new kind of consumer protest that erupted in the late 1920s in Chicago, considered the economic capital of black America, and spread like wildfire into other northern cities during the 1930s. "Don't Buy Where You Can't Work" or "Spend Your Money Where You Can Work" campaigns demanded that white store owners hire black employees if they wanted patronage, and profits, from black customers. According to St. Clair Drake and Horace R. Cayton, authors of *Black Metropolis*, a landmark study of Chicago's African-American community during the 1930s, "The first organized reaction [to the Depression] within Black Metropolis was a movement directed against white men who did business in the Black Belt. A group of ragged pickets walking in front of a Black Belt chain store in the fall of 1929 signalized the beginning of a movement which stirred Black Metropolis as nothing had since the Race Riot." When that grocery chain relented, the target shifted to Woolworth's, which eventually agreed that a quarter of its employees in "Negro neighborhoods" would be black; Sears, Roebuck, A & P, Walgreens Drugs, and other stores followed suit, welcoming back customers with "We Employ Colored Salesmen" signs in their windows. Over three thousand new, mostly white-collar jobs resulted, a victory achieved through ordinary people's determination, and financial and moral support from black churches, lodges, community organizations,

The Citizens' League For Fair Play

requests all self-respecting people of Harlem to

Refuse to Trade with
L. M. BLUMSTEIN
230 West 125th Street

¶ This firm, acknowledging its large proportion of Negro business, has refused to employ Negro Clerks.

Stay out of Blumstein's!
Refuse to buy there!

This Campaign is endorsed and receiving cooperation from the following churches and organizations:

Abyssinian Baptist
Beulah Wesleyan Meth.
Ephesus Seventh Day
   Adventists
Good Samaritan
   Independent Episcopal
Grace Gospel
Hubert Harrison
   Memorial
Mother A.M.E. Zion
Mt. Calvary M.E.
Mt. Olivet Baptist
Refuge Church of God
Shiloh Baptist
St. Martin's Episcopal
St. Mathew's Baptist
St. James Presbyterian
St. Paul's Baptist
Transfiguration Lutheran
United Seventh Day
   Adventists
Union Baptist
African Patriotic League
African Vanguard
Afro-American Voters'
   Coalition
Aster Social and Literary
   Club
Dunbar Literary Club

Business and Professional
   Men's Association
Col. Young Memorial
   Foundation
Central Harlem Medical
   Association
Cosmopolitan Social and
   Tennis Club
Day Worker's League
Dumont Literary Club
Eureka Lodge of
   Oddfellows
Excelsior Lodge, No. 4,
   Preston Univ
Excelsior Literary Club
Garvey Club of N. Y., Inc.
Junior Fellowship,
   St. Philip's
Harlem Women's Ass'n
Keystone Lodge, I.U.O.M.
Ladies & African
   Patriotic League
Manhattan Civic Center
Mills Citizens Voters
   League
New York Age
N. Y. Chapter of Nat.
   Ass'n for College
   Women

N. Y. Chapter, U. N. I. A.
Neptune Lodge Elks,
Negro Youth Progressive
   Ass'n
New York News
Harlem Com. Center
Political Voters
Premier Literary Circle
Progressive Negro Youth
   of America
Progressive Political Ass'n
Charles Romney Fusion
   Rep. Club, 11th A.D.
J. A. Rogers Historical
   Research Society
The Sentinels
Students' Literary Ass'n
   St. Mark's Epis. Church
The Interse Social Club
Undergraduate Chapter of
   Phi Beta Sigma
United Negro Progressive
   Ass'n
Unity Democratic Club
Unique Musical Club
Unison Social Club
Yoruba Literary Club
Young West Indian
   Congress

Don't fail to be in line in the Grand Parade and Demonstration on Saturday, July 28th. All persons are requested to form on 138th Street between Lenox and Seventh Avenues at 10 o'clock.

Harlem residents, like African Americans in many other cities, used their purchasing power as consumers to pressure merchants to hire blacks as store clerks, not just as janitors and elevator operators, and to demand fairer treatment as customers. (Courtesy of Programs and Playbills Collection, Manuscripts, Archives and Rare Books Division, Schomburg Center for Research in Black Culture, New York Public Library, Astor, Lenox and Tilden Foundations) and particularly the militant *Chicago Whip* newspaper. Chicago Black Belt residents, moreover, not only demanded that African-American salesclerks be hired, but that their skin be dark enough for their racial identity to be unmistakable.[55]

Before long, the movement spread to Baltimore, Washington, Newark, Detroit, Toledo, Cleveland, St. Louis, Los Angeles, Oakland, and even south to Richmond, Virginia, in each city promoted by a different, often fragile alliance of self-interested black capitalists, the black middle-class establishment, and black nationalists with predominantly working-class followings.[56]

In the spring of 1934, the campaign finally made its way to Harlem, where protesters targeted the community's largest department store, L. M. Blumstein's, in the center of Harlem's famed 125th Street shopping district. Although Blumstein's made 75 percent of its sales to blacks, the store's owners had refused to hire them as clerks or cashiers, only as elevator operators and porters. After weeks of facing picketers, attacks by the *New York Age* newspaper, and a successful boycott waged by more than three hundred allied churches, clubs, and house-to-house delegations urging "stay out of Blumstein's," the owners capitulated, to the elation of thousands of picketers who marched in a victory parade through heavy rain and then moved on to their next target.

At the end of 1934, however, local courts ruled in merchants' favor that picketing in the absence of a labor dispute was illegal, and the "Don't Buy" campaign was forced to retreat. By the following March, Harlemites remained so incensed about the racial discrimination surrounding consumption that when a sixteen-year-old boy was apprehended for stealing a cheap pocketknife from S. H. Kress's Five-and-Dime store on 125th Street (where picketing had led to the grudging hiring of a few black clerks, who were subsequently transferred to the lunch counter), the rumor spread that he had been beaten and then that he had been killed. Within hours, a full-scale riot broke out, an attack by upwards of ten thousand people upon the mostly white-owned businesses that lined 125th Street. Three deaths, scores of arrests, hundreds of broken windows, and the looting of hundreds of thousands of dollars' worth of goods resulted. The small number of black-owned stores, and even a few white-owned ones known to employ blacks, were spared.

Three years later, after the legality of consumer boycotting and picketing was affirmed by a United States Supreme Court ruling, the Reverend Adam Clayton Powell, Jr., who had supported the Blumstein's boycott from the pulpit of the Abyssinian Baptist Church, revived the campaign under the auspices of a new organization, the Greater New York Coordinating Committee for Employment. Together with other community groups, it brought enough consumer pressure to bear (Powell claimed over 200 organizations and 170,000 members) to secure an agreement with the Uptown Chamber of Commerce that all Harlem stores under its jurisdiction would increase the proportion of blacks among their white-collar workers to at least one-third and promote them equitably with whites.[57]

By then, Harlem consumers were flexing their economic muscle in other ways as well. Tenants undertook rent strikes and looked to the recently founded Consolidated Tenants League of Harlem to push grievances against white landlords; riders boycotted the Fifth Avenue Bus Company for refusing to hire black drivers and conductors; Consolidated Edison was forced to employ its first black workers in nonmenial jobs after Powell's coordinating committee shut off Harlem's lights one night a week, urging people to burn candles instead, and led "billpayers' parades" to pay bills in pennies.[58] In far-flung parts of the country, African-American consumers likewise extended their boycott targets from stores to other public sites and services, such as movie theaters and public utilities, though their smaller share of a theater or telephone company's market often limited their leverage.[59]

While the "Don't Buy" campaigns succeeded in creating thousands of new positions, hundreds of thousands of urban blacks remained un- or underemployed. Nonetheless, this very visible strategy had enormous symbolic impact. People became convinced that African-American purchasing power truly meant power, and other efforts to tap it emerged. Most notable was a resurgence of interest in founding black businesses and a renewed confidence that black consumer spending could keep them viable. Supporters included not only established leaders of the black business community and the growing number of individuals who were setting their hopes, along with their meager savings, on a small business; new voices also emerged. W.E.B. Du Bois proposed new consumer strategies as part of his fundamental shift from the NAACP's traditional emphasis on integration to black separatism, a move that so alienated many of his NAACP colleagues that he consequently resigned membership in the organization that he had helped to found. Du Bois argued for supporting independent black economic enterprises through a policy of "voluntary segregation." It was a mistake, he wrote in 1931, "to think the economic cycle begins with production, rather it begins with consumption." Later he expanded, "The consuming power of 2,800,000 Negro families has recently been estimated at $166,000,000 a month—a tremendous power when intelligently directed. . . . With the use of their political power, their power as consumers, and their brain power . . . Negroes can develop in the United States an economic nation within a nation, able to work through inner cooperation, to found its own institutions, to educate its genius."[60]

Despite the poverty and unemployment rampant in northern black communities during the depression, the total number of black retail stores aimed at black consumers grew from about 23,000 in 1935 to almost 30,000 in 1939, nurtured through a mixture of entrepreneurial self-interest and a more broadly held ideological commitment to economic separatism. Over the same period, service establishments like cleaners and beauty parlors rose from 22,000 to 27,000. Although profits fell for many black, as for white merchants, more individuals chose to try their luck at the "depression businesses" they often set up in their houses or basements. "If worst came to worst, I would at least have something to eat," one black entrepreneur explained.[61]

In Chicago, a fervor developed around black business during the second half of the 1930s. New journals were launched, such as the *Southside Business and Professional Review* and *Colored Merchant and Caterer*. Black ministers preached from their pulpits on behalf of the "Double Duty Dollar" that simultaneously purchased a commodity and advanced the race. Their message: "Patronize your own, for that is the only way we as a race will ever get anywhere." Owners of black businesses in Chicago even sponsored a two-day Exposition of Negro Business in 1938, as *Time* magazine put it, "to spur Negro business and arrange a program to fight 'fleecing' by whites." After heavyweight boxing champion Joe Louis cut the entrance ribbon, 110,000 attendees "watched fashion shows, fingered fancy caskets, saw demos of pressing kinks out of Negro hair, listened to church choirs, and hot bands, munched free handouts or purchased raffle tickets from 75 booths."[62] All the excitement, however, was not enough to overcome the longstanding impediments to black business success. It was estimated in 1940 that black enterprises controlled fewer than 20 percent of total retail business in Chicago's black neighborhoods, although that surpassed the national average of 5 to 10 percent.[63]

One of the major obstacles to black business success that the National Negro Business League boldly addressed during the early 1930s was the growing threat of chain stores to independent groceries, the largest category of black enterprise. In a bold initiative, the league launched a nationwide effort to organize independent stores into a "voluntary chain," the Colored Merchants' Association (CMA). To help small-store owners compete more successfully against the grocery chains, the CMA purchased goods in volume to get lower prices from wholesalers, offered grocers training in modern merchandising methods, installed a uniform system of accounting in member stores, and advertised cooperatively. For these services, members paid dues of $5 a week. CMA's stores spread from its birthplace in Montgomery to Birmingham, Selma, Jackson, Dallas, Atlanta, New York, Brooklyn, Philadelphia, Richmond, Hampton, Winston-Salem, Nashville, Louisville, Detroit, Chicago, Tulsa, and

Omaha. Each city had a minimum of ten stores and many had substantially more. After operating for two years in Harlem, for example, CMA had twenty-three member stores and two model stores. The next year, 1932, the CMA opened a warehouse there to sell canned goods, coffee, flour, and other products with the CMA label to its New York stores. Despite the CMA's seeming success, however, by 1936 it was bankrupt, victim to a complicated combination of woes including the depression economy, wholesaler pressure on small grocers, and the difficulties of running a national retail cooperative of regionally diverse and often inexperienced grocers.[64]

Not all proponents of a separate black economy were comfortable championing capitalism, arguing that an exploiter with a black face differed very little from one with a white face. They advocated black-owned cooperatives, a kind of retail structure that was popular in other progressive circles as well during the 1930s. Du Bois was the best-known proponent of black cooperatives as a strategy for achieving black economic power without collaborating in the corruptions of capitalism. Long sympathetic to cooperatives in theory, Du Bois became a committed promoter as he searched for ways of coping with the devastations of the Great Depression. "The habit and order of cooperation," he argued in 1936, would help the black race build a new social order based on consumers' cooperation, democracy, and socialism and provide a "guide for the rise of the working classes throughout the world." Du Bois's commitment went beyond rhetoric to concrete efforts to establish cooperatives. He was frustrated with the demise of the CMA, which he blamed on its failure to tap into black "buying power [that] could only be held in loyalty to business if it shared the profit." To promote cooperativism, he traveled around the country speaking at symposia like one in Chicago entitled "Cooperatives—A Way Out for the Negro?"[65]

The Chicago area already had several cooperatives. Three were operating in the city: the most successful, the People's Consumer Co-operative; the Open Eye Consumer's Cooperative, affiliated with the Pilgrim Baptist Church; and the Citizen's Non-Partisan Cooperative Organization of Olivet Baptist Church, a study group and buying club. In nearby Gary, Indiana, a flourishing cooperative, Consumers' Cooperative Trading Association, boasted two thousand members, two food stores, and a full program of study groups and classes on cooperativism. Within a few years, the Ladies Auxiliary of the Brotherhood of Sleeping Car Porters, based in Chicago, would give black cooperativism an added boost when it promoted Brotherhood Consumer Cooperative Buying Clubs in that city and among Ladies Auxiliary locals elsewhere, as, in Brotherhood founder A. Philip Randolph's words, "the best mechanism yet devised to bring about economic democracy."[66]

Harlem saw cooperatives come and go over the decade, though by the late 1930s and early 1940s survival rates improved as people with stabler incomes showed more interest. Harlem was also the headquarters of the Young Negroes' Cooperative League (YNCL), founded by journalist George Schuyler, which established stores, buying clubs, and other cooperative ventures in black neighborhoods throughout the nation. The league's national director was a young Ella Baker, later, in the 1940s, to become a staff member of the NAACP and later still, in the late 1950s, the executive director of the Southern Christian Leadership Conference and a founder of the Student Nonviolent Coordinating Committee. In fact, cooperativism provided a fertile training ground for civil rights activist Baker. Her vitae from the late 1930s lists, in addition to her league stint, "Special Studies in Consumer Problems, Community Building, and Housing" at Columbia University, the New School for Social Research, and New York University; a scholarship to the Cooperative Institute of the Cooperative League of America; service as director of the Consumer Education Division, Works Progress Administration; chairman of education and publicity for the successful Harlem's Own Cooperative, Inc.; and a multitude of other speaking and organizing activities around cooperativism and consumer issues more broadly. For activists searching for creative ways to promote black self-determination in the 1930s, cooperatives generated much hope and excitement, if not huge memberships. They offered a more radical alternative to black capitalism. Combined with consumer boycotts, they made "organizing at the point of consumption" a viable racial strategy.[67]

The influential role played by the Sleeping Car Porters' Ladies Auxiliaries and civil rights activist Ella Baker in establishing cooperatives highlights the importance of African-American women in consumer organizing during the 1930s and early 1940s. Black women, like their white equivalents, held the purse strings in their households, so much so, that black merchants felt women customers controlled their fate: "They shop for the whole house and they easily influence the men in their spending. . . . Negro women are responsible for the success or failure of Negroes in business," complained a Chicago business leader.[68]

But black women's influence as consumers went beyond that. Throughout the country during the 1930s, they established Housewives' Leagues, sometimes under the auspices of local Urban Leagues, whose major focus was consumer organizing. The Detroit Housewives' League was the first to be founded and the largest. Organized with fifty members in June 1930 by Fannie B. Peck after she had been inspired by a lecture describing how Harlem housewives had supported local CMA stores, the Detroit league swelled by the end of 1935 to over 12,000 members who were divided into sixteen neighborhood units. Members pledged to support black businesses and professionals, buy black-produced products, and help train Detroit's young people for careers in business.[69] The Baltimore Housewives' League, with its reported membership of 2000, was a key coalition participant in that city's "Buy Where You Can Work" boycott.[70] In New York, the "Don't Buy" campaign was initially launched by the Harlem Housewives' League, which claimed over a thousand members as early as 1931. The league undertook a preliminary survey of black patronage of white stores to expose the unfair return in jobs, and lobbied Harlem housewives to trade only at CMA stores or other businesses that employed blacks. Later in the 1930s, Harlem's Dunbar Housewives' League sponsored the Harlem's Own Cooperative on West 136th Street.[71] Housewives' Leagues flourished as well in Chicago, Washington, D.C., Cleveland, and Pittsburgh, featuring in many of these places a mix of working- and middle-class members in a notable break with the middle-class-dominated black women's club movement. A National Housewives' League of America was established in 1933 and promoted its own nationwide "Don't Buy Where You Can't Work" campaign, but its influence was considerably weaker than that of locally based leagues.[72]

Black women, already mobilized as consumers in their own communities, united with white women to carry out the meat boycotts of 1935. In June of that year, on the heels of the March riot, black women in Harlem joined the meat boycott launched in Jewish neighborhoods and brought by Communist Party members to Harlem. Moving from butcher shop to butcher shop in "flying squadrons" of between three hundred and a thousand women, they threatened butchers with a "repetition of March 19" if they failed to reduce their prices. More than three hundred Harlem butcher shops agreed to close for four days at the angry women's insistence to help put pressure on the packers. Not surprisingly, the Communist *Daily Worker* reported that the meat strike in Harlem "was carried through more successfully than in any other section of the city," and indeed the inflated meat prices of Harlem's butchers were reported to have declined by as much as 50 percent after the protests.[73] Accounts of the meat boycott in most major cities refer to the participation of black women, many of whom were probably members of Housewives' Leagues or similar organizations. In fact, black women's prior experience with grassroots consumer boycotts through the "Don't Buy" campaigns very likely helped inspire the larger female mobilization during 1935. When African-American consumer activist Ella Baker and others like her participated in mainstream consumer organizations such as the Consumers' National Federation, the Cooperative League of America, and the New York Consumers Council, they undoubtedly made a crucial link between races.[74]

Black women protesters were also pivotal in pushing consumer demands beyond jobs. For example, in Brooklyn, a female-dominated organization committed to fighting job discrimination by store owners in the neighborhood of Bedford-Stuyvesant challenged as well their disrespectful behavior toward black customers. In 1933 they collected a large number of signatures accusing the manager of the local Bohack Supermarket of sexual harassment. When top management refused to fire him, they retaliated with a boycott.[75] In Pittsburgh, the Housewives' Cooperative League made breaking down Jim Crowism a top priority alongside supporting black business, pressuring white business to employ blacks, and facilitating cooperative buying. Business concerns that refused service to blacks were to be denounced on lists distributed "to every Negro home in the city."[76] These consumer actions lend good support to historian Elsa Barkley Brown's notion that politicized African-American women often exhibited a "womanist" consciousness that seamlessly interwove their gender and racial identities.[77] Black female consumer activists of the 1930s were neither more black nor more female in their loyalties; they blended both. Feminist hopes for securing good salesclerk jobs for women and demonstrating female political solidarity were inseparable from the effort to improve working and living conditions for the race through "directed spending."

When a young Ella Baker addressed the first national conference of the YNCL in 1931 on the topic "What Consumers' Co-operation Means to Negro Women," she anticipated that African Americans' new assertiveness as consumers during the 1930s would require a special commitment from black women.[78] Consumer activism among African Americans was less of an exclusively female activity than among whites, but black women's organizational skills and experience certainly ensured its success, propelling it more into the mainstream of politics in African-American communities than in white ones.

African-American grassroots consumer activism in the 1930s differed from the predominantly white consumer movement in significant ways. Whereas white, usually female, activists sought to protect consumers' rights to everything from lower prices to reliable product information to protection from hazardous goods, blacks used consumer power primarily as a means to secure their rights as producers. Blacks, moreover, aimed less at representing some general public interest and winning the federal government's support for their demands than at improving concrete economic conditions in northern black communities. Long used to solving problems on their own, African Americans brought tremendous economic pressure to bear on local white capitalists, while favoring black businesses wherever possible, turning familiar strategies of economic self-help and self-sufficiency into a new kind of black mass politics during the thirties. It was a mass politics, furthermore, aimed at taking advantage of the de facto racial segregation of urban communities. Although carried out as protests against white exploitation, "Don't Shop Where You Can't Work" and black capitalism and cooperativism nonetheless depended on residential segregation. The concentration of black consumers in specific neighborhoods was required to make their market pressure felt.

At the same time, black consumer activism shared common ground with other grassroots consumer movements. Despite a lack of attention to shaping federal policy, grassroots consumer campaigners felt part of national efforts to maximize their spending power. "Don't Buy," the CMA, and the Housewives' Leagues were all local efforts with strong national connections. At a planning meeting for a Pittsburgh Housewives' Cooperative League in 1937, for example, participants referred frequently to the experiences of leagues elsewhere, such as St. Louis's success getting black milkmen, Cleveland's support for black-owned gasoline stations, and Los Angeles's lobbying for General Electric and five-and-ten-cent stores in the black district.[79] Moreover, blacks' initial concern with jobs, much like female consumer activists' original protests over meat prices, broadened to include other kinds of consumer discontents, such as indignities suffered from racist white clerks, discrimination in other public places, and unfair rent and utility rates. But in the case of both blacks and women consumer rebels, discontents rarely involved challenging the legitimacy of capitalism. Except for ideologically committed cooperators and the relatively small, though influential coterie of Communist Party members active in consumer organizing, participants simply sought a fairer shake.

Most significantly, by mobilizing as consumers, African Americans participated in a broader political culture of dissent where "the consumer" became viewed as a legitimate and effective agent of protest, particularly for women and blacks who were marginalized from the mainstream of politics and the labor movement. In contrast to electoral and producer power, the strength of consumer power lay not so much with permanent organizations as with the potential for mobilizing mass action by individual consumers. Although depression-era blacks did not link the economic rights of the consumer to the political rights of the citizen nearly as much as women consumer activists did or as they would a few years later in the context of World War II, the seeds were planted: a slogan in the Chicago buying campaign was "Use your buying power as you use your ballot," while the Harlem group that led the boycott of Blumstein's called itself the Citizens' League for Fair Play and appealed for the support of the "self-respecting citizens of Harlem."[80] Demanding that the state defend citizen consumers' rights in the economic and political spheres was an obvious next step that the heightened expectations of wartime would encourage.

THE PURCHASER CONSUMER ALTERNATIVE

Despite many policymakers' and ordinary Americans' embrace of the ideal of the citizen consumer over the course of the 1930s, progress toward making it a reality was mixed, with ideological commitment often outpacing concrete achievement. The other way that the New Deal gave new importance to consumers—by encouraging purchaser consumer behavior as the key to economic recovery—gradually emerged as an alternative vision of consumer power. The conviction grew that consumers held the present and future health of the American capitalist economy in their hands, and that what mattered most was their aggregate purchasing power, not their right to be protected in the marketplace or to be heard in government chambers.

Enhancing consumer purchasing power was long a goal of New Deal recovery programs beginning with the NRA and AAA, and it similarly informed the institutionalization of collective bargaining through the National Labor Relations Act (NLRA) and the creation of social security, both in 1935. Unionized workers in secure jobs, it was argued, would use their greater earnings to boost consumption, while Americans guaranteed a state-funded retirement provision would have more to spend both as earners and retirees.[81] But the authority of classical economics, with its primacy of the producer, was hard to displace. Not until government policymakers grew to accept Keynesian economic theory, particularly after the economic nosedive brought on by the "Roosevelt depression of 1937–38," did they systematically begin to experiment with pump priming, in rejection of Say's Law of Markets holding that supply and demand were always naturally in balance. Beginning with Roosevelt's first cautious request in 1938 for an emergency appropriation for economic stimulus, government spending began to aim at expanding mass consumption to restabilize the American economy.[82]

The Keynesian paradigm was most thoroughly articulated in John Maynard Keynes's *The General Theory of Employment, Interest, and Money* of 1936, although it was popular in some reform circles before then.[83] (Harvard economics professor Galbraith recalls that while in 1936, the embrace of Say's law was "a litmus by which the reputable economist was separated from the crackpot," by the 1936–37 academic year, with shocking speed, "Keynes had reached Harvard with tidal force," polarizing younger and older economists in its wake.)[84] Keynesianism also became widely accepted by government economists by the late 1930s, although many New Dealers, including the President himself, remained reluctant for the nation to spend beyond its means. Keynesianism shared the New Deal's initial conviction that underconsumption was the root cause of the depression and that increased purchasing power was the key to recovery. What differed, however, was that under Keynes's influence economists began to argue that private investment and self-regulating markets alone could not remediate a stagnant "mature" economy like America's. Rather, the government would have to play a major role in fueling aggregate demand—through such strategies as jobs programs, public works, or progressive tax policies—and thereby raise the level of production and employment. Whereas proponents of classical economics, including FDR in his first term, had worried about balancing the budget, Keynesians argued that deficit spending by government was often necessary to fuel sufficient consumer demand and did not endanger the overall health of the economy. With the Keynesian revolution, then, consumers were becoming responsible for higher productivity and full employment, whereas a decade earlier that role had uncontestedly belonged to producers.

The purchaser consumer paradigm gradually permeated the thinking of economic planners in the government, key corporate managers seeking new customers for their products, and consumers themselves. Ernest Erber, a regional planner, reminded a younger colleague years later, "The prosperity of this nation is built upon spending, not saving. You might be too young to recall the campaign waged by Chambers of Commerce against money hoarding during the 30's. During those grim days, the man who spent freely was extolled as a national hero and the one who saved his money as a public enemy."[85] Americans of all ranks began to respond to this exhortation to buy. Detroit autoworker Gerald Corkum told a *Fortune* magazine reporter in the mid-1930s, for example, that instead of saving, he put any extra cash into buying things on installment, first a radio, then an electric refrigerator and washing machine, all of which gave his money "real" value and his family a superior quality of life. By the late 1930s he might very well have added that his purchases also benefited the nation's economy, keeping workingmen like himself in jobs.[86]

As New Dealers embraced a Keynesian policy of boosting demand in the late 1930s, they justified it as nurturing some of the same political goals that proponents of the citizen consumer ideal sought: the enhancement of American democracy and equality. Keynes and his followers argued that the survival of democracy in the world as an alternative to revolution (communism) and reaction (fascism) rested on America's success in reviving capitalism. Within the United States, moreover, Keynesianism was thought to encourage greater economic egalitarianism because dynamic consumer demand depended on a wide distribution of purchasing power. Concentration of wealth in a few hands, in contrast, led to excessive saving and only minimal spending. Fueling "mass consumption"—enhancing the ability of the mass of

Americans to purchase goods—promised not only a route to economic recovery, but also a more democratic and egalitarian America for all its citizens. As Franklin Roosevelt accepted the renomination for the presidency in Philadelphia in June 1936, he assured Americans, "Today we stand committed to the proposition that freedom is no half-and-half affair. If the average citizen is guaranteed equal opportunity in the polling place, he must have equal opportunity in the market place."[87] Whereas at the time, FDR's linkage of consumers to voters likely referred to protecting their rights as citizen consumers to fair treatment in mass consumer markets, subsequently "equal opportunity" would come to mean equal access to the fruits of those markets as well.

In 1941, on the cusp of World War II, Roosevelt made another promise to the American public, that his policies were designed to secure their "Four Freedoms," including "freedom from want" and the "enjoyment of the fruits of scientific progress in a wider and constantly rising standard of living." Two years later, the mass circulation magazine *Saturday Evening Post* would immortalize Roosevelt's Four Freedoms in illustrations by Norman Rockwell. Conveying a common understanding of FDR's message, Rockwell depicted "freedom from want" not as a worker with a job, nor as government beneficence protecting the hungry and homeless, but rather as a celebration of the plenitude that American families reaped through their participation in a mass consumer economy. Rockwell's Americans free from want were members of a large extended family gathered around an overabundant, elegantly set Thanksgiving table in their own private home.[88] Despite an enormous mobilization on behalf of the citizen consumer ideal in liberal government circles and in communities throughout the country during the 1930s, the less politically threatening conception of the consumer—as a purchaser consumer buying his or her way to "freedom from want"—held growing appeal to those wielding economic and political power in American society.

THE BUSINESS VIEW OF CONSUMERS

By the end of the 1930s, the importance of the consumer in public policy and in civic life was indisputable. Perhaps the best testament to the consumer's newfound authority came from American business owners, who increasingly found themselves in the position of battling citizen consumers and trying to figure out how best to take advantage of the growing attention to purchaser consumers. Most businessmen worried that too Keynesian a national economic policy would intrude on the prerogatives of the private sector and destabilize the economy through budget deficits. And

Roosevelt's New Deal, with its pandering to the "common man," had certainly proved no friend to American business. Business leaders, particularly manufacturers, much preferred to think of consumers as purchasers creating demand for their products than as citizen consumers impinging on corporate autonomy by securing protections in the marketplace and leverage in the government.

Business leaders advised one another on how to cope with the new, powerful threat of entitled consumers—for that is indeed how most of them saw it. As early as 1935, on the tail of the meat strikes, *Babson's Reports,* a business letter, warned its subscribers, "We say, and earnestly, that merchants who laugh off these consumers' crusades are sitting on dynamite. In the same spot are sitting our producers, bankers and investors. Merchants would get the shock first, but in the end it would swing to every business and financial interest in the nation." By 1939 there was no denying the challenge mounted by newly assertive consumers. *Business Week* reported to its readers that "the consumer movement has spread like wildfire across the country in the past decade and it's gaining in force and vigor every day." The next year *Advertising Age* elaborated, "It embraces every shade of political and social belief, from deepest red to purest white; it takes in every stratum of economic life, from the richest to the poorest, but its principal roots lie in the middle classes. . . . It is . . . real and important and influential." From a "very tiny blot on the horizon," it has grown to "THE major problem facing business—and particularly advertising—as they enter the fifth decade of the twentieth century."[89]

It particularly unsettled business that women, political neophytes who had once been among their most trusted customers, should be asserting themselves so militantly as consumers. When *Nation's Business* complained that "a great Consumer Movement is now tramping out the vintage in the American economic scene. Its battle hymns are heard in every forum," it expressed most alarm at forums identified as traditionally female: women's clubs that "have put aside Oriental Travel and the poetry of Edna St. Vincent Millay" for speakers on consumer education, and women's magazines where readers "want fewer recipes for summer salads and more information on consumer goods specifications or social consciousness." Moreover, the editors seemed particularly resentful that women were moving from managing their family economies to overseeing the national economy. "Woman, the guardian of the national purse strings" evoked disdain. *Nation's Business* and like-minded publications recognized that women, as empowered consumers, were gaining a new role representing the public interest, and they didn't like it.[90]

Business leaders came up with various strategies to battle the consumer threat. Where they could, when they needed to, they fought consumer groups

This street hawker sold copies of the *Consumers Bureau Guide* in the midst of the heavy foot traffic at the corner of Madison Avenue and Forty-second Street in midtown Manhattan. His presence suggests how ubiquitous attention to protecting the rights of consumers had become by 1939. Dorothea Lange. (Courtesy of Library of Congress)

seeking product standardization or stricter food and drug legislation. They also responded with consumer committees of their own to manage demanding customers, through cooperation at some moments and co-optation at others: for example, the American Standards Association established a Committee on Ultimate Consumers' Goods in 1934, the National Consumer-Retailer Council was formed in 1937, the National Association of Better Business Bureaus launched its Business Consumer Relations Conference in 1939, and about the same time the American Association of Advertising Agencies sponsored the Committee on Consumer Relations in Advertising. At times, even the Consumers' National Federation was hard-pressed to distinguish between bona fide consumer organizations and ones created as part of business's co-optive strategies, bearing as they did deceptive names like the Consumers' Foundation, the Foundation for Consumer Education in the Pacific, and the National Consumers' Tax Commission.

While the existence of these organizations reveal that business felt pressure from the consumer movement, they hardly represent evidence of any real collaboration at work. Consumer representatives were often handpicked to avoid the most militant activists, and few of these committees had real authority within the business associations that created them. Robert Lynd had only contempt for the "plans under way to organize the women of the country as consumers who can be marshaled conveniently as occasion arises as a 'front' behind which trade associations can fight for what they want."[91]

Business also remained suspicious of government's role as protector of citizen consumers. A postwar economics text put matter-of-factly, with an implication of disapproval, what many businessmen were feeling by the end of the 1930s: "With the depression and subsequently there has come the growth of a belief that the government has a final responsibility in making the economic system operate to the satisfaction of its citizens. The belief seems to be prevalent that if the economic system does not operate well through businessmen, then the government must step in and provide the means of satisfactory operation."[92]

There was one more way that some business organizations attacked the maturing consumer movement by the late 1930s, and it confirms how threatened they felt by its rise. Through trade publications of their own and in collaboration with the anti-communist witch-hunts of Congressman Martin Dies's House Un-American Activities Committee, they set out to discredit the consumer movement as "red." In this crusade businessmen ironically were assisted by the stalwarts of Consumers' Research—Frederick J. Schlink, his wife, M. C. Phillips, and J. B. Matthews—who after the split with the pro-labor Consumers Union did everything imaginable to red-bait progressive consumer organizations, including publishing articles like "Half-way to Communism with the League of Women Shoppers" and providing distorted evidence to Dies himself in 1939.[93] Business also undertook its own anti-communist campaigns. A January 1938 issue of *Nation's Business* "exposed" the left-wing sympathies of the League of Women Shoppers, declaring, "The pinks have really crashed the parlor at last!"

An organization calling itself the Pacific Advertising Clubs Association was founded in 1940 explicitly to fight the "threat to business" by consumer organizations who are "wholly subversive, financed by foreign money or by

misguided Americans who would junk our American Institutions for the com-
munistic system." Because "advertising is the voice of business," Communists
had targeted it as the way to make buyers distrustful of business. "Rampant for
several years, their work has already destroyed consumer confidence in many
directions." A 1941 report commissioned by the Association of National
Advertisers, *The Movement for Standardization and Grading of Consumer
Goods,* argued that regulation of price and quality by government officials was
for Communists "a step in the direction of 'production for use,' which is their
favorite slogan." "Government ownership and operation of all business enterprises" would inevitably follow.[94] These are but a few examples of how powerful voices in the business world hoped they could undermine the consumer
interest by tainting it red. Communists and fellow travelers surely were
sprinkled throughout progressive consumer organizations like the League of
Women Shoppers and Consumers Union, but the vast majority of citizen consumers aimed to reform American capitalism and democracy, not to overthrow them.

Rather than create phony consumer committees or red-bait real consumer organizations, companies increasingly recognized the power of consumers in another way. For corporations like Chevrolet, whose film *From
Dawn to Sunset* was discussed at the beginning of this chapter, the best alternative to the consumer movement was to give consumers "the pleasure of buying" while tapping "the purchasing power of pay packets" to fuel "a prosperity
greater than history has ever known." With that last line, Chevrolet hinted at
what would become a new orthodoxy in the postwar era: that purchasing
power might do more than stabilize a stagnant economy in depression. It
could create historic levels of economic growth.[95]

A political battle over a pavilion at the New York World's Fair of 1939
captured the tension that sharpened at the end of the decade over the best way
to incorporate consumers into the New Deal order. In this microcosm of the
fair, citizen consumer and purchaser consumer conceptions battled for dominance. By intention, the World's Fair was a collaboration between business and
government to attract capitalist and consumer dollars to New York to help the
city recover from the depression. Under the motto "Building the World of
Tomorrow," the fair promoted a vision of the future where American industry,
particularly major exhibitors such as General Electric, General Motors, Westinghouse, and Radio Corporation of America, would create prosperity and
material comfort for the consuming masses. In recognition of the importance
of consumers in this new order, plans were made for a "Consumers Building"
to be the focal exhibit of the Production and Distribution Zone of the fair.
About two dozen leaders of the consumer movement were invited to serve on

a hundred-member Advisory Committee on Consumer Interests to oversee the building, intended to have exhibits on product testing, factual advertising, and proper methods of merchandising. Two months before the fair was scheduled to open, however, the consumer activists resigned en masse, charging that they had been duped into lending their names to a project that promoted consumer exploitation rather than consumer welfare.

Indeed, the exhibits that opened in the Consumers Building by industrial designer Egmond Arens offered an upbeat message that things were getting better for consumers all the time. A large concave movie screen showed how ordinary activities, such as powdering a woman's nose or ordering food at a shop, depended upon a multitude of far-flung businesses, and argued that everyday consumption behavior by millions of people kept American mass production viable. In another exhibit, the Dark Ages of Scarcity were contrasted with the New Age of Abundance. Boxes represented how families of four different income levels coped with eight categories of living costs. After lamenting that a third of the nation's families still earned less than the subsistence level, the exhibit concluded with a quintessential purchaser consumer endorsement: "As mass production depends upon mass purchasing power, we cannot hope to build lasting prosperity under such conditions of inadequate purchasing power." But, it continued, with "the techniques and the power to produce abundance" within our grasp, soon all Americans should be able to live "the good life." Smaller exhibits sponsored by individual manufacturers filled out the hall, such as a glass column in which water-resistant Kem's Playing Cards got drenched and survived. Consumers Union was offered a spot, but only if it refrained from endorsing any particular brand names in its exhibit or literature. What mattered to the exhibit's planners was only that consumers purchase, not which brand they chose.

When the fair reopened in 1940 to try to recoup the financial losses of 1939, even that much pandering to consumer protection was abandoned. The Consumers Building metamorphosed over the winter into the uncontroversial "World of Fashion." If there had ever been any doubt, in this newly renovated world of tomorrow the ideal of the purchaser consumer, as aggregate buying power supporting the latest fashions, had beat out the citizen consumer, concerned with protecting the rights of individual consumers in the capitalist marketplace and the democratic polity.[96] In the real world of tomorrow, the conflict over the fate of the consumer interest would take longer to play out. The needs of the home front would favor the citizen consumer impulse during wartime, but as postwar recovery loomed, this conflict from the 1930s would return to center stage, and its resolution would shape the character of postwar America.

CHAPTER 2

War: Citizen Consumers Do Battle on the Home Front

The outbreak of World War II complicated the triangular relationship that had evolved by the late 1930s between consumers, the government, and business. Policymakers in Washington tread very carefully during the half decade of world war, balancing on the one hand consumer advocates who argued that wartime made it more important than ever that government view consumers as representing the public interest and in need of protection from the excesses of private enterprise, and on the other hand a business world whose major interest in consumers was as purchasers capable of kindling recovery. Conflicting ideals of citizen consumers and purchaser consumers would trouble everyone on the home front, from government officials on down to individuals caught between patriotically cooperating with wartime restrictions and avoiding them to indulge long pent-up consumer desires. As this tension played out from the national policy stage to the family circle, women became even more pivotal than they had been in the 1930s when they began to agitate on behalf of "the consumer interest." Suddenly, women's ordinary responsibilities as chief household purchasers put them in the eye of the storm of war: their recycling of metals made ammunition plentiful, their limited consumption of sugar and shoes fed and dressed the army, their adherence to tight restrictions on automobile tires and gasoline kept American tanks advancing across Europe. Their involvement in government consumer campaigns to "Produce & Conserve, Share & Play Square," moreover, gave them newfound political influence in their communities and in the nation. Although Rosie the Riveter and Winnie the WAC (Women's Army Corps) may have dominated the official record of women's contribution to the Second World War, many more millions of women achieved new civic authority through their power as consumers.[1]

The realm of consumption would become so pivotal to the success of the war effort that to an even greater extent than in the 1930s it would provide a crucial arena in which African Americans would experience—and contest—the discrimination they met in their efforts to participate fully in American life. And in the end, consumers would prove as crucial to defining the nature of America at peace as they had America at war. As V-E and V-J Days finally became reality in 1945, the exigencies of war that had kept the tension between citizen consumer and purchaser consumer under control no longer held sway. An intense struggle raged over the nature of the postwar order, in particular the relationship of consumers, business, and government within it.

CITIZEN CONSUMERS VERSUS PURCHASER CONSUMERS ON THE HOME FRONT

The outbreak of war in Europe at first was just the Keynesian jump start that a still economically depressed America desperately needed. U.S. government commitment to becoming the "arsenal of democracy" translated concretely into the expenditure of billions of dollars for armaments; after the defeat of France in June 1940, Congress appropriated at one stroke more than the nation had spent in total on World War I. With relief, Americans celebrated restaffed factories and restuffed wallets for the first time in years. Those favorable conditions in turn produced others: booming demand for consumer products, record-breaking retail sales, and the creation of even more jobs to manufacture and to sell long coveted goods. Production of refrigerators increased 164 percent in the first six months of 1941 over the average for 1935–39; automobiles were up 55 percent and other consumer durables followed suit. Department store profits reached a new peak during 1941, with the bombing of Pearl Harbor casting only a small shadow over Christmas gift-buying that December.[2]

This Keynesian manna of public spending feeding consumer demand and in turn reviving production might have carried America into full economic recovery had there not been a war to fight. But producing for war meant favoring military needs over civilian ones, directing scarce materials to armaments not appliances, and worrying that the resulting consumer shortages would encourage rampant inflation, with all of its destructive, spiraling

With production for the European war creating jobs and putting extra money in consumers' pockets for the first time in years, Americans enthusiastically began to buy goods like the electric ranges and refrigerators displayed in this appliance store showroom of 1941. American entry into the war would end the buying spree, however, as manufacturers retooled to make armaments instead of appliances. John Deusing. (Courtesy of Carpenter Center Photography Collection, Harvard University)

effects. By the Japanese attack on Pearl Harbor in late 1941, inflation was more than a worry. Wholesale food prices had shot up 29 percent in the first two years of European war, with farm products up 43 percent. Textile prices had risen 29 percent. As America entered the war, the Roosevelt administration recognized that a stronger government hand regulating the wartime economy was critical to military victory, even if many prospering businesses objected.[3]

The story of federal management of the consumer economy during World War II was one of growing government intervention in the private transactions between customers and retailers. At first, beginning in May 1940, price stabilization and consumer protection were assigned to separate divisions of the National Defense Advisory Commission, under the administration of Leon Henderson and Harriet Elliott, respectively. Elliott's Consumer Office, charged with identifying and protecting the needs of civilian consumers as the nation mobilized its defenses, had no equivalent in World War I; it was a measure of how central the "concept of consumer" had become over the last twenty years, Elliott claimed, that one of the six members of President Roosevelt's first National Defense Advisory Commission "must represent his interests." But advisory meant just that. Elliott had no authority to prevent skyrocketing prices, product shortages, or quality deterioration, only a mandate to somehow encourage consumers, manufacturers, wholesalers, and retailers to solve problems voluntarily, by exercising what she called their "economic citizenship." Elliott struggled valiantly for a year and a half, and then quit in frustration.[4]

President Roosevelt had already acknowledged the need for more decisive action by establishing the Office of Price Administration and Civilian Supply in May 1941 (later simply OPA, under the War Production Board), with Henderson in charge, and had moved Elliott's Consumer Office into it, but it wasn't until after the attack on Pearl Harbor that the Emergency Price Control Act of January 1942 put teeth into the OPA. Rationing went into effect, first of rubber, automobiles, and sugar, and gradually over time of gasoline, fuel oil, coffee, shoes, processed foods, meat, butter, rayon hose, milk, soap, and many other scarce commodities. By May 1942 the OPA issued the General Maximum Price Regulation—what became known as "General Max"—requiring merchants to set ceiling prices for goods at the highest price they had charged during March and granting the OPA specific powers of enforcement. By the war's end, nearly six thousand commodities—90 percent of goods sold—would come under price control administered by what had become the largest of the civilian war agencies. Maximum rentals were likewise set in "selected defense areas" covering territory where a majority of Americans lived. The Emergency Price Control Act also granted the OPA authority to stabilize wages, and in July, services such as laundry and shoe repair were slated to be frozen as well. A year of confusion and dislocation followed, necessitating yet stronger legislation in October 1942. Finally, by mid-1943, American consumers for the most part had adjusted to making market transactions with the government looking over their shoulders as it never had before. They coped surprisingly well with limited goods, price ceilings, rationing and recycling of scarce products, and perhaps most annoying, constant revisions in the price control system, from ration certificates and coupons to "point" ration stamps to supplemental ration tokens.[5]

But even as the necessity for price controls became irrefutable, many manufacturers, retailers, and advertisers gave them only grudging support. They were quick to complain that they cut disastrously into profits and favored some producers and distributors over others. At bottom, the pro-consumer orientation of the OPA angered these business interests. One retail trade journal railed that the consumer movement was using the war emergency "as the wedge for the introduction of long-advocated and so-called reforms for consumer welfare"; the advertising industry's annual convention in 1941 lambasted nearly every top-ranking Consumer Division official, from Elliott on down, by including them on its "roll call of arch enemies." The next year OPA director and mastermind Leon Henderson, one of the "unsung heroes of World War II" according to his assistant, economist John Kenneth Galbraith, and "the toughest bastard in town," according to Roosevelt, was forced out of his job by sniping congressmen, many of them doing business's bidding, who viewed the OPA as "Henderson's Gestapo." But despite resistance to mandatory price controls and other marketplace regulations by OPA opponents who argued that voluntary ones had proved just fine during World War I, in general the controls worked, mostly because American consumers supported them as a necessity in mobilizing for war. In contrast to an inflation rate of 62 percent in World War I, prices rose less than 8 percent during the last two years of World War II, and crucial military materiel found its way to the front.[6]

The successful mobilization of the consumer home front owed a great deal to a later OPA chief, Chester Bowles, whose advertising background prepared him well to reach American consumers' hearts even while depriving their stomachs.[7] Both to build public support and to work around the skimpy enforcement budget a skeptical, business-influenced Congress had allocated, Bowles turned to the free labor of community-entrenched volunteers to monitor OPA regulations. With this simple idea, Bowles mobilized civil society at an unprecedented scale to carry out Washington's directives. From the smallest of towns to the largest of cities, citizen volunteers served on War Price and Rationing Boards (about 5500 "Little OPAs" operated nationwide) and Consumer Interest Committees of state and local Defense Councils, organized consumer centers in their neighborhoods (135 operated in New York City alone), handed out ration books at local schools, and investigated reported violations. The OPA calculated that three out of four persons working for the agency were volunteers, more than 100,000 serving as board members and another 88,000 as assistants. At critical moments, such as when war ration books had to be issued, the OPA estimated that "more than three million gave their services."[8] Within a month of taking over as chief in November

1943, Bowles also established a Consumer Advisory Committee of the OPA, inviting twenty-six consumer leaders to play an influential if advisory role. On the activists' part, they seized the opportunity to complete their prewar project and steered the OPA as much as possible toward pro-consumer policies. The following June, at his advisory committee's recommendation, Bowles created the Office of Consumer Relations Advisor within the OPA administrative structure and appointed committee member Dr. Esther Cole Franklin to the job.[9]

Bowles's strategy of aligning the OPA with veterans of the depression-era consumer movement at the top and implanting it in the rich soil of community voluntarism at the grass roots mobilized citizen consumers on the home front. OPA Consumer Advisory Committee member Caroline Ware—a well-credentialed consumer activist since the 1930s in her own right as well as through her husband, New Deal economist Gardiner Means—claimed in her book, *The Consumer Goes to War: A Guide to Victory on the Home Front* (1942), that not only did the war require "a strong consumer front," but "we, the privates of the civilian army back home" were proving ourselves in greater numbers than ever before to be "consumers as citizens." She claimed that until the launching of the defense program, consumer interest and organization had attracted mostly middle- and upper-income consumers. But with the war, she said, "consumer consciousness has spread rapidly. Organizations of predominantly low-income consumers, such as neighborhood houses, labor unions, Negro organizations, as well as church and civic groups, have developed consumer programs." She went on to recount cases of spontaneous consumer organization, such as in Syracuse, New York, where one woman's small ad in local newspapers galvanized several thousand women within a few short weeks to establish the Organized Housewives of Syracuse committed to combating waste and inflation on the home front. Speaking in the language of the consumer movement of the thirties, she concluded, "Today, the public interest may well be identified with the interest of people as consumers."[10]

In Syracuse, as across the nation, Americans learned that one of the chief ways to support the war on the home front was as responsible consumers. New rituals of patriotic citizenship evolved—obeying OPA price, rent, and rationing regulations and reporting violators; participating in recycling, scrap, and waste fat drives; planting Victory Gardens and "putting up" the harvest—all enforced through pacts of allegiance such as "The Consumer's Pledge for Total Defense" and the "Ten Commandments for Consumers."[11] Suddenly tasks that had been viewed as private and domestic were brought into the civic arena and granted new political importance. Many shared the patriotic sentiments of the citizen who, soon after price controls went into effect, wrote a

"Consumer's Pledge Song" to be sung to the tune of the "Battle Hymn of the Republic":[12]

> *There's a simple way in which to serve the country you love best,*
> *Just read and listen to the U.S. Government's request;*
> *By taking the Consumer's Pledge—the best way to invest, in Peace*
> *   and Victory.*

> CHORUS
> *"I will be a wise consumer,*
> *Gladly do so with good humor,*
> *That's the way to win the sooner*
> *To Peace and Victory!"*

> *You can eat fresh fruits and vegetables, and thus save tons of tin,*
> *Do not be extravagant and waste, for wasting is a sin,*
> *And budget your allowances for food so we can win, the Peace and*
> *   Victory.*

> REPEAT CHORUS

> *Take the best care of your wearables, and mend them when they*
> *   tear,*
> *You can swap the children's outgrown things for things that they*
> *   can wear,*
> *You can be your own repairman when there's something to repair,*
> *   for Peace and Victory.*

For Americans new to consumer activism, becoming a good citizen consumer required some reorientation in thinking. "The principle of share and share alike is contrary to many of our traditional ways of thinking, our urge to get ahead in this world's goods, to outsmart the other fellow," an announcer on the WNYC radio program *Mrs. Consumer Speaking* acknowledged.[13] But the case for market regulation was so powerful, and the argument for fairness so convincing, that Americans for the most part fell in line. When President Roosevelt justified the rationing of all essential scarce commodities "so that they may be distributed fairly among consumers and not merely in accordance with financial ability to pay high prices for them," he seemed to be invoking a more admirable set of traditional American values: commitment to democracy and equity.[14] Gallup polls consistently documented Americans' support for OPA market regulations in the 80 and 90 percent range. The OPA's Consumer Advisory Committee concluded that "rationing in general is one of the best understood and most popular civilian programs."[15] The remarkable redistribution of income taking place due to wartime employment and market regulation, moreover, only reinforced the sense that the war emergency was promoting the long-held ideal of greater equality in America. Between 1941 and 1944 family income rose by over 24 percent in constant dollars, with the lowest fifth gaining three times more than the highest fifth, essentially doubling the size of the middle class. Even *Business Week* labeled the war a "great leveler."[16]

But even as committed and sacrificing citizen consumers seemed to be ruling the homefront roost, their nemesis, profligate purchaser consumers—ruled only by the almighty dollar—were never completely forgotten. Not everyone, at every moment, abided by price controls and rationing regulations. Some people paid over-ceiling prices. Others made secret arrangements with their grocers to buy scarce goods like sugar and meat. Black markets, often as simple as a local butcher putting a little extra beef aside for a regular customer, flourished. Consumers sometimes hoarded goods, like clothing, that they feared stores would quickly run out of. Especially by the end of the war, exhausted consumers could not always be trusted to do the right thing.[17] Indeed, Americans were not so much divided between civic-minded "good" consumers and self-interested "bad" consumers; rather, all wrestled with conflicting pressures within themselves, striking their own shifting balances between citizen and purchaser.

There were occasions, too, when a still politically influential purchaser interest aggressively threatened the citizen interest. When consumer activists in the OPA tried to implement their longstanding goal of quality standards in 1943—by grading canned goods A, B, and C—to facilitate value comparisons and protect consumers against the inevitable deterioration of goods under price ceilings, business, led by the National Canners' Association, balked, denouncing this "undercover campaign" as a "war" against brand names "in which our system of private enterprise is at stake." The outcry prompted Congress explicitly to prohibit the OPA from requiring any grade labeling from manufacturers, clipping the agency's reformist wings in a deep affront to Bowles.[18]

The survival of prosperity amid sacrifice more than anything else kept the purchaser consumer alternative alive. Even when observant of salvaging, rationing, and other market regulations, Americans managed to live better during the war than they had during the Great Depression. In 1944 the Department of Labor calculated that the average factory worker's weekly pay had increased 80 percent over 1939, while living costs were only 24 percent higher, providing a good deal more discretionary income (and deepening anxiety over inflation). Although Americans experienced conspicuous deprivations, their spending on nondurable goods—meals in restaurants, movie-going and other entertainment, clothing, drugs, liquor, flowers, and the like—climbed during the war years. Even meat consumption grew, particularly for the poorest third of the population, despite all the strict controls on its distribution. "Customers, who have never enjoyed the luxury of club steaks, are now requesting them in five-pound cuts for roasts," the manager of the Great Eastern supermarket chain worried. "Never in the history of human conflict has there been so much talk of sacrifice and so little sacrifice," OPA staffer Galbraith remarked cynically.[19]

This spreading affluence in spite of extensive market controls fed business leaders' and government officials' optimism that "a peacetime economy of abundance" would follow the war, as the president of the Studebaker Automobile Company assured a National Association of Manufacturers meeting in 1944. The same year, the research director of the magazine publishing giant Macfadden stressed to advertisers just how critical the newly prospering working class was to a postwar prosperity built around mass consumption: "As every manufacturer knows . . . there can be no high levels of production and employment unless the products of industry are bought by the workers," with their growing share of national income and stash of wartime savings. As the war wound down, the purchaser consumer armature of mass buying, erected in the 1930s to stabilize a depression economy, provided a support structure for a more expansionist postwar economy.[20]

To ensure the speedy arrival of this postwar utopia of abundance, patriotic citizen consumers were urged to save today (preferably through war bonds) so that they might become purchaser consumers tomorrow. Although the impending danger of wartime inflation required strategies to curb consumer appetites—such as restricting purchases, discouraging installment and credit spending, promoting war bond buying, and reducing spendable incomes through a much expanded mass income tax—their fulfillment was postponed rather than abandoned. Visions of postwar material prosperity did double duty, then, restraining purchases—and thereby inflation—now, and encouraging them at war's end, helping, hopefully, to avoid dreaded postwar recession by revving back up the Keynesian engine of purchasing power. During wartime, anticipating future consumption became a part of how, according to historians Robert Westbrook and Mark Leff, Americans viewed the stakes of war: fighting to preserve an "American Way of Life" rather than some lofty political ideal.[21] Fantasies of new cars, new washers, new toasters—even if virtually unavailable with the curtailed production of wartime—took on

"Do the best you can with them—somebody jumped the gun on reconversion"

COLLIER'S   VIC HERMAN

Buyers and manufacturers eagerly awaited the mass production of consumer durables that would result from reconverting defense plants back to ordinary factories at war's end. Victor Herman for *Collier's* magazine. (Courtesy of Virginia N. Herman)

patriotic significance and motivated citizens to save. Surveys of civilian finances during the war consistently reported that savings accounts and war bond purchases were mushrooming. A study of war workers' spending habits in Cleveland, for example, indicated that as early as July 1942, workers were investing approximately 8 percent of their income in defense bonds and stamps, while savings accounts in banks near plants had increased 15 percent since the beginning of the year. By 1945 personal savings had reached an average of 21 percent of personal disposable income since 1941, compared to a mere 3 percent in the 1920s.[22]

While consumers accumulated savings for future purchases, business lost little time suggesting how they should be spent, "Lining Up After-the-War Buyers" as the *Wall Street Journal* succinctly put it in 1944.[23] "WHAT THIS WAR IS ALL ABOUT," explained a Royal typewriter ad, is the right to "once more walk into any store in the land and buy anything you want." Likewise, a public service ad placed by Macy's in the *New York Daily News* in September 1943 to promote the Third War Loan Drive said it all. Under the headline

It's a promise!

THAT little home sketched there in the sand is a symbol of faith and hope and courage. It's a promise, too. A promise of gloriously happy days to come . . . when Victory is won.

Victory Homes of tomorrow will make up in part at least for all the sacrifices of today . . . *and that's our promise!*

They will have *better living built in* . . . Electrical living with new comforts, new conveniences, new economies to make every day an adventure in happiness.

Plan for *your* Victory Home now . . . the one sure way is to buy War Bonds. Every Bond you buy is an investment in your future happiness and security. And . . . every dollar you put into Bonds helps bring our boys back sooner—*and safer.* Buy another Bond today.

General Electric Consumers Institute is dedicated to the service of America's homes. Research is now devoted to wartime home-making problems such as: Nutrition · Food Preparation · Food Preservation · Appliance Care · Appliance Repair · Laundering · Home Heating and Air Conditioning. Helpful booklets are available from your G-E Appliance Dealer, or write General Electric Consumers Institute, Dept. SEP 6-5, Appliance and Merchandise Department, Bridgeport, Conn.

GENERAL ⊕ ELECTRIC

Tune in on Frazier Hunt and the News every Tuesday, Thursday, Saturday evenings over C. B. S. On Sunday night listen to the "Hour of Charm" over N. B. C. See newspapers for time, station.

General Electric, convinced that its own postwar market would depend on the building and equip-ping of privately owned homes on a mass scale, ran advertisements in the popular press during World War II promoting the dream of home ownership for all. *Saturday Evening Post,* June 5, 1943. (Cour-tesy of General Electric)

"What We're Fighting For . . ." came a short paragraph with the expected orthodoxies—"defending Democracy," "battling for a better world," "struggling . . . for survival." But thereafter the ad was devoted to a long list "of little things" "we're also fighting for": "a steak for every frying pan," permission "to take a taxi to Brooklyn," "the right to have cuffs on our pants," "the return of those lively golf balls that'll go a mile," to name just a few.[24] As the war dragged on, the return to normalcy increasingly referred to a lifestyle that purchaser consumers would soon be able to buy. "After total war can come total living," a pamphlet published by Revere Copper and Brass promised consumers, shown gazing longingly over a futuristic landscape of new homes and cars. This "dream world of post-war products," as one advertising executive called it, was so prevalent and alluring that some manufacturers, advertisers, and designers worried that consumers were being led unrealistically to expect "industrial miracles" available for purchase when they cashed in their bonds at war's end.[25]

At the center of Americans' vision of postwar prosperity was the private home, fully equipped with consumer durables. By 1945 a decade of depression and half decade of war had left the country with an acute housing shortage.[26] Hence, it was not surprising that GIs bunking in close quarters and civilians doubled up with relatives would fantasize a peacetime prosperity built around more spacious and modern dwellings. But images in government publications, advertisements, and popular culture were even more specific: they overwhelmingly depicted "home" as a detached single-family house in a suburban setting. To some extent, traditional American symbolism of "home sweet home" was being invoked, but the message was more specifically geared to the times. Most influential was government and corporate commitment to new suburban home building as a pump primer for the postwar economy. Already during the war, home ownership had grown spectacularly, with an increase of 15 percent in owner-occupied dwellings, outpacing any previous comparable period on record. Defense housing programs, moreover, had given residential builders and contractors experience building projects of several hundred units; "the housebuilding industry [has] matured substantially," a Department of Labor study of 1945 concluded approvingly, making feasible big increases in the potential volume of postwar residential construction. Chester Bowles expressed less confidence in the building and real estate industry at war's end, but he, too, was adamant that "in the construction industry lies perhaps our greatest single opportunity, not only to correct our shocking lack of decent homes, but to increase the purchasing power of our people."[27]

Government war propaganda designed to boost homefront morale further reinforced the Americanness of the single-family home. For example, the Office of Civilian Defense's V-Home Award, a certificate designed for posting in windows as "a badge of honor for those families which have made themselves into a fighting unit on the homefront" (consuming responsibly, salvaging vital materials, buying war bonds and stamps regularly, and complying with air raid regulations), visually portrayed "home" as a suburban-style house. A Civil Defense brochure promoting the V-Home program appropriately featured "The Joseph C. Gardiner family of Bethesda, Md., a suburb of Washington" as role models.[28]

Home builders and related industries also promoted house construction through such strategies as "Post-War Home" exhibitions designed to whet the public's appetite and to convey the message that the housing crisis would best be solved through building private, not public housing. Exhibits featured large-scale models, floor plans, and posters like the one that read, "Millions of new homes needed after victory—Our American system—private enterprise—will provide them—making jobs for millions." Similarly, home-decorating magazines like *Better Homes and Gardens* prodded readers to "Buy Bonds Today for 'Your Home of Tomorrow,' " and treated them to house plans, decorating tips, and seductive advertisements plugging exciting new products. An ad for Eureka vacuum cleaners not only promised women better machines at war's end, but assured them that in "fighting for freedom and all that means to women everywhere, you're fighting for a little house of your own, and a husband to meet every night at the door."[29] If all that was not enough, other aspects of popular culture contributed to putting the suburban house at the heart of the imagined postwar landscape. A popular wartime song promised, "Goodbye Dear, I'll be back in a year, We'll buy that cottage right out of town." The GI who began his testimonial about "What I Am Fighting For" in the *Saturday Evening Post* had the same dream, only on a more ambitious scale: "I am fighting," he fantasized, "for that big house with the bright green roof and the big front lawn."[30]

What evidence exists suggests that like this GI, Americans did indeed buy into the promise of improving their postwar homes. A survey of the consumer requirements of some 4500 households released in June 1944 indicated greatest demand for washing machines, followed by electric irons, mechanical refrigerators, stoves, toasters, radios, vacuum cleaners, electric fans, and hot water heaters. Yet large numbers of families were willing to forgo the purchase of appliances like these in order to use savings to buy or build a home.[31] In another survey late in the war, this one of war bond holders, the 48 percent who had definite plans for purchases prioritized expenditures on home or farm above anything other than providing for their children. One woman confided in a letter to *Better Homes and Gardens,* "I can see our house going up, stamp by stamp, bond by bond, joist by joist."[32] By joining consumer desire with the obligations of citizenship in looking ahead to peacetime, the OPA and other defense agencies began to construct a political culture that bridged the gap between citizen consumers and purchaser consumers. Although the two impulses coexisted in tension during the war, and even within individuals— between conserving and consuming patriotically, on the one hand, and purchasing freely, on the other—industry and government planners increasingly seemed to suggest that successful postwar reconversion from a war to a peace economy should be built on their convergence. The good citizen who had the public interest at heart would restrain consumption now and indulge it later.

WOMEN WARRIORS

World War II enhanced the claim of women who had argued in the 1930s that their role as chief household consumer granted them civic authority as guardians of the common good. The war emergency, even more than the depression and the New Deal, called on women to define new, consumer-based terms of citizenship and to patrol public allegiance to them. The moral judgment of "good citizen" took on new, gender-specific meaning in wartime. Loyal male citizens were defined in productivist ways, "serving their country" by laboring in the military or, if not possible, in defense industries. Loyal female citizens were defined in consumerist ways, as keepers of the homefront fires through their own disciplined, patriotic market behavior as well as through the enforcement of high moral standards in others. Despite women's growing presence in the military—still minuscule—and in defense industries—26 percent of wives worked for pay during the war— they were hailed most consistently as the standard-bearers of homefront consumerist citizenship, to an extent they had only hoped for during the 1930s. Typical was the invocation on the OPA's "Anti-Inflation Shopping List," a form designed to help consumers compare price tags to ceiling prices: "As a SMART WOMAN and a GOOD CITIZEN."[33]

From the OPA's Consumer Advisory Committee down to the "Little OPAs" and Consumer Interest Committees in states and municipalities and even further down into individual households, women shaped and implemented policies that linked the viability of a nation at war to the responsible action of female citizen consumers. Posters and billboards with messages like "You Can Help Shorten This War—and Save American Lives—right in your kitchen!" and "Keep the Home Front Pledge" by "pay[ing] no more than top legal prices" and "accept[ing] no rationed goods without giving up ration points" (part of a massive "Food Fights for Freedom" campaign by the OPA

KEEP THE
HOME FRONT PLEDGE

Pay no more than Ceiling Prices
Pay your Points in full

The Office of Price Administration launched an extensive, nationwide "Home Front Pledge Campaign" in Fall 1943, with First Lady Eleanor Roosevelt and her housekeeper the first to sign on from the front door of the White House. Designed to make price control and rationing more effective, the campaign ultimately collected signatures from over twenty million Americans. On all the posters, stickers, and informational material that blanketed the nation, a white female consumer represented the patriotic citizen. (Courtesy of the National Archives)

that garnered the signatures of twenty million shoppers) clarified how women could best serve the Allied cause. Almost always a woman was the subject of the didactic image, and if not, the viewer's gaze was assumed to be female.[34] When one government food preparation pamphlet exhorted, "Lady, it's your war, win it!" it sought to make the kitchen a crucial theater of the military front. But veteran consumer activists were also waging a related struggle, their longstanding one to legitimize female citizen consumers as the embodiment of the public interest.[35]

The central importance of consumption to the smooth operation of the home front meant that women—perceived as the power behind purchasing—gained new political authority, first in Washington and then in states and localities. Although the injunction to do battle from their kitchens could be viewed, and may have been intended by some, to prescribe traditional roles for women, there is no doubt that women seized the opportunity to propel themselves into positions of influence in the civic arena. As the general director of the American Association of University Women, Dr. Kathryn McHale, scolded President Roosevelt when he omitted consumer representatives from the newly founded Economic Stabilization Board in the fall of 1942: "At no time have the citizens of this country [read women] been so conscious of their problems as consumers, so well organized, so well informed and articulate, and so ready to participate responsibly in developing sound public policies."[36]

Men may still have run major wartime agencies like the OPA, but women were much more visible politically than they had been in the heyday of the New Deal, when Eleanor Roosevelt and Frances Perkins were notable exceptions. The OPA's predecessor organization was headed by Harriet Elliott, and Bowles's twenty-six-member Consumer Advisory Committee was made up entirely of distinguished women long identified with the consumer cause, including Dr. Hazel Kyrk, professor of economics and home economics at the University of Chicago, as chairman; New York settlement house and consumer leader Helen Hall as vice chairman; and Dr. Caroline Ware, Vassar College professor, as executive committee head. Committee member Ruth Lamb Atkinson recalled that although some speculated that Bowles had set up this female advisory panel as "window dressing," "he soon found he had a bear by the tail. In time he came to have a good deal of respect for us."[37] Moreover, the Consumer Advisory Committee went out of its way to encourage the recruitment and appointment of women to other consumer panels and boards, and it often succeeded. When Bowles initiated consumer advisory committees in district offices of the OPA in 1944 to improve communication between OPA operations and local communities, he specified that members be drawn from the various women's organizations of the area.[38] Women who had been thorns in

Whenever a new ration program went into effect, hundreds of thousands of volunteers—mostly women, as shown in this scene from Madison, Wisconsin—helped register consumers for their new allotment. (Courtesy of Library of Congress)

the side of New Deal agencies or a Congress debating food and drug legislation were suddenly sitting next to the seat of power, if not in it.

Women's new authority was most evident on the state and local level, for here they served as key administrators, both volunteer and paid, of the vast new bureaucracy that operated the home front according to directives from Washington. These directives created an astounding number and elaborate structure of offices, committees, and programs, reaching from state capitals down to every municipality and from there to neighborhoods and even blocks. Given the drain of men into the war and the enormous demands of a fully mobilized home front, women occupied positions ranging from top paid officials to the rank and file of volunteer OPA price checkers and Office of Civilian Defense block captains.[39] As in previous wars, women in World War II continued to staff chapters of nongovernmental volunteer organizations, old ones like the American Red Cross and new ones like the American Women's Voluntary Services.[40] They also expanded their ongoing community organizing activities to encompass new wartime regulations such as rent control; tenant advocacy got a boost when government rent ceilings could be invoked.[41] Even women's mundane daily war work—such as buying and selling war bonds, turning in stockings for powder bags, and collecting everything from toothpaste tubes for scrap metal to bacon grease for ammunition—earned women official recognition. But what was most remarkable about the World War II home front was that the government's attention to regulating consumption converged with the prevailing conception, carried over from the 1930s, of women consumers as the legitimate representatives of the public interest to elevate women to a new, official level of civic authority.

A closer look at New Jersey, a state whose enormous industrial capacity and strategic location meant it mobilized extensively for war, reveals how women propelled their responsibilities as consumers to a new level of influence, what even the *Woman's Home Companion* magazine, steeped in traditional gender roles, called "the job of Economic Director of the Homefront . . . a man-sized job."[42] New Jersey's shipyards, petroleum refineries, and diverse manufacturing base stocked the military's warehouses with radios and radar, ships, munitions, uniforms, chemicals, food, airplane engines, and much more. Between June 1940 and June 1941 this state that ranked forty-sixth out of forty-eight states in geographical size received 9 percent of all prime war contracts, trailing only California and New York. By war's end, New Jersey would rank fifth in the nation in war contracts.[43] With industrial mobilization, moreover, came more than half a million new jobs and an influx of new populations to fill them, to work with the women who had heeded the New Jersey War Manpower Commission's appeal, "All Women Called! All Women Called!" Alongside the tons of materiel and thousands of defense workers moving through the state's train terminals and shipping piers were crowds of soldiers, making their way to and from training at Fort Dix and Fort Monmouth, or abroad to the theaters of war. In this highly mobilized environment, women, whether employed in defense or not, donated their time and skills in dozens of ways that women in wartime always had—sewing bandages, knitting hats, and running canteens for servicemen—but in some new ways as well.[44]

It was through their power in the realm of consumption that New Jersey women gained political authority on the home front, in many cases, full partnership with men. In the first war since women had gained full citizenship rights as voters, they played a more official role in the state's warfront apparatus than they ever had before. When New Jersey's Civilian Defense director instructed local communities how to establish the Community War Services Division of their local defense councils, he explicitly specified that in jobs ranging from the very top position of chairman to the very grass roots of block leader, the officeholder should be "a man or woman," the most important criteria being not gender but "a capacity for leadership," "respect of the community," and sense of responsibility. Commitment to women sharing authority started symbolically at the state level; the deputy director of the state's Office of Civilian Defense in charge of this Community War Services Division was a woman, and four out of its nine subcommittees were chaired by women.[45] Women's perceived expertise as consumers and knowledge of their communities also earned them positions on New Jersey's State Defense Council, created on orders from Washington; on the local defense councils instructed to carry federal and state policies to every municipality; and on the long roster of state and local committees reporting to the defense councils, particularly the ubiquitous Committees on Consumer Interests.[46]

By the fall of 1941 the New Jersey State Consumer Interests Committee had been formed, made up of twenty-five women and one man and chaired by Mrs. Harriman Simmons of the New Jersey Consumers League and administered by a paid, full-time executive secretary, Mrs. Eleazer Barth, an active member of both the Consumers League and the League of Women Voters.[47] In justifying all the attention to consumers on the New Jersey home front— which, according to Caroline Ware, was a model program—the state's Defense Council explained in a 1941 publication, "For the first time, the American consumer is made a part of the defense program. . . . Back of the armed forces there must be a citizen army convinced that its Government is committed to preserve the privileges and elevate the living standard of the whole people."[48] Parallel and interlocking with the Defense Council's hierarchy was the OPA, itself functioning at the federal level, in regional offices, and through local price control boards, and often a partner in organizing community consumer centers. In both Defense Council and OPA structures, women were everywhere, wearing the official hat of government as they staffed the enormous infrastructure that was organizing communities to regiment the nation's wartime consumption.

Of course, women also exerted political influence through their traditional voluntary organizations, but even these involvements promoted women as citizen consumers with new responsibilities outside the home. At one end of the political spectrum, the progressive League of Women Shoppers of New Jersey completely shifted its strategy for improving American living standards from agitating for the unionization of women workers to protecting consumers, through activities ranging from organizing a conference rather drolly entitled "Victory...—And Vitamins: What Is the Consumers' Role in Defense?" to monitoring rent control regulations to patrolling the fairness of ceiling prices.[49] Among the many war-related activities of the more mainstream New Jersey League of Women Voters was the production of radio programs for popular broadcasting that explicitly linked good citizenship to women's war work, particularly in the consumer realm. One such program depicted a fictional encounter between Mrs. Homebody (castigated as the "motherly type, Home and family are her world") and the more activist Mrs. Earnest, a committed league member, who visits Mrs. Homebody to convince her to join. When Mrs. Homebody demurs, claiming that "politics just isn't my line. Leave that to the politicians," Mrs. Earnest replies that the war has made that impossible: now government comes right into your home and is a part of your daily life, as homemaker, parent, and citizen. In a multi-part soap opera for radio, built around the lives of two female residents of the town of Leaguesboro, Mrs. Goodwin and Mrs. Paine, Mrs. Goodwin is the model wartime woman; she knows and observes price control regulations, works for the OPA as a volunteer price assistant, and condemns the market abuses of her more selfish friend, Mrs. Paine.[50] So whether it was at the urging of more traditional female voluntary organizations or by newly empowered female government officials, New Jersey women were admonished that "good citizenship" (a concept invoked frequently by the women themselves) meant not just protecting the economic and nutritional health of their own families, but also playing an active public role.

New Jersey's largest city, Newark, revealed even more clearly the extent to which women ran the homefront show through their authority as consumers. On the simplest level they were the shock troops for the OPA. When the OPA announced in the summer of 1942 that it needed price checkers to visit eight thousand Newark stores, hundreds of women volunteered, offering to work longer hours than administrators had ever expected. On a daily basis, two hundred volunteers, most of them women, kept Newark's OPA office functioning, and five hundred others checked each day on scarce apartments or rooms offered for rent.[51] But even more telling, women fully participated in the city's elaborate warfront bureaucracy, particularly in such agencies as the Newark Defense Council's Consumer Interests Committee, which established a Consumer Information Center in January 1942 and consumer corners throughout the city soon thereafter, and the Defense Council's Fair Rent Committee, which

Sixty percent of the staff shown here processing applications for fuel coupons in the New Jersey State OPA headquarters in Newark were women. In many OPA offices, women workers were even more prevalent. Note the two African-American women on the right. Black staff and volunteers were scarce in most OPA offices. (Courtesy of the Newark Public Library)

met weekly to adjust alleged unfair increases in rents.[52] When the Office of War Information introduced a "block plan" in the fall of 1942 to train volunteer block leaders to go house to house conveying crucial war information, Newark lost no time selecting 5 sector, 50 zone, and 349 district leaders, and an army of block leaders who were recruited through registration booths in the city's department stores. By design, all were women. After fifty hours of service, women earned membership in the "United States Citizen [Service] Corps." Revealing through her choice of language how much women were claiming the block plan as their own, chief Newark block leader Mrs. Edward Fitzpatrick told a radio audience, "We like to call [the block plan] the Mother of all Plans for it stands ready to meet the needs of its child, the community."[53] When Newark's Consumer Interests Committee sponsored a "housewives battalion" in the city's Victory Parade in August 1942, its radio appeal to the women of northern New Jersey articulated just how pathbreaking women felt their management of the World War II home front was. "Never before in history have women played so large a part in war as now. Formerly men went to battle while the womenfolk stayed at home. But now we are in a 'total' war. Everybody is in it. For every *front* line fighter there are the many *home* fighters."[54]

Though some historians have stressed the entry of women into defense work as the cutting edge of their wartime contribution, and others have dismissed the consumer activities of women on the home front as reinforcing traditional gender roles, both perspectives miss the extent to which women themselves turned a customary responsibility into a new political opportunity. Living creatively and nutritionally with shortages, observing price controls and rationing regulations, recycling and collecting scrap and fat, and fighting inflation through restraint and savings were all crucial warfront activities that required female cooperation, but they got female direction as well. Assertions during the 1930s about women consumers as guardians of the public interest provided the basis for women's expanded claim to political authority during the war. In the context of World War II, good citizenship and good consumership were promoted as inseparable, and women gained special stewardship over both.[55]

AFRICAN AMERICANS CLAIM CONSUMER CITIZENSHIP

*a*nother measure of the extent to which World War II linked the rights and obligations of citizens and consumers comes through in the new ways that African Americans experienced—and protested—their exclusion from the mainstream of American life. Although historians have generally rooted the black struggle for a "Double V[ictory]"—freedom at home as well as abroad—in the demand for equality in defense jobs and the military, many of the frustrations voiced by African Americans in wartime revolved around their exclusion from sites of consumption, from restaurants, bars, hotels, movie theaters, stores, pools, buses, and other so-called public accommodations (so identified because they supposedly catered to all, whether privately or publicly owned).[56] As African Americans embarked on proving themselves loyal Americans on the home front by heeding the regulations of the OPA or journeying to new territory as soldiers and defense workers, they consistently met discrimination as consumers. In a wartime atmosphere where good consumer and good citizen increasingly were intertwined, that unfair treatment in the marketplace took on new political significance.

Whereas in the 1930s and earlier, asserting their rights as consumers was part of a strategy to achieve economic power, in the context of war African Americans recognized that their political equality as citizens was at stake as

These African-American students from Fairfax County, Virginia, learned to shop with point stamps at a play store in their classroom. Rationing and price control had a special appeal to these children and their families, despite the hardships they imposed, as the government's oversight of prices promised protection from exploitative merchants thought common in black neighborhoods. (Courtesy of the National Archives)

well. Every time that blacks were excluded from OPA price boards or refused service at stores or restaurants, both the assumed universality of citizenship and the supposed freedom of the free market were violated. As war administrators increasingly moved consumption into the civic realm, African Americans, like white female citizen consumers, made it a new ground upon which to stake their claim to fuller political participation. Citizenship came to be defined more broadly to encompass new kinds of political rituals beyond traditional voting and military service, and in the process the potential for political discontent and the grounds for mobilizing against discrimination grew. "The concept of representative government," the author of *Consumers in Wartime: A Guide to Family Economy in the Emergency* instructed his readers, "includes your freedom as a consumer to choose whatever you wish in the way of economic goods or services to satisfy your wants."[57] That black Americans did not enjoy that freedom increasingly rankled them. World War II mobilized African Americans as consumers to claim their rights as citizens, much as it did white women. But the ways it did so, the success that was achieved, and the war's legacy for the postwar era all differed.

African Americans supported price and rent controls and the rationing of scarce goods even more enthusiastically than did the average white American, recognizing in them the potential not just for fair treatment during wartime, but also for redress of the overcharging and other market exploitation that was their common lot in the hands of inner-city storekeepers and landlords.[58] Moreover, as writer Ralph Ellison pointed out in his profile of a Harlem widow struggling to feed and house her family on the wages of a domestic worker, the demon inflation particularly threatened "the Mrs. Jacksons" of black America. "Their very lives demand that they back the President's [price and rent] stabilization."[59] Accordingly, black newspapers, radio, neighborhood movie theaters, and community organizations went out of their way to guide their audiences through the complicated rules of price controls and rationing. And if they found maximum protection lacking, they agitated for it, as when New York City Councilman Adam Clayton Powell, Jr., mobilized supporters to collect 100,000 signatures on a petition to declare Harlem a "war rental area" and hence subject to rent control.[60] Although zoot-suited young men with their baggy pants and padded and pleated jackets rebelliously defied the fabric limitations imposed on clothing by the War Production Board, more common was the patriotic attitude toward government regulation of consumption expressed by Langston Hughes in his poem "Speaking of Food," published by the *Afro-American* newspaper chain in 1943.

> I hear folks talking
> About coffee's hard to get,
> And they don't know how
> They're gonna live without it.
>
> I hear some others saying
> They can't buy no meat to fry,
> And the way they say it
> You'd think they're gonna die.

If I was to sit down
And write to Uncle Sam,
I'd tell him that I reckon
I can make it without ham.

I'd say, "Feed those fighting forces
For they're the ones today
That need to have the victuals
To wipe our foes away!"

Looks like to me
That's what we ought to say.[61]

Not surprisingly, African-American witnesses gave the OPA a ringing endorsement when the agency came up for congressional reenactment in 1944, even calling for expansion of its powers to include grade labeling, so as to prevent ghetto retailers from palming off inferior merchandise at top ceiling prices.[62] Market regulation that may have seemed burdensome to some whites was viewed by many blacks as the protection they long had sought.

Blatant inequity in the implementation and enforcement of OPA regulations, however, left African Americans frustrated at the denial of their rightful protection, and participation, as American citizens. Consumer citizenship was held out as an ideal, and then made unattainable. To begin with, blacks were seriously underrepresented on the OPA's price boards and in its volunteer ranks. Fifty-nine out of every sixty local boards were lily white, and fewer than one-fourth of one percent of the agency's half million volunteers were black. Calculated another way, for every 10,000 non-blacks, 11.2 volunteered with the OPA, while only .9 blacks out of 10,000 did.[63] One might be tempted to put the blame on the reticence of the black community itself were there not so much evidence of discrimination in the OPA's recruitment. Although the original draft plan for the OPA mentioned the need to include representatives of minority groups where they lived, that provision was removed by staff members who feared opposition in the South and overly black panels in the North. When organized labor was also omitted from mention, protest resulted in its inclusion, but a similar objection from black organizations had little effect, until more than a year later when the CIO took up the issue. The absence of a clear mandate had an impact. When the chairman of the St. Louis Price Board was asked why a city with a black population of some 100,000 had no representatives on its board, he responded dumbfoundedly, "I never thought of it," and then added sincerely, "It wasn't in the directive, was it?"[64]

The OPA's Consumer Advisory Committee called for investigation of black underrepresentation, but even with more surveillance, field officials apparently continued to resist. With black involvement nationally at less than seven hundred members on war price boards and approximately fifteen hundred OPA volunteers by the end of the war, black women in particular, who made up about a quarter of those board members, were deprived of the political authority that white women gained in their communities during the war.[65] Instead, black men and women were more likely to participate in the war effort through their own organizations: church auxiliaries, fraternal orders, sororities and fraternities, church choirs, the National Council of Negro Women and the Federation of Colored Women's Clubs, and the newly organized Women's Army of National Defense for middle-aged women and the Joe Louis Service Guild for younger ones.[66] The blue-eyed, blond-haired women who smiled out from OPA posters, authoritatively instructing Americans how to fight the war on the home front, were seeking eye contact primarily with other white women.[67]

To make matters worse, enforcement of price controls in black neighborhood stores proved notoriously poor. Despite the setting of price ceilings nationwide, African Americans continued to pay from 3 to 12 percent more for groceries than whites in comparable neighborhoods. "Food Costs More in Harlem," the NAACP's first extensive wartime price survey asserted angrily in 1942. The following year, the Chicago branch made the same point in "Food Costs Negroes More in Chicago." Partly, the problem rested with the way price ceilings were set. When they were calculated according to the highest price charged in March 1942, Jim Crow overcharging was perpetuated, not attacked.[68] Whether price ceilings compared fairly to white stores or not, black consumers further encountered the problem of low compliance among merchants in their neighborhoods, with little threat of OPA enforcement. Surveys of the percentage of stores in full compliance with OPA regulations in Chicago, Detroit, and Philadelphia revealed from 10 to almost 40 percent variation between white and black neighborhoods.[69]

When the OPA was not immobilized by fear of southern anger at paying too much attention to black consumers, or not oblivious of violations in neighborhoods where few price panelists or price assistants lived, it sought to remedy the inequity with ineffective, even insensitive pamphlets like the one entitled *Negroes, Too, Are Consumers,* or with calls to the black community to solve the problem itself. The booklet *A Negro Community Works in Behalf of Its Families,* which was aimed at instructing blacks how to improve their wartime economic condition, featured the fictional family of the Andrews, living on a limited budget. "Mrs. Andrews was definitely patriotic.... But she didn't know there was anything that poor people were supposed to do." That "anything" turned out to be following food sales more carefully, planning purchases and menus better, planting a garden and preserving its harvest, and learning about nutrition. No mention was made of the need to monitor more stringently the compliance of local storekeepers with price controls and rationing regulations.[70] In a similar vein, OPA official Dutton Ferguson wrote to Walter White of the NAACP that the best solution to black underrepresentation would come from NAACP members volunteering on price panels and as price assistants, not from OPA remedial action and pressure on local and district boards.[71]

Only after violence in Harlem during the summer of 1943 did the OPA admit its responsibility for the mistreatment of blacks under price control. Within a week of the rebellion, it announced it would open a branch office at 135th Street to keep better track of rents and prices, and over the next two weeks the OPA issued more than one hundred summonses and warnings to Harlem merchants. Several months later the OPA relented and declared New York City a war rental area, finally establishing the rent control for which Harlem tenants were desperate.[72] By the time OPA administrator Chester Bowles reached out to African Americans in November 1944 with a major policy statement declaring greater commitment to impartial administrative practices, increased authority to a special assistant for Negro affairs, and the naming of more black staff and advisory committee members, African Americans had seen their enthusiasm for price and rent controls repaid with repeated discrimination as they sought to fulfill their obligations as citizen consumers.[73]

On an even more profound level, the interweaving of consumer and citizen in World War II reminded African Americans of their second-class citizenship and shaped the way they registered their anger. As hundreds of thousands of blacks struck out for new places and new opportunities through military service and defense jobs—southerners north and west, and northerners south and west—and as expectations grew that joining the nation's attack on fascism and racism abroad would mean better treatment for its victims at home, they became sorely disappointed at how little things were changing.[74] After A. Philip Randolph's threat of a black March on Washington in July 1941 was silenced by President Roosevelt's signing of Executive Order 8802 establishing the Fair Employment Practices Committee (FEPC), more and better jobs did become available in war industries, albeit often at lower wages than— and over the opposition of—white co-workers.[75] And voting was a legal right that blacks outside of the South enjoyed, and were continuing to exercise.

But what was not improving in wartime, and indeed was worsening in many places, was the way African Americans were treated on a daily basis in public, not just in the legally segregated South, but in the North and West as well. In seeking decent housing, in walking freely down streets and into parks, in patronizing stores, restaurants, theaters, and the other commercial establishments that increasingly defined public space by the 1940s, blacks were discriminated against. Polls taken during the war of black public opinion consistently confirmed that frustration with the war effort grew out of three major sources: economic discrimination in jobs and income, inadequate housing choices, and the segregation of public accommodations. In a truly free capitalist marketplace, blacks rightfully argued, the last two venues should have been open to all consumers with Uncle Sam's green money in their pockets.[76] In World War II America, housing and public spaces—even on military bases—were not.[77]

Certainly, controversy over black access to public accommodations was not new. It had long been inseparable from basic civil rights. Once the Civil War ended slavery, the principle that African Americans should be treated as "persons" rather than "property," with the freedom to move around at will, inspired the Thirteenth and Fourteenth Amendments to the U.S. Constitution and the Civil Rights Acts of 1866 and 1875. Legally, blacks gained equal access to all public accommodations—schools, parks, conveyances, inns, theaters, and other commercial establishments—but before long the Supreme Court validated state and local efforts to undermine that access. In the civil rights cases of 1883 the Court ruled the public accommodations sections of the 1875 law unconstitutional and the due process protections of the Thirteenth and Fourteenth Amendments applicable only to states, not individuals. Segregated facilities themselves were upheld in the Court's *Plessy* v. *Ferguson* decision of 1896. By the end of the nineteenth century, Congress had repealed or the courts had voided most of the federal guarantees of full and equal access to public accommodations. A Jim Crow world of separate black and white public spheres was alive and well, North and South. African Americans responded by seeking protective legislation at the state level, and eighteen states passed or amended existing civil rights acts. But even with these laws on the state books, local discriminatory practices were ubiquitous, as landlords and proprietors seemed to have decided that the most profitable way to operate a free market involved freeing it from the interference of racial prejudice—by limiting access solely to whites.[78] And as more blacks journeyed north during and after World War I, discrimination often worsened. As Langston Hughes recalled from his youth, at the end of that war, "In Cleveland, a liberal city, the color line began to be drawn tighter and tighter. Theaters and restaurants in the downtown area began to refuse to accommodate colored people. Landlords doubled and tripled the rent at the approach of a dark tenant."[79]

By the time African Americans were enlisting or being drafted into another world war during the 1940s and making all the requisite sacrifices expected of supporters on the home front, their access to public accommodations was severely limited in the South and not much better in the North. When, for example, the NAACP surveyed moving picture theaters in thirty-nine states in 1944–45, only ten states reported no evidence of segregation or exclusion.[80] Likewise, the black press regularly, and even the mainstream press occasionally, reported complaints about cab companies that refused to give blacks rides, department stores that refused to wait on black customers or to let them try on clothes, and downtown hotels and restaurants in major northern cities that refused rooms and service to distinguished black guests.[81] But most insulting of all was the treatment accorded the men and women devoting their lives to America's defense, in the military and in war industries. That discrimination became the subject of thousands of stories, narratives of exploitative war service told by soldiers and workers to their relatives, passed along to friends, printed in the muckraking black newspapers of wartime, and denounced from pulpits and lecterns. As these tales of discrimination and humiliation passed from mouth to mouth, the anger they articulated reverberated beyond the individual victims of the incidents to the larger black community. By war's end, a cacophony of complaints about the violation of black rights as citizen consumers would greet the arrival of peace, binding citizen and consumer ever more tightly in the African-American quest for equality as Americans.

Segregation in the armed forces during World War II has been well documented. Blacks were assigned to all-black units, usually under white officers, and those units generally provided the cooks, porters, and laborers that kept the American military functioning. Black soldiers and sailors slept in segregated barracks, ate in segregated mess halls, worshiped in segregated church services, and recreated on segregated teams, playing against neighboring black high schools or even, when there were no alternatives, black inmates of penitentiaries.[82] The stories servicemen and -women told excoriated segregation in the military's operation, but their greatest rage was reserved for their exclusion from the social settings of daily existence, the parts of camp and neighboring town life that they expected to be outside of the military's obsession with rank and hierarchy. At the heart of what many black servicemen sought in this "free" zone were commercial, leisure pursuits—movies, canteens, and social clubs on military bases, and restaurants, bars, and theaters in adjacent communities—and when *they* turned out to discriminate, the contradiction between the morality trumpeted by the Allied cause and the immorality of its defenders infuriated them.

One might be tempted to blame this disjuncture between expectation

This photo documents an inquiry into a deadly gun battle between black soldiers and white Military Police at Fort Dix, New Jersey. A disagreement between white and black soldiers over who could use a pay telephone in the Military Sports Palace adjacent to the base left one white MP and two black soldiers dead and five black soldiers wounded. Although the post commander ruled the shooting "merely a brawl with no racial significance" (*New York Times,* April 4, 1942), black soldiers surely were angered at being denied access to a commercial service, particularly in a northern state. Acme Newspictures, Inc., April 3, 1942. (Courtesy of Bettmann/CORBIS)

and reality on the fact that many black soldiers were northerners coping with southern segregationist mores at the multitude of military bases clustered in the South. Certainly, white southerners went out of their way to enforce Jim Crow "to impress colored soldiers from the North who may get the wrong interpretation of racial equality in Mississippi," as the mayor of Jackson put it, when he banned "all colored persons" from the main floor of the City Auditorium during performances of the light opera *Porgy and Bess,* despite its almost totally black cast. With the same goal in mind, Governor Eugene Talmadge of Georgia ordered all bus drivers to carry guns to help force black GIs to comply with Jim Crow seating.[83] But such an analysis would miss how widespread this disjuncture was, with the relatively virgin territory of the West in particular adopting many segregationist practices where they had not existed before.

Much the way the color line tightened in the North during the First

World War, the influx of southern black soldiers into the West brought "We Do Not Solicit Colored Trade" signs to the region's main streets for the first time. National Urban League staffer Reginald Johnson returned from a two-month tour of the Pacific Northwest and California to confirm that segregation and discrimination in public accommodations were indeed on the increase, even, to his amazement, in a place as obscure as the lunchroom on the ferryboat between Seattle and Bremerton. He felt the "situation is particularly acute with respect to Negro servicemen who find themselves humiliated and restricted in the eating places and places of recreation," often thanks to base commanders like the one in Walla Walla, Washington, who cooperated with local proprietors by ruling their premises "off limits" to black GIs.[84] When African-American leaders and organizations expressed outrage that the military was condoning the imposition of southern patterns of behavior on hitherto "free" communities, the official response (until all bases were officially, though not often in practice, desegrated in 1944) was that because the War Department could have only one rule to apply to the army as a whole, it had to be a Jim Crow one acceptable to North and South alike.[85]

The stories of discrimination that black servicemen told are abundant and repetitious; over and over they recount "colored-only" PXs and movie showings on military bases; segregated officers' clubs, USO dances, and "rest and recreation" resorts; and off-duty trips to nearby towns reached from a seat at the back of the bus, where upon arrival they were barred from most bowling alleys, theaters, restaurants, and taverns. A few testimonials will suffice. General Benjamin O. Davis, Jr., the son of the first black general in the U.S. Army and a West Point graduate himself who had endured the "silent treatment" in his dorm and at every meal for four years, became commander of the prestigious Tuskegee Airmen fighter pilots in 1940. Despite that achievement and a lifetime of other successes, he looked back years later on his rejection by the Fort Benning Officers' Club as the most insulting action taken against him during his entire career. Another Tuskegee Airman and later mayor of Detroit, Coleman Young, recalled getting himself and a hundred other black noncommissioned officers arrested for forcing entry into an all-white officers' club, the center of social life for men of rank.[86]

Dempsey Travis, an inductee from the South Side of Chicago, was younger and greener than these officers, but when he arrived at Camp Shenango, Pennsylvania—via a Jim Crow troop train—he was no less horrified at his treatment. The black soldiers were hidden "back up against the woods someplace," prohibited from attending any of the five theaters until a makeshift one could be raised in the center of the black area, and limited to an inferior PX. When one of his rank insisted on entering the white PX for a beer, he had his eye kicked in, and in no time a caravan of six trucks arrived filled with armed white soldiers in battle fatigues to ensure that no such mistake would occur again. They began firing on a crowd of black soldiers, hitting Travis three times and putting him in a nearby hospital, in isolation, as it too was segregated. When he recovered, he was sent to Camp Lee, Virginia, where he was housed in the camp's "black belt" of tents rather than barracks and forced to watch movies with other black officers and enlisted men behind a rope at the back of the theater.[87]

One theme reappeared again and again in black GIs' wartime stories, partly because of its prevalence in lived experience and partly because it highlighted so powerfully the injustice they suffered. The infuriation that worked its way into so many memories of World War II service was the preferential treatment given to white German prisoners of war in commercial establishments where blacks were excluded. Lloyd Brown recalled going to a lunchroom on the main street of Salina, Kansas, and being told by the owner, "You boys know we don't serve colored here." Of course they knew it; a "colored" wasn't served anywhere in town, "there was no room at the inn . . . there was no place he could get a cup of coffee." They ignored him and just stood inside the door "staring at what we had come to see—the German prisoners of war who were having lunch at the counter. . . . If we were *untermenschen* in Nazi Germany, they would break our bones. As 'colored' men in Salina, they only break our hearts."[88] Dempsey Travis recalled bitterly that in his western Pennsylvania military camp, "I saw German prisoners free to move around the camp, unlike black soldiers, who were restricted. The Germans walked right into the doggone places like any white American. We were wearin' the same uniform, but we were excluded."[89] A twist on the POW story that took on mythic proportions in black soldiers' recounting of war experiences involved their pride that popular black singer Lena Horne, sent to entertain the troops in a combined black and POW performance followed by a separate white one, carried out the first and then left, inverting the hierarchy and relegating her white audience to the lowest possible status, below both African Americans and prisoners of war.[90]

Keen observers at the time recognized that the humiliations black GIs encountered on a daily basis as consumers of goods and services was undermining their commitment as citizens and soldiers. Mary McLeod Bethune, an important African-American adviser to President Roosevelt, worried in June 1942 that "when she looked into the eyes of Negroes" she saw a soulful "questioning" that she attributed to such rejections as "soldiers in uniform denied food for 22 hours because no restaurant would serve them." Roy Wilkins of the NAACP concurred. "It is pretty grim . . . to have a black boy in uniform get an

This cartoon, probably drawn for an African-American newspaper, captures the humiliation of black soldiers and veterans when white German prisoners of war received better treatment in commercial establishments than they did. C. W. Johnson, 1946. (Courtesy of Chicago Historical Society)

orientation lecture in the morning on wiping out Nazi bigotry, and that same evening be told he can buy a soft drink only in the 'Colored' post exchange!"[91] Bethune's and Wilkins's conviction that blacks' rejection in the realm of consumption symbolized for them the full depth of their exclusion testifies to the extent to which African Americans linked the freedoms of consumer and citizen in the America of World War II. Revealingly, when Roland Fallin set out to write a poem addressing the question "Is There Democracy?" from the perspective of a black GI limited to KP (kitchen police) duty, he began the first stanza:

> I like to believe in democracy,
> But I don't think I can,
> When jim-crowed in restaurants,
> In stores and movieland.[92]

African-American civilians who journeyed north and west to claim their share of the thousands of new defense jobs created by the war found themselves facing much the same discrimination in public places as men and women in the military. In Oakland, California, for example, blacks had enjoyed access to some downtown eateries, theaters, and dance halls when their numbers were small, but once the war boom attracted thousands of migrants to nearby shipyards and defense plants, the white establishment became nervous. The conservative *Oakland Observer* complained that in "downtown Oakland restaurants where formerly no Negro ever dreamed of going, now we see Negroes all over the place." It proceeded to warn blacks against "butting into the white civilization instead of keeping in the perfectly orderly and consistent Negro civilization of Oakland." Incidents like the stabbing of a black man who refused to give up his restaurant booth to a white patron or a street melee in front of the Oakland Auditorium prompted white businesses to introduce explicit segregation in commercial settings. "White Trade Only" signs began appearing in storefront windows, bowling lanes kept the races separated, and dances at the auditorium took place on alternate nights for "colored" and white audiences.[93] Likewise, when a huge defense plant was erected in Baraboo, Wisconsin, in 1942, "We Do Not Serve Colored People" signs followed close behind the first black workers hired.[94] Enticed by new economic opportunities, southern blacks moved north and west in hopes of escaping Jim Crow, only to discover that they had brought him along with them.

Finding decent and affordable housing in the new communities where blacks were employed proved equally if not more difficult than buying a restaurant meal or a theater ticket. As Roosevelt's black adviser Robert Weaver pointed out, wartime mobilization weakened the color line in jobs while strengthening it in housing.[95] A terrible squeeze on housing options for blacks resulted. The private real estate market closed off many white neighborhoods and offered inferior housing at outrageous rents in black ones, while government war housing was inadequate and segregated (out of respect for local mores).[96] The irony was cruel. Having secured well-paying industrial jobs as a result of the war that should have provided them with the financial resources to buy a better quality of life on the open market, blacks discovered that with each passing day that market was less open. Anger exploded in violence. In mid-1943 racial rebellions broke out in forty-seven cities, from Detroit to Los Angeles to Mobile to Harlem. Catalysts varied, but at root all these rebellions reflected blacks' disillusionment over their inability to turn the prosperity of wartime to their advantage, whether because of continued job discrimination or inferior treatment in housing and other consumer markets.[97]

African Americans' frustration as spurned consumers suggested a strategy of revenge. Black defense workers in Detroit, angry at opposition to their entry into the first public housing project, the Sojourner Truth Houses, as well as other discrimination, looted "stores of decidedly exploitative character," according to a white civic leader.[98] In Harlem, rumors that a white policeman had killed a black soldier sparked a rampage of window smashing and looting along 125th Street, with vandalism totaling $3 million to $5 million. Stores known to be black-owned were spared. Community leader Adam Clayton Powell, Jr., contended that the uprising came out of "blind, smoldering and unorganized" resentment at oppression, particularly "the unusual high rents and cost of living forced upon Negroes in Harlem."[99] Sociologist Harold Orlansky concurred, claiming that looters felt justified seizing what in their view had been unfairly denied them: children took food and toys, men clothing and liquor, women garments and household goods.[100] A participant interviewed by psychologist Kenneth Clark described an orgy of material consumption. While some "people was fittin' on shoes and stuff," others were ripping vests and suits off of racks and even mannequins. "As I was stealin' I had a croaker-sack [burlap bag] load with soup to nuts. I have a radio at the bottom of the sack." In a grocery store, people helped themselves to everything from flour to bacon, suddenly free of the wartime controls that normally restricted their food consumption. "They messed up in sugar, walking in it, pissed in it, and one woman come up there with a bag and just pushed the messed up sugar aside with her hands and filled up her bag. She said, 'Sugar is scarce, you know.' "[101] As the nearly six hundred men and women arrested for looting were booked in a nearby police station, their booty made an enormous pile in the station lobby, "clothing, and household furnishings and food— particularly food," reported one observer.[102] Harlem had also exploded eight years earlier, in the midst of the Great Depression, but that time anger was directed more at merchants' refusal to hire blacks. This time, African-American wrath targeted those who brought undue suffering to consumers:

Three boys, ages twelve, thirteen, and fourteen, show off tuxedos looted from a formalwear shop during the Harlem rebellion of August 1943. Black consumers, frustrated with the deprivations of wartime, as well as the special inequities they felt they suffered from exploitative merchants even with government-supervised price control, took revenge. (Courtesy of Bettmann/CORBIS)

retailers who charged "two prices for the same article . . . the colored customer paying the higher price," as the NAACP's Roy Wilkins was told; landlords who scalped desperate renters; and government price controls that unfairly penalized African Americans.[103]

Blacks' frustration as consumers fed their sense of inequity as well as provided strategies for combating discrimination. While the rebellions of 1943 left a wake of injuries, deaths, arrests, and property destruction, they did attract the OPA's attention to black mistreatment under price control. A more peaceful but still confrontational kind of protest to emerge from the thwarting of black citizen consumers during the Second World War broached the first tentative steps toward the postwar civil rights movement, one that would be built around demands for full access to public accommodations. Military personnel, defense workers, and ordinary citizens, emboldened by the wartime climate of seeking a "Double V," carried on an impressive degree of everyday resistance to traditional Jim Crow practices. Particularly in the South, public buses became the site of guerrilla warfare, with black customers asserting their entitlement as consumers by refusing to move to the back of the bus, complaining they were overcharged, and cursing out the driver. Few of these incidents ended as tragically as the killing of Private Ned Turman by an MP (military police) for "talking back" on a bus to Fort Bragg, North Carolina, or the beating of three black WACs for using a white restroom in a railroad depot in Kentucky.[104] Yet black protesters began to sabotage the legitimacy of segregation—on buses in Tennessee, in movie theaters in Denver, at a skating rink in Syracuse, in restaurants in Detroit—and demonstrate their growing insistence that, in the language of a little pamphlet put out by the Chicago Civil Liberties Committee, "YOU have the right to enter every place . . . that is open to and invites the public, and there to buy at the same prices, receive the same attentions, and enjoy the accommodations and services the same as other persons, regardless of your 'race' or color."[105]

Although small incidents of protest occurred throughout the nation, two substantially organized efforts, one in Washington, D.C., and the other in Chicago, provided the first sustained flares of the burst of civil rights activism that would follow the war. Washington, long functioning like a segregated southern city, still in wartime prohibited African Americans from entering hotels, restaurants, movie theaters, libraries, and taxicabs. Disgraceful incidents in the nation's capital were legion. Richard Wright, in town for the opening of the stage adaptation of his novel *Native Son*, was prevented from entering a restaurant with his white producers and was forced to eat in the car. Judge William Hastie, former dean of the Howard University Law School and former aide to the secretary of war, was refused service at the National Press Club. The Loews Capital Theater canceled a Red Cross pageant because young black nurses would be attending an event intended to honor and recruit nurses for war service.[106]

Finally, in February 1943, three female students at Howard University decided they had had enough and initiated the first sit-in of the twentieth-century civil rights movement when they sat down at a segregated soda fountain in a United Cigar Store and ordered hot chocolates. The waitresses refused to serve them, they refused to leave, and when they were finally served and charged double the normal price, they refused to pay and were dragged off to jail. The campaign continued against other segregated restaurants. While the Greek owner of Little Palace Cafeteria begrudgingly acknowledged a link between democratic citizenship and freedom to consume when he insisted, "I'd rather close up than practice democracy this way," protesters outside based their demand for service on that same linkage as they waved signs that read "Our boys. Our bonds. Our brothers are fighting for you. Why can't we eat here?" and "We Die Together; Let's Eat Together."[107] In Chicago, the Congress of Racial Equality, a biracial, pacifist organization, committed itself to direct-action sit-ins at public accommodations like restaurants and theaters. Celebrated events included breaking the color line at Jack Spratt's and Stoner's Restaurants, despite the management's best efforts to discourage the demonstrators by serving meat covered with eggshells, oversalted food, and garbage sandwiches.[108]

Substantial protests like those in Washington and Chicago happened relatively rarely during the war years, but the stage was being set. The NAACP, whose Legal Defense Fund devoted itself tirelessly to challenging discrimination in public accommodations, watched its membership grow from 50,556 in 355 branches in 1940 to 450,000 in 1073 branches by 1946.[109] The war had disrupted the "old and established racial etiquette," in the language of St. Clair Drake and Horace Cayton, as they closed their mammoth history of Chicago's "Black Metropolis" in 1945. "The change in the Negro's mentality came about so rapidly that few people, even Negroes, realized its extent," they argued. "Most fundamentally, it was expressed in the Negro's refusal to accept segregation without complaint. . . . But underneath all this was the Negro's determination to become a full citizen, to plan and think for himself regardless of past friends and old leaders. He began to make demands not for concessions, not for small gains, but for *equality*."[110]

As they waged war on two fronts, African Americans tested that full citizenship and equality not just in the military, but in the markets that shaped the contours of daily life: the job market, the housing market, and the consumer market. The message, if not the reality, of wartime seemed to be that full citizenship entitled blacks—even obligated them through market regulation—to equal participation in the economic sphere. After all, weren't capitalist marketplaces, by definition, color-blind? Time and again black accounts of discrimination turned on the outrage that their dollars did not buy the same goods and services as the white guy's. Although seeking the integration of markets and public accommodations may sound conservative in the racial categories of today and hence be dismissed as the political agenda of a liberal-minded black middle class, the struggle for access to what was deemed "public" in America had a radical demand for equality at its root, which appealed to lowly army privates and defense workers no less than the black bourgeoisie. If the realm of mass consumption offered a ready setting for political action by African-American citizen consumers, the goal was as much to claim equal citizenship as to consume material goods or services. Whereas the unspoken "rules of the game" of homefront consumption elevated (mostly white) women to new political status, they served to remind African-American men and women of their sorry lack of it.

THE FINAL ROUND

*a*s World War II ended, preparations began for a last battle, this one on the home front, over how postwar "normalcy" should be defined. "How" was not at all clear, since times had not been normal for quite some time. Before the war, America had suffered through the Great Depression, a crisis which had also discredited the previous decade of the twenties, the "normalcy" following World War I. In important respects, World War II had provided a culmination of the New Deal, as it expanded the state's power to shape the economy by granting it the right to regulate prices, rents, and wages in the interests of the nation and greater fairness to citizens. "It has been a long fight to put the control of our economic system in the hands of the government," Eleanor Roosevelt wrote approvingly in her syndicated column soon after the war ended.[111] Consumer activists promoted this agenda, and many Americans rallied to the wartime call for citizen consumers who would prove their loyalty to the nation and commitment to equity by cooperating with these state controls. Women often went a step further and participated actively in the implementation and enforcement of controls in their role as guardians of the public interest. African Americans, despite the discrimination they encountered from federal agencies like the OPA, recognized that state involvement in the economy potentially offered them protection from exploitation in the private market and greater political rights as citizen consumers. And the labor movement not only valued the wage controls of wartime, but when faced with the constant threat of inflation, particularly intense at war's end, showed much more investment in consumer regulation than it had in the 1930s.

As the end of the war emergency loomed, many members of these interest groups—consumer activists, women, African Americans, organized labor, and also some veterans groups—and their supporters in the Democratic

Party and in political blocs further to the left imagined a postwar order where the state would continue to play a role regulating the consumer marketplace, and where the good citizen would continue to be defined as one who consumed responsibly with the public interest in mind. Essential to the success of this conception was the extension of price and rent controls beyond victory into peacetime, so as to prevent the spiraling effects of inflation that had proved so damaging after World War I and to protect the progress toward economic equality made during wartime. A regional OPA director wrote in a letter to the *New York Times,* "Like many other examples of social progress, the time for price control has arrived and no arguments can dispel that towering economic reality."[112] Continued consumer market regulation would complement a parallel initiative to keep the state's hand in the employment market by guaranteeing full employment, underwritten by government spending if necessary, through the proposed Full Employment Act of 1945.[113]

On the other side of the battlefield stood champions of the purchaser consumer paradigm who defined quite differently what it meant to consume with the national interest in mind after the war emergency had ended. This conception of the postwar order was articulated most fully by members of the business community involved in mass production and mass retail—from corporate executives on down to small-store owners—and their Republican and conservative Democratic political supporters. In this vision, free enterprise—functioning in a free market, free of government intervention—would collaborate with purchaser consumers pursuing individualistic goals to secure a larger prosperity for the nation, "A Better Tomorrow for Everybody," as the National Association of Manufacturers (NAM) promised. The lifting of price controls was the crucial first step. "Remove price controls on manufactured goods and production will step up *fast* . . . and goods will pour into the market. Within a reasonable amount of time, prices will adjust themselves naturally," full-page NAM ads (prepared, ironically, by Benton & Bowles, the advertising firm that Chester Bowles had helped found) blared from daily newspapers nationwide during the debate over the OPA's future.[114]

Business argued, moreover, that a flourishing mass consumption economy with competitive, unregulated pricing of new cars, new suburban homes, and new products to fill them would better protect the general good than the state controls—and inevitable shortages—of what they dismissed as a European-style, socialistic planned economy. A higher and more equitable standard of living for all, derived from economic growth, was the best route to the fulfillment of the nation's longstanding commitment to equality and democracy. High consumption, a growing economy, robust employment, and social and political equality would go hand in hand. For the champions of a postwar order empowering purchaser consumers, personal and national fulfillment converged, making unbridled mass production and consumption not just an economic panacea but a political one as well. The American cycle of "mass employment, mass production, mass advertising, mass distribution and mass ownership of the products of industry," the conservative *Saturday Evening Post* reminded its end-of-war readers, had made, and would continue to make, the United States "the last bulwark of [democratic] civilization."[115]

During the almost thirty months from the renewal of the OPA in June 1944 through its effective dissolution in December 1946, a pitched battle raged between the forces defending and opposing the continuation of price controls, carried on in the media, in Congress, and wherever else there were forums for political debate. OPA chief Chester Bowles rather immodestly called it "the battle of the century," and Americans could barely escape listening to skirmishes such as "Should the OPA Be Continued Without Restrictions?" on the radio, or reading debates like "Price Control—Good or Bad?" and a face-off between Ira Mosher, president of NAM ("Price Control Must Go!") and Chester Bowles ("Price Control Must Stay!") in magazines and newspapers.[116] The June 1946 struggle over OPA extension provoked a major showdown. The war had been over for ten months, demobilization had advanced significantly, and competing economic strategies for how to engineer a successful "reconversion" vied for dominance. Previous votes for extension in June 1944 and June 1945 had proved increasingly charged, as opponents had rallied to weaken the OPA's effectiveness, and supporters, showcasing the public's overwhelming support for price controls, had paraded in one defender after another—consumer advocates, housewives, veterans, African-American leaders, and so forth. That early experimentation with removing items from rationing and price control had led to inflation and shortages in 1944 and 1945 only raised the stakes for the June 1946 vote.[117]

With interests so vested, emotions so intense, and expert economic advice so conflicting, the decision whether or not to extend price controls did not get made definitively in June 1946, but rather took six more months of prolonged struggle to resolve, and even then some stalwarts worked to reverse the outcome. In early spring 1946, as the June 30 deadline for OPA expiration approached, the vast majority of the public continued to register support for price controls on every opinion poll taken—in proportions as high as 73 and 82 percent, many advocating extension beyond June 1947.[118] Most Americans seemed to share Bowles's conviction that to eviscerate OPA anytime in the near future would mean "we are about to throw away all the fruits of our four-year battle against higher rents and prices, and embark on an inflationary joyride."[119] As the opposition mounted its assault, orchestrated by a powerful

NAM allied with the National Retail Dry Goods Association and supported by congressmen representing agricultural and industrial interests champing at the bit for release from government price restraints, consumers at the grass roots moved into gear. They organized rallies to "Save the O.P.A." that attracted thousands at a time, marched under banners declaring such sentiments as "The National Association of American People Wants OPA" and "Save OPA from Getting the Boot," and threatened buyers' strikes should their opponents succeed. A consumers' group in Washington created a spectacle by unrolling at a Senate hearing a mammoth ball made up of petitions signed by 40,000 people pledging not to spend over sixty cents a pound on meat.[120] Consumers' commitment so impressed the business-oriented *Wall Street Journal* that it warned readers that the consumer can only be " 'pushed so far.' What happens when aroused consumers assert their sovereignty, albeit salutary, is invariably unpleasant."[121]

But alas, a vote of Congress, not a plebiscite, determined the OPA's fate. Two days before the existing price control bill was slated to expire, Congress passed a much weakened version that President Truman, predicting "bonanza" price hikes, immediately vetoed, in hopes that he would get a stronger bill in its place. Instead, the clock ran out on the OPA at the end of June, shutting down price ceilings, rent control, and all the rest along with it. Over the next month, Truman's predicted "bonanza" came true: food prices jumped 14 percent, with meat doubling, and overall living expenses increased 6 percent, the equivalent of more than 100 percent over a year. "This means a dollar a day wage cut. It is not a matter of opinion," a worker and war veteran angrily explained to a New Jersey radio audience.[122]

Defiance threatened the previous spring now became a reality. Pledging a "buyers' strike such as this country has never known," Walter Reuther, president of the United Automobile Workers Union (UAW)-CIO, mobilized labor's ranks around the country to join with consumer groups in protest. In Washington, thirty-two national organizations formed the Citizens' Price Defense Committee. Although the intensity of protest varied from place to place, almost everywhere demonstrators picketed against high prices and the abandonment of price control, and urged boycotts. In the New York metropolitan area, for example, the scale ranged from demonstrations in a dozen shopping districts in four boroughs orchestrated by the New York City Consumer Council (an umbrella organization of sixty-five civic, labor, veterans, and social welfare groups) to a campaign of housewives and community leaders in the upper-class suburb of Princeton, New Jersey, who dubbed themselves the "militant marketers." At the New York City rallies, protesters chanted "Too high, don't buy" and "Bring back the OPA," while distributing paper lapel tags

These women picketing outside a butcher's shop in the summer of 1946 not only demanded a lower price for meat, they also wanted the OPA revived and the government back in the business of regulating the marketplace. (Courtesy of Bettmann/CORBIS)

reading "Strong OPA or I Won't Buy." In Detroit, 60,000 autoworkers assembled at Cadillac Square in a sea of slogans such as "No Ceilin'—No Floor—Nothing Any More" and "Inflation Today—Depression Tomorrow" as orange and black balloons bearing the words "OPA prices" lifted over their heads.[123]

Feeling pressure from this groundswell of popular support, "Congress finally considered breathing new life into the OPA's still-warm corpse," as

Newsweek put it, and by the end of July passed a bill not appreciably stronger than the one Truman had vetoed a month earlier. On July 25 the President signed it, arguing that he had no alternative. *Newsweek* pulled no punches in analyzing the new bill for its readers. "The new price control bill is actually a price-decontrol act designed to liquidate, by degrees, the system set up for the wartime emergency." It left the OPA with "less than a third of its former power," in the newsweekly's estimation. As predicted, prices continued to rise and shortages to reign, particularly in meat, as packers chose to punish the public's insistence on price control by withholding meat from market. By mid-September slaughtering had dropped 80 percent below 1945 production. Truman, frightened that the Democrats would take the rap for the deepening consumer crisis in the upcoming November election if goods did not reappear on the market, lifted most price controls, by now many of them hardly enforceable, on October 14. But the damage had already been done. Voters registered their disgust with a President and a Congress implementing reconversion at consumers' expense by voting out the incumbents, thus returning control of both houses of Congress to the Republicans for the first time since 1930, or in the case of ten million Democratic voters of 1944, by not voting at all.[124] Four days after the Democratic defeat, Truman removed almost all the remaining price and wage ceilings. The OPA was authorized through one more June 30, but many of its local offices and price boards shut down or consolidated by the end of December, with only rent control and ceilings on sugar, rice, solid fuels, and some heavy consumer durables left to oversee.[125]

Consumers still exerted market influence in the "normalcy" that prevailed from the end of 1946 through the rest of the 1940s, even without price controls. A ritualized pattern of producer-consumer interaction developed, of rising prices provoking consumer protests, which in turn served to discipline producers and retailers from imposing even greater price hikes. When controls ended in 1946, prices rose. The Consumer Price Index increased 8 percent in 1946 and 14 percent in 1947. The Bureau of Labor Statistics figured the price rise as even higher for moderate income families in large cities: an enormous 47 percent increase in prices from June 1946 to June 1948.[126] A sampling of news headlines captures well how a kind of give-and-take developed between consumers and producers during the late 1940s, as continuing consumer protests served to keep some lid on prices in the absence of government controls, culminating in a national boycott of meat in August 1948: "BUYING: The Customer Begins to Resist" (*Newsweek,* November 4, 1946); "Store Sales Slide: Customers Shop Around as More Goods Appear; Wait for Lower Prices" (*Wall Street Journal,* February 13, 1947); "Abnormal Decline in Building Shown; Unseasonal Shrinkage in Home Construction in City in April Is Laid to 'Buying Strike'" (*New York Times,* May 11, 1947); "Bakers Battle Growing Consumer Resistance as Their Prices Hit Peak" (*Wall Street Journal,* January 15, 1948); "Rebellion at High Prices of Meat Spreads as Men and Dealers Join Women" (*Easton Express,* August 4, 1948).

Advocacy of price controls continued to serve as a political litmus test through the 1940s. The business-oriented *Kiplinger Letter* dismissed price controllers as "left-wingers" who "want to reform the whole system," while political progressives saw price regulation as a sacred cause.[127] The constant harping of consumer groups provoked President Truman to try on several occasions to reinstate government authority over pricing, but he either failed to win congressional support or backed down. The best he managed was the appointment in fall 1947 of a Citizens' Food Committee under the leadership of the president of Lever Brothers to run a voluntary program organized around the slogan "Eat Less—Waste Less," but, not surprisingly, it had little impact on prices, inventory, or the supply of grain available for shipping to a hungry Europe. The committee petered out by summer 1948.[128] Rent control was the sole survivor of the massive wartime price control machinery. Responsibility for it was transferred to the Office of the Housing Expediter when the OPA died, and although local tenant councils and leagues remained remarkably mobilized throughout the 1940s as watchdogs of rent control legislation in Washington and landlord abuses at home, Congress consistently watered down tenant protections, shifting the struggle over rent control to states and municipalities.[129]

The consumer activists of wartime proved themselves crucial players in the postwar battle to save price control. Most visible was the consumer movement itself, made up both of regulars like the OPA's Consumer Advisory Committee, the League of Women Shoppers, the American Association of University Women, and local consumer councils and tenant organizations nationwide, as well as newcomers to the fold, newly created organizations such as the Citizens' Price Defense Committee and existent groups that had come recently to embrace the consumer cause, most notably the American Veterans Committee and Veterans and Wives. When consumer activist Caroline Ware testified before Congress in support of extending price controls, she spoke on behalf of twenty-five national organizations with a combined membership in the millions.[130] The effective ending of price control in December 1946 inspired the establishment of several new organizations, most important the National Association of Consumers, founded by leaders of the recently disbanded OPA Consumer Advisory Committee, to organize consumers to "make their voices heard and actions felt in the highest councils of government, business and agriculture."[131] But the unambiguous defeat of price control would have serious consequences for the consumer movement's long-term influence, except perhaps in places like New York City, where rent control remained an important fact of life and inspired an advocacy infrastructure to protect it.

In the long-drawn-out drama over high prices and the authority of government to control them, women were the stars, handling everything from the lead roles to the walk-on parts in the campaigns for OPA renewal in 1944, 1945, and 1946, and in the continued protests against price hikes throughout the rest of the 1940s. As the leaders of consumer organizations, they staged a wide variety of performances ranging from baby carriage parades for "Buy Nothing Days" during the summer of 1946 to a mock trial in public entitled "The People of the State of New York Against High Prices" in June 1947 to organizing—by what became known as the "chain-telephone method"—an effective nationwide meat boycott in the summer of 1948, dubbed the "petticoat rebellion" by dismissive meat interests and "the revolt of the housewives" by those more sympathetic.[132] In these as well as less dramatic day-to-day activities such as testifying at hearings, circulating petitions, and running mass meetings, women built on expertise dating back to the national meat boycotts of 1935 and honed on homefront consumer organizing during the war. Highest tribute to their effectiveness came from a cartoon of September 1948 depicting a corporate board meeting where the chairman informs his associates, "The company is suffering from lack of advertising, gentlemen! How can we get the housewives to boycott us?"[133]

In every battle to extend price controls in 1944, 1945, and 1946, to reinstitute them in 1947 and 1948, and to roll back prices to 1946 levels throughout the late 1940s, African-American organizations like the NAACP were the most reliable allies women consumer activists had to count on. Citing food cost differentials that made the wartime exposés pale in comparison, "rent robbery" in black neighborhoods, and the "stranglehold" of low wages and spiraling prices, African-American witnesses pleaded for "real price control machinery across the board on food, clothing, and shelter," "even with its limitations."[134]

In Bowles's "battle of the century" to save the OPA, consumer activists gained a new ally that delighted them: the labor movement. When Reuther rallied his autoworker ranks in Cadillac Square to support a buyers' strike in July 1946 to "terrorize profiteers," his call represented a crucial turnaround for labor, which came out of the war at the peak of its strength before or since, with union membership at 36 percent of all non-farm American workers.[135] After relegating consumer issues mostly to AFL and CIO women's auxiliaries during the intense unionizing years of the 1930s and during wartime, suddenly labor leaders assessed their position in reconversion and recognized how intertwined and mutually endangered wages and prices were.[136]

As labor unions agitated for substantial wage increases to compensate for losses in overtime and other wartime job advantages, they realized how quickly these wage gains would evaporate if prices rose. The major goal of the historic 1946 strike wave in auto, steel, electrical, meatpacking, mines, and railroads—the greatest year for strikes since 1919—actually was to exert pressure on the Truman administration to keep the price control apparatus intact as workers sought wage increases from their employers.[137] Otherwise, as a United Steelworkers of America study, *The Braddock Steelworker,* tried to convince industrialists and federal policymakers, steelworkers' savings would not be spent "to help turn the wheels of industry. His savings will have to go for living essentials and not consumer durable goods—like washing machines, electric iceboxes, automobiles."[138] Already by the OPA battle of summer 1946, Reuther's UAW had lost its demand that GM grant a 30 percent wage increase out of corporate profits, without raising the price of cars. The Truman administration had given in to corporate pressure against its price stabilization program and allowed price increases based on higher labor costs. By July, when labor and consumers locked arms, workers were watching the wage increases they had won by striking negated by inflated prices. Labor's strategy in reconversion depended on winning both at the bargaining table and in the chambers of government, and loss of the OPA would doom it to a game of price-wage catch-up for years to come.

The evisceration of the OPA removed a major prop supporting the ideal of consumer citizenship that had emerged during the 1930s and flourished during the war. In this conception, being a consumer carried the rights and responsibilities of citizenship. Consuming, in safety and with full and fair access to markets, became a right to which all Americans supposedly were entitled, an intrinsic part of the "economic security and independence" that Roosevelt promised the nation in his "Second Bill of Rights" of 1944.[139] With that right, moreover, came the patriotic obligation to consume with the general good at heart, to observe price controls and other market regulations aimed at protecting consumers and preserving equity. Even African Americans, who were kept by discrimination from enjoying full consumer citizenship, recognized that vesting consumption with civic virtue could yield benefits in their quest for equality. Women, certainly, had propelled their responsibility as consumers into new kinds of political authority on the home front. War, meanwhile, kept the competing conception of the purchaser consumer—one who consumed in pursuit of personal gain—in check, at least until the end of war when alternative visions of postwar America vied for dominance.

As the government withdrew its hand from market regulation in 1946, it was not certain what kind of postwar order would emerge, and what place the consumer would have within it. But these things were clear: whatever reconversion came to mean, it was in no way an inevitability but rather would emerge out of the real contests won and lost during depression, war, and its immediate aftermath. Struggles played out over a decade and a half would set the stage for at least the next three. In addition, it was highly likely that consumers would remain central to conceptions of the "good (i.e., prosperous and moral) society," as they had during the New Deal and World War II. In the 1930s the consumer represented the public good in an age of emerging—and conflicting—countervailing powers. During World War II the consumer embodied the loyal, self-sacrificing citizen on the home front. In all likelihood, given the competing postwar visions at play in the battle over price control, the consumer would continue to figure centrally in the way American political culture evolved in peacetime.

How the tension between citizen consumers and purchaser consumers was resolved would have far-reaching consequences for postwar life. It would redefine gender roles, how women and men exerted influence in their families and communities and how that influence was recognized by the state. It would reshape class politics, as the labor movement began to embrace mass consumption as a legitimate terrain for organizing and collective bargaining. Racial life, too, would be affected, as the wartime campaign for a "Double V" set the direction for the postwar civil rights movement. And the nature of reconversion would even determine the physical reconstruction of metropolitan landscapes, both residential and commercial. At stake was nothing less than the future contours of American democratic society. In wartime, the government-sponsored OPA, the major vehicle for consumer citizenship, was praised by its supporters—many of whom sought its continuation into peacetime—as "that great democratic organization" and "the people's program." At war's end, mass producers proposed an alternative route to democracy, a mass consumption utopia that would benefit all purchaser consumers by raising everyone's standard of living. In the wake of the OPA's destruction, it was not at all clear how America's historic democratic mission would be fulfilled.[140] "Reconversion to what?" became the question of the day.

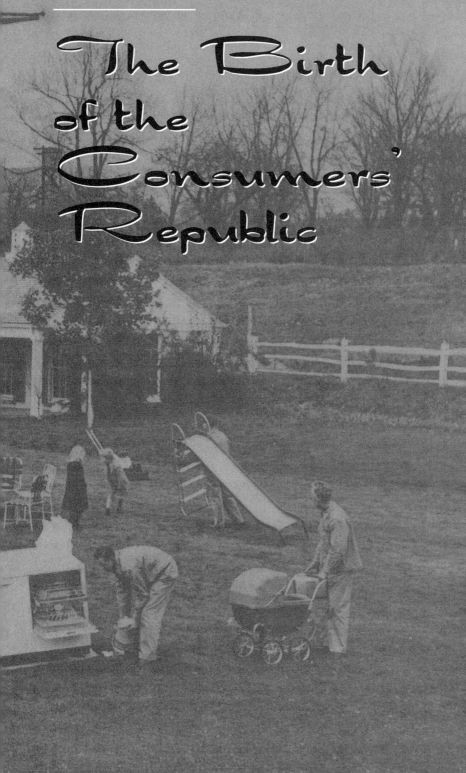

PART TWO

The Birth of the Consumers' Republic

CHAPTER 3

Reconversion: The Emergence of the Consumers' Republic

When readers opened up the May 5, 1947, issue of *Life* magazine, they beheld what was fast becoming the prevailing answer to the question "reconversion to what?" In a classic *Life* photo-essay—the magazine's distinctive style of using the lives of ordinary Americans to explore complex contemporary phenomena—readers observed the Hemeke family's adjustment to the postwar era. Entitled "Family Status Must Improve: It Should Buy More for Itself to Better the Living of Others," the story followed Ted and Jeanne Hemeke and their three children from their old, run-down house, where Ted arrived home in the clothes of a workingman and Jeanne struggled with the "dirty coal furnace" in the kitchen, to their symbolic entry into the new postwar order when they visited a modern ranch-style home that they—and the magazine's editors—clearly wished they could buy. In this imagined new life, Ted wore the middle-class badge of a suit, the children were fashionably dressed, and Jeanne approvingly surveyed

Overleaf: In "Family Utopia," *Life* magazine's editors presented "an honest representation of the dream of most U.S. families," based on consumer surveys and retail orders. With this feature, *Life* endorsed the increasingly common view that the health of the postwar economy would depend on Americans aspiring to own more commodities, here a suburban home, a convertible car, an electric stove, a washing machine, a television, and even a personal helicopter. *Life,* November 25, 1946. (Courtesy of Bernard Hoffman/TimePix)

If couples like Ted and Jeanne Hemeke purchased a new home and new consumer durables to put in it, a study sponsored by the Twentieth Century Fund predicted, they would not only improve their own lives but also make possible a higher standard of living for all Americans. *Life,* May 5, 1947. (Left, courtesy of Werner Wolff/Blackstar/TimePix; right, courtesy of Albert Fenn/TimePix; text courtesy of *Time*)

a kitchen stocked with shiny new appliances. In the accompanying text, *Life*'s editors asserted that realizing this fantasy would benefit more than the Hemeke family. Citing a Twentieth Century Fund projection for the economy in 1960, *Life* argued that "a health and decency standard for everyone" required that every American family acquire not only a "pleasant roof over its head" but all kinds of consumer goods to put in it, ranging from a washing machine and a telephone to matching dishes and silverware. As each family refurbished its hearth after a decade and a half of depression and war, the expanded consumer demand would stoke the fires of production, creating new jobs and, in turn, new markets. Mass consumption in postwar America would not be a personal indulgence, but rather a civic responsibility designed to provide "full employment and improved living standards for the rest of the nation."

    Life's concern with "everyone" and "the rest of the nation" bespoke a commonly held conviction that the revved-up engine of mass consumption promised to fulfill the long-sought goal of delivering an adequate standard of living to all Americans.[1] Another summary of the 875-page Twentieth Century Fund report prepared specifically for merchandisers of electrical products confirmed that equality of condition was anticipated by arguing for its potential to expand markets: "Shifts in the distribution of income will be even more important, from a marketing standpoint, than the general increase in over-all consumer income."[2] Reconversion after World War II raised the hopes of Americans of many political persuasions and social statuses that a more prosperous and equitable American society would finally be possible in the mid-twentieth century due to the enormous, and war-proven, capacities of mass production and mass consumption. The new growth economy of the Consumers' Republic promised more affluence to a greater number of Americans than ever before.

FOUNDERS OF THE NEW POSTWAR REPUBLIC

a wide range of economic interests, ranging from strident anti–New Deal big businessmen to moderate and liberal capitalists to labor and its allies on the left, endorsed the importance of mass consumption to making a successful reconversion from wartime to peacetime, although each came to value mass consumption for its own reasons. All of these interest groups feared a postwar depression with rampant unemployment as had followed World War I, and hence whatever their particular vision of reconversion, they favored taking immediate action to promote prosperity. Surprising caution among postwar consumers still fearful of profligate spending, despite pent-up demand and flush savings accounts from cashed-in war bonds, made quick action all the more crucial.[3] But from here priorities diverged. The conservative business interests that the National Association of Manufacturers (NAM) and the U.S. Chamber of Commerce represented sought to build on their hard-won defeats of price control and the Full Employment Act of 1945, which would have obligated the state to provide jobs if the private sector failed to create them (as the compromise Employment Act of 1946, which passed, did not). Business conservatives continued their efforts to dismantle New Deal–inspired government intervention in the operations of free enterprise. For them, more private investment leading to increased productivity was the route to economic growth and postwar prosperity, but the profits they sought from more efficiently produced and cheaply priced goods still depended on a dynamic mass consumer market.[4]

Moderate businessmen, represented by the Committee for Economic Development, which spun off from the Department of Commerce's Business

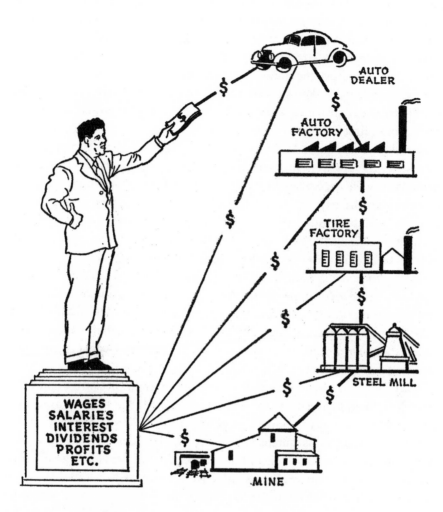

Spending Creates Jobs and Prosperity

In his book *Mobilizing for Abundance,* published in 1944, New Deal economist Robert Nathan considered consumer spending the key to activating a cycle of consumer markets fueling growth in industrial production and jobs, which in turn would create greater prosperity and more markets. Elsewhere in the book, he argued that new investment also depended on higher consumption, as "lagging consumption makes for excess capacity and stops investment." (Courtesy of The McGraw-Hill Companies)

Advisory Council during the war, had, in many cases, shared the conservatives' opposition to price control, but they also shared with liberal capitalists more openness to business-government cooperation and a sympathy for strengthening the demand side of the economy through full employment and wage hikes, so as to improve the standard of living of as many Americans as possible and, not incidentally, their purchasing power. Mass consumption, for the liberals particularly, provided a way of reconciling capitalist growth and democratic commitments, without endorsing too planned an economy or too powerful a welfare state. As liberal economist Robert R. Nathan put it in his treatise for the postwar era, *Mobilizing for Abundance,* "Only if we have large demands can we expect large production. Therefore . . . ever-increasing consumption on the part of our people [is] . . . one of the prime requisites for prosperity. Mass consumption is essential to the success of a system of mass production." Vitality in both realms, he argued, promised "abundance for all." Former OPA chief Chester Bowles echoed Nathan's perspective in his own forecast, *Tomorrow Without Fear:* "It is in the increase of consumer spending on the things that consumers want and need that we must look for the basic and lasting solution to our economic future." And, as Bowles told his former colleagues in advertising, the resulting mass markets, where "the janitor's appetite for a sirloin steak is as profitable as the banker's," would democratize the benefits of prosperity.[5]

Labor and others on the left were the most Keynesian in approach, seeking full employment at high wages; big markets for high-volume, low-unit-cost production of goods; and whatever government intervention was needed to sustain mass purchasing power. For them, a thriving mass consumption economy that workers fully participated in provided the essential key to national stability and mass affluence. As early as November 1944, the Congress of Industrial Organizations (CIO) made the plea, "Our economy feeds and grows on purchasing power as a baby does on milk. . . . The CIO knows that the baby will sicken if he does not have milk, that the whole community will suffer if purchasing power is not maintained." About the same time, the other major labor organization, the American Federation of Labor (AFL), registered a similar vision of postwar reconversion. George Meany, AFL secretary-treasurer, argued that "without adequate purchasing power in the form of wages we cannot get full postwar employment. Yes, we have the machinery to build all of the automobiles, all of the radios, washing machines and such things; we have the workers to build all of the houses that we could possibly use. But we will not make those things unless there is purchasing power available to buy them." Soon after V-J Day, Walter Reuther, soon-to-be-president of the United Automobile Workers-CIO, asserted to the influential

It Depends on How You Run the Machine

Securing high purchasing power for workers was the centerpiece of labor's postwar agenda, as jobs, wages, and high production were all thought to depend on it. "Economics to Keep the Peace," *Economic Outlook* (publication of the Congress of Industrial Organizations) 7 (March 1946). (Courtesy of the AFL-CIO)

readership of the *New York Times* that the route to reconversion was so obvious that only "our fear of abundance" could possibly keep us from speedily converting war plants to civilian production in the interest of creating jobs for workers and expanding consumer markets for manufacturers.[6]

Despite a divergence in how these groups viewed the proper role for government in the postwar economy—with, at the extremes, the NAM conservatives opposing any intervention in the free market and the unions welcoming as much as possible—the federal government in its postwar policies gave crucial support to the emerging consensus favoring a mass consumption–driven economy. To begin with, the Employment Act of 1946, the Magna Carta of postwar economic planning, defined the federal government's responsibility as "promot[ing] maximum employment, production, and purchasing power," with purchasing power providing the fulcrum for activating the other two.[7] Furthermore, all these interest groups, with the exception of the small political left of the late 1940s, supported complementary defense spending by the federal government, recognizing that a mass consumption economy would only benefit; consumer Keynesianism and military Keynesianism would go hand in hand in the era of the Cold War. Not only were companies like General Electric, Westinghouse, Goodyear, and Chrysler engaged in both kinds of production, facilitating the transfer of government-funded research from military to consumer applications, but predictable government spending on defense lent security to the consumer economy, and particularly to jobs.[8]

Other federal expenditures, such as the Servicemen's Readjustment Act of 1944 (better known as the GI Bill of Rights) and government support for housing and highway construction, likewise contributed to the emergence of a postwar "mixed economy" of public and private spending that kept mass consumption as its heart for a quarter century. Even social programs, such as unemployment insurance, social security, public assistance, and minimum wage legislation, it was recognized, helped maintain purchasing power. So pervasive was this view that Republican President Dwight D. Eisenhower, generally assumed to have been more cautious about government spending than Democratic presidents, hailed these "transfer" payments as crucial in fighting the recession of 1957–58 through "maintain[ing] personal income and consumption expenditures."[9]

As Eisenhower's statement reveals, Democratic and Republican administrations may have differed in the balance they sought between public and private spending, but they shared more common ground than not. Note these characteristic statements by Presidents Truman and Eisenhower. Deeply convinced of "the importance of purchasing power in keeping our economy fully employed and fully productive," President Harry Truman insisted to an audience in Oregon in 1950, "The uses of the powers of Government to achieve a higher living standard and a fair deal for all the people is not statism and it is not socialism. It is part of the American tradition." Eight years later, President Dwight Eisenhower, faced with a deepening recession, advocated his own version of the private-public mix. He asserted that an upturn in the economy would result from "millions of citizens making their purchases, having greater confidence," which the federal government would help by supporting more home and highway building, easing credit, and accelerating other spending projects.[10] The public, regardless of party affiliation, concurred with the postwar presidents. When surveyed in June 1954 as to whether "the Government can do anything to keep unemployment low and maintain prosperous times," about 70 percent answered in the affirmative. In 1960 more Americans looked to the government than business "to help sustain prosperity."[11]

Hence, despite vicious fighting over the extension of price controls in 1946, and struggles thereafter over the balance of power in industrial relations, the tautness of government regulation, and the extent of income redistribution through taxation, minimum wage, and other policies, *Life* magazine was right to proclaim a developing consensus by the late 1940s that a vital mass consumption–oriented economy provided the most promising route to postwar prosperity, even if the major economic interests disagreed over how best to achieve it. As a result, once again, as during the New Deal and World War II, consumers found themselves key players in the political economy, and in a way that reconciled wartime tensions between citizen and purchaser consumers.

In a resolution first hinted at by the federal government when it urged consumers to delay inflationary purchases during the war, and then perpetuated by opinion shapers like *Life* after the war had ended, the new postwar order of mass consumption deemed that the good purchaser devoted to "more, newer and better" was the good citizen. Out of the wartime conflict between citizen consumers, who reoriented their personal consumption to serve the general good, and purchaser consumers, who pursued private gain regardless of it, emerged a new postwar ideal of the purchaser as citizen who simultaneously fulfilled personal desire and civic obligation by consuming. As *Bride's* magazine told the acquisitive readers of its handbook for newlyweds, when you buy "the dozens of things you never bought or even thought of before . . . you are helping to build greater security for the industries of this country. . . . [W]hat you buy and how you buy it is very vital in your new life—and to our whole American way of living." Much as during the struggle against the Great Depression of the 1930s, excessive saving by consumers was

In the postwar Consumers' Republic, even the bride's acquisition of a new electric coffeepot promised to benefit the public good. Robert Burian. (Courtesy of Carpenter Center Photography Collection, Harvard University)

excoriated. Not coincidentally, Walt Disney's miserly Scrooge McDuck, self-ishly wallowing in his stockpiles of gold coins, made his entry into popular culture in 1947. A decade later, *Fortune* editor William H. Whyte would still proclaim, "thrift is now un-American." Wherever one looked in the aftermath of war, one found a vision of postwar America where the general good would be best served not by frugality or even moderation, but by individuals pursuing personal wants in a flourishing mass consumption marketplace. Only fear of inflation, as prices skyrocketed after the lifting of price controls and then again with the Korean War, and occasional business concerns over the nation's low savings rate cautioned any restraint.[12]

Within a city like Newark, New Jersey, when the Chamber of Commerce and other local business groups sat down to plan for postwar recovery, their prescription for prosperity—entitled "Newark Will Have Money to Spend!"—mirrored the national one. Carefully charting and graphing the exploding purchasing potential of consumers in Newark and surrounding Essex County as a result of the war, community leaders forecast that consumers "in a mood to buy in the post war period" would create record levels of employment and business profits, as well as guide the nation from the potential "chaos of peace" to "a safe and stable postwar position." For Newark's planners, as for their counterparts throughout the country, purchasers as citizens held the fate of the postwar economy—and of cities like Newark—in their hands.[13]

A thriving mass consumption economy was more than the panacea of postwar planners. For the next quarter century consumer spending indeed helped secure an historic reign of prosperity, longer lasting and more universally enjoyed than ever before in American history. National output of goods and services doubled between 1946 and 1956, and would double again by 1970, with private consumption expenditures holding steady at two-thirds of gross national product (GNP, the total market value of final goods and services produced by the nation's economy) over the era.[14] Certainly there were downturns, such as the recessions of 1953–54, 1957–58, and 1960–61, when unemployment edged up and growth slowed. But, inevitably, recessions were followed by recoveries that each time lifted Americans' wage scales and living standards a little higher. During the quarter century of great prosperity from 1949 to 1973, median and mean family income doubled. As the service sector boomed over the postwar period, moreover, expenditures within it—such as for travel, recreation, education, and medical services—were considered part of the thriving consumer budget, and thereby contributed to the power of mass consumption in creating affluence.[15]

As predicted during the war, new house construction provided the bedrock of the postwar mass consumption economy, both through turning "home" into an expensive commodity for purchase by many more consumers than ever before and by stimulating demand for related commodities. As today, the purchase of a new single-family home generally obligated buyers to acquire new household appliances and furnishings, and if the house was in the suburbs, as over 80 percent were, at least one car as well. The scale of new residential construction following World War II was unprecedented, as the nation coped with a "housing shortage of unparalleled magnitude," according to one government study. The *Kansas City Star* described the cramped conditions more caustically: "Slogan for 1946: Two Families in Every Garage." At war's end, somewhere between 3.5 and 5 million new homes were required immediately to house all the individuals and families in need, and by some estimates as many as 50 percent of existing homes needed replacement or major repairs. The remedy put the mixed economy to the test. As President Truman told the American people in a radio broadcast on reconversion in January 1946, this was "a job for private enterprise to do," while "the Government is determined to give private enterprise every encouragement and assistance to see that the houses are produced," and, he might have added, "consumed." That encouragement and assistance came through government mortgage guarantees with low interest rates and no down payment directly to buyers as part of the package of Veterans Administration (VA) benefits funded by the GI Bill, and indirectly to buyers through mortgage insurance to lenders and developers through the Federal Housing Administration (FHA) to lower their risk and encourage them to lend or build more generously and cheaply.

Suddenly, with the availability of less expensive, mass-produced homes, the need for only small or nominal down payments, lower interest rates for longer-term mortgages, and income tax advantages from mortgage interest and property tax deductions, millions of Americans concluded it was cheaper to own than to rent. And even if they did not start off so inclined, they soon reconsidered as they discovered the scarcity of decent rentals; rental-type housing represented no more than one-eighth of privately owned units constructed between 1950 and 1956, for example, in contrast to two-fifths in the 1920s, when many investors built housing to generate rental income.

Preference for private market solutions that would boost the mass consumption economy—even if heavily subsidized by the federal government—over more statist solutions like government-built housing, turned a dire social need for shelter into an economic boon.[16] While the nation's total economic output increased between 1952 and 1960 by close to 25 percent, and the use of goods and services for consumption about 30 percent, expenditures on residential construction rose more than 40 percent. One out of every four homes standing in the United States in 1960 went up in the 1950s. As a result of this explosion in house construction, by the same year, 62 percent of Americans could claim that they owned their own homes, in contrast to only 44 percent as recently as 1940, the largest jump in homeownership rates ever recorded. And in another turning point, suburban residents of single-family homes came to outnumber both urban and rural dwellers.[17] Home building became so central a component of postwar prosperity that beginning in 1959, the Census Bureau began calculating "housing starts" on a monthly basis as a key indicator of the economy's vitality.[18]

Buying homes, particularly new ones, motivated consumers to purchase things to put in them, and thereby helped stoke the crucial consumer durables market. Billions of dollars were transacted in the sale of household appliances and furnishings, as refrigerators, washing machines, televisions, and the like became standard features in postwar American homes. Most remarkable was the jump in American families owning a mechanical refrigerator: from 44 to 80 percent between 1940 and 1950. Consumer expenditure studies furthermore concluded that purchases of new household appliances represented a net increment, not a shift in spending from one kind of durable good to another.[19] Automobile sales boomed as well, with new-car sales quadrupling between 1946 and 1955, until three-quarters of American households owned at least one car by the end of the 1950s. Proving the logic of a demand-based economy, by the time the domestic auto industry reached its peak of production in 1965, turning out 11.1 million cars, trucks, and buses that year, one out of every six American jobs could be linked to this enormous consumer market. Residential construction produced a similar ripple effect.[20]

But a prosperity built so much on consumer demand raised a challenge: how to keep demand growing once war savings had been exhausted and the delayed purchases of wartime satisfied. Postwar population growth—by nearly half between 1945 and 1970—and rising incomes helped, and merchandisers invented some ingenious strategies for stimulating consumer demand. But more than anything else, the explosion of consumer credit and borrowing kept the postwar mass consumption economy afloat. Mortgage debt, fueled by VA and FHA lending, expanded along with home ownership, but so too did other forms of credit and borrowing. The value of total consumer credit grew almost elevenfold between 1945 and 1960, and installment credit—the major component of the total by the postwar era—jumped a stunning nineteenfold, with car purchases responsible for a major portion of that. When *Life* magazine gave "A Hard Look at Consumer Credit" in 1955, it identified a "revolution in consumer purchasing," where "instead of saving for years to afford major purchases, customers buy on credit and enjoy the goods while they pay for them." At least half of all major household appliances and 60 percent of car sales involved credit, and somewhat alarmingly to *Life*'s editors, the rate at which families were going into debt was rising faster than income. That remarkable growth in consumer debt worried others as well: "When businessmen generally talk confidently of a continued upsurge in sales," the *Wall Street Journal* fretted, "many an American has pushed his credit close to the limit."

Another major contributor to the explosion of consumer credit in the postwar era was the expansion of credit cards from the limited number of retail store and gasoline company charge cards available before the war to their much greater use, and in particular, the development of third-party universal cards. First to appear was Diners Club in 1949, the success of which inspired American Express, Hilton Hotels, Bank of America, and Chase Manhattan Bank to mount competitors in 1958. Many others would follow, all putting more and more credit at the disposal of consumers.[21] "The democratization of credit was proceeding at a gallop," is how one historian of finance describes the atmosphere of the era. And a 1959 Department of Labor study, *How American Buying Habits Change,* confirmed that ordinary workers had radically changed their mode of financing by the 1950s, from striving to save to incurring substantial debt. A year earlier, in fact, the National Retail Credit Association had announced that whereas in the heart of the depression in 1935, 35 percent of the 70,000 personal bankruptcies were by wage earners, now 85 percent of an 80,000 total were. Not surprisingly, by 1957, two-thirds of American families carried some kind of debt, about half of all families owing from installment buying.[22] Without a doubt, credit became an admission ticket that granted purchasers as citizens full entry into postwar mass consumer prosperity—and retailers and third-party lenders additional profits.

The flourishing of mass consumption was first and foremost a route to recovery and sustained health of the economy, but it also provided a ready weapon in the political struggles of the Cold War era. No sooner had World War II ended than this new war raged, fought with ideological swords as much as stockpiles of armaments and bombs. As the United States justified its superiority over the Soviet Union both at home and abroad, the mass consumption economy offered an arsenal of weapons to defend the reputation of capitalist democracy against the evils of communism. Three rather typical "sponsored films" produced from the late 1940s to the mid-1950s by private corporations and nonprofit foundations for public viewing in movie theaters, community meetings, and workplaces, each about ten to fifteen minutes in length, captured the dominant ideas in circulation linking mass consumption to the "American way of life." Although each film had its own specific agenda, from promoting free enterprise to selling oil, all three—and scores of films like them—assumed the centrality of mass consumption to American supremacy.

The most common way that mass consumption figured in the defense of American capitalist democracy was as evidence of the economic egalitarianism it made possible, a distribution of American abundance that beat the Soviets at their own game of creating a classless society. Widespread American home ownership and high living standards, the argument went, put to rest Soviet charges that capitalism created extremes of wealth and poverty, and secured a firm foundation for American freedom. The documentary film *Despotism,* produced and distributed by Encyclopaedia Britannica in 1946 and re-released in 1954, argued that the broader the distribution of land and other property in a community or nation, the greater the potential for democracy. If wealth proved too concentrated—including in the hands of one state or industry—and information too controlled, then despotism threatened.[23]

The claims of *Despotism* that mass consumption was creating a more egalitarian American society echoed everywhere during the 1950s. Popular magazines hammered the point home: "Our houses are all on one level, like our class structure," *House Beautiful* asserted, while *Life* celebrated how a rising standard of living meant that "people are getting more and more on a level with each other."[24] A Labor Department study of American consumer patterns claimed, "Certainly the automobile has aided wage earners . . . in breaking down barriers of community and class." Likewise, Presidents Truman and Eisenhower on many occasions praised the economic equality accompanying mass consumer prosperity. "During the last 50 years," Truman claimed in his State of the Union message to Congress in 1950, "our nation has grown enormously in material well-being." In particular, he stressed, "the income of the average family has increased so greatly that its buying power has doubled." A decade later, Eisenhower was even more confident. At the National Automobile Show industry dinner in Detroit, he praised "the great spread, throughout the peoples of our nation, of the benefits of the American system." In concrete terms that meant "an American working man can own his own comfortable home and a car and send his children to well-equipped elementary and high schools and to colleges as well. They [the Soviets] fail to realize that he is not the downtrodden, impoverished vassal of whom Karl Marx wrote. He is a self-sustaining, thriving individual, living in dignity and in freedom."[25]

A second film, *How to Lose What We Have,* presented by the American Economic Foundation and "made possible by" Inland Steel Co. and Borg-Warner Corporation, reinforced Eisenhower's link between a wide distribution of the fruits of American prosperity and political freedom by contrasting them to Soviet impoverishment in both categories.[26] This dramatization, made in 1950, depicted a community facing a plebiscite between American-style limited government with an unregulated free market economy and a "master plan" of unlimited government with a planned economy. Soon after the Soviet-style "master state" wins, a pickup truck arrives at one family's comfortable suburban home to move the original owners out and two other families in, not very subtly conveying the inferior standard of living under communism. When "average Joe" householder protests, "You can't do this to me," the "party man" responds that he has orders to move him three hundred miles away to a new job and to take away his home and car. As the truck drives off with family and possessions crammed into the open back and Joe's wife complaining that she didn't even have a chance to finish hanging curtains, the film equates political freedom with exchange in a free market economy: Americans live "far better off than the rest of the world," "freely buy and sell," and have "free choice as customers," "right down to the brand of cigarettes [they] smoke or don't smoke."

This yoking of free choice as consumers with political freedom was made frequently during the Cold War. Probably best known is the "kitchen" debate between Vice President Richard Nixon and Soviet Premier Nikita Khrushchev at the American Exhibition in Moscow in 1959, where Americans flaunted their latest model homes, appliances, cars, fashions, and free Pepsi as embodying, in Nixon's words, "what freedom means to us." Nixon boasted that with three-fourths of America's 44 million families owning their own homes, along with 56 million cars, 50 million televisions, and 143 million radios, "The United States comes closest to the ideal of prosperity for all in a classless society." He likewise sanctified the variety of goods available to American consumers as symbolic of "our right to choose. We do not wish to have decisions made at the top by government officials," whether about "the kind of house" or "the kind of ideas."[27] Demonstrating the ubiquitousness of this perspective, voices much more liberal than Nixon's, such as New Dealers David Lilienthal and Chester Bowles, shared his equation of freedom with, in Lilienthal's words, "a maximum range of choice for the consumer when he spends his dollar."[28]

A third film, *Destination Earth,* produced by the American Petroleum Institute in 1954, suggested how the link between freedom and mass consumer affluence provided a strategy for recruiting developing countries into the American sphere of influence.[29] In this animated, pseudo-science-fiction film, a space explorer from a repressive communist Mars, under the dictatorship of a Colonel Ogg, visits Earth to learn how to operate the state limousine service more efficiently. Finding himself in the United States of America, the explorer encounters an astonishing prosperity created by competitive enterprise and cheap oil, where "almost everybody has one of those automobiles" of his own. He returns to Mars armed with the tools to remake it in Earth's image, and in no time Martians overthrow Colonel Ogg for a life of free enterprise, free speech, and universal auto ownership.

In real life, the potential power of American consumer goods to win the hearts and minds of people in the so-called developing world while also fattening American manufacturers' purses was not lost on the postwar presidents. Eisenhower reminded Americans that they must continue to meet Khrushchev's challenge—"We declare war upon you in the peaceful field of trade"—with continued "leadership in world trade" and "unprecedented generosity . . . in helping to protect freedom and to promote rising levels of well-being in all nations wishing to be independent and free." Kennedy took up the mantle of encouraging American consumer exports with a sharper eye on developing markets, arguing that "too little attention . . . has been paid to the part which an early exposure to American goods, American skills and the American way of doing things can play in forming the tastes and desires and customs of these newly emerging nations." Not only would American products appeal in their own right, but their obvious superiority to shoddy Soviet manufactures would dramatize the superiority of capitalism over communism.[30] Undergirding this Cold War foreign policy of fostering capitalist democracy through marketing American goods abroad was an assumed hierarchy of material and political development that placed the United States, in its "high mass consumption stage" in contemporary economist Walt W. Rostow's terminology, at the pinnacle of modernization.[31]

Faith in a mass consumption postwar economy hence came to mean much more than the ready availability of goods to buy. Rather, it stood for an elaborate, integrated ideal of economic abundance and democratic political freedom, both equitably distributed, that became almost a national civil religion from the late 1940s into the 1970s. As ever present as this paradigm was, however, it bore no specific label at the time, so for convenience sake I will dub it the Consumers' Republic. For at least a quarter century, the ideal of the Consumers' Republic provided the blueprint for American economic, social, and political maturation, as well as for export around the globe.

The Consumers' Republic had many appeals, not the least of which was the substantial prosperity it fostered, but perhaps most attractive was the way it promised the socially progressive end of economic equality without requiring politically progressive means of redistributing existing wealth. Rather, it was argued that an ever growing economy built around the dynamics of increased productivity and mass purchasing power would expand the overall pie without reducing the size of any of the portions. When President Truman

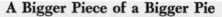

A Bigger Piece of a Bigger Pie

SHARE OF LOWEST THIRD IN THE NATIONAL INCOME

A Bigger Pie and a Thicker Slice, Too

SHARE OF MIDDLE THIRD IN THE NATIONAL INCOME

A Thinner Slice from a Bigger Pie Still Means More Pie

SHARE OF TOP THIRD IN THE NATIONAL INCOME

In what the book jacket described as "a forward-looking, optimistic plan for the nation," former OPA chief Chester Bowles argued that a postwar prosperity built on high consumer spending promised a more egalitarian America by expanding the economic pie without requiring reallocation of any of its portions. (Reprinted with the permission of Simon & Schuster from *Tomorrow Without Fear* by Chester Bowles. Copyright © 1946 by Chester Bowles.)

challenged Americans in 1950 to "achieve a far better standard of living for every industrious family" within a decade, specifically "an income of $4,000 a year," he reassured them that "raising the standards of our poorest families will not be at the expense of anybody else. We will all benefit by doing it, for the incomes of the rest of us will rise at the same time." Eight years later, John Kenneth Galbraith would bemoan in his classic work, *The Affluent Society,* how much liberals and conservatives, businessmen and economists, rich and even poor were deceiving themselves that an expanding economy was bringing not only "material improvement for the average man," but also "an end to poverty and privation for all." They were blind, he scolded, to "a self-perpetuating margin of poverty at the very base of the income pyramid" that "goes largely unnoticed, because it is the fate of a voiceless minority." Despite critical acclaim for Galbraith's book, his remained an unheeded cry in the wilderness, and the prevailing wisdom persisted that continued economic growth in the Consumers' Republic could sow the seeds of a natural egalitarianism.[32]

THE FATE OF THE CONSUMER MOVEMENT IN THE CONSUMERS' REPUBLIC

a consensus may have emerged among powerful interest groups by the late 1940s around the desirability of a mass consumer economy and the influence of consumers within it, but not everyone with the interests of consumers at heart was pleased. Activists in the consumer movement that had flourished through the economic doldrums of the Great Depression, the war emergency, and its immediate aftermath found themselves and their organizations increasingly marginalized as the Consumers' Republic gathered momentum.[33]

A variety of factors converged to stall consumer activism after the meat boycotts of the late 1940s. Although consumers were still very much on everyone's minds, the growing dominance of Keynesian economics within influential business, government, and labor circles put more emphasis on the power of total consumer spending—to determine everything from employment to economic growth—than on the need to protect the rights and interests of individual consumers, the traditional mission of consumer organizations. "Consumers in the economy" gradually displaced "the consumer in the marketplace." Quietly, the consumer interest programs of the New Deal and the war were dismantled, so by the time the Korean War brought price control back in 1950–51, a mere half decade after World War II, no consumer participation was even included, until popular agitation resulted in the reluctant cre-

ation of a weak Consumer Advisory Committee to the Office of Price Stabilization. Although the President's Council of Economic Advisers (CEA), created under the Employment Act of 1946 to assist the President in the
preparation of economic reports to Congress, appointed a National Consumer
Advisory Committee, it too had little authority, few means to initiate action,
and was not even renewed by President Eisenhower's CEA in 1953.

The increasing prosperity of the postwar era, moreover, made it hard
for consumer organizers to transcend the mainstream discourse celebrating
consumer purchasing power and to politicize consumers, who no longer felt as
vulnerable as they once had to burdensome shortages, spiking prices, and
inadequate product grading and labeling. Rather, larger economic concerns
like inflation, consumer credit, and housing scarcity were the compelling consumer issues of the day. Relatedly, the ascetic side of the consumer movement
that had promoted government regulation and consumer restraint seemed out
of step with these more bounteous times. Needless to say, consumer organizer
Caroline Ware's call for the replacement of "conspicuous consumption" to
"keep up with the Joneses" with "an American Standard" of "decent living"
premised on "keeping down with the Joneses" did not excite enthusiasm. Nor
did it help that the depression-scarred reputations of business and industry
had been resuscitated through their indisputable contributions to the war
effort, making it harder to mobilize public opinion against them.

Confidently reasserting its authority, business also went out of its way
to portray itself as a responsible agent in American economic life, serving customers to their own best advantage. The Household Finance Corporation of
Chicago, for example, published a series of booklets on "better buymanship,"
recommending a twenty-point checklist for fulfilling "good consumer citizenship." The premier trade journal of the advertising industry, Printers' Ink, put
special emphasis on counseling advertisers and businesses on ways to "demonstrate that the company is striving to serve the best interests of the consumer."[34]
And where co-optation of the consumer movement failed, intimidation often
prevailed. Red-baiting of consumer activists and their organizations by conservative business and congressional forces that had raged in the late 1930s
and retreated during wartime resurfaced with the anti-communist hysteria of
the late 1940s, destroying effective organizations like the League of Women
Shoppers by fingering "known Communists" active in their ranks. The hardly
radical Consumers Union was not cleared of "red charges" by the House Un-
American Activities Committee until 1954, after extensive hearings.[35] Finally,
and perhaps most important, the moral claim previously asserted by the consumer movement—to represent the general good—had shifted to the Consumers' Republic itself, which promised that consumers' purchasing power
would improve the lives of all Americans.

Consumer organizing in the best of times presented a unique challenge, as consumers' ranks could include both everyone and no one. On the positive side, everyone was a potential recruit, but in reality, mobilizing such a range of individuals to recognize their common interests as consumers could be difficult. In the prosperous era after the war, the task proved monumental. "When the emergency is alleviated," longtime consumer activist Persia Campbell lamented in 1958, "interest and action tend to decrease." Updating of congressional legislation during the 1940s and 1950s only protected consumers from the worst abuses in new chemical pesticides, additives in food and cosmetics, "miracle" drugs, and highly flammable fabrics, much of it monitored by a loose and poorly funded organization of existing consumer-oriented agencies, the Consumer Clearinghouse, formed in 1943. Many other new initiatives languished, despite some spectacular revelations during legislative hearings. Not until the mass of Americans perceived threats to their health and safety in the 1960s and 1970s could consumer organizations successfully inspire them to reassert their right to better protection as consumers.[36] Although a major consumer organization, Consumers Union, would flourish during the postwar era, with the readership of its magazine, *Consumer Reports,* mushrooming from 55,000 during World War II to 700,000 in 1954, it would increasingly stray from its original militant commitment (which, for example, incorporated ratings of corporate-labor relations in its evaluation of products) to become a kind of buying guide to consumer durables for a more and more affluent, educated, professional middle-class audience.[37] *Consumer Reports* became a fitting manual for the purchasers as citizens who peopled the Consumers' Republic.

The fate of the most activist organization of the era reveals something of the infertility of the postwar soil for cultivating consumer consciousness. Committed consumer activists founded the National Association of Consumers (NAC) in late 1946–early 1947, as their previous platform, the OPA's National Consumer Advisory Committee, disbanded. They envisioned an umbrella organization representing individuals and local and national consumer groups, many of them created on the wartime home front, so that "all groups of people" will "organize a strong consumer consciousness," "function more effectively in their own communities[,] and . . . be heard more clearly in Washington and in their state capitals." The NAC's masthead was a veritable "who's who" of the consumer movement, with Chester Bowles's wartime consumer advisers at its nucleus: Helen Hall, former vice chair of the OPA committee took on the chairmanship; OPA staff members and advisory committee members like Esther Cole Franklin, Caroline Ware, Colston Warne, Persia Campbell, Hazel Kyrk, and Ella Baker became board members; and prominent individuals ranging from Eleanor Roosevelt to original OPA chief Leon Henderson to Columbia sociologist Robert Lynd served as advisers. Initially committed to continuing the OPA's fight against skyrocketing food prices, the NAC's long-term mission was to lobby on behalf of consumers for long-sought goals such as product grading, rent and price control, better milk pricing and dating, regulation of chemical additives in food, school lunch programs, and permanent administrative structures like a committee on consumer interests in Congress, a cabinet-level consumer agency in the executive branch, and an official voice in the United Nations. To reach its members and chapters, the NAC published a newsletter, *Consumers on the March*, with reports on lobbying efforts and educational campaigns.[38]

Although the NAC's logo symbolically conveyed a diversity of determined consumers on the march past urban tenements, suburban homes, and rural farms, in fact the association was beset with financial and organizational problems from the start. Worried about its future as early as the late 1940s, Persia Campbell decried the difficulty of "pulling together individuals prominent in the consumer field, and representatives from different groups, into a working team," a tension not helped by the "current fear of 'communist infiltration,' which tends further to divide leaders on questions of organization."[39] But it was a lack of grassroots support that really sealed the NAC's fate. Aware of the public's market-basket concerns, the NAC tried to sell itself as committed to "raising the standard of living of the American people through consumer action." The effort failed. When membership, which was never enormous, took a further nosedive in the early 1950s, down from a high of 2400 members and 17 chapters to fewer than 300 members and 2 chapters by 1954, what had been precarious became unviable. The newsletter ceased publishing in 1953, and four years later the NAC itself went defunct.

But even as the consumer movement stagnated from the late 1940s through the 1950s, consumers themselves retained the keen attention of economic planners and business interests committed to boosting demand. Ironically, as consumers' own organizations and initiatives were faltering, they were becoming the subject of an increasing number of studies aimed at understanding how their attitudes and perceptions as consumers affected the vitality of the American economy, what an article in the *New York Times Magazine* in 1947 called "the subtle interplay of psychological and economic processes." As survey methodology gained in sophistication during and particularly after the war with improved sampling and open interviewing techniques, analysts were no longer content solely with measuring consumers' financial status or patterns of past purchases. Rather, they sought to understand the psychology of consumers in order to predict future consumer behavior upon which the well-being of the Consumers' Republic so clearly rested. The pioneer in this effort was the Survey Research Center at the University of Michigan, which began in

1946 under the direction of George Katona to investigate consumer expectations for their own finances as well as the nation's economy on a monthly basis for the Federal Reserve Board. Many other efforts to gauge consumer confidence followed, prominent among them the *Fortune* "Consumer Outlook" beginning in 1947; the Princeton Research Service's quarterly opinion studies, "Economic Trends," beginning in 1949; and a major study by the National Bureau of Economic Research in 1959 analyzing annual surveys of Consumers Union members from 1946 to 1958 to track the relationship between buying plans and actual buying over time in order to improve forecasting of consumer spending.[40]

In this sense, then, postwar concern with aggregate consumer demand had not erased the significance of the individual consumer's needs and wants. But rather than focus on what consumers thought about product safety, grading and labeling, and just prices—as the consumer movement had—survey experts investigated how the individual consumer's subjective frame of mind boded for the nation's economy. Scientifically understanding when and why people bought automobiles and appliances, or chose not to spend at all, became the key to orchestrating greater economic stability and growth without galloping inflation. "Consumer demand," as Katona and his co-author, Eva Mueller, put it, "is a function of both *ability to buy* as measured by data on income, assets, debts, and the like, and *willingness to buy* as measured by attitudinal and expectational questions in surveys." Business leaders concurred. Facing an economic downturn in 1953, one went so far as to argue that "the psychological reaction of consumers would largely determine whether business would keep on booming or slip into recession." Even President Eisenhower appreciated how much the psyche of the consumer affected America's economic fate. "In a free economy, people do not always buy just because they have money," he reflected in 1958. "Theirs is the sovereign right of choice. One of the hopeful developments of recent years is that new knowledge is rapidly being accumulated about the aspirations and wants and motivations of our people."[41] By the 1960s, in fact, the many new insights gained into the complexity of consumers' motives would lead marketers to revise basic strategies for maximizing profits in the mass consumption economy.

CHANGING THE GENDER RULES OF THE GAME

When Irving Berlin's musical *Annie Get Your Gun* opened its spectacularly successful run on Broadway in May 1946, theater audiences could identify with sharpshooter Annie Oakley's confused state of mind about what entailed appropriate female and male behavior. One moment the show's protagonist was swaggering to her male competition "Anything You Can Do I Can Do Better," the next moment confessing "You Can't Get a Man with a Gun."[42] The big question of the day—"reconversion to what?"—probed not only the character of the postwar political economy, but also the nature of social relations within a world being reconstructed after the disruptions of war. As the Consumers' Republic evolved in the postwar period, it brought with it new "rules of the game" that redefined gender, class, and racial norms. Those new rules, conceived to deliver economic prosperity to as many Americans as possible through a flourishing mass consumer market, often had unintended effects that advantaged some social groups over others and created new inequalities while addressing old ones. Overall, Americans prospered between 1945 and 1975, but the infrastructure erected to deliver that prosperity contained biases that made it more some people's Consumers' Republic than others'.

The vicious battle over the survival of the OPA in 1946 set the stage for the rewriting of gender rules with the return to peace. Pro–price control forces—overwhelmingly female, black, working-class, and progressive—were painted by the victorious opposition as weak, dependent, and feminine, while proponents of ending governmental regulation of the consumer marketplace portrayed themselves as strong, independent, and masculine. Throughout the definitive struggle of spring and summer 1946, both sides associated women with the forces seeking control and men with decontrol. For example, in May when two professors at the New York State College of Agriculture at Cornell criticized the way they felt politics was prevailing over sound economics in unwisely prolonging the life of the OPA, they characterized the sides as follows: "the advocates are primarily buyers over retail counters and predominantly women. The opponents are primarily sellers in wholesale markets and are mostly men. . . . To placate the women, the House on April 17 refused to kill OPA outright . . . and the next day voted to extend price controls by the overwhelming vote of 355 to 42. To placate the men, they voted 245 to 150 to remove the food subsidies without which price control is impossible." Defenders of the OPA, including President Truman, similarly portrayed suffering consumers as female—as housewives struggling to feed their families—and price control opponents as male businessmen, farmers, merchants, and congressmen beholden to selfish interests.

In August, after Congress rejected and then halfheartedly reinstated the OPA, observers were still depicting the struggle in gender terms. Recounting a hearing of the OPA Decontrol Board, *New York World Telegram* columnist Frederick C. Othman described the decontrollers as "portly," "inscrutable in gray tie and gray suit," and spinners of "visions of white bread again, cake, beer, and bonded bourbon whisky," and the key witness advocating the reimposition of price controls, "talking for the housewives of America," as "a handsome little woman in a dress of blue and black stripes and a blue straw hat to give us dreamers a jolt."[43] After price control went down to defeat, the linkage between women, advocacy of government regulation, and political weakness only grew. By the late 1940s even liberal supporters of price control in the Democratic Party came to fear that sustaining this position would obligate the party to new, and undesirable, forms of economic regulation, and make it too politically vulnerable.[44]

As the price control struggle foreshadowed, the policies pursued and the values embraced in the Consumers' Republic circumscribed gender roles in such a way as to delegitimate the civic authority that women had gained on the home front during World War II. Like women who lost lucrative skilled industrial jobs at war's end, women who had enhanced their political authority on the home front through their influence as citizen consumers found themselves marginalized from public life during reconversion. The defeat of price control was a slap in the face to the tens of thousands of women who mobilized for its extension, and a warning of changing times.[45]

The pejorative labels of "female" and "weak" also undermined the consumer movement more broadly. Whereas its reputation as female-dominated had once given it prestige as a voice of morality and the public interest, in the new postwar world female identification only tainted the consumer movement as out of step with the times and, accompanied by a decline in ordinary women's consumer activism, contributed to its decline. Even when some female consumer leaders, such as the founders of the NAC, persevered in the postwar era, the changing commitments of their grassroots supporters limited activists' national effectiveness. In 1946–47, for example, the Consumer Conference of Greater Cincinnati's monthly members' programs continued to address the kinds of topics that had occupied female citizen consumers during the war: in October, "Your Country's Welfare Needs Your Wise Buying"; in March, "Trade Barriers"; in April, "Consumer's Responsibility to Themselves and Other Consumers." By the next year, however, a shift in programming toward lessons in maximizing consumer purchasing power was already discernible. In 1947–48 panel discussions addressed such topics as "Do You Have Drycleaning Troubles?," "The Cost of Eating Out," "Know Your Plastics," and "Oh Lady Does Your Dress Fit?" In 1950 and 1951 the Consumer Conference's annual program schedule featured two new slogans that reflected the organization's growing emphasis on household budgeting and prudent shopping: "Make Your Dollars Have More Cents" and "Belong to the Consumer Conference to Protect Your Pocketbook." The Consumer Conference of Greater Cincinnati may have survived longer than many other prewar consumer organizations, but its postwar preoccupation with "consumers' interests" would have been barely recognizable to the female activists who had founded it in 1934 to protect "*the* consumer interest."[46]

In short, soon after the war's end, female consumers withdrew from the civic arena as wartime citizen consumers and even to some extent as postwar purchasers as citizens. Sorting out whether this was imposed on women or chosen by them as they devoted themselves to long-neglected family needs is difficult. Certainly, very quickly they were less identified as public-minded citizens than during the war. When in 1948, for example, President Truman addressed a Department of Labor conference commemorating the 100th anniversary of the Seneca Falls Women's Rights Convention, he deliberately welcomed "homemakers, workers, citizens," in that order, because "if it were not for the homemakers, we would have neither the citizens nor the workers." Clearly, his "homemakers" were female, his "workers" and "citizens" male.[47] When Mrs. Raymond Sayre, a postwar proponent of a greater public role for women "as citizens of the world," addressed an international meeting in 1947, she recognized that if women were to gain public visibility, they must "think of themselves first of all as citizens, not as homemakers or consumers." Acknowledging that "the homemaker most often thinks of herself as consumer," Mrs. Sayre argued that this role, as currently understood, conferred too narrow a concern with prices; deliberately identifying as citizen would give women "a sense of responsibility to the general welfare," what not very long before, it should be noted, "consumer" itself implied. By testifying to the severing of the link between activist citizen and consumer that had prevailed throughout the Great Depression and World War II, Mrs. Sayre and other like-minded postwar advocates of greater female civic engagement prepared the way for politically active women—albeit a decided minority—to assert themselves as peace activists, union organizers, civil rights boycotters, even political party faithfuls, but rarely any longer as consumers.[48]

Women may have made different choices in peacetime than depression and war, but there is no denying that the options they had to choose from were constricted by the gender assumptions prevailing in the Consumers' Republic. And given the centrality of consumption to the postwar economy, women's loss of civic authority through that realm reduced the average woman's political activism. The photographs in *Life* magazine's 1947 profile of the Hemeke family proved more prophetic than the editors probably understood at the time. In every image, Ted stood at a distance from the house, having just arrived from the outside world, while Jeanne strayed no farther than the front door and mostly remained inside. The camera made the link between the text's call for a mass consumption–driven economy and confining women to the home, even if the article did not explicitly articulate it.[49]

More than anything else, federal policies supporting reconversion—especially the GI Bill of Rights and new income tax codes—shaped the new gender norms of the Consumers' Republic, much the way consumer representation in New Deal agencies had during the depression and the OPA did in wartime. As the United States prepared itself for peace and prosperity, the government buttressed a male-directed family economy by disproportionately giving men access to career training, property ownership, capital, and credit, as well as control over family finances, making them the embodiment of the postwar ideal of purchaser as citizen and limiting their wives' claim to full economic and social citizenship. This discrimination against women may not have been intentional, but the way influential postwar policies were structured and then implemented nonetheless had that effect.

The chief policy instrument favoring men over women was a powerful new Keynesian program, the GI Bill, that fulfilled multiple postwar goals at once through a trio of benefits—unemployment pay while looking for a job, tuition and subsistence allowances for further education or training, and loans to purchase homes or farms or to start a business. The GI Bill rewarded the sixteen million servicemen and -women who had served their country in wartime by helping them restart their lives after an average of two and a half years away. It aimed to avoid the severe economic disruption, massive unemployment, and political unrest that had followed World War I and threatened again. And it sought to jump-start the postwar economy by expanding purchasing power, by injecting new capital into existing institutions ranging from colleges to banks to the housing industry, and by creating higher-earning and homeowning consumers who would make secure credit risks for future buying. "By increas[ing] demand for all the things a family needs in daily life," *The American Legion Magazine* bluntly put it, one could say that "the landscape architect of post-WWII America has been the VA loan guarantee officer." The magnitude of returning veterans affected and the enormity of the dollars spent have encouraged commentators at the time and since to stress the tremendous impact the GI Bill had in establishing an affluent postwar society. "One of the most significant pieces of social legislation ever passed by Congress" or "legislation that helped to build a new kind of America" is typical of the praise heaped upon it.[50] Yet the expenditure of billions of state dollars to facilitate upward mobility through education and property ownership does not mean that the GI Bill was available to all. By its very structure, the bill favored some Americans over others, and even some veterans over others, spawning consequences not necessarily anticipated by its framers and supporters.

The most obvious inequality that the GI Bill created was between veterans and non-veterans. Study after study has documented that World War II veterans achieved substantially higher median incomes, educational attainments, home ownership rates, and net worths than non-veterans of comparable age, or for that matter, than vets who failed to take advantage of GI Bill benefits. And the largest segment by far of excluded non-veterans was women, more than half the adult population. One could argue that women profited through their veteran husbands and fathers, but wives, mothers, and daughters did not share benefits equally with the male veterans in their families. Most conspicuously, widows of veterans received fewer and poorer benefits than their husbands had received, particularly for the tickets to upward mobility—education and home and business loans—until reforms began in the late 1950s. So whether in veteran or non-veteran households, women in postwar America found themselves deprived of the GI Bill's backing and thereby forced into new dependencies that limited their life options.[51]

Even women who were veterans themselves—and about 2 percent of military personnel in the Second World War were female—took much less advantage of GI benefits than their male counterparts. The reasons were multiple, ranging from inequalities and ambiguities in their entitlements to their lack of integration into veterans organizations (or even acceptance, in the case of the Veterans of Foreign Wars [VFW]), where a good deal of benefit counseling took place. Typical discriminatory policies against female vets deprived them of the same unemployment benefits as their male counterparts—they had to prove their independence from a male breadwinner—and the same living allowance for a dependent spouse while pursuing an education. For example, when college students and vets Anne Bosanko and Ken Green married in 1946 and pooled their GI Bill stipends, they had $145 a month—$90 from him, $55 from her.[52] Some of the unfair treatment of female vets stemmed from the ambiguous status of two of the women's services, the Women's Army Auxiliary Corps (WAAC) and the Women's Air Force Services Pilots (WASP), neither of which were full-fledged military units delivering equal benefits in war service and after. Congress had partly insisted on making the WAACs a civilian rather than military unit at its founding in 1942 to avoid paying the same disability benefits and pensions assured servicemen, or the same monthly allotments to WAAC husbands, whether they needed them or not, that service wives received. But even when the WAACs dropped the "Auxiliary" and became legitimately military as WACS in 1943, entitlements remained ambiguous.[53]

Women vets' abandonment of their military identities upon discharge—sometimes chosen, sometimes imposed—also kept them from claiming their fair share of GI benefits. When in 1989 in New Jersey, for example, a
state Advisory Commission on Women Veterans attempted to locate the
34,000 women who had served in the armed forces to remind them of their
rightful benefits, it found the task formidable. "Women's sense of themselves
as veterans seems to be different from that of men," explained commission
member and Navy Nurse Corps veteran Veronica Durkin. "We had enormous
pride in having served . . . but somehow many of the women didn't place their
contributions on an equal level with men." Linda Caldwell, head of the commission, concurred that female veterans were reluctant. "They don't categorize
themselves as veterans. They don't feel entitled to any benefits." Undoubtedly,
greetings to returning World War II vets such as "The Open Door to
Belleville," published by the town fathers of this community neighboring
Newark, didn't help when it welcomed home "you [who] have been doing a
man's job." And once settled back home, women found much less cultural support for perpetuating their identification with the military—fewer invitations
to share war stories, to hang out at the local American Legion hall, or to receive
medical care at VA hospitals, notoriously ill equipped to handle female
patients. Women also learned the hard way that vet status could actually invite
discrimination from potential employers, rather than the preference enjoyed
by men.[54]

Hence, it was mostly male veterans who found their transition back to
civilian life eased by government largesse. The first advantage that a returning
male vet had over, say, a laid-off civilian defense worker, male or female, was a
cushion while looking for a new job. "Readjustment Benefits" of $20 a week for
up to fifty-two weeks, dubbed the "52-20 Club," to tide him over, and the assistance of the Veterans Preference Act of 1944 in getting hired, put the veteran in
a more favorable position than the non-veteran, who had to negotiate the
uncertainties of the postwar economy on his or her own. But many veterans
opted to use the time and resources offered by the GI Bill not to seek employment at all but rather to pursue further education or training in order to enter
the job ladder later at a higher rung. Dual motives, both to compensate veterans for interruptions in their normal educational and occupational advancement and to keep many of them out of a job market flooded with returning
servicemen, motivated the GI Bill's framers to offer veterans a year of full-time
tuition or training plus a period equal to their length of service up to forty-
eight months, along with subsistence pay for themselves and dependents (the
latter in the case of male vets only). Of the more than 15 million eligible veterans, about half took advantage of these educational benefits: 2.2 million

This "former Navy fighter pilot" returned to Princeton in the fall of 1945 to finish his last two years of college, a wife and baby in tow. With the GI Bill paying tuition and a living allowance for his family, this college junior had the government's help in preparing for a comfortable position in postwar society. As a man who had already enrolled in an elite university for two years, he was more likely to benefit from the GI Bill's largesse than women or less-educated Americans. (Courtesy University Archives, Department of Rare Books & Special Collections, Princeton University Library)

attended college or post-graduate study, 3.5 million enrolled in other schooling, 1.4 million chose on-the-job training, and 700,000 sought farm training.

The hundreds of thousands entering colleges and universities grabbed the biggest headlines. Never before had so many young Americans sought higher education. Whereas only 10 percent attended in 1940, by 1948 it was 15 percent and climbing, with vets half the undergraduate population.[55] Not only were most women excluded from this educational subsidy because they generally were not veterans, but the entry of male vets on college campuses often came at their expense, as many schools scaled back female admissions to permit male attendance to more than double. Cornell, where women had been in the majority during wartime, cut female enrollment by 20 percent in 1946, while the proportion of Seattle women eighteen to twenty-four in school declined from 20 percent in 1940 to 14 percent in 1947. Many medical and engineering schools that had begun admitting women for the first time during the war now slammed the door in their faces. And even when women remained on campus, they lost the authority to run things that they had claimed during the war—whether campus newspapers, yearbooks, or governance bodies—much like their mothers and sisters in society more broadly.[56] In sum, the GI Bill helped ensure that veterans had an educational edge over non-veterans, and that college-educated veterans, mostly male, were best prepared to undertake the high-earning, white-collar work of the new postwar economy.[57] The fabled "corporation man" of the 1950s, then, was as much a product of federal policy as corporate priorities and was by no accident a man.

Veterans found another classic route to upward mobility—property ownership—greased by the GI Bill through low-cost loans to assist in the purchase of homes, farms, and businesses. Rather than provide a cash bonus as in other wars, the bill's framers favored the loan guaranty program because it was cheaper, helped alleviate the enormous housing shortage, boosted the banking and construction industries, and provided an investment outlet for wartime savings. Not only did the loan program help the veteran secure property—a much desired goal in itself—but in a world where credit had become so important to personal prosperity, a customer who either owned property or was responsibly paying off a mortgage or loan was eagerly invited to incur more debt. A VA home loan was a gift of collateral. Hundreds of thousands of loans were backed, almost 2.5 million VA home mortgages between 1944 and the passage of the Korean GI Bill in 1952. Put more meaningfully, between the end of World War II and 1966, one-fifth of all single-family residences built were financed by GI Bills; in California the FHA and VA together insured one half of all new home mortgages. Twenty-eight percent of Second World War vets used VA home loans.[58]

Not only did the GI Bill help make 42 percent of World War II vets homeowners by 1956, in contrast to 34 percent of non-vets of comparable age, with the gap rapidly growing, but looking closely at a particular place, such as the New York–Northeastern New Jersey Standard Metropolitan Area, reveals even more clearly how the GI Bill discriminated against female home ownership. Whereas women owned 9.8 percent of all mortgaged owner-occupied properties and 12.6 percent of properties with conventional first mortgages (not government-insured), they only owned 8.5 percent of all government-insured first mortgages (FHA and VA combined) and, most revealing, no VA-insured homes. Only the 10 percent female ownership of FHA-insured properties brought the overall government-insured rate anywhere near the nongovernment rate, and there were still 50 percent more women holders of private sector mortgages than of public-sector insured ones.[59] Further exacerbating the advantage that the federal government was giving male veteran homeowners, in this area of the country at least, the state of New Jersey granted property-owning vets $50 off their property tax every year in lieu of the cash bonus offered by some other states, as the tax rebate was easier to push through this penurious state legislature than a cash outlay. Not only did this property tax forgiveness discriminate against non-vets and all renters, but as further punishment, the tax burden on them grew as homeowning veterans paid less.[60]

The GI Bill's promise of a loan of up to $2000 to start a business gave male veterans the additional advantage of capital as they sought their fortunes in the postwar world. States, moreover, often supplemented this federal loan; New Jersey guaranteed bank loans of up to another $3000 to help vets get established in business. Senator Ernest McFarland of Arizona, sometimes dubbed "the father of the GI Bill," went out of his way in drafting the bill to buttress small business. In a frequently delivered speech, "Small Business, the Necessity for its Preservation, and Its Relation to the Rehabilitation of Returning Servicemen," McFarland linked small business with "the roots of our life ideals," particularly "the preservation of independence and self-reliance," in contrast to "the huge impersonal corporation" characterized by a "very real gap . . . between the owner and both the employee and the customer."[61] But even without applying for small-business loans, all servicemen and -women left the military with more capital than they had entered with: "mustering out" pay of $500 from the federal government, often supplemented by additional cash bonuses ranging from $300 to $500 from their home states.[62] And when that cash ran out, some states made more available. New Jersey added another bank loan provision to the business loan program, this one to assist veterans in purchasing household furnishings and appliances "with favorable time and instalment terms." By 1951, New Jersey veterans had used about 40 percent of the state's loans for these purchases, in contrast to 60 percent for establishing or reestablishing themselves in business, still a substantial proportion.[63]

The easy credit that New Jersey made available to its veterans for purchasing consumer durables fit well with the explicit goal of the federal GI Bill to expand veterans' consumer purchasing power now and improve their credit standing for future spending, thereby enriching returning military personnel and the larger economy in one fell swoop. The (General Omar) Bradley Commission's review of veterans' benefits, requested by President Eisenhower in 1956, clearly articulated how concern with credit had motivated the bill's authors. "Credit was viewed as one of the cornerstones of the program to aid the veteran in his efforts to readjust himself to civilian life. . . . This concept arose because of the feeling that veterans . . . had missed an opportunity to establish themselves in business or professions, and to establish a credit rating which could be the basis of borrowing to acquire a home or establish a business."[64] But although bank loans and easy credit may have been intended to place veterans on a par with their non-veteran counterparts, the Bradley Commission ultimately concluded—quite controversially—that in this respect, as in others, the GI Bill had unfairly favored veterans. It contended that except in the case of service-related disabilities, state resources should have been—and still should be—more equitably distributed to all citizens through more universal social programs.

The particular plight of women did not concern the Bradley Commission, except for how they figured in the non-veteran population discriminated against in reconversion. But had the commission paid attention to sex discrimination in the realm of credit, it would have noticed how women, both veterans and not, were uniquely stigmatized. Until 1968, for instance, if a married woman veteran applied for a VA loan, her own income was not even considered among the criteria used to determine the couple's eligibility as a good credit risk, despite her vet status; she was treated no differently from the non-working or working wife of a male vet, whose income, if she had any, was viewed as supplemental and unstable. Even with the passage of reforms beginning in 1968, much discretion in considering married women's income was still left to regional VA offices.[65] Only with enforcement of the federal Equal Credit Opportunity Act of 1974 was credit discrimination against women more fully addressed.

With access to capital and credit, as with unemployment pay, education, and home and business loans, the transformative GI Bill of Rights advantaged male Americans over females, due to men's greater numbers as veterans of World War II and to outright discrimination against women who were vets or married to vets. The GI Bill, as a Keynesian bulwark of the Consumers' Republic that directed government spending toward increasing consumer demand to fuel the economy, empowered some purchasers as citizens over others—veterans over non-veterans, men over women, and heterosexuals over homosexuals. The tens of thousands of men and women dismissed from the military with a maligning "blue discharge" for being homosexual also were denied any rights under the GI Bill.[66] Rather than expand the social provisions of the American welfare state as some early liberal supporters of the act had hoped it would, the GI Bill targeted those citizens defined as deserving according to the narrow tests and prejudices of a traditionally defined military.

The other major federal policy that set new gender rules for the Consumers' Republic was the expansion of the income tax to a mass scale with World War II.[67] The demands of financing the war and restraining inflation had moved the government to broaden the taxpayer base far beyond the wealthy few who had been paying since the income tax's adoption in 1913. Whereas only 7 million Americans filed income tax returns in 1940, by 1945, after the Revenue Act of 1942 made all incomes over $624 taxable, more than 42 million did. Not only did the income tax burden become more broadly distributed across society as the percentage of the workforce filing expanded from 26 percent in 1940 to 87 percent in 1946, but its progressive structure also made it more egalitarian, in that the rate of taxation grew as income increased.[68] The narrowing gap between high-, middle-, and low-income earners during World War II resulted in part from this progressive tax code, though it should be noted that business profits were never taxed as fully as personal income.

In 1948, and less dramatically in 1951 and 1954, Congress passed amendments to the tax code that adapted wartime tax policies to postwar normalcy, articulating the fiscal underpinnings of the Consumers' Republic. Instituting policies less progressive than in wartime, tax liability for a household with four exemptions and a net income of $5000 fell from 15.1 percent in 1945 to 10 percent with the postwar amendments (although it had been only 1.5 percent in 1940). Revised tax codes assumed, in keeping with the Consumers' Republic more broadly, that affluence would spread through a prospering economy rather than extensive redistribution of income. Announcing $5 billion of tax savings slated for 1954 to help Americans "increase their purchasing power," President Eisenhower congratulated the nation on the "wide diffusion of wealth and incomes and the strong urge of Americans to improve their living standards" that made returning tax dollars to consumers' pockets such a good investment.[69] Revised tax laws also encouraged consumers to spend and borrow on credit by expanding tax deductions for sales tax, interest and installment payments, and by taxing savings and investment income. An advice column on "Handling Your Money" that appeared in a local New Jersey newspaper in 1958, for example, advised that not only is "credit largely responsible for the high standard of living you enjoy" by keeping "factories humming, stores jammed, counters full of things you want and need," but it can "save money on your income tax in the bargain if you take a tip from business and pay as little as possible by cash." Building this inducement to spend into the American tax code prompted a recent critic to argue that the way the income tax developed in the 1940s gave the United States "one of the most pro-consumption, anti-saving tax codes among the big industrialized countries."[70]

But the most important evolution in the Internal Revenue Code by the late 1940s was the way it reinforced the GI Bill in favoring the traditional male breadwinner–headed family and the male citizen over the female within it. The adoption of the income-splitting joint return in 1948 allowed a married couple to lower its tax liability by becoming one taxpaying unit that could total the couple's taxable income, divide that total in half, and then compute a tax based on that half, which was then doubled to produce the couple's joint tax; in a progressive tax structure, the tax rate arrived at this way was inevitably lower than if each individual had filed separately. Ironically, this innovation arose out of an effort to equalize tax liability between community property and common law states at a time when all taxes were assessed on an individual basis, and yet in promoting equity across states it introduced new inequities between married and single taxpayers, and between men and women in marriages. Before the joint return, one of the major strategies for achieving the tax-reducing advantages of income splitting had been for a state to convert to a community-property system, which a growing number of states undertook in the 1940s; but the alternative of a joint federal tax return proved much more attractive to patriarchal lawmakers seeking tax reductions in that it offered tax relief to couples without requiring husbands to share legal rights to income and property with their wives, as stipulated with community property.

In particular, the joint return favored traditional married couples where the wife did not work, as here the income shifting from husband to wife—and hence tax rate reduction—was most dramatic, prompting historian Alice Kessler-Harris to term this prevailing idealization in tax law of the male provider household as "normative masculinity." Its endorsement, she argues, inevitably discouraged women's wage work and thus helped "to restrict women's aspirations, training, and job opportunities."[71] Stanley S. Surrey, a tax legislative counsel involved in amending the Internal Revenue Service's code in the late 1940s could not have been any more explicit in articulating the joint return's major benefit: "[One implication of the split-income plan is that] [w]ives need not continue to master the details of the retail drug business, electrical equipment business, or construction business, but may turn from their partnership 'duties' to the pursuit of homemaking."[72] Not all women had the luxury or desire to quit work; although women's participation in the labor force declined by the end of the 1940s from its height during the war, it was still higher than in 1940 and would continue to climb through the postwar period. But part-time and low-paid clerical and sales work would become the norm for many wives, and the tax code offered little incentive to married women or employers to do otherwise. When the increased tax liability was added to the greater costs of housekeeping and child care incurred when a married woman went to work, many determined "it just didn't pay." In contrast, the British tax code reduced the taxable income of a married couple when the wife was gainfully employed. American wives and mother received no similar invitation to work from a government that ironically, not many years before, had insisted that the nation's very survival in wartime depended on their wage labor.[73]

There were other ways that the Internal Revenue Code by the late 1940s reinforced patriarchal authority in the family. As tax rates were raised with the war, and as more and more American taxpayers became homeowners after it, the mortgage interest deduction became increasingly important; the proportion of federal tax returns claiming interest deductions rose from 2.8 percent in 1950 to 30.6 percent by 1960 and to 39.3 percent in 1970.[74] In addition to being an enormous subsidy to the homeowning middle class, the mortgage interest deduction favored men over women just as mortgages themselves did, in that until legislation barring sex discrimination in granting credit passed in the 1970s, mortgage acquisition usually required male income and proof of male credit standing. A single woman or a married woman who filed a tax return separately from her husband was twice penalized for not carrying a mortgage: once in trying—and often failing—to secure it, and again in not reaping its tax benefits. With the Revenue Act of 1951 came a further boon to homeowners—profits from the sale of a home were exempted from capital gains tax if the proceeds were reinvested in another one—along with new exemptions and exclusions for veterans and GIs from income and estate taxes, which also favored men in the ways discussed.

The Consumers' Republic developed a structure of taxation that rewarded the traditional household of male breadwinner father and homemaker mother, thereby making women financially dependent on men at a time when the transformations of depression and war might have encouraged alternatives. Even today, despite changes in the tax code in 1969, 1986, and 2001 and public hand-wringing about a "marriage penalty," many traditional, one-earner families still enjoy a "marriage bonus," two-earner families continue to face tax discrimination and get no deductions or credits for child care, and unmarried mothers with children suffer the most bias, though they often can afford it least. Concluding a long, careful analysis of the way the modern American tax structure has come to operate, tax law expert Edward J. McCaffery has despaired that even with a majority of mothers working today, "the forces of patriarchy have [not] been defeated. Far from it. . . . The tax system in context is deeply biased against working wives and mothers, and this bias becomes a part of the lived experience for women of all income classes." However he calculated it, he was forced to conclude, "We are taxing women."[75] With the GI Bill, the American government bestowed privileges on men as veterans, and then reinforced them in the new postwar income tax code.

This deeply gendered infrastructure of the Consumers' Republic contributed to a different definition of the consumer than had reigned during the Great Depression and World War II. In those earlier periods, being a "consumer" carried with it certain rights and responsibilities of citizenship that women in particular claimed, as they propelled their economic role as shopper into a moral and political mandate to represent the general good in a nation reeling from depression and then war. Increasingly over the postwar period, however, the consumer became redefined as a purchaser whose economic behavior also supported the general good, but more through fueling aggregate demand in a mass consumption–dependent economy than through asserting and protecting the rights of the individual consumer in the marketplace. As the nation moved into the mass consumption economy of the postwar era, the critical goods became less the consumer perishables of meat, milk, canned goods, and other food that female shoppers doggedly pursued in depression and wartime, and more the consumer durables of cars, houses, and appliances that men played a larger role in acquiring. The gendering of the "consumer" thus shifted from women to couples, and at times to men alone. The female citizen consumer evolved into the male purchaser as citizen who, with the help of state policies, also dominated as head of household, breadwinner, home-owner, and chief taxpayer.

As credit purchasing increasingly became the currency of the Con-sumers' Republic, moreover, women found themselves at a further disadvan-tage. Store credit cards, national credit cards like Carte Blanche and American Express, and mortgage lenders all systematically discriminated against women, favoring single men over single women and insisting that a married woman's husband be the legal holder of any credit account, regardless of whether she had possessed her own card when single or currently earned income, even if her husband was financially dependent on her. When Carte Blanche solicited a household, for example, the card always bore the husband's name, although "a special HERS card to give your wife all the credit she deserves"—in shocking pink—was offered to wives. Divorced, separated, and widowed women were worse off than single women, as their husbands took all the credit standing with them when the marriage ended and left them with no credit rating of their own, "poor risks" in the eyes of lenders who, to make things worse, usu-ally refused to consider alimony and child support as income.

Mortgage lenders, including those trading in government-backed FHA and VA loans, were no better, reluctant to lend to single women or to take into account the full—or in some cases any—income of married women. In fact, the VA perpetrated some of the worst abuses, such as encouraging lenders into the 1970s to require "baby letters" from applying couples who sought to count the wife's earnings for eligibility, including a doctor's statement that the couple was (a) sterile, (b) used an approved method of birth control, or (c) promised to get an abortion; even then, the wife's income often was dis-counted 50 percent or more. Ironically, what little evidence was collected indicated that women were more likely to pay off their debts than men. Much like the authors of the GI Bill and the income tax code, creditors assumed that virtually all women married, had children, left the workforce, and met their financial obligations only through their provider husbands. In structuring laws and regulations with that assumption, they only exacerbated the situation, depriving women of alternatives that might have come their way through easier access to what credit could buy: education, independent livelihoods, home ownership, entrepreneurship, and investments.[76]

Although on a daily basis women carried out a preponderance of the family shopping, in this postwar cornucopia of consumer goods, who— husband or wife—made the decisions about what to buy became critical. Two studies of consumer decision-making that appeared in the *Journal of Marketing* during the 1950s highlighted the growing importance of men's authority over the family purse. The first study argued in 1956 that even in areas where women were traditionally assumed to be boss, such as in expenditures for food, men were playing a surprisingly significant role. A bare majority of wives bought groceries on their own, prompting supermarket chains like A & P to mount advertising campaigns aimed specifically at male grocery shoppers. Many fewer women decided which car to buy, how much life insurance the family needed, and even whether or not to work outside the home. Choosing a new residence or a vacation spot, in contrast, was usually a joint decision. A second study in 1958 moderated that stance a bit, finding that although men still dominated car selection, women often took the lead in appliances, and couples made many purchasing decisions together. When the Department of Labor published its study, *How American Buying Habits Change,* in 1959, a photo of a couple shopping together at a supermarket portrayed postwar consumers as a family team, what one marketing expert called "the husband-wife dyad." Another study in the same year identified the team as particularly prevalent in middle-class households: "It might be said of the middle class husband that he serves as 'architect of the family's fiscal policy,'" while "the wife, on the other hand, serves as the purchasing agent with the limitation that her degree of authority over purchases is in an inverse ratio to the expensiveness of the item." Meanwhile, in working-class households, according to Mirra Komarovsky's *Blue-Collar Marriage* of the early 1960s, male dominance remained alive and well. Only with the 1970s, as women became greater contributors to family income, did studies begin to appear that argued both for more extensive joint decision-making (including car selection and residence) and greater spousal specialization in purchasing (groceries for women, insurance for men).[77] Nonetheless, documentation of a persistent male presence on what often is assumed to have been purely female terrain, particularly during the Consumers' Republic's prime before the 1970s, is significant.

PACKAGING AND FROZEN FOODS—The old-fashioned grocery store has yielded to supermarket efficiency. Today's shoppers choose personally what they want from a tremendously varied stock of packaged and frozen foods. To collect their purchases, they are allowed the use of wire baskets, which they wheel out to the family car on the shop's parking lot.

A couple shopping together became a widespread ideal and reality during the 1950s, as can be seen in this 1959 report by the Department of Labor. Janet L. Wolff's *What Makes Women Buy* (New York: McGraw-Hill, 1958), a handbook for advertisers, retailers, and manufacturers serving female customers, concurred that more and more women were shopping accompanied by their husbands. Wolff cited a recent three-state survey indicating that 20 percent of supermarket customers were couples, and a Tulsa Broadcasting Company study in which 71 percent of married women claimed they bought appliances in the company of their husbands. U.S. Department of Labor, *How American Buying Habits Change* (Washington, DC: U.S. Government Printing Office, 1959).

As the acceptance of a Keynesian demand-driven economy made consumption more and more central to the nation's economic planning and public policies in the postwar era, men as consumers played an ever greater role. A treatise explaining the new demand economy to the readers of the *New York Times*, entitled "That Key Man, the Consumer," concluded "there is no doubt that the man who foots the bills, 'the consumer,' could do a lot to help restore the stability of the economy." *Life* broadcast the same message from the cover of a special issue, "The American and His Economy," which featured a portrait of the Welling family with dad Dale towering over wife Gladys and their three young children as they all peered out from a window of their newly purchased $15,000 home.[78] In real life, families were reminded of "the key man" whenever they applied for a mortgage or a new charge card, and symbolically every day when they heard male announcers speak with authority about the design and value of consumer goods on new, extraordinarily popular television quiz shows like *The Price Is Right* with host Bill Cullum, *Let's Make a Deal* with Monty Hall, and *Queen for a Day* with Jack Bailey (where Bailey bestowed gifts of big-ticket consumer merchandise on women with the most tragic personal stories). Likewise, authoritative male voice-overs taught incompetent housewives the merits of everything from kitchen floorwax to headache medication on the myriad of commercials that filled every crevice of time within and between TV programs.

Popular situation comedies found fodder for humor in the recalibrating of gender norms in the Consumers' Republic. A much-loved episode of *I Love Lucy* revolved around Lucy and Ethel disastrously buying a freezer for their apartment house basement, along with a side of beef to go in it, to prove—unsuccessfully, of course—to husbands Ricky and Fred that they were capable of making wise and economical purchases. Other popular situation comedies—such as *The Adventures of Ozzie and Harriet, Father Knows Best, Leave It to Beaver,* and *The Donna Reed Show*—similarly amused audiences by playing on the new expectations and anxieties about female dependency and retreat from the public sphere bred by the Consumers' Republic. An episode of *The Donna Reed Show* dramatized the shifting terrain of what constituted acceptable female behavior from wartime home front to postwar homemaking: Donna runs for town council and then cheerfully abandons the campaign as soon as her doctor husband complains that he needs her more than her potential constituents.[79] Norms, whether conveyed through ideals presented on television or via government tax policies, of course, are not the same as social realities. Women could—and did—break with those norms every day. But even as they held jobs or undertook unconventional roles outside their homes in the heyday of the Consumers' Republic, they inevitably did so in the shadow of these norms, which made it that much harder to negotiate a different path.

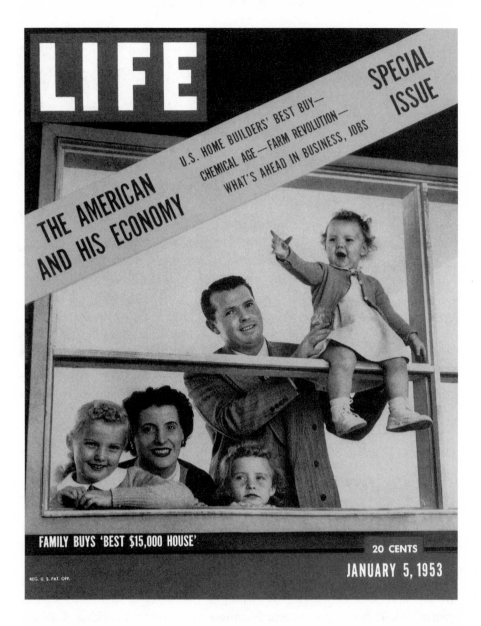

Not only did this *Life* cover affirm the importance of home building to postwar prosperity, but it also conveyed through physical positioning the dominance of men over women in "His Economy." As breadwinners like Dale Welling reigned over wives and children, however, they found themselves newly domesticated in their postwar homes. In June 1951, *Esquire* magazine instructed its male readers, "Your place, Mister, is in the home," in an article titled "Home Is For Husbands, Too." *Life,* January 5, 1953. (Courtesy of Nina Leen/TimePix)

This advertisement selling insurance to the exploding market of new homeowners clearly assumed that prospective customers were male, and that wives and children were almost a part of the property to be protected. Robert Burian. (Courtesy of Carpenter Center Photography Collection, Harvard University)

LESSONS IN CLASS

The Consumers' Republic not only fostered new rules of the game for gender roles, but for the class structure as well. Implicit in the commitment to deliver equality and democracy through mass prosperity was the desire to elevate workers to middle-class status, encapsulated in *Life*'s example of Ted and Jeanne Hemeke, for whom a middle-class suburban lifestyle marked social mobility. President Eisenhower endorsed the making of a mass middle class when he addressed the first joint AFL-CIO convention upon the merger of the two national labor federations in 1955: "The Class Struggle Doctrine of Marx was the invention of a lonely refugee scribbling in a dark recess of the British Museum. He abhorred and detested the middle class. He did not foresee that, in America, labor, respected and prosperous, would constitute— with the farmer and businessman—his hated middle class."[80] Eisenhower's words may have been only rhetoric, but postwar federal policies supported his commitment by rewarding workers for displaying the middle-class conscious-ness of aspiring consumers over the working-class consciousness celebrated by a militant labor movement during the 1930s and World War II. What historian Samuel Hays has labeled a "social service state for the benefit of the mass mid-dle class" evolved in the postwar era, distributing individual benefits by way of the GI Bill, government subsidies, and tax breaks accrued to homeowners, consumers of durable goods, credit borrowers, and male-breadwinner tax-payers.[81] In contrast, the alternative—empowerment as a unionized, class-conscious working class—was hindered, even delegitimized, by Congress's passage of the Taft-Hartley Act of 1947.

A counterrevolution with long-lasting consequences, the act reestab-lished much of the managerial authority that the New Deal's pro-labor Wag-ner Act of 1935 had challenged and put new shackles on labor. Taft-Hartley expanded the list of prohibited "unfair labor practices" to include such critical organizing strategies as mass picketing, sympathy strikes, and secondary boy-cotts, where a union takes action against a company not itself involved in a labor dispute in order to pressure another firm with which the union is dis-puting. The act empowered employers—and even the government—to acquire anti-strike injunctions and to resist the union shop through state "right-to-work" laws. The act barred the organization of supervisory person-nel like foremen and purged communists, many of them members of the founding generation of the CIO, from union leadership. By all these measures, Taft-Hartley set out to torpedo the wartime explosion of union power, and to a large extent it succeeded. American union membership never surpassed its end-of-war height of 35 percent of the workforce and remained largely con-tained within the economic sectors and regional territories that it had con-quered during its rise in the 1930s.[82]

The actions and words of postwar unions themselves seemed to rein-force this shift from militant workers to the more middle-class purchasers as citizens desired in the Consumers' Republic. To begin with, labor was obsessed with expanding workers' purchasing power; hardly a publication or speech failed to hail it as the ideal route to—and outcome from—full employment, high wages, and economic growth. By injecting workers so centrally into the macroeconomics of the postwar mass consumption economy, CIO and AFL labor leaders like Philip Murray, Walter Reuther, and George Meany inevitably drew attention to workers as consumers with material desires and ambitions. In the wake of the 1946 strikes and the restrictions imposed by Taft-Hartley a year later, labor leaders reoriented their bargaining objectives away from demanding a greater say in shopfloor operation and company decision-making from employers and more extensive social provision from government toward maximizing workers' purchasing power, by pegging wages to consumer prices through automatic cost-of-living adjustments (COLAs) and to productivity through annual improvement factors (AIFs). By the early 1960s the COLA/AIF principle had spread from the auto industry to more than half of all union contracts nationwide.[83] Meanwhile, unions focused within their own organizations on programs such as credit unions and consumer counseling clinics that better equipped members to participate in the commercial marketplace.[84] They also relentlessly called on the government to aid their consuming rank and file, if not through an expanded welfare state then more modestly through implementing price controls and loosening credit controls during the Korean War, cutting taxes for lower-income filers, and improving housing provision through greater federal spending, higher construction standards, and the extension of rent control.[85]

Another way that unions supported the Consumers' Republic was by endorsing its gender prescriptions, in particular using the growing emphasis on consumption to strengthen male authority in the family. Labor had long endorsed a traditional ideal of the family through its demand for a "family wage": adequate earnings for the male breadwinner to support non-wage-earning dependents. After a depression that had undermined the ability of many male breadwinners to provide adequately for their families, and a war that had lured more women than ever before into the industrial labor force, unions were eager to reestablish the principle of the "family wage." "The American standard of living is based upon the earnings of the main breadwinner," the United Steelworkers of America asserted emphatically in 1945. "[I]t rejects the concept that other members of the family have to work in order to provide the family with the necessary living essentials."[86] Thus, as labor's attention to consumer matters grew during and after World War II, unions made sure to move their management out of the female realm of the auxiliaries, where it had been parked in the 1930s and early 1940s when more concerned with consumer rights and protections, and into the more male-dominated territory of mainstream union business. Precious purchasing power became inseparably linked to the family wage. "Unless a worker's earnings can support his family, we [will] find our whole capitalistic set-up deprived of the market for the great production of which it is capable," was how the New Jersey State CIO Council put it in 1947.[87]

CIO women's auxiliaries that had begun the postwar era boasting that "we manage the family pay envelope" soon were shifted to a new assignment: assisting the CIO's political action committee in recruiting "the family voter," meaning other women, to strengthen labor's influence at the polls. While the more traditional craft-oriented AFL auxiliaries continued to promote union label–buying campaigns and consumer cooperatives, their merger with the

CIO auxiliaries in the mid-1950s put a damper on these activities.[88] Under male unionists' control, invigorating purchasing power became not only the best route to prosperity for workers and the nation but also a sign of successful masculine stewardship within families. Headlines like "Can Mr. Consumer Hold His Own?" and cartoons depicting male worker-consumers carrying market baskets and towering over their buying-unit families littered the post-war labor press. Walter Reuther of the United Auto Workers skillfully inter-wove the interests of men, workers, and the nation with mass consumption when he exhorted the 1946 CIO convention: "We make this fight in the CIO not only because Joe Smith needs more money to buy his kids food and get them adequate clothing and provide decent shelter, but in the aggregate mil-lions of Jones[es] and Smiths throughout America need this greater purchas-ing power because the nation needs this greater purchasing power."[89] As unions increasingly sought to put female shoppers under the supervision of newly important male consumers, they extended the patriarchal reach of reconversion across class lines.

It is not hard to see how many observers at the time, and scholars since, have concluded that the era of the mass middle class had indeed arrived. More equitable distribution of home ownership, household equipment, apparel, and automobiles seemed to have broken down the "barriers of community and class" that the Department of Labor claimed in its *How American Buying Habits Change* of 1959 had characterized the prewar nation. The Labor Department went on to assert: "The wage-earner's way of life is well-nigh indistinguishable from that of his salaried co-citizens," with which the busi-ness press enthusiastically concurred. A *Business Week* headline blared "Worker Loses His Class Identity," while *Fortune* gushed that "the union has made the worker to an amazing degree a middle-class member of a middle-class society."[90] What social scientists have since labeled the "embourgoise-ment" of workers also implied a trade-off: rewards of material prosperity and social integration in return for ceding shopfloor control and company gover-nance to management, and for accepting private corporate welfare such as pensions and health insurance in place of an expanded and more social demo-cratic welfare state. Whether called a "Fordist compromise," the "new social contract," or the "Treaty of Detroit" in reference to the United Auto Workers paradigmatic contract with General Motors in 1950, the deal was supposedly the same: corporate America got industrial stability, and workers learned to derive increasing satisfaction and status from the lives they created outside of work, thanks to high wages and generous fringe benefits. The well-paid steel-worker in Pittsburgh or Youngstown, Ohio, enjoying all the accouterments of middle-class life, became the icon of the postwar "affluent worker."[91]

The ideal promoted by the Consumers' Republic, however, should not be confused with the actual lives of American workers during the postwar period. What the Eisenhower administration's Department of Labor and the business press claimed were the new rules of the game—essentially, the integration of working-class Americans into a mass middle class—did not necessarily reflect the reality of working-class life, nor how working people viewed it. Uncovering the "real rules" requires deeper investigation into how the structures of the Consumers' Republic, intended to facilitate upward social mobility, actually worked.

The vehicle most often credited with moving working-class Americans into the postwar middle class through higher education and easy capital—the GI Bill—orchestrated much less social engineering than it promised and has been given credit for.[92] Despite the rampant rhetoric of social mobility surrounding the bill, evidence overwhelmingly indicates that the better off a GI was going into the war, the better off VA benefits made him after it. The reasons were twofold: first, the programs themselves favored vets who already had educational and financial resources; and second, the joint public-private structure of the GI Bill meant that the federal government channeled its dollars through existing institutions—the real estate industry, banks, private colleges—and thereby underwrote rather than challenged longstanding discriminatory practices. A closer look at education programs and financial benefits, the core GI Bill programs, reveals how they worked—or didn't—to make workers middle class.

A number of factors converged to make it difficult for working-class GIs, many of whom did not hold high school diplomas, to use their benefits to propel themselves into middle-class occupations. To begin with, multiple investigations confirmed that veterans who had graduated from high school or had some college education before the war were more likely than their less educated comrades-in-arms to be among the half of all veterans who took advantage of GI educational benefits, and when they did, they overwhelmingly favored academic over trade education. Sixty-five percent of World War II vets had been working full-time in a regular job before entering service. About 20 percent had been attending school full-time. But among the students, demand for GI educational benefits was much higher than among the workers: 70 percent made use of them, broken down into 71 percent of high school graduates, 82 percent of those who had been enrolled in college, and 55 percent of those who already were college graduates. The GI Bill thus helped many vets already on the college track to return to it. Among 10,000 vets enrolled in select colleges soon after the war, only 10 percent told investigators that they "definitely" could not have attended college without the GI Bill, and another 10 percent said "probably" not.[93] Given that 55 percent of World War II vets had less than a high school education at discharge, not surprisingly three times as many vets used their benefits for vocational training as for formal schooling, but that got them better-paid working-class jobs, not middle-class ones. A Louis Harris survey of aging veterans in 1983 confirmed that twice as many vets had worked as better-paid skilled craftsmen or foremen than factory operatives or unskilled laborers, a revealing reversal of the balance in the general male population.[94]

Moreover, the structure of the GI Bill in World War II, whereby the government made payments directly to schools approved by the states (a system changed with the Korean War because of flagrant abuses by proprietary schools), worked against the vocational student. It was much harder for vets seeking apprenticeships, skill instruction, and on-the-job training to find acceptable, quality placements than for college- and graduate school–bound vets, whose tuition payments went uncontested to reputable institutions. Colleges, too, proved to be much better equipped and more reliable in educating veterans than other, often fly-by-night and for-profit, schools and programs.[95] Furthermore, in contrast to later wars, when less generous benefits would force most vets into public, particularly community colleges, the amount allocated under the Second World War's GI Bill was sufficient to pay tuition at a high-prestige college, granting even more privilege to those who already enjoyed some. "Why go to Podunk College, when the government will send you to Yale?" *Time* magazine only half joked, as 50 percent of all vet students enrolled in private institutions of higher learning, which only 21 percent would do by the Vietnam era.[96] This is not to say that no working-class veterans expanded their career possibilities. A comparison of the Rutgers University class of 1942 and 1949, for example, found the latter to be more plebeian than the former. But most often, it was the already better educated, middle-class veteran who parlayed GI benefits into a college or graduate degree and a middle-class occupation, while his less educated, lower-class fellow serviceman advanced only within the working class.

Monetary benefits through mustering-out pay, bank loans, and home mortgages proved no more effective than education in giving working people the greater life options that middle-class Americans enjoyed. Burdened with inflated living costs after the lifting of price controls, working-class veterans without any other financial cushion found themselves forced to use up their mustering-out pay quickly. When the New Jersey CIO surveyed vets in its ranks in 1947, it discovered that only one veteran in ten could afford to let his terminal leave bonds remain uncashed, drawing interest; three-quarters had to apply the proceeds to current living expenses, and half had to use at least part of the funds to pay debts incurred over the past year.[97]

Securing new capital was not much easier for working-class vets than holding on to what little they already had. Many unions and veterans complained that the GI Bill's business and home loan program, administered as it was through private banks and savings and loan associations, gave government backing to profit-seeking lending institutions, which then proceeded to discriminate against those who did not qualify as traditionally defined "good credit risks." As one union leader cynically put it, "The GI Bill of Rights is a wonderful piece of legislation but it is meaningless. . . . Take loans for instance. A fellow has to be a Philadelphia lawyer to go in there and ask for a loan. Then he has to fill out about 999 forms and, in the end, he doesn't get anything." Max Roller of the liberal American Veterans Committee agreed, recalling that from newspaper articles promoting VA business loans he had thought "all the GI had to do was to go to the bank, present his discharge, and get $2000. So I came home. I spoke to the bank about it. . . . They asked me: 'What security can you offer?' Well, frankly, the average GI hasn't got any security for he doesn't make any money in the army."

Banks' admission that they turned down a majority of veteran loan applicants—purportedly to protect vets from ruinous debt—only substantiated the limited effectiveness of VA loans in facilitating upward mobility. For example, the thirteen member banks of the Newark Clearing House Association, which coordinated VA loan applications in the city, complained that government propaganda had created a widespread belief among GIs that loans were "a sort of reward for their military service," granted solely on that basis. Faced with 6052 loan applications already by December 1946, "Newark decided to put on the brakes for the veterans' own protection," the Newark War Veterans Service Bureau explained to City Hall. After reviewing candidates "courteously but searchingly," only 605 loans were granted, 10 percent of total applications. "Newark bankers were deeply interested in government loans to veterans, but not at the expense of the veterans' inexperience and folly," or, they might have added, at too much risk to themselves![98]

Labor saw the hand of the real estate and banking industries all over the GI Bill's loan program, but had little success challenging their powerful Washington lobbies. Groups such as the National Association of Home Builders opposed any government involvement to spur low-cost homes other than loan guarantees as "socialized housing." By 1953, when banks were less "veteran-conscious" and less attracted to the lower rate of interest stipulated for government-guaranteed loans, many even stopped bothering with them, which left needier borrowers with still fewer alternatives to rising commercial interest rates. It came as no surprise that the Bradley Commission concluded in 1956 that use of the loan guaranty had been highest among veterans who had worked in fairly well-paid occupations before entering service—professional and technical workers, craftsmen, and salesworkers—or if in school, had finished a year or more of college.[99]

A remarkable document, an in-depth study of an anonymous "typical small midwestern city" in the aftermath of World War II by the University of Chicago's Committee on Human Development, confirmed that the GI Bill offered little social mobility to working-class veterans. *The American Veteran Back Home: A Study of Veteran Readjustment,* published in 1951, substantiated that by and large, those who entered colleges or universities were young men who would have gone on to higher education anyway. Others did take courses at trade schools, but a number who dropped out, as well as men who failed to claim any education or training benefits at all, identified as their chief reason the limited subsistence offered a man with a family to support. "What good is the GI Bill going to do me? No married man could afford it, unless he's got lots of dough," one ex-serviceman grumbled, while another observed, "Except for the fellows that want to go to school, it seems to help very few." Nor, the interviewers concluded, was full-time schooling an option for less privileged veterans, as "a large majority had not completed their high school education." For older, poorly educated vets in particular, the "years of adult living that separated them from their last experience with school made the possibility of further education a vague, difficult, and even unpalatable consideration." Not surprisingly, very few vets in this city founded businesses or bought homes with GI Bill loans either; six veterans with good collateral had managed to, leaving "the overwhelming majority of veterans . . . convinced that the Midwest banks 'were not in favor of it, because they didn't make as much on their money.' "

The Chicago researchers told a story of dashed hopes. "Although a great number of these men had returned with a higher level of vocational aspiration, relatively few of them were able to make the necessary emotional or familial or financial adjustments involved in obtaining more education. . . . It would seem that GI Benefits, while they *might* have played an important role in giving veterans advantages . . . in climbing the socioeconomic ladder, actually played a very minor role."[100] Further evidence that working-class vets quickly scaled back their ambitions comes from a study of almost 100,000 enlisted men processed through Fort Meade in Maryland at their separation from the army between June and November 1945. When men were asked what they were planning to do upon discharge, over the course of six months the proportion of those seeking a new job and those willing to return to an old job completely switched, while those voicing uncertainty remained constant at about 20 percent. Whereas at first, half the returning vets came home bursting with new ambitions, it seems within six months, a decrease in job opportunities, the immediate necessity of making a living, and a declining confidence in the possibility for upward mobility inverted the statistics. By late 1945 half of the vets told separation counselors they would settle for getting their old jobs back.[101] So as the clock ticked within the lives of individual working-class vets as well as in historical time, reentry into civilian society involved coming to terms with less class mobility than the designers of the GI Bill had seemed to promise.

The assumption that workers' and their unions' growing concern with consumption marked their automatic ascension into the American middle class falters on more than the structural limitations of the GI Bill of Rights. Even after the initial difficulties of reconversion, workers' opportunity to achieve middle-class affluence—to acquire a home, the latest-model car, and a credit card or to send their children to college—was constantly dampened by economic uncertainty. Wages of unionized workers grew, even doubled in some cases, but still earnings for many fell short of minimum requirements for a "moderate standard of living" as defined by the Department of Labor Statistics, while even more undermining, workers could never put worries about plant closings and job layoffs far out of mind. During the recession of 1957–58, one of the worst of the postwar era, layoffs were rampant. With 300,000 autoworkers unemployed, it took almost seventeen years of seniority to retain a job in Detroit's auto plants. Nor did COLA contract provisions always keep up with inflation. During the raging inflation of the Korean War, workers' ability to consume suffered from climbing prices, as well as from the Federal Reserve's raising of interest rates to curb credit purchase and hence inflation. In the mid-1960s inflation again ate into workers' buying power, despite rising wages. And it hardly need be said that workers outside of the unionized manufacturing sector—often young, minority, and female—found employment even less stable and lucrative.

In 1955, the same year that President Eisenhower hailed working-class Americans as members of the respected and prosperous middle class, *Life* magazine profiled the travails of John and Sophie Michalewicz of Detroit, who had almost lost the home they were building after a Chrysler layoff in 1948, had barely held on to their new television in 1950 when short work weeks cut earnings, minimally celebrated Christmas in 1954 due to another layoff, and now had just learned that John's department at Chrysler was shutting down temporarily. For families like the Michalewiczes, credit dried up along with wages during layoffs, the combination severely constricting workers' participation in the Consumers' Republic. As embittered Whirlpool employees in Findlay, Ohio, explained as late as 1974, after seven years of living with seasonal layoffs, "It's hard for the ordinary worker to get credit in town because everyone knows that the company hires and fires every year. Try buying or renting when no money comes in for three or four months!"[102] As employers prized flexible payrolls and controlled costs above all else, intentionally or not they subverted workers' purchasing power and upset the fragile underpinnings of the demand economy that they themselves, as well as labor and government, had in principle endorsed.

Even when workers had sufficient money to spend, consuming did not necessarily require a trade-off between working-class identity and material aspirations. In the late 1950s several pioneering studies by marketing researcher Pierre Martineau and sociologists Lee Rainwater, Richard Coleman, and Gerald Handel identified distinctive patterns in working-class purchasing, an insight that marketers would seize upon in the 1960s and 1970s. Extensive interviewing led Rainwater, Coleman, and Handel to argue that "the saving and spending habits of the working class differ. . . . Here is a vast group of consumers who have their own special dreams and desires, their own value systems, their own way of reacting to products, to advertising, or to sales messages."[103]

When two other sociologists—Ely Chinoy and Bennett Berger—set out in the 1950s to test how participation in a mass consumer society affected the class identity of automobile workers, they too concluded that workers displayed a distinctive constellation of values and choices that differed from middle-class ones. Chinoy argued that workers in "Autotown, USA" (Lansing, Michigan), finding work meaningless, sought personal fulfillment through consumption outside of work, shunning opportunities for upward social mobility on the job: "as long as possessions continue to pile up, the worker can feel that he is moving forward." As one welder interviewed by Chinoy put it, "My next step is a nice little modern house of my own. That's what I mean by bettering yourself—or getting ahead." Lest Chinoy's findings suggest that workers who shunned advancement on the job nonetheless became middle class through purchasing homes, the experience of Berger's Ford workers indicated otherwise. For these autoworkers dwelling in suburban homes, surrounded by consumer goods, in Milpitas, California, buying a house in a "working-class suburb" reinforced rather than undermined working-class identity. A year later, Rainwater and Handel confirmed Berger's findings. After interviewing working-class Americans in five metropolitan areas (Camden, Gary, Chicago, Louisville, and Denver), they concluded that "one indication that the worker's increased prosperity which enables him to buy a new house is not being utilized as an effort to become middle class is the fact that many of these new housing areas are largely working class." Working Americans could enjoy a decent standard of living, even purchase a home, without abandoning an awareness that they had more in common with workers on the next shop machine than those in the upstairs office, nor forgetting that their economic interests differed substantially from their bosses'.[104]

Other evidence, moreover, confirms that consumption was not always an escape from work that "tamed" American workers, in the language of sociologist Daniel Bell writing in the early 1960s.[105] Rather, workers often appreciated the interconnectedness of their lives as consumers and assertive workers. For example, Local 410 of the International Union of Electrical, Radio, and Machine Workers (IUE), which represented production and maintenance workers at the Westinghouse Lamp Division plant in the industrial town of Bloomfield, New Jersey, launched a buying campaign to pressure local stores to carry Westinghouse-made products, particularly the electric lightbulbs manufactured in their own plant. As the local wrote to the chairman of the board of The Great A & P Company, "It is most disappointing to us, after purchasing our food at our favorite A & P, not even to have a choice of buying in your stores the very product which pays for our groceries. We sincerely believe that your handling of our lamps will contribute to the industrial growth of the community." The union even went so far as to contact the top Westinghouse lamp salesman when A & P stressed the importance of stronger personal contact between Westinghouse salesmen and A & P store buyers: "We sincerely hope that *you* will be able to swing A & P. We are depending on you—we are all on the same team in this." Similarly, when a Bamberger's Department Store ad featuring thirteen appliances, none Westinghouse, appeared shortly thereafter in the *Newark News*, the local's president, Richard Lynch, penned a poisonous rebuke: "I am shocked at the inconsideration of Bams for the 10,000 Westinghouse workers in New Jersey." The next month, Lynch reminded his own executive board, "The greater the total sale of Westinghouse products— the greater the profit and the job security for Westinghouse union members. And the greater the profits, the greater the opportunity for additional and overdue benefits in next year's contract."[106] Although weekly issues of *The Torch*, the local's newsletter, were filled with postwar labor's "party line" of the necessity of sustaining worker purchasing power, shopfloor concerns such as foremen abuses, illegal subcontracting of work, too frequent layoffs, and encroaching automation of the production process regularly appeared as well, as did frustrations with national politics and limitations in state social and labor policy on occasion.[107] Buying power may have become an obsession with members of Local 410 IUE, but they did not sell out their commitment to improving their work lives—or advocating a more progressive government—in the process.

At this rally in downtown St. Louis in 1950, unionized workers demanded price controls, which the government seemed slow to institute after war broke out in Korea. Their call to "Repair the Old . . . *Don't* Buy the New" revealed how much they still viewed consumer action as part of their arsenal of weapons, and not necessarily a renouncement of a class-based political agenda. Jack Gould. (Courtesy of Carpenter Center Photography Collection, Harvard University)

Workers who owned homes and bought televisions not only worried about workplace issues in the privacy of their union newsletters, they were sometimes willing to stand up to employers by striking, and even by "wildcat striking," unauthorized job actions that violated the union contract. As workers risked the wrath of their union leaders as well as their bosses when they undertook these protests over such issues as shop conditions, pay scales, production standards, staffing, and health and safety provisions, they confirmed the fallacy of assuming worker contentedness during the supposedly prosperous and pacific era of the Consumers' Republic. At Ford in 1953, for example, in the heyday of the Treaty of Detroit, 127 wildcat strikes occurred, involving 20,603 workers and 7,120,056 lost production hours. By 1960, 60 percent of a sample of 150 major employers listed workers' wildcat striking over local plant issues as one of the most serious labor relations problems they faced.[108]

Government, corporate, and labor interests that collaborated in designing the Consumers' Republic may have rhetorically promised working-class Americans that social integration and material equality as members of a mass middle class would accompany their expanded purchasing power, but other aspects of state policy and social reality continued to reinforce class distinctiveness: labor legislation like the Taft-Hartley Act kept organized labor in a straightjacket; the GI Bill offered only limited upward mobility; the tax structure became increasingly less progressive as the postwar era went on; and evolving residential and commercial patterns would increasingly reinforce class segmentation rather than class integration. Even as the white-collar job sector grew, so that by 1957 for the first time it outnumbered the blue-collar sector of 25 million by half a million employees, many Americans held on to their working-class identity. According to polls, in 1952 only 37 percent of Americans identified as middle class, and as late as 1964 it was still only 44 percent.[109]

The ideology of the Consumers' Republic that provided the blueprint for reconversion may have heralded the arrival of class integration while it implicitly endorsed gender differentiation and even inequality, but in the end working-class Americans suffered from some of the same discrimination as did women of all classes. The universal prosperity and equality assumed to be intrinsic to a vital mass consumption economy succeeded more in making promises than in ensuring delivery. Even where a rising standard of living increased workers' capacity to consume, doing so did not necessarily mean mass mobility into the more secure life of the middle class.

In many ways African Americans would fare as inequitably from reconversion as workers and women, and not surprisingly, since many of their numbers consisted of workers and women. But the power of the Consumers' Republic would also have a unique impact on the black community of the North, both singling out its members for special abuse and inspiring them to turn its promise to their own advantage. Women and workers bore the brunt of a postwar ideal that made aspirations for equality and democracy dependent on the strength of private consumption, with all its inconsistencies, rather than on a political commitment to a more redistributive and equitable welfare state. African Americans, so long discriminated against in consumer markets, could at least advance their status by rightfully demanding equal access to private consumption. Keeping alive the consumer movement's commitment to mobilization at the point of consumption to protect the general good, African Americans would come out of World War II and into the reconversion era more determined than ever to fight for equality in the consumer marketplace.

CHAPTER 4

Rebellion: Forcing Open the Doors of Public Accommodations

mericans' embrace of the Consumers' Republic had a paradoxical effect on African Americans. On the one hand, vesting so much power in the private marketplace constricted blacks' opportunity in postwar America. Key components of the Consumers' Republic's infrastructure, most notably the GI Bill, discriminated against blacks even more insidiously than against women or the white working class. Whereas many women were excluded from benefits by virtue of not being veterans, black vets, like white workers, were legitimately entitled but penalized by the way the GI Bill operated through state-level regulatory agencies and entrenched private institutions such as colleges, banks, building and loan associations, and the real estate industry. When seeking benefits, both white working-class and African-American vets met economic discrimination as poor credit and loan risks, but black ex-GIs faced the added insult of watching the government's dollars sanction the racial prejudice they routinely experienced whenever they applied for a job or vocational training, admission to college, or a mortgage or bank loan to start a business.

On the other hand, the firm connection that the Consumers' Republic established between citizenship and consumption presented African Americans with new opportunities for fighting the discrimination in public places that had so angered them during wartime. Throughout the North, and less visibly in the South, the ten years between the war and the Montgomery bus boycott of 1955 saw an explosion in black challenges to exclusion from public accommodations, many of them sites of consumption and leisure, given that much of public life transpired in commercial venues by the postwar era. By the time of Montgomery and the lunch-counter sit-ins and boycotts of the early 1960s—usually credited with launching the modern civil rights movement through disciplined consumer action—and the passage of the federal Civil Rights Act of 1964 barring discrimination in public accommodations nation-wide, politicized black consumers had already spent years agitating at the grass roots for, literally, a place at the table. That attacking segregation in public places became the focus of many local civil rights struggles after the war, par-ticularly in the North, testified to the widespread appeal of the inclusive ideals of the Consumers' Republic. At least until the mid-1960s, political efforts aimed at gaining equal access to mass consumer markets would prevail over alternatives that challenged more fundamentally the economic and cultural status quo.

JIM CROW MEETS EX-GI JOE

a benefit program like the GI Bill, aimed at honorably discharged veterans, put African Americans at a disadvantage from the start. Deficiencies of health and education had kept the mostly southern and rural black population's representation in the armed forces below its proportion in the nation. And African Americans who did serve were disproportionally, and often unfairly, given dishonorable discharges at dismissal, making them ineli-gible for GI benefits. Between August and November 1946, 39 percent of black soldiers and only 21 percent of white soldiers were dishonorably discharged from the service. The eligible black vets remaining—often poorly educated and without financial resources—next encountered the class discrimination in who benefited from GI educational, training, and loan programs. Like white working-class veterans, blacks had come home ambitious about redirecting their lives: a third sought new homes away from their prewar residence, almost half hoped to attend school, and two-thirds desired a new line of work, with a full four-fifths wanting nothing to do with the job they had left behind. But despite these hopes for building a new life, like their white peers, African-American vets soon discovered how difficult achieving it could be.

Along with the obstacles that all working-class Americans faced in making the promise of the GI Bill of Rights a personal reality, eligible blacks encountered racial prejudice at every turn.[1] To begin with, getting help negoti-ating one's way through the Veterans Administration (VA) bureaucracy was not easy. Like female vets, blacks were barred from full membership in the

As Staff Sergeant Herbert Ellison explained the GI Bill of Rights to this quartermaster trucking company stationed in Italy during World War II, the assembled African-American soldiers listened attentively to the benefits they were told they could expect upon discharge from the army. (Courtesy of the Library of Congress)

most established veteran organizations: the American Legion, the Veterans of Foreign Wars, and the Disabled American Veterans. They could participate only in Jim-Crowed, and underresourced, black posts. Some black vets joined small, local veterans' clubs, more social than anything else, or the few national veterans' organizations that did not discriminate—the liberal American Veterans Committee (AVC) and the mainly black and more radical United Negro and Allied Veterans of America (UNAVA)—but many vets resisted affiliating with these, fearing they were too marginal or politically left. In the anti-communist postwar climate, the UNAVA soon found itself accused of being an affiliate of the Communist Party, U.S.A., was labeled "disloyal," and lost its accreditation as a veterans' organization, despite broad-based support in the black community, including from the establishment National Baptist Convention of America. A helpful voice reaching out to black vets was thereby silenced.[2]

The federal agencies charged with implementing the GI Bill were hardly more helpful to blacks than veterans' organizations. Both the VA and the United States Employment Service (USES) had ignored NAACP and other pressure to hire black employees, making Atlanta's VA office, with only seven blacks out of 1700 personnel, fairly typical of the South and even the North. White counselors tended to channel black vets into the low-level jobs and training opportunities that so many vets had hoped to escape. In Arkansas, for example, 95 percent of the black placements made by the USES were for service and unskilled jobs. A New Jersey CIO representative likewise reported, "I found from Trenton headquarters of Selective Service a reluctance . . . and refusal to develop a program . . . to go beyond the stereotyped concerning Negroes." Faced with limited employment opportunities and low wages, many more blacks than whites entered the "52-20 club" offering up to a year of $20 a week readjustment allowances. For the first year after V-J Day, an average of 15 percent of all black veterans opted for what was popularly known as "rocking chair" money, compared with 4 percent of white veterans, while another 35 percent of blacks made no further headway toward employment stability, shifting jobs every few months. Even a federal benefit as presumably universal as terminal pay became captive to racial prejudice. The UNAVA accused local U.S. postmasters in southern states of failing to deliver application forms to African-American veterans, and countered this subterfuge by running its own underground operations to distribute forms. Furthermore, because much of the GI Bill's educational, training, and job placement work was channeled through state-level agencies like departments of education with little federal oversight, applicants found themselves even more victimized by unscrupulous and useless training programs than white workers, particularly—but by no means exclusively—in the South, where training was explicitly segregated by race.

A college education, one of the few available routes for African Americans out of unskilled work, likewise eluded many black vets who sought it, either because they were not educationally prepared or could find no available place, as most white colleges refused them admittance or had strict quotas, and the relatively few black colleges were overflowing with students and underequipped with resources. By early 1947, of the 100,000 black veterans eligible to attend college under the GI Bill, only 20,000 had gained admittance, while 15,000 applied but could find no place and another 50,000, it was estimated, might have tried had there been any hope. Upwards of 70 percent of those enrolled attended black institutions. A survey of the twenty-one leading black colleges, enrolling 11,043 veterans, indicated that 55 percent of all veteran applicants had to be turned away for lack of space, twice the rate for veterans as a whole. The competition proved even worse for professional training: more than a thousand prospective doctors applied for seventy slots at Howard University Medical School. For all these reasons, when the VA surveyed black veterans nationwide in 1947, it discovered that only 5 percent of them were enrolled in courses and programs under the GI Bill's educational benefit.[3]

A haunting letter to the *Washington Post* in November 1946 so captures the despair of a black ex-GI that it is worth quoting at some length. A decorated combat war veteran, this once idealistic GI, "inspired with the desperate hope that out of this war against the bigotry of Hitler and Mussolini would come a better world to live in, a better America to return to," arrived home "to find myself what I was before—a second-class citizen. What is more, the fact that I was now a veteran, instead of buttressing my wartime hopes, actually was held against me. Now that I was a veteran, I was considered to be not merely a Negro, but a cocky one to boot." Relieved at first not to be returning to the South "to be greeted by the Ku Klux [Klan] and the Columbians," he looked to the touted GI Bill for help making a new life up north. But although "the GI Bill of Rights draws no color line," he soon discovered "how many schools are there willing to accept me as a GI student? My color bars me from most decent jobs, and if, instead of accepting menial work, I collect my $20 a week readjustment allowance, I am classified as a 'lazy nigger.' On-the-job training is admittedly a fine thing, but how many opportunities are there for Negro veterans?" Organizing to protest exclusion only meant "we are called 'Communists' or fomenters of trouble." Sorrowfully he concluded, "No, this is not a gripe. It's a cry in the wilderness."[4]

Although this anonymous letter writer did not mention it, he might justifiably also have despaired at the extreme housing crisis that engulfed black vets when they returned home. As late as the spring of 1947, 53 percent of all married black veterans, compared to 39 percent of all whites, were living doubled up with relatives, in trailers, or in small rented rooms. The few housing remedies discriminated against African Americans. The racial segregation in scarce federal housing projects meant that the few existing emergency facilities limited blacks to small quotas, and the VA mortgage insurance program required vets to qualify at private banks and building and loan associations, which discriminated against blacks on several fronts. Not only was it difficult for blacks to pass muster at lending agencies and to secure the lowest interest rates, but VA and FHA financing respected, even reinforced, a hierarchy of neighborhoods that "red-lined" areas where many blacks lived and hoped to buy, coloring them red on government maps to mark them as poor investments. Red zones were usually urban, old, and perceived as deteriorating simply by virtue of having minority residents. Even blacks who somehow managed to qualify personally as mortgagees often found their applications rejected by banks because the property they sought to buy was considered too high-risk. A black vet in Corpus Christi, Texas, enlisted the help of his local NAACP branch when several attempts to take advantage of his GI benefits proved futile because "all the districts that we [Negro veterans] may choose to live have been ruled out." He concluded, "Under the present set-up, *NO NEGRO VETERAN* is eligible for a loan." Nearby in Mississippi, discrimination proved much the same. An *Ebony* magazine survey of thirteen cities in the state revealed that by the summer of 1947, black vets had received only two of the 3229 loans that the VA had guaranteed.

The situation was not much improved up north. The white executive secretary of the East Paterson, New Jersey, Chamber of Commerce wrote to the branch director of the Paterson NAACP in 1950 offering his help challenging the outrageous denial of "rights and privileges" to "Negro service men and civilians" resulting from "lending institutions refusing to make loans on Negro properties." A firm believer in the promise of "home ownership" to go "far toward harmonizing the diverse interests of our widely separate and scattered racial and cultural groups," he despaired at "the almost total lack of opportunity for negro service men to buy and finance homes at prices and terms available to qualified white service men." Although the VA refused to keep racial records, a sympathetic administrator in the central office told the NAACP's special assistant for housing in 1955 that "it is my educated guess that less than 30,000 colored veterans have benefited from the provisions of the GI loan program," and even if this estimate was somewhat off, he had no doubt about the "unfavorably disproportionate participation by colored veterans."

Statistics on mortgage characteristics in the New York–Northeastern New Jersey Metropolitan Area in 1950 confirm that exclusion: of the 449,458 mortgaged properties where the race of the owner was reported, only 1.7 percent belonged to "nonwhites," the rest to whites. A closer look at these figures reveals that non-whites owned 2.1 percent of the properties with conventional first mortgages, .9 percent of the FHA mortgaged ones, and only .1 percent of those with VA mortgages, when total VA mortgages amounted to 15.5 percent of the total mortgaged properties. These poor mortgage showings were particularly disappointing in light of a study by the Bureau of Labor Statistics in 1947 that exposed the eagerness of black veterans to purchase homes. In New York City, a third of the black veterans had taken some steps preparatory to home buying, and most could afford the expected monthly payments. What they couldn't find were mortgages and houses. Because the VA channeled resources through private banking and real estate interests, African Americans found the Consumers' Republic's promise of mass home ownership eluding them.[5]

All in all, the GI Bill was hardly the ticket to upward mobility for African Americans that many had hoped and patriotic lore has enshrined.

Dominating the complaints of this New York City chapter of the United Negro & Allied Veterans of America in 1948 about their treatment upon returning home after the Second World War was the inadequate housing available to them. Although the GI Bill had promised all veterans assistance in buying homes, African Americans found it particularly difficult to convince private banks that they qualified for the government's VA mortgage guarantees. (Courtesy of Culver Pictures Inc.)

Still, African-American vets did what they could to secure a footing in postwar America, some simply by choosing to leave the South. By 1950 more than half of all black veterans were living in a different region (usually the North and West) from where they had been born, in contrast to about a third of their age cohort who had not served in the military.[6] Furthermore, the GI Bill, despite a record of discrimination, raised expectations that later would fuel the civil rights movement. For example, the struggle of a black vet, Herman Sweatt, to use his GI benefits in 1946 to attend the University of Texas Law School in Austin led the NAACP, and eventually the United States Supreme Court, further down the path toward the historic *Brown* v. *Board of Education* decision of 1954, which required the desegregation of the nation's schools. When in 1950 the Supreme Court supported Sweatt's rejection of the makeshift "separate-but-equal" Texas State University Law School for Negroes—in reality three basement rooms off campus—the ambitions that the GI Bill had fed in this particular vet helped further the ambitions of a generation.[7] And in a less public but nonetheless personally significant way, Lowell Steward, a member of the select, all-black Tuskegee Airmen, left the service armed with his GI benefits and intent on becoming a commercial airline pilot and buying a home for his young family. When he was turned down for civilian flying jobs as well as a home in Beverly Hills "advertised for sale for veterans" that he had "the qualifications and the financing" to purchase, he immersed himself in studying real estate. "My main reason for going into real estate was to find a good home for myself," but thirty years later he found himself still at it, "finding neighborhoods and homes that blacks could buy." Here again, expectation first fed—and then thwarted—by the GI Bill inspired Steward to a lifetime struggle for racial equity in housing.[8]

MAKING PUBLIC ACCOMMODATIONS PUBLIC

Like Lowell Steward, many African Americans came out of the World War II experience expecting that a crucial test of "victory at home," half of the desired "Double V," would be their fair access to the promised material fruits of peacetime, that long-sought "piece of the pie." If in wartime the responsible consumer and the good citizen had proved synonymous, reconversion America was reinforcing the link in asking people to tie their own prosperity to the nation's by mass consuming, thereby buttressing the democratic and egalitarian society for which the war against fascism had been waged. Blacks like home buyer Steward, law student Sweatt, that anonymous *Washington Post* letter writer, and the residents of Paterson, New Jersey, and Corpus Christi, Texas, soon discovered, however, that it took more than will or money to participate in the Consumers' Republic. The doors to schools, neighborhoods, and a vast array of public places would have to be forced open if African Americans were to be allowed in. Nationally, black leaders pushed for a permanent Fair Employment Practices Committee (FEPC), long overdue anti-lynching legislation, and court rulings favoring black representation on juries, black ridership on interstate buses, and the unconstitutionality of restrictive covenants barring blacks from certain neighborhoods. In the South, where black voting rights were still widely abrogated, activists fought hard for voter registration and against the poll tax and whites-only primaries. Above all, in community after community north and south during the late 1940s and the 1950s, ordinary people waged the first stage of the postwar civil rights struggle at the grass roots by demanding access to public accommodations—to the stores, restaurants, hotels, housing developments, theaters, bowling alleys, and other sites of consumption where consumers were expected, and black Americans increasingly expected, to fulfill the rights and obligations of purchasers as citizens.

Though the civil rights movement would gradually become viewed, particularly among whites, as a struggle for racial integration, what first drove blacks who challenged discrimination in public accommodations after World War II was a demand for equality of access. The war played a crucial role in moving African-American consumers from using their dollars to demand jobs, as in the "Don't Shop Where You Can't Work" campaigns of the 1930s, to using them to demand recognition as equal citizens. Now, as the ideal of a Consumers' Republic spread, blacks' broader and fairer participation in mass consumption seemed elemental to achieving a more equitable American society. Hence, when members of Lorraine Hansberry's Younger family—the protagonists of her award-winning 1959 play, *A Raisin in the Sun*—sought to use a $10,000 insurance payment to escape the ghetto of South Side Chicago, they set out not to integrate a racist white neighborhood—"We don't want to make no trouble for nobody or fight no causes"—but rather in search of what Mama described as "the nicest place for the least amount of money for my family. . . . Them houses they put up for colored in them areas way out all seem to cost twice as much as other houses."[9]

Many real African Americans, like the fictional Youngers, believed that full citizenship in the Consumers' Republic entitled them to equal rights to consume in a truly free market. Writing in 1948, black housing expert Robert C. Weaver, who years later would become President Lyndon Johnson's first secretary of the new Department of Housing and Urban Development (and the first black cabinet member ever), expressed outrage that "Negroes (and certain other colored minorities) [were] . . . excluded from freely competing in the open market," particularly for housing, one of the most "basic consumer goods." The result was an "artificially limited quantity and quality of housing being offered to them," so contrary to the way the system of free enterprise, with its "guaranteed free access" to total supply and demand and hence to the best price for buyer and seller alike, was supposed to work. Although Hansberry's and Weaver's own middle-class backgrounds undoubtedly influenced the symbolic importance they placed on fair access to housing markets, Hansberry wrote out of a radical political commitment, suggesting how widespread was the conviction that citizenship required equal access.[10]

Looking closely at the way blacks in New Jersey struggled to claim their full civil rights from the 1920s into the 1950s reveals the importance of the battle for access to public accommodations, most often commercial enterprises, in one racially polarized but hardly unusual northern state. Although it is commonplace to assume that Jim Crow reigned primarily within the South, to a surprising extent blacks who went north also found themselves closed out of jobs, neighborhoods, and what were supposed to be "public" accommodations. In fact, exclusion generally grew with the expansion of northern or western black communities, as dominant white societies came to perceive blacks as a mounting threat. New Jersey's story was no different. Despite civil rights laws on the books dating back to the 1880s, black residents faced growing discrimination in a state that by the 1930s had become known as "the Georgia of the North" for its climate of prejudice and the terror wreaked there by the Klan and German-American Bund.[11] As in many northern states, the southern part of New Jersey shared a special affinity with the South's regime of Jim Crow, but discrimination by no means flourished only there. Throughout New Jersey, black residents were relegated to the most deteriorated housing, whether in the state's industrial cities of Newark and Camden or in its resort towns of Atlantic City and Asbury Park. Schools, too, were segregated, with a third more all-black schools existing in 1940 than in 1920, despite a statute dating from 1881 prohibiting exclusion from any public school on account of nationality, religion, or race. Even when children were enrolled in the same schools, as in the northern county of Bergen, often they were taught in separate classrooms. And the relatively few black teachers employed in the state were frequently treated like permanent substitutes.[12]

But as devastating as this discrimination was, a state report, *The Negro in New Jersey,* released in 1932, singled out for special censure the blatant—and growing—exclusion of blacks from public and commercial places: "Segregation instead of lessening has increased. Thus, because of a tremendous increase in population, the Negro group has noted tendencies toward an increasing social separation in housing, theatres, restaurants, hotels, swimming pools, beaches, and other public accommodations." In 1940, on the eve of World War II, New Jersey's black residents—who at 5.4 percent of the state's population made up a greater proportion than in any other northern or border state—experienced many kinds of discrimination, but their greatest humiliation came from being denied on a daily basis a legitimate place in the public life of New Jersey, which as the century passed, was increasingly played out in commercial settings.[13]

Other than an impressive though unsuccessful campaign rallying some two thousand residents to fight Jim Crow seating in Atlantic City's movie theaters in 1937–38, sustained challenges to Jim Crow's public face were rare before the war.[14] In the largest center of New Jersey's black population—the

The visible presence during the 1920s and 1930s of the Ku Klux Klan in Newark, shown here at a Klan funeral in Fairmont Cemetery, contributed to the hostile environment encountered by the increasing number of African Americans who migrated to New Jersey from the South. Newark's black population almost quadrupled between 1910 and 1930. Harry Dorer. (Courtesy of The New Jersey Historical Society)

old industrial city of Newark in the northeastern corner of the state—African Americans mostly carried out their daily lives within the constraints of this northern-style segregated society. When they protested during the 1930s, it was usually to demand economic power within their own separate communities, in support of black-owned businesses and against white storekeepers who refused to hire African Americans. So, for example, although Newark became a mecca for black jazz in the thirties and forties (which not incidentally provided hundreds of black jobs), African-American customers were resigned to their exclusion from the major "whites only" clubs along the city's thoroughfares of Broad and Market Streets and their banishment to the balconies of downtown theaters (referred to as "nigger heavens") if they wanted to see first-run movies or hear black greats such as Eubie Blake, Ella Fitzgerald, and Duke Ellington, or even hometown stars like vocalist Sarah Vaughan and tenor saxophonist Ike Quebec. Until the opening of the black-owned Coleman Hotel in the 1940s, African-American entertainers who played Newark were themselves forced to stay at black rooming houses or with friends. "Downtown was for whites," Bill Roberts, a well-known bartender at black nightspots, put it bluntly.[15] Downtown department stores were more willing to take black customers' money than clubs, but often they refused to let them try on garments before purchasing them. Restaurants often declined to serve them. Casualty insurance companies likewise refused to take money from black auto owners, out of fear that in the case of an accident judges and juries would discriminate against black defendants in awarding damages.[16]

Nor were Newark's private businesses the only ones to resist having black customers. During the Great Depression, when Newark's black residents suffered so terribly that at one point they made up almost a third of all relief cases though only a twelfth of the population, private charities like the Salvation Army, the Goodwill Mission, and the local Red Cross refused them help, and even the city-owned lodging house offered only segregated accommodations.[17] Other exclusions of blacks also bore the government's imprint. Most perniciously, no black doctors, nurses, or patients were allowed in Newark's tax-supported public hospital or affiliated nursing school, only in the wholly inadequate thirty-bed Booker T. Washington Community Hospital, which, when coupled with the exclusion of blacks from all private hospitals, put an already disease-prone poor population at even greater risk.[18]

World War II brought New Jersey's black residents both new opportunities and new discontents. The war attracted even more blacks to New Jersey, increasing the black population some 40 percent between 1940 and 1950. New migrants came to staff the state's extensive defense plants, as New Jersey's war production ranked fifth in the nation, and on assignment to the state's substantial share of military bases. With the help of the war economy, African Americans in New Jersey had money in their pockets for the first time in years. But as blacks' presence and prosperity grew on New Jersey's home front, the private humiliations that blacks had experienced during the 1920s and 1930s became more infuriating—and more public—due to a receptive black press and a politicized black population. When shipyard worker Charles Edwards found himself forced to sit in the back of a bus riding from New York to Camden, or when the Casino Skating Rink on Asbury Park's boardwalk refused to let black GI Lawrence Gelzer skate, or when a public roadhouse in Little Ferry, located in northern New Jersey, shut the door on black motorists ordered off Route 46 during a practice air raid, commercial settings—restaurants, bars, movie theaters, hotels, and the like—became the new front line of the battle for "Double V" in New Jersey. The state legislature's narrow response to the Little Ferry episode, incidentally—to make the specific act of refusing anyone shelter during an air raid a crime punishable by fine or imprisonment—only highlighted how deeply entrenched was discrimination in public life through-

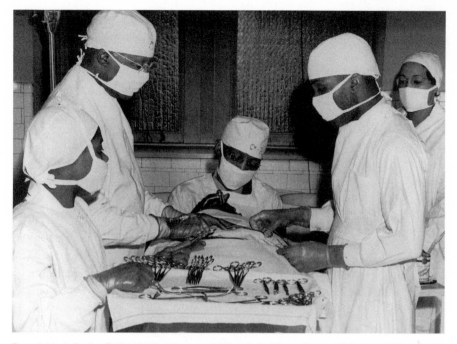

The all-black Booker T. Washington Community Hospital of Newark, established in 1927, was the only place in Newark where African-American doctors and nurses could work and black patients could receive medical treatment. Not until 1946 did the tax-supported Newark City Hospital begin to welcome blacks. The Community Hospital remained open until 1953. (Courtesy of Department of State, New Jersey State Archives)

out the state. By 1945, New Jersey's black population, now grown larger and angrier, was poised to greet peace with a declaration of war.[19]

Newark's homefront story mirrored this mix of fortune and frustration at the state level. Having been 10 percent of the city's population in 1940, blacks constituted 17 percent by 1950, as Newark increasingly looked like a city where blacks could make a decent living. In the 1940s, there were jobs to be had in industry, long closed to black workers, and in government agencies like the federal Office of Dependency Benefits, whose staff in its downtown Newark headquarters was a quarter black. Labor shortages in the city meant that blacks finally could find jobs downtown as cooks and waiters in restaurants, and in department stores. But despite this progress on the job front, African Americans still could not eat in many of those downtown restaurants, the department store positions offered them were more often as elevator operators and janitors than as clerks on the sales floor, and paying the same admission as whites at Newark's movie theaters still only bought blacks seats in the balcony or in isolated side sections. African Americans' inequality as consumers on the home front, moreover, was only reinforced through their virtual exclusion from the work of the critically important Office of Price Administration, where they were only 7 of the 305 paid staff and only 2 out of 510 local OPA board members in the northern Jersey district of which Newark was the heart.[20]

What most distinguished Newark's wartime from prewar eras was the way black residents reacted to their exclusion as consumers. Everywhere one looked, individuals and organizations were demonstrably resisting longstanding Jim Crow practices. When the Far Eastern Chinese Restaurant refused to seat a customer in its main dining room, a scuffle resulted because the banished customer refused to acquiesce. A taxi driver refusing a ride to a black man who turned out to be the president of the activist Essex County Equality League got more publicity than he bargained for. The Savoy Theater found itself sued for refusing to seat white members of the Equality League in the blacks-only balcony section. As plans were developing for a separate USO center for African-American troops, sixteen local organizations protested it as an injustice not just to the soldiers but to local black volunteers as well. Other angry volunteers manned booths and canvassed door-to-door collecting signatures on a petition challenging the American Red Cross's segregation of blood plasma. And when the black owner of the Golden Inn Tavern was refused a liquor license as he tried to move his business to the "colored Broadway" of the Central Ward, where Jewish tavern owners had long enjoyed a monopoly, black residents launched a boycott of Jewish businesses. They also picketed to protest the overcharging of black customers. Newark's own riot in June 1943, although smaller than the violent cataclysms of Detroit and Harlem, registered enough black discontent to cause the death of one black youth and the injury of several blacks and Italians.[21]

Not surprisingly, when writer Curtis Lucas set out to capture the feel of Newark during the war in his novel *Third Ward Newark,* discrimination in job and retail markets became a crucial backdrop to his plot. Faced with the unsolved murder of a young black woman, his Third Ward residents responded: "White bastards! . . . A colored girl is too black to work in their offices, or in their department stores downtown. But she ain't too black for one of them to go to bed with on Saturday night." When the police failed to arrest any white suspects, "that night they started breaking store windows on the hill," a spontaneous protest against "the white man's stores, where they were overcharged."[22]

William M. Ashby, social worker and founder of the Newark Urban League in 1916, eloquently described this new defiance toward the Jim Crow marketplace among Newark's blacks who, like him, had long put up with the burdens of living within a segregated Newark. His own memoir abounds with prewar frustrations securing restaurants for all-black and interracial events, coping with segregated theater seating, fruitlessly searching for decent jobs for Newark's black workers, and administering—albeit with great discomfort— the segregated welfare programs that were often the only way to secure help for the needy, such as city children eager to attend summer camp. "This was a unique period for Negroes in this country," he observed of the early postwar period. "In mind, body and soul they became starkly aware that they were feeling something which was entirely new, or if not new, certainly with a driving and reckless force. They said: 'I'm tired of all this goddam crap. Tired of hearing the white man say, "I can't serve no niggers in my restaurant," tired of being told, "I ain't got no place for colored in my hotel." Why, hell, I've been to Europe. Hitler levelled his bullets at me. Missed. I went to the Pacific. Mr. Hirohito sent his madmen at me to blow me to hell in their planes. I'm still here. Why don't I tell the white man, "Take your goddam boots off my neck! Get the hell out of my road so I can pass! I know now how to run around you or jump over you." ' "[23]

And as wartime shifted into reconversion, Newark's black residents did indeed run harder and jump higher in pursuit of what they considered crucial endorsement of their rights as full citizens. Membership in the local NAACP boomed; protests at Jim Crow restaurants, theaters, bars, skating rinks, and swimming pools continued with even greater frequency; and vocal outrage greeted new injustices, such as the discovery that only 623 black families, in contrast to 2113 white ones, were housed in the city's seven low-income projects, four of which were entirely reserved for whites, despite overwhelming evidence that at least half of Newark's black population was living in "unhealthful and unwholesome quarters." Some expressions of outrage did finally yield results. After years of complaints about the Newark City Hospital's exclusion of blacks, in 1946 two black physicians (the first, a woman) received staff appointments and black women were enrolled in its nursing school.[24]

Not only was blacks' politicization as consumers during wartime a critical prerequisite to their civil rights achievements soon thereafter, but the convergence of their ever louder protests with widely held expectations for the postwar Consumers' Republic made progress in the realm of public accommodations more substantial than in other spheres of civil rights. While discrimination would continue to prevail in jobs, housing, schools, and political representation far into the postwar era, a far-reaching commitment to expanding the ranks of purchasers as citizens made the struggle for equal treatment in the realm of public accommodations more successful. Often overlooked, predating as it did the better known southern campaign of the mid-1950s to mid-1960s, this first—and northern—phase of the postwar civil rights movement triumphed through a strategic mix of agitation and legislation.

Amid the many markers of the war's end in New Jersey was the publication of a landmark report by the Urban Colored Population Commission to the state legislature, *Discrimination in Public Places and the Civil Rights Laws of New Jersey*. Over the next decade it would become the blueprint for a wholesale upgrading of the state's legal protections against racial discrimination. "After extensive study, this Commission has concluded that no phase of discrimination directed against the State's urban population has a wider or more dangerous influence than discrimination in public places," the report's authors insisted. "This type of discrimination embraces every class of the colored population, irrespective of means, education, culture, character, position or behavior and in actual application and execution, subjects all, without distinction, to extremes of embarrassment, humiliation and injustice . . . and excites an increasing and bitter resentment among the colored population because the continuous injustices, flagrantly perpetuated, are commonly accepted and ignored, despite the existence of the New Jersey Civil Rights Laws." Undoubtedly spurred by the unrelenting demands of the state's black residents during the war years, the commission continued that the time to accord the black population more than " 'second class' citizenship" was now, when "every resource must be utilized in an uncompromising campaign to make the virtues of democracy mean something more than empty, insincere words."[25] By 1950 the state of New Jersey would establish a new legal infrastructure that despite many limitations, particularly with enforcement, better protected the rights of all citizens to participate in everything that was deemed "public" in state life.

Refurbishing New Jersey's ineffectual laws against discrimination in public accommodations entailed a many-step process that culminated in the passage of the Freeman Civil Rights Act of 1949. Before the war ended, in April 1945, the state passed a state-level Fair Employment Practice Law (later renamed the New Jersey Law Against Discrimination when it became the supporting trunk for a series of civil rights branches), aimed at providing state support for the continuation of the FEPC when the wartime federal law expired. Although prohibiting employers, labor unions, and employment agencies from practicing job discrimination proved extremely difficult without the federal government's club of wartime defense contracts or later affirmative action policies, the law established a state administrative structure missing in previously passed civil rights laws, which had put all the burden of court costs and publicity on the victim. The newly created New Jersey Division Against Discrimination (DAD) was housed within the state's Department of Education and charged with enforcing the law in response to aggrieved parties' complaints, first through conciliation and then, if necessary, by holding hearings and issuing cease-and-desist orders that carried fines and jail terms when violated. Despite many weaknesses in its administrative structure—the DAD did not have the statutory power to initiate complaints, received limited funding, and was forced to operate within a Department of Education more oriented toward peaceful resolution than rigorous enforcement—the state nonetheless made an important statement and some progress toward requiring respect for all its citizens' civil rights.[26]

The next step in establishing a more effective legal infrastructure was the adoption of a new state constitution in 1947, which included a provision making New Jersey the first state constitutionally forbidding segregation in its public schools and state militia, a more powerful impediment against discrimination than simple legislation. As pressure to reform New Jersey's corrupt and inefficient policymaking machinery had mounted in the 1930s, groups committed to governmental improvement had turned to revision of the state's archaic constitution as the only possible route around dominant rural interests and urban machines like Mayor Frank Hague's of Jersey City. With the new constitution's hard-won civil rights protections in hand, integration of the state's National Guard proceeded in the late 1940s, complementing that of the U.S. military in 1949, as did the dismantling of some of the most flagrant segregation in New Jersey's schools, though integrating the state's schools would remain a much more complex and elusive goal for many years to come.[27]

Finally, with the constitution setting an important precedent, racial liberals submitted another report to the governor in 1948, *Civil Liberties in New Jersey*, taking on the remaining major area of infringement against civil rights in public. They argued: "There are still frequent violations. . . . Negroes, for example, can never be sure when they leave the vicinity of their homes what conditions they will encounter in unfamiliar areas." The culprits were familiar: restaurants, hotels, skating rinks, bowling alleys, and other kinds of public accommodations.[28] Within a year, thanks to energetic lobbying by a broad coalition of state organizations under the Joint Council for Civil Rights dominated by black, Jewish, and labor interests and the energetic support of Republican Governor Alfred Driscoll, a bill introduced by Newark-area assemblywoman Grace Freeman passed; it was, in essence, an amendment to the 1945 civil rights law expanding the DAD's responsibility to include the monitoring of discrimination in public accommodations. Governor Driscoll viewed its passage with satisfaction as the fulfillment of his campaign pledge to the state's NAACP to deliver "full citizenship" to all, testimony to the widely accepted linkage of consumption and citizenship.[29]

Although violations of the Freeman Act persisted, by the late 1950s African Americans in Newark attested to the sea change in their circumstances. An optimistic report by the Newark Interracial Council in 1957 asserted, "Discrimination in public accommodations is regarded by Negroes in Newark today as a very minor and rapidly vanishing problem." One informant was quoted as testifying, "Within the past seven or eight years [since the Freeman Act passed], I do not recall receiving so much as a sidewise look in any of the better places." More guarded responses stressed how fear of poor treatment still kept many African Americans from venturing beyond familiar spots; as another witness explained their caution, "We have not become accustomed to this situation in Newark even yet. We have run into so many nasty situations in past years that we have difficulty in believing that change has really occurred."[30] And change wasn't universal. Thirteen out of forty-five motels surveyed by the DAD in northern New Jersey in 1955 acknowledged never having housed a black guest, while half the motels in the state said they refused to rent to non-whites.[31] Nonetheless, a *Newark News* investigation in April 1956 concluded that the situation had greatly improved, even if black customers were not always warmly received.

With entry into jobs, schools, housing, neighborhoods, and even some hospitals still stubbornly resistant to legislative remedy, expanding and monitoring access to public commercial spaces in New Jersey's cities proved easier. With the fullest protection of the law, black consumers now could sit freely on any bus, shop in any store, eat in any restaurant, drink at any bar, and settle anywhere in any theater. By demanding the opening up of what was already expected to be a free and "mass" consumption marketplace, as the Consumers' Republic promised, black and white civil rights reformers achieved more than when they invoked blacks' social entitlement to attend any school or live in any community, asserted their economic right to hold any job, or made a moral bid for entry into worlds clearly circumscribed as private. A broad societal commitment to the ideal of the Consumers' Republic meant that "even where there was no legal duty," commercial institutions "which once discriminated against Negro customers in various ways now solicit their increasingly valuable trade and treat them with utmost courtesy," according to the NAACP Legal Defense and Educational Fund's director-counsel Jack Greenberg in 1959.[32]

Black trade was not welcomed everywhere, of course. Most of the ambiguity that remained around blacks' access to public accommodations by the late 1950s revolved around how to define what was "public" and hence legally subject to state laws against discrimination, and what was "private" and thereby exempt.[33] This issue was of particular interest to the Jewish individuals and organizations in New Jersey who took a lead role in agitating for civil rights reform and who linked discrimination against blacks to anti-Semitic exclusion of Jews from private facilities with "gentlemen's agreements."[34] One of the reasons that swimming pools, bowling alleys, and skating rinks persisted as the most frequent violators of civil rights legislation was that they could make the most cogent case for themselves as private clubs granting admission only to members. The courts, however, when in a position to rule, generally applied a strict standard in defining "private," requiring convincing evidence that the club was indeed closed to many and depended on a genuine system of dues paying.

Not coincidentally, many of these facilities that sought to hide behind the shield of "private" were sites of intimate bodily contact among users, not unlike the barbershops and beauty parlors exempted from New Jersey's civil rights laws altogether. These "club" owners were more concerned with losing white customers fearful of contamination than gaining new black customers. For years, for example, Palisades Amusement Park fended off protests like pool "stand-ins" and extensive litigation resulting in stormy court battles for refusing to let blacks swim in its pool. In time, the least capable of keeping up the charade of a private club, such as skating rinks and bowling alleys, succumbed to social, legal, and economic pressures to open their doors. But swimming pools, like barbershops and beauty parlors, continued to resist through at least the 1950s, defending their status as private and remaining bastions of irrational fears of racial impurity. The *Newark News* even identified a rise in the number of private pools and swimming clubs during the mid-1950s, which "most Negroes and inter-racial leaders," it punned, attributed to "the reluctance of many whites to get into the swim with Negroes." A follow-up investigation by the DAD of eighty-seven inland swimming facilities confirmed rampant discrimination, much of it in facilities accused of misrepresenting themselves as private clubs. With so many of these persistent violators of civil rights legislation being recreational facilities, the New Jersey State Recreation Commission recommended a strategy of providing more adequate public facilities so that people would be less dependent on private enterprise. Enhancing the public sphere made great sense but was a formidable challenge in a state whose 128-mile coastline had not one public beach in 1950.[35]

New Jersey's postwar achievements in opening up access to public accommodations paralleled what happened elsewhere throughout the North. Almost everywhere, African Americans' demands to be treated as equals in restaurants, stores, theaters, parks, pools, buses, hospitals, and the like—to buy anything from a beer to a house to a swim wherever they chose—led to the breakdown of many longstanding racial barriers to blacks' full participation in public life. Hundreds of municipalities established interracial committees to shepherd along the process after the war. By 1948, eighteen northern and western states had passed some sort of civil rights legislation barring discrimination; by 1955, New York, Massachusetts, Rhode Island, and Connecticut had state commissions like New Jersey's authorized to hear complaints of discrimination and to take administrative action to enjoin them.[36] Meanwhile, one of the most visible public accommodations—major league baseball—provided a powerful symbol for the new era when Jackie Robinson broke through the color line in 1947. Other historic firsts followed him through the hole in the ballpark fence, most notably the full desegregation of the armed forces in 1949, the only policy implemented, however, of the far-reaching recommendations made in the final report of President Truman's Committee on Civil Rights.[37]

Even the South felt some of this pressure for change in the consumer marketplace, particularly in the years before the emergence of the full-blown civil rights movement of the early to middle 1960s. It was no accident that alongside the gradual but frustrating campaigns to register blacks to vote and then, after the *Brown* decision, to integrate segregated schools, so many local actions revolved around blacks strategically wielding their buying power to claim full citizenship. Historians are just beginning to discover how much skirmishing took place in segregated cities like Birmingham, Alabama, over delineating seating on buses and in theaters, access to stores and parks, and boundaries between black and white neighborhoods in the decades before the more publicized events of the 1960s.[38] Already well known are the Montgomery bus boycott of 1955–56, when a groundswell of grassroots support kept blacks off the city's segregated buses for thirteen months, and the lunch-counter sit-ins of 1960, launched by four black freshmen at North Carolina Agricultural and Technical College in Greensboro. Their sit-in at a local Woolworth's to demand service spread so swiftly and so widely that by the end of that year, student campaigns had swept every southern and border state, plus Nevada, Illinois, and Ohio, and involved some 70,000 black and white supporters, all demanding that African Americans not be discriminated against at this one counter at Woolworth's, Kress's, or Grant's when their money was gladly accepted at every other counter in the store. Lunch-counter sit-ins soon expanded in Greensboro, Nashville, Clarksdale, Savannah, Atlanta, Dallas, Birmingham, Jackson, Natchez, and on and on throughout the South to encompass boycotts of downtown stores that discriminated against blacks as

Pickets outside the southern Robert E. Lee Hotel during the 1950s protested against their exclusion from a public accommodation. Their placards conveyed how much African Americans at the time linked the right to participate fully in the commercial marketplace—here, to rent a room from a hotel—to "full citizenship." (Courtesy of the Library of Congress)

customers in restaurants, dressing rooms, restrooms, and beauty parlors. "Close out your charge account with segregation, open up your account with freedom," was the slogan of Atlanta's boycott, designed to pressure Rich's Department Store, and later others, to desegregate.[39]

Complementing these grassroots southern efforts, the northern-based Congress of Racial Equality (CORE), pioneer of wartime and early postwar efforts to integrate downtown eating places, theaters, and roller-skating rinks in the North, orchestrated national consumer actions to force desegregation—of F. W. Woolworth's stores for refusing to serve blacks at its southern lunch counters, of interstate buses and bus terminals in the Journey of Reconciliation of 1947 and the Freedom Rides of 1961, and of highway restaurants like Howard Johnson's in the Freedom Highways campaign of 1962.[40]

Southern whites might not have liked it, but they were getting a clear message that the consumer marketplace could not easily be preserved as segre-

Civil rights activists in New Jersey carried their campaign for equal rights at sites of consumption into the 1960s. These picketers outside a New Jersey Woolworth's in 1963 showed their support for Martin Luther King, Jr.'s demonstrations in Birmingham, Alabama, by urging consumers to boycott Woolworth's because of its record of prohibiting black customers from eating at the lunch counters of its southern stores. (Courtesy of Special Collections and University Archives, Rutgers University Libraries)

gated space. Civil rights activists regularly were mounting boycotts and other consumer actions both to achieve the end goal of desegregation and as a political strategy to put pressure on the racial status quo at its weakest link, white economic dependence on black consumers. They understood that downtown merchants in southern cities could hardly afford to lose black customers when whites were fast relocating to the suburbs. Southern whites came to appreciate the strategic importance of the consumer marketplace so well that increasingly they used it to discipline their own racial ranks. Southern white liberal Virginia Durr recalled the fate of those like her and her husband, Clifford, who supported the Montgomery bus boycott: "The first thing that happened to whites like us . . . was that we lost our businesses. People didn't come to us." By the mid-1960s white supremacists were countering black consumer boycotts with "buy-ins" designed to support spurned merchants and their own boycotts of white retail businesses owned by those considered race traitors. The White Citizen's Council of Montgomery prepared placards for picketing that read, "The management of this store has shown a preference for the colored trade. Please cooperate."[41] By the time that President Kennedy introduced a national civil rights bill in 1963 that would become the Civil Rights Act of 1964, and called upon Congress "to enact legislation giving all Americans the right to be served in facilities which are open to the public—hotels, restaurants, theaters, retail stores, and similar establishments," consumers in local communities from Newark to Birmingham had been waging a grassroots struggle in the consumer marketplace for two decades, had made breakthroughs in many localities, and at least in the northern case had won on the state level stronger protections than the national act would itself deliver, limited as it was to businesses in some way involved with the federal government or interstate commerce.[42]

The orientation of the Consumers' Republic to the marketplace made blacks more vulnerable to discrimination in some respects, as with the GI Bill, but in other ways it gave them tools to demand more equal treatment. Their experiences in the war and its aftermath taught them to speak a language that was understood in postwar America, where the individual's access to the free marketplace was a sacred concept. In this sense, the Consumers' Republic had its liberating side, as it offered the protection of a mass market whose success depended on attracting consumers previously excluded from it. The middle-class black drive to consume that sociologist E. Franklin Frazier so excoriated in his 1957 classic polemic *Black Bourgeoisie* for leading to self-hatred and opportunism thus had a more socially subversive impact than he recognized.[43]

On the other hand, this focus on winning access to public accommodations and markets inevitably limited the civil rights movement, particularly in the North, because it favored those demands that grew out of, and intersected with, the mainstream discourse and assumptions of the nation, braiding the experiences of black Americans with those of whites. Alternative approaches—more black nationalist, or simply sympathetic with the separate black economy of the "Don't Shop" campaigns of the 1930s, or more invested in an activist social democratic state regulating for greater economic equality—found much less encouragement. African Americans who focused in the postwar era on affirming political rights through ensuring equal access to sites of consumption certainly gained the momentum, which not inconsequently had the side effect of channeling black consumer ambitions toward white commercial enterprises (to the eventual devastation of many black ones). Articulating black discontent in the language of a liberal struggle to pursue individual rights in a free capitalist marketplace and then successfully securing those rights, moreover, only reinforced the legitimacy of the capitalist order as a way of organizing economic life.[44]

Many scholars of the civil rights movement have argued that, particularly in its early postwar manifestations, the movement promoted a liberal notion of rights within an economic status quo. But the story told here complicates that traditional account in a number of ways. First, it points to a broader and more politicized popular base for the struggle to desegregate public accommodations than the usually credited black middle-class reformers and their constitutionally oriented organizations, like the NAACP. As exclusion from participation in sites of consumption became a searing mark of unequal citizenship during a war fought to protect democracy and a reconversion promising fuller integration through mass consumption, blacks with a wide range of political views came to demand greater inclusion. As John Lewis, a leader of the militant Student Nonviolent Coordinating Committee (SNCC) in the 1960s, explained, the fact that "we couldn't even get a hamburger and a Coke at a soda fountain" became an infuriating measure of blacks' lack of freedom "in what we believed was a free country." Likewise, James Baldwin's frustration, "At the rate things are going, all of Africa will be free before we can get a lousy cup of coffee," conveyed the powerful symbolic value even for radical critics of getting served as consumers.[45]

Furthermore, the NAACP, so often the only game in many towns in these early postwar years, cannot be viewed monolithically as responding only to a middle-class constituency with an agenda limited to fighting legal battles in the courts. The files of the NAACP reveal the extent to which ordinary African Americans throughout the country chafed at their exclusion from public accommodations and pleaded with the NAACP's New York headquarters to support their local struggles, which pleased, even as it overwhelmed, the national staff. The legal masterminds of the NAACP, Charles Hamilton Houston and Thurgood Marshall, never intended judicial activism to define the movement; they always considered litigation a tool to educate, politicize, and recruit the larger public into the black freedom struggle.[46]

Yet grassroots mobilizations against Jim Crow exclusion from public accommodations could—and did—have more radical agendas for challenging racial inequality than the liberal NAACP could comfortably endorse. Journalist Louis Lomax wrote in *Harper's Magazine* after the lunch-counter sit-ins of 1960, "Negroes all over America knew that the spontaneous and uncorrupted student demonstrations were more than an attack on segregation. They were proof that the Negro leadership class, epitomized by the NAACP, was no longer the prime mover in the Negro's social revolt. The demonstrations have shifted the desegregation battles from the courtroom to the marketplace."[47] Ella Baker, involved with consumer organizing from the 1930s until well into the 1960s, and at the time of the sit-ins the executive director of Martin Luther King, Jr.'s Southern Christian Leadership Conference (SCLC), also understood the radical potential of building a mass movement out of the direct action possible in the consumer marketplace. Reflecting back on the student conference she had helped organize in the wake of the lunch-counter sit-ins, which led directly to the birth of SNCC, she wrote how it was "crystal clear that the current sit-in and other demonstrations are concerned with something bigger than a hamburger. . . . The Negro and white students, North and South, are seeking to rid America of the scourge of racial segregation and discrimination—not only at the lunch counters but in every aspect of life."[48] The Consumers' Republic, in prizing broad participation in mass consumer markets, provided a wide range of black Americans—differing in locale, class, and ideology—with an available and legitimate recourse for challenging racial discrimination, particularly as other avenues—such as desegregating neighborhoods, schools, voter registration lists, and jobs—were often blocked. Mass consumption begot a mass civil rights movement.

Despite the radical potential of consumer organizing appreciated by the Ella Bakers of the civil rights movement, attention to democratizing the marketplace reinforced the Consumers' Republic's orientation toward "expanding the pie" to make it larger and more encompassing, and disinterest in redistributing economic resources to achieve more fundamental socioeconomic equity. The legal and commercial right to participate drew more attention than the economic right to a fair share. In the same vein, emphasizing the liberating effects of the entitlement to spend income as whites did rather than how income was earned played down the importance of African Americans' access to rewarding, quality jobs. It became easier to integrate black Americans into a shared postwar culture by facilitating their purchasing of the abundant fruits of a growing economy than by tearing down the formidable barriers to job equality put up by employers and unions alike, particularly after anti-communist fervor purged the labor movement of many racial progressives. While the white establishment welcomed blacks as consumers more enthusiastically than as workers, black voices of protest raised against Jim Crow contributed as well, complaining less about whether blacks could afford dinner in a restaurant or a ticket to the movies than about how they were treated once they got there. True to the ideology of the Consumers' Republic, expanding mass consumption—getting more people to buy the same things, now in racially shared spaces—bore the burden of making postwar America more egalitarian and democratic. As a headline in the *Newark News* blared in 1956, the passage of the Freeman Act in 1949 had made it possible for "The Negro in Essex," enjoying "Money and the Vote," to be "Equal with Whites."[49]

Blacks' entry into public accommodations previously off bounds was part of a larger restructuring of physical space that accompanied the establishment of the Consumers' Republic during the postwar era. As a consensus emerged that privately owned, single-family homes, usually in suburban locations, offered the best solution to the severe housing crisis after World War II, and that privately owned, decentralized shopping centers better served these new suburbanites as centers of commerce than did urban downtowns, the very landscape of metropolitan America got recast over the long reign of the Consumers' Republic.

Although desire for a more egalitarian society made up of homeowning and mass consuming citizens motivated the planning of this new landscape of mass consumption, these new settings soon took on a life of their own, with the imperatives of the market often undercutting any social commitment to the well-being of the mass that had fueled their creation in the first place. As these new suburbanized spaces adapted to the changing social and economic conditions of postwar life, their status as private markets of housing and commerce put them outside government regulation and made them ill disposed to protect universal rights. Although promoters of the Consumers' Republic may have aimed to integrate all Americans into a more inclusive world defined by mass consumption, its reality would prove quite otherwise. In particular, African Americans' hard-fought gains in access to public accommodations would become jeopardized when the new landscape of mass consumption moved people, and increasingly public accommodations, out of the urban centers where blacks congregated and into suburbia, where their presence was often discouraged. With residential suburbanization and commercial decentralization remaking the face of New Jersey, as well as many other states, blacks' investment in a strategy of demanding equal access to the mass consumer marketplace would face new challenges.

PART THREE

The Landscape of Mass Consumption

CHAPTER 5

Residence: Inequality in Mass Suburbia

In 1957 the mass circulation women's magazine *Redbook* released a film entitled *In the Suburbs* to persuade national advertisers that it had its finger on the unique pulse of a massive new market—the young adults who had been streaming out of cities into mass-built homes in the exploding suburban communities of postwar America. Through an ethnographic portrait of the newly evolving suburban lifestyle, the film captured the distinctive sights and sounds of fifties suburbia: the happy, high-pitched voices of a huge new postwar generation of children being born and raised there; the buzzing sociability at neighborhood parties where young residents built worlds of peers to replace family and other ties left behind in the city; the endless home improvement schemes undertaken by proud and ambitious new homeowners; and, most important to the magazine and its advertisers, the proliferation of voracious consumers who have "come into their purchasing stage and are off on a wild non-stop ride" in a "happy-go-spending world." Having geared its articles to the life concerns and material interests of this new young adult suburban market of more than 2.5 million families—who not coincidentally were buy-

---

Overleaf: Subdivisions of single-family homes and strategically located regional shopping centers, like the Garden State Plaza which opened in 1957 in Paramus, New Jersey, dominated the new postwar landscape that emerged out of an economy oriented around mass consumption. (Courtesy of Garden State Plaza Historical Collection)

ing 70 percent of all homes sold—*Redbook* invited its prospective advertisers to join ranks to reach this "buy-it-now" generation.[1]

Although *In the Suburbs* was an unambiguous marketing tool that simplistically stereotyped suburbanites, the link it identified between mass consumption and suburbanization was broadly recognized in postwar American society, as suburbia became the distinctive residential landscape of the Consumers' Republic, that commitment to rebuild the American economy and society after World War II around the mass consumer market. At an astonishing pace, the futuristic highways, suburban "Pleasantvilles" surrounding "Centerton," and appliance-equipped, single-family homes showcased in the New York World's Fair's model "Democracity" of 1939–40 were becoming a reality.[2] Between 1947 and 1953 the suburban population increased by 43 percent, in contrast to a general population increase of only 11 percent; over the course of the 1950s, in the twenty largest metropolitan areas, cities would grow by only .1 percent, their suburbs by an explosive 45 percent. And as *Fortune* magazine excitedly informed its business readers in its own exposé on the "lush new suburban market," suburbanites' buying power was even greater than their numbers. The 30 million Americans that *Fortune* counted as suburban residents in 1953 may have represented 19 percent of the U.S. population, but they spent 29 percent of its income, with their higher paychecks and homeownership rates and more children fourteen and under than the rest of the metropolitan population, all indicators of high consumption.

Just as the framers of the Consumers' Republic had hoped, privatized mass consumption—much of it linked to suburbanization—was proving itself an ideal strategy for boosting national recovery and prosperity. Annual consumer expenditures for housing and automobiles alone, without appliances and other furnishings, more than tripled between 1941 and 1961, rising to $2513 from $718 per household in constant dollars. When homeownership rates jumped from not quite 44 percent in 1940 to 62 percent in 1960, the suburban home itself became the Consumers' Republic's quintessential mass consumer commodity, capable of fueling the fires of the postwar economy while also improving the standard of living of the mass of Americans.

In a special issue on "The New America" in 1957, *Newsweek* magazine explained the way that suburbia benefited both the larger economy and individuals within it. It pointed to a consensus among economists that "the suburbanite is tomorrow's best customer and a firm foundation for future national prosperity." It went on to praise suburbia's success in offering ordinary Americans a bigger piece of the pie. The typical suburbanite, *Newsweek* asserted, is fast becoming "a man of property. His savings may be in the form of equities in house and appliances, but month by month he is becoming a man of sub-

Rows of look-alike houses, often varying only by exterior color and a few decorative details, sprouted practically overnight on what had until recently been farmland outside American cities. Due to these large-scale developments, ownership of single-family homes grew more in the decade following World War II than it had in the previous 150 years. Robert Burian. (Courtesy of Carpenter Center Photography Collection, Harvard University)

stance" as "his goods, his desires, his income, his numbers—all are going up and up."[3] As suburbanization gave a majority of Americans for the first time ever the opportunity to become people "of property," it also seemed to promise a surefire way of incorporating a wide range of Americans into a mass consumption–based middle class. "Suburbia is the exemplification of the new and growing moneyed middle class . . . bound, sooner or later, to become *the* American market . . . socially and economically more uniform," *Fortune* exulted. A long-sought more egalitarian America seemed to be arriving via rows of "raised ranches" on 5000-square-foot lots.

This was not the first time in American history, of course, that purchasing a home, particularly one away from the city's business center, offered owners a way of securing middle-class status. Victorian streetcar and garden suburbs and the bungalow building of the 1920s provided important precedents. But the links to established networks of train and trolley transportation required in an era before mass auto ownership and federally funded highways, the much smaller scale of building possible before the postwar "merchant builders" introduced mass production–type construction, and the absence of government mortgage assistance to broaden the potential consumer market made these earlier suburban expansions less inclusive in their promise and appeal. Rather, late-nineteenth- and early-twentieth-century suburbs often housed wealthy commuters alongside lower-income vassals to serve them; twenties' bungalow developments attracted more middle-class residents, but on a smaller scale than in the postwar era. With annual housing starts ballooning from 142,000 in 1944 to more than a million in 1946 to a height of almost 2 million in 1950—after which it stabilized at around 1.3 million a year— "mass suburbia" is an apt description.[4]

The state of New Jersey offers an ideal setting in which to analyze the distinctive residential landscape of mass suburbia. In this quintessential postwar suburban state, where overall population grew by almost 2 million between 1940 and 1960—what amounted to a 50 percent increase over the two decades—every major city except Paterson lost population, and Paterson gained a mere 4000 residents due to an unusually large in-migration of low-income people with many dependent children, offsetting a dramatic out-migration of higher-income residents. Increasingly, people from long-established, often highly industrialized, and, by the end of the war, congested and deteriorating urban centers—whether neighboring New York City or New Jersey's own Newark, Paterson, Passaic, Jersey City, and Elizabeth—left homes near jobs, relatives, and long-established ethnic and religious communities to move to newly built houses farther out, first in Bergen, Essex, Union, Passaic, and Morris Counties, and later in Burlington, Middlesex, Monmouth, and Somerset, much the way Americans of an earlier era had left farms and small towns for beckoning cities. In time, 70 percent of the state's total land area would qualify as suburban, so that by the turn of the twenty-first century New Jersey and Connecticut shared the distinction of being the nation's most suburbanized states.[5] Whereas once work and family had dictated residence, now increasingly consumption—of homes, goods, services, and leisure—did. With the government subsidizing highways and home purchases and consumers contributing their pent-up demand and savings from the war, large numbers of urban residents packed their bags and their cars and headed for suburbia. Typical were Cele Roberts and her husband, who, expecting their first child, left a one-room apartment on the Lower East Side of Manhattan in 1949 for "that suburban dream life," where "a hundred dollars down" bought "a house that had venetian blinds, a washing machine, a refrigerator."[6]

Postwar highway construction, especially limited-access roads, proved particularly crucial to New Jersey's suburban development. In one striking example, the construction of the 118-mile New Jersey Turnpike and the 164-mile Garden State Parkway by the mid-1950s turned the rural area of Wood-

Map illustration: Judith Rew Design

	nonsuburban counties, 1976
——	county boundary
•	places mentioned
—·—·—	New Jersey Turnpike
– – –	Garden State Parkway
·········	Routes 80 & 280
—··—··—	Route 78

10 MILES

SUBURBAN DEVELOPMENT IN NEW JERSEY

bridge Township, where these two north-south highways intersected, into a
community of 100,000 within a decade. Later construction of Interstates 80,
280, and 78 running east-west would further open up outlying areas for residential development. Before World War II, the major urban centers in the
northern part of the state had largely remained self-contained, with little

interconnection or access to their hinterlands, as roads were limited, the rail network focused primarily on New York City, and interurban trolleys had never succeeded in tying the region together early in the century. Resident labor forces were largely employed locally.[7] When new postwar highways extended the possible travel distance from home to job, breadwinners were able to commute back into the cities for work. As time passed, more of them worked outside the cities as well, as businesses moved outward in search of newer, cheaper, and more spacious facilities. Hence, despite all the population increase in New Jersey's suburbs between 1950 and 1960, the number of trans-Hudson passengers headed for New York increased only 15 percent. Reflective of the new importance of highways was the dramatic decline over the decade in rail and ferry use by Hudson crossers, and the subsequent rise in autos and buses, from 60 percent to a full 80 percent of the total, with private car commuters outnumbering bus riders 2 to 1.[8]

By 1960, New Jersey had distinguished itself as a highly suburbanized state, particularly within the New York metropolitan area, where New York City's intensely urban character lowered homeownership rates for the region as a whole. Whereas 57 percent of families in the metropolitan New York area were tenants renting anything from a couple of furnished rooms to a luxury apartment, the renting population in the New Jersey portion replicated the lower national rate of 42 percent. And in a region where 35 percent of families owned a single-family detached house, 49 percent of New Jerseyites did, with another 3 percent owning single-family attached homes. Single-family houses themselves mushroomed from 7 percent of New Jersey's housing stock in 1950 to 64 percent a decade later. To bring the suburban character of most of northern New Jersey into even sharper focus, a city like Newark in 1960 dramatically defied the state's prevailing pattern of single-family home ownership, with 73 percent of its families—many of them poor—renting, thereby indicating that home ownership was even higher in the non-urban areas of northern New Jersey. So recent was this suburban built environment that in 1960 a full quarter of the dwelling units in the northern New Jersey region, as in the nation, had been constructed since 1950, most outside of city boundaries, fulfilling the preference of Federal Housing Administration (FHA), Veterans Administration (VA), and private mortgage lenders for homes that were new and single-family.[9] Here was a vast suburban residential landscape freshly carved out of what only yesterday had been farmland and settled by what would soon be a majority of New Jersey residents, who were purchasing on the private real estate market the ultimate mass consumer product of the postwar era, a house. The "garden state" was fast becoming the "backyard garden" state, as the housing subdivision became the New Jersey farmer's final crop.[10]

The New Jersey case, while in so many ways typical of the national trend in mass suburbanization, also offers some special analytical advantages. The diversity of the state's population—across class, given its industrial history, and across race, given the substantial African-American presence by 1950—permits a more nuanced portrait of the remaking of metropolitan America. More serendipitously, an activist New Jersey Supreme Court in the postwar period made the state a testing ground for the most pressing controversies to arise out of postwar residential suburbanization, such as who could—and could not—live in suburbs; how much disparity in spending for basic services like schools would be tolerated between cities and suburbs; and what kind of rights citizens should enjoy when often public space in suburbia consisted primarily of privately owned shopping centers. The highly suburbanized state of New Jersey—today forty-fifth in size and ninth in population—was among the first to thrash out the licenses, liabilities, and limits of the new landscape of mass consumption, and thereby warrants our attention.[11]

SEGMENTING SUBURBIA

Suburbia was home to affluence, and to inequity, too. Much the way access to mortgages, credit, and tax benefits through the supposedly universal GI Bill of Rights and the mass income tax ultimately favored some social groups more than others—men over women, middle class over working class, and whites over blacks—so, too, postwar suburbia disappointed those invested in its potential to equalize through mass abundance. There is no denying that moving to suburbia improved the quality of life of many Americans, but the extent to which private real estate markets shaped postwar suburban communities over time exacerbated inequality by establishing new kinds of hierarchies.

Postwar suburbia started off much the way its idealistic promoters envisioned it. In the late 1940s available housing supplies fell so short of need that everyone—engineer or factory foreman, teacher or state trooper—was simply relieved to find a home to buy. The "creation myths" of postwar suburbia often told of eager buyers from all walks of life lined up outside a developer's office the day it opened, hoping to claim the best lots and earliest move-in dates. For the most part, the stories were true. In 1950 sociologist William Dobriner found a social-class mix among the early settlers of Levittown, Long Island, where 62 percent held white-collar occupations and 38 percent blue-collar, each with corresponding educational levels and incomes. The case of Sam Gordon and his family, who moved in 1952 from a rented apartment in a so-called changing neighborhood of the Bronx to a split-level house in Harbor Isle, a new subdivision on Long Island not very different from nearby Levittown, was typical. Sam was an electrician, and when he left the Bronx, he claimed he wasn't looking to break away from the lower classes. He still thought of himself as a "workingman," and, in the words of family chronicler Donald Katz, "If he sought social distance from those poorer than himself, it was only to get away from people who might hurt Eve or the kids. He didn't want to emigrate to one of the vast tracts of prefabricated housing out of some desire to assimilate or to lose his ethnic roots, or even to 'conform'—a word that had lately filtered down to mahjongg tables and coffee breaks from complex sociological analyses of changing national character like David Riesman's *The Lonely Crowd.*"[12]

On Long Island, Sam's electrician's business thrived, and in time he would start to identify his children and eventually even himself as middle class. "You know what it means to be middle class?" Sam would joke with his friends. "It means that your kids look out the front window to keep track of who's got more," instinctively endorsing that popular notion of the era that mass consumption, beginning with consuming a new house, helped suburbanites of varying economic circumstances identify as middle class. But just as Sam was coming around to feeling like a middle-class resident of his suburban community, Harbor Isle was changing. By the late 1950s he began to notice that many of the accountants, lawyers, and other white-collar suburban pioneers were moving to bigger homes in more affluent towns.

Sociologist Dobriner confirmed that by 1961 Levittown had lost a significant portion of its white-collar residents while the overall occupational characteristics of Nassau County had not changed. Now, 50 rather than 62 percent of Levittown's residents had white-collar occupations, 45 rather than 38 percent blue-collar ones, and the trend was clear. Meanwhile, neighboring Garden City had a male labor force that was 83 percent white collar, far exceeding the county's 56 percent, while more than half of its newcomers between 1955 and 1960 had moved there from other suburbs. Not far away in Woodbury, Long Island, "sprawling acre" lots distinguished it from Levittown, now "passé," according to an upwardly mobile househunter in 1960. Put simply, ambitious, educated, and high-earning Harbor Isle and Levittown families left these communities when they could for more upscale suburbs like Garden City and Woodbury. Dobriner concluded that "selective recruitment" was homogenizing the Levittowns of Long Island as they "drifted down from middle to working class."[13] The increasingly class-segmented character of Nassau County on Long Island was replicated in suburban New Jersey and throughout the nation. Moreover, alongside and further complicating this growing community differentiation by class was community differentiation by race. In testimony to the U.S. Senate's Select Committee on Educational Opportunities in 1970, New Jersey–based regional planner Ernest Erber despaired that a collaboration between home buyers, the real estate industry, and suburban municipal officials had created a situation where "vast areas of New York's suburbs are now one-class, one-race (often one-religion) in residential composition."[14]

As Erber suggested, between 1950 and 1970, while suburbia mushroomed in territorial size and in the number of Americans it harbored, it became highly stratified socioeconomically. Ironically, it was this bond between suburban living and mass consumption—the source early on of egalitarian hopes—that was largely responsible, as it made market concerns paramount in decisions about how and where one lived. As home in the suburbanized Consumers' Republic became a mass consumer commodity to be appraised and traded up like a car rather than a longstanding emotional investment in a particular neighborhood, ethnic community, or church parish, "property values" became the new mantra. Of course, people still chose the communities they lived in from a range of alternatives, but increasingly they selected among homogeneous suburbs occupying distinctive rungs in a clear status hierarchy of communities. "Upgrading, the continuing movement toward bigger houses, better neighborhoods, and more possessions as incomes rise and more children arrive," was the way *Newsweek* described this new suburban ritual. A corporate wife interviewed by sociologist William H. Whyte, Jr., in *Fortune* revealed how it worked: "First, in a couple of years, we'd move out of Ferncrest Village (it's really pretty tacky there, you know). We wouldn't go straight to Eastmere Hills—that would look pushy at this stage of the game; we'd go to the hilly section of Scrubbs Mill Pike. . . . Then, about ten years later, we'd finally build in Eastmere Hills." Fast disappearing were the early-twentieth-century suburbs where employers and employees had lived alongside each other. New housing developments were particularly easy to peg at a particular consumer market through home prices, lot sizes, and community amenities, giving new suburban areas instant socioeconomic, and therefore market, identities.[15]

Home pricing served as the most obvious class sorter in the increasingly segmented postwar metropolitan housing market. Many working-class people were kept out of middle-class suburban communities simply by virtue of their expense. One calculation of the annual income needed in the early 1960s to buy a home in New Jersey's new Morris County suburbs of Parsippany–Troy Hills, about twenty miles northwest of Newark, figured that to carry a $15,000 mortgage, and pay taxes, maintenance, utilities, and commuting costs, would require $12,000 a year income, when policemen and firemen in Bergen County earned $7500 to $9800 as late as 1970, and only 17 percent of all Newark families—and only 9 percent of non-white families—earned over $9000. Purchases of homes in older, established middle-class suburbs could cost even more, as resales often required higher down payments than new-home purchases.

Home prices in some suburban communities were so high as to prevent manufacturing workers from moving closer to their jobs when plants relocated to outlying sites. With the average weekly wage for manufacturing workers in New Jersey at $116.62 in 1966, even in the unlikely case of a full fifty-two weeks a year employment, workers could not afford homes in the areas where most industries moved. "The result," according to the New Jersey Committee of the Regional Plan Association, "is to confine all but the highest paid strata of manufacturing employees to housing in the cities and older suburbs, or to induce them to buy beyond the fringe of suburban development where one family homes are built at marginal standards on inexpensive land and poorly served by community facilities."[16] But even if they could not settle in the Parsippany–Troy Hills of the state, many working-class Jerseyites nonetheless moved to suburbs they could afford, helping to shape the "cops and firemen" sector of the suburban real estate market and populating the "working-class suburbs" studied by sociologists Bennett Berger, Lee Rainwater, Richard Coleman, and Gerald Handel. The roster of the officers and shop stewards of the International Union of Electrical, Radio, and Machine Workers (IUE)-CIO's local at Westinghouse Electric's Bloomfield plant in the mid-1950s reveals a substantial number still living in Newark, but more of them were spread out among the less expensive suburbs of Essex County, some new, others old. A national AFL-CIO poll in 1966 confirmed that union members were increasingly becoming suburban residents, many workers driving long distances to work. The trend worried labor leaders, as nearly 50 percent of all union members and 75 percent of those under the age of forty now lived outside the traditional reach of central labor bodies based in cities.

In an effort to reconnect workers' jobs and residence while at the same time providing affordable, quality housing, the United Auto Workers Housing Corporation, a subsidiary of the autoworkers' union, tried to build federally assisted housing within the price range of the 5200 decently paid, unionized workers employed at a large Ford assembly plant that had moved to Mahwah in Bergen County in 1955. But the town of Mahwah refused the union's request to rezone to permit more affordable alternatives to the single-family homes with a 975-square-foot minimum, on one- or two-acre lots, required by local ordinance. A complaint to the New Jersey Division on Civil Rights that low-income workers were "discriminatorily barred from living in Mahwah solely because of their income" went nowhere. By 1970, Ford would complain that the long distances its Mahwah plant workers were forced to travel led to unusually high absentee and turnover rates. Likewise, although a large IBM installation was welcomed in the same county's Franklin Lakes as a lucrative tax-paying ratable, the garden apartments sought to house employees locally typically met with the response, "There is lots of empty land and cheap housing further out—there's no reason why people should feel that they have to live in Franklin Lakes just because they work here."[17] One of the starkest reminders of the formidable class barriers dividing metropolitan New Jersey by 1960 took place every day in the Newark area, where 50,000 blue-collar city dwellers—a third of the resident labor force in this increasingly working-class and poor city of 400,000—left for jobs outside Newark where they could not afford to live, while 200,000 white-collar workers commuted to corporate jobs in Newark from outlying middle- and upper-class suburbs.[18]

If suburbanization encouraged a class segmentation of the metropolitan landscape, the market orientation and differential wealth of consumers were not the only factors responsible. The federal dollars allocated for mortgage assistance and guarantees beginning in the 1930s with the New Deal's Home Owners' Loan Corporation (HOLC) and continuing with increased FHA and VA spending after the war favored not only new, single-family houses, but also their location in homogeneous middle-class communities. From the mid-1930s until at least the late 1950s, when this discriminatory redlining came to light and supposedly ended, neighborhoods and towns having what was considered too much "lower class occupancy" or "inharmonious racial and nationality groups" were rated poorly and treated as too high risk for mortgage investment. Because private lenders adopted the HOLC's "Residential Security Maps" as the basis for their own decisions, prospective home buyers suffered the same consequences whether they sought government-backed loans or not. The newly built postwar housing tracts, particularly those priced for middle-class consumers, fit the desired bill perfectly and got more than their share of Uncle Sam's largesse; approximately one-half of all suburban housing nationwide had received FHA or VA financing by 1962.

A simple comparison of VA home loans guaranteed between 1945 and 1960 in four New Jersey counties—two of them areas of new suburban growth, Bergen and Middlesex, and the other two, Essex and Hudson, older, more urbanized regions around declining Newark and Jersey City and their first-ring suburbs—tells the story. Bergen County, with a population increase between 1950 and 1960 of 45 percent, and the newer yet Middlesex County, with a population increase of 64 percent, received VA home loans at the rate of one loan per 15 and 12 residents, respectively, based on 1960 population totals. In contrast, established Essex County, with its population increase of a mere 2 percent, and Hudson County, with its population loss of 6 percent, received VA home loans only at the rate of one loan per 36 and 64 residents, respectively. FHA appraisers so effectively wrote off Hudson County that by 1960, more than twenty-five years after the federal government's entry into the mortgage market, residents there had received only $12 of mortgage insurance per capita, the second lowest total in the nation after the Bronx, in sharp contrast to Nassau County, home of suburban Levittown and Garden City, where residents had received $601 per capita. Not surprisingly, from the start in the 1930s, not one neighborhood in Newark ever received a top "A" rating from FHA appraisers. Even "high class Jewish" and elite Protestant sections earned only "Bs," given their dangerous proximity to "hazardous" urban neighborhoods. The sole "A" ratings went to prime neighborhoods in Newark's suburbs of Millburn, Maplewood, Montclair, West Orange, and the like. The United States government clearly considered newly built homes in the more homogeneous—meaning white and middle-class—booming suburbs of Bergen, Middlesex, and Nassau Counties to be better investments than older houses within long settled, and more class and racially diverse, Essex and Hudson Counties. When private banks followed that lead, investment money accompanied middle-class residents out of New Jersey's cities. The FHA's blunt response to criticism of its discriminatory policies, that its purpose was not to help cities but rather to stimulate home building and home ownership, reaffirmed the founding principles of the Consumers' Republic, that the health of the American economy and society depended on the vitality of mass consumption markets.[19]

As the Mahwah and Franklin Lakes cases suggested, once middle-class

Table 1. VA HOME LOANS GUARANTEED IN FOUR COUNTIES OF NEW JERSEY, 1945–1960

County	1950 Population	1960 Population	Population Change, 1950–1960	Total No. VA Loans, 1945–1960	Population Per VA Loan, 1960
BERGEN	539,139	780,255	45%	53,103	14.7
ESSEX	905,949	923,545	2%	25,758	35.9
HUDSON	647,437	610,734	–6%	9,533	64.1
MIDDLESEX	264,872	433,856	64%	37,037	11.7

Source: Computer run of New Jersey counties receiving VA home loans, 1945–1960, provided by Paul Nehrenberg, Department of Veterans Affairs, Washington, DC; *United States Census of Population, 1950* and *1960*.

suburbs were established, residents utilized zoning ordinances—a power dele-gated to individual municipalities by the state back in 1927 and strongly reaf-firmed in the new 1947 New Jersey Constitution—to shape the character of future postwar growth and to keep the New Jersey landscape's hardening class boundaries intact. Whereas for a few years right after the war suburban towns built garden apartments to ameliorate the severe housing shortage, soon many zoned against their construction, seeking to distinguish more clearly between communities of buyers and communities of renters. For example, when the Borough of Englewood Cliffs withdrew all land from multiple-family dwelling use and limited its residential use to one-family in the late 1940s, the state supreme court ruled that the citizens and elected officials were acting within their rights to define their community as they wished.

Likewise, zoning restrictions requiring minimum house and lot sizes became more and more common in postwar New Jersey suburbs. When a developer wanted to build small houses in Wayne in 1949, a booming suburb (whose population would grow 147 percent between 1950 and 1960) located twenty miles west of New York City and near the city of Passaic, the township established stringent minimum-size requirements for dwellings, including a larger living space in those houses built without an attached garage in order, supposedly, "to protect the health and safety" of residents but more likely to ensure a minimal house value. When in 1952 the developer challenged the zoning ordinance in court in *Lionshead Lake, Inc.* v. *Township of Wayne,* a lower court ruled it unconstitutional, asking, "What are the families of ordi-nary means to do and where are they to go?" But the New Jersey State Supreme Court, in a precedent-setting decision, upheld the township on appeal, bluntly agreeing that "the size of the dwellings in any community inevitably affects the character of the community and does much to determine whether or not it is a desirable place to live." Acknowledging the validity of residents' fears of declining property values and class status, the decision continued, "Without such restrictions there is always the danger that after some homes have been erected, giving a character to a neighborhood, others might follow which would fail to live up to the standards thus voluntarily set."[20]

During the 1940s and 1950s, New Jersey suburban communities, backed by the state's supreme court, increasingly utilized zoning law to enforce economic stratification. Reviewing that record in 1953, Harvard law professor Charles M. Haar despaired that the legitimate goal of zoning—to regulate, and usually separate, different kinds of land usage within a municipality in the broad public interest—was being overridden by "real estate interests" for whom zoning was a tool to "preserve rigidly the character of certain neighbor-hoods in the interest of preserving property values." At the other end of the

RESIDENTIAL SEGREGATION BY INCOME CLASS has been fostered by Federal regulations, restrictive codes, and fiscal zoning. Developers catering to buyers of $50,000 to $100,000 homes, as in this small plat with 29 swimming pools, can neglect the need for balanced communities.

The report of the National Commission on Urban Problems, *Building the American City,* which was submitted to Congress and President Lyndon Johnson in 1968, stated bluntly that residential communities had become stratified by social class. The report called for major improvements in housing for the poor, a challenge in an economy where "housing is the most important consumer good." As a result of a thriving real estate market, "the housing industry has shown a remarkable ability to provide housing for those whose incomes are sufficient to afford it." (Courtesy of J. R. Eyerman/TimePix)

market, older towns like Bergenfield, whose zoning continued to allow small lot sizes and modest, affordable homes, worried about how much harder it had become to attract the upper-middle-class home buyers who traditionally had played leadership roles in the community.[21]

The massive scale of suburban home building also lent itself well to this process of increasing class differentiation, as newly constructed houses easily bore class markings. For many prospective home buyers, drives in the quickly suburbanizing "countryside," punctuated by stops at fully furnished model homes in new subdivisions, became a popular weekend pastime. While banners and billboards blared the price range of a new development, the homes themselves embodied the details of each market niche. House size was the first critical factor, and its evolution over the postwar period confirmed the pattern of growing class diversification. A survey in 1950 revealed that at that early date, the typical new home had 983 square feet of floor area, only one-third had three or more bedrooms, and fewer than one out of twelve was built with more than one bathroom, evidence for a fairly undifferentiated suburbia immediately after the war. Already by the first quarter of 1955, however, the typical non-farm single-family home under construction had 1170 square feet of floor area, three-fourths had three or more bedrooms, and almost half had more than one bathroom. Accompanying this overall increase in house size was greater variation, divided roughly at a little less than a third with under 999 square feet, another near-third with between 1000 and 1199 square feet, and somewhat more than a third with 1200 and up square feet, thereby heightening class distinctions in the suburban housing stock.

Greater style differentiation developed as well, giving clear class identities to new homes. The same surveys revealed that while in 1950, 89 percent of exterior wall construction used cheap and simple wood, by 1955 more prestigious facing materials were gaining ground: about one-third of new homes were faced with brick, 9 percent used a combination of brick and wood, and other specialty materials, such as asbestos shingle, stone, and stucco, were growing in popularity.[22] That year, an unusual and fascinating collaboration between a Philadelphia-area developer, Ralph Bodek, and a marketing professor at the University of Pennsylvania, William T. Kelley, resulted in a study based on a random sampling of recent purchasers of the split-level homes in Bodek's large Lawrence Park development in Marple Township, Delaware County, Pennsylvania. Seeking to understand better how and why people selected different style homes, they discovered that new homeowners made clear social-class associations with particular house types. These solid middle-class residents of Lawrence Park—schoolteachers, office workers, sales workers, and the like who had explicitly sought a community of middle-class neighbors "as much like themselves as possible," where they wouldn't "have to keep up with the Joneses" or worry that "certain minorities will get in"—gave consistent responses to their interviewers: they linked row houses and two-family "twin houses" with low-middle-income buyers, such as laborers and lower-white-collar workers; ranch houses with lower-middle- or middle-income buyers who were deemed advanced, sporty, but less than respectable for choosing to live on one level; split-level houses, their own choice, as solidly middle-income, appealing to young couples with children who were also modern but more conventionally so; and two-story colonial houses, without exception assigned to "upper-income professional people and executives," conservative, respectable, and moneyed buyers at the top of the social scale.[23] These Lawrence Park homeowners thus lived in a suburbia where communities were class coded by house type, as new developments typically featured one style or another.

The allocation of space within suburban homes likewise carried class messages. The disappearing dining room provides a good case in point. When developers promoted new "open-plan" designs for more informal living that eliminated traditional dining rooms (and not incidentally saved space and hence cost), many consumers objected. Middle-class women testified before a federal housing hearing in 1956 that they considered kitchen counters and combination living-dining rooms poor replacements for real dining rooms; similar discontent expressed in Bodek and Kelley's survey suggested to them that separate dining rooms, along with a second bathroom, might be worth incorporating into future homes. Thus, a house with a separate dining room, in flaunting practicality and cost cutting, carried prestige, as did more bathrooms, a recreation room, and an attached garage.[24] In the Wayne zoning case, the presence of an attached garage added enough to a house's value and status to allow it to be smaller than one without.

But not all class distinctions in new homes stemmed from middle-class consumers being able to afford more "desirable features" than working-class consumers. Often, their priorities simply differed. A marketing survey for Macfadden Publications, based on extensive interviewing of working- and middle-class housewives, for example, revealed that the desires of middle-class homeowners—plenty of room to entertain, distinctive architecture particularly on the exterior, multiple bathrooms, and separate bedrooms to provide privacy to all members of the family—mattered less to working-class consumers, who entertained less formally at home, valued being well equipped with appliances inside over how their homes looked on the outside, and cared much less about protecting personal privacy. As magazines like *Good House-keeping* helped their middle-class readers strike a careful balance between

Row House

Twin House

A team of a developer and a marketing professor used these renderings to probe how consumers differentiated the owners of five popular house styles. With in-depth interviewing, they established that home buyers associated distinctive social-class statuses with each house type. Comfortable with subdivisions where one style house—and hence population—predominated, buyers' greatest worry was "that certain minorities will get in, which would destroy property values." The surveyors concluded, "It is interesting to note that people prefer to live near others as much like themselves as possible—they do not seem interested in the possibility of new stimulating associations with people different from themselves." Ralph Bodek, *How and Why People Buy Houses* (Philadelphia: Municipal Publications, 1958). (Courtesy of Steven M. Rosen, Esq., Attorney in Fact for Ralph Bodek, deceased)

Ranch House

Split Level

Two-Story Colonial

stylish "open-plan" public space and "privacy for everyone—a master bed-room a bit remote from the children's area, a separate bedroom for each child, and at least two bathrooms to avoid traffic jams at rush hours"—working-class homeowners put their money into time-saving appliances and gadgets, and had fewer qualms about their children sharing bedrooms.[25] New homes marketed to elite, middle-class, and working-class markets thus differed in how they allocated interior space as well as in their sizes and styles.

When in 1959 Vance Packard wrote his best-selling exposé, *The Status Seekers,* about the persistence of class hierarchies amidst America's celebrated classlessness, he drew attention to "mass produced suburbs" as a crucial set-ting. "We have recently been seeing the outpouring of tens of millions of peo-ple" to new communities "geared to specific economic levels and, in some instances, to people of specific religious and ethnic groups." He disparaged the result: "the creation of many hundreds of one-class communities unparalleled in the history of America. . . . There is no need to rub elbows with fellow Americans who are of a different class. The more expensive of these one-layer communities, where homes cost $50,000, import their teachers, policemen, and store clerks from nearby communities in a lower price range." Packard then went on to denounce another way that suburbia fostered divisions within postwar America: by intensifying racial segregation in these new "develop-ment 'communities,'" "much more sweeping . . . than in established, old-fashioned-type communities" simply because "by dictate of the builders" they can become "100 percent white."[26] As Packard accurately observed, superim-posed on an evolving class grid of metropolitan America in the postwar era was an evolving racial grid that kept African Americans and other minorities locked in cities and a few older suburban communities, while whites predom-inated in most of the booming newer suburbs.

Race was intrinsic to the process of postwar suburbanization, as the steady influx of African Americans to northern and western cities during the war, and the Second Great Migration out of the South that followed it, helped motivate urban whites to leave. Nationally, as three whites moved out for every two non-whites who moved in, nine of the ten largest cities lost population between 1950 and 1960 while all metropolitan areas grew. In New Jersey, while the suburban population mushroomed, the non-white population of Newark grew steadily from 11 percent of the total population in 1940 to 17 percent in 1950 to 34 percent in 1960 to 56 percent in 1970, an overall increase of 466 percent during a period in which the city's white population declined by 56 percent. Jersey City, Paterson, Passaic, Elizabeth, Camden, Atlantic City, and most of New Jersey's other cities experienced similar increases in black and decreases in white residents.[27] Whites left because they feared living near

blacks, whom they considered culturally different and in some vague way bea-
cons of greater poverty and crime.

But racial prejudice alone does not adequately explain the intensity of
postwar residential segregation. Accompanying, and further encouraging, this
prejudice were new kinds of market pressures introduced by the dynamic suburban real estate market flourishing in the Consumers' Republic. Most important, as a majority of white Americans invested most of their life savings in a
home by 1960, fear of racial mixing moved beyond a simple white discomfort
with sharing neighborhoods and public institutions. The presence of black
neighbors threatened to depress property values and hence to jeopardize people's basic economic security, or so homeowners were convinced. "Segregur-
bia" has flourished, the director of Newark's civil rights agency, the Mayor's
Commission on Group Relations, cynically put it in 1962, because "the free
enterprise system lurking in many American hearts has provided more moves
to all-white suburbs than the billion words of love have promoted the spiritual
advantages of economic and integrated city living."[28]

As Vance Packard had predicted, the market forces that created mass
suburbia—the large-scale housing entrepreneurs, the increasingly socioeconomically differentiated housing market, the highly mortgaged consumers—
made racial mixing there much less prevalent than in urban America. New
Jersey's cities had long had racially diverse populations, occasionally even
within neighborhoods, as did a few select prewar suburbs—such as Plainfield,
Montclair, and Englewood—where the presence early on of black service and
domestic workers living close to their well-off employers provided a magnet
for further settlement. In contrast, the racial boundaries of New Jersey's postwar suburbia grew even more impermeable than its class ones. Northern New
Jersey, host to much of the state's suburban expansion, evolved into a complicated mosaic arranged in a pattern of solid white only occasionally punctuated
by distinct, and intense, areas of black.[29]

A closer look at Essex County confirms just how racially polarized the
postwar landscape of mass consumption became. While only 13 percent of the
residents of towns in that county outside of its seat in Newark were African
American in 1970, when the county as a whole was 30 percent black, 89 percent of those black suburbanites lived in only three municipalities: East
Orange, Orange, and Montclair, where they made up 42 percent of the total
population (though twice as high a proportion in East Orange than in Montclair). Outside of this suburban "black belt," in the other eighteen suburban
communities in Essex County, only 2 percent of the population was black.[30]
Although some of this racial differentiation between suburbs can be attributed
to the class segmentation previously discussed, given the low income of many

African Americans, the case of Clifton in Passaic County illustrates the undeniable significance of race. Clifton, a suburb of the old industrial cities of
Paterson and Passaic and an employment center for manufacturing and other
commerce in its own right, boasted a population by 1960 of almost 90,000,
primarily made up of construction workers, truck drivers, craftsmen, factory
operatives, clerks, and laborers. Working people found Clifton an affordable
community. In 1960, 35 percent of its households were renters—42 percent
paying $80 or less a month—and 65 percent owned the town's moderate-
priced homes, a rate above the national average. And yet, despite its affordability, 99.9 percent of Clifton's population was white, while neighboring, and
more urban, Paterson and Passaic had growing numbers of black and Puerto
Rican residents, many of whom worked in Clifton.[31] Essex County likewise
boasted all-white, working-class suburbs, such as Nutley and Bloomfield.

Clearly, race dictated where people lived, relegating African Americans
and, in time, Puerto Ricans, primarily as renters, to core urban areas and the
few suburban communities where they either had long-established roots or
had spilled over from nearby cities, while allowing whites to purchase homes
freely in suburban towns, their options restricted only by what they could
afford. When black and white Newarkers were surveyed in 1959 about their
intentions to move within the next year, about a fifth of each race responded
"yes," roughly comparable with the mobility of the U.S. population as a whole.
But whereas two-thirds of the blacks indicated they would relocate within
Newark's boundaries, more than half the whites said they planned to leave
Newark proper, moving either to the suburbs or away from the area entirely.
The redistribution of Newark's population into solid areas of urban black and
suburban white was well under way.[32]

The same governmental forces that stratified suburbia by class helped
segment it by race, and did an even better job. Federal mortgage guarantee
agencies—the HOLC, FHA, and VA—adopted and elaborated the discriminatory practices of private lenders by considering the presence of racial groups
other than whites the greatest obstacle to assigning neighborhoods a favorable
rating; a stable community promising minimal defaults on mortgage loans
was assumed to be a segregated, white one. Although not all its discriminatory
guidelines were known to the public, by 1955 housing reformer Charles
Abrams had figured out enough to assert that "the FHA [has] adopted a racial
policy that could well have been culled from the Nuremberg laws," setting itself
up as it did "as the protector of the all white neighborhood." At a Governor's
Housing Conference held in Trenton, New Jersey, that year, participants
referred openly and frequently to FHA and VA discrimination as an indisputable fact of life that necessitated passage by the state of anti-discrimination
legislation like that which New York had recently enacted.[33]

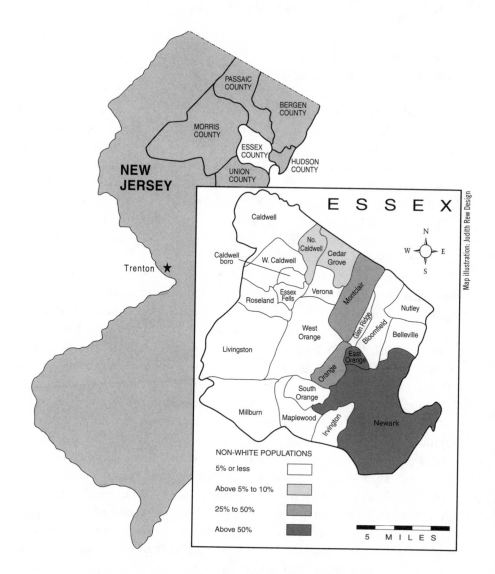

NON-WHITE POPULATION IN MUNICIPALITIES OF ESSEX COUNTY, NEW JERSEY, 1970

Note: No municipalities in Essex County had non-white populations of more than 7 percent and fewer than 25 percent. Also, note that this map shows non-white population, which was made up overwhelmingly of African Americans. According to the 1970 census, only 1.1 percent of Essex County's population was not black or white, and it was largest in the three municipalities with the highest number of African Americans (Orange, East Orange, and Newark). Forty-three percent of "other" was identified as Asian; the rest were probably Latinos, with most coming from Puerto Rico.

Source: U.S. Bureau of the Census: Census of Population, 1970.

Zoning, too, played its part. Just as postwar suburbia was taking off, the U.S. Supreme Court ruled in *Shelley* v. *Kraemer* (1948) that restrictive covenants—a major zoning strategy in use since the 1920s for keeping non-whites and other undesirables like Jews out of particular neighborhoods—were unconstitutional. Coming of age just when these covenants were no longer viable as a tool, mass suburbia developed alternative approaches to enforcing segregation, such as class-based zoning against multiple dwellings and inexpensive housing. New Jersey regional planner Ernest Erber found local land-use controls and building regulations so successful in excluding blacks from suburban housing that, he argued at a U.S. Senate hearing in 1970, this "misuse of legal instruments" of zoning was constituting a new form of de jure segregation, supposedly outlawed by recent civil rights legislation and Supreme Court decisions.[34]

Another zoning-related approach, practiced by older suburban communities fighting to hold on to white populations attracted to newer whiter suburbs, sought to use newly available urban redevelopment legislation to purge existing black settlements. Soon after the war, for example, East Orange invoked New Jersey's Preiser Act to condemn as "blighted" the area where almost all of the town's blacks lived and replace their homes, many of them owner-occupied, with garden apartments far too expensive for the displaced to afford. One might assume that the redevelopment plan's motive was simply the civic improvement of a depressed area had it not so boldly justified the proposed actions as a deliberate effort to stem white residents' exit from East Orange due to "excessive inter-mixture of economic or cultural forces." To eliminate such forces and "retain its attractiveness as a place in which a high type population will want to live," the plan's authors recommended that property owners be encouraged to "join neighborhood organizations." Because "unity of neighborhood action can best be achieved if the families are somewhat similar in economic and social respects," they insisted, "each neighborhood must encourage the retention of its type of population."

When neighboring Montclair proceeded to hire the same planning firm of Harland Bartholomew & Associates to prepare its housing redevelopment plan, Marian Wynn Perry of the national office of the National Association for the Advancement of Colored People (NAACP) angrily warned Montclair's NAACP branch, "Unless we can fight the plan in East Orange, Mr. Bagby [representative of the firm] will march successfully over the whole of suburban New Jersey imposing his segmented pattern of life upon heretofore democratic communities."[35] Needless to say, even the most vicious of redevelopment plans could not keep East Orange white, wedged as it was along Newark's northwestern borders with so few other exit doors open and with white residents of East Orange so opposed to integration. During the 1950s alone, the town's non-white population surged a whopping 120 percent. By 1970 it had become over 50 percent African American, which included many black middle-class former Newarkers frustrated with the larger city's deterioration. By the mid-1990s, at 95 percent, it had the highest concentration of black population in the nation other than East St. Louis, Illinois.[36]

Other strategies of exclusion employed to do the job of the outlawed restrictive covenants depended on the power of real estate market gatekeepers—developers, brokers, mortgage lenders, and, of course, property owners. Builders made blanket policies to exclude blacks that would take years of test cases, court challenges, and courageous purchases to undo. The Levitts provide a classic example. Despite considerable interest among blacks in buying homes in the new Levittowns, developer William Levitt refused to sell to them, and even tried to bar resales, arguing that it was not his role to solve society's racial problems. Because he was convinced his white customers did not want black neighbors, to do otherwise would mean "we'd lose millions. . . . We could not afford to take such losses." And indeed, the arrival of the black Myers family in his Pennsylvania development on a house resale in 1957 provoked whites to vicious violence replete with rock throwing, cross burnings, and Confederate flag waving, leading to mass arrests. Attesting to the extent to which fear of declining property values underlay this resistance, one Myers neighbor told a *Life* magazine reporter: "He's probably a nice guy, but every time I look at him I see $2000 drop off the value of my house." For years, Levitt successfully fought off lawsuits in all his communities, until his public announcement at the press conference opening his Burlington County, New Jersey, development in June 1958 that he would not sell to black buyers made him vulnerable to a newly enacted New Jersey law prohibiting discrimination in federally subsidized housing (which included Levittown by virtue of FHA- and VA-guaranteed bank loans made directly to the developer). In 1960 the New Jersey Supreme Court definitively ruled against Levitt.

But despite the occasional historic breakthrough in the color line by brave home buyers like the Myerses, Levitt's initial assumption that he was building segregated communities continued to shape them. In 1953, when Levittown, Long Island's population reached 70,000, it was the largest community in America with no black population. By 1960, Levittown included only 57 blacks and 163 of "other race" out of a total of 65,276 residents, bringing the non-white population to a minuscule .3 percent. By 1980, despite extensive anti-discrimination legislation and court challenges throughout the nation, the situation had barely improved: 45 blacks and 646 "others" put the total of non-whites still at only 1.2 percent.[37] Another postwar developer

In August 1957, William and Daisy Myers bought for $12,150 a ranch-style house that had lan-guished on the market for more than two years in Levittown, Pennsylvania. They were the first black family to break into this five-year-old community of 60,000. When they arrived with their three young children, they were greeted by jeering crowds, rocks thrown through their picture windows, and an offer to buy back their house for $15,000. Local and state police provided protection during months of harassment, which receded only when ringleaders were served with court injunctions. Within a year, a second black family moved in without incident. (Courtesy of AP/Worldwide Photos)

whose impact on West Coast suburbia rivaled Levitt's on the East, Joseph Eich-ler, took a more liberal position, becoming the first large-tract builder to declare his willingness to sell homes to minorities who could afford them, even offering to buy back homes from whites uncomfortable with their new neigh-bors. According to Eichler lore, possibly apocryphal, he once told some dis-gruntled owners, "If, as you claim, this will destroy property values, I could lose millions. . . . You should be ashamed of yourselves for wasting your time and mine with such pettiness."[38] The point, however, is that whatever the developer's particular position on residential integration, his will could deter-mine the racial composition of an entire community, and in more cases than not, he was convinced that his profits depended on keeping it white. Changes in the home-building industry from small-scale builders to community devel-opers contributed substantially to greater residential segregation in an era when other racial barriers, such as exclusion from public accommodations, were receding.[39]

Other guardians of racial segregation, the real estate brokers, discriminated outright against African Americans seeking to buy suburban homes—refusing to help black customers, withholding listings, and distorting house appraisals—as well as employed more subtle schemes like "steering" black buyers away from white communities into blacker ones to preserve the color line. In doing so, they were upholding the National Association of Real Estate Boards' Code of Ethics that "a realtor should never be instrumental in introducing into a neighborhood a character of property or occupancy, members of any race or nationality, or any individual whose presence will clearly be detrimental to property values in the neighborhood," though the phrase "members of any race or nationality, or any individual whose presence" was officially dropped in 1950 as a result of the *Shelley* v. *Kraemer* decision. The realtors of racially mixed Montclair hence were model professionals. As investigators for the "Montclair Community Audit," a much acclaimed and probing assessment of the assets and liabilities in the town's racial status quo, discovered in December 1947, "in regard to both sales and rentals there are certain areas of Montclair in which houses are to be sold or rented only to certain persons. To achieve this end there is in existence between the real estate operators the so-called gentleman's agreement." Without it, realtors insisted, "property values would go down."

Within cities, realtors were often responsible for fueling white flight to white suburbs. In a plea to the mayor of Newark to expand the Mayor's Commission on Group Relations in 1962, for example, the chairman and director argued, "It is a tragic commentary on the inadequacy of our services that we do not even have enough intergroup specialists to meet with families and whole neighborhoods which are in a state of panic and consequently fleeing from Newark because one or two blockbusters have told them: 'Sell now before it's too late.' " Although their ranks were much smaller, black realtors joined white ones in "blockbusting," turning the first racial break in a neighborhood into a profitable new market by scaring white owners into selling at low prices and then turning around and raising the sale price for black buyers hungry for decent homes.[40]

But realtors should not shoulder all the blame for victimizing black house seekers. White homeowners did their share of damage as well. Although the record is full of white harassment of prospective black neighbors, occasionally to the point of cross burnings and arson, more typical was what happened in Somerset, in central New Jersey, in the mid-1960s. After a four-year search, a young professional black couple managed to find a house that an elderly white couple was willing to sell them. When the neighbors learned of the pending deal, however, they pressured the sellers to withdraw, got together

The arrival of African-American neighbors could divide a white community. In July 1955 a group of white families launched a campaign in their northeastern Teaneck, New Jersey, neighborhood to urge 309 white families to resist realtors' calls to "sell while the selling is good," now that 57 black families had moved in from adjacent Englewood over the previous two years. Several weeks into the campaign, block meetings and delegations distributing "Not for Sale" signs door-to-door had convinced 90 families not to sell, while 51 had refused to sign, many putting their homes on the market. The campaigners sought to preserve a stable neighborhood "where home values do not decrease because of integration." *New York Times*, July 3, 1955. (Courtesy of Phillip A. Harrington/*Look* Magazine Photograph Collection, Library of Congress)

and bought the property themselves, and eventually put the house back on the market for purchase only by whites. Often, no matter how hard black buyers tried to convince sellers and neighbors of their good character, the deals never even got this far.[41] White homeowners' conviction that the presence of non-whites inevitably depressed property values ran so deep that even when academic sociologists and progressive housing policy experts documented how rarely this happened, many whites stubbornly held on to the faith, mostly out of fear of the consequences of being wrong.[42]

For their part, mortgage lenders vigilantly redlined against black neighborhoods and black buyers, contributing through the withholding of their dollars to the deterioration of black neighborhoods, the preservation of all-white communities, and the severe limiting of options available to black house seekers. Not only were minority applicants more likely to be refused mortgages, but when they got them they often were smaller than a comparable white buyer would receive and came with higher down payments, interest rates, commission fees, and home insurance premiums, and shorter terms of amortization. Although the VA kept no accounting of the race of its loan recipients, its records did show that almost half of its 5291 mortgage guarantees granted for multi-dwelling suburban developments in Essex County between World War II and 1956, when the *Newark News* investigated, went to Livingston and Cedar Grove, where there were no black residents in 1956. Livingston, the fastest growing of the county's twenty-two communities, led with 1418 VA guarantees in twenty-five developments, in stark contrast to older Newark and Montclair, the communities with the largest black populations, where a total of only 55 comparable dwellings were VA guaranteed. A study of savings-and-loan and commercial bank lending in Newark from 1960 to 1965 showed private institutions acting much the same way.[43]

Not until the 1970s would enough pressure build in Washington to pass open housing and anti-redlining legislation—such as the federal Fair Housing Act of 1968, the Equal Credit Opportunity Act of 1974, the Home Mortgage Disclosure Act of 1975 (toughened in 1989), and the Community Reinvestment Act of 1977, along with New Jersey's own Anti-Redlining Statute of 1977 and fair housing legislation in 1985—making possible effective challenges to discriminatory real estate sales and mortgage-lending practices. But even thereafter, unequal treatment persisted. An analysis of mortgage and home-improvement loan lending in Essex County during the mid-1970s, based on the disclosure of loan data now required by law, concluded that the thirty lending institutions with their main offices in the county not only gave more than half of all Newark loans to the two most prosperous areas of the city and greatly favored Essex County suburbs above its cities, but they were also making many more loans outside of Essex County, presumably to whiter suburban pastures, than inside, by a ratio of 3 to 1. In 1989, Urban Institute researchers claimed that half of all black and Latino home seekers nationwide continued to face discrimination as buyers. And still in 2000, another study revealed, minority homeowners paid higher mortgage rates than whites of comparable income. Small wonder that homeownership rates among blacks and Latinos continued throughout the postwar era to lag significantly behind whites. Racial patterns have become so indelibly set after years of the color coding of metropolitan America, moreover, that despite somewhat greater

Table 2. HOMEOWNERSHIP RATES AMONG WHITES, BLACKS, LATINOS, AND URBAN WORKING FAMILIES IN THE UNITED STATES, 1940 TO 2000

Population Group	1940	1950	1960	1970	1980	1990	2000
Whites	46%	57%	64%	65%	67.8%	68.2%	73.8%**
Blacks	24%	34.5%	38%	41.6%	44.4%	43.4%	47.2%
Latinos*	na	na	na	43.7%	43.4%	42.4%	46.3%
Urban working familes, est.***	30% (1934–36)	44%	56%	57% (1972–73)	na	56% (1986–87)	na
All U.S. homeowners	43.6%	55%	61.9%	62.9%	64.4%	64.2%	67.4%

* = The definition of what we now refer to as Latino has shifted with each census. The 1970 Census restricted Hispanic to "householders of Spanish language," those who reported Spanish as their mother tongue. In the 1980 Census, the group was understood as "Spanish Origin." Beginning in the 1990 Census, total "Hispanic Origin, of any race," included Mexicans, Puerto Ricans, Cubans, and "Other Hispanic."

** = 2000 Census defines this category as "White, nonhispanic"

*** = These figures come from cost-of-living surveys carried out by the Department of Labor, as discussed in "How Family Spending Has Changed in the U.S.," *Monthly Labor Review* 13 (March 1990): 23–24.

Sources: *1970 Census of Housing, Vol. 1, Part 1, United States Summary,* p. S6; *1980 Census of Housing, Vol. 1, Chapter A, General Housing Characteristics, Part 1: United States Summary,* pp. 1–7; *1990 Census of Housing, General Housing Characteristics, United States,* "Table 2: Occupied Housing Units by Race and Hispanic Origin of Householder: 1990," p. 2; "Housing Vacancies and Homeownership Annual Statistics: 2000, Table 20: Homeownership Rates by Race and Ethnicity of Householder," http://www.census.gov/hhes/www/housing/hvs/annual00/ann00t20.html; "Historical Census of Housing Tables, Homeownership," http://www.census.gov/hhes/www/housing/census/historic/owner.html; "Historical Census of Housing Tables, Ownership Rates, 1950–1990," http://www.census.gov/hhes/www.housing/census/historic/ownrate.html.

purchasing power and access to real estate and mortgage financing today, blacks for the most part continue to cluster where others of their race already live or in newer all-black suburbs. Although in New Jersey, as in much of the nation, every census finds more minorities living in suburbs, suburbia, like America's cities, remains highly segregated. Minority suburbanization has hardly proved synonymous with racial integration.[44]

The lives and literary production of two talented native sons of Newark—writers Philip Roth and Imamu Amiri Baraka (a.k.a. LeRoi Jones)—testify to how this city, once an intense tangle of different classes, ethnicities, religions, and races, "a majority composed of competing minorities" in Roth's words, became over the course of the postwar period a black urban core surrounded by a white suburban periphery.[45] Through Roth's memoirs and highly autobiographical fiction, we watch first the process of white, and in particular Jewish, class segmentation within the Greater Newark Area during the 1940s and 1950s and then the flight of most whites, regardless of class, to the suburbs during the 1960s and 1970s. Roth's 1959 autobiographically inspired novella, *Goodbye, Columbus,* captures through a clash of urban and suburban imagery the vast class gulf in the summer romance between working-class Neil Klugman, Newark resident and commuter to local Newark College (predecessor to Rutgers's Newark campus), and the upper-class Radcliffe student Brenda Patimkin, who was born in Newark but soon wisked off to the elite suburb of Short Hills (part of Millburn). As Neil heads out to Short Hills to visit Brenda for the first time, he muses:

> Once I'd driven out of Newark, past Irvington and the
> packed-in tangle of railroad crossings, switchmen shacks,
> lumberyards, Dairy Queens, and used-car lots, the night grew
> cooler. It was, in fact, as though the hundred and eighty feet
> that the suburbs rose in altitude above Newark brought one
> closer to heaven, for the sun itself became bigger, lower, and
> rounder, and soon I was driving past long lawns which seemed
> to be twirling water on themselves, and past houses where no
> one sat on stoops, where lights were on but no windows open,
> for those inside, refusing to share the very texture of life with
> those of us outside, regulated with a dial the amounts of mois-
> ture that were allowed access to their skins.[46]

Roth's own family could not afford to leave Newark's lower-middle-class Jewish neighborhood of Weequahic for a well-off suburb, and instead, when Roth was seventeen, they moved to another urban neighborhood in nearby Elizabeth where his mother had grown up. That failure only reinforced Roth's identification of suburbia with upward social mobility. By the late 1950s he had created the Patimkins to represent those offspring of Newark's Jewish immigrant generation who had prospered and then "moved further and further west . . . up the slope of the Orange Mountains, until they had reached the crest and started down the other side, pouring into Gentile territory as the Scotch-Irish had poured through the Cumberland Gap." As recently as 1998 the theme was still with him, as he had the protagonist of *I Married a Communist* drive during the late 1940s through "the quiet Maplewood streets, past all the pleasant one-family houses where there lived the ex-Newark Jews who'd lately acquired their first homes and their first lawns and their first country club affiliations."[47] When profiled in the *Newark News* in 1958 on the eve of the publication of *Goodbye, Columbus,* Roth hardly minced words: "My work concerns the geographical dispersion of Jews, what happens when they move from Prince Street to West Orange—it really is the story of immigrant to 'nouveau riche.'" And at that moment in time at least, Roth saw his own future in this dispersion, as he led the interviewer to conclude, "He is enamored enough with New Jersey to want to live in the suburbs—'preferably Glen Ridge' [a suburb of Newark not far from West Orange or Short Hills]—when he gives up bachelorhood."[48]

As time passed, Roth's writing began to chronicle not just the departure of upwardly mobile Jewish Newarkers, but the exit of all Jews from a city becoming more and more black. In his memoir, *Patrimony,* Roth recounted taking his father after his mother's death to the Jewish Federation Plaza in West Orange in search of a senior residence for him. When his father tried to place a woman they met, asking, "Berkowitz from where?" she replied, "Where else? Newark." It turned out that the home was full of elderly exiles from their old lower-middle-class neighborhood. Already by the period at the heart of Roth's Pulitzer Prize–winning novel, *American Pastoral,* the late 1960s and early 1970s, his protagonist Swede Levov distinguished himself by being among the very last white, Jewish holdouts in Newark, where he stubbornly insisted on keeping his glove factory operating despite deteriorating conditions after the 1967 race rebellion and great family pressure to close it down.[49] The departure of the Jews from Newark gave Roth a transcendent subject for a lifetime of writing, and he, in turn, has brought an extraordinary literary incisiveness to Newark's ethnic, class, and racial dispersal.

Poet, playwright, novelist, and essayist Baraka's life and writing chart Newark's evolution into a poorer and blacker city from the very different perspective of an African American who has remained there. Born in the city a year and a half after Roth, in 1934, also to lower-middle-class parents, Baraka grew up in a "mixed neighborhood" of blacks and Italians in a wartime environment where the enemy was more often Germans or Japanese abroad than anyone at home. By high school, however, this world grew less harmonious, as he and his friends matured and as more blacks moved into the Italian territory where his family had been pioneers. As he wrote in *The Autobiography of LeRoi Jones*:

> I could tell that something was happening in the whole of Dey Street/Newark Street/Lock Street world, bounded by Central and Sussex Avenues, when Augue began to say certain things. Like one time we were sitting on the auditorium steps in the playground bullshitting about something and he was combing his hair. . . . So I says to Augie to lemme use the comb. . . . But Augie nixes me and says, "Don't mix the breeds." . . . Sure I knew exactly what my best white friend Augie was saying, and I knew instinctively that his mother had probably put that shit into his head.[50]

Although his family would soon move back to the much blacker Central Ward, Baraka continued to travel across town to the virtually all-white college preparatory Barringer High School and then on for a year to Newark College, perpetuating a little longer his involvement with white Newark. But then, at the point when Roth left Newark College for all-white Bucknell, Baraka headed for all-black Howard University. After two more stints in interracial worlds—the air force and the integrated artistic and political milieux of Greenwich Village in the late 1950s—by the mid-1960s, Baraka had left his white wife and moved first to Harlem and then back to Newark, where he married a black dancer and passionately devoted himself to the nourishment of black arts and black nationalist politics within the city of his birth. There he has remained for more than thirty years, a powerful and persistent voice fighting for Newark's future, alternating between weapons of writing and political action, inside and outside the electoral system. Baraka gained notoriety as the bard of the '67 rebellion; his poem "Black People!" was used against him in court when he was charged and convicted of unlawfully carrying firearms and resisting arrest, a sentence that was reversed on appeal.[51]

Although Baraka has taken pride in Newark's determined survival as a black city, not surprisingly he has often lashed out at the suburbs whose prosperity regularly rubs salt in his city's wounds. "Newark banks take black money to invest in the suburbs . . . to build housing projects or shopping malls," he typically complains. Or, on another occasion: "Downtown is a ghost town after 5 because the Crackers live off somewhere WestOrange-SouthOrange-Teaneck-Montclair-Bloomfield-Maplewood, &c.&c.&c., a hundred suburbs dripping with money taken out of Newark. And the downtown's for white people in daylight, long gone by fingerpoppin night. . . . Newark is a *colony* . . . where white people make their money to take away with them." The unlikely truce that Baraka forged in the late 1960s with another Newark community leader, Tony Imperiale, voice of white "law-and-order" Newark, was based, in the words of journalist Stewart Alsop, on a "balance of terror," sustained by a mutual "contempt for the liberalism of white suburbia."[52] For the persevering Baraka, as for the self-exiled Roth, Newark's ill fate could not be separated from the robustness of its suburbs.

Roth and his family are long gone from Newark, he to return in person only for occasional celebrity appearances, though more frequently in his memory-driven imagination, prompted by a worn reference book about Newark that he keeps at his elbow as he writes.[53] In contrast, Baraka, despite his artistic and economic success, had made a lifelong commitment to remain in Newark, commuting for years from there all the way to his teaching job at the State University of New York at Stony Brook. Just as white abandonment of Newark has preoccupied Roth, so the trials and possibilities of black urban persistence have driven Baraka's writing and life choices.

Where these two brilliant native sons, both still producing art deeply inspired by Newark, have ended up building their lives into the early twenty-first century—Roth in the exurbia of Connecticut and Baraka still resolutely tied to the city of his birth—has everything to do with their respective races' fates within the metropolitan landscape of mass consumption, particularly as it was most brutally played out in Newark. Although the once upscale suburban ideal of the early twentieth century had certainly been democratized after World War II, mass suburbia still fell short of its initial promise to equalize the pieces of an expanding pie of prosperity. Commodifying "home" within a booming suburban real estate market meant accepting the imperatives of that market; the rational pursuit of profit seemed to require class and racial separation.

Frustrated observers like Newark civil rights activist Harold Lett could not help pointing out an embittering irony, however. While white householders, real estate brokers, lenders, and developers insisted that they had no choice but to submit to the market forces that sustained property values, even if they led to segregation, they created for blacks "a highly controlled market, where the natural laws of supply and demand are distorted, limited, and twisted. . . . You can get the finest car that's made, at home or abroad; you can purchase the very finest of clothing; foods of all sorts and description are available to you . . . in what purports to be a free enterprise market." Except for one very big exception—housing. "Forced to buy in a 'rigged' . . . market, where their demand for housing always exceeds the supply available to them; where the supply available, most frequently, is a marginal supply, is composed of shoddy or shabby goods, and proportionately is more costly than the better variety of goods on the market," all minorities but particularly blacks "are placed in the peculiar position in the American economy of being able to put a sign up, almost anyplace, with respect to the housing market, a simple little sign that says, 'blight for sale,' limiting the market to which this offer is being made." And as Lett spoke at Rutgers University in July 1959, he exposed another troubling irony: "the exploitable minorities whom they [the white public] have been taught to fear actually serve the housing industry in a very profitable manner," artificially inflating property values for whites, "but, at a great cost to society itself." In that sense, Lett concluded, the real estate market was far from a pure free market. Rather, it was rigged for everyone, with whites benefiting at blacks' expense.

Although Lett did not remark on it, the interweaving of class and race exclusion in metropolitan America made circumstances all the worse for most prospective black suburbanites. Working-class blacks found their options limited not only by what their low median incomes could buy, but also because the most affordable suburbs were settled by white working-class residents not very upwardly mobile themselves and hence often vigilantly opposed to any social change in their stable communities. Middle-class blacks who in principle should have enjoyed more residential choice faced obstacles too in joining white suburbia, some of their own making and others erected by their white middle-class peers. When the alternative existed, middle-class black suburbanites often preferred to live in blacker middle-class suburbs. But where that was not an option or a desire, they had a difficult time gaining entry into the neighborhoods of ambitious middle-class whites, who avoided risks that might compromise their real estate investment and, in turn, their own geographical mobility. In the sixteen metropolitan areas with one-quarter million or more black residents in 1980, the degree of black-white residential segregation barely varied across educational level from high school dropout to college graduate and across income from $10,000 to above $50,000.[54]

THE LOCALISTIC POLITICS OF MASS HOME OWNERSHIP

The class and racial fragmentation of metropolitan New Jersey, and America more generally, reinforced inequality of residential opportunity, but the story does not end there. Rather, this fragmentation had consequences that deepened and broadened the nature of that inequality over the course of the postwar period. First, the socioeconomic hierarchy of communities that arose from the commodification of "home" intensified the inequitable effects of the "localism" that had long been a feature of American, and particularly New Jersey's, political culture. As residents retreated into suburbs defined by the homogeneity of their populations and the market values of their homes, the barriers they erected against outsiders grew higher, and their conception of "the public good" correspondingly narrowed. Second, as the communities Americans identified with thus constricted, the inequities of postwar life expanded beyond housing to include public services provided and paid for by municipalities, the most important being the provision of education through local schools. Suburbs designed to deliver the promises of the Consumers' Republic to a wide range of postwar Americans ended up creating many local republics varying in socioeconomic makeup and in the privileges they bestowed upon their citizens. State efforts to overcome this discrimination or inequality fostered on the local level, moreover, often foundered on that same stubborn insistence on local control. A hard-won state commitment to protecting civil rights through the Freeman Act of 1949, for example, faced dangerous dilution from a demand for local implementation. In a compromise with resistant southern counties of New Jersey, the final version of the act substituted municipal commissions on civil rights, to be appointed by mayors, for more vigilant county councils appointed by the state council. Not surprisingly, many of the state's 567 independent municipalities stalled as long as possible in creating these bodies, jeopardizing the act's effectiveness.[55] The same kind of local resistance to fulfilling state mandates to equalize housing opportunity and educational spending also persisted into the twenty-first century. Control over zoning and education had long been the prerogative of local governments, and they were determined to keep it that way.

Localism has a long history in the United States, and particularly in New Jersey. Some have traced it all the way back to the many separate settlements of different religious groups in the state, who, in the absence of one dominant ethnic or religious power as in other colonies, sought to curb central authority to enhance freedom of worship and local customs.[56] Other contributing factors included constitutionally weak governors unable to rise above local interests, the early acquisition of power in the state legislature by anti-city, rural interests, and the related, longstanding difficulty cities had in annexing adjacent land. In the absence of that capability, cities lost residents— most often wealthy ones—to outlying municipalities when urban congestion and decline drove them outward. While cities in other states were expanding through annexation and consolidation in the late nineteenth and early twentieth centuries (New York pulling off the greatest extension with its addition of 250 square miles in 1891), New Jersey's Newark remained only 23.5 square miles with no buildable land, and hence began to lose residents and resources quite early to new jurisdictions that landowners and real estate interests eager for more local control had organized from the mid-nineteenth century on. In time, it should be noted, other older American cities began to suffer Newark's fate and encounter opposition to further expansion, and it was only the newer cities of the Sunbelt, in such states as Florida, Texas, and California, that managed to continue annexing and consolidating as the twentieth century progressed due to liberal state annexation laws.[57]

Citizens who prized the independence of their local governments not surprisingly had little interest in sharing power with more distant levels of political authority, be it county, region, or state. For at least a century before the mass suburbia of the postwar era, New Jersey residents had opposed granting too much authority to governmental bodies that transcended local boundaries. New Jersey was not alone. Other states may have been less extreme, but nationwide Americans linked democracy to local government and brought a skeptical eye to efforts to centralize political authority. Even when the post–New Deal expansion of the federal government might have been expected to lure Americans from their provincial perches, that repudiation of localism failed to happen, thanks in large part to the impact of postwar suburbanization and mass home ownership. Although they lived with and benefited from a more powerful federal government, postwar suburbanites were simultaneously attracted to what they considered the responsive, democratic character of local self-rule. They set out not just to replicate the New England small town but to improve upon it. As the "cult of localism" rose again in suburbia, political scientist Robert Wood wrote in 1959, "the institutions and political processes . . . long established but rusty in disuse become the basis for creating new . . . kinds of small communities." "Suburban legal independence," built on "our longstanding conviction that small political units represent the purest expression of popular rule, that the government closest to home is best," became a vehicle for achieving a "degree of homogeneity . . . that was not possible before . . . and [for] escaping the greater community."[58]

Even an effort to remedy an undesirable condition like traffic congestion could face local resistance if it required cross-community cooperation. When in 1957 the traffic from two new regional shopping centers so aggravated existing road jams from other highway stores that it pushed the thoroughfares of Bergen County's Paramus far beyond their capacity, Paramus's Planning Board chairman still had to struggle to convince municipal officials countywide to collectively build the fifty to one hundred miles of new highways needed, despite federal grants available to help pay for them. Soon he was fuming that municipal boundaries were nothing but lines on a map stopping a cooperative approach to mutual problems.[59]

In the late 1950s, Robert Wood and Raymond Vernon undertook a Harvard-based study of the New York metropolitan region for the Regional Plan Association, under the revealing title *1400 Governments: The Political Economy of the New York Metropolitan Region.* Despairing at the fragmentation of authority between so many jurisdictions in the tri-state region, which made coordinating metropolitan development like building those new highways in Bergen County a nightmare, they called for the agglomeration of "one of the great unnatural wonders of the world . . . a government arrangement perhaps more complicated than any other mankind has yet contrived or allowed to happen."[60] New Jersey's long tradition of local political autonomy probably made it the worst offender in the region, as localism there became not just a matter of policymaking but also of economic independence. A decade later, at two conferences called to ponder the future of New Jersey, prominent state leaders were still despairing that citizens' commitment to "home rule" had so fragmented the state that "joint political action for the state's welfare" and "rational solutions" to the state's many problems had become virtually impossible. Somewhat in vain they argued for a reorganization of power away from the state's 567 municipal units toward stronger counties, a more assertive state legislature and executive branch, consolidated services, and larger taxing districts.[61]

That is not to say that before the proliferation of locally conscious, socially stratified communities with mass suburbanization in the postwar era, cities did not have socioeconomically distinct neighborhoods, offering unequal services to their residents. But the critical difference was that all neighborhoods still had to negotiate with each other within a single political structure, making deals over spending tax dollars and dividing other spoils of city rule. True, Progressive Era reformers had established a commission form of government in New Jersey cities like Newark, as elsewhere in the United States, to minimize that negotiation by replacing ethnic machine bosses with more "efficient"—and elite—commissioners selected through citywide, not ward, elections. But ethnic and black politicians still found ways to get some of what they wanted. During the 1920s and 1930s, Newark's black Democratic political leaders allied with politicians supported by the organization of mobster Abner "Longie" Zwillman, who, according to a politician of the era, "provided more jobs for blacks than city government," with all the "plants and contractors that they controlled." And in the 1940s and 1950s, as more opportunities arose through mainstream party politics, blacks traded their votes for securing the political goals they cared most about. The integration of Newark

City Hospital in 1946 finally succeeded, for example, through an exchange of black voters' support for the reelection of City Commissioner Meyer C. Ellenstein in 1945 from the once Jewish and increasingly black Hill District, in return for Ellenstein's help securing the admission of a black physician at the hospital.

By the 1950s another cycle of municipal reform restructured Newark government to bring back a strong mayor and a nine-member city council, with five of those representatives elected by wards. Although by no means an equal partner within the city's Democratic machine, Newark's swelling black population did gain a greater voice in city government, culminating with Kenneth Gibson's election as mayor in 1970.[62] This give-and-take of social groups and urban neighborhoods on one city's political stage receded, however, as the postwar metropolitan region became a congeries of autonomous municipalities with unequal bundles of municipal services, each now free to tax, spend, and legislate as it wished with little concern for the others.[63] Similarly, New Jersey's urban and suburban communities had displayed significant local consciousness in the prewar period, but with less socioeconomic stratification among them localism created less inequality than it did in postwar mass suburbia.

As postwar suburbanization marched on, zoning fulfilled another function within communities beyond building barricades against outsiders considered different from themselves: to keep down both the demand for local services and the property taxes needed to fund them. The most prevalent kind of postwar zoning became "upzoning," or "large lot zoning," a strategy of requiring substantial plots for home construction to preserve high property values but also to cap a municipality's population and thereby control the demand and cost of local services. If one house was built on a large lot instead of three or four on smaller ones, fewer children would enroll in school, fewer residents would need police and fire protection, and fewer cars would wear down local roads. Furthermore, upzoning heightened inequality between suburbs and cities and among suburbs by ensuring that in newer, wealthier, and less densely settled suburbs the quality of services grew higher while the per capita costs of operating and paying for them became lower than in poorer cities and in older, more diverse suburbs with no such way of gatekeeping. By 1968 three-fourths of all vacant land in New Jersey's nine northeastern counties was zoned for minimum lot sizes of a half acre and upward, much of it one and two acres, with only a tiny portion of the remaining quarter reserved for multi-family housing, thus creating two societies: a sparser, wealthier, and better serviced New Jersey, on the one hand, and a denser, poorer, and overburdened New Jersey on the other.[64]

At the same time that local zoning was keeping down municipal costs in suburbia, cities were facing rising ones. As middle- and upper-income citizens, as well as the commerce and industry they supported, fled the cities, those left behind became saddled with the increasing burden of keeping them running on declining tax revenues. Fewer taxpayers—and particularly fewer wealthy ones—and rising costs of servicing commuters and a growing, needy poor population usually led to higher tax rates for those left behind. In 1961, for example, Newark's tax rate on full property values was 4.6 percent, while the rest of Essex County averaged 3.4 percent. Likewise in Passaic County, Paterson's was 4.2 percent, the rest of the county's 2.3 percent, and the disparity only worsened over time. To make the point even more sharply, in 1964 a New Jersey resident who owned a house worth $20,000 would have paid on average $622 in municipal property taxes, but if the homeowner lived in Newark, the bill would have been $1184 or in Hoboken, $1608.[65] Moreover, despite these higher tax rates, urban services frequently declined. Hence lower-income people with substantial need for public services—in health, education, police, housing, transportation, and welfare—who remained in New Jersey's cities and older suburbs were saddled with paying higher taxes on their less valuable property and getting poorer services in return than their better-off suburban neighbors. It proved increasingly difficult to keep a middle-class homeowner in troubled Newark, Paterson, or Jersey City when moving a few miles over the city line yielded substantially lower taxes and superior services.

The localistic orientation of New Jersey's citizens led to other disparities in how urban and suburban residents supported state services. After World War II, when New Jersey's population and settled land area were expanding rapidly, and broad-based taxation (all taxpayers paying into the state's coffers) was becoming more and more necessary to support adequate state infrastructure and services, resistance to it persisted, both to keep down the tax burden and to limit the intrusiveness of government beyond the locality. As the Regional Plan Association put it succinctly in its analysis of New Jerseyans' resistance to statewide taxation, "there was no better way of keeping state government weak than by keeping it poor."[66] Instead of broad-based taxes that supported trans-local governmental entities and services and redistributed some wealth throughout the state, New Jerseyans continued to insist on the primacy of local property taxes: taxes on individual property, set, collected, and spent by self-contained municipalities to keep power and resources in local hands. By definition, however, property taxes produce vast inequalities between localities, as property values and tax rates vary by community and put unequal amounts of revenue per capita at towns' disposal. In particular, they discriminate against urbanized areas faced with large demands for services and against individuals with low or fixed incomes, in both cases because of a lack of relationship between tax assessment and ability to pay. In addition, in this postwar era of the mass income tax, the property tax deduction on a tax-payer's federal income tax benefited homeowners, most often suburban, over renters, more likely urban, much the way the mortgage interest deduction did.

New Jersey voters long had resisted broad-based taxation, despite hav-ing one of the highest per capita personal incomes in the nation. In 1935, in the midst of the crisis of the Great Depression, the state passed its first statewide tax, a 2 percent sales tax, but the outcry that greeted it led to its repeal within three months. Aside from a three-cents-a-package cigarette tax imposed in 1948 and other excise taxes on liquor, gasoline, and horse racing added later, it would take until 1966 for a general sales tax—at a mere 3 per-cent with many exemptions—to become permanent, and even then, the income tax proposed to accompany it was shelved. Already by the mid-1950s, 31 states had a state income tax, 33 states had a general sales tax, and only 3 states, of which New Jersey was one, had neither. At this time, New Jersey's statewide taxes were half the national average (although property taxes were the highest in the nation), contributing to making the state's per capita rev-enues and expenditures the lowest in the country. Progressive forces in the state like the League of Women Voters kept pushing for broad-based taxation. Its Paterson branch performed a biting skit in 1963, "To Beat the Bond: or Oh, State, Poor State, You're Hung Up on Finances and It May Be Too Late," to urge voters that "the graduated personal net income tax is what it's got to be!" rather than unrealistically depending on turnpike revenues to bail them out or falling back yet again on bond issues that "saddl[ed their] children and grand-children with such a big debt."[67] But other interest groups hailed the status quo. The Newark Chamber of Commerce, for instance, sought to recruit new firms in the 1950s by bragging that "Newark's compact, conveniently-reached business center offers the 'white collar' side the advantage of work near transit lines and stores . . . and living in income-tax-free New Jersey." But while white-collar commuters were saved from paying into Newark's coffers, Newark's mostly blue-collar residents were staggering under the load of a property tax bill responsible for providing over 80 percent of the city's total revenues.[68]

Only after urban rebellions in Newark, Plainfield, and Englewood in July 1967 did the chorus of voices demanding that the state bail out its crum-bling cities by sharing more of its suburban wealth grow sufficiently powerful to support a change in tax policy. But despite the angry denunciation of the status quo by the Governor's Select Commission on Civil Disorder—"the State has left local governments [particularly core older cities] to fend for themselves," spending less per capita than any other state to aid local govern-

Table 3. PERCENTAGE OF TOTAL MUNICIPAL REVENUES (INCLUDING
INTERGOVERNMENTAL REVENUES) DERIVED FROM LOCAL PROPERTY TAXES,
SELECTED CITIES IN THE UNITED STATES AND IN NEW JERSEY, 1970

United States Cities	Total Revenues from Local Property Tax	New Jersey Cities	Total Revenues from Local Property Taxes
Milwaukee	35.1%	BAYONNE	75.6%
San Francisco	33.2%	PASSAIC	74.9%
Cleveland	32.2%	NEWARK	62.1%
New York City	26.0%	TRENTON	61.8%
St. Louis	25.9%	CAMDEN	58.0%
Phoenix	16.7%	JERSEY CITY	53.0%

Source: Division of State and Regional Planning, Department of Community Affairs, State of New Jersey, "The Housing Crisis in New Jersey, 1970," Newark Public Library, New Jersey Documents.

ments—the meager result was an increase in sales tax to 5 percent and the creation of a state lottery.[69] Not until 1976 did New Jersey pass an income tax, and then only after its state supreme court had actually closed down the public schools because the state had failed to respond adequately to the court's mandate to fund school districts more equitably as part of its 1973 decision in the landmark case of *Robinson* v. *Cahill*.[70]

But since the state income tax, so begrudgingly adopted, remained low and delivered little state aid to municipalities, property taxes continued to be the major source of revenue for New Jersey's localities, which meant that serious inequalities persisted between cities and suburbs and between wealthier and poorer suburban communities even after acceptance of the income tax. Well into the 1990s, New Jersey relied more heavily on the property tax than any other state with both a sales and income tax, keeping its property taxes per capita the highest in the nation. Citizens' continued resistance to paying taxes encouraged the state to search for alternative sources of revenue, with the 1970 lottery and a 1978 casino tax proving the most promising. Whether through taxes on property, sales or legalized gambling, or income from the state lottery, however, New Jersey was raising a major portion of its revenues through regressive means, based on consumer purchases, that perpetuated—even heightened—inequality, as all consumers, whatever their wealth, paid the same tax. And because neighborhoods with old rental housing and with elderly, low-income, and large black and Latino populations proved to be the prime markets for the lottery, poorer, urban residents of the state were disproportionally contributing to that revenue stream as well.[71]

The economic and political autonomy of New Jersey's postwar suburbs, and the inequality it fostered, did not go uncontested. Even as the momentum gathered, individuals and organizations who recognized the dangers accompanying excessive localism sought to contain it. Some carried out fair housing campaigns, others fought for a state income tax, and probably the most effective mounted suits in the state's courts challenging the way the landscape of mass consumption was shaping the life options of New Jersey's citizens. Early suits in the late 1940s and 1950s, previously discussed, challenging the use of restrictive zoning in Englewood Cliffs and Wayne, and others in Bedminster, Hasbrouck Heights, and Gloucester, failed in the courts.[72] But the growing housing crisis in the state became the fulcrum for a more successful challenge by the late 1960s. Construction was running some 30 to 45 percent behind the annual rate of new housing units needed to meet projected demand for the rest of the century. In particular, people with low and moderate incomes were suffering, as only about 20 percent of households could afford the going rate by the late 1960s of at least $30,000 a house.[73] State housing experts by then were explaining publicly how interlocking in a single system of exclusion were the obstacles to a viable housing solution. As one state report put it in 1970, the glaring shortage of affordable housing was precipitated by large-lot zoning requiring single-family homes on at least half an acre: "large-lot zoning is often in large part a by-product of high tax rates, which are in turn a result of the dependence on the local property tax (to a degree greater than in any other state), which in turn prevents all but nominal development in core cities, which is (to some degree) the result of antiquated and arbitrary municipal boundaries resulting in extremely limited amounts of developable land in the center cities."[74] A single chain of shortsightedness linked the longstanding crises of New Jersey's cities to the growing unaffordability of its suburbs.

The breakthrough would come in the late 1960s when the one branch of government somewhat shielded from the wrath of New Jersey voters, the courts and particularly the state supreme court, courageously responded to the challenges brought before them. In a series of decisions, culminating in the nationally historic Mount Laurel rulings, justices of the New Jersey Supreme Court struck down zoning laws that zoned out poor people and mandated that wealthy suburbs bear more of the burden of housing the less affluent in their regions. No longer could they foist that responsibility on the already overcrowded and financially pressed cities. Instead, suburbs would have to assume their "fair share" of the region's growth and make "an affirmative effort" to provide low- and moderate-income housing, in the process diversifying their populations. Not only was this a matter of meeting "the needs, desires, and resources of all categories of people who may desire to live within [a town's] boundaries." The court also recognized that as employers moved their workplaces out of cities into suburbs, suburban residence had become a necessity for many people's economic survival. Communities that zoned to reserve land for industrial and commercial "ratables," prized for generating tax dollars without requiring many services, would now have to "permit adequate housing within the means of the employees involved in such uses." To do anything less than the court was mandating meant depriving New Jerseyans of their constitutionally protected "general welfare." A more penetrating critique of all that had transpired to undermine social and economic equality in two decades of postwar suburbanization was hardly imaginable.[75]

The setting for the New Jersey case that generated the most far-reaching condemnation of exclusionary zoning in postwar America was the Township of Mount Laurel, a fast-growing community outside of Camden and twenty-one miles east of Philadelphia. As the township turned from farmland into suburb between 1950 and 1970, quadrupling in population, it put into place all the standard exclusionary zoning tricks of the trade to ensure that its transition would attract middle-income residents and light industry to enhance, not drain, its property tax base: large lot zoning, single-family detached housing with minimum floor space requirements, and a ban on apartments, attached townhouses, and mobile homes except for a small number of multi-family units where expensive amenities and tight limits on bedrooms and school-age children promised upper-class and childless occupants. Given its location close to Camden, by now one of the poorest cities in the United States and primarily black and Puerto Rican in population, Mount Laurel not only wanted to keep its tax rate down but its undesirable neighbors to the west out. By the late 1960s the town's small but longstanding black community—tenant farmers for decades on what had been white-owned farms—realized that Mount Laurel was headed in a direction that would exclude its own future generations if no action was taken. With the help of housing advisers, black residents requested that the town rezone thirty-two acres for thirty-six low-income garden apartment rental units. When Mayor Bill Haines informed black community leaders in their small church one Sunday afternoon in 1970 of the town's refusal to rezone, shocking people with roots going back five, six, and seven generations with the retort, "If you people can't afford to live in our town, then you'll have to move," the legal challenge that would become *South Burlington County N.A.A.C.P. v. Township of Mount Laurel* was born.

The class-action suit pursued by Ethel Lawrence, a Mount Laurel resident who traced her own ancestry back seven generations, produced three key decisions by the New Jersey Supreme Court: in 1975, 1983, and 1986. Taken together they confirmed both the highly stratified character of the state's postwar landscape and the tremendous obstacles to changing it. *Mount Laurel I* (1975) asserted the illegality of exclusionary zoning and obligated localities like Mount Laurel to "plan and provide for an appropriate variety and choice of housing" but established no mechanism for enforcement. Not surprisingly, few suburbs, including Mount Laurel, responded by building any low- or moderate-income housing. By 1983, however, Robert Wilentz had become chief justice and the court resolved to put teeth in its ruling. *Mount Laurel II* required proof that municipalities were meeting their "Mount Laurel obligation." The court specified exactly how many units of affordable housing Mount Laurel had to build and instructed lower court judges to set similar goals when other towns were challenged. Developers were required to set aside a portion of new housing for low- and moderate-income inhabitants, and if towns refused to comply, builders could take them to court, assured that if they won they gained the right to build more market-priced units than present zoning permitted. For a few years the "builder's remedy" contributed to significant progress, as it put the private-market developer in the public service, making him, in the words of legal historian Richard Briffault, "a kind of private attorney general for the economic and social integration of New Jersey's suburbs."[76]

But it wasn't long before the "builder's remedy" inspired an antidote of its own. When a scared and angry suburbanized electorate voted in a nonbinding state referendum to abolish the court's Mount Laurel decisions, the legislature was finally goaded into action. The resulting Fair Housing Act of 1985 accepted *Mount Laurel I and II* in principle but moderated their effects. The zoning authority of localities received more protection, a new state Council on Affordable Housing (COAH) set less stringent affordable housing guidelines for localities that respected "the established pattern of development in the community," and municipalities could discharge their Mount Laurel obligations by using Regional Contribution Agreements (RCAs) to buy their way out of up to half their "fair share" housing responsibility through contributions to other communities in their region, usually cities already housing low-income residents. Between 1987 and 1998, $120 million was transferred from suburban to urban areas to build and rehabilitate housing as a result of RCAs. The city of New Brunswick, 40 percent black and Hispanic, for example, gained funds from neighboring suburbs to build 306 new housing units and rehabilitate one hundred more. The well-to-do suburban community of Princeton, in contrast, reduced its obligation from 800 to 215 units, although after facing Mount Laurel lawsuits, the Borough and Township of Princeton both developed court-approved housing plans that have increased the supply of low- and moderate-income housing appreciably.[77] Despite outrage from "fair share" housing advocates, the supreme court in 1986 accepted the state's program in *Mount Laurel III* as constitutional, trading a dilution of *Mount Laurel I and II* for at least some assumption of responsibility by the state.

Three decades after Ethel Lawrence brought her suit against the Township of Mount Laurel, consciousness about the need for affordable housing has been raised in New Jersey, and the suburbs have made some concessions to condominiums and apartments, as much in response to an exorbitant housing market as to court injunctions. But the deeply etched class and racial contours of the state have proved hard to change. By transferring resources for new housing to poorer cities and suburbs, wealthier communities have been able to escape relatively unscathed while urban populations have become reanchored to old cities. Just the way cities, and not suburbs, have been the chief recipients of public housing projects since they began in the late 1930s, as legislation establishing the United States Housing Authority respected local choice by putting the initiative to assess a need, establish a housing authority, and apply for federal assistance solely on the municipality, so today cities, and not suburbs, are building the lion's share of affordable housing for the poor who are still with them.[78] In addition, better-off suburbs have fulfilled their required Mount Laurel obligations as much as is allowed by building affordable housing for sale—often as condominiums—rather than for rent, a more privileged market, and for senior citizens rather than for the low income, carrying the double benefit of less class diversity and less pressure on the schools. Some communities, moreover, have embraced anti-growth, open-space conservation as a defense against any new development at all, including "fair share" housing.[79] And in an era of little federal investment in subsidized housing, the money that might have made a difference when Ethel Lawrence first brought her suit, or even when *Mount Laurel I* was decided, no longer is available.

Altogether, these factors have given New Jersey more affordable housing than it surely would have had otherwise, but not nearly enough to alter the state's segmented class and racial landscape. Affordable housing advocates have long estimated the need at 500,000 or more units, the supreme court mandated 240,000 in 1984, COAH scaled that number back to 145,000 in 1987 and again to 85,000 in 1993, and as of 2001, not quite 25,000 units had been built.[80] Racial segregation in particular persists, as most of the people moving into "fair share" subsidized housing in the suburbs have been young, working class, and white. Although Lawrence's original suit cited racial discrimination, the court chose to propose remedies based on economic classifications and not worry about racial representativeness within them. The African-American residents of Mount Laurel finally got their long-awaited "fair share." It took a full fourteen years after the legal victory of 1983 for a proposal for a low- and moderate-income complex of rental townhouses—now called the Ethel R. Lawrence Homes in honor of its deceased champion—to assemble land and financing and win approval by the town's planning board. After that high hurdle was cleared in 1997, construction moved ahead and the first families moved into their new homes at the end of 2000.[81]

Mount Laurel may well be the Roe v. Wade or Brown v. Board of Education of exclusionary zoning, as the authors of one study of the New Jersey decisions have put it, but similar cases—many of them inspired by Mount Laurel—have rocked zoning boards and courts throughout the nation. Everywhere postwar suburbanization has intensified class and racial segregation, and in many places "fair share" advocates have challenged the "natural"—and exclusionary—workings of the private marketplace in housing. While a majority of states have left local land-use authority untouched, state supreme courts in California, New York, Pennsylvania, and a few other states besides New Jersey have reviewed and overturned some local zoning practices, while urging their states to assume a stronger role in land-use planning. In a handful of states, like Massachusetts, "anti-snob" zoning legislation has made its way onto the books.

A few affordable housing efforts on a smaller scale have also proved successful. In Montgomery County, Maryland, the Moderately Priced Housing Law, enacted in 1974, requires that all new developments include some housing affordable to people making 65 percent or less of the county's median income, and developers get a "density bonus" of more market-price units in exchange for building the affordable ones. Ten thousand units have been built, enough to begin to erode some of the class segregation in suburban Montgomery County. Counties in California, Connecticut, Florida, New Jersey, Oregon, and Vermont have undertaken similar programs, recognizing the advantages of a countywide effort that transcends municipalities and thereby closes escape hatches. The Chicago area has hosted another successful experiment thanks to a United States Supreme Court ruling in Hills v. Gautreaux that the U.S. Department of Housing and Urban Development discriminated racially by putting all its public housing in black neighborhoods of the city. Now some minority public housing residents receive vouchers to rent apartments in outlying white suburbs.[82] Almost everywhere, however, even when the highest courts of the land have given their blessing, the task is gargantuan and the progress snail-like. "Fair share" housing decisions like *Mount Laurel* cannot be considered important because they have radically altered suburban landscapes but rather because they attest to how deeply entrenched socioeconomic stratification, and the local authority that supports it, remains in the early twenty-first century.

SCHOOLING INEQUALITY

Because localities fund so many basic services in America, their staunch autonomy has created other kinds of inequality beyond the housing exclusion admirably condemned by the courts. Most significant has been inequality of educational opportunity. Education in the postwar period, more than in any previous time, became tightly linked to economic and social success. A high school degree, and particularly a college education—which requires adequate secondary school training—substantially raised household income and net worth. By 1960 a man with a college education earned about three times more than someone who had dropped out of school in the lower grades.[83] As Americans pursued the promises of the "affluent society," a good education became a ticket, an inferior one a hindrance.

Schooling in particular fell victim to the inequities of excessive localism because throughout America, states traditionally have granted local communities the authority to provide and pay for their own schools through taxing real property within their borders. Although New Jersey's dependence on property taxes has been extreme, even in states with higher levels of state contribution to school funding the rule remained: the wealthier the community, the more it had to spend on its schools. Moreover, abundant tax revenues went further per pupil in exclusive communities where upzoning controlled school enrollment growth. Assuming a relationship between school spending and educational quality—and it would be hard to deny the advantages of more money for teachers' salaries, school facilities, smaller classes, and instructional materials—inadequate school budgets inevitably compromised the future life chances of a municipality's children.[84] With the tremendous population growth experienced in states like New Jersey between the end of World War II and the 1970s, the race to keep up with the demand for more schools, classrooms, and teachers put poorer communities at a distinct disadvantage.[85]

Essex County, New Jersey, provides a clear-cut case of how school spending per pupil, and, subsequently, educational quality, varied according to the socioeconomic profiles of postwar communities. The higher the median income, adult educational and job status, white presence in the population, homeownership rate, and house value, and the lower the population density—all characteristics of wealthy suburbia—the greater a community's per pupil spending on schooling for its children, and most unfairly, the lower the local tax rate its residents were assessed to pay for it. So, for example, among the four communities listed in Table 4, urban Newark, a third non-white in 1960, had the lowest median family income, level of education, representation of white-collar workers, homeownership rate, single-family house value, and amount of wealth per pupil potentially available for property tax assessment, while wealthy and all-white suburban Millburn had the highest rankings in every social category. But when it came to school spending, Newark's per pupil expenditure was only three-quarters as high as Millburn's, despite the fact that its equalized tax rate—based on true market value of property—was two and a third times higher. White, working-class Bloomfield, dense with small owner-occupied houses, spent the next lowest amount per pupil, 13 percent less than Millburn, but paid taxes at a rate that was a third higher, confirming that class as well as racial stratification was alive and well in Essex County in 1960. And Montclair, a racially and class-mixed community with income and educational disparities within its own borders, paid for its suburban-like per pupil spending with high property tax rates akin to a city. Disparities in educational spending within Essex County not only resulted from different property values and tax rates, but also were created by the competing claims on a municipality's tax revenues—many more in a Newark than a Millburn—and the preference of ratables such as shopping centers and industrial parks for the high purchasing power and amenities of a well-off community like Millburn over a working-class town like Bloomfield.

As with housing, individuals and groups savvy and disapproving of the localistic, and inequitable, approach to postwar school funding have brought repeated challenges in New Jersey and around the nation. If exclusionary zoning became one Achilles' heel in the high hopes for a democratic postwar suburbanization initiated by the Consumers' Republic, school finance has proved the other. For years administrators in states like New Jersey attacked the very fragmented structure of school funding and provision, urging consolidation of small districts to save money through eliminating the administrative duplication that long has kept the state's total school spending high despite its maldistribution and low state contribution. But in New Jersey, as in many other places, pleas for consolidation fell on deaf ears. When in 1957 Bergen County considered consolidating some of its fifty-four local school districts into regional ones to cut back on the half a million dollars being spent for each to have its own superintendent, the answer from the grass roots was a

Table 4. WEALTH, SCHOOL SPENDING, AND PROPERTY TAXATION IN SELECTED COMMUNITIES OF ESSEX COUNTY, NEW JERSEY, 1960

Municipality	Median Family Income	Completed 4 Years High School or More; Age 25 and Over	Employed Persons Working in White-Collar Jobs	Population White (vs. Non-White)	Population Density Per Acre	Homes Owner-Occupied/ Median Value of Single-Family House	Per Pupil Expenditure/ Equalized Property Valuation Per Pupil*	Tax Rate Per $100 Valuation: Total/School/ Equalized Property Tax Rate**
Newark	$5,454	27.2%	31%	65.6%	26.2	22.6%/ $13,500	$424.31/ $22,084	$10.25/ $3.39/ $4.94
Bloomfield	$7,557	44.8%	54.5%	98.5%	15.0	58%/ $17,400	$481.43/ $32,862	$8.15/ $3.53/ $2.84
Montclair	$8,423	61%	56.5%	75.9%	10.9	55.7%/ $22,300	$501.71/ $34,851	$8.14/ $3.32/ $3.27
Millburn	$14,145	73.2%	74.7%	99%	2.9	83%/ na	$551.83/ $62,981	$6.73/ $3.02/ $2.13

Essex County	$6,651	49.7%	44.8%	80.2%	11.3	na/ $18,400	$452.89/ $28,707	na
New Jersey	$6,786	40.7%	44.9%	91.3%	9.4	61.3%/ $15,600	$391.37/ $29,292	na

na = not available

* = "Equalized Property Valuation" is a measure of school district wealth. It is the value of taxable property in a district adjusted to reflect 100% of market value, which facilitates comparison between districts with different rates of property assessment. The total Equalized Property Valuation is then divided by the average daily enrollment of resident pupils, 1959–60.

** = "Equalized Property Tax Rate" is also adjusted to reflect an assessment ratio of 100% of market valuation to facilitate comparisons between districts where the percentage of market value at which property is assessed differs.

Sources: U.S. Department of Commerce, Bureau of the Census, *County and City Data Book, 1962; Census of Population: 1960, Vol. 1, Characteristics of the Population, Part 32, New Jersey; General Social and Economic Characteristics, New Jersey; Census of Housing, New Jersey, 1960;* U.S. Census Bureau, "Census of Housing, Ownership Rates," www.census.gov/hhes/www/housing/census/historic/owner/html/; State of New Jersey, *Ninth Annual Report of the Commissioner of Education: Financial Statistics of School Districts School Year 1959–60;* "Tax Rate, Income and Per Capita Real Property for Essex County Municipalities—1960," Ernest Erber Papers, Box B, Folder 6, Newark Public Library; "1960 Population and Housing Density Analysis," Essex County, November 1963, Ernest Erber Papers, Box B, loose papers, Newark Public Library; League of Women Voters of Millburn, *Know Your Township,* 1965, p. 38.

resounding "no." Communities have usually explained their resistance as a defense of local control, but often not far beneath the surface have lurked fears of class and racial mixing, as wealthy, white districts in particular have denounced regionalization. New Jersey today still boasts over 600 school districts, a third of them with fewer than 500 students.[86]

The most serious challenge to this localistic approach to school funding, and the inequality it has fostered, has been waged in state courts, and as with the attack on exclusionary zoning, New Jersey has led the pack both as blatant offender and heroic champion of equity. Much the way housing reformers challenged the right of affluent towns to exclude lower-income residents through zoning policies, so education reformers have challenged the system of funding education through local property taxes—which weds quality of education to local wealth—and have pushed the state to assume greater fiscal responsibility for public schools. Once again, as in housing, New Jersey's activist state supreme court has blazed an historic, if still contested, path of national significance, condemning the educational inequalities inherent in metropolitan localism. Once the United States Supreme Court in the 1970s rejected all federal constitutional challenges to the way education was financed, as it had also done with exclusionary zoning, the action shifted to state courts to determine if current school funding formulas violated rights guaranteed under state constitutions.[87] Although the battle for equity in school finance would in time become a political hot potato in New Jersey and elsewhere, like its twin struggle against exclusionary zoning, the most decisive skirmishes would be fought in courtrooms a step removed from voters, taxpayers, and state legislators. As states continued to suburbanize and exurbanize over the last third of the twentieth century, their courts became the conscience of the nation, reminding Americans of the harmful costs that accompanied the advantages of mass suburbanization.

The thirty-year attack on New Jersey's localistic system of school finance for violating the state's constitutional guarantee of "a thorough and efficient education" to all its children began in February 1970 when Kenneth Robinson, a sixth grader in Jersey City's public schools, sued the State of New Jersey in Hudson County's superior court.[88] The suit, *Robinson* v. *Cahill* (William T. Cahill, governor 1970–74), argued that because educational quality affects social and economic mobility and is a fundamental right of citizens, the state had an obligation to equalize quality across communities, whatever the local financial resources. In 1973 the state supreme court ruled that New Jersey's heavy reliance on local property taxes discriminated against poor districts, and it called for massive tax reform with the goal of raising more state revenues to ensure every child a "thorough and efficient" education through parity in spending. New Jersey's contribution to local school spending had long been notoriously low. In the 1940s it ranged between 3 and 6 percent, when neighboring New York's was a third. By the late 1960s New Jersey was still contributing less than a third of all non-federal school revenues, putting it toward the bottom of the list of states.[89]

But it was one thing for the court to respond to a suit brought by education reformers and mandate a greater state role in overseeing and financing local schools, and quite another to convince mainstream voters and their state legislators to pass the broad-based taxation required to achieve it. Given the deeply rooted antagonism to statewide taxation within New Jersey's political culture, dependence on the property tax continued; and even after the eleventh-hour adoption of a small state income tax in 1976 following the court's shutdown of the state's schools for its failure to enact a new, permanent funding structure, disparity between affluent and poor districts persisted. As it turned out, the Public School Education Act of 1975, passed in response to the *Robinson* v. *Cahill* decision and the new income tax of the following year, made more state revenues available to school districts but failed to reduce disparities between them, as wealthier districts could use the state contribution to boost school spending to new heights, while hard-pressed and tax-conscious municipalities pared local contributions to the bone to finance other municipal services or even to reduce the property tax rate. In concrete terms, this meant that for the struggling city of Paterson the difference in actual dollars between its own per pupil spending and New Jersey and Passaic County averages doubled with the 1975 act.[90] So in 1981 the nonprofit Education Law Center brought a second lawsuit—*Abbott* v. *Burke* (Fred Burke, New Jersey Commissioner of Education 1974–78)—on behalf of Raymond Arthur Abbott, an eleven-year-old from Camden, a community by now 70 percent non-white and devastatingly poor with more than half the population living below the poverty line, and nineteen other children from there and the similarly impoverished cities of East Orange, Irvington, and Jersey City.[91]

This new class-action suit that expanded to encompass 285,000 students in 28 poor school districts charged that the remedies proposed to respond to *Robinson* v. *Cahill* in the Public School Education Act of 1975 failed to fulfill the "thorough and efficient" requirement of the state constitution in New Jersey's most impoverished cities. Low-wealth, property-poor, and high-tax school districts were not receiving enough of the increased dollars in state aid to education to catch up, and spending gaps were actually growing. After a long, contentious process of documenting disparity in school spending and educational programs between New Jersey's cities and suburbs and wrangling over responsibility and remedy, the state supreme court unanimously decided in

Table 5. SCHOOL SPENDING AND PROPERTY TAXATION IN SELECTED
COMMUNITIES OF ESSEX COUNTY, NEW JERSEY, MID-1970S, AFTER PASSAGE OF
PUBLIC SCHOOL EDUCATION ACT OF 1975

Municipality	School Population White (vs. Non-White), 1975–76	Per Pupil Expenditure, 1977	Equalized Property Valuation Per Pupil, 1977*	Equalized Property Tax Rate Per $100 Valuation, 1977**
NEWARK	9.8%	$1,912.05	$24,722	$5.77
BLOOMFIELD	94.2%	$1,844.51	$89,189	$4.43
MONTCLAIR	56.9%	$2,490.96	$84,261	$5.01
MILLBURN	98.5%	$2,593.84	$184,782	$3.38
ESSEX COUNTY	44.7%	$1,998.13	$56,507	$4.74
NEW JERSEY	76.2%	$1,990.74	$78,164	$3.01

* = "Equalized Property Valuation" is a measure of school district wealth. It is the value of taxable property in a district adjusted to reflect 100% of market value, which facilitates comparison between districts with different rates of property assessment. The total Equalized Property Valuation is then divided by the average daily enrollment of resident pupils, 1976–77.
** = "Equalized Property Tax Rate" is also adjusted to reflect an assessment ratio of 100% of market valuation to facilitate comparisons between districts where the percentage of market value at which property is assessed differs.

Sources: State of New Jersey, Department of Education, "New Jersey Public School Racial/Ethnic Enrollments, 1975–76," Newark Public Library; New Jersey Education Reform Project, "Newark School Finance Profile, 1977–1978," Principal Researcher Earl Preston Thomas, March 1978, Newark Public Library, "Q" Files—Greater Newark Urban Coalition.

1990, nine years after the suit was filed, in favor of Raymond Abbott, agreeing that he had indeed been denied a "thorough and efficient education." "Under the present system," the court found, "the poorer the district and the greater the need, the less the money available, and the worse the education." As if to clinch the case for differential educational opportunity, plaintiff Abbott, by now a high school dropout, learned of his victory while serving time in the Camden County Jail for violating parole from a previous burglary conviction. By then, the average disparity between rich and poor districts had grown to $1400 a student, from $248 in 1975 when the New Jersey State Legislature passed the Public School Education Act. At one extreme was Princeton, spending $7725 per pupil, and at the other, Camden, making do on $3538, less than half as much.[92]

But compliance with the court's 1990 order demanding parity in spending between New Jersey's wealthiest and poorest districts continued to provoke persistent, passionate conflict within the state, particularly to the extent that it required taxpayers to pay higher state income taxes or put caps on school spending by better-off suburban districts. Within a month of the *Abbott* ruling, the legislature passed a higher income tax under the Quality Education Act (QEA) intended to raise another $1.1 billion a year for state education aid, and allocated portions of the new revenue directly to thirty troubled "Special-Needs Districts."[93] But shortly thereafter, confronted with voter outrage, the legislature turned around and siphoned off about a third of the new tax revenues for statewide property tax relief and school tax reduction. If taxpayers were supporting schools with income taxes, then property taxes should decline, it was argued. The result of the diversion, however, was that now there were fewer income tax and property tax dollars to spend on schools. In 1993 the ongoing, intense controversy precipitated the defeat of incumbent Democratic governor Jim Florio, who had pushed progressive tax reform and a more redistributive system of school aid through the original QEA, by Republican challenger Christine Todd Whitman, whose campaign pledge to cut the state income tax by 30 percent won her—and the Republicans who swept both houses of the state legislature—the election.[94]

Since then, the Education Law Center has repeatedly returned to the courts waving the banner of spending equity. In 1994 it argued successfully that the QEA was unconstitutional for its failure to assure parity. In 1997 it convinced the state supreme court to strike down an attempt by Governor Whitman to define parity based on curricular standards, a strategy that aimed to deliver "a thorough and efficient education" across municipalities without substantially raising state spending on education.[95] Controversy has continued to rage over whether equity requires capping spending in wealthier districts or simply increasing state assistance to poorer districts to bring them up to an average minimal spending level, based on what the wealthiest towns spend. Within a month of taking office as New Jersey's governor in 2002, Democrat James McGreevey denounced over thirty years of state foot-dragging and announced that he will abide by the supreme court's *Abbott* ruling, spending the money required to reconstruct the thirty special-needs districts. But having also inherited a historically high $6 billion budget shortfall, it remains to be seen if McGreevey's good intentions will lead to better schools. In the meantime, rural and middle-income suburban districts have filed suits arguing that New Jersey's school aid formula discriminates against them, plagued as they are by low commercial and residential property tax bases and less state assistance than urban special-needs districts.[96]

With an electorate dominated by suburban voters and a disparity between districts in educational spending, program, and performance that in truth defies easy remedy, the stalemate persists. So long as New Jersey remains overly dependent on the property tax, the problems of schooling and housing equity continue to be intractable and intertwined. The most vocal critics of approving the Ethel R. Lawrence Homes in Mount Laurel in 1997, according to the chairman of the local planning board, based their objections to low-income housing on the calculation that "140 units, figure two children per unit, and do the arithmetic and come up with about $2 million a year in extra education costs." If those children remained in Camden or some other municipality, the thinking went, their education would be someone else's responsibility.[97] As with the court battle over equitable housing, New Jersey's landmark school finance cases have admirably sought to break the iron grip of excessive localism, but it remains a powerful shaper of mass suburbia.[98]

Much like *Mount Laurel, Robinson* v. *Cahill* and *Abbott* v. *Burke* have had analogs in other states, New Jersey simply providing an early and intense challenge to the constitutionality of inequitably funding public schools through the property tax.[99] In almost all fifty states, struggles have raged over how schools should be financed. But whether particular school finance suits have won in the courts or not, as a result of greater consciousness about inequitable funding and mounting political pressure to remedy it, almost everywhere in the nation the proportion of school funding provided by the states rather than localities has gradually increased. While nationally in 1970 state portions totaled 41 percent, by 2000 they came to 50 percent, although recalcitrant New Jersey was still contributing only 40 percent of the cost of public education, while its average property tax bill of $4000 remained the highest in the nation, making equalization of spending and program quality that much harder to achieve.

Moreover, according to the Harvard Project on School Desegregation (now the Civil Rights Project), New Jersey's schools consistently ranked as the fourth most segregated in the nation, and more recently the sixth (as other states have become more segregated), ensuring that inequality between school districts with different economic bases has meant deep disparity of opportunity between the races. Where New Jersey has been for a while, the rest of the nation has now arrived. Over the last decade, school resegregation dividing white from black and Latino students has intensified everywhere, thanks to court decisions freeing urban school districts from desegregation orders and the ongoing residential segregation of America's suburbs.[100] Throughout the nation, the traditional "common school," the cornerstone of American democracy in its inclusiveness, has regrettably splintered into many different

Table 6. STATUS OF CONSTITUTIONALITY OF STATE SCHOOL FINANCE SYSTEMS AND THEIR REFORM, 2001

States Where Property Tax–Based School Finance System Ruled Unconstitutional	States Where School Finance System Has Been Challenged and Upheld, Though in Some Cases, Reform Was Introduced	States That Have Undergone Some School Finance Reform Without Major Court Cases	States with No Known Action
Alabama	Colorado	Florida	Alaska
Arizona	Georgia	Illinois	Delaware
Arkansas	Idaho	Indiana	Hawaii
California	Louisiana	Iowa	Indiana
Connecticut	Maryland	Kansas	Nevada
Kentucky	Michigan	Maine	
Massachusetts	Minnesota	New Mexico	
Montana	Missouri	Utah	
New Hampshire	North Carolina		
New Jersey	North Dakota		
New York	Oklahoma		
Ohio	Oregon		
Rhode Island	Pennsylvania		
Tennessee	South Carolina		
Texas	South Dakota		
Vermont	Virginia		
Washington	Wisconsin		
West Virginia			
Wisconsin			
Wyoming			

Sources: "The Courts and Equity: A State-by-State Overview," *Funding for Justice: Money, Equity, and the Future of Public Education* (Milwaukee: Rethinking Schools, 1997), pp. 61–67; "The National Context: Rulings on Other School Systems," *New York Times*, July 13, 1994; "Pulse: School Financing," *New York Times*, Nov. 27, 1995; "Ohio Funding Struck Down," *Rethinking Schools*, Summer 1997; "N.H. Court Overturns Funding of Schools," *Boston Globe*, Dec. 18, 1997; "In the 'Live Free or Die' State, An Unpalatable Tax Decision," *New York Times*, June 29, 1998; Richard Briffault, "Our Localism: Part I—The Structure of Local Government Law," *Columbia Law Review* 90 (January 1990): 24–39; "With Ruling, New York Joins States Revamping School Financing," *New York Times*, Jan. 13, 2001.

schoolhouses where "common" refers more to the family incomes and racial identities of students than to a shared experience crosscutting social divides.[101]

The delivery of other kinds of services in New Jersey besides school spending has likewise suffered from the state's inequitable tax structure. In the area of categorical assistance—such as Aid to Families with Dependent Children and Old Age Assistance—New Jersey has required its counties to carry more than a quarter of the cost, greater than in any other state, thereby penalizing communities and taxpayers in counties with heavy caseloads. Not surprisingly, in 1965, the mayor of upper-middle-class Livingston urged his town to secede from Essex County and join less burdened Morris County.[102] In the case of general assistance welfare programs, New Jersey's municipalities have borne 40 to 60 percent of the cost. As with schooling, wealthier suburbs, with more resources to spend and generally lighter demand for services, have paid at a lower rate than needier, poorer places. In white, working- and lower-middle-class Clifton, for example, inhabitants each paid only 6 cents through their property taxes in 1965 toward general assistance benefits, while in Newark the cost was $14.84 per inhabitant and the tax rate was three and a half times higher.[103] Whether a matter of educating their children or supporting elderly or impoverished fellow citizens, New Jersey taxpayers have borne the costs of delivering essential services in a way that has widened rather than narrowed the gulf between the haves and have-nots, the opposite outcome from what many social programs were designed to achieve.

The educational inequality created by the local funding of public schooling has particularly disadvantaged African Americans in New Jersey, and then compounded the problem by leaving them with few ways of fighting against it. Segregated schools had long existed within the state's cities and towns, but thanks to the added confidence gained with World War II and the civil rights movement of the 1940s and 1950s, black parents began to challenge the racial gerrymandering in their communities that assigned their children to "Negro schools" with inferior facilities and resources. First in Trenton (1944) and Asbury Park (1946) and later in Englewood (1955 and again in 1963), Newark (1961), Montclair (1961), Orange (1962–63), Teaneck (1963), and elsewhere, celebrated protests—marches, rallies, picketing, sit-ins, boycotts, and lawsuits—drew attention to discrimination and in some cases even redressed it.[104] But when mass suburbanization encouraged the dispersal of metropolitan residents out of multi-racial towns and cities and the fragmentation of metropolitan government, what had already been a difficult enough task of battling local school boards, municipal governments, and fellow citizens to create integrated, equitable schools became an impossible one, as whole cities and towns, and all schools within their borders, became increasingly all-white or all-black. When the United States Supreme Court justices ruled in the landmark *Brown* v. *Board of Education* decision of 1954 that segregated schools were inherently unequal, they expected that greater social equality would come to America from children attending the same schools. Now, a half century later, the failure to integrate, in fact the tendency to resegregate, bodes poorly for our progress toward a more racially just society. *Brown* v. *Board of Education,* the cornerstone of postwar America's effort to overcome a century of racial inequality following slavery, became increasingly meaningless as growing residential segregation kept whites and minorities apart and persistent localism, fortified by a stratified real estate market and substantial municipal property taxes, made remedying inequality extremely difficult.

LIVING IN "SPREAD-CITY"

W hen young white families packed up their belongings and hit the roads leading out to suburbs in the late 1940s and 1950s, their expectations did not differ very much from those of *Redbook*'s marketing department, producers of the film *In the Suburbs.* The "happy-go-spending" world of mass suburbia was a new frontier beckoning them, promising the same opportunity and prosperity that earlier American frontiers had offered their settlers, this time through the miracle of mass consumption. Their own plot of land, with a single-family house bought on the private real estate market and stocked with all the material goods that they could afford, provided a foundation for both their own rise and, through the collective power of a democratic mass market, the nation's recovery after World War II. What an exciting revival of the American dream this was, after a decade and a half of frightening depression and paralyzing war. But before too long, it would become clear that this dream belonged to some people more than others, as class and racial stratification and a localistic embrace of exclusionary zoning and inequitable school finance fed economic and social inequality in postwar metropolitan areas, threatening the egalitarianism hoped for. Although by 1965 suburbs would replace cities as home to a majority of Americans, they attracted the most prosperous ones: nationally, 60 percent of metropolitan families with incomes under $3000 remained in core cities, while 55 percent of those whose incomes surpassed $10,000 lived in the suburbs.[105] And within suburbia, people with different income levels were sorted into particular communities by home prices, house types, zoning laws, and the like.

Economic discrimination, moreover, was not the only, nor the most obstructive, barrier; race was. White working-class people may not have been able to afford the most exclusive suburbs, but they found welcoming communities nonetheless. In contrast, even for African Americans with financial means, like Gretchen Sullivan Sorin's family, pursuing the suburban dream was fraught with obstacles. Although the Sullivans owned a substantial Victorian house in Newark, deteriorating services (particularly schools her parents feared would fail to provide their children with "the route to success and acceptance") persuaded her teacher mother and engineer father, like other upwardly mobile middle-class Americans, to seek a home in the suburbs in 1965. With their hearts set on a single-story, modern ranch house, the Sullivans found just the one in affluent, predominantly white Westfield, known for its excellent schools. But right before the deal was sealed, the owner contritely revealed that "the neighbors think you will drive property values down . . . and don't want us to sell it to you." Crestfallen, the Sullivans found another house in Colonia, in a kind of nowhere's land on the boundary with Edison that seemed more rural than suburban. With more than an acre of land surrounding the house, neighbors were at arm's length, although a few other families nearby were also black. Here the Sullivans got their new ranch house, with all the standard markings of affluence: an expansive front lawn, an exterior faced with pink and gray rough-cut stone, a formal dining room and breakfast nook, a finished basement, a back patio, and a two-car garage. Although Gretchen made a success of herself in school, it was never easy. Out of the 1700 students at Colonia Senior High, only about fifty were African American. Nearby towns like Rahway with larger black populations provided the Sullivan family with a welcoming church and Gretchen with boys to date.[106] The determined Sullivans did find a way to break through the exclusionary walls of suburbia, but their story only highlights the enormous obstacles confronting blacks who tried to do so.

Although a case like the Sullivans' is specific to New Jersey, it represents a national phenomenon. New Jersey, with its extreme manifestations of the gains and losses in postwar suburbanization and its activist state supreme court that for three decades did not shy away from adjudicating the consequences of increasing socioeconomic segmentation, was at the tip of a very large iceberg. As should be evident by now, most other states have similarly encountered and struggled with the inequalities promoted by the rise of mass suburbia.

A postwar suburbanization built upon private real estate markets and sustained through local taxation, rather than through greater state oversight and funding for housing and schooling as the courts would eventually demand, further reinforced the inequality of economic well-being fostered by other infrastructures of the Consumers' Republic, such as the GI Bill and amendments to the mass income tax. Despite an early confidence in the universal benefits of selling to the "mass," symbolized by the enormous market in single-family suburban homes, before very long a postwar economy built on mass consumption divided consumers into distinctive market—and social—sectors. Soon, advertisers and marketers would reinforce these divisions as they, too, forsook the mass market for the greater profits to be made segmenting it into distinctive submarkets built around differences of gender, class, race, age, and lifestyle. Still today, housing remains a foundation of the American economy, with home construction accounting for 5 percent of the nation's economic activity, 10 percent with furnishings and appliances, and home ownership constituting the largest portion of Americans' portfolios.[107]

But while purchasers as citizens—the rank and file of the Consumers' Republic—may have pursued their individual economic interests in the housing marketplace under the assumption that they thereby were serving the general good as well, that pursuit did not benefit the larger public nearly as much as originally expected. Rather, the power of property values dictated new kinds of risks and loyalties, in particular discouraging suburban homeowners from undertaking more class and racial integration of their communities. When Robert Wood investigated American suburbs in 1959, he exposed the logic operating in a world where "the drive for . . . high-value property" determines all: "to be liberal in their attitude toward lower-income newcomers, to strive for heterogeneous neighborhoods, to welcome citizens regardless of race, creed, or color . . . is to invite financial disaster."[108] Hence, the landscape of mass consumption evolved into a disaggregated metropolis where community identity and benefits marked people as different and deserving of unequal privileges rather than fostering a common stake in a metropolitan region, a state, and, at times, even a nation.

This tendency toward hierarchy and exclusion, represented most powerfully through upzoning, ironically has even kept suburbia from fulfilling the fullest economic growth possible, as more housing could have been constructed there, given the demand. During the 1960s the National Association of Home Builders, their state affiliates, and individual builders nationwide recognized that large-lot zoning and other restrictive and exclusionary tactics seriously threatened the vitality of the construction industry, and hence their own livelihoods, and took strong stands against them. Capped populations and home building, intended by suburban residents to keep down the cost of services and taxes, won out over new house construction, creating tremendous shortages as well as high resale prices.[109] Not surprisingly, advocates of Mount Laurel–type reform of suburban zoning found allies among builders. Although today a low-growth suburban policy is often applauded as environmentally smart, the democratic promises of the Consumers' Republic were premised on the social benefits of unbounded mass consumption. Respecting both people's needs for housing and the future health of the environment requires honest and open balancing of one against the other, not the strategic use of one to hinder the other.[110]

That Americans embraced localism to the extent they did during the postwar era may seem surprising. Most studies of the nation after World War II focus on the federal government, putting it, even as its popularity ebbed and flowed, at the center of the postwar story. This examination of the political culture of postwar suburbanization reveals another realm of governmental authority that mattered greatly to Americans. As suburbanites determined that their basic security increasingly rested on protecting their major financial investment—a home—and that decisive control often had to be exerted at the local level, municipal government became a high-stakes game in the late-twentieth-century suburb as much as in nineteenth-century America and in twentieth-century cities, where its importance was indisputable. This continued investment in the locality and suspicion of political authority outside it would prove to have significant consequences for people's more general attitudes toward government as the postwar era progressed.

Interestingly, in a social democratic country like Sweden, in contrast to the United States, policymakers more ideologically committed to egalitarianism and social mixing recognized the threat raised by a suburbanization rooted in private home ownership. As a result, the Swedes insisted on meeting their equally dire postwar housing shortage with an urban policy that radically restricted the growth of single-family, privately owned homes on the outskirts of cities like Stockholm. Instead, they supported multi-unit housing in already built-up areas fully served by mass transportation. As one Social Democratic Party leader perspicaciously put it, "Suburbs of private houses mean social segregation." Elaborated another, voicing a perspective that would not have sat very well with Americans, "We cannot allow people to preserve their differences. People will have to give up the right to choose their own neighbors." As late as the mid-1970s, consequently, homeowners made up only 30 percent of the Swedish population. It should be noted that as Sweden has become less committed to social democracy in recent years, the American model of segmented suburbanization has been gaining ground, with wealthy Swedes pursuing suburban single-family homes and automobile commutes, and less affluent Swedes abandoning state-owned urban housing to new immigrant populations with even fewer options.[111]

Residential suburbanization contributed to the emergence of a social landscape in the postwar period where the mass of Americans shared less and less common physical space and public culture. Although cities are often thought of as atomized spaces, and suburbs as a reembrace of community, the places where that happened in suburbia—such as kitchen coffee klatches and cul-de-sacs—were more private, or at least insulated, than public parks or city streets. Moreover, if in moving to the suburbs, residents participated in more homogeneous, stratified communities, the contact they did have with neighbors connected them to less diverse publics. Over time, the lure of the nearby more eclectic city itself receded. By 1978 a *New York Times* survey of suburban New Yorkers already found that 54 percent did not feel they belonged to the New York metropolitan area at all and 76 percent thought that events occurring in the city did not affect them. With only 21 percent of the household heads queried working in New York City, more than half of the surveyed visited the city less than five times a year, and a quarter never went.[112]

As low-density suburbia gained ground, by the early 1960s planners dubbed it "spread-city" for the great distances now required to support schools, stores, theaters, doctors, newspapers, and the like, and despaired that "life in the spread-city is privatized." Typical was the observation: "Large lots encourage private outdoor activities as opposed to use of public recreational areas: the backyard cook-out rather than a picnic, gardening instead of hiking." Growing distance from urban entertainment centers "makes television more attractive relative to movies or theatre or concerts. Radio or television replaces the public meeting."[113] When Jane Davison, who came from two generations of suburbanites in well-off Summit, New Jersey, near Millburn, and raised her own family in a single-family house in suburban Massachusetts during the 1960s, reversed her grandmother's journey and moved into an apartment complex in the city of Boston, she insightfully reflected that because she had been "designed for a suburb," living in a city required learning about "collective consumption, about enjoying public space as if it were my own."[114]

Although planners in the sixties paid it less heed, Davison would have understood as well that privatized suburbs sustained the postwar domestication of women, as their time and labor were required to protect these residential havens, not least of all to physically navigate their families through "spread-city." And yet, as a marketing study of female consumers recognized in 1958, when it argued that "the car is almost a second home for women," reality was not so simple. It also acknowledged that "the automobile is in greatest part responsible for today's women's mobility," a mobility that gave women "broader views and contacts" and made them "generally better informed."[115] As new public spaces emerged in suburbia, the most significant of which was the regional shopping center, it is important to consider how they fit into the stratifying, privatizing world that was evolving, and that women presumably were helping to sustain. When marketplaces moved from urban downtowns to suburban shopping centers, did the power of the mass market break through the exclusionary barriers crisscrossing suburban America or reinforce them? And how did African Americans fare, who, despite judicial victories against restrictive covenants in *Shelley* v. *Kraemer* and segregated schools in *Brown* v. *Board of Education,* and despite growing legal protections on the state and federal levels through civil rights legislation, had been effectively barred from many suburbs? The regional shopping centers of northern New Jersey can provide some answers.

CHAPTER 6

Commerce: Reconfiguring Community Marketplaces

By the 1950s the shopping center . . . had become as much a part of suburbia as the rows of ranch houses, split-levels, and Cape Cods," political scientist Robert Wood stated matter-of-factly in his *Suburbia: Its People and Their Politics* of 1959. And indeed, attention within the Consumers' Republic to promoting consumer spending reshaped much more than the character of residential communities in the postwar metropolitan landscape. The physical arrangement of American commercial life became reconfigured as well. As existing suburban town centers proved inadequate to support all the consumption desired by the influx of new residents, as suburbanites more and more attached to their cars increasingly viewed returning to urban downtowns to shop as inconvenient, and as retailers came to realize that suburban residents, with their young families, new homes, and vast consumer appetites, offered a lucrative frontier ripe for conquer, the regional shopping center emerged as a new form of community marketplace. Wood underscored the tremendous increase in suburban share of total metropolitan retail trade from 4 percent in 1939 to 31 percent by 1948; by 1961 it would total almost 60 percent in the ten largest population centers. But as significant as the volume of commerce transacted in suburbia was the setting where that consumption took place.[1]

The development of a new, distinctive kind of metropolitan marketplace suited to mass suburbia lagged behind the construction of residences. New suburbanites who had themselves grown up in urban neighborhoods walking to corner stores and taking public transportation to shop downtown had to contend with inadequate retail options until at least the mid-1950s. Only in the most ambitious suburban tracts built after the war had developers incorporated stores into their plans. In those cases, developers tended to place the shopping district at the core of the residential community, much as it had been in the prewar planned community of Radburn in Fair Lawn, New Jersey, and in the earliest shopping centers such as Kansas City's Country Club Plaza of the 1920s. These precedents, and their descendants in early postwar developments in Park Forest, Illinois, Levittown, New York, and Bergenfield, New Jersey, replicated the structure of the old-style urban community, where shopping was part of the public space at the settlement's core and residences spread outward from there.[2] But most postwar suburban home developers made no effort to provide for residents' commercial needs. Rather, suburbanites were expected to fend for themselves by driving to the existing "market towns," which often offered the only commerce for miles, or by returning to the city to shop. Faced with slim retail offerings nearby, many new suburbanites of the 1940s and 1950s continued to depend on the big city for major purchases, making do with the small, locally owned commercial outlets in neighboring towns for minor needs.

It was not until the late 1950s that a new market structure appropriate to this suburbanized, mass consumption society prevailed. Important precedents existed in the branch department stores and prototypical shopping centers constructed between the 1920s and 1940s in outlying city neighborhoods and in older suburban communities, which began the process of decentralizing retail dollars away from downtown. But the scale required now was much larger. By 1957, 940 shopping centers had already been built. That number more than doubled by 1960, and doubled again by 1963; by 1976 the 17,520 shopping centers in the nation would represent an almost nineteenfold increase over twenty years.[3] With postwar suburbanites finally living the motorized existence that had been predicted for American society since the 1920s, traffic congestion and parking problems discouraged commercial developers from expanding in central business districts of major cities and smaller market towns, already hindered by a short supply of developable space.[4] Rather, retailers preferred catering to suburbanites on the open land where they now lived and drove, deeming it a unique opportunity to reinvent community life with their private projects at its heart.[5]

Merchandisers at first built stores along the new highways, in retail "strips" that dispersed consumers could easily reach by car. By the 1950s, however, commercial developers—many of whom owned department stores—devoted themselves to constructing a new kind of marketplace, the regional shopping center, aimed at satisfying suburbanites' consumption *and* community needs, which had similarly been paired in the old town centers. Strategically located at highway intersections or along the busiest thoroughfares, the regional shopping center aimed at attracting patrons living within half an hour's drive who would come by car, park in the abundant lots provided, and then proceed on foot (although there was usually some bus service as well). Here was the "new city" of the postwar era, a community center suited to an economy and society built around mass consumption. Well-designed regional shopping centers, it was thought, would provide the ideal core for settlements that grew by adding residential nodes off major roadways rather than concentric rings from downtown, as in cities and earlier suburban communities. After spending several months in the late 1950s visiting what he called "modern-day downtowns," Women's Wear Daily columnist Samuel Feinberg was moved to invoke Lincoln Steffens's proclamation on his return from the Soviet Union in the 1920s: "I have seen the future and it works."[6]

Although the shift in community marketplace from town center to shopping center was a national phenomenon, Paramus, New Jersey, a postwar suburb seven miles from the George Washington Bridge that became the home of the largest shopping complex in the country by the end of 1957, provides an illuminating case.[7] Within six months, R. H. Macy's Garden State Plaza and Allied Stores Corporation's Bergen Mall opened three-quarters of a mile from each other at the intersection of Routes 4, 17, and the soon-to-be-completed Garden State Parkway. Both department store managements had independently recognized the enormous commercial potential of Bergen and Passaic Counties. Although the George Washington Bridge had connected the area to Manhattan in 1931, the Great Depression and the war had postponed major housing construction until the late 1940s. By 1960 each shopping center had two to three department stores as anchors (distinguishing it from many prewar projects built around a single anchor), surrounded by fifty to seventy smaller stores. Attracting half a million patrons a week, these shopping centers dominated retail trade in the region.[8]

The Paramus malls have special significance because of their location adjacent to the wealthiest and busiest central business district in the nation. If these malls could prosper in the shadow of Manhattan, the success of their counterparts elsewhere should come as no surprise. Furthermore, the Paramus case illuminates three major effects of shifting marketplaces on postwar American community life: in commercializing public space, they brought to community life the market segmentation that increasingly shaped commerce and residence; in privatizing public space, they privileged the rights of private property owners over citizens' traditional rights of free speech in community forums; and in feminizing public space, they enhanced women's claim on the suburban landscape while circumscribing the power they wielded there.

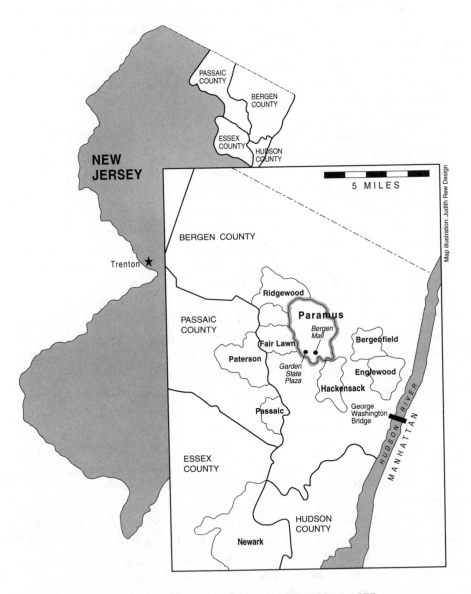

PASSAIC
COUNTY

BERGEN
COUNTY

ESSEX
COUNTY

HUDSON
COUNTY

NEW
JERSEY

Trenton ★

5 MILES

Map Illustration: Judith Rew Design

BERGEN COUNTY

PASSAIC
COUNTY

Ridgewood

Paramus

*Bergen
Mall*

Fair Lawn

Bergenfield

Paterson

*Garden
State
Plaza*

Englewood

Hackensack

Passaic

George
Washington
Bridge

ESSEX
COUNTY

HUDSON
COUNTY

Newark

HUDSON RIVER

MANHATTAN

LOCATION OF SHOPPING CENTERS IN PARAMUS, NEW JERSEY, 1957

COMMERCIALIZING PUBLIC SPACE

Developers, department stores, and big investors such as insurance companies (who leapt at the promise of a huge return on the vast amounts of capital they controlled) built shopping centers to profit from what seemed to be ever rising levels of consumption. As Macy's board chairman, Jack Isidor Straus, who oversaw the development of the Garden State Plaza, confidently explained in 1965, "Our economy keeps growing because our ability to consume is endless. The consumer goes on spending regardless of how many possessions he has. The luxuries of today are the necessities of tomorrow."[9] Why not, then, situate new stores as accessible as possible to the most dynamic sources of demand fueling the thriving economy of postwar America—the new, high-consuming suburbanites? Already a decade earlier, an article in the *New York Times Magazine* marking the growing interest in building shopping centers had concluded, "There is a widely held belief that American households are ready to do more buying than they presently do. . . . They would do it more readily but for the difficulty of getting to the 'downtowns' where the full range of goods is available." The solution proposed: "Bringing the market to the people instead of people to the market."[10]

Focusing on the obvious economic motives developers and investors shared in constructing shopping centers, however, can mask the visionary dimension of their undertaking, which led them to innovate a new retail form. When planners and shopping center developers envisioned this new kind of consumption-oriented community center in the 1950s, they set out to perfect the concept of downtown, not to obliterate it, even though their projects directly challenged the viability of existing commercial centers like Hackensack, the political and commercial seat of Bergen County adjacent to Paramus.[11] They felt that they were participating in a rationalization of consumption and community no less revolutionary than the way highways were transforming transportation or tract developments were delivering mass single-family housing. "Shopping Centers properly planned by developers and local communities are the rational alternative to haphazard retail development," the International Council of Shopping Centers explained.[12]

The ideal was still the creation of centrally located public space that integrated commerce with civic activity. Victor Gruen, one of the most prominent and articulate shopping center developers, spoke for many others when he argued that shopping centers offered dispersed suburban populations "crystallization points for suburbia's community life." "By affording opportu-

Postwar shopping centers like the Garden State Plaza presented themselves as an improvement over the typical downtown, with their landscaped, open-air walkways; centralized and efficient administrations; ideal mix of stores; private security forces; and ample parking. (Courtesy of Garden State Plaza Historical Collection)

nities for social life and recreation in a protected pedestrian environment, by incorporating civic and educational facilities, shopping centers can fill an existing void."[13] Not only did Gruen and others promote the private construction of community centers in the atomized landscape of suburbia, but their earliest shopping centers idealized—almost romanticized—the physical plan of the traditional downtown shopping street, with stores lining both sides of an open-air pedestrian walkway that was landscaped and equipped with benches. Regional shopping centers would create old-style community with new-style unity and efficiency; statements like "the shopping center is . . . today's village green" and "the fountain in the mall has replaced the downtown department clock as the gathering place for young and old alike," dominated planning for new centers.[14]

Designed to bring many of the best qualities of urban life to the suburbs, these new "shopping towns," as Gruen called them, sought to overcome the "anarchy and ugliness" characteristic of many American cities. A centrally owned and managed Garden State Plaza or Bergen Mall, it was argued, offered an alternative model to the inefficiencies, visual chaos, and provinciality of traditional downtown districts. A centralized administration made possible the perfect mix and "scientific" placement of stores, meeting customers' diverse needs and maximizing store owners' profits. Management kept control visually by standardizing all architectural and graphic design and politically by requiring all tenants to participate in the tenants' association. Common complaints of downtown shoppers were directly addressed: parking was plentiful, safety was ensured by hired security guards, delivery tunnels and loading courts kept truck traffic away from shoppers, canopied walks and air-conditioned stores made shopping comfortable year-round, piped-in background music replaced the cacophony of the street. The preponderance of chains and franchises over local, independent stores, required by big investors such as insurance companies, brought shoppers the latest national trends in products and merchandising techniques.

Garden State Plaza and Bergen Mall provide good models for how shopping centers of the fifties followed Gruen's prescription and became more than miscellaneous collections of stores. B. Earl Puckett, Allied Stores' board chair, went so far as to boast that Paramus's model shopping centers were making it "one of the first preplanned major cities in America," an urban innovation that also maximized profits.[15] As central sites of consumption, they offered the full range of shops and services that would previously have existed downtown. They not only sold the usual clothing and shoes in their specialty and department stores—Stern Brothers and J. J. Newberry at Bergen Mall, Bamberger's (Macy's New Jersey division), JCPenney's, and Gimbel's at Garden State Plaza—but also featured stores specifically devoted to furniture, hardware, appliances, groceries, gifts, drugs, books, toys, records, bakery goods, candy, jewelry, garden supplies, hearing aids, tires, and even religious objects. Services grew to include restaurants, a post office, Laundromat, cleaners, key store, shoe repair, bank, loan company, stock brokerage houses, barbershop, travel agency, real estate office, "slenderizing salon," and Catholic chapel. Recreational facilities ranged from a 550-seat movie theater, bowling alley, and ice-skating rink to a children's gymnasium and playground.

Both shopping centers made meeting rooms and auditoriums available to community organizations and scheduled a full range of cultural and educa-

Local residents brought their own lawn chairs to the "Music on the Mall" summer concerts at the Bergen Mall in 1960, one of the many activities that the shopping center sponsored to establish itself as the hub of community life. (Courtesy of the Newark Public Library)

tional activities to legitimize these sites as civic centers, while also attracting customers. Well-attended programs and exhibitions taught shoppers about such "hot" topics of the fifties and sixties as space exploration, color television, modern art, and civics. Evening concerts and plays, ethnic entertainment, dances and classes for teenagers, campaign appearances by political candidates, and community outreach for local charities were some of the ways that Bergen Mall and Garden State Plaza made themselves indispensable to life in Bergen County.

In sum, it was hard to think of consumer items or community events that could not be found at one or the other of these two shopping centers in Bergen County. (In the 1970s a cynical reporter cracked that "the only institution that had not yet invaded" the modern shopping mall was the funeral home.) To a regional planner like New Jersey's Ernest Erber, these postwar shopping centers represented a new kind of urbanism appropriate to the automobile age: the "City of Bergen," he dubbed the area in 1960. Seven years later the New Jersey Federation of Planning Officials was still encouraging its members and their communities to use "appropriate zoning and site development controls to encourage this desirable trend" of making centers "real downtowns for the surrounding area." In time, the *New York Times* would proclaim Paramus's commercial complex the real thing: "It lives a night as well as a day existence, glittering like a city when the sun goes down." In fact, shopping centers prided themselves on their greater "night existence" than most downtowns, as their stores and services were open to patrons from 10 a.m. to 9:30 p.m., at first four nights a week, and by the 1960s six nights.[16]

Making the shopping center a perfection of downtown entailed more than building idealized pedestrian streets, showcasing a full range of goods and services, and staying open long hours. Developers and store owners also set out to exclude from this new public space unwanted urban elements, such as vagrants, prostitutes, disruptive rebels, racial minorities, and poor people. Market segmentation became the guiding principle of this mix of commercial and civic activity, as the shopping center sought, perhaps contradictorily, to legitimize itself as a true community center and to define that community in exclusionary socioeconomic and racial terms.

The simple demographics of postwar America helped, as metropolitan areas were becoming polarized between poorer, blacker cities and more prosperous, whiter suburbs.[17] But shopping centers did not inadvertently exclude simply by virtue of their suburban location. Rather, developers deliberately defined their communities through a combination of careful site selection, marketing, and policing. Locating a center in a prosperous area was the first priority. As the chairman of the board of Bamberger's New Jersey put it bluntly in 1964, "There are many kinds of people, and we must, therefore, consider the qualitative as well as the quantitative composition of the population." Once established in an affluent community, moreover, centers needed to be respectful of their neighbors. "A shopping center which fails to consider its relationship to residential areas," the shopping center developer Victor Gruen warned, "will soon be surrounded by blighted and slum neighborhoods and will find itself with a greatly reduced business potential."[18]

Once well situated, most branch department stores and new shopping centers worked to secure a white middle-class clientele. Macy's reminded its stockholders in 1955 as it was building its first shopping center, Garden State Plaza, "We are a type of organization that caters primarily to middle-income groups, and our stores reflect this in the merchandise they carry and in their physical surroundings."[19] By the late 1950s retailers were getting expert advice from publications such as the *Journal of Marketing* to ensure that the "tone and physical character of the[ir] advertising permit the shopper to make social-class identification." As suburbs were "quickly becom[ing] stratified along social-class and mobility dimensions," this article elaborated, it was imperative that stores "acquire a status definition." Almost all suburban shopping centers built in this early period sought to appeal to what Macy's called the "middle-income groups," who, it was widely assumed, would also be white.[20] Baltimore's Planning Council exposed the racial overtones to commercial reconfiguration under way in this era more explicitly than merchants ever would: "Greater numbers of low-income, Negro shoppers in Central Business District stores, coming at the same time as middle and upper income white shoppers are given alternatives in . . . segregated suburban centers, has had unfortunate implications for Central Business District merchants."[21]

When shopping centers located in prosperous communities, moreover, their presence only augmented that prosperity, exacerbating the inequalities that already characterized suburbia. As one bank assured its investors, property values in residential communities are "enhanced by the presence of a regional shopping center," while location at a distance from stores lessened a town's desirability. Nor did the benefit end there. The bank's monthly newsletter continued, "Regional shopping districts are surplus areas yielding far more in taxes than they cost in municipal services." Imposing "no costs for schools, parks or recreation areas and a minimum of cost per dollars of assessed value for street maintenance, police or fire protection . . . at least three-fourths of the taxes received are a net surplus to the city or taxing district." And, indeed, Paramus boasted in 1960, three years after Bergen Mall and Garden State Plaza had opened, that "business pays taxes accounting for 43 percent of the town's total revenue."[22] In other words, a town well enough off to attract a shopping center was rewarded with higher property values and a big boost to its property tax and sales tax revenues, resulting in improved local services and potentially lower tax rates for residents.

Carefully controlled access to suburban shopping centers further supported the class and color line. The operating assumption in planning centers was always that patrons would travel by car. The debate among developers, played out in retailer trade journals and planning conferences, revolved instead around how long that drive could feasibly be; articles like "The Influence of Driving Time Upon Shopping Center Preference" were legion.[23] But not everyone living in metropolitan areas had cars. A survey of consumer expenditures in northern New Jersey in 1960–61 revealed that while 79 percent of all families owned cars, fewer than one-third of those with incomes below $3000 did, and that low-income population included a higher percentage of non-white families than the average for the whole sample.[24] Although bus service was available for non-drivers, only a tiny proportion arrived that way (in 1966 a daily average of only 600 people came to Garden State Plaza by bus compared to 18,000 to 31,000 cars, many carrying more than one passenger). The small number traveling by bus was not surprising, as bus routes were carefully planned to serve non-driving customers, particularly women, from neighboring suburbs, not low-income consumers from cities like Passaic, Paterson, and Newark. Meanwhile, studies of African-American mobility as late as the 1970s documented their great dependence on public transportation to get to work or to stores.[25]

Whereas individual downtown department stores had long targeted particular markets defined by class and race, some selling, for example, to "the carriage trade" at the upper end and others to the bargain hunters at the lower, shopping centers took market segmentation to the scale of a downtown, much the way suburbs converted distinctive urban neighborhoods into homogeneous municipalities. In promoting an idealized downtown, shopping centers like Garden State Plaza and Bergen Mall tried to filter out not only the inefficiencies and inconveniences of the city but also the undesirable people who lived there.

If developers and retailers envisioned the regional shopping center as the new American city of postwar suburbia, what actually happened? How successful were shopping centers in attracting the patrons they sought and displacing existing urban centers? The behavior of consumers, on the one hand, and retail businessmen, on the other, reveals the impact of Bergen Mall and Garden State Plaza on the commercial and community life of Bergen County.

Consumer surveys of the late 1950s and early 1960s, carried out by sociologists and market researchers interested in evaluating the changes wrought by the new regional shopping centers, provide a remarkably good picture of consumer behavior in the era. Before Bergen Mall and Garden State Plaza opened in 1957, Bergen County shoppers satisfied their immediate needs on the Main Streets of Hackensack and of smaller surrounding towns like Ridgewood, Fair Lawn, Bergenfield, and Englewood. For more extensive shopping, people went to branches of Sears and Arnold Constable in Hackensack; Meyer Brothers and Quackenbush's department stores in Paterson; Bamberger's, Hahne's, and Kresge's in Newark, and quite often to the big stores in Manhattan. Even before the regional shopping centers opened, the huge influx of new suburban dwellers had raised retail sales in Bergen County from $400 million in 1948 to $700 million in 1954, an increase of 75 percent. By 1958 sales had increased another 23 percent to $866 million. Nonetheless, Bergen County residents in 1954 were still spending $650 million outside the county, almost as much as inside.[26]

Samuel and Lois Pratt, professors at Fairleigh Dickinson University, surveyed Bergen County consumers living within a ten-minute drive of the two new shopping centers in 1957, 1958, and 1959 to follow changes in their shopping habits over time. Prior to the opening of the shopping centers, seven in ten of the suburban families surveyed shopped in New York City to some extent. One year after the centers opened, the numbers shopping in New York dropped to six in ten, and two years after, fewer than five in ten families shopped there at all. In other words, one-fourth of the entire sample formerly had shopped in New York City but had now entirely stopped. The loss was even more substantial than that; the 15 percent of suburban families who formerly did most of their shopping in New York City—people the Pratts labeled "major shoppers"—showed the sharpest decline, 50 percent by 1958, 80 percent by 1959. Moreover, those who continued to shop in New York City were spending much less money there; the average annual expenditure in New York by suburban families dropped from $93 to $68 after the regional shopping centers opened. Furthermore, consumers were much less likely to shop in the New York stores that had opened suburban branches. By the end of the first year, the number of Bergen County families who had traded in the New York Macy's or Stern's dropped by half.

A similar study of 1100 shoppers by the New York University School of Retailing confirmed the Pratts' findings: shoppers for women's wear were half as likely to go to New York and a third as likely to go to Hackensack just one year after the shopping centers had opened. By the early 1960s a survey of New York area shoppers by a Harvard Business School professor concluded that more than 80 percent of residents of the New Jersey suburbs were most likely to shop close to home for clothing and household items, while only 20 percent went most often to Manhattan and 38 percent to New Jersey cities. (Some multiple answers brought the total over 100 percent.) Nationwide the trend was the same. Retail sales in central business districts declined dramatically between 1958 and 1963, even while overall metropolitan sales mushroomed from 10 to 20 percent.[27]

The reasons consumers routinely gave for shifting from downtown stores to shopping centers varied, but the overwhelming motivation they articulated was convenience—the ability to drive and park easily, more night hours, improved store layouts, increased self-service, and simplified credit with the charge plate, more available at suburban stores. The Pratts concluded that shoppers were not so much dissatisfied with New York and Hackensack stores as attracted to the ease and "progressiveness" of shopping center shopping. They seemed to share the developers' sense that shopping centers were the modern way to consume.[28]

While overall patronage of stores in surrounding downtowns declined as shopping center patronage increased, researchers discovered that the story

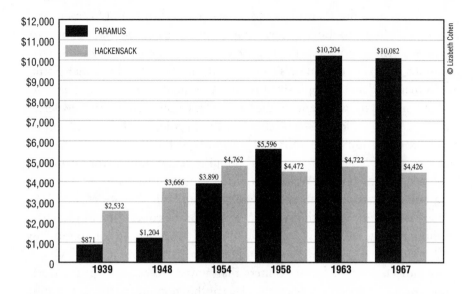

**PER CAPITA ANNUAL RETAIL SALES, 1939–1967,
PARAMUS AND HACKENSACK, NEW JERSEY**

Source: U.S. Census of Business: Retail Trade-area Statistics, 1939, 1948, 1954, 1958, 1963, 1967;
U.S. Bureau of the Census: Census of Population, 1940, 1950, 1960, 1970.
Calculated as: (Total Retail Sales/Consumer Price Index)/Population for Nearest Year.

was not so simple. Some local stores were benefiting as Bergen County residents became less dependent on New York. Small purchases that shoppers would have made alongside larger ones in New York were now handled closer to home, often in locally owned shops in small downtowns. A Hackensack, however, did not benefit as much as a Ridgewood or Englewood, since it was being displaced as a major shopping site by the shopping centers, and its stores were less likely to foster the same kind of loyalty to merchants as shops in small towns. In fact, within a year of the shopping centers' opening, major shoppers used Hackensack a third less; as a consequence, 50 percent of the retail establishments on Main Street reported they had done less business than in the previous year. By 1960 the competition had caused 10 percent of the stores on Hackensack's Main Street to close. Bergen County residents were restructuring their consumption patterns by substituting the new shopping centers for New York and for closer, large shopping towns like Hackensack, while continuing to shop—mostly for convenience goods and services—in the small town centers near their homes.[29]

While it is hard to evaluate the extent to which people viewed the shopping centers as more than places to shop—as the community centers that developers aimed to build—anecdotal evidence suggests that many did. Reporters writing stories in the late 1950s and 1960s on the way malls were becoming central to the nation's culture made this point, and routinely introduced their readers to people like Ernest J. Weinhold, a retired designer, who said that he and his wife came to the Cherry Hill Mall in southern New Jersey four days a week. "I love it here—there are things going on that you don't find anywhere else. I don't shop every day but what I do buy I get here."[30] The general manager of Willowbrook Mall, a shopping center not far from Paramus, explained that the Ernest Weinholds of the suburban world made it easy to program activities about forty-five weeks a year. "Whether it's charity fairs, 4-H exhibits, meetings of the Weight Watchers or the concert by the local barbershop quartet, we find that people respond—and that's what counts." By 1973 a *U.S. News & World Report* study reported that Americans of all ages spent more time in shopping centers than anywhere else, except for work, school, or home.[31] In the new public place of the shopping center, consuming and leisure were becoming inseparably intertwined, constructing community experiences around the cultural tastes of white middle-class suburbanites.

The response of businessmen in the existent town centers of northern New Jersey provides further evidence of the crisis confronting local retailers with the arrival of the shopping centers in the late 1950s. As the openings of Bergen Mall and Garden State Plaza neared, and particularly once they were a reality, main street retailers in Hackensack, Paterson, and other shopping towns told interviewers that they knew they had to improve their own stores and work cooperatively with other merchants to promote downtown. In 1957, Hackensack's Chamber of Commerce launched the first of many campaigns to make shopping there more attractive, featuring the covering of downtown parking meters at Christmastime so customers could park free. Paterson, four miles away, formed a Commercial Development Fund for Paterson's Future, which raised $65,000 to promote downtown through marketing and advertising. At the same time the Municipal Parking Authority issued $1.8 million in bonds to double the capacity of Paterson's parking lots, raising the total to 800. (By contrast, each shopping center offered parking for more than 8000 cars.)

Despite the best of intentions to ease parking and traffic, make downtown safer, improve customer service, cooperate in promoting downtown shopping, expand merchandise, modernize stores, and strengthen community ties, merchants in Bergen County's town centers had a tough time. Organizing cooperative campaigns of merchants who by identity and practice were independent was extremely difficult. Chambers of Commerce and similar entities lacked the coercive, centralized authority of shopping center managements.

One downtown's promotional campaign, unfortunately, was more likely to draw shoppers away from another town in crisis than from the shopping centers. Paterson's gain through the Commercial Development Fund for Paterson's Future, for example, turned out to be neighboring Fair Lawn's loss, as retail sales there dropped by half their 1954 level by the end of 1958. In the specific case of Hackensack, moreover, the Pratts found in a study of Bergen County retailers that even before the shopping centers opened, the city was in relative decline. Although total retail sales grew along with the exploding suburban population, Hackensack's share of the county market decreased from about 20 to 16 percent between 1948 and 1954. Hence, the shopping centers were only the latest blow to local merchants who had not figured out how to prosper in a world undergoing so much social and cultural change.[32]

Recognizing the limits of what they could do alone or through their volunteer merchants' organizations, established Bergen County retailers endorsed two strategies for improving their situation, both of which mobilized the authority and resources of government on their behalf. First, they joined a coalition of other interests, including churches and citizens concerned with traffic congestion, to pass blue laws prohibiting Sunday sales. If the shopping centers were allowed to open on Sunday, small, family-run stores for whom a seven-day week was a great hardship would suffer a handicap. If all stores were required to close, the score would be more even. "It's easy for the big stores to open, but it's different for the independents," explained the owner of a men's clothing store in Hackensack, adding that he and most of his staff of ten worked six days a week. "We are truly a service store, which consists of all full-time people. If you open seven days, you might have to hire part-timers. Our customers want to find a familiar face. They don't want to hear that the person they expect to see is off today."[33] The best defense that downtown retailers had against the shopping centers—service—would thus be jeopardized.

Losing no time, Paramus prohibited Sunday sales of virtually all goods except "necessities" (food, drugs, gasoline, newspapers) in 1957, the year the shopping centers opened. Violators were subject to a $200 fine per offense or ninety days in jail, or both, which finally put teeth in a longstanding statute on the state books. Although merchants in highway shopping centers protested and sued to have the ordinance revoked, arguing all the way to the New Jersey Supreme Court that their ability to compete with stores in neighboring towns was undermined, they lost. Meanwhile, agitation continued for an effective statewide restriction of Sunday shopping so that locales with blue laws would not be penalized, and the New Jersey legislature finally agreed to allow counties to hold referenda on the question. In November 1959 voting took place in fifteen of the state's twenty-one counties; twelve counties, including Bergen, voted a Sunday ban into law. Although highway discount stores appealed, the state supreme court eventually upheld the law, as did the United States Supreme Court indirectly when it ruled in 1961 on four companion cases concerning the constitutionality of Sunday closing laws in Maryland, Massachusetts, and Pennsylvania. The Supreme Court held that such laws did not violate freedom of religion as protected under the First Amendment or the equal protection guarantees of the Fourteenth Amendment, and thereby left it to individual states and localities to regulate Sunday selling as they wished. Due, no doubt, to strong advocacy by influential local businessmen, Bergen County was reputed to have made the greatest effort at enforcing blue laws of any county in New Jersey. A local magistrate even ordered that cigarette vending machines in a Howard Johnson chain restaurant be unplugged on Sundays. Nationwide during the late 1950s and early 1960s, retailers skirmished over Sunday closing laws, not so much defending traditional mores as using the language of church and state to veil intense struggles over the extent to which discount stores, shopping centers, and chain stores could capture millions of dollars in retail business through restructuring consumer markets.[34]

The second way that downtown businessmen sought to harness the power of the state in fighting the shopping centers involved the use of federal funds for urban renewal. The 1954 National Housing Act and the 1956 Federal Highway Act made it possible for cities to use urban renewal grants for rehabilitation of commercial areas; the federal government pledged from two-thirds to three-quarters of the cost of acquiring land and demolishing structures. Paterson proved the most aggressive of Bergen and Passaic Counties' cities in pursuing this strategy, joining with at least sixteen other communities in the metropolitan New York area. Dissatisfied with the gains from the Commercial Development Fund's promotional and parking efforts, civic leaders founded PLAN (Paterson Looks Ahead Now) in the early 1960s to redevelop 121 acres at the core of downtown. PLAN implemented a design by Victor Gruen, who had become an early advocate of the revival of downtowns through careful commercial planning, much as he had pioneered the development of regional shopping centers, themselves the source of many cities' economic ills.

Bringing many features of Bergen County's shopping centers to the Paterson city center, Gruen designed wide, landscaped pedestrian areas, accessible through loop roadways tied in with six parking garages accommodating 4500 cars. With Uncle Sam committed to footing three-quarters of the $24 million bill, local civic leaders headed by PLAN president Raymond J. Behrman, owner of a downtown luggage and women's accessories store, worked to reverse a drastic decline. By 1962 the number of Paterson shoppers was half what it had been in 1940, despite all the population growth in the region. Soon, Hackensack was talking about applying for urban renewal funds as well. But even this injection of federal dollars failed as a remedy. By 1971 shopping centers in the Paterson/Passaic metropolitan area had captured 79 percent of all retail trade, well beyond the average 50 percent share for shopping centers in the nation's twenty-one largest metropolitan areas. In 1950, Paterson was a major shopping district, while retail in Paramus hardly existed. Twenty years later, Paterson found itself suffering from long-term economic decline, ignored by recently constructed parkways, turnpikes, and interstates, and facing growing competition from shopping centers, while Paramus was well on its way to becoming one of the largest retail centers in the world. As the segmentation of consumer markets became the guiding principle in postwar commerce, no amount of revitalization could make a city whose population was becoming increasingly minority and poor attractive to the white middle-class shoppers with money to spend.[35]

While local merchants in Bergen and Passaic Counties struggled, the big New York and Newark stores developed their own strategy for dealing with the competition from the new suburban shopping centers: they opened branch stores. Rather than be eclipsed by the postwar shift in population, they followed it. By the late 1950s branch stores—once a rarity—had become a national trend among large department stores and specialty shops. Among department stores with annual net sales of $10 million or more, the percentage of branch sales skyrocketed from 4 percent of total sales in 1951 to 32 percent by 1959. By 1966 over half of all department store sales would be made in branch stores. Specialty stores with sales over $1 million made a comparable shift from 6 percent of sales through branches to 33 percent between 1951 and 1959. By the 1960s the very success of a regional shopping center like Bergen Mall or Garden State Plaza depended on the quality of the department store branches that served as its anchors. Branch stores had evolved from small outlets of Fifth Avenue flagship stores into full-fledged department stores carrying a wide range of merchandise. In the early 1970s, in fact, Bergen Mall's Stern Brothers took the dramatic step of closing its New York City stores, investing everything in its more profitable shopping-center branches. Stern's was not alone. By 1976 branch sales amounted to nearly 78 percent of total department store business nationwide. The department store trade's huge postwar investment in suburban stores had consequences for consumers, for local retailers, and, as will soon become apparent, for department store employees as well.[36]

By the 1960s the mass consumption economy had brought about a major restructuring of consumer markets. As retail dollars moved out of major cities and away from established downtowns within suburban areas, regional shopping centers became the distinctive public space of the postwar landscape. Suburban populations increasingly looked to the mall for a new kind of community center—consumption-oriented, tightly controlled, and aimed at purchasers as citizens who preferably were white and middle class. This commercialization of public space during the postwar era had profound consequences, perhaps the most important of which was the struggle to define what kind of political behavior was permissible in the new, privately owned public place of the shopping center.

PRIVATIZING PUBLIC SPACE

Whereas, at first, developers had sought to legitimize the new shopping centers by arguing for their centrality to both commerce and community, over time they discovered that these two commitments could conflict. The rights of free speech and assembly traditionally safeguarded in the public forums of democratic communities were not always good for business, and they could undermine the rights of private property owners—the shopping centers—to control entry to their land. Beginning in the 1960s, American courts all the way up to the United States Supreme Court struggled with the political consequences of having moved public life off the street and into the privately owned shopping center. Shopping centers, in turn, began to reconsider the desirable balance between commerce and community in what had become the major sites where suburbanites congregated.[37]

Once regional shopping centers like the Paramus malls had opened in the 1950s, people began to recognize them as public spaces and to use them to reach out to the community. When the Red Cross organized blood drives, when labor unions picketed stores in organizing campaigns, when political candidates ran for office, when anti-war and anti-nuclear activists gathered signatures for petitions, they all viewed the shopping center as the obvious place to reach masses of people. Although shopping centers varied in their responses—from tolerating political activists to monitoring their actions to prohibiting them outright—in general, they were wary of any activity that might offend customers. A long, complex series of court tests resulted, culminating in several key Supreme Court decisions that sought to sort out the conflict between two basic rights in a free society: free speech and private property. Not surprisingly, the cases hinged on arguments about the extent to which the shopping center had displaced the traditional "town square" as a legitimate public forum.[38]

The first ruling by the Supreme Court was *Amalgamated Food Employ-*

ees Union Local 590 v. *Logan Valley Plaza, Inc.* (1968), in which Justice Thurgood Marshall, writing for the majority, argued that refusing to let union members picket the Weis Markets in the Logan Valley Plaza in Altoona, Pennsylvania, violated the workers' First Amendment rights, since shopping centers had become the "functional equivalent" of a sidewalk in a public business district. Because peaceful picketing and leaflet distribution on "streets, sidewalks, parks, and other similar public places are so historically associated with the exercise of First Amendment rights," he wrote, they should also be protected in the public thoroughfare of a shopping center, even if privately owned. The *Logan Valley Plaza* decision likened the shopping center to a company town, which had been the subject of a previously important Supreme Court decision in *Marsh* v. *Alabama* (1946), upholding the First Amendment rights of a Jehovah's Witness to proselytize in the company town of Chickasaw, Alabama, despite the fact that the Gulf Shipbuilding Corporation owned all the property in town. The "Marsh Doctrine" affirmed First Amendment rights over private property rights when an owner opened up his or her property for use by the public.[39]

The stance taken in *Logan Valley Plaza* began to unravel, however, as the Supreme Court became more conservative under President Richard Nixon's appointees. In *Lloyd* v. *Tanner* (1972), Justice Lewis F. Powell, Jr., wrote for the majority that allowing anti-war advocates to pass out leaflets at the Lloyd Center in Portland, Oregon, would be an unwarranted infringement of property rights "without significantly enhancing the asserted right of free speech." Anti-war leaflets, he argued, could be effectively distributed elsewhere, without undermining the shopping center's appeal to customers with litter and distraction.[40]

The reigning Supreme Court decision today is *PruneYard Shopping Center* v. *Robbins* (1980). The Supreme Court upheld a California State Supreme Court ruling that the state constitution granted a group of high school students the right to gather petitions against the U.N. resolution "Zionism is Racism." The Court decided that this action did not violate the San Jose mall owner's rights under the U.S. Constitution. But, at the same time, the Court reaffirmed its earlier decisions in *Lloyd* v. *Tanner* and *Scott Hudgens* v. *National Labor Relations Board* (1976) that the First Amendment did not guarantee access to shopping malls, and it let the states decide for themselves whether their own constitutions protected such access.

Since *PruneYard*, state appellate courts have been struggling with the issue, and mall owners have won in many more states than they have lost. Only in six states—California, Colorado, Massachusetts, New Jersey, Oregon, and Washington—have state supreme courts protected citizens' right of free speech in privately owned shopping centers. In New Jersey, the courts have been involved for some time in adjudicating free speech in shopping centers. In 1983, Bergen Mall was the setting of a suit between its owners and a political candidate who wanted to distribute campaign materials there. When a Paramus municipal court judge ruled in favor of the mall, the candidate's attorney successfully appealed on the familiar grounds that "there is no real downtown Paramus. Areas of the mall outside the stores are the town's public sidewalks." He further noted that the mall hosted community events and contained a meeting hall, post office, and Roman Catholic chapel. In this case, and in another one the following year over the right of nuclear-freeze advocates to distribute literature at Bergen Mall, free speech was protected on the grounds that the mall was equivalent to a town center.[41]

In two more recent decisions, in December 1994 and June 2001, the New Jersey Supreme Court reaffirmed that the state constitution guaranteed free speech in shopping malls. In the first case, *New Jersey Coalition Against War in the Middle East* v. *J.M.B. Realty Corp.*, opponents of the Persian Gulf War wanted to distribute leaflets at ten regional malls throughout the state. Writing for the majority, Chief Justice Robert N. Wilentz confirmed how extensively public space had been transformed in postwar New Jersey:

> The economic lifeblood once found downtown has moved to suburban shopping centers, which have substantially displaced the downtown business districts as the centers of commercial and social activity. . . . Found at these malls are most of the uses and activities citizens engage in outside their homes. . . . This is the new, the improved, the more attractive downtown business district—the new community—and no use is more closely associated with the old downtown than leafletting. Defendants have taken that old downtown away from its former home and moved all of it, except free speech, to the suburbs.

Despite the New Jersey Supreme Court's endorsement of free speech in 1994, it nonetheless put limits on its exercise, reaffirming the regional mall owners' property rights. Its ruling allowed only the distribution of leaflets—no speeches, bullhorns, pickets, parades, demonstrations, or solicitation of funds. Moreover, the court granted owners broad powers to regulate leaflet distribution by specifying days, hours, and areas in or outside the mall permissible for political activity. Mall owners were also allowed to require leafletters to carry million-dollar liability policies, which were often unobtainable or prohibitively expensive.[42]

In 2001 the New Jersey State Supreme Court clarified its position with a ruling in *Green Party of New Jersey* v. *Hartz Mountain Industries*. The Mall at Mill Creek had imposed restrictions on the Green Party of the sort presumably allowed under the court's 1994 decision—such as requiring a $1 million liability policy and limiting access to one day a year—as the party attempted to collect signatures in support of Ralph Nader's presidential run in 1996. In a unanimous decision, the state supreme court reaffirmed the notion of the mall as the "functional equivalent" of the Main Street of yesterday and called for a "balancing test" that more positively weighed the importance of individual liberties like leafletting "in our system of political discourse." Although the judges did not void all restrictions, New Jersey remains a beacon of free speech. In many more states, shopping centers have retained the right to prohibit political action altogether, much as they control the economic and social behavior of shoppers and store owners.[43]

An unintended consequence of the American shift in orientation from public town center to private shopping center, then, has been the narrowing of the ground where constitutionally protected free speech and free assembly can legally take place. As Justice Marshall so prophetically warned in his *Lloyd* v. *Tanner* dissent in 1972, as he watched the Berger Court reverse many of the liberal decisions of the Warren Court:

> It would not be surprising in the future to see cities rely more and more on private businesses to perform functions once performed by governmental agencies. . . . As governments rely on private enterprise, public property decreases in favor of privately owned property. It becomes harder and harder for citizens to communicate with other citizens. Only the wealthy may find effective communication possible unless we adhere to *Marsh* v. *Alabama* and continue to hold that "the more an owner, for his advantage, opens up his property for use by the public in general, the more do his rights become circumscribed by the statutory and constitutional rights of those who use it."[44]

As Marshall's dissent predicted, the privatization of what had de facto become public space in suburban shopping centers had ominous implications for the preservation of democratic freedom in cities as well. For example, the explosion over the quarter century since Marshall's dissent of self-taxing Business Improvement Districts (BIDs)—supported by urban merchants to clean, upgrade, and police their neighborhoods to compensate for what they considered inadequate government attention, but worrisomely free of municipal oversight or public accountability—suggests some of the troubling directions

American society may be headed as once-public spaces and services become privatized, in cities and suburbs alike.[45]

FEMINIZING PUBLIC SPACE

*a*long with commercialization and privatization, the shift from downtown to shopping center entailed a feminization of public space. For decades if not centuries, women had been the major shoppers in their families. That pattern continued in the postwar era, with marketers estimating that women did anywhere from 67 to 92 percent of the shopping and spent a great deal of their time at it.[46] What made the birth of the shopping center a noteworthy departure from earlier periods, however, was that significant public space—in private hands—was now being tailored to women's needs and desires as consumers. While the department store born of the nineteenth century created similarly feminized space, the urban commercial district of which it was a part catered as much to male consumption, leisure, and associational life—through bars, clubs, pool halls, and smoke shops, to say nothing of the male-dominated street resulting from the mix of commercial and corporate culture downtown. The early shopping center, in contrast, created the equivalent of a downtown district dedicated primarily to female-orchestrated consumption.[47]

The first shopping centers were planned with the female consumer in mind. As women patrons increasingly drove their own cars, they found parking spaces at the shopping center designed wider than usual for the express purpose of making it easier for them—many of whom were new drivers—to park.[48] Women then entered a well-controlled "public" space that made them feel comfortable and safe, with activities planned to appeal especially to them and their children. From the color schemes, stroller ramps, baby-sitting services, and special lockers for "ladies' wraps" to the reassuring security guards and special events such as fashion shows, shopping centers were created as female worlds. "I wouldn't know how to design a center for a man," admitted Jack Follet of John Graham, Inc., a firm responsible for many shopping centers. And if New Jersey resident Mrs. Bonnie Porrazzo was any indication, designers like Follet knew what they were doing. Four or five times a week, she visited a shopping center three minutes from her suburban home because "It's great for women. What else is there to do?" The reported shopping priorities of women like Bonnie Porrazzo—convenience to home, one-stop shopping, big stores, self-service, and evening hours—fit well with what shopping centers had to offer.[49]

But for all the attention that early shopping centers lavished on women, their growing presence in the suburban landscape did not increase women's social and economic power in postwar society. Consumers' growing interest in shopping as families even when orchestrated by women, the increasing use of credit in purchasing, and the kind of jobs that women secured at shopping centers all conspired to limit the gains in domestic and public authority that a feminized suburban space might otherwise have encouraged.

Whenever suburban and downtown shopping were compared in the 1950s and 1960s, shopping centers were singled out for their greater family appeal. In typical fashion, *Redbook's* 1957 film *In the Suburbs* depicted the "happy-go-spending," "buy-it-now" generation passing great amounts of time together as a family in the local shopping center: "Like the rest of life in suburbia, shopping has a family flavor," the narrator observed while footage showed couples buying while their children trailed along or played nearby. These young adults, he went on, "have a 'let's-go-see quality' that bring crowds to community events and promotions" sponsored by the centers. A study comparing family shopping in downtown Cincinnati with its suburban shopping centers found that while 85 percent of downtown patrons shopped alone, only 43 percent of shopping center patrons did; most of them were accompanied by family members. Other surveys showed as many as two-thirds of female suburban customers shopping with someone else. Women shoppers in Bergen County surveyed by the Pratts conformed to these patterns. In the first few years after the centers opened, four in ten families were spending more time shopping, three in ten were making more shopping trips, two in ten were taking the children more often, and two in ten were including husbands more often than before the malls were built.[50]

When "the whole family [was] shopping together," as marketer Pierre Martineau put it in 1958, men played a greater role in household purchasing. Survey after survey documented husbands' increasing presence alongside their wives at shopping centers, which made evenings and weekends by far the busiest time there, creating peaks and valleys in shopping that had not affected downtown stores nearly as much. In many suburban centers more than half the volume was done at night. At Bergen Mall the peak traffic count was at 8 p.m., and shopping was very heavy on Saturdays as well. A May Company executive described how this imbalance created special problems in branch-store operation: "The biggest day in the suburban store will be ten times the poorest day, instead of five as it usually is downtown." The manager of the Tots 'n Teens toy store in Shoppers World in Framingham, Massachusetts, tried to explain to less experienced mall sellers how the new-style suburban shopping actually worked: "It's a curious thing about a shopping center. Most of our

Large, open, well-lighted departments
with year-round air conditioning
permit Bamberger's to handle
large crowds easily.

Do-it-yourself delivery is popular
with suburban customers — and so is the
"togetherness" of family shopping.

This page from Macy's annual report to shareholders the year its Garden State Plaza opened conveyed the prevalence of women shoppers but also hinted at the growing importance of the "togetherness of family shopping," referred to in the bottom caption. Reproduced from R. H. Macy & Co., Inc., *1957 Annual Report*. (Courtesy of Robert F. Wagner Labor Archives, New York University, from its Department Store Workers, Local 1-S Collection)

daytime shoppers are women who are just looking around. It's hard to sell them during the day but if they're at all interested, they'll be back at night—with their husbands. That's when we do the real business."[51]

Shopping centers responded to suburban couples' growing tendency to shop together with stores and programming specifically designed to further encourage families to turn shopping chores into leisure time spent at the mall. William M. Batten, board chair of JCPenney, for example, recalled "the broadening of our lines of merchandise and our services to encompass a fuller spectrum of family activity" as the company began building stores in shopping centers rather than on Main Street in the late 1950s and 1960s. Only then did Penney's start selling appliances, hardware, and sporting goods, and offering portrait studios, restaurants, auto service, and Singer sewing instruction. *Business Week* reported that department stores were scurrying to respond as well: Federated Department Stores started a new Fedway chain to attract the whole family and in its F. & R. Lazarus store in Columbus was "making a real effort to take the curse of femininity off the big store" by selling more male-oriented merchandise. Atlanta-based Rich's Department Store added a "Store for Men" adjoining its main store. Automobile shows, Saturday "kids' movies," student art exhibits, and circus clowns were only a few of the many events designed to attract men and children. In time, shopping centers themselves would be constructed as less feminized space, with all family members, not just women, in mind. As families strolled and shopped together at the mall, more and more they engaged in a form of activity that may have been female-directed, but reflected greater sharing of responsibility for household purchasing between husbands and wives.[52]

The huge expansion of credit that accompanied the rise of suburban shopping centers contributed to men's increased involvement in, even control over, female purchasing. In 1950 the ratio of credit to disposable income among American consumers was 10.4 percent, with $21.5 billion worth of debt outstanding. By 1960 the ratio had grown to 16.1 percent, the debt to $56.1 billion; a decade later they had reached 18.5 percent and $127 billion, respectively, as credit became an essential pillar in the Consumers' Republic's infrastructure. Retailers with both downtown stores and suburban branches observed directly how shopping center expansion fueled that growth: Jack Schuster opened two toy stores in 1962, one in downtown Rochester, the other in the suburban Pittsford Plaza; not only were unit sales four times higher in Pittsford, but charge accounts were opened and used there at twenty-five times the rate of downtown.[53]

The credit trend was also apparent in Bergen County. Bamberger's promoted its Garden State Plaza store as offering "A Credit Plan to suit every need," a choice among Regular Charge Accounts, Budget Charge Accounts, and Deferred Payment Accounts. Once customers came into the store, an innovative Teletype hookup with the Bergen County Credit Bureau enabled charge accounts to be established quickly. When another Garden State Plaza anchor store, JCPenney, which had long built its identity around low-price, cash-and-carry purchasing, opened its first shopping-center store in 1957, it finally accepted that credit was expected, even demanded, by consumers, and became the last of the large nationwide retailers to introduce a store credit card. By 1962 national credit facilities and systems were operating with the latest electronic data-processing technology, and charging had become the standard way to buy. Both customers and stores claimed they benefited. Consumers felt better able to stretch their dollars, while retailers carefully documented that shoppers buying with credit spent more, particularly in the stores where they had charge accounts. As a credit manager at Sears, Roebuck told a sales meeting, "A credit customer is yours—a cash customer is anybody's."[54]

As credit cards increasingly became the legal tender of shopping center purchasing, they expanded women's access to family income from spending the domestic allowance assigned from the weekly or monthly paycheck to committing the family's present and future savings. But at the same time, credit cards deepened women's economic dependence on men, as qualifying in almost all cases depended on husbands' income, even when women earned money of their own. An investigation of sexual discrimination in consumer credit as late as 1973 found that JCPenney was typical of retailers in granting credit solely to single women; once married, divorced, separated, or widowed, only husbands could qualify for a charge account. When in the same year a member of Essex County, New Jersey's branch of the National Organization for Women pressed Penney's regional credit manager for an explanation, he replied in writing, "In not directing our monthly statements and correspondence to the husband's attention, we could be accused of conspiring with the wife to keep the knowledge of the existence of the account from him." Of course, women had been financially subservient to their breadwinner husbands much earlier in the twentieth century, running their households on the money they got by asking (and in some cases begging and stealing), through the more progressive weekly allowance, and in the most egalitarian marriages, via the joint account. But before the era of family shopping and the charge card, wives probably encountered less scrutiny from their husbands about either their expertise as shoppers or their household budget allocations.[55]

As evident in the rise in family shopping and the expanded use of credit cards, even as women benefited from the emergence of shopping centers, so too their horizons were limited by them. Even women who took jobs in shopping centers like Bergen Mall and Garden State Plaza, many working for the first time in their married lives, did not find their fortunes much improved. As the department stores established branches, they increasingly turned to suburban housewives as retail clerks. The fit seemed perfect. Many women were interested in part-time work, and the stores were looking for part-time labor to service the notorious peaks and valleys in suburban shopping. As a Stanford Business School professor advised branch managers in the year the Bergen County shopping centers opened, "Fortunately, most of these suburban stores have in their immediate neighborhood a large number of housewives and other nonemployed women who have been willing to work during these evening and Saturday peak periods. . . . Many of these women apparently work as much because of interest as because of economic necessity, and, as a rule, they have proved to be excellent salespeople." The Paramus malls took heed. Shortly after opening in 1957, Stern Brothers in Bergen Mall reported that "housewives make up the greatest proportion of the new personnel"; by the mid-1960s the part-time employment of women had swelled the malls' combined employee ranks to almost six thousand, two-thirds of them part-time and many of them local residents.[56]

But according to New York–area labor unions like Local 1-S, RWDSU (Retail, Wholesale and Department Store Union), which represented employees at Macy's and Bamberger's, and District 65, RWDSU, which represented them at Gimbel's, Stern's, and Bloomingdale's, the department stores had another motive for hiring so many part-timers in their new suburban branches: they were trying to cut labor costs and break the hold of the unions, which had organized their New York stores successfully enough to make retail clerking a decent job. Indeed, retailers gave a lot of attention to keeping labor costs down, judging them to be the greatest obstacle to higher profits. Suburban branch managers sought to limit the number of salespeople needed by depending more on customer self-service and "pipe-racking," putting goods on floor racks rather than behind counters. Some stores, such as Sears, Roebuck, Montgomery Ward, and JCPenney, expanded their catalogue operations.[57] But the basic strategy of the suburban department store was to control wages through hiring more part-timers at minimum wages and benefits.

Organizing the new suburban branches became a life-and-death struggle for the unions beginning in the 1950s. They recognized that not only was the fate of new branch jobs at stake, but as retail dollars left the city for the suburbs, jobs in the downtown stores were threatened as well. The branch store was becoming, in effect, a kind of runaway shop that undermined the job security, wages, benefits, and working conditions of unionized downtown workers. Local 1-S and District 65 tried all kinds of strategies, such as demanding

Bamberger's Department Store prepared an employee handbook, of which this is the cover, for the opening of its Garden State Plaza store in 1957. Hoping to recruit part-time female employees among housewives in neighboring suburban towns, the store offered them "new friends," while male applicants were promised "a new career." (Courtesy of Robert F. Wagner Labor Archives, New York University, from its Department Store Workers, Local 1-S Collection)

contract coverage of the new branches when renegotiating their existing contracts with downtown stores; getting permission from the National Labor Relations Board to split the bargaining units within particular branch stores (such as into selling, non-selling, and restaurant) to facilitate organization; assigning downtown store workers to picket suburban branches during strikes and organizing campaigns; and gaining the right for city-store employees to transfer to branches without losing accumulated seniority and benefits.

But still, successful labor organization of the suburban branches proved extremely difficult. Branch-store management at Stern's, Bamberger's, and a Bloomingdale's that opened nearby took an aggressive stand against unionization, harassing and firing employees who showed the least inclination to organize, particularly women. Bill Michelson, executive vice president of District 65, pointed to the mentality of part-timers, who so dominated branch-store employee ranks, as another obstacle to successful organizing: "The part-timer, usually a housewife in a suburban town, is interested in picking up extra money and does not have deep roots in her job." The large turnover among part-time workers—through layoffs as well as voluntary resignation—made organizing them all the harder.[58]

Despite the determined efforts of Local 1-S and District 65 to organize all department store workers in the Paramus shopping centers, Gimbel's was the only store to sign a union contract that covered its Paramus store, in exchange for a lesser wage increase and the cancellation of a threatened strike. At all the rest, an overwhelmingly female labor force worked part-time at minimum wage, with few benefits, no union representation, and limited opportunities for career advancement. Work became a way for women to maintain their status as consumers, but it did not significantly empower them as producers who could contribute substantially to—or be independent of—male earnings. At Bamberger's, in fact, the handbook for new employees urged them to use their staff discount to purchase store merchandise (20 percent off for apparel worn on the job, 10 percent on other items) so that they could serve as model consumers for customers. The shopping center, then, contributed to a segmentation not only of consumers but of workers as well in a postwar labor market that offered new jobs to women but marked these jobs as less remunerative and more dead-end.[59]

Furthermore, as a workplace, much like as a public space, the shopping center constricted the rights available to the people who frequented it. That women came to dominate the ranks of workers, as they already did consumers, meant that their political freedom was particularly circumscribed. The shopping center thus posed a contradiction for women in the 1950s and 1960s: although it created a new community setting initially catering to female needs and desires, it increasingly contained them as consumers and part-time workers. In this era before equal credit protection, feminist revolt, and affirmative action opened other opportunities, women's choices were limited not simply through peer pressure and personal priorities, as is often claimed, but also through the larger economic restructuring taking place in the metropolitan marketplace of the Consumers' Republic.

SUBURBANIZING CITIES

ass consumption in postwar America created a new landscape, where public space was more commercialized, privatized, and feminized within the regional shopping center than it had been in the traditional downtown center. This is not to romanticize the city and its central business district. Certainly urban commercial property owners pursued their own economic interests, political activity in public spaces was sometimes restricted, and the priorities of women and men did not always coexist peacefully. Nonetheless, the legal distinction between public and private space remained significant. Urban loitering and vagrancy laws directed against undesirables in public places have repeatedly been struck down by the courts, while privately owned shopping centers have been able to enforce trespassing laws.[60] Overall, an important shift from one kind of social order to another took place between 1950 and 1980, with major consequences for Americans. A free commercial market attached to a relatively free public sphere (for whites) underwent a transformation to a more regulated commercial marketplace (where mall management controlled access, favoring, for example, chains over local independents) and a more circumscribed public sphere of limited rights.

Not by accident, public space, like residential settlement patterns, was restructured and segmented by class and race in New Jersey, as in the nation, just as African Americans gained new protections for their right of equal access to public accommodations. Although civil rights laws had been on the books in New Jersey since the late nineteenth century, not until the Freeman Bill of 1949 passed were African Americans finally guaranteed equal access to schools and commercial venues including restaurants, retail stores, hotels, public transportation, movie theaters, and beaches, with violators subject to fines and jail terms. Throughout the 1940s and 1950s, African-American citizens of New Jersey and other northern states vigilantly challenged discrimination by private property owners. Yet larger structural changes in community marketplaces were under way, financed by private commercial interests committed to

This two-page spread from "The Story of Avon . . . A Product and an Opportunity," a recruiting note-book from Avon Products, shows how the company assumed that potential saleswomen sought work to buy desired consumer goods, not to provide basic support for their families. 1957–58. (Courtesy of Hagley Museum and Library)

profits they thought depended on socioeconomic and racial segmentation. While African Americans and their supporters were prodding courts and legis-latures to eliminate legal segregation in public and private places, real estate developers, retailers, and consumers were collaborating to shift economic resources to new kinds of segregated spaces like shopping centers.[61]

The rise of shopping centers threatened African-American job oppor-tunities as well. Right after the war, influential civil rights organizations such as the National Association for the Advancement of Colored People, the National Urban League, and the Congress of Racial Equality, assisted by pro-gressive white groups like the American Jewish Congress and the League of Women Shoppers, had pushed the neighborhood-based "Don't Shop Where You Can't Work" campaigns of the 1930s into the mainstream retail economy and mounted an all-out effort to get blacks hired as downtown department store clerks, not just in low-level wrapper, porter, and elevator operator jobs. A 1946 survey of the hiring practices of New York City department stores revealed shockingly low numbers of black salespeople: 9 out of 3000 at Macy's, 1 out of 600 at Gimbel's, 3 out of 1000 at Bloomingdale's. Two years later the numbers had barely risen.[62]

But over the next two decades, concerted efforts were made to chal-lenge retailers' claims that hiring black clerks would cost them white patron-age, and gradually the number of African Americans employed in sales and clerical jobs in New York and Newark department stores grew. By the late 1960s a third of the more than 8000 people working in Macy's Herald Square store in Manhattan, for example, were black and Puerto Rican, employed across the full spectrum of jobs. When metropolitan retail markets underwent restructuring, however—so that between 1959 and 1965 95 percent of new retail jobs in the New York metropolitan area were located in suburbs outside New York City—blacks and Puerto Ricans lost out. A two-year study of employment and housing opportunities for racial minorities in suburban New York, released in 1970, concluded that "participation in retailing by minority employees in the larger establishments in suburban counties of the Region is minimal." In Bergen County, the retail labor force included only 4.6 percent blacks and 1.1 percent with Spanish surnames. None of the causes cited were surprising: hiring discrimination, inadequate transportation, few suburban housing options, low pay, and "the sea of white faces which a black prospect encounters upon entering a suburban store."[63]

The landscape of mass consumption created a metropolitan society where people no longer left their residential enclaves to enter central market-places and the parks, streets, and public buildings that surrounded them, but, rather, were separated by class, race, and less so gender in differentiated com-mercial subcenters. Moreover, all commercial subcenters were not created equal. Over time, shopping centers moved beyond simply aiming at "middle-income groups" to become even more class stratified, with some like Bergen Mall marketing themselves to the lower-middle class, while others like Garden State Plaza went upscale to attract upper-middle-class consumers.[64] If tied to international capital, some central business districts, such as New York and San Francisco, prospered, although not unscarred from recent retail mergers and leveraged buyouts. Other downtowns, such as Hackensack and Elizabeth, New Jersey, became "Cheap John's Bargain Centers" serving customers too poor and deprived of transportation to shop at malls. Even in larger American cities, poor urban populations shopped downtown on weekends while the white-collar workers who commuted in to offices during the week patronized the suburban malls closer to where they lived. Some commercial districts were taken over by enterprising, often newly arrived ethnic groups, who breathed new life into what would otherwise have been in decay, but they nonetheless served a segmented market.

Worst off were cities like Newark, where the effects of long-term retail decentralization were exacerbated by white reactions to the racial problems of the 1960s. Once the largest shopping district in the state, Newark saw a 24 per-cent decline in department store sales between 1963 and 1968, every one of its major department stores close between 1964 and 1992, and much of its retail space remain abandoned, leaving residents like Raymond Mungin to wonder, "I don't have a car to drive out to the malls. What can I do?" Mass consump-tion in the Consumers' Republic was supposed to bring about greater equality in material life and in opportunities to pursue consumption. Instead, diverse social groups became less integrated into central consumer marketplaces and more frequently consigned to differentiated retail institutions, segmented markets, and new hierarchies.[65]

Finally, the dependence on private spaces like shopping centers for public activity and the more recent privatization of public space with BIDs have gravely threatened the government's constitutional obligations to its citizens. Cities, in responding to their own steadily worsening retail crisis, have endorsed some strategies that suburbanize urban shopping, importing the suburban center's wariness about free speech along with a retail model that has inspired the creation on Main Street of pedestrian and transit malls (often failures), and privately owned, enclosed shopping centers linked to parking garages. Nor have new privatized retail centers been the only urban public places facing disputes over how much freedom of speech and public assembly will be tolerated. In New York City, for example, Penn Station sought the right to eject homeless people from the station, while City Hall tried to limit the number of protesters allowed to assemble on its steps; both efforts were successfully challenged in the courts.[66]

When Jürgen Habermas theorized about the rise and fall of a rational public sphere, he recognized the centrality in the eighteenth and nineteenth centuries of accessible urban places—cafes, taverns, coffeehouses, clubs, meeting houses, concert and lecture halls, theaters, and museums—to the emergence and maintenance of a democratic political culture. Over the last half century, transformation in America's economy and metropolitan landscape expanded the ability of many people to participate in the mass market. Likewise, that mass market helped African Americans mount a civil rights movement around undeniable claims to equal access to the public, often commercial venues where goods and services were dispersed. But the commercializing, privatizing, and segmenting of physical gathering places that has resulted from allowing the unfettered pursuit of profits to dictate a new metropolitan landscape has made more precarious the shared public sphere upon which democracy depends. Monsignor James Linder, a Roman Catholic priest in Newark, described to a *New York Times* reporter the state of public space in downtown Newark in 1997: "Prime office space is that with garage parking, and they are all built like fortresses, with their lobbies up on the second floor and retail space in atriums and courts. They were all built with the riots in mind, and it's not very pedestrian-friendly and inviting. The result is you have two cities downtown: the one in and around the offices and the one on the streets where the people are."[67] Not only did the reconfiguration of community marketplaces in the Consumers' Republic move retail out of downtown into the suburbs, but Newark and other struggling cities responded to suburbia's challenge by mimicking its solutions, replicating the exclusions and inequities of metropolitan fragmentation within their own borders.

PART FOUR

The Political Culture of Mass Consumption

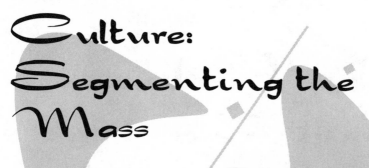

CHAPTER 7

Culture: Segmenting the Mass

hen in 1945 the *New York Herald Tribune* introduced the readers of its Sunday magazine to the exploding field of market research and what it was predicting about American consumer desires once the war ended, the paper stressed that the inquiry into "what you want" assumed a unified "you." Statements like "nine out of ten of you want," "three times as many of you hope," "most of you have decided" ran through the text.[1] "The rich man smokes the same sort of cigarettes as the poor man, shaves with the same sort of razor, uses the same sort of telephone, vacuum cleaner, radio and TV set," and drives a car with only minor variations, *Harper's Magazine* concurred a couple years later.[2] In the aftermath of World War II, mass consumer markets that delivered mass-produced goods to a wide swath of Americans seemed the best route to prosperity. By the mid-1950s an unprecedented number of Americans were participating in what chronicler Thomas Hine has

Overleaf: Maggie Kuhn—founder of the Gray Panthers, a civil rights group for senior citizens—led a demonstration outside the national headquarters of the U.S. Chamber of Commerce in October 1977 in support of a congressional bill authorizing a new federal agency to serve as consumer watchdog. This advocacy by the Gray Panthers illustrates how the consumer movement of the 1960s and 1970s mobilized supporters within the narrow interest groups that had emerged through a mix of identity politics and market segmentation since the early sixties. (Courtesy of Julie Jensen/Photography)

called "one of history's great shopping sprees" to acquire multitudes of material goods in the style he has aptly labeled "Populuxe": fashionable and luxurious, yet affordable to many.[3]

But how, marketers soon began to worry, could they ensure continued profits? As more and more Americans bought a house, car, refrigerator, and washing machine, wouldn't markets get saturated and consumption ebb? True, the baby boom was creating larger potential markets among, for example, those "happy-go-spending" young suburban families celebrated in *Redbook* magazine's promotional film, but their children would not become consumers in their own right until the late 1960s. Moreover, wouldn't a booming economy create more business competition along with more prosperous consumers? After all, the number of operating businesses had increased 45 percent between 1945 and 1959, according to *Printers' Ink*, a trade journal of advertisers, and that did not even take into account growth in foreign competition.[4] Manufacturers and retailers all producing for the same mass market ran a serious risk of putting each other out of business. Already by 1956 marketing expert Wendell Smith, past president of the American Marketing Association and director of marketing research and development for Radio Corporation of America (RCA), was warning of the "recent ascendency of product competition to a position of great economic importance. An expanded array of goods and services is competing for the consumer's dollar," intensified by advancing technology "creating competition between new and traditional materials."[5] Recession in 1957 alarmed manufacturers and marketers all the more, casting the nation's sluggish economy since 1954 as the origins of a looming crisis.

Marketers invested in the promises of Populuxe experimented with a variety of remedies to stimulate demand. They developed new products for consumers to buy, making television sets, for example, more portable, larger screened, and, by 1961, capable of displaying color. They tried pricing sought-after goods like appliances at higher prices to bring in greater revenue. And most commonly, they encouraged product obsolescence by regularly changing the wings on cars, the colors on refrigerators, and the hemlines on skirts. "Basic utility cannot be the foundation of a prosperous apparel industry," B. Earl Puckett of Allied Stores instructed four hundred leaders of the fashion world in 1950. "We must accelerate obsolescence," he insisted, and over the decade the garment industry would prove itself a model, according to *Printers' Ink*.[6] Industrial design as a profession had developed in the 1930s with the promise of redesigning the objects of everyday life. In postwar America, the practice and profession exploded together, and increasingly its Bauhausian-inspired mission to raise the aesthetic standards of the mass of Americans—

Automobile manufacturers were among the most enthusiastic practitioners of "planned obsolescence," a strategy for expanding demand by continually redesigning goods to encourage consumers to trade in yesterday's model for tomorrow's. Jean Raeburn, 1950. (Courtesy of Carpenter Center
Photography Collection, Harvard University)

what visionary industrial designer Charles Eames in 1950 described as design
"to bring the most of the best to the greatest number of people for the least"—
easily fed into the strategy of planned obsolescence, with designers regularly
restyling mass consumer goods. The head of styling at Ford, George Walker,
explained the challenge: "We design a car to make a man unhappy with his
1957 Ford 'long about the end of 1958." His counterpart at competitor General Motors was even more ambitious: "In 1934 the average car ownership
span was 5 years; now it is 2 years. When it is 1 year, we will have a perfect
score."[7]

　　Even as these innovations squeezed greater profits out of existing
demand, they continued to assume the existence of a unified, often referred to
as "middle-class," market where the mass of consumers shared a consistent set
of Populuxe tastes and desires. As a study of Philadelphia department store
customers concluded in 1950, "The leveling of incomes since 1940 has pro-

vided a great stimulus for stores to move toward the middle of the middle." Article after article in the trade publication the *Journal of Retailing* between 1945 and 1960 promoted the viability of selling to the "average consumer," frequently referred to as "Mr. or Mrs. Consumer," the same customer being targeted by the shopping centers popping up all over suburbia.[8] To the extent that goods were aimed at anything but this average middle-class market, those markets were usually understood as steps along a continuum of "income groups" capable of more or less discretionary spending but unlikely to diverge much from the accepted set of consumer preferences.

When Wendell Smith warned of the growing danger of product competition in 1956, he proposed an alternative to mass marketing that made his article in the *Journal of Marketing* a landmark: market segmentation. He argued that in place of mass markets, goods would "find their markets of maximum potential as a result of recognition of differences in the requirements of market segments." As "many companies" are finding that "their *core* markets have already been developed . . . to the point where additional advertising and selling expenditures [are] yielding diminishing returns, attention to smaller or *fringe* market segments, which may have small potentials individually but are of crucial importance in the aggregate," Smith advised, can yield greater consumer satisfaction, continued profitability, and "a more secure market position."[9] Two years after Smith's article, Pierre Martineau, a University of Chicago–trained sociologist and marketing director of the *Chicago Tribune* (long a leader in market research), elaborated the rationale for market segmentation in another groundbreaking article in the *Journal of Marketing*. Martineau attacked the prevailing assumption that "a rich man is simply a poor man with more money and that, given the same income, the poor man would behave exactly like the rich man," by insisting "this is just not so." A member of a market segment defined by social class or other criteria, Martineau argued, is "profoundly different in his mode of thinking and his way of handling the world. . . . Where he buys and what he buys will differ not only by economics but in symbolic value."[10] From their different perspectives, Smith and Martineau together advanced a new axiom of marketing, whether applied to cigarettes or refrigerators: homogeneity of buyers within a segmented market, heterogeneity between segmented markets.

Although Smith and Martineau are officially credited in the annals of marketing with conceptualizing the modern notion of market segmentation in the late 1950s, it was not an entirely new idea. Before the Second World War, different industries had begun to take variation in consumer tastes into account at different times. The first major success has usually been attributed to General Motors' assault on Ford's unchanging Model T in the late 1920s, promoting annual model changes and some customer discretion within that.[11] But in keeping with how mass markets themselves were understood to be divided in the era before widespread market segmentation, by differentiating more between products than users, General Motors and other early segmenters tended to vary their products to appeal to different "price classes," income groups that, like the indistinguishable poor man and rich man rejected by Martineau, were separated more by ability to buy than by taste. For example, when in 1940 GM surveyed 10,000 prospective buyers about their interest in an early version of the automatic transmission, the Hydra-Matic Drive, income level was assumed to be the decisive factor.[12] It would not be until Smith and Martineau in the late 1950s, followed by scores of other marketing innovators, espoused the new concept of market segmentation that segments would emerge as unique markets to be sold substantially different products.

By the time Thomas Robertson of the Harvard Business School published his marketing text, *Consumer Behavior*, in 1970, he would conclude a key chapter with the statement, "The basic dilemma, in summary, is whether to adopt a policy of market segmentation or aggregation—whether to build generalized or ambiguous appeals into a product so that consumers can perceive it as they choose, or whether to concentrate on a specific segment, thus deliberately excluding a given proportion of consumers. Will 80 percent of a small market segment produce more revenue than 10 percent of a mass market?" The thrust of his book—and other writing of the era—was a resounding "yes."[13] Note that although Robertson still entertained a mass market option in 1970, he acknowledged sufficient variation in consumer preferences to urge mass marketers to fashion "generalized or ambiguous appeals."

By the 1970s, with the success of historic campaigns such as Pepsi-Cola's "Pepsi Generation" challenge to mass-marketed Coca-Cola, market segmentation had become the indisputable rule in marketing and was well on its way to achieving ever greater dominance and sophistication. A survey of medium-size and larger Fortune 500 firms in the mid-1960s concluded that already by then most manufacturers were incorporating the market segmentation concept into product development and sales. The family-owned cosmetic company of Estée Lauder, for example, began segmenting in 1965 by adding to its core products a new male line of Aramis toiletries, soon followed by Clinique for young women, Prescriptives for older, wealthier, more professional women, Origins for men and women interested in natural, environmentally responsible products, and, finally in 1991, Prescriptives All Skins for darker-toned, minority women. Likewise, department stores and the shopping centers they anchored increasingly shifted their marketing strategy during the 1960s and 1970s away from selling to the "middle of the middle" toward catering to

In this friendly, freedom-loving land of ours... Beer Belongs—Enjoy It!

BEER and ALE—AMERICA'S BEVERAGES OF MODERATION
Sponsored by the United States Brewers Foundation ... Classified 1684

You only go around once in life.
So grab for all the gusto you can.
Even in the beer you drink.
Why settle for less?
When you're out of Schlitz,
you're out of beer.

Market segmentation in beer was part of a larger transformation of the beer industry in the post-war period. Beginning in the 1940s, a few large brewers selling packaged beer prevailed in a national market that previously had been dominated by local and regional brands mostly distributed on draft through neighborhood taverns. In 1946 the seven leading beers controlled just 20 percent of the market; by 1970 the ten largest controlled 70 percent. While the industry underwent concentration, its fewer, bigger brewers embraced market segmentation, gearing their numerous beer brands to different consumer segments. In 1954, before market segmentation, the United States Brewers' Foundation sought a mass market with an image of men and women, of all ages, drinking beer (left; *Look*, August 24, 1954). But soon, Pabst was selling Schlitz to rugged outdoorsmen (right; *Look*, February 10, 1970), while Anheuser-Busch was asking readers of *Ebony*, "When Do You Say Bud? After the work is done or right in the middle of the fun," in an ad featuring a black construction worker drinking Budweiser while relaxing in a local bar and playing basketball with his buddies (November 1977). Later, Coors promoted Coors Light to female readers of *Ms.* magazine with the message "You don't have to be a man to appreciate a great beer" (September 1987). (Courtesy of the Beer Institute and Pabst Brewing Company)

segments defined by age, affluence, and lifestyle, in the process drawing sharper distinctions between themselves and their competitors. Retailers were finally heeding advice offered by a farsighted Martineau back in 1957, the same year that he wrote his classic article on social-class segmentation, that retailers must develop more store "personality," or "image," to fill a particular "niche in the marketplace," not try "to be all things to all people." *Business Week*, in taking stock of product marketing at the start of the seventies, concluded that the "breakout of consumers by age group, income, education, geography, ethnic background and use patterns" through "selective selling or market segmentation" had accelerated to such a degree that the "the terms 'mass market' and 'mass media' have almost become misnomers."[14]

The move from mass to segmented markets promised greater, steadier profits through expanding the pool of potential consumers: a wider variety of products, each tailored to a specialized population, would create more buyers in total and less cutthroat competition to win them. The shift from mass to segment had consequences, moreover, not just for merchandising but also for the political culture of postwar America more broadly, as its influence spread. How, then, did marketers and advertisers come to shift ground so decisively between 1945 and 1970? And what brought about this reconceptualizing of mass markets as discrete communities of consumers with distinctive needs, wants, and product preferences?[15]

ORIGINS OF THE SHIFT FROM MASS TO SEGMENT

a variety of forces converged to move profit-seeking marketers away from assuming a unified mass market. Fears of declining consumer demand alone would not necessarily have led to an embrace of market segmentation, no matter how persuasive a Smith or Martineau, had not other developments been under way. Probably most significant was the postwar explosion of market researchers' interest in consumer motivation, prevalent enough to attract scathing condemnation for its manipulative dangers from social critic Vance Packard in his best-seller of 1957, *The Hidden Persuaders*.[16] As researchers like George Katona of the Survey Research Center at the University of Michigan, Ernest Dichter, founder of the Institute of Motivational Research, and Herta Herzog of New York's Tinker Group shifted the focus from "who" and "what" to "why" people bought, they opened the door to the possibility of greater diversity in consumers' behavior and attitudes.[17] Their research, consisting of depth interviews, Rorschach inkblot tests, thematic apperception tests, and other techniques borrowed from psychology and psychoanalysis, focused on how an individual's psyche shaped the decision to buy: how a home freezer could appeal to an emotionally insecure consumer by providing the abundance of food often associated with a mother's love or how a shiny new and more powerful car could reassure a man of his masculinity. The overall impact of this work was to make it harder to sustain the fiction of a unified mass market.[18] If individuals brought unique psychological motivations to the marketplace, wasn't it likely that they set different priorities in consuming as well? Market segmentation provided a way of classifying those priorities.

By the 1970s continued interest in the psychological dimension of consuming would lead to the emergence of "psychographics," a term coined to mean the combining of demographic and psychological factors to define market segments. Increasingly, lifestyles, behavioral traits, and buyer attitudes earned a place in consumer profiles alongside age, income, education, race, ethnicity, religion, and other demographic data. In a famous early article, Daniel Yankelovich divided wristwatch and automobile customers into three attitudinal groups: those who bought the product for the lowest possible cost; those who bought for product quality, styling, and durability; and those who bought for prestige and out of other emotional needs.[19] "Psychographics" would become so sophisticated that by 1985 the chief executive of Spiegel Company would boast that armed to the teeth with information, the marketer became "the friend who knows them [consumers] as well as—perhaps better than—they know themselves," paving the way for many of today's most aggressive marketing trends: "target marketing"—often singling out children and minorities for pointed appeals; "life-style branding"—selling products by attracting consumers to a particular way of life rather than the good itself; and categorizing consumers with statistical precision (such as in sixty-two distinctive "clusters" of buyers, given labels like "Blue Blood Estates," "Shotguns and Pickups," and "Hispanic Mix Residents") for direct marketing, telemarketing, and Internet shopping solicitation.[20] Rather than aim to sell commodities in as much volume as possible to the mass, modern-day marketers, equipped with advanced psychographic tactics, identify clusters of customers with distinctive ways of life and then set out to sell them idealized lifestyles constructed around commodities.

As marketing advanced in the postwar era, links extended to social science disciplines other than psychology, helping further to conceptualize buyers as heterogeneous. When the *Journal of Marketing* began publishing in 1936 and the American Marketing Association (AMA) was founded six months later, both committed themselves to what the journal billed as "the advancement of science in marketing." Increasingly, scholars rather than marketing executives defined and refined the field through the pages of the journal, and symbolically the directorship of the AMA passed from the president of Stop & Shop Supermarkets to an academic economist from the University of California on the eve of the market segmentation revolution. The budding scholarly field of sociology in particular became the provider of a major body of research and a steady supplier of researchers. Over the course of the 1950s and 1960s, sociological categories of analysis—"social class" and "status hierarchies," "reference groups" and "subcultures," "opinion formation," "pressure groups," and "cognitive dissonance"—entered the world of marketing, much

*"According to my Zip Code, I prefer non-spicy foods, enjoy tennis more
than golf, subscribe to at least one news-oriented periodical, own between thirty and
thirty-five ties, never buy lemon-scented products, and have a power tool
in my basement, but none of that is true."*

In 1966 an article in the *Journal of Marketing* quoted an executive of a major advertising industry as saying, "The isolation of particular target segments is standard operating procedure here. It has become practically impossible to enter the national market on a broad, undifferentiated basis with any real hope of success." Thirty years later the science of segmenting had become so elaborate that it was ripe for spoofing. *The New Yorker,* September 6, 1993. (Courtesy of © The New Yorker Collection 1993 Roz Chast from cartoonbank.com. All rights reserved.)

---

of it theory aimed at explaining social differentiation. Sociologists soon made the same transition from academia to marketing, beginning with Paul Lazarsfeld of Columbia and continuing with Pierre Martineau and Lee Rainwater, who both trained at the University of Chicago under W. Lloyd Warner, author of the classic *Social Class in America* (1948). The *Chicago Tribune*'s Martineau, in fact, provided an important link between motivational research and social-class categorization in marketing, supporting with the *Tribune's* substantial research budget studies that probed the distinctive mind-sets of different social classes.[21] As time went on, scientific and technical advances in survey research, increasingly achieved through the use of computers, gave marketers new quantitative capabilities "to improve the match between product and segment," in the words of University of Chicago Business School professor William Wells.[22]

The growing influence of social science on marketing prepared the way for market segmentation and, in turn, gave practitioners more precise tools for identifying and catering to segments of consumers. A 1966 volume, *Consumer Behavior and the Behavioral Sciences,* edited by Steuart Henderson Britt, psychologist and professor of marketing at Northwestern University and editor of the *Journal of Marketing,* epitomized the marriage of social science and selling. Organized through a two-part structure of, first, presentation of relevant concepts from psychology, sociology, and anthropology, followed by articles documenting their application to marketing, this book drew attention to segments of class, race, ethnicity, religion, and age, making clear the extent to which market segmentation was the offspring of this marriage.[23]

The technical sophistication that market researchers and scholars pioneered together reinforced another factor contributing to segmentation's rise: the desire of advertisers and marketers to raise the profile and profitability of their own profession. Advertising expenditures tripled between World War II and 1959, when they reached $11 billion, up $3 billion from 1955 alone, raising the visibility of the profession along with its earnings. Among the many factors contributing to that growth were big postwar sales for heavily advertised products like automobiles, the arrival of television as a new advertising medium, and expansion among advertising agencies, whether newly merged mega-firms on Madison Avenue or suburban upstarts capitalizing on the postwar boom in suburbia.[24] Denouncing the misplaced priorities of "the affluent society" in his book of that name in 1958, economist John Kenneth Galbraith lambasted the "institutions of modern advertising and salesmanship" for "creat[ing] desires—to bring into being wants that previously did not exist," but he nonetheless recognized how integral the growth of the advertising industry was to the whole postwar project of increasing private production and consumption to achieve national prosperity.[25]

By embracing segmented markets, advertisers and market researchers made themselves even more indispensable, as manufacturers and retailers required more sophisticated guidance to sell to a splintered purchasing public than to an undifferentiated one. New developments in retailing also helped the advertising profession use market segmentation to build influence. When retail stores revolutionized selling by adopting more self-service to save labor costs, it meant, according to Wendell Smith, "providing less and less sales push at point of sale." The resulting "premium placed by retailers upon products that are presold by their producers and are readily recognized by consumers" meant a windfall for advertisers hired to promote products directly to distinct market segments.[26]

The emergence of television as a beckoning new frontier for advertising also helped foster a climate receptive to market segmentation. As early as 1953, two-thirds of American households owned televisions; by the mid-1960s, 94 percent had at least one, and many had more. Given that the average American watched TV five hours a day, viewers could hardly have been more captive to the "selling machine in every living room," as it was called in an NBC instructional film coaching advertisers on how to sell through television.[27] By the end of the 1950s, that confidence made TV the source of more than half of all revenues at most big advertising firms, where total earnings mushroomed with television. Selling commodities was critical to the new technology's viability, more important to broadcasters and advertisers than the entertainment itself.[28]

While network television was, of course, a mass medium aimed at a mass market, its need to sell bred almost from the start a receptivity to "narrowcasting," or targeting programs at demographically specific audiences.[29] Once the very early years of limited programming had passed, advertisers and broadcasters lost no time conceiving of future profitability in terms of market segmentation, even before Wendell Smith gave it that name. This was necessary if television was to expand beyond evening prime time, as the rest of the day and week was most profitably programmed with distinctive audiences in mind: children in the early mornings and on weekends, homemakers during the day, teenagers in the late afternoons, various adult audiences in the evenings, families on Sunday nights. Commercials could then be appropriately pitched to relevant viewers. Already by the mid-1950s, television marketing studies by firms like Daniel Starch and Staff were probing the distinctive viewing and purchasing patterns of daytime and evening audiences, men and women, and specific age groups, such as "children 10 to 17." Networks undertook their own research, too, with such studies as NBC's "Children's Television Survey" of 1955 and "Daytime Rendezvous . . . with the Women Who Buy" of 1959. Both identified profitable market segments and the "selling power" of the shows they watched by documenting greater recognition and usage of a sponsor's products by viewers than non-viewers.[30]

Market segmentation got a further boost when the struggle between the networks and advertising agencies over who would actually produce televi-

These children planted in front of the television in December 1954 might have been watching early-morning cartoons or late-afternoon kiddie shows, but the allocation of broadcast time just for them—as well as for other specialized audiences—testified to the importance of narrowcasting almost from TV's start, which only intensified with the arrival of cable in the 1970s. (Courtesy of the Minnesota Historical Society)

sion programs was resolved in favor of broadcasters. At first, in a carryover from radio, advertising agencies and their clients rather than the networks themselves controlled production of TV programs as well as commercials, and shows were often broadcast under the name of the sponsor, such as *Texaco Star Theater, Colgate Comedy Hour,* and *Goodyear TV Playhouse.* In many early programs, furthermore, advertisements were not very subtly woven into scripts, as when some member of the Nelson family drank milk on every episode of *Ozzie and Harriet* to promote its sponsor, the American Dairy Association, or when children in the "peanut gallery" on the *Howdy Doody Show* sang along with the commercials for Welch's grape juice, Wonder Bread, and Royal Pudding. Gradually, networks assumed control over program creation and sold time to "participating sponsors" who shared the cost of a show that the network produced; by 1958 networks controlled over 75 percent of all programming, and shows normally had multiple sponsors. Breaking the link between sponsors and their own shows, which companies had often funded to promote a corporate image through the "gratitude factor" rather than to sell particular products, served to free more advertising dollars for targeting specialized consumers at different times on different stations and gave networks more control over the broadcasting day and week. New rating systems based on viewership set a price for each program's advertising independent of the cost of production, ensuring that the most popular shows earned the networks the highest profits (and discouraging creative innovation in programming out of fear of jeopardizing the now all-important ratings). More now than ever, daytime soap operas and game shows were sponsored by makers of detergents and floor cleaners, children's programs by manufacturers of kids' food and toy products, and weekend sports by shaving companies. Automobile makers focused on evening adult shows, coordinating annual model changes with the start of the fall television season and provisioning network shows with the latest cars. Over time, broadcasters became more and more proficient at fine-tuning their programming to appeal to profitable market segments and then attracting advertisers to well-defined sponsorship niches.[31]

Networks gained control of program production and began selling commercial time to sponsors just when market segmentation was taking off in advertising more broadly. Through intensifying the segmentation of the television market, broadcasters helped sponsors diversify their investment in television—by inviting, for example, targeted "spot" commercials—with the goal of selling more products and thus making larger profits for the networks. By 1961, one marketing executive was convinced, "The postwar onset of television has furnished a most convenient springboard for market segmentation as a strategy to be more widely and systematically applied," because "Spot TV is a powerful, well-adapted medium for promoting new products in selective markets."[32] Five years later a survey of media directors at advertising agencies by *Media/Scope* magazine concluded that a majority of marketing plans for consumer products were now built around "target audiences . . . tailor-made for each product." Combining demographics, product-use patterns, psychological analyses, and other increasingly refined markers of segments, media planners crafted sponsorship campaigns along the lines spelled out by one media director: "For toys and games we go right to children audiences. For a household product to women. For a fragrance to a high per cent of men. In fact, within the toy and game category, we even have breaks according to the age of children."[33]

The arrival of cable television in metropolitan markets in the 1970s with its expanded range of viewer options only exacerbated the carving up of television programming and audiences into market niches, and moved segmentation to a whole new level. Cable had existed since the 1940s as Community Antenna Television serving out-of-the-way communities, but it did not become a viable commercial venture until three decades later. The original conception of cable was that it be funded by subscription and not commercials, but the attractiveness of self-selecting, finely tuned cable audiences to advertisers hungry to sell to market segments finally became irresistible. From total advertising revenues of $58 million in 1980, cable jumped seventeenfold to $993 million by 1986, and another twenty-onefold to $21.1 billion by 1989, catapulting cable's share of all cable and broadcast advertising dollars to 42 percent. Although still below broadcast advertising revenues, cable's profits continued their rise, built around a marketing strategy that sold cable based on its highly differentiated audiences.[34]

Cable's success, so tightly linked to market segmentation and its close descendant, psychographics, put intense pressure on the networks, whose longstanding commitment to segmenting was still no match for cable. Every year since the late 1970s, the networks watched in alarm as their audience share declined. By the fall of 1998 high hopes for stemming the tide once again fizzled with another 9 percent decline from their 37 percent total audience share of the previous season. Prime-time network audiences, while not as drastically reduced, were still plummeting—from 91 percent of all viewers in 1977–78 to 62 percent by 1996–97 and then down again, a loss of a third over two decades.

Media analysts blamed the climate of extreme market segmentation for much of the networks' decline. Not only had the total television audience become excessively segmented, with cable channels siphoning off entire cohorts such as blue-collar male wrestling enthusiasts or young fans of rock videos, but the obsession of mainstream advertisers, and hence the networks, with targeting affluent, urban younger adults with programs featuring clones of themselves had misfired: "The young, upscale viewer doesn't watch enough television to build a seven-night-a-week schedule around them," grumbled one observer. By the end of the century, marketers' sophisticated knowledge of buyers, combined with the determination of cable and network television to target the most profitable—and profligate—audiences, had created a highly fragmented television world where networks, saddled with big production costs and a structure less conducive to narrowly defined niches than cable, found themselves dangerously squeezed. As media commentator Steven Stark has aptly put it, just the way Ed Sullivan's once enormously popular Sunday night "Really Big Show" (a.k.a. "Rilly Big Shew")—where the juggler performed before the rock star and the borscht-belt comedian after the concert violist—became unimaginable, so increasingly "Really Big Networks" serving multiple audiences were a creature of the past. *Washington Post* television critic Tom Shales put a similar spin on the shift from network to cable niche:

"We're splintered. We're not as much 'we' as the 'we' we were. We're divisible."[35] The television program that once gathered all members of the family along with neighbors and friends around the living-room set rarely exists anymore, although it must be said that even in the 1950s, the overwhelmingly white, middle-class, and suburban orientation of television programming meant that many Americans watched characters unlike themselves. Today, household members are more likely to view their own shows on their own TVs, in the privacy of their own rooms, linked more to market clusters defined by their age, race, class, gender, and lifestyle than to each other.

Finally, none of these pulls toward market segmentation—from motivational and social science research to advertiser's professional ambitions to the rise of television—would have been imaginable in the late 1950s and doable in the 1960s and 1970s had not the industrial production process become more flexible, making it possible to respond with smaller product runs to diverse consumer demand. Mass production had developed based on the principle of lowering production costs by producing standardized products in large bulk for sale to a broad range of customers. But by the mid-1950s the mass market had become larger than necessary to achieve economies of scale, while new production technology and methods of handling information had made diversity of product offerings technically possible and economically profitable.[36] Wendell Smith understood that market segmentation depended on production innovation. In his 1956 treatise he attributed its potential for success to a "decrease in the size of the minimum efficient producing or manufacturing unit required," providing "release from some of the rigidities imposed by earlier approaches to mass production . . . [such as] the necessity for long production runs of identical items."[37] In time, more and more manufacturers, faced with crushing mass market competition and armed with new technological capabilities, would embrace small batch production as their salvation.

Ironically, despite concern among cultural critics of the fifties that the standardization inherent in mass consumption was breeding social conformity and homogeneity, the Madison Avenue that they reviled was moving by the end of the decade in the opposite direction: toward acknowledging, even reifying, social differences through an embrace of market segmentation. While Vance Packard was caricaturing "Mrs. Middle Majority," David Riesman proclaiming the peer orientation of growing numbers of "other-directed" metropolitan Americans, and C. Wright Mills, Sloan Wilson, and William H. Whyte calculating the hidden costs of entrapment in bland corporate jobs and predictable suburbs for many a "White Collar," "Man in the Gray Flannel Suit," and "Organization Man" and their families, advertisers were in fact shifting strategy.[38] Rather than seeking to appeal to what they once assumed was a homogeneous mass market, they were segmenting markets into communities of consumers with distinctive traits and psychologies, in the process shifting their attention from product to user. Identifying and catering to diversity among purchasers became the watchword of many highly visible marketing campaigns by the late 1950s.

The transition from the paradigm of the mass market to the paradigm of the market segment emerged in *Life* magazine's ambitious study of consumer expenditures published between 1957 and 1960, right on the cusp of the market segmentation revolution. *Life* undertook a massive investigation of the buying behavior of 10,000 households as part of its strategy to retain profitability, the challenge facing most mass market–oriented sellers by the mid-1950s. With its circulation pushing 6 million, further spectacular growth in readership seemed unlikely. Instead, executives decided to survey their readers with an eye to increasing the profits of *Life*'s advertisers, in hopes that their higher earnings would yield greater willingness to advertise—and at higher rates. In summarizing this monumental seven-volume report for its own readers, *Business Week* noticed some surprising, even contradictory trends that signaled the sea change about to take place. On the one hand, consistent with the ideology of mass marketing prevailing at the time, "*Life* stressed hard the homogeneity of the U.S. market," noting little divergence across income groups in the proportion of income spent on different categories. At the same time, *Business Week* observed, the report contained "some intriguing statistics on variations within the market," associated with such factors as a family's stage in the life cycle, suburban residence, education, occupation, and gender.

What *Business Week* found intriguing, *Life* hoped would be revolutionizing. As its manager of market research, himself a Columbia-trained economist, pronounced to the profession through the *Journal of Marketing* early in 1958, "What this study provides, in essence, is the basis for determining the relationship and importance of different household characteristics (income, age, education, etc.) in the demand for various goods and services." Without invoking "market segmentation" by name, *Life*'s executives had come to recognize that future profits—for their advertisers and hence for themselves—depended on identifying market difference rather than assuming market uniformity.[39] Of course, this was not the end of mass marketing altogether; even segmenters still lumped people together into common markets. But increasingly the consumer marketplace differentiated Americans from each other on the basis of class, gender, age, race, personality, and lifestyle, rather than trying to encompass everyone in one cohesive mass market. Much the way suburban residential communities and shopping centers, originally conceived to be widely accessible new postwar spaces, became increasingly stratified by class and race as they targeted distinct populations, so too as the postwar era progressed did the mass market itself fracture into numerous constituent parts.

The shifting orientation within the marketing and advertising professions from mass to segment may have given the impression that the emergence of market segmentation was solely a top-down process, with all initiative coming from Madison Avenue and the corporate headquarters of its clients. But this was far from the case. Rather, it was a much more interactive process, with potential consumers exerting decisive influences on the marketing field, helping to convince marketers that groups with increasingly independent identities offered new opportunities for cultivation as segments. An obvious case was the "happy-go-spending" new suburbanites, but populations much less explicitly market-oriented became prime candidates for segmentation as well. It was no accident that the rise of market segmentation corresponded to the historical era of the 1960s and 1970s, when social and cultural groups such as African Americans, women, youth, and senior citizens began to assert themselves in a way that came to be called "identity politics," where people's affiliation with a particular community defined their cultural consciousness and motivated their collective political action. Marketers who, had they not been in search of ways to avoid saturating the mass market, might have despaired at the splintering of the mass in the 1960s, soon seized the new opportunities for selling it offered. When Wendell Smith elaborated his notion of market segmentation in the late 1950s, he spoke of "segments-within-segments, some quite sizeable, others smaller but still all potentially profitable—all waiting to be located, identified and sold," suggesting even then his awareness that segments existed in society prior to being "discovered" by marketers.[40]

By the late 1960s advertisers and marketers had fully absorbed the message. Russell Haley, vice president and corporate research director for D'Arcy Advertising in New York, argued that the only issue for debate was "which of the virtually limitless alternatives is likely to be the most productive" as "the idea that all markets can be profitably segmented has now received almost as widespread acceptance as the marketing concept itself," and concluded that the first rule of thumb should be "it is easier to take advantage of market segments that already exist than to attempt to create new ones." The next year, Prentice-Hall's best-selling marketing text went so far as to list subcultures that held out "the promise of becoming an important market segment."[41] From identification, it was only a short step to intensive market surveying of subcultures, with members sometimes serving as consultants to segmented marketing campaigns, as when the Liggett Group impaneled a group of young men and women to try to get a better fix on the youth market for cigarettes.[42]

What it meant for members of subcultures to be subjected to appeals from mainstream marketers is complicated. In some ways, their attractiveness as markets granted them legitimacy, even authority, as when the youth panel cockily told Liggett's executives to "show [us] your ideas and [we]'ll appraise them." Segmenting the mass market thus helped democratize it, allowing subcultures to shape markets around their own priorities. For example, Tom Wolfe brilliantly tracked how Detroit automakers in the early 1960s had discovered a youth culture of California car customizers and southern stock car racers and then lost little time delivering their translucent paint colors and super speeds to "a whole generation as . . . yours." On the other hand, when the marketplace geared itself to the unique cultures of segments, groups like these "custom car kids" who often had defined themselves in reaction to the mainstream were now drawn further into the commercial market, and could at times be co-opted by it, even when they brought their own meanings to the exchange. After all, when marketers recognized—and catered to—diversity in the cultural values of consumers, or unconventional consumers provided their own subversive readings of the advertising message, existing power relations were rarely altered. Most fundamentally, ownership usually remained concentrated in large corporate merchandisers. A "customized" car from General Motors, the healthy natural foods "boutique" line of General Foods, or Miller Brewing Company's hip "Red Dog" micro-brew label still rang up profits for Fortune 500 firms. Likewise, blue jeans inevitably lost much of their power as a personalized symbol of youthful rebellion when department stores began selling them preshrunk, bleached, and torn.

In sum, by the late 1960s and early 1970s the conjunction of marketers seeking alternatives to mass marketing and consumers asserting their independence from what they perceived to be mainstream American culture bred an explosion of market segmentation. What resulted was a new commercial culture that reified—at times even exaggerated—social difference in the pursuit of profits, often reincorporating disaffected groups into the commercial marketplace.[43]

THE ELABORATION OF MARKET SEGMENTS

Marketers' conception of a mass market had encouraged them through the 1950s to emphasize what united American consumers. Their embrace of market segmentation thereafter lent marketplace recognition to social and cultural divisions among Americans, making "countercultures" and "identity politics" more complex joint products of grassroots mobilization and marketers' ambitions than is often acknowledged. Indeed, as mass markets increasingly splintered, individuals gained more opportunity to express their separate identities through their choices as consumers.[44] Key market segmentations—by class, gender, age, race, and ethnicity—suggest the give-and-take process between marketers and potential segments that accentuated differences among and within social groups.

The oldest form of market division, predating the era of market segmentation, was by some version of social class. In the days of mass marketing, differentiation—to the extent it existed—usually meant dividing consumers by income groups, with variation in consumption patterns more often explained by what a person could afford than by what he or she preferred. In economist Thorstein Veblen's influential conceptualization at the turn of the twentieth century, what most divided the "leisure class" from lower classes "on a scanty subsistence" was "conspicuous consumption." When those below the leisure class managed to consume, Veblen assumed their tastes had "trickled down" from above.[45] Standard-of-living surveys of the early twentieth century continued to link significant consumer choice with disposable income, the amount of that income understood to dictate expenditures beyond necessities.[46] Accordingly, in the heyday of mass marketing from the 1920s through the 1950s, it was thought that success depended on maximizing the middle-class market to reach the growing number of Americans with enough discretionary income to support the mass production and distribution of goods.[47]

With the shift to market segmentation and particularly the rise of psychographics by the 1960s, marketers turned class differentiation from an income to a lifestyle distinction. Interest now grew in defining a much more complicated constellation of values and preferences to distinguish one class's consumption choices from another's. *Chicago Tribune* marketing research czar Pierre Martineau described the challenge in 1957 as uncovering "the sharp differences in attitudes and motive forces, in codes, even in communication abilities between social classes." He went on: "While America is a political democracy and while theoretically all men are equal in the eyes of the law, yet realistically we observe a very definite social-class order. The friends we choose, the neighborhoods we live in, the way we spend and save our money, the educational plans we have for our children are determined in large degree along social-class lines." He concluded that "social class is a major factor shaping the individual's style of life." Three families with the same $8000 a year income but from different social classes, another theorist of class segmentation explained a few years later, would spend their money in radically different ways.[48] As lifestyle usurped the more traditional class markers of income, and even education and occupation, what consumers bought—a Cadillac over a Chevrolet, a ranch house instead of a Cape Cod, *The New Yorker* over *True Story* magazine—became indicators of their class identity. Consumer choices, moreover, reconfirmed individuals' membership in a class community; a marketing study of early owners of color television sets referred to them as "Colortown," suggesting simply by its title that a purchase bonded this "luxury market" together.[49]

With the steady rise in Americans' standard of living during the 1950s and 1960s, marketers paid particular attention to the working class. Here was a hugely profitable market whose maximization required a thorough understanding of working people's distinctive tastes and desires. As Martineau asserted in 1957, "the evidence of the blue-collar worker's buying ability is overwhelmingly apparent," making him "not only the center of political power but a center of purchasing power." Martineau cited a three-year study of the class structure of metropolitan Chicago carried out under the supervision of famed University of Chicago sociologist Lloyd Warner, dividing the area into five class categories and pointing out that the last two—considered the working classes—included almost two-thirds of this typical metropolitan area's population: Upper Class (.9 percent), Upper Middle Class (7.2 percent), Lower Middle Class (28.4 percent), Upper Lower Class (44 percent), and Lower Lower Class (19.5 percent).[50]

But sophisticated marketers knew that targeting the burgeoning blue-collar market meant taking more than income into account. Manufacturers and sellers of goods ranging from furniture to clothing to magazines hired marketing researchers to help them figure out what working people wanted. Social Research, Inc. (SRI), established in 1946 with backing by Sears, Roebuck by social anthropologist Burleigh Gardner, a former business professor at the University of Chicago who had worked closely with Warner, undertook many comprehensive studies of working-class taste, the most well known being Workingman's Wife: Her Personality, World and Life Style (1959). Macfadden, publisher of True Story and three similar "Family Behavior Group" (FBG) magazines, commissioned a number of these studies in the late 1950s and early 1960s to help advertisers successfully sell appliances, clothing, furniture, and other products to the FBG's primarily working-class readership. Sprinkled with the new vocabulary of class segmentation—"taste cultures," "blue collar aesthetic," "habit lags"—these studies document SRI's learning and then teaching other merchandisers how "to talk most effectively to the members of the blue-collar class."[51] Rather than share the earlier assumption of mass marketers that prosperity would draw workers into some homogeneous middle-class market, market segmenters at SRI over and over again asserted quite the opposite:

> More money to spend does not necessarily make a working class person middle class; both groups may buy many of the same things, but often for different reasons; there are important differences between them as people.

Working class people want to enjoy in their own way the boun-
tiful American Life that has become increasingly available.

Let us emphasize again here that the traditional working class
life has not only *not* disappeared but that it continues to have
recruits from the younger generations, some of whom live in
new houses in suburbs.[52]

By the 1980s, as income inequality in America grew and working-class
people had less money to spend, marketers and manufacturers shifted their
prime target to upper-class consumers with more disposable cash. Wealthy
segments became the new market frontier. As the president of USA cable
bragged to potential advertisers in 1983, the competing networks not only suffered from declining numbers of viewers, but they were also stuck with the
wrong kind: "Cable TV is attracting the upscale suburban viewer." Within
that upscale market, many marketers made subtle differentiations—such as
dual paycheck, inherited wealth, sophisticated, retired—each characterized by
a unique lifestyle. For example, one of the best-known market segments—
Yuppies ("young, urban professionals," and their black counterpart, Bup-
pies)—represented a complex interweaving of age, urban residence, and class.
Here, too, marketers defined the Yuppie not only through psychographic
analysis, but also by what he or she bought. The consumer purchase became
both the objective of and the evidence for social-class segmentation.[53]

How much was the emergence of social-class segments an interactive
process, where the distinctive values and behavior of class subcultures attracted
the attention of marketers? Class in some form had already mattered to marketers earlier in the century, but their continued attentiveness to class segmentation lends support to arguments that although the rhetoric of the
Consumers' Republic was broadly inclusionary, people's lives continued to
show enough class difference over the postwar era to convince marketers that
it was profitable to segment by social class. In particular, the realities of working-class life—limitations in the upward boost from the GI Bill and the mass
income tax; economic insecurities resulting from frequent layoffs and inflationary pressures; suburban residential and commercial development that
reinforced rather than broke down class boundaries; the continued politicization of the workplace, even in eras of no-strike union contracts or declining
unionization; and distinctive purchasing patterns—sustained class barriers.

Marketers like SRI and clients like Macfadden understood this differentiated class landscape, both spatial and structural, and rested their market
segmentation strategy upon it. In so doing, however, they contributed to fram-

ing social class in the postwar period increasingly as a set of lifestyle preferences rather than an economic and power relationship, a reorientation encapsulated in an influential marketing essay of 1974 entitled "Life Style: The
Essence of Social Class." The era of market segmentation helped make smoking a Camel, listening to country music, or driving a pickup as much a badge
of working-class identity as a union membership card. Likewise, upper-class
identity became more than ever a status one could buy—through acquiring a
certain kind of home, car, exotic vacation, and other accouterments widely
popularized by the 1980s as "the lifestyle of the rich and famous." One marketer predicted in the mid-1960s that with "New" money having climbed
within the last generation to the top of the financial structure, integration with
"Old" money would be only a matter of time because its children increasingly
were sharing the same lifestyles as the old elite.[54]

When marketers began segmenting by gender, they were categorizing
consumers in a way that was even more pervasive in the development of
marketing science than was the case with social class, because marketers had
envisioned the consumer as female since the early days of mass marketing at
the beginning of the twentieth century. As an ad in *Printers' Ink* succinctly
expressed it in 1929, "The proper study of mankind is *man* . . . but the proper
study of markets is *woman*." In the 1920s and 1930s women were conceptualized by ad agencies as "purchasing agents" for their families—an extension of
their newfound status as household experts—assumed to be responsible for
about 85 percent of total consumer spending. World War II only reinforced
the authority of female consumers on the home front.[55]

But with the rise of the Consumers' Republic after the Second World
War, attention shifted to the consuming household or family unit as men
gained more influence over consumption, accompanying their wives more frequently on shopping expeditions and exerting new control with the expansion
of credit. Consequently, marketers no longer assumed a dichotomy between
male producer and female consumer. In the heyday of mass marketing during
the late 1940s and 1950s, the average household was conceived as presided
over by a male "head of spending unit" or a "husband-wife dyad" with respective areas of expertise—not a sole female purchasing agent. A survey of ads
featuring women as primary buyers in the trade journals *Advertising and Selling* and *Printers' Ink* documented a decline by half in female-oriented appeals
between 1946 and the mid-1950s. That calculation was no accident. As early as
1947, trade journals began instructing merchants about "Appealing to Men
Customers" now that men were "becoming an increasingly important factor in
that traditional 'No Man's Land,' the American market place. Whereas in former times the majority of the family buying was done by women, today mer-

chants the Nation over are recognizing a trend on the part of the so-called stronger sex to do an additional share of the purchasing." Businessmen who in the past had concentrated on selling to female customers "will now have to devote some energy to appealing to the male sex if they would realize maximum sales." Some merchandisers viewed the married couple as an increasingly important purchasing unit. In *The Feminine Mystique*, Betty Friedan cited a typical postwar marketing survey that described marriage as "more consciously and more clear-headedly than in the past ... a partnership in establishing a comfortable home, equipped with a great number of desirable products." Young couples were found to center their conversations and dreams "around their future homes and their furnishings." Other advertisers emphasized the newfound market significance of the purchasing family, a concept *McCall's* magazine termed "togetherness." One *McCall's* ad seeking potential advertisers for the magazine pictured a backside view of a nuclear family in dungarees with the jingle: "This togetherness applies, to what the family wants or buys. Before they realize a dream, They huddle—like a football team."[56]

When market segmenters revolutionized advertising after the late 1950s, however, they initiated yet another shift: men and women increasingly became viewed as separate, profitable market segments with distinctive desires and responsibilities, no longer a single family market. Market segmenters distinguished between both the buying behavior of male and female shoppers and the objects they chose to consume. Behavioral differences between the sexes had origins, they argued, that extended beyond the social and cultural to the psychological and even physiological. In 1958, for example, Janet Wolff claimed in *What Makes Women Buy: A Guide to Understanding and Influencing the New Woman of Today* that women were marked as shoppers by their biology—reproductive systems and sexual characteristics, size and muscular power, proportions and acute senses—mediated by distinctive personality traits like intuition, compassion, loyalty, and irrationality. Hence, according to another researcher, it was women's strong visceral, sometimes to the point of physical response to the "fresh, creamy surface of a newly opened shortening can" that inspired motivational researcher Ernest Dichter to redesign the label for Snowdrift shortening.[57]

While marketers subjected female consumers to this kind of psychological analysis, often aimed at their insecurities, they credited men as a market segment with authority and financial resources but spared them the same mental probing. In fact, the authors of a 1972 text on market segmentation noted that "male buyers have been to a large extent a neglected-market segment." "Despite the tremendous sums of money controlled, spent, and influenced by this segment on the purchase of products both for their own use and for their families, little is known about the specific characteristics of male buyers." Although periodic articles like "There's a Male in Your Market" reminded advertisers of the importance of understanding the male shopper, it was only in the 1980s that men came in for anything like the scrutiny applied to women shoppers. But then the dissection began in earnest. In one instance, the growing number of men aged twenty-one to fifty-five living without female partners were classified as "pup tenters" versus "settlers," while in another, married men were divided between "progressives"—comfortable with changing male and female roles—and not.[58]

Products too were increasingly categorized by who had primary responsibility for their purchase, with advertising campaigns appropriately designed to sell automobiles, life insurance, or filter cigarettes with a new "man-sized flavor" to men, and furniture, cosmetics, or laundry detergent to women. In 1959, NBC market segmenters had delighted at the "womanpower" demonstrated when its daytime television viewers favored sponsors' products over others. By the turn of the twenty-first century, the market strength of "womanpower" made possible several cable networks aimed solely at women, complemented by dozens of websites, all backed by big corporate money such as America Online and the French luxury goods manufacturer LVMH. Although "manpower" had reigned through most of the postwar era, marketing pitches built on a more complex understanding of men's distinctive tastes and priorities took longer to appear.[59]

Gender segmentation provides a good example of how segmenting the market not only differentiated the basic categories of female and male, but also subdivided them into smaller fragments. The most common partition was by class. When marketers segmented by social class, women were often singled out for epitomizing the values of a particular class segment. For Martineau, women provided the purest evidence for a class's consumer profile; he claimed that while the average man has opportunities "to brush shoulders with people up and down the social scale, a woman is much more sheltered classwise." Hence, the justification for a study like SRI's *Workingman's Wife*. One marketing text of the 1970s, drawing on research by SRI and other investigators, developed class-oriented marketing strategy based on judgments about wives, such as "upper-middle-class women's elegant taste in clothing," "lower-middle-class women's conscientious home-orientation," and "upper-lower-class women's dissatisfaction with their lives apart from mothering."

By the mid-1980s this subdivision of the female market by social class assumed the lifestyle emphasis gaining in class differentiation. One consulting firm classified women in eight lifestyle clusters, ranging from the "Good Life" (working, married, no children) to "The Challenge" (working, married, children) to Dependent (not working, unmarried, children). Other researchers developed their own taxonomies for female consumers, though most made a key distinction between women who worked outside the home and those who did not. Consumer products could then be positioned precisely to appeal to segments defined not only by gender, but fine-tuned by age, class, occupation, family situation, lifestyle, and feminist consciousness, thereby complicating any essentialist male-female dichotomy. As *Business Week* reminded the readers of its weekly marketing feature in 1961, "Any mere man knows women are different. Sometimes, though, men—even marketing men—forget a vital addendum to that dictum: Women are even different from other women."[60]

In a model of how subcultural protest could inspire new strategies of market segmentation, feminism in the 1960s and 1970s, with its challenge to traditional female roles and gender bias in the media, was turned by marketers to their advantage: the creation of a new feminist market segment. Had advertisers and marketers remained stubbornly tied to the strategy of mass marketing, rising feminist consciousness, with its rejection of the mainstream media's sex stereotyping of women, would undoubtedly have presented a commercial threat. And of course, some protests by women's liberation activists against exploitative advertising surely did. Feminist actions against CBS, *Ladies' Home Journal,* and select Madison Avenue advertising agencies were probably not good for business.[61]

But with the diversity of appeal possible—even encouraged—under market segmentation, feminists soon became a new market for everything from douches appropriate for "Women's new freedom" to a feminist television character named Maude. In typical fashion, after pressure from women led Congress finally to prohibit sex discrimination in the credit market in 1974, the United States League of Savings Associations did an about-face and began looking at the women they long had scorned as "an untapped market," in the words of its spokesperson. Though marketers sometimes misjudged what would appeal to feminist consumers, the women's liberation movement at least inspired them to try to turn feminist defiance into consumer compliance. A special advisory panel of the trade's National Advertising Review Board, reporting back to its general membership in 1975 on "Advertising Portraying or Directed to Women," concluded that responding constructively to feminist criticism of derogatory images of women would accomplish two goals: "First, it will provide a greater measure of fair treatment for women," and "second, it will be an intelligent marketing decision." The lesson was learned quickly. Within two years, *Business Week* reported that a review of business travel, life insurance, and credit card advertising indicated that female executives "have started to achieve capitalism's ultimate accolade: They are now treated as a distinct marketing segment."[62]

Find the $25,000 executive without life insurance.

She's the working woman. And she needs life insurance as much as anyone else in the picture.

If you're single, life insurance is a solid, sensible way to get ready for the future. Because The Equitable's whole life insurance plans give guaranteed cash values that you can borrow against. For a house. For retirement. For emergencies.

And if you're married, you also need life insurance to protect your contribution to your family's income and lifestyle.

The Equitable has a booklet for you that talks life insurance. Woman to woman. It's filled with quotes from a recent panel discussion. And it could answer some of your questions about life insurance.

It's free. And it's important you read it.

Because you need life insurance as much as a man.

EQUITABLE

It's time you figured out how much your life is worth.

This ad from the November 1976 issue of *Ms.* magazine reveals how the women's movement of the 1970s encouraged mainstream advertisers to recognize and target a new feminist market. (Courtesy of Equitable Life Assurance Society of the United States)

Whereas social class and gender were marketing categories with histo-ries that stretched back to the early twentieth century, two other kinds of mar-ket specialization—by age and by race or ethnicity—required the postwar revolution in market segmentation to flourish. Teenage, child, senior, black, and ethnic became more than labels for visible social groups; they became marketing segments that advertisers determined were well worth catering to.

If any kind of segmentation epitomized the hopes and success of the postwar marketing profession, it was segmenting by age, where stages of life, linked to patterns of purchasing, reshaped the mass market. One typical overview of the life cycle and buying behavior, published in 1966, identified nine categories, stretching from "Bachelor stage" and "Newly married couple" to "Full Nest I through III" (differentiated by children's ages), and culminating in "Empty Nest I and II" (distinguished by whether the head of household was working or retired) and "Solitary survivor," both "in labor force" and "retired." Each stage featured unique market behavior, with, for example, the Newly Married and Full Nesters at their peak in consumption of homes and con-sumer durables, while Empty Nesters shifted priorities to travel, luxuries, and medical care. Complementing this life cycle analysis, moreover, were intensive studies of certain key age markets. A special report in *Printers' Ink* at the dawn of market segmentation concluded that it was not just a question of marketers suddenly seeing age segments where once they had pictured only a family unit. Rather, whereas "a generation ago . . . purchases tended to reflect the needs of the family as a whole," the meteoric rise of discretionary income in the post-war period had given each segment of the family more influence on purchase decisions, "and—to an extent that would have been considered unlikely in 1939—certain members of the family now have personal purchasing power." Increasingly, the postwar family was becoming a collection of variously aged individuals with discrete consumer desires and capabilities.[63]

The first age cohort to attract marketers' attention was teenagers. The discovery of this teen market actually preceded the embrace of market seg-mentation, as promoters began experimenting with the idea in the 1940s, and its success contributed to the appeal of more extensive segmentation a decade or so later. A 1949 issue of Daniel Starch's marketing research newsletter, for example, was devoted to convincing advertisers of what today seems obvious: that greater profits would result from "writ[ing] special copy for magazines with special audiences" like the teenage readers of *Seventeen* magazine rather than using a standard sales pitch. Although "adolescence" had been labeled since the nineteenth century to signify a developmental stage, and "youth cul-ture" referred to a select group of eighteen- to twenty-four-year-olds in the 1920s, it was not until a majority of teens were graduating from high school in the 1940s that the teenage period of life—from ages thirteen to eighteen—took on the attributes of a mass cultural experience.

What began as an awareness during and after World War II of a distinctive "teenage" stage of life, with its own language, customs, and emotional traumas, very quickly developed into a consumer market. Most often credited with pioneering this notion of a teenage market was a Chicago-born advertising pioneer named Eugene Gilbert. Barely out of high school himself in the mid-1940s, he launched a variety of schemes: advising local department stores on young men's clothing, undertaking a nationwide survey of teen taste, and writing two monthly fashion columns: "Girls and Teen Merchandise" and "The Boys' Outfitter." By the early 1950s, Gilbert had moved his Youth Marketing Company to New York and was publicizing his research findings widely, particularly the enormous potential profits at stake when the average teenager spent $3.03 a week, he figured. Gilbert's achievement—what he, in 1959, described as "our salient discovery ... that within the past decade the teenagers have become a separate and distinct group in our society" with control over $9.5 billion of income (almost all of it discretionary) and influence over much more—soon spawned a huge industry cashing in on the teen market. A magazine like *Seventeen,* which debuted in 1944, prided itself on catering to "the needs, the wants, and the whims" of teenagers, translating as many as possible into consumable goods. Marketing firms like Gilbert's and the Student Marketing Institute advised companies how to sell an exploding range of products to youth, the largest age group in America by the early 1960s thanks to the "baby boom."

Before long, being a teenager became defined as a unique consumer experience: buying certain kinds of things—records, clothes, makeup, movies, and fast food—in certain kinds of places—shopping centers, drive-in theaters, and car-hop restaurants. By the 1960s even manufacturers of mainstream merchandise like RCA (record players and records) and Pepsi-Cola saw their future profits—even survival—linked to how well they managed to insert their product into the fantasy world of the teenage market segment, dubbed by the latter producer, in an extraordinarily successful advertising campaign from 1961 to 1966, the "Pepsi Generation." Celebrating Pepsi drinkers as all-American youthful rebels against the "establishment," implicitly linked to Coke, Pepsi marketers cleverly demonstrated both that the marketing of teen rebellion against conventional values could yield big profits and that it could appeal beyond the age cohort by defining youthfulness as a state of mind—"for those who think young."[64]

The era of market segmentation also put children in a more powerful position as consumers. Children had long provided a market for toys and clothes, but television made it more possible to appeal to them independently of their parents. Until the mid-1950s the promotion of toys and games was limited and poorly funded ($1 million annually), and what existed was directed mostly at parents. But by the early 1960s marketers were rethinking their selling plans, most importantly involving child-development experts and children themselves in extensive research on the likes and dislikes of the child segment. Now sponsors of programs like *Howdy Doody, Disneyland,* and the *Mickey Mouse Club* urged young viewers to "be the first on your block" to buy a particular sugary breakfast cereal, packaged snack food, or new toy, all boldly enough displayed on the television screen for even the non-reader to identify on a supermarket shelf or in a toy store window.

Not accidentally, advertisements targeting children as a segment in the 1950s and 1960s sought to lay the groundwork for a lifetime of consumption, preparing the way for their voyage from child to teen to adult male or female segment. Mattel's teenage Barbie with her closets full of fashionable outfits and accessories taught the importance of how you dressed and what you owned. Cardboard grocery stores stocked with miniature replicas of brand-name goods; child-size Easy-Bake Ovens, Bissell's "Little Queen Carpet Sweepers," and Kenner's "Girder and Panel Build-a-Home and Subdivision Set"; shopping board games like Milton Bradley's "Acme Checkout Game, the exciting new supermarket shopping game"; and the latest-model toy cars—all instructed children how to function in the adult world of consumption. Amsco, a leader in what were called brand-name "tie-in" toys, made no secret of this strategy, candidly acknowledging that "leading manufacturers of consumer products" viewed them "as an effective and relatively inexpensive method of brand indoctrination of children who constitute tomorrow's many millions of consumers for their products." By the 1970s shrewd toy manufacturers were developing yet another marketing innovation, special "kidsvid infomercials" on television, such as "He-Man and the Masters of the Universe" and "G.I. Joe," constructed around a featured toy. Now a child's favorite show was not only linked to a product, it was *about* that product. Over the last forty years, the American toy industry has propelled itself into the multi-billion-dollar global giant it is today through its marketing ingenuity, built more than anything else on making children, not their parents, its best customers.[65]

By the late 1960s "seniors" became the newest frontier of age-based segmentation. In 1968 the *Journal of Marketing* ran a speculative piece, "The Aged Segment of the Market, 1950 and 1960," predicting that as the number and income of older Americans continued to rise, opportunities for selling to them would multiply. A decade later *Business Week* pronounced that the segment's day had arrived. In a 1979 article entitled "Discovering the Over-50 Set," the

Christmas morning brought toys to girls and boys designed to introduce them to the consumer life of adult women and men. As markets increasingly segmented by age, companies invested in the trade-name toy business. In an article, "Big Business Goes Tiny" in November 1953, *Life* magazine featured manufacturers who "figur[ed] that the child who plays with a toy Bathinette or a Euclid dump truck today will buy a real one tomorrow." Lucian Brown. (Courtesy of Carpenter Center Photography Collection, Harvard University)

editors asserted that after two decades of concentrating on selling products and services to young people, "Madison Avenue . . . now . . . has awakened to the existence of a growing market referred to as the 'oldsters,' '50-plus,' or 'maturity,' market." " 'We've been ignoring a group almost twice as large as the total population of Canada,' " one advertising leader observed, " 'simply because we had blinders on to anyone who wasn't young, raising a big family and in the 'age of acquisition.' " Suddenly, major manufacturers like Procter & Gamble and Bristol-Myers were noticing gray-haired consumers, while magazines like the new *Prime Time* and the older *Modern Maturity,* published by the American Association of Retired Persons for twenty years without advertisements, and a new cable station for viewers over fifty all now offered attractive advertising opportunities. A population that had until recently been written off as too fiscally cautious and conservative suddenly promised rich dividends, and in no time marketers were meticulously dissected it into subsegments by age, gender, physical ability, income, and lifestyle.[66]

Although some of the impetus to carving out this new marketing segment came from analyses showing a slowdown in the growth rate of younger segments of the population, here again, like with so many other market segments, a burgeoning grassroots movement of "senior power" inspired Madison Avenue's response. When seventy-year-old Maggie Kuhn was forced to retire in 1970, she and some friends formed a national organization dedicated to banning mandatory retirement and championing the rights of older citizens. Dubbed the Gray Panthers—after the militant Black Panthers—by a New York talk-show host, they sought to make "ageism" as compelling a rallying cry as racism and sexism. Meanwhile, existing national organizations like the American Association of Retired Persons and the National Council of Senior Citizens became powerful lobbies for senior interests such as partial property tax exemptions, Medicare and social security benefits, and the right to work. Consumer watchdog Ralph Nader even set up a Retired Professionals Action Group to be the voice of an "old people's liberation movement." Not only had the political mobilization of this social group alerted marketers to its existence, but the "maturity media," including the likes of *Modern Maturity* and *Mature Outlook,* had gone out of their way to lure advertisers' dollars to help underwrite the group's influence. Preening for potential advertisers, they stressed the financial advantages of a cohort free of mortgage and school tuition responsibilities and swimming in high salaries, pensions, and savings. They even went so far as to emphasize that "the sense of familial obligation has changed and it's now acceptable to take from the family savings and spend," according to one influential marketing executive. In 1987, *Advertising Age* approvingly alerted its readers to the popularity among seniors of a new bumper sticker that announced, "I'm spending my children's inheritance."[67]

Finally, the era of market segmentation transformed the way marketers related to populations defined by race and ethnicity, with the most significant segment consisting of African Americans. The consumer marketplace had long been a crucial site of African-American political assertiveness, in the effort during the 1930s to secure employment opportunities within black communities and, by the 1940s and 1950s, as a route to demanding access to public accommodations, viewed as a symbolic threshold to equality in the larger society. In those early years of the civil rights movement from the 1930s through the 1950s, when full integration into white society was the chief goal of most black activists, the black media—newspapers, magazines like the Johnson Publishing Company's *Ebony* and *Jet*, and a growing number of marketing companies—set out to convince mainstream advertisers to incorporate the "Negro Market" into their selling campaigns, both for the symbolic recognition and the expected boon to their own coffers. Typical was the effort by a black marketing firm, the Research Company of America, hired in the late 1940s by the *Afro-American* newspaper chain to survey black households in three northern cities to prove to potential advertisers that "colored Americans read and believe in their race paper," as many as 97.6 percent of all black families in Baltimore, it was claimed. Moreover, after surveying "Negro Uses of Specified Items, by Brands," the study confirmed a longstanding finding that "the Negro is very brand conscious . . . and unusually 'brand loyal,'" as well as likely to spend a higher proportion of income on consumables than whites.[68]

Despite such evidence, the challenge of convincing mainstream marketers to reach out to black consumers remained daunting. As one prominent market researcher acknowledged in 1949, "America's Negro population today is our largest and most important underdeveloped market. In buying power and numbers it has grown rapidly. Yet until recently national advertisers paid little attention to this segment of our population though it is larger than the population of the entire Dominion of Canada." In 1948, when Pepsi-Cola became one of the first mainstream advertisers to "discover" the Negro market and mount an advertising campaign in over fifty black newspapers, it set a precedent that would continue through the 1950s of major companies increasingly pursuing African Americans' rising spending power, but without substantively reorienting their "one-size-fits-all" mass marketing campaigns. For the black media soliciting their attentions, however, color-blind advertising symbolized social acceptance and progress beyond the racist stereotyping traditionally associated with black advertising characters like the bandanna-clad Aunt Jemima and wide-eyed, mop-headed "Topsy" child.[69]

With the reorientation to market segmentation in the early 1960s, however, marketers shifted their approach. Now they sought not only to attract African-American consumers' substantial purchasing power but also to appeal to the distinctive values and concerns that they assumed blacks brought to the marketplace. Building on a wealth of racial segmentation studies generated by the booming postwar field of market research, they got extensive advice on "The Marketing Dilemma of Negroes," "Black Buyer Behavior," "Why the Negro Market Counts," and "Dimensions of the Negro Market," to name only a very few.[70] Sometimes the products being marketed were made specifically for black buyers, such as a black Barbie doll or a specialized hair product or a black radio station. More often, the advertised items were mass-marketed goods—cigarettes, liquor, cars—but with marketing carefully tailored to attract African-American consumers. In 1963, for example, Coca-Cola sponsored *The Alma John Show* on a hundred black radio stations, a ten-week series of five-minute programs aimed at African-American teenagers. Hosted by a well-known black radio broadcaster, it featured, according to publicity, "short interviews with leading Negro personalities, along with etiquette, grooming, dating, health and party tips," thereby associating Coke with the life of the party as well as the lives of young African-American partygoers.[71]

Advertisers' embrace of a market segmentation strategy for selling to blacks by the 1960s resulted from a combination of the larger change in marketing practice and the impact of a civil rights movement that continued to mobilize blacks at the point of consumption—through sit-ins, selective buying campaigns, and boycotts—as an effective means by which to demand rights.[72] Hence, as in other cases of market segmenting, assertiveness by this racial subculture fueled marketers' willingness to treat it as a viable market segment. *Business Week*'s first article addressing "The Negro's Force in [the] Marketplace" in 1962 warned readers of the urgency, as "business will have to reckon increasingly with this forced identity in the days ahead. . . . For in the market, as in the schools, the restaurants, and the hiring halls," alluding to all the contested ground of the civil rights movement, "the Negroes are on the march."

Later in the decade, black marketing expert D. Parke Gibson confirmed in his handbook for selling, *The $30 Billion Negro,* that the civil rights movement had—and should—inspire mainstream marketers' appeal to African-American consumers. "At one time, perhaps, the American Negro could be led through white-oriented leadership, white-oriented media, and through the spill-off of some public relations effort. It is doubtful if such could be accomplished today." He went on, "After the summers of 1964, 1965, 1966, 1967, and the spring of 1968 [significant moments of racial protest], it is, no doubt, hard for anyone to believe there is not an effective, almost automatic, unidentifiable 'channel of communication' among Negroes." Gibson urged advertisers to take into account Negroes' new pride in blackness. Allaying some marketers' fears that racial segmentation could be mistaken for a revival of segregation, he assured them, "Customer-oriented programs aimed at Negro consumers are not segregation in reverse but simply provide the Negro with what he wants—recognition." Catering to race consciousness, he argued, would not only win black consumers who were discovering their powers of selective purchasing, but would also bring marketers rewards at the bottom line.

Johnson Publishing Company's founder, John H. Johnson, who in the 1940s and 1950s had encouraged mainstream advertisers to reach out to the "Negro market" with standard appeals, now made the case for considering blacks a separate market segment. "The Negro market . . . is not a special market *within* the white market—it is, on the contrary, *a general market* defined, precisely, by its exclusion from the white market. . . . Negro consumers tend to think, buy, and act in significantly different ways than white consumers," and in the shadow of the civil rights movement "are growing not less self-conscious but more self-conscious," he asserted in an opinion piece in *Advertising Age* in 1964. Over the next decade, understanding of the black market would grow in complexity, making internal class differences, for example, more prominent, but even black media experts promoting these differentiations would insist that class operated within blackness, not apart from it.[73]

The shift from incorporating blacks into mass markets to setting them apart through racially based market segmentation, then, paralleled the larger evolution of civil rights from integration to black power. In the era of "black is beautiful," a race-conscious marketing effort was expected to go beyond reaching black consumers by minimally adjusting mainstream advertising campaigns to acknowledging greater black uniqueness by, for example, showcasing models with dark skin and Negroid features who spoke in black slang. Even as establishment a magazine as *Ebony* told potential advertisers in its own ad in *Advertising Age* in 1969, "You can't rely on your usual advertising media to win us," referring to the "4.4 million black people who do their shopping" through *Ebony.* "You can understand why we can't feel a total involvement with anything that appears in the mostly white media."

Commitment to that separate black market by advertisers and consumers alike persisted long after the heyday of the civil rights movement. In the early 1990s the president of the African American Marketing and Media Association told *Time,* "It's not a question of *if* firms should market to blacks, it's *how*." How to customize products and sales pitches to black tastes occupied marketers from Kmart and JCPenney to Hallmark, Mattel, and Reebok for almost forty years, though sometimes to black consumers' detriment. When G. Heilman Brewing Company developed a potent malt liquor for primary

These three hair-care ads that appeared in *Ebony* magazine chart how mainstream manufacturers shifted their strategy of appealing to African-American consumers over the postwar period. The first (top left), which appeared in 1956, shows the white-owned Godefroy Company running its standard mass circulation advertisement, with a white model, despite *Ebony*'s overwhelmingly black readership. The second (top right), from 1961, reveals how Clairol's embrace of market segmentation led to the substitution of a middle-class-looking black model for the white ones who appeared in mainstream ads, without changing the text. Finally, in 1970 the rise of the Afro-centric "black-is-beautiful" movement convinced a company like Clairol that targeting the black market meant more extensively tailoring its message and image to African-American consumers. Ironically, mainstream white-owned companies' greater responsiveness to black culture and more effective marketing to black segments contributed to a dramatic rise in their share of the black personal-care business, a sector that had once been dominated by black-owned companies. (Courtesy of Lamor Inc. and Clairol Inc.)

sale to black males and R. J. Reynolds was caught promoting a high-nicotine cigarette designed to hook black smokers, critics cried that they had taken market segmentation to a dangerous level.[74]

Market segmentation around race, moreover, has had a complicated impact on the economics of African-American communities. In an irony that has been much lamented in recent years, the growing responsiveness of mainstream, usually white manufacturers, marketers, and retailers to black demands for recognition in the marketplace often contributed to the demise of separate black business districts, stores, and even products. Black makers of beauty aids, for example, long dominant in this market sector, virtually collapsed when mainstream cosmetic companies like Revlon, Avon, and Clairol began aggressively pursuing African-American consumers. With the concept of a segmented black market, often serviced by white companies, taking the place of a separate black economy, blacks may have received more recognition in the white world, but at the cost of investment in a black one. Between 1969 and 1984 the proportion of black income spent in black-owned businesses dropped by half, from 13.5 percent to just 7 percent; most shocking over this period, blacks' retail hair-care purchases from white-owned general-market firms shot up from essentially nothing to 70 percent of all sales. By 1992 only 3 percent of spending by black consumers went to black-owned companies. As MaVynee Betsch, longtime resident of a black beach resort in Florida that virtually disappeared with the civil rights revolution, lamented, "Now you go to the motel. You don't own it. You eat at the restaurant. You don't own it. No, the white man owns it, and you go to his place and you give the white man his money."[75]

Meanwhile, white marketers' embrace of market segmentation, in relaying distinctive messages to black consumers through black media venues, did little to integrate mainstream white society beyond hiring a handful of black employees to serve as inside experts. A New York Times assessment of the state of marketing to blacks in 1961 found that while 90 percent of the models used in Ebony advertisements were now black, up from 50 percent just five years earlier, resistance remained great, even in the North, to employing them in mainstream advertising. Mostly, marketers feared a white backlash, even though research suggested their worries might be unfounded. Thirteen years later, in 1974, a survey of blacks in advertisements appearing in mass circulation magazines such as Time, Newsweek, Reader's Digest, and Esquire still found that fewer than 7 percent of ads with people in them included blacks. A parallel survey of advertisements in the New York Times put the number at fewer than 5 percent. Often, the African Americans appearing in mainstream ads tended to be celebrities from sports or entertainment.[76] By welcoming racially segmented marketing—black ads for black audiences—as politically progressive, African-American leaders may have inadvertently taken the pressure off mainstream marketers to integrate their campaigns and nurture a vision of America that was racially mixed.

Some politically conscious black consumers and organizations like the NAACP and the Reverend Jesse Jackson's Operation PUSH, recognizing that African-American faces smiling out from ads in the black media were only enriching white corporations, demanded that producers, retailers, and advertisers repay the black community for their dollars, much the way consumer activists like W.E.B. Du Bois, Ella Baker, and the Reverend Adam Clayton Powell, Jr., had in the 1930s. The expansion of billboard advertising in urban black neighborhoods during the 1980s made this racial disjuncture between market and marketer all the more disturbing to many critics, as larger-than-life images of black consumers enjoying cigarettes, alcohol, and other mainstream products now towered over communities. An issue of *Black Enterprise* magazine as recently as 1999 urged readers to flex their financial muscles in support of companies that invested in the African-American community, such as the few supermarket chains with stores in cities, and highlighted the Reverend Al Sharpton's initiative against what he charged was a "blackout" of minority media outlets by Madison Avenue.

One new development in recent years has been the emergence of a new generation of black entrepreneurs determined to reverse the race's historic lag in entrepreneurship through marrying sophisticated market segmentation techniques to the old commitment to separate black business. Robert L. Johnson, for example, took an idea for a cable channel aimed at elderly audiences and adapted it for black viewers in 1979, creating the extraordinarily successful Black Entertainment Television: "You don't have to reinvent the wheel. You've just got to paint it black," is how he described his approach. A more recent ambition, to create a black airline, faced the challenge of linking consumers' black identity to their choice of air carrier. Many African-American entrepreneurs and consumers continue to hope, much as proponents of black business did earlier in the century, that "buying black" will keep investment dollars in black communities, but every day white competitors wield ever more sophisticated tools of market segmentation as well.[77]

Whether practiced by black or white marketers, the success of market segmentation on the racial front has made the capitalist marketplace more respectful of—and one could even argue has further inspired—the distinctive identity of black consumers. In just one example, the findings of the Batten Barton Durstine & Osborn (BBDO) advertising agency in April 1992 made for a shocking headline in the television world: "Black TV Audience Picking Its

Own Top 10." For the first time ever, the Top 10 prime-time television pro-grams, and most of the Top 20, were completely different for black viewers than for white ones. The news was welcomed by a BBDO spokesperson, who explained that this solid documentation of the racial divergence of television audiences, combined with the fact that television was watched almost 50 per-cent more in black households than non-black ones, would make the sale of ads aimed at black viewers all that much more profitable.[78] Whereas before the 1960s marketers either ignored or sought to incorporate black consumers into a homogeneous color-blind mass market, after that, in the era of segmenta-tion, successful marketing to blacks meant delivering to them a unique set of options, or, in some cases, the same options packaged especially for them. Marking certain products and sales appeals as black, and then encourag-ing African-American consumers (and the not-so-small number of whites attracted to both the goods and the image) to acquire them, has made blacks a more legitimate and lucrative market, but increasingly over the postwar era, a separate one.

Having honed their skills on the black market, market segmenters beginning in the 1970s extended their reach to other ethnic populations. Whereas before then only small immigrant manufacturers and retailers had pitched goods to ethnic markets, usually through the pages of the foreign-language press, now major American corporations began spending millions to ensure that minority customers stocked their cupboards with their products. Here again, rising assertiveness by ethnically defined subcultures—Chicano and Indian power modeled after black power, a rediscovery of immigrant her-itages by many second- and third-generation Americans during the 1970s, and the new markets created by recent arrivals from Asia and Latin America after the immigration reform of the 1960s—helped convince Madison Avenue that buying habits of the Irish, Italians, Poles, Jews, Chinese, Mexicans, and other ethnic consumers were sufficiently idiosyncratic and hence segmentable. Gen-eralizations like this one from a marketing text as early as 1972—that second-generation Italian housewives continued to favor fresh over packaged foods, whereas Puerto Ricans led all ethnic groups in their preference for frozen food dinners and cake mixes—became legion. As marketers surveyed and resur-veyed ethnic populations in search of profitable marketing precepts and broke segments down into subsegments—of the "assimilated" versus the "tradi-tional," for example, and by social class—they continued to perfect how and what to sell to ethnic Americans.[79]

The Latino market has proved to be the most recent high-stakes game for segmenters. Exploding in size from ongoing immigration, a high birthrate, and marketers' unification of a number of Spanish-speaking populations—

Mexicans, Puerto Ricans, Cubans, and other Latin Americans—into one single national Spanish-speaking culture, "Hispanic" or "Latino/a" has become the fastest-growing portion of the American population and will soon overtake blacks as the nation's largest minority. That alone would make targeting profitable, so other favorable developments—a fast-growing middle class, buying power that rose 65 percent between 1990 and 1998 alone, and a geographical concentration in California, Texas, New York, Florida, and Illinois—have made Latinos only more attractive as a market segment. The television market has itself been divided into Spanish- and non-Spanish-speaking households, recently putting the ratings company, Nielsen Media Research, in the middle of a virulent struggle between Univision, the nation's largest Spanish-language broadcaster, and television executives at English-language stations in the enormous New York market over how many meters to place in Spanish- as opposed to English-speaking households. The proportion in dispute, supposed to reflect accurately each group's percentage of television viewers, inevitably will affect the ratings of shows, and consequently the amount that stations can charge for commercials. Following close on the heels of the Latino market is another conglomeration of diverse immigrant populations—the "Asian-American market"—which, although smaller, holds out great promise to marketers due to the quickly expanding size and high earnings of its members.[80]

At the start of the twenty-first century, recognition of racial and ethnic difference through bilingual education or affirmative action may be under siege in some corners of American society, but Madison Avenue remains convinced that carving up the nation into distinctive racial and ethnic subcultures still pays. If a commitment to the economic and social benefits of mass consumption underlay the Consumers' Republic of the postwar period, it was not an unchanging conception. At the dawn of the era, corporate America, ranging from manufacturers to marketers, assumed that success in building mass markets depended on minimizing differences of class, gender, age, race, and ethnicity and maximizing any and all commonalities in consumers' tastes and buying behavior. By the late 1950s, however, marketers, fearing market saturation, began taking a different tack, one soon endorsed by social groups looking to differentiate themselves from the conventional mainstream. The imperatives of profit-making for the former and political assertiveness for the latter combined to support "market segmentation," dividing the mass market into distinctive segments, each marked by its own values, priorities, and patterns of purchasing. Now, reinforcing social differences—not emphasizing sameness—paid dividends at the bank.

This shift in marketing from mass to segment affected American consumers in diverse ways. On the one hand, it recognized and reinforced subcultural identities, giving often disempowered Americans, such as workers, feminists, teenagers, African Americans, and Latinos, a kind of legitimacy through proving their worth in the consumer marketplace. In the case of blacks in particular, their demand for attention as a market segment provided another way to use the realm of consumption as a battleground in the struggle for civil rights. In contrast, the ambivalence of mainstream marketers toward embracing homosexuals as a market segment denied them a desired sanction. Advertisers have most commonly targeted the gay market through a dual marketing approach, what they call "gay window dressing," where the ad avoids explicit reference to homosexuality but sends clear signals to gay males and lesbians.[81]

On the other hand, as market segmentation gave capitalists and rebels alike a shared interest in using consumer markets to strengthen—not break down—the boundaries between social groups, it contributed to a more fragmented America. The marketplace became more like other fractured places in post–World War II America, most notably residential communities and commercial centers, where an investment in mass consumption ironically also propelled Americans away from the common ground of the mass toward the divided, and often unequal, territories of fragments, accentuating in the process everything that made these places different from each other. For when marketers singled out teenagers or African Americans for special appeals, they were taking action not inconsistent with landlords and shopping center managers who tried to bar these groups, despite the fact that on the surface marketers seem to have reached out and landlords and managers to exclude. Both were more comfortable segregating rather than integrating the postwar public sphere. Furthermore, although individuals are complex composites of multiple identities—of class, gender, age, race, ethnicity, religion, geography, sexual preference, and lifestyle—the reinforcement by marketers and other cultural boundary makers of some fault lines over others—in privileging race over class, for example, or age over geography—gave them a strong hand in shaping the contours of postwar consumer culture.

SEGMENTING VOTERS IN POLITICAL MARKETS

How far-reaching was the impact of this fundamental shift from mass marketing to market segmentation? Did marketers' commitment to fragmenting the mass market have consequences for other realms of postwar American experience, particularly politics? Given the centrality of mass consumption to the larger political culture we have been calling the Consumers' Republic, one might very well expect a spillover. And indeed, astute observers of American society after World War II noticed that mass marketing was becoming more and more entangled in other aspects of life, especially politics, illuminating a potential connection between market structure and political structure. In the 1940s, Paul Lazarsfeld and his Bureau of Applied Research at Columbia University hypothesized strong similarities between political campaigns and advertising campaigns, testing a "consumer preference model" of politics that stressed the impact of the mass media on individual choice and applied marketing research techniques like repeated depth interviews to voters. In 1950 sociologist David Riesman argued in *The Lonely Crowd* that Americans were increasingly becoming "consumers of politics," responding to the packaging of leaders or events as they did products, valuing charisma and glamour over more rational self-interest.

Seven years later, Vance Packard elaborated Riesman's critique in his diatribe against advertisers and marketers, *The Hidden Persuaders*. What really frightened Packard was the way that motivational researchers and symbol manipulators were transferring strategies from selling products to consumers to selling politicians to voters. Dividing his book in two parts, "Persuading Us as Consumers" and "Persuading Us as Citizens," he devoted careful attention in the latter section to exactly how over the course of the 1950s mass marketers had made "spectacular strides in changing the traditional characteristics of American political life." For Packard, the danger to American democracy was encapsulated in the strategy of advertising executive Rosser Reeves, who, before masterminding Eisenhower's 1952 television blitz, had built his reputation through a series of celebrated ad campaigns—for Wonder Bread ("helps build strong bodies twelve ways"), M&M's ("melt in your mouth, not in your hands"), Colgate ("cleans your breath while it cleans your teeth"), and Anacin ("FAST-FAST-FAST relief"). As Reeves put it bluntly, "I think of a man in a voting booth who hesitates between two levers as if he were pausing between competing tubes of tooth paste in a drugstore. The brand that has made the highest penetration on his brain will win his choice."[82]

The application of mass marketing techniques to the political arena dates back to the turn of the century, though it reached a new level of intensity in the 1930s. Nineteenth-century political campaigns had used the language and paradigm of disciplined military campaigns: "cadres" of party workers, presided over by party "captains," "mobilized" "armies" of "loyal" voters and punished "traitors" on the electoral "battlefield." With the new century came the gradual atrophy of political parties and the rise of a new political paradigm of the marketplace, where voters became consumers, candidates and issues products, and campaigns advertising pitches overseen by mass marketers.[83] Beginning in the 1890s, political parties hired public relations experts and then "ad men" to enhance candidates' images. During World War I the federal government employed experienced advertisers to build public support for the war effort, and in the 1920s the League of Women Voters' "Get-Out-the-Vote" campaigns employed every advertising technique known to Madison Avenue to boost voter turnout.[84] But all that was mere warm-up for the 1930s, when New Dealers heavily marketed recovery programs like the NRA, with its Blue Eagle logo; when the Democrats and their Republican challengers, Alf Landon and Wendell Willkie, made history hiring advertising men as "public relations directors"; and, most important, when the techniques of market research advanced sufficiently to make them reliable predictors of voters' attitudes, not just buyers' preferences. When surveyors George Gallup, Elmo Roper, and Archibald Crossley accurately forecast Roosevelt's landslide in 1936, consumer research had successfully spawned public opinion polling, and American politics changed forever.[85]

At about the same time, a husband-wife team of marketing consultants in California, Clem Whitaker and Leone Smith Baxter, established Campaigns, Inc., the first company devoted exclusively to managing political campaigns, and with it the concept of entrusting an election campaign entirely to a political consultant. But despite these critical innovations that brought consumer marketers into the political arena, their influence through the 1940s remained limited enough that in 1950, the Committee on Political Parties of the American Political Science Association could still conclude that "relatively little use has been made by the parties of social survey techniques as a basis for political campaigns." Likewise, other experts concluded that in comparison to the subtle manipulation of public opinion ubiquitous in commercial advertising, political propaganda remained crude. In most campaigns, longstanding party operatives were still calling most of the shots, even when they bought advice from advertising and marketing experts.[86]

Ironically, it was the campaigns of down-home, grandfatherly Dwight D. Eisenhower in 1952 and again in 1956 that brought mass marketing fully into the political arena, sounding the death knell for campaigning by whistle-stop tours, street parades, and grassroots organization. Now, convinced that, in the words of Republican Party chairman Leonard Hall, "you sell your candidates and your programs the way a business sells its products," the Republican Party hired three major New York advertising agencies, BBDO, Young and Rubicam, and Ted Bates and Company, to bring their full bag of advertisers' tricks to the campaign, particularly the magic of television. Madison Avenue did not disappoint. Ted Bates's ad whiz Reeves came up with the ingenious idea of buying time at the very end of top-rated programs like *This Is Your Life. The $64,000 Question,* and *The Jackie Gleason Show* to capture already tuned-in, prime-time audiences for Ike. And rather than have Eisenhower deliver predictable political speeches, Reeves produced a forty-spot ad campaign, "Eisenhower Answers America," featuring twenty-second and one-minute commercials of Ike answering ordinary people's questions with what came across as honesty and empathy. For the three weeks before election day, the spots saturated the airwaves in key states at a cost of millions of dollars. The campaign—in both the advertising and electoral sense—culminated with an election-eve BBDO-produced extravaganza (promoted in an ad in the *New York Times* as "one of the great hours in radio and television history . . . an hour you and your family will remember the rest of your lives"), filled with testimonials by representative Americans about why they were voting for Ike. In addition, the GOP in 1956 hired Hollywood actor and MGM public relations director (and later California senator) George Murphy to make its convention in San Francisco appear more like a television commercial for party and candidate than its undisciplined predecessors ever had. Vice presidential candidate Richard Nixon, of course, was no stranger to promoting himself through television either; when charged with fundraising improprieties in 1952, he saved his spot on the ticket through delivering his famous "Checkers" speech, emotionally defending himself, his family, and their dog on prime-time television directly following the popular *Milton Berle Show*.

The Democrats, caught off guard by the Republican media onslaught in 1952, which left them embarrassingly stuck with a glut of outdated, half-hour, late-night broadcasts of candidate Adlai Stevenson pontificating, scrambled to catch up to the Republicans in 1956. They sought help from the ad agency Norman, Craig and Kummel, known for its successful "I Dreamed I Went Walking in My Maidenform Bra" ad campaign, which introduced negative political commercials against Eisenhower and Nixon and, along with the Republicans, a new five-minute TV spot format, and they hired another MGM director, Dore Schary, to orchestrate their convention. What wasn't working in the Democrats' favor, however, was their candidate. Stevenson purportedly protested to party handlers: "The idea that you can merchandise candidates for high office like breakfast cereal, that you can gather voters like box tops—is, I think, the ultimate indignity to the democratic process." While Eisenhower had initially voiced doubts in 1952, he quickly deferred to Republican Party chieftains thoroughly sold on the miracle-making of Madison Avenue in business and politics.[87]

A best-selling novel, *The Golden Kazoo*, by retired adman John G. Schneider, published in 1956, provides a remarkable document of how well people at the time understood the way that mass marketing was transforming American politics. The novel satirizes Madison Avenue's growing influence over the electoral process by following the schemes of Madison Avenue's boy wonder, Blade Reade, principal of Reade & Bratton, Inc., as he takes total control over the presidential campaign of Republican candidate Henry "Hank" Clay Adams, former governor of Kansas. Schneider's satirical brush limns it all: the ad executive's scorn for old-fashioned pols, including the chairman of the Republican National Committee and the candidate himself; the packaging of the candidate for television audiences as a "*simple* picture—a beautiful, powerful, appealing but simple picture"; a mass-marketed campaign aimed at what Blade calls "a real, low-down Lowest Common Denominator," or LCD for short; and growing dependence on scientific pollsters—the agency's Flying Survey Squad deceptively introducing itself to interviewees as the American National Research Council, Inc.—who daily put samplings into electronic calculating machines and watched them come out as "market analyses."

The plot revolves around Blade's search for "a big, spectacular, strictly 1960 idea" to propel his lagging candidate to victory. Blade knows the solution doesn't rest with articulating positions on issues. As he tells his number one copywriter, "Sell me a bill of goods, Joe. Look, I don't want you to come back and tell me what our boy should do or say about farm policy, foreign affairs, tariffs, taxes, or civil rights. Don't sell the welfare state, the free enterprise system, or whatever screwball Utopia you've got figured out for the U.S.A. Henry Clay Adams is your product. He's a can of beer, a squeeze tube of deodorant, a can of dog food. Sell him." Blade and his team come up with a scheme to portray Adams's forty-something wife, Zelpha, as "a kind of TV Mrs. America." They script her doing everything from advertising "Mizzus Henry Clay Adams's Old Harvest Table Recipes" (as polls showed higher readership ratings for recipes than political ads) to pretending that she is pregnant to win audience sympathy.

When in mid-October polls still reveal that Adams's Democratic opponent has the advantage, Blade pulls out all the stops, applying everything he has learned as a product marketer to politics. He mounts a major promotional giveaway, explicitly appealing to voters as consumers by dispersing to them the $16 billion worth of food that the government has stockpiled from farmers through agricultural price supports, "a truckload of food for every family" worth $350. Blade launches this last-ditch campaign through a Broadway-type telecast broadcast live in front of 40,000 at the New York Coliseum that is reminiscent of BBDO's 1952 election-eve show for Eisenhower. In it, Hank Adams comes to the rescue of a tragedy-burdened "Typical American Family" by bringing them bushel baskets of food. As the novel closes and Blade watches Adams squeak through to victory, he articulates the adman's simultaneous dependence on, and contempt for, the consumer-voter: "It's the revolution. The consumer. The poor, dumb, beat-up, oppressed, cheated, neglected, ignored and humiliated consumer. The stupid, unorganized, helpless, name-less, faceless, numberless consumer. The ridiculous, prat-falling clown, the almighty slob!"[88]

What novelist Schneider could not predict in 1956, when he so cyni-cally imagined the election of 1960, was that the advent of market segmenta-tion later that decade would change the rules of the game for political marketing, as it had for product marketing, pushing campaigns and election-eering away from selling to Blade Reade's "Lowest Common Denominator" mass market toward crafting special messages for distinctive segments about whom more and more was becoming known through increasingly sophisti-cated polling. The change was first visible in the 1960 presidential election, already famous for making television the kingmaker through the televised debates between a telegenic John Fitzgerald Kennedy and a Nixon who, despite his experience as a debater, proved no match as a television celebrity. Further-more, in an eerie version of Schneider's novel, market researchers from Social Research, Inc. helped the Kennedy campaign improve JFK's image as an inde-pendent head of his own household, rather than as a subordinate to his pow-erful family, by building up through televised interviews wife Jacqueline as a capable, intelligent, and mature partner.[89]

But that election is also noteworthy for Kennedy's new attention to voter segments, rather than solely appealing to the mass of Americans as Eisen-hower had. Kennedy hired Louis Harris to do private state-level opinion polling for him and used his findings to tailor his messages, such as on civil rights, to the occasion of his speechmaking. A marketing company, Simulmat-ics, provided the Kennedy campaign with a computerized mathematical model of the U.S. presidential electorate that, along with polling, likely helped his managers identify sufficient support in West Virginia to deliver his "upset" pri-mary victory there over Hubert Humphrey, which propelled him toward the Democratic nomination. Furthermore, Kennedy's Catholicism drew intense attention to the religious identity of voters, while his physical attractiveness, so visible on television, made female voters a segment for wooing.

Upon taking control at the Democratic convention, the Kennedys quickly discovered that apart from a Civil Rights Division on paper, the Democratic National Committee had no structure through which to make pointed appeals to special interest groups. Kennedy brother-in-law Sargent Shriver was promptly dispatched to reach out to as many of these groups as possible, and soon a range of special units emerged: the Nationalities Division, with four main sections of German, Italian, Polish, and Spanish, as well as twenty-six special committees; an additional Spanish-language operation of Viva Kennedy clubs; special interest groups like Businessmen for Kennedy, Farmers for Kennedy-Johnson, and Labor's Committee for the Election of

These two photographs record John F. Kennedy appealing to crowds in northern New Jersey. At the top, he is campaigning at Paramus's Bergen Mall in 1960, addressing an all-white audience assembled at one of the main centers of suburban public life, the shopping center. On the bottom, he is driving through the streets of Newark, enthusiastically welcomed by the increasingly black and Latino population that lived there. During the postwar era, the growing residential segregation of metropolitan America by race and class reinforced the segmentation of voters brought about by the application of marketing techniques to the political sphere. An electorate splintered into segments with separate, and narrower, political concerns resulted. (Courtesy of the Newark Public Library)

Kennedy and Johnson; and Senior Citizens for Kennedy, Youth Citizens for Kennedy-Johnson, and a reinvigorated Civil Rights Division. Pioneer segmenters Kennedy and Johnson also paid more attention to geographical targeting, allocating most of their time to doubtful states, while mass marketers Nixon and running mate Henry Cabot Lodge, Jr., trudged around the country trying to fulfill their promise "to carry this campaign to every one of the 50 states." Republican efforts at courting specialized interest groups likewise proved less effective than the Democrats'.[90] While the Republicans had pushed politics into the age of mass marketing in the 1950s, in 1960 the Democrats, under the wing of the sophisticated and well-oiled Kennedy marketing machine, took the initiative in recognizing the benefits of breaking that mass electorate apart.

But in 1964 the leadership in segmenting political campaigns swung back to the Republicans. Television played an even greater role in the race that year between Lyndon Baines Johnson and Barry Goldwater, who broadcast 10,000 television spots between them including several celebrated ones produced for LBJ by the Doyle Dane Bernbach agency, of Levy's rye bread, Avis, and Volkswagen ad fame, to scare voters with the nuclear danger of a Goldwater victory—one of a little girl innocently licking an ice cream cone that the narrator warns could be made from milk contaminated by fallout and another of a child pulling the petals off a daisy in a countdown that ends with a thermonuclear explosion.[91] But the major advance in applying market segmentation techniques to politics to come out of this election would be on the ground, not on the air. It was the development of a direct-mail strategy by Richard Viguerie and other political conservatives that made targeting audiences with particular messages much more precise than was possible with television advertising and other traditional media.

Although the Nixon-Lodge ticket had experimented with direct mailing to various address lists in 1960 with mixed results, it was Goldwater's campaign that launched the first successful large-scale direct-mail solicitation, posting more than 15 million fundraising appeals and raising $5.8 million. Viguerie further refined the methods of direct mail by taking the names of the 12,500 Americans who had contributed more than $50 to Goldwater's campaign and building from there. He first used his list to fundraise for the conservative youth organization, Young Americans for Freedom, and as his meticulously assembled lists grew over the sixties and seventies, so too did the right-wing candidates and causes he helped promote. George Wallace's success in 1972 in particular was credited to Viguerie's sharpshooting with his computerized letters. (By 1977, Viguerie had compiled more than 30 million names of conservative-leaning individuals and employed three hundred people at the Richard A. Viguerie Company and its various subsidiaries.) Political organizations of other conservative candidates, most notably Ronald Reagan and Pat Buchanan, and issue-driven political action committees (PACs, such as Gun Owners of America, the Moral Majority, and the National Tax Limitation Committee) perfected the science of direct mail, delivering specially tailored messages ever more accurately to the most appropriate constituents. In time, Democratic candidates such as George McGovern and liberal groups such as Common Cause and the National Organization for Women would mount successful direct-mail campaigns as well. When Reagan assured recipients of his invitation to join the Republican Presidential Task Force, at an annual price tag of $120, with the compliment, "I'm not asking everyone to join this club—only proud, flag-waving Americans like you," he did more than flatter. Likely they had been carefully selected through cross-tabulating of their income, residence, age, past political views, magazine subscriptions, church affiliation, and so forth.[92]

Republican campaigners expanded the basic strategy of market segmentation—identifying demographic and lifestyle clusters—beyond direct-mail fundraising to recruiting potential voters in Richard Nixon's 1968 campaign for president. Determined not to replay the defeat of 1960, Nixon and his campaign team—noteworthy for its experienced talent drawn from television and advertising—used the latest polling and market research techniques to divide the American electorate into voter blocs that could be sold different images of the candidate, images conveyed especially well through new-style television ads made up of emotion-grabbing collages of still photographs and other iconography set to dramatic soundtracks. Televised commercials targeting the South, where Nixon was in a dogfight with independent candidate and racial extremist George Wallace, spoke in "regional code words" and images about "busing," "crime," and the "Supreme Court," according to his southern campaign manager, Fred LaRue, and hence were used "very selectively," never in the North. In another segmentation scheme, Nixon's campaign hired nationally famous country-and-western artists to record ballad-type songs for broadcast on radio and television, arranged so that stanzas addressing different issues could be added or dropped as the local situation required. Citing a basic principle of market segmentation, LaRue cautioned, "You could spend a million dollars on songs like that and it's wasted money unless you get them played in the right spots. You got to get that on or adjacent to country and western programs. Either that or wrestling. That's a special kind of audience. . . . What you do for those people would not appeal to other kinds of people and vice versa." Similarly, Nixon's "ethnic specialist," twenty-seven-year-old Kevin Phillips, devoted himself to identifying "where the

Senator McGovern thinks your vote is in the bag.

President Nixon doesn't believe it—look at his record.

He has made possible more loans to black businesses than any President before him.

He is the first President to ask for governmental funds to fight Sickle Cell Anemia.

He asked for $2.5 billion to raise the quality of education in disadvantaged schools.

He opened up jobs through Federal Manpower Programs for 1.2 million blacks and minority members last year alone.

He has budgeted $602 million for Civil Rights Enforcement, a 700% increase over the previous administration.

He is making free or reduced-price lunches available to more than 8 million children.

He is spending $371 million to combat drug abuse this year.

He drafted a bill which would give any black student Federal Aid to go to college.

He has appointed more blacks to top government posts than any other President in history.

He is helping nearly 12 million people with his Food Stamp Program.

Deeds, not words. That's why President Nixon deserves your support. Don't be taken for granted. Make your vote count. All Americans need President Nixon. Now more than ever.

THE RECORD	LAST YEAR OF PREVIOUS ADMINISTRATION	CURRENT YEAR OF NIXON ADMINISTRATION
Aid to Black Colleges	$108 Million	$200 Million
Aid to Minority Bank Deposit Program	(Did not exist)	$245 Million
Aid to Minority Business Enterprise	$200 Million	$700 Million
Civil Rights Enforcement Budget	$75 Million	$602 Million
Equal Employment Opportunity Commission Budget	$8.2 Million	$30.5 Million
Fair Housing Enforcement Budget	$2 Million	$8.2 Million
	TOTAL ADMINISTRATION	TOTAL ADMINISTRATION
Executive Level Appointments	49	62
Sub-cabinet Appointments	3	9
White House Staff	2	7
Generals /Admirals	2	12
Supergrade Appointments	63	150
Presidential Appointments to Commissions/Advisory Boards	60	89

President Nixon. Now more than ever.

Paid advertisement—published and paid for by the Finance Committee to Re-elect the President, M. H. Stans, Chairman, C. L. Washburn, Deputy Chairman, P. E. Barrick, Treasurer, 1701 Pennsylvania Ave. N. W., Washington

When Richard Nixon's campaign committee placed this advertisement in *Ebony* magazine in November 1972, it addressed the special interests of black voters. Like direct-mail appeals and radio and television commercials, targeted advertising campaigns such as this one urged Americans to vote their self-interest rather than to subordinate it to the common good. (Courtesy of the Richard Nixon Library & Birthplace)

groups are and then we decide how to reach them. What radio station each listens to, and so forth." Fearing he had started too late in the '68 campaign to nail down what he called "group susceptibility," he predicted that "by 'seventy-two I should have it broken down county by county across the whole country so we'll be able to zero in on a much more refined target."[93]

Market segmentation techniques were not only implemented in candidate campaigns in the 1960s and 1970s; they were also called on to help mobilize voters around controversial issues. For example, in what proved to be a successful battle defeating an anti-union "right to work" referendum in Missouri in 1978, a cluster system was used to identify union sympathizers. According to a disapproving *U.S. News & World Report*, "Missouri's labor leaders worked together under a campaign plan that was designed for them by a Washington political consultant. . . . With advertising, direct mail, telephone contacts and door-to-door solicitations, the unions directed their message only into favorable areas—union households, blue-collar neighborhoods and the black community. This strategy means that they place[d] their local TV commercials around tough-guy shows like 'Baretta.' "[94] Carefully pitched campaigns by California conservatives in the late 1970s helped collect the necessary signatures to put Proposition 7, a pro–death penalty measure, and Proposition 13, Howard Jarvis's massive property tax cut, on the ballot. The latter particularly targeted senior citizens.[95]

Mass marketing has obviously had a tremendous impact on the practice of twentieth-century American politics. Campaign duels between televised advertisements, packaged candidates known more by image than substance, and party conventions that are no more than infomercials are not creations of the last two decades, when their presence has been much commented on, but rather have deep roots in the earliest years of the Consumers' Republic. Since the 1960s, moreover, politicians' embrace of market segmentation has promoted additional trends. Attention to matching voters to candidates much like products to consumers has encouraged perpetual dependence on pollsters, what a recent observer has called "government of the polls, by the polls, for the polls," the turning of campaigns over to political consultants with the technology and expertise to target specialized voters with tailor-made messages, and the gradual decline of political parties, as increasingly "independent" voters become mobilized through direct appeals by individual candidates and single-issue campaigns. Political segmentation substitutes narrower identities with narrower interests for the broader constituencies to which "big tent" parties most effectively respond. Certainly, the extensive feedback mechanisms from voters to candidate that political marketing has put in place have had benefits. No recent candidate could convincingly plead ignorance of who the voters are and what they want. To the extent that market segmentation of the electorate has made politicians more responsive to voters' diverse concerns than when they searched for the "Lowest Common Denominator," which inevitably favored some groups over others, it has enhanced democracy in America.[96]

But in other ways, this thrust dangerously threatens democratic government. To start with, the enormous expense of hiring the media and marketing expertise now required to mount an even run-of-the-mill campaign has made seeking office feasible only for the wealthy or their agents; from 1912 to 1952 each national party spent about the same amount of money per vote cast in national elections, only to see the expenditure skyrocket over the next sixteen years until by 1968 each vote cost three times as much. Furthermore, as polling, direct mail, and other strategies have helped candidates adapt their images flexibly to multiple audiences, campaigns have moved further and further away from appealing to a shared political agenda, what John Schneider's Blade Reade, for all his cynicism, called the critically important "Lowest Common Denominator." Rather than try to convince voters of some common good, as Roosevelt, Truman, and Eisenhower all struggled to do—from FDR's Four Freedoms to Ike's prime-time "Eisenhower Answers America"—more recent presidential candidates, as well as many running for lower office, at best construct a composite vision out of the specialized interests of their distinct constituencies, and at worst avoid discussing any common good at all.

With the new practitioners of political marketing embracing something they call the "law of minimal effects," they have become convinced of the limited ability of a campaign to change people's attitudes and hence of the necessity for candidates to appeal to voters' existing views without offending them with contrary positions. According to one study of political consulting, "slicing and dicing" the electorate has become a chief strategy for achieving "high interest, low backlash" communication with voters. On the very same block in Miami, one homeowner with children might receive a mail piece addressing mortgage tax deductions and federal aid to education, while her neighbor, a renter without children and with a Latino surname, would get a message about relations between the United States and Cuba with no mention of mortgage tax breaks or education. Exacerbating this fragmentation of the electorate through targeted appeals, moreover, is the kind of discourse direct-mail campaigns employ to capture recipients' attention. Political observer James Davison Hunter has noted that the simplified analysis, demonized enemies, and sensationalized claims commonly found in direct-mail appeals further polarize the public beyond their ideological differences. With candidates establishing direct links to constituents, moreover, those citizens identified as not important, either because they are not likely to vote or wield little influence, are easily ignored. On the voters' part, just as segmented buyers of goods seek the best match for their distinctive tastes and desires with what is available in the commercial marketplace, so segmented citizens have similarly come to expect the political marketplace—consisting of candidates, government agencies, and PACs—to respond to their needs and interests narrowly construed.

When the far-reaching implications of the shift from mass to segment are combined with the other kinds of social differentiation under way over the postwar period, the consequences for American political culture in the last decades of the twentieth century are monumental indeed. In a Consumers' Republic constructed around the expectantly broad-reaching rewards of mass consumption, the imperatives of profit-making soon motivated marketers to segment the mass, rather than reinforce it, everywhere from the commercial marketplace to the political arena, much the way mass home builders and shopping center owners became invested in the stratification of metropolitan areas. Likewise, individuals soon learned that their own good fortunes as homeowners, shoppers, and voters depended on identifying with special interest constituencies with clout—for example, localistically minded suburbanites, Yuppies, African Americans, senior citizens, or gun owners. Although mass markets, mass culture, and mass politics by definition did not promise positive political outcomes, and could render some social groups invisible, they also could make new political achievements possible for the first time through forging alliances across class, race, ethnicity, and region.[97] America's retreat from the aspiration to appeal to the mass, which accelerated in the 1960s, combined with the ongoing stratification of residential communities and the privatization of public space, made the achievement of a broad-based political agenda difficult.

Americans' growing recognition that social and consumer identities could have strategic political value fueled the return in the 1960s of a reborn politics of consumption, embraced from the bottom up through the consumer movement sparked by Ralph Nader's crusade against General Motors, and from the top down by Presidents Kennedy, Johnson, Nixon, and Carter, and by Congress and state legislatures. Much as novelist Schneider uncannily predicted in *The Golden Kazoo* in 1956, consumer rights became a new battle cry of citizens and elected officials alike. In some ways, this late-twentieth-century consumer movement harked back to the 1930s and 1940s, linking the consumer interest to the larger public interest and reviving the mandate of the citizen consumer to serve as protector of the general good. But in other, more disturbing ways, all the social, economic, and political changes since the late 1940s altered its significance and broadened the territory in which the Consumers' Republic's more self-serving purchasers as citizens operated. In what in many ways became, by the end of the twentieth century, a "consumerization of the republic," not only were citizens still assured that they fueled their own and the nation's prosperity simultaneously through their private consumption. Increasingly they were bringing market expectations to their appraisals of the government itself, judging it and its policies by the personal benefits they, as segmented purchasers as citizens, derived from them.

CHAPTER 8

Politics: Purchasers Politicized

On March 15, 1962, President John F. Kennedy sent a special message to Congress declaring a Consumer Bill of Rights—the right to safety, to be informed, to choose, and to be heard—and calling for specific executive and legislative actions to protect these rights. With that action, Kennedy launched a third wave of the consumer movement in the twentieth century, reminiscent of the two previous waves during the Progressive Era and the New Deal but ultimately more influential. Asserting that "Consumers, by definition, include us all," he decried in the first message by a president explicitly addressed to consumer issues that although they are responsible for "two-thirds of all spending in the economy," "they are the only important group . . . who are not effectively organized, whose views are often not heard." Since 1872, when legislation was enacted to protect the consumer from frauds in the U.S. mail, Kennedy reminded lawmakers, the federal government—Congress and the executive branch—had borne responsibility for protecting consumers' interests in the economy. With powerful new technologies creating new hazards as well as new opportunities, and mass marketing "utilizing highly developed arts of persuasion," new action was required "for more effective protection of the consumer and the public interest."[1] Actually, Kennedy was fulfilling a promise he made on the campaign trail in the fall of 1960, when his rhetorical pledge—"The consumer is the only man in our economy without a high-powered lobbyist. I intend to be that lobbyist"—met with unexpected enthusiasm from audiences.[2]

For the next decade and a half, through the administrations of the four presidents who served until 1980, this third-wave consumer movement would affect national, state, and even local politics and policies. Not long after he became president, Lyndon Baines Johnson would affirm his commitment to the slain Kennedy's agenda for consumer protection in a special address to Congress in 1964, and again in his State of the Union in 1968.[3] Richard Nixon would release his own Buyers' Bill of Rights in October 1969 soon after he came into office, and Presidents Ford and especially Carter would remain concerned with the consumer interest.[4] And although explicit presidential support for the consumer movement would decline with President Ronald Reagan's election in 1980, in other subtle ways policymaking justified as being in the consumer's interest would become even more deeply entrenched in American political culture as the twentieth century became the twenty-first.

The commitment to represent consumers better in government decision-making and to protect them in the consumer marketplace went far beyond presidential rhetoric. Through the 1960s and 1970s, the executive, legislative, and judicial branches of government oversaw the enactment of dozens of federal laws and regulations to protect consumers from harmful food, drugs, and cosmetics; unsafe manufactured products and vehicles of transportation; misleading labeling, packaging, and advertising; discriminatory banks and credit agencies; unfair monopolies; toxic water and air; and other threats to consumer well-being. In addition, by 1975 all fifty states had designated some sort of agency to be responsible for consumer protection, while thirty-nine had passed consumer protection statutes. Commissioners of Consumer Affairs became legion in cities, counties, and states alike.[5] In the popular media, whether magazines, newspapers, or television news, investigative reporters devoted themselves through special features and regular advice columns and segments to exposing problems encountered by consumers.[6] Moreover, consumers began to see themselves as a class of individuals sharing particular rights and entitlements, and they formed new organizations to lobby in their common interest. At all levels of power—from Main Street to the corridors of Congress—consumers suddenly became a force to be reckoned with, as a rank-and-file movement reconstituted after almost two decades of retreat after World War II. For the next decade and a half at least, a new protagonist—the victimized consumer—would attract the spotlight in the president's cabinet room, the congressional hearing room, the public courtroom, the corporate boardroom, and the community meeting room.

Why, one has to wonder, did concern with the consumer revive when it did? How did it evolve over time? Above all, what was its impact? Did a revived consumer movement, commonly referred to as "consumerism," bring with it the return of the publicly minded citizen consumer of the Roosevelt era and the repudiation of the postwar purchaser as citizen, whose pursuit of private consumption was considered adequate contribution to the common good in the booming Consumers' Republic? How did the Consumers' Republic itself fare in a political climate where the good of the nation now seemed to require protecting the rights of individual consumers, not just encouraging mass consumption by millions of purchasers?[7]

THE EMERGENCE OF THIRD-WAVE CONSUMERISM

ennedy did not pull concern for the consumer out of thin air. It had been gently circulating there, thanks to the efforts of muckraking author Vance Packard (*The Hidden Persuaders* [1957] and *The Waste Makers* [1960]), periodic articles in Consumers Union's *Consumer Reports* that went beyond being a buyers' guide, and a few determined, though more often than not unsuccessful senators and congressmen who, beginning in the mid-1950s, held hearings and pushed new legislation to protect consumers from the bounty of new products flourishing in the Consumers' Republic: chemicals like food additives and pesticides, potentially dangerous goods like flammable fabrics and refrigerators without safety door handles, "miracle drugs" like the birth-defect-inducing tranquilizer thalidomide, and debt-threatening financing innovations like credit cards. A few long existent products came in for scrutiny as well, most notably tobacco and automobiles. The Federal Trade Commission (FTC) ordered Philip Morris to stop advertising the unsubstantiated claim that its cigarettes were "recognized as being less irritating to the nose and throat by eminent nose and throat doctors." The result, however, was only to encourage the tobacco industry to invest heavily in filter-tip cigarettes, which it promoted deceptively as offering greater protection to a smoker's lungs, particularly after the mass circulation *Reader's Digest* published an article in July 1954 suggesting a possible link between smoking and cancer.[8] And beginning in 1956, a Special Congressional House Subcommittee on Traffic Safety chaired by Alabama Congressman Kenneth Roberts conducted extensive hearings on automobile design, publicizing but unable to do anything about many of the flaws leading to highway casualties that Ralph Nader would later expose to an avalanche of popular outrage.[9]

The previous consumer movement of the 1930s and World War II era had collapsed by the late 1940s. Although the Employment Act of 1946, in the spirit of wartime commitment to the consumer interest, had called for consumer consultation to the newly created President's Council of Economic

Advisers, that representation had atrophied during the 1950s.[10] What advocacy for consumers persisted through the 1950s, then, was undertaken by maverick (and sometimes opportunistic) lawmakers such as Congressman Roberts, Illinois Senator Paul Douglas—a champion of truth-in-lending—and Tennessee Senator Estes Kefauver, who, as chairman of the Senate Antitrust and Monopoly Subcommittee, went on the attack against the prescription drug industry, rather than by any bottom-up mobilization of consumers, with the major exception of civil rights activism.[11] African Americans had boycotted, picketed, and otherwise protested in the 1950s and early 1960s on public buses and beaches and in commercial establishments like movie houses, restaurants, and skating rinks to secure their full participation in the Consumers' Republic. That aside, unorganized consumers were the "forgotten men" of the federal government, according to the author of a major consumer economics textbook in 1953 who went on to lament that "all the New Deal consumer interest programs of the federal government were quietly eliminated. Even in the 1950–51 policy-making meetings for price control, no consumer participation was included."[12]

So what changed by the 1960s to launch a new consumer movement and who took the initiative? As is usually the case with significant cultural and political shifts, a number of factors converged to inspire this third wave of consumer activism, as was recognized by the Chamber of Commerce when it tried to explain the onslaught to its members: "The very forces which have shaped the changing American environment of the Sixties have influenced the revival of renewed concern for the American consumer and have stimulated the resurgence of a consumer movement dormant since the . . . Thirties. These include population growth, affluence, rising educational levels, economic growth, technological advance, mass marketing, changing social values and personal attitudes, and institutional changes in business, government, and the marketplace."[13] Several of these forces deserve elaboration.

Despite challenging the Consumers' Republic's avoidance of regulating the marketplace, the consumer movement of the 1960s and 1970s nonetheless grew out of the success of the Consumers' Republic. As more and more Americans had discretionary income and aimed to improve through their consumption of mass-produced goods the quality of their own lives and the vitality of America's economy and democracy, they increasingly sought a "fair shake" as consumers. Michael Pertschuk, who worked for two early consumer advocates—Oregon Senator Maurine Neuberger and Senate Commerce Committee Chair Warren Magnuson of Washington State—before President Jimmy Carter appointed him chair of the FTC in 1977 has argued that products themselves did not become appreciably worse or more dangerous or more poorly labeled and packaged, but rather that Americans, "having for the first time acquired those goods for which they had worked and saved and dreamed . . . had unrealistically high expectations." Senate consumer champion Philip Hart, ironically adapting a popular cigarette advertising slogan, offered a similar analysis: "Consumers today are spending more but enjoying it less."[14]

The growing complexity of the flourishing marketplace also made new kinds of demands on consumers that they sought help managing; advanced technologies, new synthetic materials, alluring consumer credit, computerized billing, and many other innovations within the Consumers' Republic fueled consumer agitation as well as appetite. Betty Furness, special assistant to President Johnson for consumer affairs, testified accordingly, "You gave us nylon but didn't tell us it melts. You gave us insect spray, but you didn't say it would kill the cat. You gave us plastic bags, but didn't warn us that it could, and has, killed babies. You gave us detergents, but didn't tell us they were polluting our rivers and streams. And you gave us the pill, but didn't tell us we were guinea pigs." Furness's representation of consumers in the Johnson White House in itself symbolized how the promises of the Consumers' Republic ultimately fed consumerism. David Halberstam has described well Furness's pre-Washington career in his sweeping history of the 1950s: "If there was one figure who came to symbolize the dazzling new American kitchen and all its astonishing appliances, as well as the revolution in selling and advertising that was taking place, it was Betty Furness—the Lady from Westinghouse." After years of selling refrigerators and vacuum cleaners on television by assuring viewers, "You can be sure if it's Westinghouse," Furness took her credibility with Americans to Washington, and helped shift consumer expectations for quality and dependability from manufacturers to government.[15]

The emergence of market segmentation within mass marketing also helped fuel consumerism. Consumer protection analyst Laurence P. Feldman has argued that the reorientation in marketing of the late 1950s from simply developing a product and selling as much of it as possible to consumer motivation and market segmentation—targeting a product at the identified need of a distinctive segment of consumers—contributed to increased consumer discontent. "Theoretically, the application of the marketing concept and market segmentation should lead to more perfect consumer satisfaction," Feldman acknowledged, but "ultimately . . . under competitive pressure, continual refinements of segmentation tended to lead to an emphasis on the satisfaction of needs."[16] By making appeals around more specific consumer desires, manufacturers, retailers, and marketers raised expectations and hence the risk of disappointment.

Highlighting consumer discontent was not the only way that the explosion of market segmentation in the 1960s fed the consumer movement. The population segments that marketers catered to became, in a more politicized environment, consumer interest groups pursuing special safeguards from the government and, in some cases, corporations. For example, children and senior citizens, both big discoveries as market segments, became important interest groups seeking consumer protection. Consumer products associated with vulnerable children, such as flammable pajamas and unsafe cribs, became the centerpiece of consumer product safety campaigns, while the controversy over aiming television commercials directly at children, which often promoted low-nutrition foods and poor-quality toys, became one of the fiercest struggles of the era. Critics like Action for Children's Television condemned the exploitation of children as a violation of parents' rights to educate their own offspring, thereby assaulting advertisers' new strategy of selling directly to children.

Likewise, senior citizens brought their newfound influence in the marketplace to bear on consumer advocacy. In a telling case in 1973, elderly delegates to the first annual convention of the Citizens Action Program in Chicago, a group of blue-collar and lower-middle-income city residents, protested soaring food prices and demanded a 50 percent reduction in telephone charges and cuts in electricity rates for the elderly. "With our senior powers we'll send Charlie Brown [the president of Illinois Bell Telephone] to the showers," they chanted at every opportunity, mimicking for their own purposes the kind of advertising jingle usually aimed at them. On a larger scale, organizations like the American Association of Retired Persons, the National Council of Senior Citizens, and the Gray Panthers lobbied hard to protect the special interests of senior consumers. In time, their grievances became a critical topic of discussion at many a conference, such as when the New Jersey Consumers Conference in 1967 considered ways to protect the aging from being defrauded and to provide them with food in smaller packages, or when the White House showcased the "elderly consumer" during its Conference on Aging in 1971.[17]

The case of senior citizens exemplifies the linkage between the consumer movement and what political scientists call "interest group politics," whose flourishing they date from the 1960s. As marketing strategies for identifying and catering to distinct segments were transferred to the political sphere, the resulting segmentation of citizens narrowed their political concerns. With the evolution of the consumer movement over the 1960s and 1970s, consumers made for a complex public interest group. In some cases, consumer mobilization grew out of and reinforced distinct population segments such as children and the elderly. At the same time, however, and often in tension with that trend, Presidents Kennedy, Johnson, and Nixon, and even activists like Ralph Nader embraced a more encompassing definition of the consumer reminiscent of the citizen consumer of the New Deal era, conveyed when JFK asserted that "consumers include us all."

This latter approach had the virtue of envisioning a broad-based constituency of consumers, one that appealed to presidents and other politicians as a universalizing, liberal alternative to emerging "rights talk" based in racial, gender, and other narrower identities thriving in the volatile 1960s. "Other issues . . . have divided the country into camps," Nader told a reporter in 1970, "but there's no split at the grassroots level [of the consumer movement]. It's a 'people's movement.'" In an increasingly postindustrial era of service sector growth and more pervasive middle-class identity, moreover, invoking the rights of consumers ideally cast a wide net over the populace, and specifically offered a more inclusive discourse about the exploitation of consumers in place of the more divisive industrial-era discourse about the exploitation of labor. It is no accident that Ralph Nader launched his extensive public interest group network, the Public Citizen—designed to counter self-serving special interest lobbies on behalf of a collective good—out of his consumer advocacy work. In all cases, however, Americans who were politicized as consumers, whether segmented or unified, increasingly resembled other interest groups where citizens claimed rights outside of traditional political party membership and voting, and empowered Washington-based advocacy organizations to lobby in their name.[18]

The Democrats' return to the White House in the 1960s created a third way that consumerism emerged out of the Consumers' Republic, by giving added stimulus to the nation's ongoing postwar commitment to Keynesianism, which made consumer demand the centerpiece of a prosperous economy. From the late 1930s through the 1950s and early 1960s, mass consumption was intended to grease the wheels of the economy, creating economic growth, high employment, and mass prosperity by sustaining demand, expanding the proverbial economic pie without any painful redistribution of its portions. Even as military expenditures grew with the Cold War buildup, commercial and military Keynesianism were seen as flourishing hand in hand. In proposing a $14 billion tax cut in 1962, finally implemented as the Revenue Act of 1964 signed by President Johnson, Kennedy recommitted his administration to fiscal action aimed at enhancing consumer purchasing power to invigorate the economy. Even the Kennedy White House's growing attentiveness to economic growth was not viewed as incompatible with a demand-driven economy. "Keynes-cum-growth," as economic historian Robert Collins calls it, still meant that private purchasing power, supported by government action, held the key to a healthy economy. As Kennedy told Congress in *The Economic Report of the President* in January 1962, "The proposed partial tax suspension would launch a prompt counterattack on the cumulative forces of recession. It would be reflected immediately in lower withholding deductions and higher take-home pay for millions of Americans. Markets for consumer goods and services would promptly feel the stimulative effect of the tax suspension." Three years later, in his *Economic Report* to Congress in January 1965, Johnson labeled 1964 "the year of the tax cut." "It was not the first time that taxes will be cut, of course, nor will it be the last time. But it *was* the first time our Nation cut taxes for the declared purpose of speeding the advance of the private economy toward 'maximum employment, production, and purchasing power.' " Later in the report, in discussing the necessity of finding employment for all young people, he explained its importance beyond providing for their livelihood: "If this challenge is met, the new workers will become eager consumers, helping to maintain high employment levels with their demands for houses, cars, and other goods and services." Not surprisingly, *Time* magazine named John Maynard Keynes man of the year for 1965, signaling his continued reign over Washington.[19]

What distinguished Democratic Presidents Kennedy and Johnson from Republican President Eisenhower's record over the previous eight years and spurred the consumer movement, however, was their greater comfort with a strong federal hand in the economy. Not only were they willing to stimulate demand through tax policy and public spending, which Ike himself did, but they also favored empowering the government to intervene in the market to protect the engine of that demand, consumers—what one might call "demand-cum-protection." As Kennedy put it in his Consumer Bill of Rights speech, "To promote the fuller realization of these consumer rights, it is necessary that existing Government programs be strengthened, that Government organization be improved, and in certain areas, that new legislation be enacted."[20] Although demand-cum-growth and demand-cum-protection became more difficult to sustain by the late 1960s without imposing unpopular new taxes as the escalating costs of the Vietnam War fed inflation, even President Nixon kept up at least a superficial commitment to the ideal of Keynes-cum-protection, despite his ingrained Republican ambivalence toward federal authority.

Conditions in this heyday of the Consumers' Republic were clearly ripe for the revival of a consumer movement. Yet it is unlikely that it would have happened without the provocation of committed activists, inside and outside of government. Presidents Kennedy, Johnson, and Nixon would probably not have seized the consumer issue if they had not felt political pressure.

Former FTC chairman Michael Pertschuk, who was at the center of activism on the Hill as counsel to Senator Magnuson's Commerce Committee from 1964 until 1977, identified five distinct groups of entrepreneurs who formed a tenuously organized but mutually reinforcing coalition behind what he calls "consumer entrepreneurial politics."[21] The first group in Pertschuk's cast consisted of "congressional entrepreneurs"—politicians drawn to consumer advocacy like Magnuson, Kefauver, and his successor on the Senate Antitrust and Monopoly Subcommittee, Senator Philip Hart; Paul Douglas and his successor on the Senate Banking Committee, William Proxmire; Senators Gaylord Nelson, Abraham Ribicoff, Frank Moss, Walter Mondale, Edmund Muskie, and the list could go on. These were lawmakers who combined a real concern for consumer exploitation with a shrewd awareness that they could use the media to market consumer issues to voters and thereby sell themselves to a broad public constituency. The election of 1958 had brought more of these liberals to the Senate, and Johnson's landslide in 1964 gave them the run of the House. Assisting these officeholders was Pertschuk's second group, a new breed of "entrepreneurial congressional staff" who tended to be liberal-minded idealists with a vaguely anti-business inclination, drawn to Washington to "do good."

The other three parties making up Pertschuk's consumer entrepreneurs operated outside of government, often lending their support to activist congressmen and their staff. The first group consisted of the media, with an aggressive core of investigative and advocacy journalists, ranging from columnists like Drew Pearson, Jack Anderson, and Sidney Margolius to *Washington Post* consumer reporter Morton Mintz and political cartoonist Herblock. All could be counted on to relish exposing the finagling of corrupt special interests to defraud innocent consumers.

Among organized interests supporting consumer activists, the most powerful was the labor movement. Having long ago recognized that its members' livelihoods depended on favorable conditions of consumption, not just production, when national consumer organizations began forming in the mid-1960s, labor unions from the AFL-CIO down to many of its constituent internationals were among the most dependable institutional members, providing essential financial and political support. In fact, before the convening of the first national Consumer Assembly in 1966 and the founding of the Consumer Federation of America in 1967, the AFL-CIO organized its own national conference in Washington, D.C., entitled "The Worker Is a Consumer" in May 1965. In addition, many unions ran their own extensive consumer education programs in-house, ranging in focus from pocketbook issues like credit counseling to larger health and safety concerns.

The fit between labor and consumerism was easy. Unions already were deeply committed to the notion of organization as the route to power, to the importance of government legislation and regulation for protecting workers, and to education as a critical strategy for winning adherents. Hardly an AFL-CIO convention passed in the heyday of the consumer movement without the kind of resolution that was adopted in 1973. Claiming that "millions of consumers are defrauded in the market place every year when they are sold shoddy products and unsafe food," it called for a "consumer protection agency, improved product warranties and no fault insurance." Some issues, of course, proved easier for labor to support than others; truth-in-lending and -packaging, auto safety, meat inspection, and the like indisputably promised improvements in the lives of workers. On the other hand, a consumer protection agency empowered to review wage settlements, strikes, and import duties from the perspective of consumers' interests, or a law prohibiting throwaway tin cans when one's livelihood depends on making them, provoked more hostility. But in general, as consumer movement analyst Lucy Creighton has pointed out, labor saw advantages in championing a consumerist agenda, both for the sake of its own rank and file and to broaden its base of support beyond workers to all American consumers. Johnson's naming of Esther Peterson, former organizer for the International Ladies' Garment Workers' Union and undersecretary of labor for labor standards under Kennedy, as his first special assistant to the President for consumer affairs reflected the intimate marriage of labor and consumer politics.[22]

Finally, we come to Pertschuk's fifth group, the "Not-for-Profit Consumer Entrepreneurs," of whom Ralph Nader was undeniably the most prominent and influential. Without Nader, crusader against environmental degradation Rachel Carson, and lesser lights like pediatrician Abraham Bergman, who campaigned for flame-resistant childrens' sleepwear, and writer Jessica Mitford who exposed corrupt funeral practices in *The American Way of Death* (1963), consumer abuses would never have gained the public notoriety they did, nor would legislative and regulatory remedies have been adopted so successfully. If anyone can be credited with moral leadership of the consumer movement in the 1960s and 1970s, it would be Ralph Nader. He began researching the blatant disregard for safety by the auto industry as a student at Harvard Law School in the late 1950s, embracing for his flagship cause the product most integral to the success of the Consumers' Republic, the automobile. By the time he published his landmark book, *Unsafe at Any Speed: The Designed-in Dangers in the American Automobile,* in 1965, which showcased what he called the "second collision" between rider and car in General Motors' sporty Chevrolet Corvair, it was just the spark needed to turn a hundred small consumer fires into a major conflagration for greater legislative and regulatory protection. Better than anyone else, Nader understood that a tipping of the scales toward the consumer and away from big business and big "do nothing" government—whose officeholders, he charged, were too often in the pockets of corporations and whose regulatory agencies became "captured" by the industries they supposedly regulated—required awakening public outrage with the startling truth. He also believed deeply that the survival of American democracy depended on sustaining that outrage, not just against a crash-prone car or industrial pollution, but consistently through viable citizens' organizations. His more than two dozen public interest organizations became civilian watchdogs over corporations and government alike, from the high-powered Center for the Study of Responsive Law with its pugnacious force of Nader's Raiders to the more decentralized Public Interest Research Groups (PIRGs), all initially funded with the $425,000 settlement he got from GM for its illegal spying aimed at discrediting him.[23]

One more contribution to the emergence of the third-wave consumer movement deserves attention: the discovery of the "low-income consumer." An important article in the *Journal of Marketing* in 1970 identified "the new visibility of the low-income consumer" as a primary catalyst in magnifying the seriousness of imperfections in the marketplace that "would probably not have generated nearly the same depth of concern in earlier periods."[24] Although African-American writers like James Baldwin had long protested market conditions for poor ghetto residents, as when he wrote about "how extremely expensive it is to be poor. . . . Go shopping one day in Harlem—for anything—and compare Harlem prices and quality with those downtown," it wasn't until the early 1960s that the concept of the "low-income consumer" emerged through social science investigations such as David Caplovitz's *The Poor Pay More* (1963). Studies like Caplovitz's exposed the worst kinds of consumer exploitation, much intentional, some due to the structural disadvantages encountered by ghetto residents often required to patronize expensive local stores because they had no access to cheaper retail outlets and often dependent on credit buying because they had little ready cash.[25] In the face of urban crisis in the mid-1960s, moreover, the concept offered a way of understanding the persistence of poverty amid America's affluence, and provided a cause and remedy for the deteriorating circumstances of the nation's urban poor. As Johnson's consumer adviser Peterson bluntly presented it, "If we are overcharged, we can absorb the loss. When a poor person overpays, he sinks that much deeper in poverty."[26]

When dozens of American cities underwent explosive urban rebellions that shattered commercial districts, beginning in 1964 in New York City and continuing over the next four years in Los Angeles, Chicago, Cleveland, Tampa, Cincinnati, Atlanta, Newark, Detroit, and elsewhere—at least 329 separate incidents in 257 American cities, involving hundreds of thousands of African Americans—efforts to understand ghetto dwellers' anger latched onto their victimization as consumers. Many new rounds of investigations were launched, into overcharging, exorbitant credit fees, exploitative installment contracts, shoddy merchandise, wage garnishment, and nefarious sales practices, such as "bait-and-switch" advertising, "pyramid selling," and fraudulent door-to-door selling schemes. The National Advisory Commission on Civil Disorders, known popularly as the Kerner Commission after its chair, Governor Otto Kerner of Illinois, concluded, "Much of the violence in recent civil disorders has been directed at stores and other commercial establishments in disadvantaged Negro areas. In some cases, rioters focused on stores operated by white merchants who, they apparently believed, had been charging exorbitant prices or selling inferior goods. . . . [I]t is clear that many residents of disadvantaged Negro neighborhoods believe they suffer constant abuses by local merchants."[27]

Although mistreatment by police, inferior schools, deteriorated housing, inadequate transportation, and a paucity of decent jobs clearly underlay protesters' frustration as well, remedying those deep-seated ills seemed an overwhelming and long-term challenge. The available discourse of the "low-income consumer" offered an appealingly simple explanation for ghetto looting—one, it might be noted, that stressed poverty over race—as well as a quick fix, concrete action on the federal level that could be implemented through President Johnson's War on Poverty. Soon, the federal government was sponsoring fact-finding studies and conferences, funding consumer education components such as Project Moneywise within ongoing poverty programs, and promoting new lower-price retail outlets in low-income neighborhoods.[28] Greater economic justice, it was felt, required educating consumers better and enforcing fairer "rules of the game" when they consumed, though not necessarily tackling the deeper inequities fostered by the consumption-based economy.

In the aftermath of racial rebellion in New Jersey, where entrenched opposition to a state income tax made implementation of a more sweeping urban reform agenda difficult, progressive organizations like the New Jersey Council on Social Issues lobbied for a state truth-in-lending law, and Newark's city government organized the Newark Office of Consumer Action with five ward headquarters. The City of Newark mandated Consumer Action to intervene in response to all kinds of complaints against public agencies and private businesses as well as to offer a comprehensive consumer education program "focusing on the problems of low-income inner city consumers," everything from "Tenants' Rights" to "Facts About Funerals" to "How to Buy Furniture." Funding came from the federal government's Model Cities Program of the Department of Housing and Urban Development and the Community Action Program of the Office of Economic Opportunity, as well as the state of New Jersey's Department of Community Affairs. In addition to this extensive complaint and investigation operation, radio programming, and a monthly newsletter, workshops and "rap sessions" around common consumer problems were held at community sites as diverse as PTA meetings, tenants' groups, neighborhood and senior centers, schools, churches, and day care centers. Thousands of consumers sought help every year. Local efforts also focused on exposing inequities in store pricing and increasing African-American ownership of Newark's businesses through the availability of special minority business loans and consultation, all expected to benefit black consumers.[29]

Much like the consumer movement more broadly, advocates for the low-income consumer understood poor people's exploitation as immoral, even unlawful discrimination in the marketplace, which responsible government intervention must rectify. In the same vein, Nader and other consumer activists urged public-supported legal assistance for the poor so that they could better defend themselves against gauging landlords, finance companies, and car dealers. This focus on the deprivations encountered by the low-income consumer testified to the persistence of the Consumers' Republic framework—that mass consumption, with fair access, offered the solution—even in the face of deep social unrest. It indicated as well a widespread confidence that the consumer movement could overcome these economic malfunctions through such remedies as a more vigilant FTC and truth-in-lending, anti-redlining, and equal credit legislation.

A BALANCE SHEET FOR THE CONSUMER MOVEMENT

The achievements of the consumer movement were extraordinary. With its accomplishments so taken for granted today, it is easy to forget just how impressive they were. In its heyday between 1967 and 1973, more than twenty-five major consumer and environmental regulatory laws passed, and hundreds remained under consideration. Regulation likewise increased noticeably. In 1965 industries subject to pervasive federal regulation accounted for roughly 7 percent of the U.S. gross national product; by 1978 heavily regulated industries accounted for over 30 percent of GNP. Between 1970 and 1975 alone, expenditure by U.S. federal agencies on "economic" regulation grew 158 percent, from $166 to $428 million. An even greater surge in "social" regulation meant that during the same five-year period, the new "social" regulatory agencies—including the Environmental Protection Agency (EPA), the Occupational Safety and Health Administration, and the Consumer Product Safety Commission (CPSC)—rose more than 200 percent, from $1.4 to $4.3 billion. A nation that had last moved to regulate food, drugs, and cosmetics in 1938 and had granted the FTC only minimal authority over advertising now specified how manufacturers must label, package, price, and advertise their goods; whether products were effective and safe enough to sell, highways safe enough to drive on, and workplaces safe enough to work in; who could be excluded from loans and credit and who could not, with full disclosure of terms required; and acceptable environmental standards for air, water and waste.[30]

Beyond cataloguing successes, however, it is important to recognize what was accomplished and what was not. Consumer activists inside and outside of government made three levels of demands, with the first two achieving more success than the third. The first level sought to pass laws to protect consumers better in the marketplace. The second level aimed to reorient the government's regulatory authority toward the public interest, in many ways reviving former commitments like the anti-trust thrust of the Progressive Era and the New Deal ideal of the independent regulatory agency as a "tribune of the people," standing between the public and "private greed," as FDR put it. The growing responsiveness of the courts to product liability suits, moreover, provided another way that consumers' interests became better protected through the vigilance of government. The third level, on which the least headway was made, aimed to give consumers a permanent voice in government through a separate department of the consumer or other such agency within the executive branch. In essence, this third level sought to broaden protection in the economic sphere to representation in the political sphere, binding consumer and citizen ever closer.[31]

All three levels of consumer advocacy assumed the viability and desirability of a system of capitalist private enterprise and markets. In that sense it was a politics compatible with the Consumers' Republic, even though it rejected entrusting the protection of the purchaser as citizen solely to the private marketplace and, to some extent, veered back toward the citizen consumer paradigm of the New Deal era. The beneficial fruits of mass production and mass consumption were never questioned, but rather their quality was to be enhanced, their dangers curbed, and their wider distribution and affordability—the idealistic promise of greater democracy and equality embedded in the Consumers' Republic—better ensured through more aggressive government intervention. As one consumer activist explained it, "The federal government is one way for us to return rational, informed choice to the marketplace—whether it's interest rates or boxes of detergent or packages of potato chips. . . . To secure one of the consumer's most basic rights—the right to choose—we need federal authority to compel lenders and food processors and soap makers to provide the kind of information and packaging that makes such choice possible."[32]

More radical consumer politics—socialism, cooperativism, anticonsumption, and self-sufficiency or the use of consumer actions as a vehicle for broader social protests such as civil rights, anti-war activism, and unionization (as when the United Farm Workers organized national consumer grape boycotts in 1968 and 1984 to pressure growers to recognize their union)—played only a minor role in shaping the ideology of the mainstream consumer movement. Consumer activists nonetheless learned from the tactics of these social movements.[33] Overall, this was a politics of Americans who banned together as consumers to protest the practice, not the ideal, of advanced capitalism. In fact, Nader was frequently criticized by the left for accepting the economic status quo. By grounding his notion of the public good in Americans' preferences as consumers, leftists charged, he ignored the ultimate oppressiveness of the pursuit of material goods, and, by not advocating the restriction of consumption, he endangered the ecological balance of the United States and even the world. Ironically, Nader provoked the wrath of the right as well, for jeopardizing capitalism by interfering too much in the competitive workings of the market through overlegislation and overregulation of business.[34]

Not a lot need be said about the first two levels of achievement. Table 7 lists the major legislation passed and the new regulatory commissions established. In addition, the consumer movement pushed existing agencies like the FTC, the Food and Drug Administration (FDA), and the Federal Communications Commission (FCC) to be more vigilant in the public interest and less "captured" by the desires of the industries they regulated. By 1970, moreover, the judicial system of torts, and product liability more specifically, had shifted dramatically from requiring proof that a manufacturer or seller had negligently violated a specific contract with a consumer to much more willingness on the courts' part to hold manufacturers liable for any malfunction and compensate injured parties accordingly. Likewise, consumer advocates were pushing the use of class-action suits against suppliers who engaged in unfair or fraudulent actions. According to legal scholar Peter Schuck, "By the late 1970s, these judicial innovations expanding the scope of a manufacturer's duty to design and produce safe products, multiplying the categories of persons entitled to sue to enforce that duty, easing the causation requirements, and

Table 7. ACHIEVEMENTS OF THE CONSUMER MOVEMENT, 1960–1978: THREE LEVELS OF ACTIVITY

Level 1: Protecting Consumers in the Marketplace

Federal Hazardous Substances Act (1960)

Color Additive Amendment (1960)

Kefauver-Harris Drug Amendments to the
Pure Food and Drug Act of 1906 (1962)

Air Pollution Control Act (1962)

Water Quality Act (1965)

Federal Cigarette Labeling and Advertising Act (1965)

National Traffic and Motor Vehicle Safety Act (1966)

Fair Packaging and Labeling Act (1966)

Child Protection Act (1966)

Wholesome Meat Act (1967)

Air Quality Act (1967)

Flammable Fabrics Act (1967)

Fire Research and Safety Act (1968)

Automobile Insurance Study (1968)

Federal Coal Miners' Health and Safety Act (1968)

Natural Gas Pipeline Safety Act (1968)

Consumer Credit Protection Act (1968)

Interstate Land Sales Full Disclosure Act (1968)

Wholesome Poultry Products Act (1968)

Radiation Control for Health and Safety Act (1968)

Child Protection and Toy Safety Act (1969)

National Environmental Policy Act (1969)

Consumer Product Safety Act (1970)

Fair Credit Reporting Act (1970)

Clean Air Act Amendments (1970)

Federal Water Pollution Control Act (1970)

Truth-in-Lending Act Amendments (1970)

Poison Prevention Packaging Act (1970)

Equal Credit Opportunity Act (1974)

Fair Credit Billing Act (1974)

Public Broadcasting Finance Act (1975)

Toxic Substances Control Act (1976)

Fair Debt Collection Practices Act (1977)

Level 2: Reinvigorating Government Regulation in the Consumer Interest

---

FTC and FDA both strengthened over the period. For example, FTC required warnings on cigarette packages (1964), soon extended to demanding equal broadcast time for anti-smoking messages, then to outlawing all cigarette advertising on radio and TV (1971); smoking limited and then banned on all commercial airline flights.

Highway Safety Bureau (1966)

Corporation for Public Broadcasting (1967)

National Commission on Product Safety appointed (1967)

Occupational Safety and Health Administration (1970)

Environmental Protection Agency, Council of Environmental Quality (1970)

Consumer Product Safety Commission (1972)

Freedom of Information Act (1974)

Magnuson-Moss Warranty Act (1974)

Federal Trade Commission Improvement Act (1975)

Courts assume more regulatory role through product liability tort system, 1960s–70s

---

Level 3: Institutionalizing the Consumer Voice in Government

Proposals to establish an independent federal consumer advocacy or protection agency to represent the consumer interest in all divisions of the federal government ignored or defeated in Congress from 1952 through 1978.

upholding unprecedented damage awards were well established." In essence, the courts became another regulator of the marketplace for dangerous or defective products, another existing arm of government retooled to curb the influence of exploitative corporations and empower consumers.[35]

Of course, this list of first- and second-level achievements omits the substantial amount of legislation that consumer activists sought but did not secure. Likewise, reinvigorated regulation had its limits; the tobacco industry, for example, successfully managed to evade lawmakers' control. When the Consumer Federation of America in 1973 called for "an immediate Federal Trade Commission investigation of the 100 most concentrated industries," such a full-scale anti-trust attack on corporate concentration never occurred. And from its inception in 1973, the Consumer Product Safety Commission never received the budget it needed to protect Americans properly from hazardous products.[36] Nor does a list like this one testify to lapses in enforcement of laws passed, which happened all too often. But overall, by the mid-1970s consumers had seen great progress in the regulation of the marketplace on behalf of their own health, safety, and economy.

It was the third level of demands—to institutionalize consumers as representatives of the public interest in government itself—that utterly failed. This effort came closest to seeking a return to the citizen consumer ideal that had prevailed during the New Deal and World War II, though even then consumer activists were unable to win the cabinet-level department they desired. Nonetheless, in New Deal agencies like the National Recovery Administration, the Agricultural Adjustment Administration, and the wartime Office of Price Administration, consumers gained a legitimate voice in the government, a recognition of their role as a counterveiling force to other organized interests, such as business, labor, farmers, and the federal government itself. Efforts to establish some kind of cabinet-level independent consumer advocacy agency with broad powers to intervene on consumers' behalf in all government units began in the 1950s, continued through the 1960s, and intensified in the 1970s. As champion Senator Warren Magnuson explained it, a fighting "pike was needed in the carp pond." As the battle heated up in the mid-1970s, Nader turned over day-to-day supervision of his Public Citizen organizations to colleagues in order to devote his full energies to securing such a consumer agency, so crucial did he consider it to advancing the consumerist agenda. As a reporter for the *Christian Science Monitor*, writing a twelve-part series on the consumer movement in March 1970, put it in the last article that cast ahead to the future: "In Washington this year, consumer efforts focus on building a loud and permanent voice in the name of the public interest. . . . What consumer advocates and Congress seem most eager to see is an organizational setup that

Charles Schulz's depiction of Lucy as a consumer advocate in the midst of the political struggle over a new federal consumer watchdog agency in 1977 reveals how visible the issue had become. Schulz gave Esther Peterson, President Jimmy Carter's consumer adviser, a personal copy of the cartoon dedicated to her, but through the Lucy character he also associated women more generally with consumer activism. (Courtesy of United Feature Syndicate, Inc.)

would ensure firm consumer representation in government decisionmaking."[37] Supporters would battle for such an agency for the next eight years.

Despite activists' tireless lobbying efforts, legislation creating a federal consumer agency went down to defeat, done in by lack of White House support under Nixon and Ford and by the increasing militancy of business groups like the Chamber of Commerce, the National Association of Manufacturers, the National Federation of Independent Business, and the Business Roundtable, newly founded in 1972 to unite the chief operating officers of leading corporations, all of whom viewed the bill as a "Trojan Horse Threat to American Business," the most serious advance yet of the destructive tidal wave of consumer protection. In 1970 the agency bill passed the Senate and not the House, in 1972 it died in a Senate filibuster, in 1974 it passed the House but was again blocked by a Senate filibuster, in 1975 it passed the Senate but lost in the House, and in 1977 and 1978, bolstered by the support of the new president, Jimmy Carter, it provoked the biggest showdown yet, but still ended up in the trash bin. Nader led a Committee for the Consumer Protection Bill backed by over two hundred consumer groups, unions, and other supporters that, among other strategies, mounted a "Nickel Campaign," showering congressional skeptics with nickels aimed at convincing them that the new agency would cost the average citizen only five cents a year, in contrast to the millions of dollars being spent by big business to fight it.[38] But, thanks to what agency supporter Congressman Benjamin Rosenthal (D-New York) considered "the most intense lobbying I've ever seen against any bill," an independent agency to defend consumers' interests before federal regulatory commissions, agencies, and courts as advocates had long hoped was not to be. The most representation that consumers achieved in the federal government during this era was an adviser for consumer affairs to Presidents Johnson, Nixon, Ford, and Carter and a supporting committee which varied in name from the Committee on Consumer Interests under Johnson to the Consumer Affairs Council under Carter. Through this office, Esther Peterson, Betty Furness, Virginia Knauer, and then Peterson again under Carter worked within clear constraints to remind presidents and their staffs to "remember the consumer" when making policy.[39]

HOW DEEP THE GRASS ROOTS?

To what extent, and in what ways, was consumerism a broad-based mass political movement? Support outside of Washington policy circles is not easily estimated, or, more precisely, taking its full measure requires looking in a variety of places: public opinion broadly, the vitality of organizations lobbying on behalf of consumers, and finally, grassroots agitation around the consumerist agenda.

Polls and other indicators suggest that public opinion widely supported the efforts of the consumer movement. As early as 1968, a confidential nationwide survey by the Opinion Research Corporation alarmed its corporate subscribers by concluding that "seven Americans in ten think present Federal legislation is inadequate to protect their health and safety. The majority also believe that more Federal laws are needed to give shoppers full value for their money."[40] Louis Harris polls over the next decade documented not only consumers' steadily declining confidence in products, services, retailers, and advertisers, but also their desire for better regulation and legislation to protect themselves. A 1973 Harris poll concluded, "A big majority of the American people say 'It is good to have critics like Ralph Nader to keep business on its toes.' "[41] In 1977, Harris collaborated with a marketing institute at the Harvard Business School on an extensive survey, "Consumerism at the Crossroads," that documented ongoing popular dissatisfaction with goods and services as well as recognition that some efforts, such as product labeling and information, had improved over the past decade. Not surprisingly, Harvard professor Stephen Greyser concluded from his study that "there is strong evidence from the public that consumerism is here to stay."[42] The debut of a Boy Scout merit badge for consumer buying in the same period confirmed that consumerism had joined the saintly ranks of motherhood and apple pie. Scouts out to earn this badge were expected to study three consumer laws, write a legislator or local paper with their view of a proposed law, critique a company's consumer services, analyze three problems for both consumers and merchants in low-income areas, and probe the helpful or misleading information conveyed in advertising.[43] Consumer consciousness had become an accepted part of the good citizenship for which Boy Scouts were being trained.

Public opinion alone would not have had much influence in pressuring for legislative and regulatory changes without formal organizations channeling that sentiment appropriately. The third-wave consumer movement bred an explosion of organizations on the national, state, and local levels: public agencies and nonprofits, newly created ones and in a few cases, such as Consumers Union, the American Cancer Society, and the National Consumers' League (NCL) and its state chapters, existing organizations now reoriented toward more consumerist goals. Established in 1967, the Consumer Federation of America (CFA) became the clearinghouse for more than two hundred consumer-oriented organizations by the mid-1970s, resembling, as control central for the third-wave consumer movement, the Emergency Conference of Consumer Organizations and the Consumers' National Federation of the second-wave movement during the New Deal era. As chief lobbyist on behalf of consumers, the CFA represented them at public hearings before Congress and regulatory bodies; provided up-to-date information to constituent organizations, many of them operating at state and local levels; and coordinated members' efforts to maximize impact. Members ranged from trade unions and local consumer agencies to credit unions and rural electric cooperatives. Beyond the CFA, additional national consumer organizations formed around specific issues, such as anti-smoking (Action on Smoking and Health), food safety (Center for Science in the Public Interest), automobile dangers (Center for Auto Safety), and health care (Health Research Group), while hundreds of others took root in states, counties, and localities.[44]

Alongside these new consumerist organizations stood some established ones, such as the NCL, which underwent a transformation in emphasis. The league, now confronted with a groundswell of interest in consumerism and a recognition that individuals' economic well-being depended on consumer as much as producer protections, shifted away from its decades-long mission of mobilizing consumer buying power and lobbying for better working conditions, wages, and social insurance toward a more consumer-driven political agenda. Although the NCL never abandoned its commitment to labor standards, it did reposition itself "to make a significant contribution to the consumer's well being today," in the words of one executive director, thereby, not unrelatedly, "reestablish[ing] a reasonably sound organizational and financial basis for the League," whose institutional viability as a workplace advocate had become increasingly precarious in an era of industrial unionization.[45]

Consumer organizations were as visible on the local and state levels as on the national one—if not more so. New Jersey provides an instructive case. A pioneer in consumer legislation and organization, it was among the first states to protect its residents against fraud and, in 1967, to establish a state Office of Consumer Protection to receive complaints and advocate on behalf of consumers in state government. By the mid-1970s the state office, now toughened as the Division of Consumer Affairs within the Department of Law and Public Safety, had established a network of over a hundred Consumer Affairs Local Assistance Officers (CALAs) to receive, and when possible to mediate, consumer complaints at the local level, referring cases of fraud to the state office for intensive investigation with a view to litigation. In 1974 the litigatory capability of the state was further enhanced when Governor Brendan T. Byrne created the Department of the Public Advocate, essentially a state-sponsored public interest law firm authorized to sue anyone in the state, including the governor himself. What Ralph Nader considered "the crown jewel of consumer and taxpayer protection in state governments"—in many ways the cabinet-level consumer beachhead that had eluded him at the federal level—had a broadly defined authority, pursuing more than two thousand lawsuits over the next twenty years to enforce state and federal laws governing everything from consumer fraud to prisoners' rights to exclusionary zoning in the suburbs. Also, New Jersey's supreme court proved to be a leader in tort reform as in other areas of judicial activism, adopting the doctrine of "strict liability" as early as 1960.

Nonprofit consumer organizations thrived in New Jersey as well. Twelve organizations were considered substantial and stable enough in 1976 to make it into the federal Department of Health, Education and Welfare's *Directory of Consumer Organizations*, including the Consumers' League of New Jersey, the Newark Consumer Project, the Gray Panthers of South Jersey, and three branches of NJPIRG. These nongovernmental consumer watchdogs provided critical vigilance over state consumer agencies, whose aggressiveness fluctuated with the governor and legislature sitting in Trenton. Consumer groups invited to participate in a day-long conference sponsored by the State Division of Consumer Affairs in May 1973, for example, used it as an opportunity to voice frustration with Governor Cahill's administration for being "less than diligent in satisfying consumer needs." The research director for NJPIRG went so far as to label it "a consumer fraud."[46] Although the state apparatus that emerged around consumer protection often failed to meet advocates' high expectations, the interplay of public and private organizations nonetheless created a new kind of political climate respectful, at least verbally, of consumers' rights.

Viable organizations were clearly not synonymous with mass support; Michael Pertschuk's "Not-for-Profit Consumer Entrepreneurs" did not require rank-and-file action to make their organizations dynamic and influential. Furthermore, rank-and-file political activity is notoriously hard to initiate and sustain, and just as hard to measure. Even in the New Deal era, when large numbers of women and African Americans identified as the rank and file of a rising consumers' movement, there were limits to its extensiveness. Now, in the heyday of the consumers' movement of the 1960s and 1970s, some organizers still expressed frustration over the difficulty of mobilizing mass support, despite Americans' stated sympathies with the cause in opinion polls. Several factors contributed. First, despite Presidents Kennedy and Johnson and activist Ralph Nader's attraction to "consumers" as a universal category that transcended narrower, more divisive identities, such a broad-based interest raised significant difficulties for organizing. As practitioners and scholars of interest group politics know well, the less defined the shared interest, the harder it is to organize constituents. Participants at the time understood this problem themselves. Robert Lampman, staff member of the Council of Economic Advisers charged with overseeing Kennedy's order to create a consumers' advisory council to implement consumers' "right to be heard," expressed concern in 1963: "Ironically, it may be easier to arrange new ways for government to do things *for* consumers than to arrange ways for consumers to participate in government and to express their point of view. . . . How do we communicate from a mass of largely unorganized consumers to those responsible for governmental decisions on numerous (some highly technical) questions?"[47] Hence, it was easier to mobilize consumers within narrower segments—as female consumers, black consumers, working-class consumers, youthful consumers, elderly consumers, and so forth—where a group's distinctive interests and comfort identifying as a population segment could be tapped. In this sense, consumer politics conformed to politics more generally after 1960, where political constituencies increasingly were segmented.

Second, many leaders, like Nader, stressed legislative achievements over building grassroots organizations. With the exception of his state-based PIRGs, Nader depended more on financial contributions from a broad base of

Americans than on their day-to-day support. In fact, Nader was quite satisfied with the adequacy of his popular base when his first direct-mail funding drive for Public Citizen yielded more than a million dollars, most from $15 memberships.[48] In many ways, Nader's Public Interest organizations were typical of the shape of civic engagement in the late twentieth century. As scholars of the subject have pointed out, participant-based organizations increasingly declined and were replaced by top-down "mailing-list organizations" offering fewer, if any, opportunities for face-to-face community interaction.[49]

But these impediments aside, significant grassroots mobilization did underlie the consumer movement of the 1960s and 1970s, with several social groups particularly active. An NCL report of 1982 reflecting back on the peak of the consumer movement argued for the formative influence of popular mobilization: "Consumerism has had a long-standing influence in the marketplace since the earliest days of commerce. In the 1960's–70's, however, consumer activism rose sharply to spur a citizens movement with national political force." Senator Frank Moss of Utah, a strong consumer advocate in Congress, similarly credited the fury of the hinterland with inspiring new policies in Washington: "There is a quiet revolt in this country. It is a revolt of people who are not violent, but who are angry—at incredibly shrinking packages and expanding prices and preposterous advertising. We in Congress, and they in the Administration, ignore this revolt at our peril."[50] Two critical constituencies who had supported the consumer movement of the New Deal era reenlisted: women and African Americans. In addition, other politically mobilized segments—young people, senior citizens, and rank-and-file unionists—joined their ranks.

Women served as the foot soldiers and the leadership of the third-wave consumer movement, much as they had for its predecessors during the Progressive Era and the New Deal. When Esther Peterson served President Johnson as his special assistant for consumer affairs, she was faced with a groundswell of grassroots agitation from "housewives" for such goals as lower supermarket prices, fewer price-raising promotional gimmicks like games and trading stamps, better inspection of consumer scales, and more honest advertising of specials. Although not as firmly planted in the historical record as the meat boycotts of 1935 and 1946, these spontaneous protests in the fall of 1966 gave women tremendous visibility at the time, monitored as they were through daily front-page stories and television news reports. What began as a boycott of five supermarket chains in Denver by approximately 100,000 members of Housewives for Lower Food Prices very quickly became a national phenomenon, with tens of thousands more women from 100 cities in 21 states organized in groups calling themselves such attention-grabbing names as

This photograph from the front page of the *New York Times,* October 29, 1966, was captioned "Housewives on the March." It showed women boycotting a supermarket in Queens, New York, as part of a national protest against high food prices and the promotional games, rampant in all but two states (Wisconsin and New Jersey outlawed them) since 1958, that consumers blamed for adding to the cost of groceries. (Courtesy of Neil Boenzi/*The New York Times*)

HELP (Housewives to Enact Lower Prices), MILK (Mothers Interested in Lower Kosts), Women on the Warpath, YELP (You're Enlisted to Help Lower Prices), We've Had It Club, and Pantry Pennypinchers, who cleverly urged women, "Stand up and be heard but not seen in chain-store supermarkets."

Although great controversy ensued over who was actually to blame for the steep jump in food prices over the previous year—farmers, wholesalers, retailers, or government spenders—to appease the protesters, many supermarket chains lowered prices on essential items like meat, milk, and butter, and ended many of the store promotions that pushed up prices. In fact, it was Peterson's enthusiastic support for the boycotters, beginning with the well-publicized hugs she gave members of the Denver Housewives for Lower Food Prices as they chanted "Down with frills, stamps, and gimmicks" that soured Johnson's close advisers on her and led them to force her resignation in early 1967. While they were trying to deflect public attention from rising inflation, manifesting itself particularly in higher food prices, to their consternation Peterson was telling a reporter from the *New York Times,* with utmost sincerity,

"I just think it's so beautiful that the gals are waking up." President Johnson's consumer initiative had been partly intended as a bid for the political sympathies of female, white, middle-class, suburban consumers, perceived as an important swing vote, but his administration was caught off guard when these women asserted themselves outside of the voting booth.[51]

As inflation continued to spiral into the 1970s, women once again turned to supermarket boycotts as a way to register their frustration with soaring prices. When alterations in President Nixon's price control policies raised rents and food costs dramatically in March 1973, women orchestrated another national boycott. As seven years earlier, the rank-and-file nature of the revolt was unmistakable. "A grass-roots explosion all over the country," is how one local New York consumer leader described it, a view confirmed by a *New York Times* reporter covering the story: "It is made up mainly of groups of tenants in apartment buildings, neighbors who shop at the same markets in small towns, block associations, and—perhaps most typical—groups of women who meet every morning over coffee." A New York City congressman who observed boycott advocates collecting signatures outside a supermarket in Queens claimed in astonishment, "I've seen rent petitions and antiwar petitions and all sorts of petitions. But I've never seen a petition like this where not one single person refused to sign." More than 500,000 consumers from New York, New Jersey, Connecticut, and Pennsylvania sent cash register tapes to President Nixon.[52] Although grassroots in origin, the boycott inspired the creation of a permanent organization, the National Consumers Congress (NCC), to coordinate boycotts nationwide.

In 1973, as in 1966, boycotts began over high prices, but soon expanded to include other consumer demands. As Betty Furness, chair at the NCC's organizational meeting April 11 reminded assembled boycott leaders laden with hundreds of thousands of petitioners' names, "Meat is just the tip of the iceberg." One of the first actions the NCC called after the meat protest was a boycott of Coca-Cola and Pepsi-Cola to help defeat pending legislation allowing the soft-drink industry to maintain a system of marketing based on exclusive territories, in violation of anti-trust laws. In a further example of the depth of the iceberg, a group of suburban Chicago housewives initially motivated by high prices successfully protested against local supermarkets' use of food freshness codes that were incomprehensible to shoppers.[53]

Women's active participation made possible another key item on the consumer movement's agenda—fairer access to credit. Inspired by the growing frustration of married, separated, divorced, and widowed women that they could not establish credit in their own names, feminist organizations like the National Organization for Women (NOW) lobbied fiercely for the Equal

Credit Opportunity Act (ECOA), finally passed in 1974 and enacted in 1976, and then monitored its implementation. In the files of NOW's Credit Task Force are thousands of furious letters documenting the discrimination women encountered as they sought to secure bank and credit cards and to qualify for mortgages, testimony to the groundswell of female anger that drove the successful campaign for equal credit. In this battle, the pen was as mighty as the placard.[54]

The third-wave consumers' movement, coinciding as it did with the birth of second-wave feminism, also offered an opening for women to work their way into government positions. Esther Peterson's and Betty Furness's posts as consumer adviser in the White House were replicated on the local and state level. Bess Myerson Grant, Miss America of 1945 who went on to become active in New York politics, became New York City's commissioner of consumer affairs, a position later filled by Betty Furness following her stints in Washington and Albany. In Chicago, future mayor Jane Byrne held the job of commissioner of consumer sales. Kay Valory served as consumer counsel to Governor Ronald Reagan of California, and Virginia Knauer was the director of the Pennsylvania Bureau of Consumer Protection before becoming President Nixon's special assistant for consumer affairs.[55] The opportunity that consumer mobilization offered women to exert influence at the grass roots and in official positions was not lost on critics. Much as during the battle over extending the OPA in 1946, opponents tried to denigrate the movement by associating it with women. Belittling the repeated food boycotts as "ladycotts" or "girlcotts," casting doubt on bachelor Ralph Nader's masculinity, disdaining consumerism as overprotective "big motherism," critics sought to diminish the significance of the movement through rendering it feminine, or by 1973, feminist.[56] During the consumer movement's peak decade from the mid-1960s to mid-1970s, American women served as the foot soldiers and many of the generals in the campaign to make markets and government more protective of consumers.

African Americans had repeatedly used their economic power as consumers for political ends, against Jim Crow discrimination in the South beginning in the late nineteenth century, as Garveyites and believers in a separate black economy in the 1920s, as supporters of the "Don't Shop Where You Can't Work Campaigns" of the Great Depression, as military personnel, home-front defense workers and civilians demanding full citizenship during World War II, and as battlers for civil rights from the late 1940s through the 1960s. At the height of civil rights activism, mobilizing consumers through sit-ins, picketing, selective buying, and boycotting provided a strategy for punishing discriminatory merchants—whether small-town southern storekeepers, northern restaurant owners, or national chains like Kress and Woolworth's—and more basically, for linking equal economic participation to equal political participation. Throughout the civil rights era, moreover, African-American consumers continued to use direct action at the point of consumption, much as they had in the 1930s, to pressure employers to hire black workers, through such famed campaigns as the Congress on Racial Equality's (CORE) picketing of White Castle Hamburger shops up and down the East Coast.[57]

By the late 1960s the increasing militance of the civil rights movement with the rise of black nationalism and black power revived the pre–World War II push for a separate black economy, ironically dovetailing at times with Presidents Johnson's and Nixon's more conservative initiatives to foster black enterprise. Black nationalist leader Malcolm X marked his own conversion to the Black Muslims with his disillusionment working at a Jewish-owned furniture store in the Detroit ghetto when he first got out of prison. He went on to advocate a Black Muslim network of grocery stores, drugstores, restaurants, and other small businesses as the key to liberation from white exploitation. As Malcolm wrote in 1964 shortly before he was killed:

> The black man in North America was economically sick and that was evident in one simple fact: as a consumer, he got less than his share, and as a producer gave *least*. The black American today shows us the perfect parasite image—the black tick under the delusion that he is progressing because he rides the udder of the fat, three-stomached cow that is white America. For instance, annually, the black man spends over $3 billion for automobiles, but America contains hardly any franchised black automobile dealers. For instance, forty per cent of the expensive imported Scotch whiskey consumed in America goes down the throats of the status-sick black man; but the only black-owned distilleries are in bathtubs, or in the woods somewhere. Or for instance—a scandalous shame—in New York City, with over a million Negroes, there aren't twenty black-owned businesses employing over ten people. It's because black men don't own and control their own community's retail establishments that they can't stabilize their own community.[58]

By the late 1960s other black nationalists, and even mainstream civil rights activists, were pushing for black-owned businesses as well, and for more patronage of them by governments and national chains. For example, the Reverend Jesse Jackson's Operation Breadbasket, an offshoot of Martin Luther King, Jr.'s Southern Christian Leadership Conference founded in 1967 with branches in thirty cities by 1970, conducted selective buying campaigns against major companies to, in Jackson's words, "help reverse the flow of dollars out of the black community." In one of its most celebrated struggles, the organization threatened black "economic withdrawal" from A & P stores in black neighborhoods if the chain refused to make deposits in black banks, to use black insurance companies, to hire black builders to construct and maintain stores, and to give prominent exposure to black-made products.[59] As they had for almost a century, African Americans continued to view the consumer marketplace as an appropriate and available arena for working out their status in American society, whether as equal to or independent from whites.

What distinguished the consumer politics of African Americans at the grass roots in this era of third-wave consumerism, however, was that in at least two ways they invoked the dominant liberal discourse of the "low-income consumer" to make new, more radical claims, transcending both the more limited, longstanding black call for equal access to the capitalist marketplace and the emergent white concern with fair marketplace practice. First, tens of thousands of participants in the multitude of ghetto rebellions from 1964 to 1968 engaged in looting local stores as a way of avenging exploitative treatment and satisfying their pent-up desires for basic consumer goods, promised but not delivered by a supposedly prosperous postwar America. Second, members of a new movement of welfare recipients, the National Welfare Rights Organization (NWRO) and its numerous state and local branches, likewise built on public concern over the problems of the low-income consumer to claim that everyone was entitled to an adequate standard of living, whether earned through a job or provided by the welfare state.

Until now, the thrust of black consumer politics had been to seek equal access to, and equal treatment in, the marketplace, and this was still the focus of many black consumer projects and support for the mainstream consumerist agenda. One of the most active members of the Consumer Federation of America, for instance, was the Consumer Education and Protective Association (CEPA), an organization based in Philadelphia's black neighborhoods that picketed merchants accused by individual consumers of exploiting them. Similarly, Operation Breadbasket's complaints against A & P included the charge of selling low-quality meats to black customers, and the Harlem Consumer Education Council orchestrated boycotts of ghetto stores on the day that welfare checks arrived and food prices predictably rose.[60] The new, more grassroots consumer activism of the third-wave era, in contrast, redefined the thrust of the movement toward a demand for economic justice measured through the acquiring of consumer goods and services, not just fairer protections in gaining access to them. As a New York civil rights activist of the period put it, "The black cat in Harlem wasn't worried about no damn bus—he'd been riding the bus for fifty years. What he didn't have was the fare."[61] And, he might have added, decent food, clothes, appliances, and furniture.

The Kerner Commission and other bodies investigating the "civil disorders" of the 1960s all concluded that retail stores—the inescapable daily reminder of ghetto residents' economic deprivation—suffered a much greater proportion of damage from trashing and looting than public institutions, industrial properties, or private residences. And given the disproportionate white ownership of stores in the neighborhoods under siege, white retailers were the ones to suffer the most from massive looting often followed by burning, not only to cover incriminating evidence but also to destroy credit records. Frequently, in fact, discriminating rebellion participants spared black businesses with "Soul Brother" signs in their windows. Investigators agreed that looters were punishing merchants who had subjected them, as "low-income consumers," to all the recently catalogued abuses.

The Kerner Commission also heard testimony that participants were satisfying pent-up desires for the consumer goods that television, movies, and advertising daily held out—made all the more enticing with the intensified targeting of the segmented African-American market in the 1960s—without offering the means to secure them. The commission's report cited a study of low-income families in New York City, documenting that as early as 1961, 95 percent had televisions, ensuring that few blacks were deprived of images of American abundance, even if denied substantial access to its fruits. The frustrating gap between aspiration and reality was obvious even to the relatively conservative president of the National Business League, formerly the National Negro Business League founded in 1900 by Booker T. Washington, when he testified to the Kerner Commission in 1967: "It is to be more than naive—indeed, it is a little short of sheer madness—for anyone to expect the very poorest of the American poor to remain docile and content in their poverty when television constantly and eternally dangles the opulence of our affluent society before their hungry eyes." Emblematic was black writer Louis Lomax's conversation with a looter in Watts. When he confronted the young man carrying a sofa from a burning furniture store by imploring, "Brother, brother, do you realize what you're doing?" the man replied, "Don't bother me now. I've got to hurry back to get the matching chair." Yet if this looter was typical, he did not view his behavior as irresponsible lust for material possessions, but rather as an entitlement of his full citizenship in affluent America. A rebellion participant in Detroit defended his actions in just these terms: "I was feeling

Men and women of all ages looted Gellers' Department Store at the corner of South Orange Avenue and Littleton Street in Newark's Central Ward in July 1967, entering and leaving through shattered store windows in broad daylight. Anger over many kinds of exclusion exploded in five days of revolt in the streets, particularly the looting of white-owned stores resented for high prices and exploitative sales practices. (Courtesy of the Newark Public Library)

proud, man, at the fact that I was a Negro. I felt like a first class citizen. I didn't feel ashamed of my race because of what they did."[62]

The revolt in the Central Ward of Newark in July 1967, one of the nation's worst in terms of bodily injury, death, and property loss, demonstrated how ghetto residents' awareness of their deprivation as consumers shaped the character of the event, even if it did not cause it. White flight had shifted Newark's population very quickly over the postwar period from 17 percent non-white in 1950 to more than 60 percent black and Latino, mostly Puerto Rican, by 1967. Accompanying this precipitous demographic change was a rapid disappearance of good industrial jobs, growing poverty, severe housing and health crises, and a political situation seething with racial tension. Although African Americans made up nearly 52 percent of the population, they had minimal representation in city government, on the police force, and in the school department. The latest confrontation grew out of the mayor's plan to condemn and turn over 150 acres in the almost all-black Central Ward to keep the expanding College of Medicine and Dentistry from leaving Newark, forcing the relocation of thousands of residents. With that crisis and others simmering in the background, the police beating of a black cabdriver who resisted arrest for a minor traffic violation on the night of Wednesday, July 12, 1967, exploded into five days of revolt in the streets. By the end, $15 million in property had been lost, including at least seven hundred stores, hundreds of people had been injured, and twenty-six were killed, all but three by the hands of the Newark Police, the New Jersey State Police, and the National Guard, who battled fiercely to reassert their control over the main shopping district of the ward.

What most struck observers over and over again was how much the hour-to-hour, day-to-day activity of the rebellion consisted of instrumental looting of stores. When Mayor Hugh Addonizio and Governor Richard Hughes toured the core of the protest area on July 14, they were most upset, according to the *New York Times,* as they "watched helplessly as men, women, and children almost gaily raided wrecked stores. . . . They saw children carrying toys and bicycles, and adults with appliances, TV sets and liquor they had taken from stores with smashed windows and broken doors." Governor Hughes declared himself "shocked and horrified" by the "holiday atmosphere." The *Newark News* reported, "Mobs raced into almost every business sector, loading television sets, appliances, furniture and other items into baby carriages and shopping carts. Numerous looters pulled cars and even trucks up to smashed storefronts, calmly walking into the debris and carefully selecting what items to take for themselves."

Lest we suspect distortion in the reporting of mainstream white newspapers, leaders of Newark's black community concurred with this picture of a mass shopping spree, in fact stressing that this was no rear-guard action of a transient underclass. A *Life* reporter quoted "a good-looking, light-skinned young Negro who heads one of the conventional action groups in Newark" as telling him, "This insurrection was supported by the vast majority of black people—that's where the mayor and the others make a mistake. Not only poor blacks but middle-class blacks were out there looting, sticking stuff in their cars." Analysis of arrest records supports that claim: of the 1426 persons arrested, 76 percent of them were charged with crimes against property (burglary, larceny, and buying, receiving, or possessing stolen property), and of those individuals eighteen or older for whom employment information was available, almost three-fourths had jobs, putting them among the more stable residents of the community. By all accounts, moreover, Newark's looters

A National Guardsman patrolling the streets of the Central Ward's commercial district on July 15, 1967, to restore order was ironically photographed in front of a store whose windows were still intact—not because of his vigilance but because looters had spared it for being black-owned. (Photo by William Clare/*The Star-Ledger*, Newark, NJ)

showed great respect for "Soul Brother," "Sister Soul," and "Black" signs in shop windows, systematically sparing them along with some white-owned stores known to treat customers fairly. When black-owned stores were damaged, later analysis invariably linked their smashed and bullet-ridden windows to vengeful white officers in the New Jersey State Police and the National Guard, who had become almost vigilante snipers by the end of the siege.[63]

Whereas the Harlem revolt of 1935 had protested merchants' refusal to hire black clerks and the Harlem rebellion of 1943 had expressed consumers' frustrations with their unfair treatment under the home-front price controls of World War II, this one in nearby Newark a quarter century later revealed the state of mind of African-American consumers no longer satisfied to be spectators rather than participants in the Consumers' Republic. A black youth who made it home with several boxes of shirts and shoes from Snyder Men's Store on Springfield Avenue revealingly told a group of admirers, "They tell us about that pie in the sky but that pie in the sky is too damn high." Another whose mother forbade him to join his friends explained to a reporter why he nonetheless thought looting was morally justified in this case: "I don't think it's right to steal. But I would have looted with my friends. We don't have anything here."[64]

Amiri Baraka, Newark's native son playwright and poet, published a poem in *Evergreen Review* while out on bail between his arrest on trumped-up charges during the 1967 rebellion and his subsequent trial. In his poem "Black People!" which the judge read aloud to support an extraordinarily harsh sentence (later overturned on appeal), Baraka angrily justified looting as a way for blacks to extract their due, free of the usual exploitation by white retailers—"get what you want what you need," "No money down. No time to pay."

BLACK PEOPLE!

What about that bad short you saw last week
on Frelinghuysen, or those stoves and refrigerators, record players, shotguns,
in Sears, Bambergers, Klein's, Hahnes', Chase, and the smaller joosh
enterprises? What about that bad jewelry, on Washington Street, and
those couple of shops on Springfield? You know how to get it, you can
get it, no money down, no money never, money dont grow on trees no
way, only whitey's got it, makes it with a machine, to control you
you cant steal nothin from a white man, he's already stole it he owes
you anything you want, even his life. All the stores will open if you
will say the magic words. The magic words are: Up against the wall mother
fucker this is a stick up! Or: Smash the window at night (there are magic
actions) smash the windows daytime, anytime, together, lets smash the
window drag the shit from in there. No money down. No time to pay. Just
take what you want. The magic dance in the street. Run up and down Broad
Street niggers, take the shit you want. Take their lives if need be, but
get what you want what you need . . .[65]

When Baraka testified before the state of New Jersey's Lilley Commission investigating the Newark rebellion in late November, he touched again on how blacks' material deprivation amid America's affluence motivated their actions: "The poorest black man in Newark, in America, knows how white people live. We have television sets; we see movies. We see the fantasy and the reality of white America every day. This is offered to us as a reason for committing ourselves to the goals of white America. The average black man knows this is a fantasy except for those few who are sent away to college to have their minds shaped into the image of white desire." In his *Autobiography,* written a decade and a half later, Baraka lamented how misguided his fellow Newarkers had been but nonetheless underscored the frustrated consumer desire that fueled the rebellion: "Families worked together, carrying sofas and TVs collectively down the street. All the shit they saw on television that they had been hypnotized into wanting they finally had a chance to cop."[66]

Tragically, the outcome of this cataclysm in Newark, as in many other American cities, isolated inner-city residents even more from the fair shake at the good life that for five days in July 1967 suddenly came within their grasp. Many agreed with the Chicago man who, surveying the blocks of burned-out, white-owned stores that scarred the city's South Side landscape after that city's own violence, told the Greater Chicago Citizens Riot Probe Commission, "Stores should put something back into the community. We should have 50 percent of the stores. We need some cooperatives." Yet the more common aftermath everywhere was the departure of white merchants and the refusal of financial institutions to loan money to or insurance companies to insure aspiring black entrepreneurs. Years would follow in Newark's Central Ward with no supermarkets and few other viable businesses in what had once been the dynamic commercial district at its heart. As late as 1982 the 1300 families living in the high-rise housing project nearby had only one grocery with limited stock and high prices, one family cafe, and a few summertime vegetable peddlers as immediate sources of food; other goods were even scarcer. Not until 1990 did 93,000 Central Ward residents finally get a supermarket, when a Pathmark store was built in partnership with a nonprofit community development corporation.[67] In sharp contrast to their plea for inclusion in prosperous America, participants in Newark's 1967 rebellion inadvertently contributed to the restructuring of community marketplaces under way in metropolitan America, adding neighborhood commercial devastation to their exclusion from suburban shopping centers and even, in some cases, new downtown retail developments.

The second way that African Americans, and to a lesser extent Latinos, mobilized at the grass roots to turn concern over the "low-income consumer" to their own ends was in organizing as welfare recipients to demand larger benefits and more respectful and just treatment. Through the National Welfare Rights Organization (NWRO), active from 1966 to 1974, and its affiliated branches, 540 at the peak in 1971, low-income consumers and their advocates argued that welfare recipients—predominantly poor black women—had rights to a decent living as citizens of an affluent America. Rather than focus on job creation, as did many other organizations advocating for poor people, NWRO sought to secure for welfare clients the money, material goods, and credit to buy the additional consumer items that they needed to live dignified and autonomous lives. Ultimately, organizers hoped, such pressure to increase

These two photographs contrast the same person at the same corner of Springfield Avenue and Prince Street in Newark's Central Ward, thirty years apart. The first, taken in the midst of the rebellion on July 14, 1967, shows a National Guardsman requesting identification from Foy Miller. Although damage to stores is visible, the vibrancy of the commercial district comes through. In the second photograph, Ms. Miller stands in the same location on July 14, 1997. Now vacant lots have replaced retail establishments, depriving the area's residents of places to shop near their homes. (Copyright Benedict J. Fernandez, top, and Ozier Muhammad/*The New York Times,* bottom)

welfare expenditures would lead Congress to pass a Guaranteed Annual Income—also championed as a Guaranteed Adequate Income—providing all Americans with a basic living above the poverty level. Welfare rights organizations employed two major strategies to achieve these long- and short-term goals: massive use of the right to a "fair hearing," a trial-like administrative procedure rarely utilized, to challenge welfare departments' frequent refusal to authorize special grants for purchases of new clothing, furniture, appliances, summer camp, and the like; and the mounting of local and national consumer actions, including picketing and boycotts, to force major retailers to grant credit to poor people, usually deprived of access to the credit that allowed other Americans to participate more fully in the era's prosperity. Much like the protesters who took to the streets in the rebellions of the 1960s, welfare activists introduced an entitlement to a higher quality of life into the discourse of the "low-income consumer," heretofore focused more on fair access to markets.[68]

It wasn't that NWRO didn't want good jobs for welfare clients. Well-paying jobs capable of supporting a family held great appeal—if welfare recipients could work. But that was a big if. Activists repeatedly pointed out that more often than not those on welfare were aged, disabled, or mothers with small children, unable to work but deserving nonetheless of an adequate standard of living: plentiful food, decent residential accommodations, respectable clothing, functional furnishings. "We believe that the way to do something about poverty is to give people the money they need to meet the basic necessities of life at least at a minimum level for health, decency, and dignity," NWRO executive director George Wiley and New York City welfare rights leader Beulah Sanders told the Joint Economic Committee of Congress in 1968.[69] The first thing NWRO and local organizations did was encourage eligible people to enroll in welfare, in most cases Aid to Families with Dependent Children (AFDC). Between 1960 and 1970 the national welfare rolls skyrocketed from 3.1 million to 7.4 million, with more of the eligible—from only 42 percent in 1967 to 87 percent in 1973—receiving benefits. In New York City, where welfare rights activity was particularly intense, total grants rose 500 percent between 1963 and 1968.[70]

NWRO's next step was to educate recipients to take best advantage of their benefits. Everywhere, recipients received counseling from savvy welfare veterans and their supporters, often socially conscious members of the clergy. Attention focused on utilizing the little-known right to a "fair hearing." The Welfare Rights Organization of Newark, for example, with help from the Scholarship, Education and Defense Fund for Racial Equality (SEDFRE), a spin-off of CORE, published a guide, Your Welfare Rights, in 1967, instructing welfare clients how to work the welfare system, particularly how to ask for a fair hearing to satisfy "special needs." This coaching typically led to hearing requests by AFDC recipients like Delores Hassell, a mother of three, who protested that "I filled out a Minimum Standard ['basic need'] household sheet asking for an iron, sheets, dishes, pots and pans, two chairs and a dresser for my daughter. I spoke to my caseworker, Miss Etman, who said that I could wait for these things."[71] The individual lodging the complaint, like Hassell, was not the only one helped by the fair-hearing strategy. By flooding the welfare appeals process, activists often succeeded in winning higher benefits and better treatment for all recipients.

Recognizing that monthly welfare checks and occasional special grants could barely provide an adequate quality of life, and that most middle-class Americans depended on access to credit to underwrite their lifestyles, local welfare groups as well as the national organization orchestrated intensive campaigns to force large retailers to make credit available to welfare recipients, thereby freeing them from dependence on exploitive ghetto merchants who preyed on low-income customers with usurious installment schemes. Protests began during the summer of 1968 against the major downtown department stores in Philadelphia, and over the next year spread to both local department stores and national chains around the country. The Brooklyn Welfare Action Council, for example, demonstrated outside, and even brazenly inside by bringing full carts of merchandise to the register and trying to charge them at the popular discount department store Korvettes. With persistence, they won more favorable credit review procedures for people on welfare there and at the higher-end Brooklyn-based store Abraham & Straus. A national campaign against Sears, Roebuck, more successful in some locales than others, brought public attention everywhere to the credit issue.[72]

To some extent, these campaigns conformed to traditional consumer organizing against the long-targeted evil of credit discrimination. Yet in advocating that poor people had the right to credit—even if it meant risking debt—welfare rights activists distinguished themselves from the more paternalistic experts dedicated to safeguarding low-income consumers from exploitative retailers as well as their own appetites as consumers. Moreover, the welfare rights position on credit conveyed a powerful message that economic justice involved ensuring that poor consumers could purchase the material goods they needed and wanted, even if they currently lacked the cash to pay for them. As Juliet Greenlaw, an AFDC recipient and Indiana state representative to NWRO, testified at a hearing on the Democratic Party's platform in August 1968, "Food and rent is not all of life. Why shouldn't we be able to buy perfume once in a while—or a ring—or even a watch? Every woman wants and needs some of these things—particularly when we see other women having them. . . .

The National Welfare Rights Organization mounted a campaign in 1969 to boycott Sears, Roebuck stores until welfare recipients were granted the same right to credit that other consumers enjoyed. The twelve-year-old daughter of the "Action Chairman" of the Sears campaign in Newark wrote, "Today we went to Sears to ask them could we have credit in there [*sic*] store they don't want any part of us welfare people. They don't know what it is to be poor and to try to have the better things in Life." Dorothy Perry, "Composition—Welfare Rights," April 8, 1969, cited in Felicia Kornbluh, "To Fulfill Their 'Rightly Needs,'" *Radical History Review* 69 (Fall 1997): 92. (Courtesy of the National Welfare Rights Organization Records, The Moorland-Springarn Research Center, Howard University)

Our children drop out of school because they don't have decent clothes, let alone the things that other children take for granted—enough school supplies, money for a class trip, a graduation suit or dress." Independent access to credit would give recipients not only the means to buy, but the ability to decide on their own what to buy. As Johnnie Tillmon, a national leader of NWRO, cautioned welfare mothers, "'The' Man, the welfare system, controls your money. 'He' tells you what to buy and what not to buy, where to buy it and what things cost." Credit, she and others argued, offered a kind of economic freedom that all Americans, including poor black women, deserved.[73]

Whereas the mainstream white consumer movement focused more on liberal protection from the abuses of the marketplace than on the economic inequalities that made some people more capable of consuming than others, some African-American activists turned one of the basic tenets of the movement—an end to discrimination against the "low-income consumer"—toward critiquing the economic inequalities rampant in American society during the 1960s. This was not a rigid color line, of course. Minority populations supported aspects of the mainstream consumer movement, and white housewives who demanded lower prices were calling for a stronger standard of economic fairness. But in a city like Newark, the growth of welfare rights organizing coincided with the July 1967 rebellion in the streets to heighten the intensity of an equity-oriented, consumer-centered politics.

With similar rumblings at the grass roots throughout urban America, it is likely that Martin Luther King, Jr.'s shift at the end of his life in 1967–68 from battling racial discrimination to championing a "Poor People's Campaign" asserting the right of the poor to a decent life was inspired by what he learned from compatriots fighting in the decaying streets of urban ghettos and the dehumanizing offices of the welfare bureaucracy. In the 1930s, African Americans had employed the boycott tactics of the consumer movement to secure good jobs in the shops of their own neighborhoods. In the 1960s once again consumerism provided a vehicle for pursuing economic justice, this time defined not so much in terms of jobs, scarcer than ever in economically troubled industrial cities like Newark, but as a right to a decent standard of living in the Consumers' Republic. In fact, leaders of the welfare rights movement went even further and linked their campaign to mainstream justifications for the Consumers' Republic. The chairperson of the Milwaukee County Welfare Rights Organization, for instance, claimed that the NWRO agenda would benefit the nation as a whole, not just individual poor consumers: "A guaranteed adequate income would put more money into our economy. Poor people spend all their money; we don't have enough to save any. If people had a decent income, they would spend it on better housing, clothes, food, and normal things needed for a decent life."[74] In arguing that bringing poor consumers more extensively into the flourishing world of mass consumption would enhance, not undermine, the viability of the economy, NWRO leaders as late as the 1970s located their radical (albeit within a capitalist framework) demand for a Guaranteed Adequate Income within the postwar consensus surrounding the Consumers' Republic.

Other social groups beyond women and African Americans—young adults of college age, senior citizens, rank-and-file unionists—also provided support at the grass roots for the consumer movement. College students in particular made up a critical base for the movement, contributing thousands of volunteer hours and dollars, as well as organizational talent. To some extent, of course, consumerism was just one cause among many that politically aware young people embraced during the 1960s and early 1970s. But Ralph Nader, who generally expressed more interest in research and lobbying in Washington than grassroots organizing, went out of his way to cultivate student support, giving youthful consumer activism a nudge that grew into a wallop. In the summer of 1968, Nader brought to Washington a small group of law students to undertake a study of the FTC that turned out to be a scathing attack. The next summer his "Nader's Raiders" multiplied, with over a hundred students of law, economics, engineering, and medicine engaged in various studies of other government agencies, including the Department of Agriculture, the FDA, the National Water Pollution Control Administration, and the Interstate Commerce Commission (ICC). By the summer of 1970, two hundred students assembled in Washington, and from there, the notion of young adults mustering their research and organizing skills on behalf of the public interest took off.

Nader's national PIRG and its loosely affiliated state and local branches—many of them supported by deductions from college students' activity fees—engaged in lobbying both the public and legislators on critical consumerist issues. By November 1972, Nader claimed that 350,000 students at more than 50 colleges and universities in 13 states had enrolled; by 1973 the totals had risen to 400,000 dues-paying members at 138 campuses in 19 states and the District of Columbia. In the typical pattern, students at a college or university voted by referendum to allocate an average of $3 from their fees to their local or state PIRG, and then elected representatives to the all-student board in numbers corresponding to the size of their financial contribution. That board selected projects and paid professional staff, including lawyers, to oversee student volunteer researchers and organizers. A full range of concerns engaged students: consumer and environmental hazards, false advertising, fair and unit pricing, decent housing, equal credit for women, tax reform, utility rates, access to medical and dental care, mass transit, even the problems of the low-income consumer. When students from twenty-five eastern colleges assembled at Villanova University in November 1970 to organize a National Student Consumer Protection Council, they decided—somewhat naively—to send students into ghetto areas to help families design weekly budgets, to advise them on major purchases, and to collect complaints about business practices to which they had fallen victim. Students also took the lessons of consumerism back home to their own campuses, leading to sit-ins at the Universities of Michigan, Massachusetts, Wisconsin, and California to demand that school stores sell books and supplies at cost, which landed more than a few protesters in jail. Although PIRGs suffered from the turnover typical of student projects, and their dues checkoff system sometimes raised opposition from college trustees, at their best they created a structure to involve thousands of young people in the third-wave consumer movement.[75]

Perhaps the most convincing evidence that the consumer movement of the 1960s and 1970s had widespread support came from the expressed anxieties of business leaders over its broad base. The creation of the CFA in 1967 was greeted somewhat hysterically by the *Kiplinger Washington Letter* as a "super-organization" planning "marches on state capitals and big letter-writing campaigns." The *National Business Woman* profiled "The Militant Shopper," who joins with "groups of ordinary citizens . . . to publicize gyps and dodges and to plump for corrective and regulatory laws and law enforcement." A panel convened at the 12th Annual Government Affairs Conference of the American Advertising Federation in 1970 warned the audience that they could no longer assume "that consumerism would go away if left alone." "No longer the well-publicized activity of the vocal minority," it now covered all income levels and was undeniably "a real grass-roots movement that is growing more sophisticated in its demands." In the last election, the panelists soberly pointed out, no candidate running for office on consumer issues was defeated.[76]

The consumer movement of the 1960s and 1970s had indeed acquired a substantial popular base and was far more than the top-down creation of advocates in Washington. Even if die-hard activists were rare, many Americans embraced a new consumer consciousness by the mid-1960s, and, in particular, social groups marginal to mainstream politics—women, African Americans, and youth—seized the opportunities for influence that consumerism offered. As in the 1930s and 1940s, political outsiders found that their politicization as consumers provided an avenue for challenging the status quo. For most adherents, the third-wave consumer movement was a way of holding the Consumers' Republic that they were living in accountable to the ideal upon which it was founded: that a flourishing mass consumption economy could be safe, democratic, and equitable. Increasingly, they had discovered, they needed to build more legislative, regulatory, and judicial protections into the marketplace so that the citizen consumer ideal of the 1930s and 1940s, committed to the common good, could coexist in greater balance with the rank-and-file purchasers as citizens of the Consumers' Republic. Often the consumer movement aimed at strengthening government power to hold corporate America more accountable, and at its best it proved an effective strategy for disciplining capitalist private enterprise in the public interest. Although many of its most celebrated campaigns seemed to revolve around lowering prices or providing people with more material goods, such as the meat boycotts of 1966 and 1973 and NWRO's campaign for credit in 1968–69, almost always a broader consciousness of the consumer interest was involved. These were moral, not just economic struggles.

That said, troubling trends also beset the third-wave consumers' movement. First, in replicating the confluence of political citizen and economic consumer that had characterized the concept of the Consumers' Republic from the start—as full economic participation in the Consumers' Republic seemed almost a right and responsibility of political citizenship—the consumer movement only intensified that blurring of lines between the two categories. In much of the discourse of the consumers' movement, for example, "citizen" and "consumer" were used interchangeably. "Every citizen can benefit from knowing more about consumer laws," pronounced President Jimmy Carter in his proclamation declaring National Consumer Education Week in October 1980. "For government to serve the people, agencies must by their own initiative interact with the citizenry. . . . All too often what separates government and consumers is a lack of knowledge," a National Consumers' League report chimed in during 1981. Even the consumer rebels in the streets merged their identities as citizens and consumers. Much like the Detroit looter who attested to feeling like a "first class citizen," an NWRO activist wrote in a letter to Sears management, "People on welfare must be allowed the same rights and opportunities as other American citizens."[77] Whereas such claims to their rights as citizens strengthened the case that consumerist advocates, ghetto rebels, and welfare recipients made for themselves as deserving consumers in the economy, it also took Americans further down a slippery slope that would in time reshape their relationship to government itself.

Second, to the extent that the consumer movement's success increasingly depended upon galvanizing people within narrowly defined subcommunities, it contributed—alongside other social shifts over the postwar period—to a restricting of Americans' common interest. Consistent with the way the policy infrastructure of the Consumers' Republic (such as the GI Bill, the income tax, and the structuring of credit) differentiated Americans by gender, class, and race, the way the commercial and residential landscapes of metropolitan America segregated along class and racial lines, and the way mass marketing evolved into segmented marketing and then carried strategic targeting of consumer segments over into politics, the consumer movement reinforced a long-term postwar trend. More often that not, identifying as a consumer meant thinking of oneself not in the broad identity terms originally intended by the promoters of consumer citizenship in the 1930s, by the framers of the Consumers' Republic right after World War II, and even by the liberal pioneers of third-wave consumerism like Kennedy and Nader, but rather in narrower ways, as part of distinct constituencies of consumers—women, African Americans, youth, labor, poor people, senior citizens—with particular rights and needs for protection.[78] The problem was less that women or blacks or younger and older Americans were articulating their own consumerist demands for protection against unrestrained private and sometimes even governmental power. Clearly, the universal category of "consumer" ran the risk of obfuscating important subgroup agendas, whereas narrower definitions of vulnerable consumers offered greater prospect for across-the-board success. The problem was more that people found little support or encouragement to think beyond their own self-interest as consumers, and the nation's agenda therefore failed to represent as much as it could have a negotiation among its constituent parts.

So long as the Consumers' Republic still thrived, and that oft-invoked economic pie continued to grow in size without shrinking each group's portion, the consequences of moving from a notion of a common consumer interest to multiple consumer interests was barely noticeable. But when the Consumers' Republic began to falter with hard economic times in the mid-1970s, citizens who barely distinguished themselves from consumers, living in a nation more fragmented than ever, increasingly severed America's common interest from Americans' individual and group self-interests so that "consumer" became more a claim to personal entitlement than a commitment to society's collective well-being.

DECLINE OF THE CONSUMER MOVEMENT

Obviously, Americans no longer live in the golden era of the consumer movement. Although they are still surrounded by vestiges of consumerism and periodic invocations of the citizen consumer—as evidenced in debates over a Patients' Bill of Rights, the safety of certain drugs, the monopolistic practices of Microsoft, and the viability of a Nader presidency—the messianic intensity of the third-wave consumer movement has surely passed. Understanding fully why, how, and to what extent consumerism has declined would require another book, since the purpose here has been to explore the movement's rise. Suffice it to say, however, that several factors precipitated the unraveling of consumerism and the Consumers' Republic that spawned it, above all the economic crisis that reached full force in the mid-

1970s, bringing an end to a quarter century of economic boom. While the spendable real income of a family of four had risen 20.4 percent between 1947 and 1957, and 13.1 percent between 1957 and 1967—providing the wherewithal for participation in the Consumers' Republic—it actually declined 1.7 percent between 1969 and 1979, mostly due to high inflation.

Inflation began rising in the mid-1960s, as President Johnson sought to pay for a war in Vietnam and expensive Great Society programs at home without raising taxes, putting his popularity above playing by the required rules of the Keynesian game. President Nixon, inheriting both Johnson's inflationary spiral and his Vietnam War, took the dollar off the gold standard and instituted wage and price controls in 1973 to curb inflation, but they in turn contributed to stagnant wages, shortages, and growing income inequality. Presidents Gerald Ford and then Jimmy Carter presided over the worsening of this severe economic crisis into what came to be called "stagflation"—a killer combination of sluggish growth and productivity, unremitting unemployment, and an inflation rate that climbed to almost 15 percent. Measured in constant prices, the annual average compound growth rate of the gross national product fell from 4 percent for 1960–73 to 1.8 percent for 1973–82. Productivity, which had grown at a 3 percent average annual clip after World War II, sagged after 1973 to only about 1 percent growth a year. Energy shortages in 1973–74, provoked by the Organization of Petroleum Exporting Countries' (OPEC) embargo on oil exports, contributed further to the damage. With all this bad news, consumer confidence plummeted from a baseline of 100 percent set in 1966 to an average of 71.3 percent in the 1970s, when the average between 1951 and 1993 was 82.1 percent. Compounding these immediate problems, moreover, was the longer-term decline in American industrial production, often referred to as "deindustrialization." As corporations systematically diverted capital from productive investment to speculation, mergers and acquisitions, and foreign investment, and as competitors from abroad encroached on America's lion share of industrial manufacturing and world markets, workers found themselves without jobs and their hometowns and cities without operating factories.[79]

For the first time in the postwar period, the Consumers' Republic as a prescription for an economy and political culture no longer seemed viable. When earlier the Consumers' Republic had promised—and delivered to a certain extent—economic and social incorporation through mass consumption, a prosperous economy lifted many boats, despite the discrimination and inequalities that made the consumer marketplace less than its ideal. Now a formula for economic health built on widespread participation in a vibrant mass consumption economy seemed ill suited to the realities of mid-1970s America. As inflationary worries kept the federal government from encouraging demand, and unemployment and declining real incomes kept consumers from buying, the underpinnings of the Consumers' Republic collapsed.

One small case study of a closed factory in Newark demonstrates the ripples of damage. When J. Wiss & Sons, a large cutlery manufacturer that had been in business in Newark since 1848, was acquired by a Texas conglomerate, it was relocated to the cheaper operating environment of North Carolina. Its departure deprived Newark of 760 manufacturing jobs, an additional 468 jobs in stores, banks, luncheonettes, taverns, and other local businesses, and more than $14 million in purchasing power, half of which, on deposit in local banks, had underwritten loans to finance mortgages, home improvements, and purchases of automobiles, televisions, and other appliances.[80] A viable Consumers' Republic required widespread purchasing power, and that, as unions had argued throughout the postwar era, meant lots of good jobs, now fast disappearing as unemployment rates climbed from 4.8 percent of the workforce in 1973 to 8.3 percent in 1975 to 10 percent in 1981, and real weekly earnings fell at a −0.4 percent annual rate during both the 1970s and 1980s.[81]

Even as President Carter staggered under the burden of stagflation, he nonetheless continued to uphold the consumerist agenda—up to a point. He brought activist Esther Peterson back into the White House as his consumer adviser, and endorsed many ongoing consumer campaigns, such as the battle for an independent, cabinet-level federal consumer department. Yet his presidency nonetheless proved a turning point for the Consumers' Republic, and consequently third-wave consumerism. What has been called Carter's "malaise speech" (despite his never having mentioned the word)—a televised address to the nation on July 15, 1979—is a critical text where he explicitly rejected the principles of the Consumers' Republic. Searching for an explanation and a remedy for the public demoralization he saw all around him, Carter targeted Americans' "worship [of] self-indulgence and consumption." Rather than viewing consumption as providing the means to a prosperous, satisfying life for all, "piling up material goods," he argued, creates "emptiness" in individual lives and "fragmentation and self-interest" for the larger society, as citizens embraced a "mistaken idea of freedom, the right to grasp for ourselves some advantage over others." As Carter broke with how "the good life" had been envisioned over the postwar period and counseled material sacrifice in place of material contentment (a message that met with enormous unpopularity at the time), he likewise explored new avenues in government policy that would make possible the more dramatic redirections in economics and politics that his successor, Ronald Reagan, would promulgate beginning in 1981.[82]

Carter's retreat from a faith in consumer spending in the face of stagflation coincided with a weakening of the consumer movement, foretold by the definitive defeat in Congress of a federal consumer agency. Partly, the political climate became much less receptive to the goals of consumerism. Businesses, long at war against the consumer movement, saw an opportunity to get the upper hand, as they struggled to stay afloat financially. They demanded greater prerogatives and often blamed their troubles on the high price exacted from them by "overprotective" legislation and "overregulating" government agencies, or at least they proposed that a retrenchment from both would help remedy the floundering economy. Meanwhile, consumerism's longtime champion, the labor unions, reeling from the twin devastations of recession and deindustrialization, were hardly in a strong position to commit much money and attention to the consumer movement's defense.[83]

Moreover, presidents and their allies in Congress across the political spectrum, beginning with Ford and Carter and escalating with Reagan, would themselves conclude that some of the policy directions of the previous era had been misguided. In particular, regulation, once a prime consumerist strategy for coercing private companies into upholding the public interest, became viewed as stifling growth and penalizing consumers through its tendency to create expensive bureaucracy and suppress healthy competition. Consumers would see lower prices and more product choice, it was argued, if firms had greater flexibility in a freer marketplace. As Virginia Knauer, back in Washington as Reagan's director of the U.S. Office of Consumer Affairs, put it, "There is a high cost to be paid for consumer protection. . . . When businesses are allowed to regulate themselves, competition will ensure that savings will trickle down to consumers." Republican Congressman William Frenzel of Minnesota was one of many critics to castigate the reformed FTC of the 1970s, the pride and joy of third-wave consumerists: "The FTC is more than just your ordinary pain-in-the-neck. It is a king-size cancer on our economy. It has undoubtedly added more unnecessary costs on American consumers who it is charged with protecting, than any other half dozen agencies combined . . . [and] it engages in witch-hunt[ing], demanding information which costs consumers dearly, for cases it never intends to complete."[84]

Many Americans who long had supported legislation and regulation to protect their interests as consumers now put less priority on the movement and more on lowering their cost of living, and they did so in a variety of ways. Some people met the havoc of inflation through continued, but carefully directed consumer organizing, enlisting in protest groups such as COIN (Consumers Opposed to Inflation in the Necessities) and the Citizen/Labor Energy Coalition, devoted to challenging skyrocketing energy costs. But at the opposite extreme, many others, particularly senior citizens on fixed incomes, joined property tax revolts—beginning with Proposition 13 in California and Proposition 2½ in Massachusetts and spreading across the nation from there—to cope with the combined threats of recession and inflation by withdrawing their dollars from government coffers. That Americans had often mobilized as consumers within narrow interest groups only encouraged them to assess their fate during recession in the same limited terms.[85]

The two major, and interrelated, policy initiatives that Ford launched, Carter embraced, and Reagan expanded were deregulation of the economy and privatization of government. Both aimed at shrinking the size and authority of the federal government, the former through weakening regulatory commissions and their mandates, the latter by moving critical government functions into the private sector. The joint Democratic and Republican parentage of these retreats from governmental control attests to the wide-based consensus that came to favor them, contrary to common wisdom that they were solely a conservative Republican strategy. Although Reagan may have embraced deregulation and privatization more exuberantly than his Democratic predecessor, it was Carter who, beginning with his presidential campaign against big government in 1976, sowed the seeds of a retrenchment from the general postwar inclination toward expanding government oversight of the public-private partnership that underlay the Consumers' Republic. Carter, moreover, joined with other prominent liberals like Massachusetts Senator Edward Kennedy and establishment liberal organs like the *Washington Post* (which editorialized against the FTC in 1978 as the "National Nanny") in mounting what Michael Pertschuk has labeled "the revolt against regulation."

Although some deregulators attacked regulatory agencies long accused by consumer advocates of being captive to industry, and in that sense promoted—rather than denounced—the consumerist program, there is no denying a more general swing against what was viewed as overzealous regulation. The combination of economic hard times, a Naderist left that had never quite abandoned its suspicion of "regulatory capture," a resurgent pro-business right, and an economics profession newly recommitted to laissez-faire ensured the end of business-as-usual both at longstanding regulatory commissions like the Civil Aeronautics Board and the ICC, and, in time, at agencies devoted to new kinds of rigorous regulation such as the FTC, the FCC, the EPA, and the CPSC. The climate seemed to change overnight from advocating regulation to championing deregulation. The director of the Office of Public Affairs at the FTC in the late 1970s, Deborah Leff, recalled how swiftly support for the commission's consumerist agenda seemed to evaporate, both in Congress and among the general public: "The turn seemed so sudden. Everything was hunky-dory, and then almost everything the FTC touched—whether children's TV, or the funeral rule, or the used car rule—fell apart, even though there would have been almost unanimous consumer opinion that used car

On August 26, 1988, the Ironbound Committee Against Toxic Waste organized a demonstration on the steps of Newark's Essex County Courthouse to demand renewed commitment to the environmental and consumer legislation passed in the heyday of activism during the 1960s and 1970s. Their tombstone props declare the death of supposed federal protections, forcing their close-knit community of Portuguese immigrants to battle for cleanups of toxic sites where Agent Orange and other dangerous chemicals had been manufactured in the past and for the rejection of a planned garbage-burning incinerator which they feared would spew pollution and carcinogens into their neighborhood. (Photo by Robert Eberle/*The Star-Ledger,* Newark, NJ)

dealers and undertakers were not always the most honorable individuals. We were caught off guard, and greatly disappointed."[86]

Most important, Ford, Carter, and Reagan all defended their new initiatives toward privatization and deregulation in the old language of serving the consumer interest. That justification was both an ideological conviction and a strategy for neutralizing the surviving consumer movement, which struggled mightily to expose the damage it felt was being done to longstanding consumerist goals through increased health and energy costs, declining product, drug and food safety standards, weakened anti-trust enforcement, and so forth, in documents such as the Consumer Federation of America's

WARNING: *Reaganomics Is Harmful to Consumers* of 1982 and WARNING: *Reaganomics Is Still Harmful to Consumers* of 1983.[87] Through the Consumers' Republic generally and the third-wave consumer movement more specifically, consumers had established themselves as significant economic and political players in the postwar economy. Even when the movement went on the defensive in the late 1970s, a rapt audience remained for investigative consumer reporting on television shows like *60 Minutes* and the evening news. Hence, innovators like Carter and particularly Reagan knew that any departure from the status quo still required taking the consumer interest into account and selling new programs as benefiting consumers. For example, they defended privatization, at least rhetorically, as forcing government to embrace private marketplace models and respect capitalist measures of success, including servicing customers effectively. As the Grace Commission Report to President Reagan, aimed at restructuring the federal government for greater efficiency, proclaimed in 1984: "A government which cannot efficiently manage the people's money and the people's business will ultimately fail its citizens by failing the same inescapable test which disciplines the private sector: those of the competitive marketplace and of the balance sheet."[88] Here private sector strategies were urged on government in the interests of citizens assumed to be some combination of consumers and stockholders.

Both the Carter and Reagan administrations also defended deregulation as serving the consumer interest. Carter told assembled Democrats in the Newark, New Jersey, area at a gala dinner in October 1980, "We believe that we ought to get the Government's nose out of the private enterprise of this country. We've deregulated rail, deregulated trucking, deregulated airlines, deregulated financial institutions, working on communications, to make sure that we have a free enterprise system that's competitive, that's competitive so that the customers get a better deal and the business community gets a better deal as well." Four years later, when the Republican platform of 1984 asserted that "the flood of regulation has been stopped," it boasted, "We have reduced the regulatory burden on Americans." The same year, Reagan consumer adviser Knauer defended the continued deregulation of airlines, trucking, railroads, intercity bus transportation, utilities, banks, broadcasting, computer-related communications, and gas and oil as fostering greater competition and producing "massive positive benefits for the consumer" who, according to the President, was "being poorly and unfairly served by the existing regulatory system." "By making their own choices in the free marketplace," Knauer asserted, consumers "become the regulators."

New York Times reporter Michael deCourcy Hinds was one contemporary observer who recognized how the Reagan administration was co-opting

By the time this cartoon appeared in national newspapers in 1988, air travel had been deregulated for ten years, and skepticism was growing that airline deregulation—originally defended as a benefit to travelers—was indeed in consumers' best interest. (Courtesy of Tribune Media Services, Inc. All rights reserved. Reprinted with permission.)

the rhetoric of consumerism. "Consumer activists and the Reagan administration alike say they represent consumers," he wrote in 1983. "While die-hard consumer advocate Michael Pertschuk may rail that 'consumers [are] bugs on the Reagan windshield of regulatory removal,' Christopher DeMuth, executive director of the Vice-President's Task Force on Regulatory Relief, tells an interviewer, 'Consumer benefit is the bottom line.'"[89] Needless to say, deregulators' and privatizers' justification of their initiatives as serving the consumer interest made refuting them more difficult for third-wave consumer advocates, much the way the consumer movement of the 1940s was undermined by the pro-consumer promises of the Consumers' Republic.

Increasingly under Reagan the test of what was in the consumer's interest became how the individual, or at most the special interest group, was faring economically. Reagan judged the deregulation of petroleum prices and natural gas a success, for example, because production increased and "energy costs for consumers" diminished, regardless of the environmental costs of increased oil drilling, much of it in wilderness areas. Businesses and consumers saved billions of dollars, Reagan's regulatory relievers claimed, from reduced enforcement of regulations—such as those requiring automatic seat belts and air bags on new automobiles, safer seats and tires on aircraft, rigorous safety tests for food and drugs, and health and safety standards at workplaces—and from reduced investigations and prosecution of violators by agencies like the EPA and the CPSC.[90] Likewise, when Reagan urged voters to decide how to vote first in the election of 1980 and again in 1984 by asking themselves, "Are you better off now than you were four years ago?" he was in his own way appealing to their consumer interest, but defining it much differently—more individualized and more in terms of financial well-being—than it had been understood in the heyday of citizen consumers, or even in the more recent drive for accountability by purchasers as citizens. Ironically, Reagan's tack was exactly what Jimmy Carter had bewailed in his "malaise speech" several years earlier when he predicted that "fragmentation and self-interest" would curse an America that worshiped self-indulgent consumption. Rather than the protection-oriented Consumer Bill of Rights of Kennedy and the Buyers Bill of Rights of Nixon, Reagan's Economic Bill of Rights defined economic freedom as an individual's right to "contract freely for goods and services," with minimal intervention by unions, regulators, or other government agents, including the Internal Revenue Service.[91] Carter in 1979 could hardly have predicted how his own policy initiatives would contribute to the ends he so feared.

Another measure of how far Reagan's administration had come from the Consumers' Republic was its rejection of Keynesian economic policy and embrace of what came to be called "Reaganomics," a substitution of "supply-side" policies for ones that previously had been demand-oriented. At the centerpiece of Reagan's economic program to counter inflation and stagnation was a massive tax cut and non-progressive reduction in marginal rates in 1981, justified not in Keynesian terms of fueling demand but rather to stimulate investment and growth. Alongside cuts in government spending, the reduction or elimination of a wide variety of entitlement programs (legacies of the Kennedy and Johnson administrations), an anti-inflationary money policy, and the already discussed moves toward privatization and deregulation, the tax cut showed the Reagan administration taking a very different approach to fostering economic health. Rather than seeking to draw all Americans into an expansive mass consumption web, Reaganites promoted capital investment, concentrated wealth, tax cutting, and personal savings over consumption, with the assumption that prosperity would "trickle down" from new corporate and private wealth to ordinary American consumers.

In reality, however, inequality of income grew enormously during the last two decades of the twentieth century, much of it traceable to Reagan's new economic policies.[92] Between 1980 and 2000 the top 5 percent of families increased their share of the nation's total aggregate income to 20.8 percent, up from 14.6 percent, a 42 percent gain. The top fifth of families saw a 15 percent increase in their share of income, while all the remaining fifths lost ground in terms of share. In 1980 corporate CEOs earned about forty times as much as the average worker; today they earn closer to 500 times as much. Over the same period, the overall wealth of the wealthiest grew even faster than their income. The top 1 percent of households currently have more assets than the bottom 95 percent combined.[93]

As Presidents George Bush and Bill Clinton perpetuated Reagan's supply-side approach through deficit reduction and a commitment to shrinking government through deregulation and privatizing public services, they helped recast the Consumers' Republic into what might be called the Consumerization of the Republic, where consumer/citizens—still permeable categories in the political culture—increasingly related to government itself as shoppers in a marketplace. When Reagan embarked on what he called "civil service reform," he had defended his administration's "proposals that will help our government give the American people what they pay for by deregulating the bureaucracy and by rewarding individual merit and achievement." Similarly, he had conceptualized citizens as customers of government when he advocated privatizing Amtrak because, shamefully, "taxpayers pay about $35 per passenger every time an Amtrak train leaves the station."[94]

Setting a related tone early in the Clinton administration was the Clinton-Gore National Performance Review Report of 1993 aimed at "reinventing government," entitled *From Red Tape to Results: Creating a Government That Works Better and Costs Less.* In keeping with a president who would soon proclaim to the country that "the era of big government is over," the report listed among its top goals "putting customers first," proposing a new-style government modeled after the efficient retail business: "Effective, entrepreneurial governments insist on customer satisfaction. They listen carefully to their customers—using surveys, focus groups, and the like. They restructure their basic operations to meet customers' needs. And they use market dynamics such as competition and customer choice to create incentives that drive their employees to put customers first." In Vice President Gore's follow-up progress report of 1995, he advocated further privatization to improve the performance of traditional government services like the U.S. Postal Service in the interests of more "customer satisfaction." Clinton's Republican opponent in the 1996 presidential race, Robert Dole, embraced the same consumer paradigm, promising all Americans, in just one example, an "education consumers' warranty" from the nation's public schools. This reconceptualization of the citizen-government relationship quickly descended the ladder of command. In New Jersey, Governor Christie Whitman promised residents a tax bill more in line with the services they were getting after her election in 1993, and by 1996, even the township council of a small town like Montclair had vowed to treat its residents more like customers.[95]

As the market relationship became the template for the citizen's connection to government, the watchdog, public-spirited citizen consumers of the 1930s and 1940s increasingly were replaced by the self-interested government customers of the 1990s, who were encouraged to bring a consumer mentality to their relations with government, judging public services and tax assessments much like other purchased goods, by the personal benefits they derived from them. Government officials responded accordingly, judging potential actions by whether or not they lowered costs for consumer/citizens. In the Clinton years, anti-trust challenges to mergers were most often undertaken if they promised cheaper goods to consumers—whether drugs or computers or office supplies—not to protect any loftier ideal of competition within industries. As a New York anti-trust lawyer advised clients inquiring whether a merger was likely to win approval in 1998, "The one thing the Government is concerned about is when customers are unhappy. They have a strong base of customers who have complained and complained loudly." Business success at winning new legislation on managed care or banking deregulation similarly depended on the persuasiveness of arguments that consumers would ultimately benefit, regardless of the larger societal costs.[96]

As the Consumers' Republic transmogrified into the Consumerization of the Republic, moreover, politicians and their customer-voters were quick to reject what, in their view, yielded an inadequate personal return on their investment, opposing policies that gave others "something for nothing," whether generous welfare benefits for those without work, universal health care to cover the uninsured, or estate taxes that transferred wealth away from big inheritors. As economic inequality proliferated in American society at the turn of the twenty-first century, the benefits long ago promised to all in the salad days of the Consumers' Republic increasingly became reserved for those who paid for them. And the message of the Consumers' Republic at its most idealistic—that the interests of individual purchasers as citizens and of the nation were one and the same—evolved into an expectation that what's best for me is what's best for America. Whereas from the 1930s to as late as the 1970s, to refer to the consumer interest was also to appeal to some larger public good beyond the individual's self-interest, the ubiquitous invocation of the consumer today—as patient, as parent, as social security recipient—often means satisfying the private interest of the paying customer, the combined consumer/citizen/taxpayer/voter whose greatest concern is, "Am I getting my money's worth?"

Aspects of the Consumers' Republic have persisted into the twenty-first century. The Bush tax cut of 2001, for example, was promoted as a way of expanding consumption to stimulate the economy. The cartoon's merger of taxpayer and consumer reflects a larger convergence of the two identities since the 1980s, as citizens have been encouraged to view themselves in a market relationship with government. (Rall © 2001 Ted Rall. Reprinted with permission of Universal Press Syndicate. All rights reserved.)

a history that extends into our own lifetimes, that continues to shape our daily lives, is hard to bring to conclusion. Although the Consumers' Republic that flourished in the aftermath of World War II went into retreat during the 1970s, its legacy remains. As I finish this book, we still judge the health of our economy by indicators such as consumer confidence and spending, and housing starts.[1] When President George W. Bush and other national leaders seek strategies to cope with threatening recession, whether as a result of a contracting economy or paralysis brought on by the terrorist attack of September 11, 2001, they crank up the machine of mass consumption through tax cuts and other stimulants in the expectation that consumer spending can bring us through, to "Keep America Rolling," in the words of General Motors' recent advertising campaign.[2] Economies where consumers fail to consume serve as negative examples. The Japanese, whose success as a new democracy after World War II was tied to their launching of a vibrant mass consumption economy, have been criticized recently for refusing to spend their nation out of an intractable economic depression.[3]

The suburbanized metropolitan environment where the vast majority of Americans dwell descends directly from the residential and commercial landscapes created in the heyday of the Consumers' Republic. The census of 2000 revealed that metropolitan areas are more racially segregated than ever, even when the overall complexion of suburbia was more diverse.[4] Challenges to exclusive localism—by requiring affordable housing in well-off suburbs or equalizing school spending across poorer and richer communities in states—continue all over the country, New Jersey included.[5] Suburban shopping centers remain a contested space caught between community expectations that they are public and property owners' insistence, backed by many state supreme courts, that they are private.[6] The spectacular growth of catalogue buying and e-commerce has further privatized shopping, removing Americans all that much more from the diverse social interactions once part of going "downtown" and even threatening the viability of the flawed but at least semi-public suburban mall.[7] The privatization of former public spaces and functions persists elsewhere as well, such as when for-profit Starbucks coffee shops open in public libraries, modeled after the increasingly ubiquitous cafe-bookstores; when the proliferation of private cell phones makes public telephones, deregulated since 1996, fewer in number and higher in cost; when self-taxing private improvement districts perform more and more of the work that public agencies once did, without municipal oversight; and when a rapidly increasing number of Americans—estimated at one in six—live under the private police protection and private services of gated or other kinds of association-managed communities, such as condominiums and cooperatives, the most recent innovation being luxury apartments built over stores in upscale private shopping centers.[8]

Other aspects of the Consumers' Republic remain with us as well. Advertisers and marketers are constantly gaining more precision in pinpointing the demographic and lifestyle trends of consumer segments, employing new tools such as Internet "cookies" to monitor the "clickstreams" of e-shoppers. Meanwhile, television watchers persist in preferring narrowcasting cable channels to the networks (though the networks have caught on and now operate on cable as well) and are experimenting with the advanced technology of "black boxes" to customize their viewing options even further.[9] Similarly, with every election, political marketers develop greater expertise, and spend more money, tailoring the messages of their candidates to narrowly defined segments of voters.[10] In the political arena, consumers and their organizations still exert influence, even as the conventional consumer movement flounders. A grassroots Bus Riders Union in Los Angeles, made up of passengers on public buses who are poor and resentful of fare hikes and service cutbacks, wins repeated court victories against a Metropolitan Transportation Authority that has favored, at their expense, rail routes designed to bring wealthier suburbanites to work in the center city.[11] African Americans in particular continue to counter discrimination in the marketplace with campaigns to punish some retailers and reward others. An NAACP-orchestrated consumer boycott challenges a discriminating hotel chain and a state that insists on flying the Confederate flag from its capital building.[12]

For all Americans, citizenship and consumership remain intertwined. Occasionally, when they push for a real Patients' Bill of Rights, for example, Americans become public-minded citizen consumers. Sometimes, such as when consumers demand government recalls of defective tires, they are accountability-seeking purchasers as citizens. And often in recent years, they function like self-interested investors in a Consumerized Republic. The commissioning of an "American Customer Satisfaction Index" to help the General Services Administration rate citizens' pleasure or displeasure with government agencies, and skirmishes over the privatization of social security are recent efforts to give consumer/citizen/taxpayer/voters a higher return on their investment.[13]

But I am a writer of history, not a contemporary critic or predictor of the future, so I would like to close this book with a few historical conclusions. First, I hope that my analysis has complicated our understanding of the so-called Golden Era of postwar prosperity that lasted approximately from 1945 to 1975. I have tried to convey that this period of unprecedented affluence did much more than make Americans a people of plenty. Undergirding the pursuit of plenty was an infrastructure of policies and priorities, what I have dubbed, for shorthand, the Consumers' Republic. In reconstructing the nation after World War II, leaders of business, government, and labor developed a political economy and a political culture that expected a dynamic mass consumption economy not only to deliver prosperity, but also to fulfill American society's loftier aspirations: more social egalitarianism, more democratic participation, and more political freedom. In their ideal America, a mass consumption–driven economy would provide jobs, purchasing power, and investment dollars, while also allowing Americans to live better than ever before, to participate in political decision-making on an equal footing with their similarly prospering neighbors, and to exercise their cherished freedoms by making independent choices in markets and politics.

But the Consumers' Republic did not unfold quite as policymakers intended. In its ambition, it helped reshape many aspects of postwar American life, most notably the nation's class and racial profile, the gender dynamics within families and workplaces, the social landscapes where Americans lived and consumed, the way economic markets were structured, the way politics was practiced, and the way the American state evolved. At times, as when African Americans and women used their influence in consumer markets to assert themselves politically or when young people and senior citizens gained greater recognition as profitable market segments and then, in turn, as political constituencies, a prosperous Consumers' Republic substantially advanced the progressive goal of social inclusion. And in its seductive ideal of democracy and equality through prosperity, it provided true inspiration to a wide range of

Americans, not only the Consumers' Republic's creators but also some of its critics, whether welfare rights activists seeking a fair shake at credit or New Jersey Supreme Court justices ruling that the decent housing and schooling provided in well-off communities needed to be more widely accessible.

But at other times, the Consumers' Republic's dependence on unregulated private markets wove inequalities deep into the fabric of prosperity, thereby allowing, intentionally or not, the search for profits and the exigencies of the market to prevail over higher goals. Often the outcome dramatically diverged from the stated objective to use mass markets to create a more egalitarian and democratic American society. Solving the nation's severe postwar housing shortage by building communities of private homes pegged to distinct sectors of the real estate market created a suburbanized metropolis more hierarchically stratifying than equalizing, as variant tax bases and property values provided localities with greatly divergent revenues to fund basic services like schools. Letting private developers dictate the nature of public space in mass suburbia through privately owned shopping centers, increasingly aimed at distinctive markets and withheld from consumers of undesirable race, age, and class, segregated customers by purchasing power, while also limiting free speech and assembly. Market segmentation and its application to politics differentiated consumers and voters along class, gender, age, race, and ethnic lines, accentuating what divided Americans and undermining common concerns. And economic inequality expanded greatly during the 1970s, 1980s, and 1990s, so that between 1979 and 1997 the average income of the richest fifth of the population jumped from nine times the income of the poorest fifth to about fifteen times, while the three-fifths in between did little better—and not just because of the regressive Reagan tax cut or the loss of well-paying industrial jobs through deindustrialization.[14] Rather, the deeply entrenched convictions prevailing in the Consumers' Republic that a dynamic, private, mass consumption marketplace could float all boats and that a growing economy made reslicing the economic pie unnecessary predisposed Americans against more redistributive actions. When, after decades of postwar prosperity, economic crisis hit in the 1970s, the inequalities that had lurked barely beneath the surface rose as a specter to haunt the rest of the century. Letting private markets reign, without adequate attention to questions of income or resource distribution or without sufficient monitoring of how well the nation's avowed values were being fulfilled, diminished the Consumers' Republic's otherwise substantial achievements.

Most ironic perhaps, the confidence that a prospering mass consumption economy could foster democracy would over time contribute to a decline in the most traditional, and one could argue most critical, form of politi-

The NAACP marked its seventy-fifth anniversary in August 1984 with an "Overground Railroad March from Richmond to New York" to inspire more African Americans to register to vote. Here supporters advance down Broad Street in Newark. Despite great efforts to get more Americans out to vote in 1984, voter turnout continued to decline steadily. In 1960, 65 percent of eligible Americans had voted. By 1984 only 55.7 percent participated, and by 1992 turnout had plummeted to just 38 percent of the eligible electorate. (In the tightly contested 2000 presidential election, turnout would rise to 51 percent.) A decline in numbers was not the only change. Wealthier, more educated segments were increasingly likely to vote. (Photo by Steve Andrascik, *The Star-Ledger*, Newark, NJ)

cal participation—voting—as more commercialized political salesmanship replaced rank-and-file mobilization through parties.[15] The increased reliance on pollsters and political consultants, in turn, further undermined the democratic character of elections, making campaigns affordable by only the wealthiest of candidates and more and more oriented toward divisive "slicing and dicing" of the electorate. Although at times scientific targeting of constituents made politicians more responsive to the will of voters, that often came at the cost of favoring special interests over common interests.

In the 1960s self-identified consumers in the Consumers' Republic would initiate a grassroots politics of their own. It began as a consumer movement of purchasers as citizens determined to create new protective legislation and regulation to hold corporations and government more accountable to the highest moral goals of the Consumers' Republic. But by the mid-1970s—thanks to growing resistance to giving consumers a permanent foothold in government, an economic recession of massive proportions, and an increasingly conservative political leadership—it led to a rejection of "big government" and an embrace of privatization, deregulation, and a more self-interested market relationship between citizens and government.

I also hope it is clear in this rendering of the postwar era that the experiences of women and African Americans cannot be isolated from mainstream history, as they too often are in the ghettoized subfields of the historical profession. In this telling, the struggles of blacks seeking full civil rights and women pursuing greater political and economic participation were inextricably entwined with the political economy and political culture of the Consumers' Republic. At times, the new postwar order boosted their efforts. When African Americans launched the modern civil rights movement by demanding equal access to public sites of consumption in the 1940s and 1950s after being shut out during World War II, or when they protested their exclusion from the society's general prosperity through urban rebellions and welfare rights organizing during the 1960s, the supposedly free markets of the Consumers' Republic helpfully provided a measure of their segregation, a justification for action, and a strategy of protest. Similarly, women were able to turn the influence they had as consumers in the marketplace toward more political ends as watchdog citizen consumers during the Great Depression, as home-front managers during World War II, and as both the rank and file and high-ranking orchestrators of the consumer movement in the 1960s and 1970s, when they finally succeeded in securing real protections for women in finance, credit, and other markets.

At other times, though, proponents of the Consumers' Republic tapped into conservative gender and racial expectations to reinforce the status quo. The architects of the Consumers' Republic first promoted it as an alternative to a wartime order that they impugned as weak through its association with female-defended price controls and other state interventions. They went on to develop an infrastructure through the GI Bill, amendments to the federal income tax, and credit practices that reinforced a male-headed breadwinner household, even as women were entering the workforce in growing numbers.

Similarly, blacks' success in using the promises of the Consumers' Republic to justify greater access to public accommodations was offset by their failure to overcome the racial and class barriers constructed by suburbanites obsessed with preserving property values. Without denying the salience of racism, it is fair to say that the huge economic investment in residential property made by a majority of Americans over the postwar era discouraged risk-taking in residential decisions.

How did the growing residential fragmentation of metropolitan America over the second half of the twentieth century matter? Here, as in several other places, I have lamented the social and political segmentation brought about by the playing out of market forces in the Consumers' Republic. In discussing the emergence of a landscape of mass consumption, I also criticize the way commercial spaces became stratified by race and class, and how the shift from downtowns to shopping centers inadequately, to my mind, substituted a privatized and fragmented suburban core for the more public and inclusive "town square" of the city. Likewise, when I examine the shift from mass to segmented marketing, and particularly the adoption of these marketing strategies by candidates and their campaigns, I observe the narrowing of common ground and the retreat from concern with the general good. Even the effectiveness of the consumer movement of the 1960s and 1970s, I argue, came to depend on its ability to mobilize consumers within narrow interest groups defined by race, class, gender, age, and so forth, propelling consumer politics further toward the pursuit of self-interest.

I tread on fragile ground in making these arguments. One must beware of promoting false or naive notions of a universal "common good" and unified "public" and thereby denying the more diverse and complicated multi-cultural America that has greeted the twenty-first century. Broad characterizations run the risk of elevating the most mainstream of identities—white, middle-class, male, heterosexual, thirty-something—and the narrowest of agendas to represent a more variegated America. Rather, "common" and "public" must derive from the true diversity of the nation's population. The task is not an easy one. For the United States, figuring out how to articulate a common set of political and social goals while becoming increasingly diverse as a nation is among the greatest challenges of the twenty-first century. This book hopefully suggests some starting points. To begin with, it is important to recognize that not all divisions among Americans are sacrosanct. It is just as much a fallacy to assume that all interest or identity groups enjoy authentic purity as to embrace as natural a unified public. We should not forget that manufacturers, advertisers, marketers, and political operatives became invested in segmenting the whole, thereby encouraging social and cultural divisions for their own profit. Moreover, it is important to distinguish between harmless and even self-

affirming segmentation of identities and interests and ones that rest on stratification and inequality. When some groups enjoy more resources and power,
and hence more life choices than others, fragmentation serves not to validate
difference but instead to facilitate discrimination.

Second, and probably most important, we can do a better job, without
denying the diversity of our constituent parts, of weighing one group's needs
and interests against another's, negotiating not just tit-for-tats but resolutions
to conflicts that seek justice and fairness for as many Americans as possible.
Similarly, the guardians of true public space must learn to tolerate multiple
claims on its use. Deliberating for the general good means not denying
inevitable differences but rather assuming collective responsibility for one
another's well-being. As the United States becomes an increasingly multicultural nation, it is more important than ever that social groups not become
competing, self-interested segments, or self-contained, oblivious islands. This
book has dwelled on the way evolving patterns of residence, commerce, marketing, and politics polarized people in the second half of the twentieth century. Only with concerted effort can we transcend these pressures to fragment
and become a nation diverse but still unified around a common national purpose that is built on something other than war.

It should come as no surprise that Americans remain identified as both
consumers and citizens. Increasingly over this century, the economic behavior
of consumption has become entwined with the rights and obligations of citizenship. More and more in the postwar era, Americans merged their aspirations for an adequate material provision and a legitimate place in the polity,
expecting the two to go hand in hand or the former to encompass the latter.
When the founders of the Consumers' Republic invested the economic marketplace with democratic promise and thereby blurred the boundary between
consumer and citizen, they were contributing to an ongoing progression that
began with a nineteenth-century conception of citizenship interweaving political participation—voting, military, and jury service—with a man's right as a
producer to earn an independent living. Over the course of the twentieth century, political citizenship increasingly brought with it the entitlement to enjoy
basic material comforts, potentially available to women as well as men, independent wage earners or not.[16] Not surprisingly, one of President Franklin
Roosevelt's basic Four Freedoms—"Freedom from Want"—became popularly
interpreted during World War II as the promise of abundance for all Americans. Not long after, Americans in the Consumers' Republic learned that consuming for personal and national benefit was not only a right but a duty of
citizenship, as America reconstructed its economy and society after World War
II to become a more prosperous, egalitarian nation.

In some ways, the Consumers' Republic was an American private-marketplace version of English economist T. H. Marshall's concept of "social citizenship," where he applied the equality of status inherent in citizenship to the inequalities of class and argued for a modern British welfare state that recognized "a universal right to real income . . . [to] modify the whole pattern of social inequality."[17] In America, though, it was the private consumer economy—not a welfare state, though on many occasions government assisted—that was charged with the responsibility of fulfilling the nation's economic obligations to its citizens. Later, leaders of the consumer movement of the 1960s and 1970s would insist that all good citizens must become politically responsible and socially conscious consumers, enlisted in a multifaceted assault on corporate and governmental corruption. Even after the decline of the Consumers' Republic, Presidents Reagan, G.H.W. Bush, Clinton, and G. W. Bush would justify their different policy orientations as efforts to satisfy citizens who were also deserving consumers, and who eventually would declare themselves consumers of government itself. By the end of the twentieth century, citizen and consumer had become interlocking identities for most Americans.

To what extent a linkage of citizen and consumer facilitates or negates a politics that champions a democratically arrived at common good is an open question. Some critics over the twentieth century, most recently and prominently Christopher Lasch and Michael Sandel, have urged the disjoining of the two categories, charging that modern liberals invested in an economy of growth have bypassed to their peril the virtuous resisters to an ascendant consumer-oriented vision—the petit-bourgeois, self-governing, morally and religiously committed, civic republican "true" citizens who lost out in the early years of this century.[18] But while Lasch and Sandel make some important points about the dangers of a political order that elevates consumer wants over civic needs, I think it is unrealistic to assume we can reverse a century-long trend of entwined citizenship and consumership. As much as I might prefer a public sphere inhabited by voting citizens rather than demanding consumers, by public-spirited taxpayers rather than self-interested tax cutters, and by communities committed to cooperation with neighbors rather than wrapped in isolated localism or destructive competition, I fear that such an alternative hopelessly resides in an unregainable past—if it ever existed at all. Separating the citizen from the consumer would involve severing a linkage that has only solidified over the course of the twentieth century.

Rather than fantasize jettisoning this Janus-faced citizen consumer who still stands guard at our gates, we might be wiser to identify a usable legacy that maximizes its benefits and minimizes its costs. We could encourage the revival of the citizen consumer ideal that prevailed during the Great Depression and World War II, with its commitment to building into the agencies of government a power base for consumers to assert their will. We could reinvigorate the liberating aspects of the purchaser as citizen tradition that provided African Americans and women with a way of protesting against exclusion and the consumer movement with a vehicle for holding corporations and governments accountable to a higher moral standard. And we could seek to reverse the trend toward the Consumerization of the Republic by not shrinking from articulating the important things that only government can do, if the interests of all the people are ever to be considered and if limits are to be put on the power granted private markets to deliver both goods and good.

There is some hopeful evidence of a reversal of the drives for privatization and deregulation that have reduced government's legitimacy. For example, legislators are having second thoughts about continuing to privatize prisons, schools, ambulance services, and libraries and to deregulate power companies, as outcomes prove disappointing and taxpayer savings appear much less than originally expected.[19] Similarly, in the wake of the tragic hijacking of four airplanes on September 11, 2001, the federal government has taken responsibility for overseeing airport safety from bottom line–oriented private airlines that have been blamed for many of the security breaches contributing to the disaster. And the Enron and WorldCom scandals have reawakened calls for government regulation of corporate finance and accounting practices. As one commentator has put it, probably a little more optimistically than the majority of Americans would, "Government suddenly looks good again."[20]

Even if we would prefer to decouple citizen and consumer, the best we may hope for is to turn this inheritance from the twentieth century to our advantage in the twenty-first. Taking nothing for granted, we can hold our mandate to be both citizens and consumers to the highest standards of democracy, freedom, and equality, dwelling not so much on whether we should simultaneously be citizens and consumers but rather accepting that, like it or not, we are. The question then becomes, United States citizen: consumer in what kind of republic?

Notes

ABBREVIATIONS USED IN THE NOTES

AA	*Advertising Age*
AAAPSS	*Annals of the American Academy of Political and Social Science*
AHR	*American Historical Review*
AIS	Archives of Industrial Society, University of Pittsburgh
AJS	*American Journal of Sociology*
Angevine	Erma Angevine Papers, Special Collections, Rutgers University Library
Anthony	Daniel Sutherland Anthony Papers, New Jersey Information Center, Newark Public Library
Atkinson	Ruth Lamb Atkinson Papers, Special Collections, Vassar College Library
Barnett	Claude A. Barnett Papers, Chicago Historical Society
BG	*Boston Globe, Boston Sunday Globe*
BR	*Bergen Record, Bergen Evening Record* (later, *The Record*)
BW	*Business Week*
Campbell	Persia Campbell Papers, Consumers Union Archives, Yonkers, New York
CHS	Chicago Historical Society
CLNJ	Consumers' League of New Jersey Papers, Special Collections, Rutgers University Library
CR	Consumers' Research Papers, Special Collections, Rutgers University Library
CSM	*Christian Science Monitor*
CU	Consumers Union Archives, Yonkers, New York
Erber	Ernest Erber Papers, New Jersey Information Center, Newark Public Library
GSD	Graduate School of Design, Harvard University, Frances Loeb Library
GSP	Garden State Plaza Historical Collection, Paramus, New Jersey
Hackensack	Johnson Free Public Library, Hackensack, New Jersey
HBR	*Harvard Business Review*
ICSC	International Council of Shopping Centers, New York City
ILWCH	*International Labor and Working-Class History*
IUE	International Union of Electrical, Radio, and Machine Workers, Special Collections, Rutgers University Library
JAH	*Journal of American History*
JAR	*Journal of Advertising Research*
JM	*Journal of Marketing*
JMR	*Journal of Marketing Research*
JR	*Journal of Retailing*
JUH	*Journal of Urban History*
Lett	Harold A. Lett Papers, New Jersey Information Center, Newark Public Library

411

Lilley	Lilley Commission Papers, New Jersey State Archives, Trenton, New Jersey
LWV-NJ	League of Women Voters of New Jersey Papers, Special Collections, Rutgers University Library
Margolius	Sidney Margolius Papers, Special Collections, Rutgers University Library
NAACP	National Association for the Advancement of Colored People Papers, Library of Congress
NAC	National Association of Consumers Papers, Consumers Union Archives, Yonkers, New York
NJAA	*New Jersey Afro-American*
NN	*Newark News, Newark Evening News*
NPL	New Jersey Information Center, Newark Public Library
NSL	*Newark Star-Ledger (later Star-Ledger)*
NYT	*New York Times*
Peterson	Esther Peterson Papers, Schlesinger Library, Radcliffe Institute, Harvard University
PI	*Printers' Ink*
POQ	*Public Opinion Quarterly*
Rutgers	Special Collections, Rutgers University Library
Ruttenberg	Harold J. Ruttenberg Papers, Historical Collections, Labor Archives, Pennsylvania State University
Schlesinger	Schlesinger Library, Radcliffe Institute, Harvard University
Schomburg	Schomburg Center for Research in Black Culture, New York Public Library
SEDFRE	Scholarship, Education and Defense Fund for Racial Equality, 1944–76, Wisconsin Historical Society
USGPO	United States Government Printing Office
WHS	Wisconsin Historical Society
WSJ	*Wall Street Journal*

PROLOGUE

1. Raymond Williams, "Consumer," from *Keywords: A Vocabulary of Culture and Society* (New York: Oxford University Press, 1985), in Lawrence B. Glickman, ed., *Consumer Society in American History: A Reader* (Ithaca, NY: Cornell University Press, 1999), pp. 17–18.

2. Thorstein Veblen, *The Theory of the Leisure Class: An Economic Study of Institutions* (New York: Macmillan, 1899); Simon N. Patten, *The New Basis of Civilization* (New York: Macmillan, 1907); Patten, *Product and Climax* (New York: Huebsch, 1909); Daniel Horowitz, "Consumption and Its Discontents: Simon N. Patten, Thorstein Veblen, and George Gunton," *JAH* 67 (September 1980): 301–17; David M. Potter, *People of Plenty: Economic Abundance and the American Character* (Chicago: University of Chicago Press, 1954), quote from p. 177; E. Franklin Frazier, *Black Bourgeoisie* (Glencoe, IL: Free Press, 1957); John Kenneth Galbraith, *The Affluent Society* (Boston: Houghton Mifflin, 1958); David Riesman, with Nathan Glazer and Reuel Denney, *The Lonely Crowd: A Study of the Changing American Character* (New Haven: Yale University Press, 1950); Riesman, *Abundance for What? And Other Essays* (Garden City, NY: Doubleday, 1964); Seymour Martin Lipset and Leo Lowenthal, eds., *Culture and Social Character: The Work of David Riesman Reviewed* (Glencoe, IL: Free Press, 1961); Herbert Marcuse, *One-Dimensional Man: Stud-*

ies in the Ideology of Advanced Industrial Society (Boston: Beacon, 1964); Daniel Bell, *The Cultural Contradictions of Capitalism* (New York: Basic Books, 1976).

3. Peter Novick, *That Noble Dream: The "Objectivity Question" and the American Historical Profession* (New York: Cambridge University Press, 1988), pp. 332–37, 345–48; John Higham, "Beyond Consensus: The Historian as Moral Critic," in Higham, ed., *Writing American History: Essays on Modern Scholarship* (Bloomington: Indiana University Press, 1970), pp. 138–56; Clinton Lawrence Rossiter, *Seedtime of the Republic: The Origin of the American Tradition of Political Liberty* (New York: Harcourt, Brace, 1953); Edmund Sears Morgan, *The Birth of the Republic, 1763–89* (Chicago: University of Chicago Press, 1956); Robert W. Rydell, "The Pledge of Allegiance and the Construction of the Modern American Nation," *Rendezvous* 30 (1996): 13–26; Gerard Kaye and Ferenc M. Szasz, "Adding 'Under God' to the Pledge of Allegiance," *Encounter* 34 (1973): 53–56. This invocation of the "republic" among consensus historians was quite different from the more radical "republicanism" that historians, beginning in the 1960s, would argue motivated many revolutionaries and artisans in the eighteenth and nineteenth centuries.

4. See Chap. 5, n. 5.

CHAPTER 1. DEPRESSION: RISE OF THE CITIZEN CONSUMER

1. Robert S. Lynd, "The Consumer Becomes a 'Problem,' " in J. G. Brainerd, ed., *The Ultimate Consumer: A Study in Economic Illiteracy, AAAPSS* 173 (Philadelphia, 1934), p. 6; also see in same volume Gardiner C. Means, "The Consumer and the New Deal," pp. 7–17; Lynd, Foreword to Persia Campbell, *Consumer Representation in the New Deal* (New York: Columbia University Press, 1940), pp. 9–10; Lynd, "Democracy's Third Estate: The Consumer," *Political Science Quarterly* 51 (December 1936): 481–515; "Business Week Reports to Executives on the Consumer Movement," *BW*, Apr. 22, 1939, p. 45; also see Lucy Black Creighton, *Pretenders to the Throne: The Consumer Movement in the United States* (Lexington, MA: Heath, 1976), p. 27; Mark C. Smith, *Social Science in the Crucible: The American Debate over Objectivity and Purpose, 1918–1941* (Durham, NC: Duke University Press, 1994), chap. 4, "Robert Lynd and Knowledge for What?" pp. 147–49.

2. Jam Handy Organization for Chevrolet Motor Company, *From Dawn to Sunset*, released June 8, 1937, 26 minutes, 35 mm, from Rick Prelinger, ed., *Our Secret Century: Archival Films from the Darker Side of the American Dream*, vol. 2, *Capitalist Realism*, Voyager CD, 1996.

3. Scholars writing on consumption before the twentieth century argued extensively about its importance in the economy, the social structure, and the culture. Those fascinating debates are too complex to go into here, but for more see Neil McKendrick, John Brewer, and J. H. Plumb, *The Birth of a Consumer Society: The Commercialization of Eighteenth-Century England* (Bloomington: Indiana University Press, 1982); John Brewer and Roy Porter, eds., *Consumption and the World of Goods* (London: Routledge, 1993); Lawrence B. Glickman, ed., *Consumer Society in American History: A Reader* (Ithaca, NY: Cornell University Press, 1999), particularly essays by James Axtell, T. H. Breen, and Joyce Appleby; and T. H. Breen, "Baubles of Britain: The American and Consumer Revolutions of the Eighteenth Century," *Past and Present* 119 (May 1988): 73–104. The literature on the linkage between independent producers and republican citizens is vast.

4. David P. Thelan, *The New Citizenship: Origins of Progressivism in Wisconsin, 1885–1900* (Columbia: University of Missouri Press, 1972); Michael J. Sandel, *Democracy's Discontent: America in Search of a Public Philosophy* (Cambridge, MA: Harvard University Press, 1996); Lorine Swainston Goodwin, *The Pure Food, Drink, and Drug Crusaders, 1879–1914* (Jefferson, NC: McFarland, 1999); Margaret Finnegan, *Selling Suffrage: Consumer Culture and Votes for Women* (New York: Columbia University Press,

1999). In his classic work *The Age of Reform: From Bryan to F.D.R.* (New York: Vintage, 1955), pp. 170–73, Richard Hofstadter asserts: "It was in the Progressive era that the urban consumer first stepped forward as a serious and self-conscious factor in American social politics. 'We hear a great deal about the class-consciousness of labor,' wrote Walter Lippmann in 1914. 'My own observation is that in America today consumers'-consciousness is growing very much faster.' . . . Vague as it was, consumer consciousness became a thing of much significance because it was the lowest common political denominator among classes of people who had little else to unite them on concrete issues."

5. Paula E. Hyman, "Immigrant Women and Consumer Protest: The New York City Kosher Meat Boycott of 1902," *American Jewish History* 70 (September 1980): 91–105; Dana Frank, "Housewives, Socialists, and the Politics of Food: The 1917 New York Cost-of-Living Protests," *Feminist Studies* 11 (Summer 1985): 255–85; Annelise Orleck, *Common Sense and a Little Fire: Women and Working-Class Politics in the United States, 1900–1965* (Chapel Hill: University of North Carolina Press, 1995), pp. 27–30. See Helen Sorenson, *The Consumer Movement: What It Is and What It Means* (New York: Harper & Bros., 1941), p. 7, on more middle-class women's protests through Housewives' Leagues against the price of eggs and apples in Chicago and Philadelphia around 1912, and Gary R. Mormino and George E. Pozzetta, *The Immigrant World of Ybor City: Italians and Their Latin Neighbors in Tampa, 1885–1985* (Urbana: University of Illinois Press, 1990), p. 157, on consumer boycotts in Tampa during World War I.

6. Lawrence B. Glickman, *A Living Wage: American Workers and the Making of Consumer Society* (Ithaca, NY: Cornell University Press, 1997); Dana Frank, *Purchasing Power: Consumer Organizing, Gender, and the Seattle Labor Movement, 1919–1929* (New York: Cambridge University Press, 1994).

The classic studies of labor boycotting date from the Progressive Era: Harry W. Laidler, *Boycotts and the Labor Struggle: Economic and Legal Aspects* (New York: Lane, 1913), and Leo Wolman, *The Boycott in American Trade Unions* (Baltimore: Johns Hopkins Press, 1916). Also see Marcel van der Linden, "Working-Class Consumer Power," *ILWCH* 46 (Fall 1994): 109–21; Gregory R. Zieren, "The Labor Boycott and Class Consciousness in Toledo, Ohio," in Charles Stephenson and Robert Asher, eds., *Life and Labor: Dimensions of American Working-Class History* (Albany: State University of New York Press, 1986), pp. 131–49.

7. Allis Rosenberg Wolfe, "Women, Consumerism, and the National Consumers' League in the Progressive Era, 1900–1923," *Labor History* 16 (Summer 1975): 378–92; Kathryn Kish Sklar, "Two Political Cultures in the Progressive Era: The National Consumers' League and the American Association for Labor Legislation," in Linda K. Kerber, Alice Kessler-Harris, and Sklar, eds., *U.S. History as Women's History: New Feminist Essays* (Chapel Hill: University of North Carolina Press, 1995), pp. 36–62; Sklar, "The Consumers' White Label Campaign of the National Consumers' League, 1898–1918," in Susan Strasser, Charles McGovern, and Matthias Judt, *Getting and Spending: European and American Consumer Societies in the Twentieth Century* (Washington, DC: German Historical Institute; New York: Cambridge University Press, 1994); Landon R. Y. Storrs, *Civilizing Capitalism: The National Consumers' League, Women's Activism, and Labor Standards in the New Deal Era* (Chapel Hill: University of North Carolina Press, 2000), chap. 1; "National Consumers' League: Memorandum for National Social Work Council," n.d. but c. 1924, Angevine, Box 5, Folder B-1; "History of Consumers' League of New Jersey (1900–1950)," CLNJ, inventory file.

8. Lynn Dumenil, *Modern Temper: American Culture and Society in the 1920s* (New York: Hill and Wang, 1995), pp. 76–97; Lizabeth Cohen, *Making a New Deal: Industrial Workers in Chicago, 1919–1939* (New York: Cambridge University Press, 1990), pp.

100–158; Robert S. Lynd and Helen Merrell Lynd, *Middletown: A Study in Contemporary American Culture* (New York: Harcourt, Brace & World, 1929); President's Research Committee on Social Trends, *Social Trends in the United States*, 2 vols. (1933; reprint, Westport, CT: Greenwood, 1970), pp. 857–911; Martha Olney, *Buy Now, Pay Later: Advertising, Credit, and Consumer Durables in the 1920s* (Chapel Hill: University of North Carolina Press, 1991). Interestingly, women active in the Ku Klux Klan during the 1920s used selective buying in their battle for racial and religious supremacy, particularly boycotting Jewish-owned stores: Kathleen M. Blee, *Women of the Klan: Racism and Gender in the 1920s* (Berkeley: University of California Press, 1991), pp. 147–53.

9. On consumer-oriented legislation during the Progressive Era and the dearth of consumer political activity during the 1920s, see Robert N. Mayer, *The Consumer Movement: Guardians of the Marketplace* (Boston: Twayne, 1989), pp. 10–19; Sorenson, *Consumer Movement*, pp. 6–9; Mark V. Nadel, *The Politics of Consumer Protection* (Indianapolis: Bobbs-Merrill, 1971), pp. 3–16; Creighton, *Pretenders to the Throne*, pp. 7–18.

10. John Kenneth Galbraith, *American Capitalism: The Concept of Countervailing Power* (1952, 1956; reprint, New Brunswick, NJ: Transaction, 1993); Ellis Hawley, *The New Deal and the Problem of Monopoly: A Study in Economic Ambivalance* (Princeton: Princeton University Press, 1966), pp. 187–90. Also see Alan Brinkley, "Prosperity, Depression, and War, 1920–1945," in Eric Foner, ed., *The New American History* (Philadelphia: Temple University Press, 1990), pp. 132–33, for helpful treatment of what he terms a "broker state."

11. Creighton, *Pretenders to the Throne*, pp. 25–27; Hawley, *New Deal and Problem of Monopoly*, pp. 198–204, 275.

12. Franklin D. Roosevelt, "Address at Oglethorpe University," May 22, 1932, Franklin and Eleanor Roosevelt Institute, "Franklin Delano Roosevelt: President of the Century," FDR Speeches, http://www.feri.org/fdr/speech07.htm, pp. 4–5.

13. Interview with Esther Peterson by Scott Bruns, Nov. 2, 1976, Columbia University Oral History Research Office, p. 5-275.

14. Mayer, *Consumer Movement*, pp. 20–22; Creighton, *Pretenders to the Throne*, pp. 19–22; Sorenson, *Consumer Movement*, pp. 31–55; President's Research Committee, *Recent Social Trends*, p. 886. See Lawrence B. Glickman, "The Strike in the Temple of Consumption: Consumer Activism and Twentieth-Century American Political Culture," *JAH* 88 (June 2001): 99–128, for the fate of Consumers' Research during the 1930s, including its spawning of a more left-wing Consumers Union.

15. Quote from Newark Consumers' Cooperative League, *Bulletin*, August 1937, "Newark Associations" File, NPL. On cooperatives generally, see "What About the Consumer Movement?" *AA*, reprint from 1940, Atkinson, Box 4, Folder 6, p. 6; "Business Week Reports to Executives on the Consumer Movement," *BW*, Apr. 22, 1939, pp. 43–44; Colston E. Warne, "Consumers on the March," *The Nation*, June 5, 1937, pp. 645–46; Sorenson, *Consumer Movement*, pp. 105, 107, 137–53; Dorothy Houston Jacobson, *Our Interests as Consumers* (New York: Harper & Bros., 1941), pp. 227–307; Hawley, *New Deal and Problem of Monopoly*, pp. 199, 201–202, 268; Pearce C. Kelley, *Consumer Economics* (Homewood, IL: Irwin, 1953), pp. 579–617, with particular attention to survey in 1940 of urban co-op members on pp. 599–602; Charles S. Wyand, *The Economics of Consumption* (New York: Macmillan, 1937), pp. 395–423; Warren C. Waite and Ralph Cassady, Jr., *The Consumer and the Economic Order* (New York: McGraw-Hill, 1949), pp. 369–87.

For an excellent case study of the emergence and growth of consumer cooperatives during the 1930s, see from the "Q" Files, NPL: Frank Eakin, "N.J.C.C.'s First Year, Being Chapter One of the Life Story of a Suburban Consumers Cooperative," 1937; "President's Report to the Third Annual Convention of the New Jersey Federation of Consumers

Cooperatives," Newark University, Dec. 10, 1938; "President's Report to the Fourth Annual Convention of the New Jersey Federation of Consumers Cooperatives" and "Who's Who on the Convention Program," Newark Athletic Club, Dec. 9, 1939.

16. Alan Brinkley, *The End of Reform: New Deal Liberalism in Recession and War* (New York: Knopf, 1995), pp. 37–40, 67–85; Brinkley's book has been of enormous help to me in understanding the importance of the consumer to New Dealers; Arthur M. Schlesinger, Jr., *The Age of Roosevelt: The Crisis of the Old Order* (Boston: Houghton Mifflin, 1957), pp. 398–403.

17. John Dewey, "The Need for a New Party," *The New Republic,* Mar. 18, 1931, pp. 115–17; Mar. 25, 1931, pp. 150–52; Apr. 1, 1931, pp. 177–79; Paul H. Douglas, *The Coming of a New Party* (New York: McGraw-Hill, 1932); Robert B. Westbrook, *John Dewey and American Democracy* (Ithaca, NY: Cornell University Press, 1991), pp. 443–50; Schlesinger, *Crisis of Old Order,* pp. 142, 198, 436.

18. Sorenson, *Consumer Movement,* p. 163.

19. On the economic thinking of the Republicans and the creators of the NRA, see Brinkley, *End of Reform,* pp. 36–39, 69–82; John Kenneth Galbraith, *The Affluent Society* (Boston: Houghton Mifflin, 1958), pp. 16–18; Alan Sweezy, "The Keynesians and Government Policy, 1933–1939," *American Economic Review* 62 (May 1972): 116–17; Hawley, *New Deal and Problem of Monopoly,* pp. 188–90; Galbraith, *American Capitalism,* pp. 13, 19, 21–23.

20. Lynd, Foreword to Campbell, *Consumer Representation in the New Deal,* p. 11. On the NRA and specifically the CAB, see Campbell, *Consumer Representation in the New Deal,* pp. 27–88; Campbell, *Bringing the Consumer Point of View into Government* (Greeley, CO: Council on Consumer Information, 1958), pp. 14–17; Sorenson, *Consumer Movement,* pp. 14–20; Hawley, *New Deal and Problem of Monopoly,* pp. 75–146; "The Consumer Movement," *BW,* Apr. 22, 1939, p. 45; Dexter M. Keezer, "The Consumer Under the National Recovery Administration," and Paul H. Douglas, "The Role of the Consumer in the New Deal," *AAAPSS* 172 (March 1934): 88–106; Ben W. Lewis, "The 'Consumer' and 'Public' Interests Under Public Regulation," *Journal of Political Economy* 46 (February 1938): 97–107. For an example of the CAB's public criticism of the NRA, see "Consumers' Board Urges NRA Changes on Conference Eve," *NYT,* Mar. 5, 1934. Widespread acceptance of the necessity of consumer representation led, after the NRA ended, to the establishment of a new Consumers Division, with a "consumers' cabinet" that included many former CAB members such as its chair, Mrs. Emily Newell Blair, Leon Henderson, and Robert Lynd: "Cabinet to Direct Consumer Division," *NYT,* Oct. 12, 1935.

21. For a detailed discussion of the Consumer Counsel of the AAA, see Campbell, *Consumer Representation in the New Deal,* pp. 194–261; Campbell, *Bringing the Consumer Point of View into Government,* pp. 17–18; Erma Angevine and Dr. Caroline F. Ware, *Effective Consumer Participation: Consumer Participation in Federal Decision Making* (Washington, DC: National Consumers' League, 1981), pp. 7–8, Angevine, Box 6, Folder E-4.

22. Mayer, *Consumer Movement,* pp. 23–24; Angevine and Ware, *Effective Consumer Participation,* p. 9.

23. Kelley, *Consumer Economics,* p. 145; Waite and Cassady, *Consumer and the Economic Order,* pp. 124–25.

24. Nadel, *Politics of Consumer Protection,* p. 21; Campbell, *Bringing the Consumer Point of View into Government,* pp. 18–19; Sorenson, *Consumer Movement,* pp. 19–20.

25. Sorenson, *Consumer Movement,* p. 19; Creighton, *Pretenders to the Throne,* pp. 27, 39; Douglas, "Role of the Consumer in the New Deal," p. 104.

26. *The Public Papers and Addresses of Franklin D. Roosevelt with a Special Introduction and Explanatory Notes by President Roosevelt,* vol. 3, *The Advance of Recovery and Reform,*

1934 (New York: Random House, 1938), p. 57; Means, "Consumer and the New Deal," p. 7.

27. Mayer, *Consumer Movement*, pp. 24–25; Sorenson, *Consumer Movement*, pp. 12–14; Nadel, *Politics of Consumer Protection*, pp. 16–18; "Business Reports to Executives on the Consumer Movement," *BW*, Apr. 22, 1939, pp. 44–45; and from Atkinson, "The FDA Museum," Box 1, File 1; unidentified speech critiquing Federal Food, Drug, and Cosmetic Act, 1938, Box 1, File 5; U.S. Department of Agriculture, Food and Drug Administration, "Digest of the New Federal Food, Drug, and Cosmetic Act," June 27, 1938, Box 1, File 5.

28. Hawley, *New Deal and Problem of Monopoly;* Elizabeth Faue, *Community of Suffering and Struggle: Women, Men, and the Labor Movement in Minneapolis, 1915–1945* (Chapel Hill: University of North Carolina Press, 1991); Cohen, *Making a New Deal.*

29. Kenneth Dameron, "The Consumer Movement," *HBR* 17 (Spring 1939): 271–89.

30. Sorenson, *Consumer Movement*, pp. 21–30, 56–81; Creighton, *Pretenders to the Throne*, pp. 74–76; James E. Mendenhall, ed., *Consumer Education: Background, Present Status, and Future Possibilities* (New York: Appleton-Century, 1943); Institute for Consumer Education, *Next Steps in Consumer Education*, Proceedings of a National Conference on Consumer Education held at Stephens College, Columbia, MO, April 3, 4, and 5, 1939; *Making Consumer Education Effective*, Proceedings, Second National Conference, Institute for Consumer Education, Stephens College, Bulletin No. 2, July 1940; *Consumer Education for Life Problems*, Proceedings, Third National Conference, Institute for Consumer Education, Stephens College, Bulletin No. 3, June 1941. Consumer economics expanded as a branch of economics during the 1930s, reflecting growing attention to the consumer interest. Women economists were influential in shaping the field. Elizabeth Ellis Hoyt, *Consumption in Our Society* (New York: McGraw-Hill, 1938); Kelley, *Consumer Economics*, passim and particularly pp. 148–50.

31. "Business Week Reports to Executives on the Consumer Movement," *BW*, Apr. 22, 1939, p. 46; Sorenson, *Consumer Movement*, pp. 195–96, also 83–84.

32. "Business Week Reports to Executives on the Consumer Movement," *BW*, Apr. 22, 1939, pp. 46–47; Sorenson, *Consumer Movement*, pp. 59–60, 69–72, 82–110; "Remarks by Caroline F. Ware on Receiving the National Consumers' League Trumpeter Award, April 11, 1978," Margolius, Box 1, folder "AFL-CIO"; from Atkinson: speech crediting women with victory of Food, Drug, and Cosmetic Act of 1938, no author, title, or date, Box 1, Folder 5; "What About the Consumer Movement?" *AA*, reprint 1940, Box 4, Folder 6, pp. 2–6; material on Women's Joint Congressional Committee, Box 5, Folder 13.

33. Sorenson, *Consumer Movement*, pp. 86–87, 102, 118–19; "Housewives Are Urged to Fight High Prices," clipping July 8, 1935, CR, General Files, Box 30, Consumerism, "Organization and Representation of the Consumer, 1931–75"; "What About the Consumer Movement?" *AA*, Atkinson, p. 4, for McHale quote to FDR; untitled and undated speech to American Home Economics Association, Atkinson, Box 1, Folder 5.

34. On the League of Women Shoppers, see Sorenson, *Consumer Movement*, pp. 127–28; Jane Filley and Therese Mitchell, *Consider the Laundry Workers* (New York: League of Women Shoppers, 1937); Leane Zugsmith, *L Is for Labor: A Glossary of Labor Terms* (New York: League of Women Shoppers, 1937); Therese Mitchell, *Consider the Woolworth Workers* (New York: League of Women Shoppers, 1940); CR, General Files, Political-Front Organizations, 1935–70, "L"—League of Women Shoppers; and in Ruttenberg, four folders on League of Women Shoppers. In *The Group*, Mary McCarthy's novel satirizing the lives of eight Vassar graduates, liberal Priss Hartshorn Crockett works for a short time for the League of Women Shoppers (1954; reprint, New York: Signet, 1963), pp. 238–39.

35. The National Consumers' League's gradual shift toward consumer issues can be traced through internal documents. For example, at an NCL board meeting in January 1934 the question of the league's policy toward consumer protection was discussed "and the board felt that the National Consumers' League and its branches should adhere to its original program of expressing the consumer's conscience rather than his interest in prices and quality of goods." By June 1938 the board indicated that the league "has come to recognize the inescapable interconnections" between fighting for minimum wages and hours and prices. "The National Consumers' League, therefore, puts itself on record as recognizing the need for including within the scope of its interest such problems of direct consumer concern as the growth of monopolistic practices and arbitrary price rises in so far as these problems bear on the achievements of direct labor legislative objectives of the League's program." By June 1940 the board was working so closely with the consumer adviser to the Defense Commission, Harriet Elliott, and her assistant, Caroline Ware, "building consumer protection into the program of national defense," that the NCL's national office was moved to Washington. From Angevine, Box 5, Folder B-4: NCL Board Minutes, Jan. 26, 1934, p. 3; NCL Board Minutes, June 14, 1938; NCL Board Minutes, June 20, 1940, p. 4. Also see Sorenson, *Consumer Movement*, p. 126, for new concerns of NCL, c. 1940.

36. "Statement on the make-up and program of the Consumers' National Federation and the consumer movement by Helen Hall and Robert Lynd," 1939, Campbell, Series II, Box 1, Folder 2; Campbell, *Consumer Representation in the New Deal*, pp. 60–61; Sorenson, *Consumer Movement*, pp. 103, 111–36; "Business Week Reports to Executives on the Consumer Movement," *BW*, Apr. 22, 1939, p. 52.

37. Consumers' National Federation press release, "Consumers Ask for More Government Services," Jan. 20, 1940, Campbell, Series II, Box 1, Folder 3. See Nancy Cott, *The Grounding of Modern Feminism* (New Haven: Yale University Press, 1987), on debates over women's political activity after suffrage; Kristi Anderson, "Women and Citizenship in the 1920s," in Louise A. Tilly and Patricia Gurin, eds., *Women, Politics, and Change* (New York: Russell Sage Foundation, 1990), p. 187, on women's suspicions of political parties; Liette Patricia Gidlow, "Getting Out the Vote: Gender and Citizenship in an Age of Consumer Culture" (Ph.D. diss., Cornell University, 1997), on voting in the 1920s; and Alexander Keyssar, *The Right to Vote: The Contested History of Democracy in the United States* (New York: Perseus, 2000), pp. 218–21, on decline in women's voting. I am grateful to Sue Cobble for helping me conceptualize this shift.

38. The best source on the housewives' protest is the work of Annelise Orleck, " 'We Are That Mythical Thing Called the Public': Militant Housewives During the Great Depression," *Feminist Studies* 19 (Spring 1993): 147–72, and *Common Sense and a Little Fire*, pp. 215–49. *WSJ* quote from "Meat Prices Decline as Resistance of Buyers Increases," June 12, 1935. Also see Sorenson, *Consumer Movement*, pp. 119–21; Colston E. Warne, "Consumers on the March, Part II," *The Nation*, June 12, 1937, p. 676; from CR, Box 30, Consumerism, "Consumer Boycotts and Picketing, 1931–1951": "Meat Price Strike Led by Radical Woman Listed as Communist," *Los Angeles Times*, Apr. 10, 1935; "Consumers: Angry Housewives Chop Meat Out of Their Diet," *Newsweek*, Apr. 6, 1935; "Price Drive Shuts Many Meat Shops," *NYT*, May 27, 1935; "Boycott of High-Priced Meat Spread by Militant Housewives," *NYT*, May 28, 1935; "Mad at Meat," *BW*, June 5, 1935; "Consumers Threaten Meat Boycott," *Food Field Reporter*, July 1, 1935; "Embattled Housewives Demand Lower Food Prices," *Journal of Electrical Workers and Operators*, July 1935, pp. 292, 307; "Detroit Joins Meat Strike; Forces 300 Markets to Close," *Farmers Union Herald*, August 1935; "Butchers Quit in Hamtramck," *Detroit News*, Aug. 3, 1935; "Mary Zuk and the High Cost of Living," *Food Field Reporter*, Aug. 26, 1935; "No Meeting of Minds," *BW*, Aug. 24, 1935; M. C. Phillips, "Communists and the High Cost of Living," *Consumers'*

Digest, February 1940, pp. 33–38; M. C. Phillips, "Communists and the Milk Strikes," *Consumers' Digest,* March 1940, pp. 49–54.

39. Quote from Wyand, *Economics of Consumption,* pp. 388–89.

40. "Consumers," *Newsweek,* Apr. 6, 1935; Orleck, "'We Are That Mythical Thing'"; Orleck, *Common Sense,* pp. 215–49; Sorenson, *Consumer Movement,* pp. 119–20.

41. Orleck, "'We Are That Mythical Thing'"; Orleck, *Common Sense,* pp. 236–39; Sorenson, *Consumer Movement,* pp. 119–20; "No Meeting of Minds," *BW,* Aug. 24, 1935, p. 11; "Woman's Work," *Journal of Electrical Workers and Operators,* July 1935, p. 292.

42. William P. Mangold, "On the Labor Front," *The New Republic,* Apr. 8, 1936, p. 250; Lynd, "Democracy's Third Estate," p. 496.

43. Faue, *Community of Suffering and Struggle,* particularly chap. 3; Cohen, *Making a New Deal,* chap. 8.

44. I am grateful to Sue Cobble for this insight. See her *Dishing It Out: Waitresses and Their Unions in the Twentieth Century* (Urbana: University of Illinois Press, 1991).

45. Campbell, *Consumer Representation in the New Deal,* p. 274; Warne, "Consumers on the March, Part II," *The Nation,* June 12, 1937, p. 676; Sorenson, *Consumer Movement,* pp. 106–107; Mark Starr, "What Labor Is Doing," in *Making Consumer Education Effective,* pp. 6–13; Steven Fraser, *Labor Will Rule: Sidney Hillman and the Rise of American Labor* (New York: Free Press, 1991), pp. 153–54, recognizes labor's general ambivalence while acknowledging that the Amalgamated Clothing Workers' "New Unionism" was exceptional in supporting a cooperative program during the 1920s. Report of Washington meeting with union leaders in "The First Bona Fide Consumer Group Interviews the President," February 1938, Campbell, Box 1, Folder 2.

46. Starr, "What Labor Is Doing," p. 8; Creighton, *Pretenders to the Throne,* pp. 72–73, argues that increasingly after World War II "as labor became more secure in its economic position, it came to see the consumer movement's goal of more efficient consumer spending as consistent with labor's own goal of greater worker income." Fraser, *Labor Will Rule,* shows how once again Sidney Hillman and his Amalgamated Clothing Workers were a decade ahead, anticipating in the 1930s what most unions would not recognize until the 1940s, much the way their "New Unionism" of the 1920s anticipated "New Dealism" of the 1930s.

47. For the importance of looking beyond the workplace and the labor union for black working-class politics, see Robin D. G. Kelley, "'We Are Not What We Seem': Rethinking Black Working-Class Opposition in the Jim Crow South," *JAH* 80 (June 1993): 75–112.

48. Frank L. Hayes, "Chicago's Rent Riot," *Survey* 66 (Sept. 15, 1931): 548–49; St. Clair Drake and Horace R. Cayton, *Black Metropolis: A Study of Negro Life in a Northern City* (1945; reprint, Chicago: University of Chicago Press, 1993), pp. 734–39; Clayborne Carson, "The Red and the Black," *The Nation,* Oct. 29, 1983, pp. 405–408.

49. *Lynchburg News,* June 9, 1906, quoted in August Meier and Elliott Rudwick, "The Boycott Movement Against Jim Crow Streetcars in the South, 1900–1906," *JAH* 55 (March 1969): 756–75; Meier and Rudwick, "Negro Boycotts of Segregated Streetcars in Virginia, 1904–1907," *Virginia Magazine of History and Biography* 81 (October 1973); Robert E. Weems, Jr., "African-American Consumer Boycotts During the Civil Rights Era," *Western Journal of Black Studies* 19 (Spring 1995): 72–73.

50. Grace Elizabeth Hale, *Making Whiteness: The Culture of Segregation in the South, 1890–1940* (New York: Pantheon, 1998); Roger L. Ransom and Richard Sutch, *One Kind of Freedom: The Economic Consequences of Emancipation* (Cambridge, Eng.: Cambridge University Press, 1977), pp. 120–48, 161–62, 182–83; Ted Ownby, *American Dreams in Mississippi: Consumers, Poverty, and Culture, 1830–1998* (Chapel Hill: University of North Carolina Press, 1999).

51. E. Franklin Frazier, "Negro Business: A Social Myth," in Edwin M. Epstein and David R. Hampton, eds., *Black Americans and White Business* (Encino, CA: Dickenson, 1971), p. 233; Gunnar Myrdal, *An American Dilemma: The Negro Problem and Modern Democracy,* 2 vols. (1944; reprint, New Brunswick, NJ: Transaction, 1996), 2:800; Meier and Rudwick, "Boycott Movement," pp. 274–75, 281; J. H. Harmon, Jr., "The Negro as a Local Business Man," *Journal of Negro History* 14 (April 1929): 116–55.

52. On the "separate black economy" movement of the 1920s, see Cohen, *Making a New Deal,* pp. 148–54. On the new "Negro market," see Drake and Cayton, *Black Metropolis,* pp. 433–36.

53. Cohen, *Making a New Deal,* pp. 149–50; Roi Ottley, *"New World A-Coming": Inside Black America* (Cleveland: World, 1945), pp. 68–81; "Marcus Garvey," in *The Oxford W.E.B. Du Bois Reader,* ed. Eric Sunquist (New York: Oxford University Press, 1996), pp. 265–76; Myrdal, *American Dilemma,* 2:746–49.

54. Cohen, *Making a New Deal,* pp. 149–52; Harmon, Jr., "Negro as Local Business Man," pp. 140–55; *The Negro Market: Published in the Interest of the Negro Press* (Chicago: Ziff, 1932), pp. 12–13; Myrdal, *American Dilemma,* 1:307–12; Cheryl Lynn Greenberg, *"Or Does It Explode?": Black Harlem in the Great Depression* (New York: Oxford University Press, 1991), pp. 27–28.

55. On consumer activism in Chicago, see Drake and Cayton, *Black Metropolis,* pp. 84–85, 295–96, 733–34; "Woolworth Employs Colored Girls; Pickets Are Removed," Oct. 6, 1930, press release, Barnett, Box 260, Folder 7; Richard Durham, "Don't Spend Your Money Where You Can't Work," n.d. but c. 1939, Barnett, Box 149, Folder 4; Cohen, *Making a New Deal,* pp. 153–54.

56. Andor Skotnes, " 'Buy Where You Can Work': Boycotting for Jobs in African-American Baltimore, 1933–1934," *Journal of Social History* 27 (Summer 1994): 735–61; Karen Olson, "Old West Baltimore: Segregation, African-American Culture, and the Struggle for Equality," in Elizabeth Fee, Linda Shopes, and Linda Zeidman, eds., *The Baltimore Book: New Views of Local History* (Philadelphia: Temple University Press, 1991), pp. 67–73; "Negroes Must Work," *New Jersey Herald News,* Aug. 20, 1938, reprinted in Clement Alexander Price, ed., *Freedom Not Far Distant: A Documentary History of Afro-Americans in New Jersey* (Newark: New Jersey Historical Society, 1980), pp. 235–36; Gretchen Lemke-Santangelo, *Abiding Courage: African American Migrant Women and the East Bay Community* (Chapel Hill: University of North Carolina Press, 1996), pp. 73, 166.

57. On the "Buy Where You Can Work" campaign in Harlem, see Vere E. Johns, "To Boycott or—Not to Boycott? A. We Must Have Jobs," *The Crisis* 41 (September 1934): 258, 274; Melville Weiss, " 'Don't Buy Where You Can't Work': An Analysis of Consumer Action Against Employment Discrimination in Harlem, 1934–1940" (M.A. thesis, Columbia University, 1941); Greenberg, *"Or Does It Explode?"* pp. 114–39; Charles V. Hamilton, *Adam Clayton Powell, Jr.: The Political Biography of an American Dilemma* (New York: Atheneum, 1991), pp. 90–94; William Muraskin, "The Harlem Boycott of 1934: Black Nationalism and the Rise of Labor-Union Consciousness," *Labor History* 13 (Summer 1972): 361–73; Mark Naison, *Communists in Harlem During the Depression* (New York: Grove, 1983), pp. 50–51; Myrdal, *American Dilemma,* 1:1261; Christopher Agee, "The Boycotts-for-Jobs Movement and Black-Jewish Relations: 1928–1935" (senior thesis, University of California, Berkeley, 1997), in possession of the author.

The United States Supreme Court decision that permitted picketing again in 1938 was *New Negro Alliance* v. *Sanitary Grocery Company,* which ruled that because blacks suffered employment discrimination due solely to their race, they could respond by making special demands, including picketing.

On the Harlem riot, see Alain Locke, "Harlem: Dark Weather-Vane," *Survey Graphic,* August 1936, pp. 457–62; Cheryl Greenberg, "The Politics of Disorder: Reexamining Harlem's Riots of 1935 and 1943," *JUH* 18 (August 1992): 395–44; Naison, *Communists in Harlem,* pp. 140–55; Ottley, "*New World A-Coming,*" pp. 151–53. Ralph Ellison powerfully captures the night of the riot in *Invisible Man* (New York: Random House, 1947), chap. 25.

58. Myrdal, *American Dilemma,* 1:313; Joel Schwartz, "The Consolidated Tenants League of Harlem: Black Self-Help vs. White, Liberal Intervention in Ghetto Housing, 1934–1944," *Afro-Americans in New York Life and History* 10 (January 1986): 31–51; Ronald Lawson with the assistance of Mark Naison, eds., *The Tenant Movement in New York City, 1904–1984* (New Brunswick, NJ: Rutgers University Press, 1986), pp. 19, 94–102, 114–16, 119–20; Greenberg, "*Or Does It Explode?*" p. 134.

59. T. Arnold Hill, "Picketing for Jobs," *Opportunity* 8 (July 1930): 216; Myrdal, *American Dilemma,* 1:1261; Durham, "Don't Spend Your Money," Barnett, Box 149, Folder 4, pp. 7–8; "New Jersey Conference (Atlantic City Theatre Discrimination Case 1937–38)," NAACP, I, G 115.

60. For an excellent analysis of Du Bois's thinking during the 1930s, see Thomas C. Holt, "The Political Uses of Alienation: W.E.B. Du Bois on Politics, Race, and Culture, 1903–1940," in Leon Fink, Stephen T. Leonard, and Donald M. Reid, eds., *Intellectuals and Public Life: Between Radicalism and Reform* (Ithaca, NY: Cornell University Press, 1996), pp. 236–56; W.E.B. Du Bois, "A Negro Nation Within the Nation," *Current History* 42 (June 1935): 265–70, reprinted in David Levering Lewis, ed., *W.E.B. Du Bois: A Reader* (New York: Holt, 1995), p. 568.

61. Vishnu V. Oak, *The Negro's Adventure in General Business* (Westport, CT: Negro Universities Press, 1949), pp. 72–94; Greenberg, "*Or Does It Explode?*" p. 84; Drake and Cayton, *Black Metropolis,* pp. 454–56; "500 New Stores Every Year," *Afro-American,* Oct. 18, 1941.

62. "Business in Bronzeville," *Time,* Apr. 18, 1938, pp. 70–71; Richard I. Durham, "Don't Spend Your Money," Barnett, Box 149, Folder 4, p. 6; "Sausage Plant, a Variety Store, Products Concern Chicago's Pride Firms; Insurance Companies Are Thriving and More Negro-Controlled Stores Are Being Developed," n.d. but c. 1938, Barnett, Box 260, Folder 6; Henry Bacon, "Chapter 1: Welcome to Bronzeville," Sept. 29, 1940, Barnett, Box 149, Folder 4, pp. 10–11; Drake and Cayton, *Black Metropolis,* pp. 430–33; Local Retail Grocers, Inc. to "The Clergy, Business and Civic Leaders," July 6, 1939, Barnett, Box 260, Folder 7.

63. St. Clair Drake, "Churches and Voluntary Associations in the Chicago Negro Community," Report of Official Project 465-54-3-386, Works Projects Administration District 3, Chicago, December 1940, p. 179; Myrdal, *American Dilemma,* 1:307.

64. Oak, *Negro's Adventure in General Business,* pp. 60–66; "Negro Chain," *Time,* May 12, 1930, pp. 47–48; from Barnett, Box 277, Folder 7: Albert Anderson (for the Associated Negro Press), "Say, What's This Thing the Business League Is Trying to Do?" n.d., and "Plan of the National C.M.A. Stores Inc.," n.d.; H. M. Foster, "Negro Chain Stores," *The Nation,* Mar. 11, 1931; Albon L. Holsey, "The C.M.A. Stores Face the Chains," *Opportunity* 7 (July 1929): 210–13; *The Negro Market,* p. 13; E. Franklin Frazier, "Negro Business: A Social Myth," in Epstein and Hampton, eds., *Black Americans and White Business,* p. 235.

65. Holt, "Political Uses of Alienation," pp. 248–51; W.E.B. Du Bois, "The C.M.A. Stores," *Pittsburgh Courier,* July 31, 1937, in Lewis, ed., *W.E.B. Du Bois,* p. 571; Drake, "Churches and Voluntary Associations," p. 211.

66. Drake, "Churches and Voluntary Associations," pp. 211–12; "The Struggle on the Consumers' Front, A Weapon for Educating the Negro People," *Daily Worker,* Nov. 27,

1935, p. 4; Paula F. Pfeffer, "The Women Behind the Union: Halena Wilson, Rosina Tucker, and the Ladies' Auxiliary to the Brotherhood of Sleeping Car Porters," *Labor History* 36 (Fall 1995): 568–71; "Brotherhood Consumers Cooperative Buying Club Rally," press release, Jan. 31, 1944, Brotherhood of Sleeping Car Porters Papers, CHS, Box 118, Folder 7; and see other material in Folders 3, 4, and 7. I am grateful to Tracey Deutsch for pointing me to these records.

67. From NAACP, II, A 572, file "Staff: Baker, Ella J., 1940–42": "Experience Sheet"; reference letter from Isabel Taylor, July 12, 1939; "Consumers' Cooperation Among Negroes," memorandum from Miss Baker to Mr. Wilkins, Aug. 12, 1941; Charles Payne, "Ella Baker and Models of Social Change," *Signs: Journal of Women in Culture and Society* 14 (Summer 1989): 885–99; "The Struggle on the Consumers' Front," *Daily Worker*, Nov. 27, 1935; Joanne Grant, *Ella Baker: Freedom Bound* (New York: Wiley, 1998), pp. 31–37. Grant points out that Bob Moses, who became a leader in the southern civil rights movement of the 1960s, worked as a milk cooperative delivery boy in the early 1940s, another example of the consumer movement of the 1930s and 1940s providing a training ground for civil rights activism later.

68. Drake and Cayton, *Black Metropolis*, p. 441.

69. Darlene Clark Hine, "The Housewives' League of Detroit: Black Women and Economic Nationalism," in Nancy A. Hewitt and Suzanne Lebsock, eds., *Visible Women: New Essays on American Activism* (Urbana: University of Illinois Press, 1993), pp. 223–41; Oak, *Negro's Adventure in General Business*, pp. 100–102; Victoria Wolcott, "'For a More Prosperous Day': Economic Self-Help, African-American Women and the Detroit Housewives' League, 1930–1941," paper presented at the Organization of American Historians, Mar. 31, 1995, in possession of author.

70. Skotnes, "'Buy Where You Can Work,'" p. 751.

71. Greenberg, "*Or Does It Explode?*" pp. 116–17; Weiss, "'Don't Buy Where You Can't Work,'" pp. 58–59; Ella Baker, "Consumers' Cooperation Among Negroes," Aug. 12, 1941, NAACP, II, A 572, file "Staff: Baker, Ella J., 1940–42"; Grant, *Ella Baker*, pp. 35–36.

72. Wolcott, "'For a More Prosperous Day,'" pp. 67, 14; Oak, *Negro's Adventure in General Business*, p. 102.

73. Naison, *Communists in Harlem*, pp. 149–50; Orleck, *Common Sense*, pp. 235, 348n67; "The Struggle on the Consumers' Front," *Daily Worker*, Nov. 27, 1935.

74. "Experience Sheet," NAACP, II, A 572, file "Staff: Baker, Ella J., 1940–42."

75. Clarence Taylor, *The Black Churches of Brooklyn* (New York: Columbia University Press, 1994), p. 81.

76. Minutes of Housewives' Cooperative League meetings, Fall 1937, in Urban League of Pittsburgh Papers (AIS 81:11), FF321, "Housewives' Cooperative League, 1937," AIS.

77. Elsa Barkley Brown, "Womanist Consciousness: Maggie Lena Walker and the Independent Order of Saint Luke," *Signs: Journal of Women in Culture and Society* 14 (Spring 1989): 610–33, cited in Hine, "Housewives' League of Detroit," pp. 224–25.

78. Grant, *Ella Baker*, p. 32.

79. Minutes, Sept. 7, 1937, and Sept. 15, 1937, Urban League of Pittsburgh Papers (AIS 81:11), FF321, "Housewives' Cooperative League, 1937," AIS.

80. Durham, "Don't Spend Your Money," Barnett, Box 149, Folder 4, p. 7; Johns, "To Boycott or—Not to Boycott?" *The Crisis* 41 (September 1934): 258; Weiss, "'Don't Buy Where You Can't Work,'" p. 59.

81. See the work of Meg Jacobs on Edward Filene for discussion of his "middle way" of using state power to create greater purchasing power: government facilitation of worker organization would fuel high wages and hence expand purchasing power, without state involvement in pump priming. Filene and his Twentieth Century Fund worked with Senator Robert Wagner, chief author of the NLRA: Jacobs, "The Politics of Purchasing

Power: Political Economy, Consumption Politics, and State-building, 1909–1959" (Ph.D. diss., University of Virginia, 1998); and "Edward Filene, the Twentieth Century Fund, and the New Science of Consumption: From Bargain Basement to Bargaining Table," paper presented at colloquium, June 7, 1996, New York University, in possession of the author. On the economic benefits of social security, see George Lipsitz, "Consumer Spending as State Project: Yesterday's Solutions and Today's Problems," *Getting and Spending*, p. 132.

82. My discussion of Keynesianism has benefited from David M. Kennedy, *Freedom from Fear: The American People in Depression and War, 1929–1945* (New York: Oxford University Press, 1999), pp. 350–62; Brinkley, *End of Reform*, pp. 65–85, 116–17, 231–35; Alan Sweezy, "The Keynesian Revolution and Its Pioneers: The Keynesians and Government Policy, 1933–1939," *American Economic Review* 62 (May 1972): 116–24; George Soule, "This Recovery: What Brought It? And Will It Last?" *Harper's* 174 (March 1937): 337–45; Galbraith, *Affluent Society*, pp. 16–18, 188–93; Daniel Bell, *The End of Ideology* (Cambridge, MA: Harvard University Press, 1988), pp. 75–80; Martyn J. Lee, *Consumer Culture Reborn: The Cultural Politics of Consumption* (London: Routledge, 1993), pp. 80–81.

83. Fraser, *Labor Will Rule*, pp. 259–70, explores how labor leader Sidney Hillman had a "proto-Keynesian underconsumptionist outlook" even before the stock market crash.

84. John Kenneth Galbraith, *A Life in Our Times: Memoirs* (Boston: Houghton Mifflin, 1981), pp. 65, 67.

85. Ernest Erber to John P. Wiet, July 28, 1964, Erber, Box B, Folder 2.

86. "Success Story," *Fortune*, December 1935, p. 124.

87. " 'We Are Fighting to Save a Great and Precious Form of Government for Ourselves and the World'—Acceptance of the Renomination for the Presidency, Philadelphia, PA, June 27, 1936," *The Public Papers and Addresses of Franklin D. Roosevelt with a Special Introduction and Explanatory Notes by President Roosevelt, 1936* (New York: Random House, 1938), 4:234.

88. Franklin Roosevelt, "State of the Union Address," January 6, 1941, quoted in Glickman, ed., *Consumer Society*, p. 5; see also Robert B. Westbrook, "Fighting for the American Family: Private Interests and Political Obligation in World War II," in Richard Wightman Fox and T. J. Jackson Lears, *The Power of Culture: Critical Essays in American History* (Chicago: University of Chicago Press, 1993), pp. 194–221. Rockwell's "Freedom from Want" from *Saturday Evening Post*, Mar. 6, 1943.

89. "Merchants May Be Sitting on Dynamite," *Babson's Reports*, Nov. 25, 1935; "Business Week Reports to Executives on the Consumer Movement," *BW*, Apr. 22, 1939, p. 52; "What About the Consumer Movement?" *AA* (reprint, 1940), in Atkinson, Box 4, Folder 6, p. 1.

90. Fred DeArmond, "Consumer Clans Are Gathering," *Nation's Business*, January 1938, pp. 40, 42.

91. Dameron, "The Consumer Movement," *HBR*, pp. 284–85; Kelley, *Consumer Economics*, pp. 146–47; Creighton, *Pretenders to the Throne*, p. 29; Persia Campbell, *The Consumer Interest: A Study in Consumer Economics* (New York: Harper & Bros., 1949), p. 635. Lynd quote from "Consumer Groups at Critical Stage," *NYT*, May 16, 1937. Membership in the Consumers' National Federation was limited to an organized body "which is not operated for profit, nor in the interest of, nor connected with profit-making organizations," as a way of keeping out business-affiliated consumer groups; membership flyer for the Consumers' National Federation, c. 1937, Campbell, Series II, Box 1, File 4.

92. Waite and Cassady, *Consumer and the Economic Order*, p. 410.

93. Sorenson, *Consumer Movement*, pp. 131–36; from CR, General Files, Political-Front Organizations, 1935–70, "L"—League of Women Shoppers: M. C. Phillips in *Consumers' Digest*: "Communists and the High Cost of Living," February 1940, pp. 33–38;

"Communists and the Milk Strikes," March 1940, pp. 49–54; "Half-way to Communism with the League of Women Shoppers," April 1940, pp. 39–44; "Are There Reds in the Kitchen?" September 1940, pp. 47–52; and from Ruttenberg, folders on League of Women Shoppers: "Statement of League of Women Shoppers on Dies Committee Report," n.d. but 1939. For more on the league's reaction, see Statement from Pittsburgh League of Women Shoppers in response to accusations from Dies Committee, n.d. but 1939; telegrams from Pittsburgh League of Women Shoppers to D.C., Feb. 1, 3, 11, 1939.

In 1939 the Consumers' National Federation prepared a long refutation of the charges made by "the Matthews-Dies report of the Congressional Committee to Investigate Un-American Activities"; Helen Hall and Robert Lynd, "Statement on the make-up and programs of the Consumers' National Federation and the Consumer Movement," Campbell, Series II, Box 1, Folder 2.

94. DeArmond, "Consumer Clans Are Gathering," *Nation's Business,* p. 42; "Threat to Business and how it is being met in the West by the Pacific Advertising Clubs Association," n.d. but c. 1941, Atkinson, Box 4, File 3; George B. Hotchkiss, *The Movement for Standardization and Grading of Consumer Goods* (New York: Association of National Advertisers, 1941), p. 26. Consumer activist Caroline Ware recalled years later that advocates of the Food, Drug, and Cosmetic Act of 1938 were called "reds, out to subvert the free enterprise system": "Remarks by Caroline F. Ware on Receiving the National Consumers' League Trumpeter Award, April 11, 1978," Margolius, Box 1, "AFL-CIO," p. 5.

95. The New Deal view of the economy as stagnant in the late 1930s, and not as oriented toward growth as it would become in the postwar period, is examined in Robert M. Collins, "The Emergence of Economic Growthmanship in the United States: Federal Policy and Economic Knowledge in the Truman Years," in Mary O. Furner and Barry Supple, eds., *The State and Economic Knowledge: The American and British Experience* (Cambridge, Eng.: Cambridge University Press, 1990), pp. 138–43. I am grateful to David Kennedy for pointing out this gradual reorientation in economic thinking from stagnancy to growth.

96. Joseph P. Cusker, "The World of Tomorrow: Science, Culture, and Community at the New York World's Fair," p. 10, and Warren I. Susman, "The People's Fair: Cultural Contradictions of a Consumer Society," pp. 19–20, in Queens Museum, *Dawn of a New Day: The New York World's Fair, 1939/40* (New York: New York University Press, 1980); David Gelernter, *1939: The Lost World of the Fair* (New York: Free Press, 1995), pp. 112–14, 116–17; "The Consumer Movement," *BW,* Apr. 22, 1939, pp. 50, 52; Richard Wurts and Others, *New York World's Fair 1939/1940 in 155 Photographs* (New York: Dover, 1977), p. 47; Sorenson, *Consumer Movement,* p. 177. On the fair more generally, see Museum of the City of New York, "Selling the World of Tomorrow," catalogue from exhibit 1989–90; John E. Findling, ed., *Historical Dictionary of World's Fairs and Expositions, 1851–1988* (Westport, CT: Greenwood, 1990), pp. 293–300.

CHAPTER 2. WAR: CITIZEN CONSUMERS DO BATTLE ON THE HOME FRONT

1. Of the 33 million women at home as housewives in December 1941, seven out of eight were still there in 1944, the peak of wartime employment. Moreover, even women laboring as defense workers purchased for their households: Michael C. C. Adams, *The Best War Ever: America and World War II* (Baltimore: Johns Hopkins University Press, 1994), p. 70. Rosie the Riveter is a well-known symbol of the new female industrial worker during World War II. The Winnie the WAC character was created by an army recruit, later professional cartoonist, Vic Herman in 1943. Not only were his cartoons distributed to base newspapers worldwide, but the army also sponsored Winnie the WAC look-alike contests; the winner was asked to help recruit for the fledgling Women's

Army Corps: "Vic Herman Was a Master of the Arts," *San Diego Union-Tribune,* Apr. 16, 1999.

2. Radio Theatre Productions, *The Home Front, 1938–1945* (Petaluma, CA: The Mind's Eye, 1985), Program 3: "Arsenal of Democracy"; "War and the Cost of Living, Address by John Cassels, Economic Adviser, Consumer Division, Office of Price Administration, at the Conference on Labor in National Defense, Harvard University, December 7, 1941," Campbell, Series I, Box 4, Folder 35, p. 4; "War Workers' Spending Habits," *Women's Wear Daily,* July 28, 1942, p. 27. The previous clipping, like many others cited in this chapter, comes from the very rich clipping files of the Consumers' Research Papers (CR), General Files, Government War Preparation, Rutgers. Hereafter I will not give the full CR reference for clippings, only for pamphlets, correspondence, and other unpublished material in the CR files.

3. "War and the Cost of Living by Cassels," address, p. 3; "The Consumer Faces Inflation," address by Harriet Elliott, Pennsylvania State Council of Defense, Harrisburg, Sept. 26, 1941, CR, General Files, Government War Preparation, "Effect of War Preparation on the Consumer, 1942," p. 6; "High Prices—Thin Purses, New York Conference on 'War and the Consumer,'" Jan. 24, 1942, Campbell, Series I, Box 3, Folder 32; "'New Rich' Change Buying Trends in Wichita Stores," *Women's Wear Daily,* Aug. 31, 1942.

4. On Harriet Elliott and the Consumer Office of the Advisory Commission to the Council of National Defense, see Ben Lewis, chief economist, Office of the Consumer Advisor, "The Consumer, the Market, and National Defense, at the Conference of National Retail Trade Organizations Called by Miss Harriet Elliott, Consumer Adviser on the Advisory Commission to the Council of National Defense, Washington, D.C.," Aug. 29, 1940, Campbell, Series I, Box 4, Folder 34; Eunice Fuller Barnard, "Guns? Yes, and Butter, Too," *NYT Magazine,* July 21, 1940; "National Defense in the American Way, Radio Address by Miss Harriet Elliott, . . . Station WBIG, Greensboro, North Carolina, November 3, 1940, 6:30 p.m., E.S.T.," Campbell, Series I, Box 4, Folder 34; from CR, General Files, Government War Preparation: "The Consumer Faces Inflation," address by Harriet Elliott, Harrisburg, PA, Sept. 26, 1941, pp. 2–3; National Council of Jewish Women, "The Consumer at War: A Leader's Guide for Five Sessions," January 1942, "Effect of War Preparation on the Consumer, 1942," p. 1.

5. On the workings of the OPA, see extensive material in CR, Government War Preparation, and Campbell, Series I, Boxes 3 and 4, particularly Office of Price Administration, "What's in the Price Control Law?" May 1, 1942, Folder 35. Also see "Exit the Can Opener," *Time,* Mar. 8, 1943, p. 18; Persia Campbell, *The Consumer Interest: A Study in Consumer Economics* (New York: Harper & Bros., 1949); John Kenneth Galbraith, *A Life in Our Times* (Boston: Houghton Mifflin, 1981), pp. 106–91; notes on article "Governmental Costs," Jan. 15, 1952, CR, General Files, Government War Preparation, "OPA, 1942–52"; Amy Bentley, *Eating for Victory: Food Rationing and the Politics of Domesticity* (Urbana: University of Illinois Press, 1998); Perry Duis and Scott La France, *We've Got a Job to Do: Chicagoans and World War II* (Chicago: Chicago Historical Society, 1992), pp. 18–24; Barbara McLean Ward, "A Fair Share at a Fair Price: Rationing, Resource Management, and Price Controls During World War II," in Ward, ed., *Produce and Conserve, Share and Play Square: The Grocer and the Consumer on the Home-Front Battlefield During World War II* (Portsmouth, NH: Strawbery Banke Museum, 1994), pp. 79–103; Meg Jacobs, "'How About Some Meat?': The Office of Price Administration, Consumption Politics, and State Building from the Bottom Up, 1941–1946," *JAH* 84 (December 1997): 911–41; Richard Polenberg, *War and Society: The United States, 1941–1945* (Philadelphia: Lippincott, 1972), pp. 30–36, 95–96; Richard R. Lingeman, *Don't You Know There's a War On?: The American Home Front, 1941–1945* (New York: Putnam's, 1970), pp. 234–70;

Hugh Rockoff, *History of Wage and Price Controls in the United States* (Cambridge, Eng.: Cambridge University Press, 1984), pp. 85, 76.

6. On business opposition to government regulation, and in particular price ceilings and controls, see "Business-Consumer Relations," *Sales Management,* June 15, 1940, pp. 68, 70; "Miss Elliott & Co.," *BW,* Dec. 6 1941; "The Retailer in National Defense by Mr. Fred Lazarus, Jr., Vice-President, The F. & R. Lazarus & Co., Columbus, Ohio, at Conference of National Retail Trade Organizations Called by Miss Harriet Elliott, Consumer Adviser on the Advisory Commission to the Council of National Defense, Washington, D.C., August 29, 1940," Campbell, Series I, Box 4, Folder 34; "Meeting on July 29th, 1942, Consumers-Retailers Conference on Price Ceilings, Manhattan," Campbell, Series I, Box 3, Folder 32; "Instalment Curb," *BW,* May 24, 1941, p. 32; "House Report Cites Danger to War Effort," *New York Sun,* Dec. 18, 1942.

On Leon Henderson, see David Brinkley, *Washington Goes to War* (New York: Ballantine, 1988), pp. 50–52, 115, 125–33; Alan Brinkley, *The End of Reform: New Deal Liberalism in Recession and War* (New York: Knopf, 1995), pp. 146–48; and interview with John Kenneth Galbraith in Studs Terkel, *"The Good War": An Oral History of World War Two* (New York: Pantheon, 1984), pp. 323–24. On inflation rates see Harvard Sitkoff, "The American Home Front," in Ward, ed., *Produce and Conserve,* pp. 39–40, and Campbell, *Consumer Interest,* p. 184.

7. On Chester Bowles, see "The Administration: 'Battle of the Century,' " *Time,* Mar. 4, 1946, pp. 18–20; D. Brinkley, *Washington Goes to War,* pp. 133–36; Andrew H. Bartels, "The Office of Price Administration and the Legacy of the New Deal, 1939–1946," *Public Historian* 5 (Summer 1983): 19–23.

8. Mrs. Nathaniel Singer to Mayor of New York City, June 1946, Campbell, Series I, Box 3, Folder 28; Office of Price Administration, Consumer Division, "Consumer Centers," February 1942, Campbell, Series I, Box 3, Folder 33; Campbell, *Consumer Interest,* pp. 143, 158; Harold G. Vatter, *The U.S. Economy in World War II* (New York: Columbia University Press, 1985), pp. 91–98. The 3 million number comes from *Handbook for War Price and Rationing Boards* (Washington, DC: USGPO, January 1944), quoted in Donald M. Dozer, "The Gap Between Government and People," *POQ* 9 (Spring 1945): 75.

9. "The OPA Consumer Advisory Committee, Preliminary First Draft—For Committee Members," December 1944, Campbell, Series I, Box 3, Folder 31; press release, Office of War Information, Office of Price Administration, Dec. 2, 1943, CR, Government War Preparation, Role of Consumer, "Consumer Advisory Committee, 1943–49"; "Mrs. Helen Hall to Serve O.P.A. Consumer Board," *New York Herald Tribune,* Dec. 2, 1943; "OPA Advisory Board Aims to Aid Public," *NYT,* Dec. 9, 1943; press release, Office of Price Administration, Feb. 2, 1944, CR, General Files, Government War Preparation, Role of Consumer, "Federal Agencies Representing Consumers, 1940–43"; Office of Price Administration, "Members of the Consumer Advisory Committee," July 1944, and "The OPA Consumer Advisory Committee and Its Work," October 1945, Atkinson, Box 5, Folder 28. Two studies undertaken right after the war provide excellent documentation for the importance of volunteers to the success of the OPA operation: Imogene H. Putnam, *Volunteers in OPA,* and Harvey C. Mansfield and Associates, *A Short History of OPA,* Historical Reports on War Administration: Office of Price Administration, Office of Temporary Controls, General Publications Nos. 14 and 15 (Washington, DC: Office of Price Administration, 1947), pp. 245–52 in the latter report.

10. Caroline F. Ware, *The Consumer Goes to War: A Guide to Victory on the Home Front* (New York: Funk & Wagnalls, 1942), pp. 1–3, 194–95, 204–205, 235. On the consumerist economics of Ware and Gardiner Means in the 1930s, see Meg Jacobs, " 'Democracy's Third Estate': New Deal Politics and the Construction of a 'Consuming Public,' " *ILWCH* 55 (Spring 1999): 27–51.

11. In Campbell, Series I: "Memorandum to 'Consumers All' from Harriet Elliott, November 1, 1941," Box 3, Folder 29, and "What's this about meat?" on *Mrs. Consumer Speaking*, radio script, WNYC, Mar. 3, 1943, Box 4, Folder 38, p. 5.

12. "Consumer's Pledge Song," June 23, 1942, Campbell, Series I, Box 3, Folder 32.

13. *Mrs. Consumer Speaking*, n.d., Campbell, Series I, Box 4, Folder 39, p. 1.

14. Helen G. Conoyer, "Government Agencies and the Consumer in Wartime," 1944, Campbell, Series I, Box 3, Folder 30, pp. 2, 8.

15. George H. Gallup, *The Gallup Poll: Public Opinion, 1935–1971*, vol. 1, *1935–1948* (New York: Random House, 1972), 1940–45, passim; "The OPA Consumer Advisory Committee, Preliminary First Draft—For Committee Members," December 1944, Campbell, Series I, Box 3, Folder 31, p. 14; also see "War Problems of Home Front Come to Nation's Bill Browns," *Newsweek*, Sept. 28, 1942, p. 29.

16. Sitkoff, "American Home Front," in Ward, ed., *Produce and Conserve*, p. 45; "The Defense Standard of Living," *BW*, Aug. 23, 1941, p. 60. See also Jeffrey G. Williamson and Peter H. Lindert, *American Inequality: A Macroeconomic History* (New York: Academic Press, 1980), pp. 82–86.

17. Office of War Information, New York–New Jersey Region, "A Fair Share for Everyone" (10-minute speech), n.d. but c. 1943, Campbell, Series I, Box 3, Folder 30. For a helpful description of how the "black market" functioned in a little neighborhood grocery store, see interview with Helen Studer in Sherna Berger Gluck, *Rosie the Riveter Revisited: Women, the War, and Social Change* (New York: New American Library, 1987), p. 189.

18. Edmond F. Maher as told to Mary Ellen Leary, "Customer's Nightmare," *Saturday Evening Post*, Feb. 5, 1944, p. 20; press release, "Consumers Ask Vinson to Restore Grade Labeling," Nov. 15, 1943, Atkinson, Box 6, folder "Grade Labelling Standards"; Jessie V. Coles, *Consumers Can Help Win the War* (Berkeley: University of California Press, 1943), pp. 74–77; Lucy Black Creighton, *Pretenders to the Throne: The Consumer Movement in the United States* (Lexington, MA: Heath, 1976), p. 30; Kenneth Dameron, "Marketing-Labeling," in Dameron, ed., *Consumer Problems in Wartime* (New York: McGraw-Hill, 1944), pp. 226–28; Bentley, *Eating for Victory*, pp. 51–55; Campbell, *Consumer Interest*, p. 160; Galbraith, *Life in Our Times*, pp. 184–86.

19. Another way of capturing the rising standard of living during wartime is the statistic that mean family income rose over 25 percent in constant dollars between 1941 and 1944; see William L. O'Neill, *A Democracy at War: America's Fight at Home and Abroad in World War II* (New York: Free Press, 1993), p. 429. Also "Huge Outlays by Shoppers, Americans Spending More This Year Than Ever Before and Mostly on Non-Durable Goods," *NN*, Aug. 7, 1944; "Shoppers Demand Highest Quality, NJ Chain Finds," *Food Field Reporter*, June 7, 1943; "Average American Eats Better and Buys More Goods Than Before War," *WSJ*, Apr. 19, 1944; "War Problems of Home Front Come to Nation's Bill Browns," *Newsweek*, Sept. 28, 1942, p. 29; "Consumers Can't Win," *Time*, Oct. 30, 1944; Jacobs, " 'How About Some Meat?' " p. 931; interview with Galbraith in Terkel, "*The Good War*," p. 323.

20. Paul Hoffman, speech to the National Association of Manufacturers, Dec. 6, 1944, Box 2, Edwin Nourse Manuscripts, Harry S. Truman Library, quoted in Robert M. Collins, "The Emergence of Economic Growthmanship in the United States: Federal Policy and Economic Knowledge in the Truman Years," in Mary O. Furner and Barry Supple, eds., *The State and Economic Knowledge: The American and British Experience* (Cambridge, Eng.: Cambridge University Press, 1990), p. 145; Everett R. Smith, *What Shall We Do About It?* (New York: Macfadden, 1944), p. 79.

21. Robert W. Westbrook, "Fighting for the American Family: Private Interests and Political Obligation in World War II," in Richard Wightman Fox and T. J. Jackson Lears,

The Power of Culture: Critical Essays in American History (Chicago: University of Chicago Press, 1993), pp. 195–221; Mark H. Leff, "The Politics of Sacrifice on the American Home Front in World War II," *JAH* 77 (March 1991): 1296–1318.

22. "War Workers' Buying Habits in Cleveland," *Women's Wear Daily,* July 14, 1942; Michael French, *U.S. Economic History Since 1945* (Manchester, Eng.: Manchester University Press, 1997), p. 41; Securities and Exchange Commission release, Sept. 21, 1944, cited in Campbell, *Consumer Interest,* p. 168.

23. "Industry Spends at a Record Rate, Lining Up After-the-War Buyers," *WSJ,* May 13, 1944.

24. Frank W. Fox, *Madison Avenue Goes to War: The Strange Career of American Advertising, 1941–45* (Provo, UT: Brigham Young University Press, 1975), p. 34, cited in Adams, *Best War Ever,* p. 130; "What We're Fighting For," *New York Daily News,* Sept. 16, 1943.

25. Revere Copper Company, "After Total War Can Come Total Living," *Revere's Part in Better Living* 10 (1943), New York Public Library, in Dell Upton, *Architecture in the United States* (New York: Oxford University Press, 1998), p. 234. Also see Revere Copper and Brass, Inc. ad in *Life,* July 20, 1942, "Beyond the war waits happiness," in Westbrook, "Fighting for the American Family," p. 214; Robert Friedel, "Scarcity and Promise: Materials and American Domestic Culture During World War II," in Donald Albrecht, ed., *World War II and the American Dream* (Washington, DC: National Building Museum; Cambridge, MA: MIT Press, 1995), p. 77. Consumers were promised that wartime research, particularly in electronics, would pay off in miraculous consumer products after the war. Shure Brothers, an amplification equipment manufacturer in Evanston, Illinois, promoted war bonds on billboards with the promise that "tomorrow you can have the new things developed from the blueprints of war!" Duis and La France, *We've Got a Job to Do,* p. 78; also see John Morton Blum, *V Was for Victory: Politics and American Culture During World War II* (New York: Harcourt Brace Jovanovich, 1976), pp. 101, 104. For concerns that consumers were being misled, see "Would Tone Down Post-War 'Dream,'" *NYT,* July 11, 1943; Francis Westbrook, Jr., "Those Post-War Miracles," *The Nation,* Sept. 18, 1943, pp. 320–22; Raymond Loewy, "What of the Promised Post-War World—Is It Just a Dream, or Will It Come True?" *NYT Magazine,* Sept. 26, 1943, p. 14.

26. Blum, *V Was for Victory,* pp. 102–103.

27. U.S. Bureau of Labor Statistics, "Effect of War Housing Shortages on Home Ownership," *Monthly Labor Review* 62 (April 1946): 560–66; U.S. Bureau of Labor Statistics, *Probable Volume of Postwar Construction,* bulletin no. 825 (May 1945); Chester Bowles, *Tomorrow Without Fear* (New York: Simon & Schuster, 1946), p. 62; Greg Hise, "The Airplane and the Garden City: Regional Transformations During World War II," in Albrecht, ed., *World War II and the American Dream,* pp. 144–83. The "Town of Tomorrow at the New York World's Fair" of 1939 consisted of fifteen houses, "a full-scale model village, representing a segment of a town of thirty-five hundred population." It looked ahead to postwar suburbia, with its cul-de-sacs and lack of sidewalks, but legitimized itself as a "new concept in community planning that will aid in re-creating the old New England type of village universally acknowledged the most perfect form of democracy": "Building Tomorrow Town," *Sketchbook Magazine* (1939 New York World's Fair Edition) (1938), 15:29, quoted in Rosemarie Haag Bletter, "The World of Tomorrow: The Future with a Past," *High Styles: Twentieth-Century American Design* (New York: Whitney Museum of American Art, in association with Summit Books, 1985), p. 92.

28. Office of Civilian Defense, *What Can I Do?* (Washington, 1942), cited in Richard Polenberg, *War and Society: The United States, 1941–1945* (Philadelphia: Lippincott, 1972), p. 133; Stan Cohen, *V for Victory: America's Home Front During World War II* (Missoula, MT: Pictorial Histories, 1991), p. 52.

29. Cohen, *V for Victory*, p. 394; Ward, "A Fair Share at a Fair Price: Rationing, Resource Management, and Price Controls During World War II," in Ward, ed., *Produce and Conserve*, p. 100; "Home Is the Strength of the Nation," cover, *Better Homes and Gardens*, July 1942, in Robert Heide and John Gilman, *Home Front America: Popular Culture of the World War II Era* (San Francisco: Chronicle, 1995), p. 71; Eureka vacuum cleaners ad, "My Heart's Overseas but My Hands Are on the Job," *Saturday Evening Post*, Aug. 21, 1943, in Westbrook, "Fighting for the American Family," p. 213.

30. Radio Theatre Productions, *The Home Front*, Program 2: "London Calling"; "What I Am Fighting For," *Saturday Evening Post*, July 17, 1943, quoted in Blum, *V Was for Victory*, p. 67.

31. Alan Roy Berolzheimer, "A Nation of Consumers: Mass Consumption, Middle-Class Standards of Living and American National Identity, 1910–1950" (Ph.D. diss., University of Virginia, 1996), p. 468; "Survey Shows Civilians Won't Rush to Buy Scarce Appliances When They Are Available," *WSJ*, June 2, 1944; Blum, *V Was for Victory*, pp. 100–101; "Women Place Washer at Top of Buying List," *Chicago Daily Tribune*, June 7, 1945.

32. "What Plans Do People Have for Using the Money from Their Bonds?" from *Men and Events* (Bulletin of the Union League Club of Chicago, 1933–42) in Duis and La France, *We've Got a Job to Do*, p. 118; *Better Homes and Gardens* quote from Blum, *V Was for Victory*, p. 104.

33. Office of Price Administration, "Anti-Inflation Shopping List," May 1945, CR, General Files, Government War Preparation, Role of Consumer, "OPA, 1945–46." On women's presence in the workforce, see Karen Anderson, *Wartime Women: Sex Roles, Family Relations, and the Status of Women During World War II* (Westport, CT: Greenwood, 1981), p. 91.

34. *To Win the War: Home Front Memorabilia of World War II* (Missoula, MT: Pictorial Histories, 1995), passim and p. 112; Ward, ed., *Produce and Conserve*, passim; Cohen, *V for Victory*, passim; Duis and La France, *We've Got a Job to Do*, passim; Heide and Gilman, *Home Front America*, passim; Jacobs, " 'How About Some Meat?' "

35. Duis and La France, *We've Got a Job to Do*, p. 23.

36. Kathryn McHale to The Honorable Franklin D. Roosevelt, Oct. 6, 1942, CR, General Files, Government War Preparation, "Role of Consumers, 1941–43."

37. Note by Atkinson, n.d., Atkinson, Box 5, Folder 26.

38. "The OPA Consumer Advisory Committee," Preliminary First Draft—For Committee Members, October 1944, Campbell, Series I, Box 3, Folder 31, p. 19. Other organizations also urged the appointment of women to war price and rationing boards. See, for example, a report of a two-day leadership conference for trade union auxiliaries: "Advocate Women on Price Boards," *NYT*, July 13, 1942. Bowles's action described in Putnam, *Volunteers in OPA*, p. 87.

39. Jacobs, " 'How About Some Meat?' " p. 925; Anderson, *Wartime Women*, p. 89.

40. O'Neill, *Democracy at War*, p. 133. The Bronx, New York, Chapter of the American Women's Voluntary Services claimed 20,000 members in 34 neighborhood units as early as April 1942. See Bertha Schwartz to Dr. Persia Campbell, Apr. 20, 1942, Campbell, Series I, Box 3, Folder 27.

41. Mark Naison, "From Eviction Resistance to Rent Control: Tenant Activism in the Great Depression," and Joel Schwartz, "Tenant Power in the Liberal City, 1943–1971," in Ronald Lawson, ed., with the assistance of Naison, *The Tenant Movement in New York City, 1914–1984* (New Brunswick, NJ: Rutgers University Press, 1986), pp. 127–30, 134–41.

42. *Woman's Home Companion* quote from "She's the Key to the Wartime Market Puz-

zle," *Advertising and Selling*, April 1943, p. 73, cited in Lori Rotskoff, "Power of the Purse: The Gendering of Consumption During the 1940s and 50s," paper for American Studies 787a, Yale University, Dec. 26, 1992, p. 21, in possession of the author.

43. John T. Cunningham, *New Jersey: America's Main Road* (Garden City, NY: Doubleday, 1966), pp. 294, 297, 299; "Jersey War Work: $12,090,197 in Major Contracts in This Area," *NSL*, Jan. 29, 1945.

44. "Hudson County Goes to War, 1940–1945: Hudson County's Contributions to the War Effort, An Exhibition by the Hoboken Historical Museum, Sponsored by the New Jersey Historical Commission," May 20, 1994, pp. 9, 13–14.

45. Office of Civilian Defense Director, "Organization and Functions of the Community War Services Division," November 1942, "TIC" Files, NPL, pp. 6, 21, 23.

46. "Final Report of the Office of Civilian Defense Director, State of New Jersey," Oct. 1, 1945, "Q" Files, NPL.

47. New Jersey Defense Council, "A Manual for Consumer Interests Committees of State and Local Defense Councils," October 1941, "Q" Files, NPL; "Report of Meeting of Consumer Interests Committees, November 6, 1941, State Home for Girls, Trenton, NJ," CR, Government War Preparation, "NJ State Defense Councils, Newark Defense Councils, Consumer Activism"; "Gets Consumer Post," *NYT*, Dec. 24, 1941.

48. New Jersey Defense Council, "A Manual for Consumer Interests Committees of State and Local Defense Councils," October 1941, "Q" Files, NPL, p. 3; Ware, *Consumer Goes to War*, pp. 284–85.

49. I found bulletins of the New Jersey League of Women Shoppers during wartime in two places: from June 1939 to February 1941 in Ruttenberg, and through the end of 1942 in CR, General Files, Political-Front Organizations, 1935–70, "L"—League of Women Shoppers. See particularly *Bulletin* for January, Feb. 16, May, June–July, and December 1942, and Program for "Victory . . . —And Vitamins." Also see "Rent Petitions," Office of Civilian Defense, *Consumers News Letter of the Consumer Interests Committee*, vol. 2, no. 6 (July 15, 1942): 5. For evidence of a parallel shift toward consumer activism among the National League of Women Shoppers and some of its branches, see "Ceiling Charts Compiled for Public by 35 Brooklyn Consumer Groups," *NYT*, Dec. 31, 1943; League of Women Shoppers of Washington, D.C., Papers, Schlesinger; League of Women Shoppers Papers in CR, as identified here and in Ruttenberg, as identified, particularly "Minutes and Reports, The Fourth Annual Convention of The League of Women Shoppers, Inc.," May 16–17, 1941.

50. Script for "Why Join the League?" Folder 12, and scripts for "Leaguesboro-on-the-Air," Folders 16, 18, 19, 23, 39, 40, in LWV-NJ, Box 21.

51. "OPA Price 'Wardens' Tour State, 7,000 Women Call on Stores in Educational Drive," *NN*, July 8, 1942; "Find Capital Favor for School Meals," *NYT*, May 21, 1943; John T. Cunningham, *Newark* (Newark: New Jersey Historical Society, 1988), p. 292.

52. See the many documents in the "Newark Defense Council" files, NPL, and New Jersey Defense Council, *Consumer News Letter of the Consumer Interests Committee*, 1941–44, passim, for discussion of Newark and particularly Newark Fair Rent Committee in CR, Government War Preparation, "New Jersey State Defense Council, Newark Defense Council, Consumer Activism." The Wartime Council of Newark Libraries published a "Directory of War Agencies" in April 1943, listing the chairs of all the city's agencies active in war work. The predominance of women is very apparent: clipping file, "Newark and World War, 1939–1945," NPL.

Women were equally active in other cities. For a sampling of the New York City scene, see "War Against High Prices Won by Bronx Consumers," *PM*, Feb. 17, 1944; "Consumers' Seal Fights Black Market," *PM*, Mar. 16, 1944.

53. "Enter the 'Block Leader,'" *Consumers News Letter,* vol. 2, no. 14 (Nov. 20, 1942): 1, 6, 7, and "The Block Leader Arrives," *Consumers News Letter,* vol. 2, no. 15 (Dec. 5, 1942), most of issue, in CR, General Files, Government War Preparation, "New Jersey State Defense Council, Newark Defense Council, Consumer Activism." Also, in "Newark Defense Council" files, Newark Document File, NPL: Community War Services Civilian Defense, "Activities of C.D.V.O.," 1944; "Newark Community War Services Block Leader (Briefing Book)"; "Block Leaders Bulletin," July 1, 1943; "Civilian Defense—and You the Citizen," transcript of radio program "The Block Leader Plan," WAAT, Feb. 1, 1943, p. 2. For a useful report on block plans in other cities, and the centrality of women to their success (in some places leaders were called "block mothers" or "Liberty belles"), see James M. Landis, "Block by Block," *Victory,* Dec. 22, 1942, CR, General Files, Government War Preparation, Role of Consumers, "Block Leader Groups."

54. "Newark's Victory Parade Today to Have Consumer Division," *Consumer News Letter,* vol. 2, no. 8 (Aug. 15, 1942): 1–2, CR, General Files, Government War Preparation, "New Jersey State Defense Council, Newark Defense Council, Consumer Activism." The OPA discovered that its dedicated volunteers, some of whom racked up hundreds, even thousands of hours as the war dragged on, desired special recognition of their service. Hence, the OPA developed a hierarchy of buttons, certificates, pins, service bars, and ribbons, which local boards usually distributed at annual ceremonies; Putnam, *Volunteers in OPA,* pp. 140–41.

55. A good deal of literature about women in World War II equates the expansion of their gender roles almost solely with their entry into defense plants. See, for example, Anderson, *Wartime Women;* Rosalind Rosenberg, *Divided Lives: American Women in the Twentieth Century* (New York: Hill and Wang, 1992), pp. 126–37; Leila J. Rupp, "Woman's Place Is in the War: Propaganda and Public Opinion in the United States and Germany, 1939–1945," in Carol Ruth Berkin and Mary Beth Norton, eds., *Women of America: A History* (Boston: Houghton Mifflin, 1979); Ruth Milkman, *Gender at Work: The Dynamics of Job Segregation by Sex During World War II* (Urbana: University of Illinois Press, 1987).

Amy Bentley has focused on what she calls the "Wartime Homemaker" in her book *Eating for Victory.* Her attention to the role of food in the war has led her to emphasize more than I do the limitations rather than the political access women gained as patriotic food providers. She views the government's message as one that constrained rather than empowered women; see particularly pp. 24–58. D'Ann Campbell, *Women at War with America: Private Lives in a Patriotic Era* (Cambridge, MA: Harvard University Press, 1984), stresses that a relatively small proportion of women were employed in war work; a much larger number supported the war as community volunteers. She, however, emphasizes the private goals and benefits they derived from their homefront activities more than the civic ones for which I argue.

56. The *Pittsburgh Courier,* the largest black newspaper in the country, launched the "Double V" campaign in 1942, which called for "victory over our enemies at home and victory over our enemies on the battlefields abroad"; quoted in Margaret Crawford, "Daily Life on the Home Front: Women, Blacks, and the Struggle for Public Housing," in Albrecht, ed., *World War II and the American Dream,* p. 110.

57. Leland J. Gordon, *Consumers in Wartime: A Guide to Family Economy in the Emergency* (New York: Harper & Bros., 1943), pp. 7–8.

58. Typical of this view was the *Indiana Recorder's* endorsement of price ceilings because "this move offers housewives the means of checking legal prices in stores": May 15, 1943, quoted in memo to "Leaders of National Organizations" from Frances H. Williams, June 17, 1943, NAACP, II, A 461, "OPA, General 1943," pp. 1–2.

59. "The Way It Is," *New Masses*, Oct. 20, 1942, in *The Collected Essays of Ralph Ellison* (New York: Modern Library, 1995), pp. 310–19.

60. Frances Harriet Williams, "Minority Groups and OPA," *Public Administration Review* 7 (Spring 1947): 125–26; Naison, "From Eviction Resistance to Rent Control," p. 129.

61. Langston Hughes, "Speaking of Food," *NJAA*, Apr. 3, 1943. On the popularity of zoot suits and their subversive message, see "The Riddle of the Zoot: Malcolm Little and Black Cultural Politics During World War II," in Robin D. G. Kelley, *Race Rebels: Culture, Politics, and the Black Working Class* (New York: Free Press, 1994), pp. 161–81; Eric Lott, "Double V, Double-Time: Bebop's Politics of Style," *Callaloo* 11, no. 36 (Summer 1988): 597–605; and Stuart Cosgrove, "The Zoot-Suit and Style Warfare," in Jennifer Scanlon, ed., *The Gender and Consumer Culture Reader* (New York: New York University Press, 2000), pp. 342–54.

62. "Statement of the National Association of Colored People Before the Senate Committee on Banking and Currency on March 31, 1944," and press releases, "Price Control Backed by NAACP Before Senate Group" and "NAACP Asks OPA Hold Rent Ceiling," Aug. 3, 1944, NAACP, II, A 461, "OPA General 1944."

63. Campbell, *Women at War with America*, p. 69; "Analysis of Reports on Negro Participation in the Work of War Price and Rationing Boards," Apr. 30, 1945, NAACP, Series II, A 462, "OPA 1945."

64. Williams, "Minority Groups and OPA," pp. 124–25, including n. 5.

65. "The OPA Consumer Advisory Committee, Preliminary First Draft—For Committee Members," Campbell, Series I, Box 3, Folder 31, p. 19; Williams, "Minority Groups and OPA," pp. 124–25, 127, 128. Black organizations also protested the lack of blacks employed by the OPA; see "Asks Negro Voice in OPA," *NYT*, Aug. 24, 1942.

66. St. Clair Drake and Horace R. Cayton, *Black Metropolis: A Study of Negro Life in a Northern City* (1945; reprint, Chicago: University of Chicago Press, 1993), pp. 746–50.

67. Bentley, *Eating for Victory*, pp. 37, 44.

68. In NAACP, II, A 461, "OPA General 1942": NAACP, "Food Costs More in Harlem: A Comparative Survey of Retail Food Prices," 1942; "OPA Will Act to Curb Jim Crow Prices," press release, Sept. 11, 1942, telegram to President Franklin D. Roosevelt, Oct. 3, 1942; "Negro Communities Worst Victims," press release, Oct. 9, 1942; "OPA Ceilings No Remedy for Food Cost Differential in Negro Neighborhoods." On overcharging in Chicago, see reference to Nelson C. Jackson, "Food Costs Negroes More in Chicago," Chicago Branch NAACP, April 1943, in "A Statement on High Prices for Consumer's Goods in Chicago, Illinois . . . Particularly as such prices obtain and relate to Negro Families," prepared by the Chicago Branch NAACP for presentation before the Sub-Committee of the Congressional Joint Committee on the Economic Report, Oct. 2, 1947, NAACP, II, A 485, "Price Control 1946–48," p. 5.

69. Williams, "Minority Groups and OPA," p. 127 n.7; Office of War Information, Office of Price Administration, press release, N-574, September 1943, and A. R. Johnson to Roy Wilkins, Nov. 5, 1943, NAACP, II, A 461, "OPA, General 1943"; "Statement of the National Association for the Advancement of Colored People Before the Senate Committee on Banking and Currency on March 31, 1944," NAACP, II, A 461, "OPA, General 1944," p. 2.

70. Jacobs, " 'How About Some Meat?' " p. 927; Consumer Division, Office of Price Administration and Civilian Supply, Office for Emergency Management, "A Negro Community Works in Behalf of Its Families," Campbell, Series I, Box 3, Folder 30.

71. Dutton Ferguson to Walter White, Aug. 28, 1943, NAACP, II, A 461, "OPA, General 1943."

72. Dominic J. Capeci, Jr., *The Harlem Riot of 1943* (Philadelphia: Temple University Press, 1977), pp. 158–59; Naison, "From Eviction Resistance to Rent Control," pp. 129–30, and Schwartz, "Tenant Power in the Liberal City, 1943–1971," pp. 140–41, both in Lawson, ed., *Tenant Movement;* Cheryl Greenberg, "The Politics of Disorder: Reexamining Harlem's Riots of 1935 and 1943," *JUH* 18 (August 1992): 430.

73. Williams, "Minority Groups and OPA," p. 126. Ella Baker's biographer drew from a report in her papers that by 1945 the number of blacks employed by the OPA had grown to 1250 in regional and district offices, out of a total of 58,507, or 2.1 percent. In the national office, blacks made up 13 percent of the staff. OPA Report, Mar. 3, 1945, Ella Baker Papers, cited in Joanne Grant, *Ella Baker: Freedom Bound* (New York: Wiley, 1998), p. 57.

74. Ross Gregory, *America 1941: A Nation at the Crossroads* (New York: Free Press, 1989), pp. 204, 215.

75. O'Neill, *Democracy at War,* pp. 238–39, 245.

76. Blum, *V Was for Victory,* p. 189; Drake and Cayton, *Black Metropolis,* p. 753.

77. For a thorough survey of African-American access to public accommodations in 1943, see sociologist Charles S. Johnson's volume prepared for Gunnar Myrdal's *American Dilemma* project, *Patterns of Negro Segregation* (New York: Harper & Bros., 1943).

78. My understanding of the black struggle for access to public accommodations is based on Joseph William Singer, "No Right to Exclude: Public Accommodations and Private Property," *Northwestern University Law Review* 90 (Summer 1996): 1286–1477; Jack Greenberg, *Race Relations and American Law* (New York: Columbia University Press, 1959), chap. 3, "Public Accommodations and Services," pp. 79–114; Valerie E. Weaver, "The Failure of Civil Rights 1875–1883 and Its Repercussions," *Journal of Negro History* 54 (October 1969): 368–82; William H. Chafe, "Providing Guarantees of Equal Opportunity," *Chronicle of Higher Education,* June 30, 1995, pp. B1–2; John P. Milligan, "Perspective on: Civil Rights in New Jersey," *NJEA Review* (March 1956), reprint in New Jersey Documents, Law and Public Safety Department, Civil Rights Division, NPL; and A. Leon Higginbotham, Jr., *Shades of Freedom: Racial Politics and Presumptions of the American Legal Process* (New York: Oxford University Press, 1996).

79. Langston Hughes, *The Big Sea* (1940; reprint, New York: Hill and Wang, 1993), p. 51.

80. Memo to Presidents and Secretaries of NAACP Branches, from Thurgood Marshall, Special Counsel, Subject: Discrimination and Segregation in Theaters, June 8, 1944; Memo to Presidents of Branches, from Thurgood Marshall, Special Counsel, Aug. 31, 1944, Subject: "Moving Picture Theaters," NAACP, II, B 67, "Discrimination Theaters, General, 1940–44," and "Discrimination Theaters, General, 1945–49."

81. "What Would You Do?" column, *NJAA,* Apr. 3 and June 12, 1943; " 'Porgy, Bess' Cast Taste Baltimore J.C.," *NJAA,* Oct. 16, 1943; "Quebec: Color Line," *Time,* Aug. 27, 1945; "Six Negro Athletes of N.Y.U. Sue Hotel in Philadelphia, Charging It Barred Them," *NYT,* June 13, 1946.

82. Gregory, *America 1941,* p. 216; O'Neill, *Democracy at War,* pp. 235–37; Harvard Sitkoff, "Racial Militancy and Interracial Violence in the Second World War," *JAH* 58 (December 1971): 32, 51; C.L.R. James et al., *Fighting Racism in World War II* (New York: Monad, 1980), p. 17; A. Russell Buchanan, *Black Americans in World War II* (Santa Barbara, CA: Clio, 1977), p. 7. Two recent books document well discrimination against black soldiers, including their efforts to partake in recreation and patronize commercial establishments on bases and in neighboring towns: Daniel Kryder, *Divided Arsenal: Race and the American State During World War II* (Cambridge, Eng.: Cambridge University Press, 2000), and Maggi M. Morehouse, *Fighting in the Jim Crow Army: Black Men and*

Women Remember World War II (Lanham, MD: Rowman & Littlefield, 2000), particularly pp. 89–96.

83. "Soldiers Walk Out on 'Porgy and Bess' Co.," *NJAA*, Dec. 25, 1943; Adams, *Best War Ever*, p. 122.

84. Memorandum to Mr. Konvitz from Mr. Wilkins, Mar. 27, 1944, NAACP, II, B 63, "Discrimination, General, 1944"; Sgt. Harold ? (unreadable) to NAACP, Mar. 21, 1944, NAACP, II, B 61, "Discrimination: Bars, Hotels, Restaurants, 1944"; Marilynn S. Johnson, *The Second Gold Rush: Oakland and the East Bay in World War II* (Berkeley: University of California Press, 1983), p. 169; Blum, *V Was for Victory*, p. 190. See Phillip McGuire, ed., *Taps for a Jim Crow Army: Letters from Black Soldiers in World War II* (Lexington: University Press of Kentucky, 1983), pp. 166–67, for more examples of discrimination near bases in the West. Even in Hawaii, where racial attitudes had been more relaxed than on the mainland, racial exclusion spread to downtown restaurants, nightclubs, and dance halls. USO dances also became an issue, until a compromise was worked out where black servicemen would dance only with female partners supplied by the USO: Beth Bailey and David Farber, "The 'Double-V' Campaign in World War II Hawaii: African Americans, Racial Ideology, and Federal Power," *Journal of Social History* 26 (Summer 1993): 827, 834–35.

85. P. L. Prattis to Judge William H. Hastie and Walter White, Apr. 14, 1942, NAACP, II, B 264, quoted in McGuire, ed., *Taps for a Jim Crow Army*, p. 166.

86. "A Black Military Hero Breaks His Long Silence," *NYT*, Feb. 20, 1991; interview with Mayor Coleman Young in Terkel, *"The Good War,"* pp. 347–48; also see pp. 343–46, 366–72, interviews with Lowell Steward and Alfred Duckett, for more testimony about segregated officers' clubs.

87. Interview with Dempsey Travis in Terkel, *"The Good War,"* pp. 151–59. Black GIs released from the front for two weeks of "rest and recreation" at the army's expense were not sent to the luxurious resort hotels at Lake Placid, Santa Barbara, Miami Beach, or Hot Springs, but rather to the Theresa Hotel in Harlem and the Pershing Hotel on Chicago's South Side: Blum, *V Was for Victory*, pp. 210–11.

88. "Brown v. Salina, Kansas," *NYT*, Feb. 26, 1973, quoted in Blum, *V Was for Victory*, pp. 190–91.

89. Interview with Dempsey Travis in Terkel, *"The Good War,"* p. 151.

90. Interview with Alfred Duckett in ibid., p. 369.

91. Albert Parker, "Signs of the Times," *Militant*, June 20, 1942, in James et al., *Fighting Racism in World War II*, p. 179; Roy Wilkins quoted in Herbert Garfunkel, *When Negroes March: The March on Washington Movement in the Organizational Politics for FEPC* (New York: Atheneum, 1975), p. 23.

92. Roland Fallin, "Is There Democracy?" *Baltimore Afro-American*, Mar. 28, 1942, quoted in Bentley, *Eating for Victory*, p. 81. This is the third poem cited in this chapter, no accident given the times. Philip Roth has noted that "high demotic poetry was the liturgy of World War II": *I Married a Communist* (Boston: Houghton Mifflin, 1998), p. 39.

93. Johnson, *The Second Gold Rush*, pp. 169–70. Also see Chester Himes's wartime novel, *If He Hollers Let Him Go* (1945; reprint, New York: Thunder Mouth, 1986), for the humiliations of a black shipyard worker in Los Angeles stores and restaurants.

94. Lillian Davenport to Gentlemen, NAACP, NYC, Mar. 3, 1942, and newspaper column, "This World of Ours," by Roy L. Matson, *Wisconsin State Journal*, Feb. 27, 1942, in NAACP, II, B 61, "Discrimination: Bars, Hotels, Restaurants, 1940–42."

95. Robert Weaver, *Negro Ghetto* (New York: Harcourt, Brace, 1948), p. 94, cited in Margaret Crawford, "Daily Life on the Homefront: Women, Blacks and the Struggle for Public Housing," in Albrecht, ed., *World War II and the American Dream*, p. 114.

96. Overcrowding in Chicago's black neighborhoods was so horrific that in 1943 Robert Taylor of the Chicago Housing Authority compared the population density of 90,000 persons per square mile to the slums of Calcutta and declared it worse: Duis and La France, *We've Got a Job to Do*, p. 54.

97. On the racial rebellions of 1943, see Sitkoff, "Racial Militancy and Interracial Violence," p. 52. Black soldiers fed up with inferior facilities and community hostility rebelled in military training camps during the summer of 1943 as well; see Polenberg, *War and Society*, p. 126.

98. Lingeman, *Don't You Know There's a War On?*, p. 327. For more on Detroit, see Buchanan, *Black Americans in World War II*, pp. 46–53; O'Neill, *Democracy at War*, pp. 239–40; and Paul D. Casdorph, *Let the Good Times Roll: Life at Home in America During World War II* (New York: Paragon House, 1989), pp. 107–13.

99. Powell quoted in Neil Hickey and Ed Edwin, *Adam Clayton Powell and the Politics of Race* (New York: Full-Fleet, 1965), p. 81, quoted in Greenberg, "*Or Does It Explode?*" p. 212. For more on Harlem, see Capeci, *Harlem Riot of 1943;* Nat Brandt, *Harlem at War: The Black Experience in WWII* (Syracuse, NY: Syracuse University Press, 1996), pp. 183–215; Greenberg, "Politics of Disorder," pp. 395–441.

100. Harold Orlansky, "The Harlem Riot: A Study in Mass Frustration," *Social Analysis* Report #1, 1943, pp. 8–9, quoted in Greenberg, "*Or Does It Explode?*" p. 212.

101. Kenneth B. Clark and James Barker, "The Zoot Effect in Personality: A Race Riot Participant," *Journal of Abnormal Psychology* 40 (April 1945): 143–48.

102. Comment by Walter White, quoted in Brandt, *Harlem at War*, p. 201.

103. A. R. Johnson, Vice-President–Treasurer of United Tenants League of Greater New York to Roy Wilkins, Nov. 5, 1943, NAACP, II, A 461, "OPA General 1943."

104. Robin D. G. Kelley, "'We Are Not What We Seem': Rethinking Black Working-Class Opposition in the Jim Crow South," *JAH* 80 (June 1993): 75–112; Albert Parker, "The Case of Pvt. Ned Turman: He Died Fighting for Democracy," *Militant*, Aug. 23, 1941, and "The Army's Version," *Militant*, Nov. 22, 1941, in James et al., *Fighting Racism in World War II*, pp. 128–32; Adams, *Best War Ever*, p. 122.

105. Chicago Civil Liberties Committee, "EQUAL RIGHTS Regardless of 'Race' or Color," NAACP, II, B 61, "Civil Rights, New Jersey."

106. D. Brinkley, *Washington Goes to War*, p. 248; *Philadelphia Afro-American*, Sept. 25, 1943.

107. Buchanan, *Black Americans in World War II*, pp. 117–19; D. Brinkley, *Washington Goes to War*, pp. 251–52.

108. August Meier and Elliott Rudwick, *CORE: A Study in the Civil Rights Movement, 1942–1968* (Urbana: University of Illinois Press, 1975), pp. 3–14; "Non-Violent Direct Action Breaks Jim Crow in Restaurant," *NJAA*, May 29, 1943.

109. Richard M. Dalfiume, "The 'Forgotten Years' of the Negro Revolution," *JAH* 55 (June 1968): 99–100; also see his book, *Desegregation of the U.S. Armed Forces: Fighting on Two Fronts, 1939–1953* (Columbia: University of Missouri Press, 1969).

110. Drake and Cayton, *Black Metropolis*, p. 761.

111. Cited in letter to the editor by Paul G. Richter, May 1, 1946, *New York Herald Tribune*, May 2, 1946.

112. Quoted in "Off the Editor's Chest," *Consumers' Research Bulletin* 26 (October 1950): 21.

113. Primary sources arguing for (and against) the extension of the OPA and price controls are voluminous in the Consumers' Research Papers. For an example of promotional material defending price controls based on the World War I experience, see Office of Price Administration, Region 2, "Reconversion: America's Number One Problem,"

n.d., CR, General Files, Government War Preparation, Role of Consumer, "OPA, 1945–46." Also see Robert Griffith, "Forging America's Postwar Order: Domestic Politics and Political Economy in the Age of Truman," pp. 65–70, and Cranford D. Goodwin, "Attitudes Toward Industry in the Truman Administration: The Macroeconomic Origins of Microeconomic Policy," pp. 99–104, both in Michael J. Lacey, ed., *The Truman Presidency* (Cambridge, Eng.: Cambridge University Press and the Woodrow Wilson International Center for Scholars, 1989).

One faction of those seeking to continue price controls was motivated by the desire to restrict American food consumption so as to feed a starving Europe. The major organization, Food for Freedom, was founded in March 1943 and disbanded in 1947. For documentation, see Atkinson, Box 5, File 26.

114. National Association of Manufacturers' advertisement "Paging Mr. Bowles," *New York Journal-American*, Apr. 18, 1946; "Battle of the Century," *Time*, Mar. 4, 1946, p. 18. Also see the anti–price control arguments in "Price Control—Good or Bad?" *Talk It Over* (Washington, DC: National Institute of Social Relations, 1946), in Anthony, "Non-Newark Material." For details on the NAM campaign against price control, see Elizabeth A. Fones-Wolf, *Selling Free Enterprise: The Business Assault on Labor and Liberalism, 1945–60* (Urbana: University of Illinois Press, 1994), pp. 33–35, 39–41.

115. Quoted in Blum, *V Was for Victory*, p. 115; also see on this page other corporate statements rejecting state planning and regulation and embracing free enterprise. For characteristic articulations of the anti–price control position, see from *WSJ*: "Lingering U.S. Controls Over Industry Threaten Free Enterprise System," Dec. 26, 1945; "Tentacles of Compulsion," Apr. 1, 1946; "The O.P.A. Cancer," Apr. 3, 1946; "Rationing—A Backward Step," May 22, 1946; "Hold the Free Market Line: Price Controls Only Drive Inflation Underground, Create Black Markets, Kill All Incentives to Produce," Sept. 30, 1947. Also "OPA Increases Inflation, Says Grocer Group," *Chicago Daily Tribune*, Jan. 24, 1946; "The Administration: 'Battle of the Century,'" *Time*, Mar. 4, 1946, pp. 18–21; "N.A.M. President Urges Congress Abolish OPA," *New York Sun*, Mar. 18, 1946; "Protests Swell Over OPA, Manufacturers and Retailers Are Angered Over Price-Adjustment Delays," *New York Sun*, Mar. 20, 1946; "NAM 'Blames OPA for Lost Output,'" *NYT*, Apr. 22, 1946.

On the negative model of Britain's Beveridge Report and the persistence of price controls in Europe, see Daniel T. Rodgers, *Atlantic Crossings: Social Politics in a Progressive Age* (Cambridge, MA: Belknap, 1998), pp. 494–508, and Jytte Klausen, "Beveridge in America: NRPB and Postwar Planning: A Comparative Perspective," Oct. 4, 1998, paper in possession of author.

116. Bowles's quote in "The Administration: 'Battle of the Century,'" *Time*, Mar. 4, 1946, p. 19; "Should the OPA Be Continued Without Restrictions?" *Bulletin of America's Town Meeting of the Air* 12 (May 9, 1946), CR, General Files, Government War Preparation, Role of the Consumer, "OPA, 1946"; "Price Control—Good or Bad?" *Talk It Over;* Ira Mosher, "Price Control Must Go!" and Chester Bowles, "Price Control Must Stay!" *Liberty*, Oct. 27, 1946, reprinted by Department of Information, Office of Price Administration, in CR, General Files, Government War Preparation, Role of the Consumer, "OPA 1945–46."

117. Thomas E. Scanlon, chairman, Congressional Committee for the Protection of the Consumer to "Dear Friend," June 26, 1944, NAACP, II, A 461, "OPA General 1944"; "The OPA Consumer Advisory Committee," preliminary first draft for committee members, December 1944, Campbell, Series I, Box 3, F 31; Campbell, *Consumer Interest*, p. 157; Casdorph, *Let the Good Times Roll*, pp. 179–223.

118. National polls cited in *Talk It Over*, p. 11; "Era of Unenlightened Selfishness," *Chicago Daily Tribune*, Apr. 11, 1946, for Chicago survey.

119. Quoted in Michael W. Flamm, "Price Controls, Politics, and the Perils of Policy by Analogy: Economic Demobilization After World War II," *Journal of Policy History* 8 (1986): 349.

120. "Rally to 'Save the O.P.A.' Goes Over the Ceiling," *New York Herald Tribune,* Apr. 18, 1946; "Mayor Sees Peril in Attacks on OPA," *NYT,* May 13, 1946; "O.P.A. Rally, Off Then On Again, Attracts 5000," *New York Herald Tribune,* May 13, 1946; "A Buyers' Strike?" *WSJ,* May 24, 1946; "Buyers' Strike Threatened at Rally for OPA," *Times-Herald of Washington, D.C.,* June 25, 1946; "Buyers' Strike Due to Cut Living Costs, Fight Food Rackets," *NYT,* June 27, 1946; "Shortage of Meat Grows Worse Here," *NYT,* June 28, 1946; Anne Stein, "Post-war Consumer Boycott," *Radical America* 9 (July–August 1975): 158–60.

121. "A Buyers' Strike?" *WSJ,* May 24, 1946.

122. "PRICES: Control Again by a Law Nobody Likes," *Newsweek,* Aug. 5, 1946, p. 19; Mansfield, *Short History of OPA,* p. 100; Station WAAT, radio script, performed Sept. 19, 1946, LWV-NJ, Box 21, p. 7.

123. "U.A.W. to Call Buyers' Strike as Prices Rise," *New York Herald Tribune,* July 16, 1946; "Buyers' Strike Growing," *The New Republic,* July 15, 1946; "Consumer Charges of 'Gouging' Denied by Retail Grocers Here," *New York Herald Tribune,* July 10, 1946; "Senate Votes to Keep Meat, Poultry and Eggs Exempt in New Price Control Bill; Buyers' Strike Will Begin July 23 in 5 Centers Here," *NYT,* July 10, 1946; " 'Buyers Strike' Pickets Fail to Reduce Store Sales Here," *Times-Herald of Washington, D.C.,* July 12, 1948; "Princeton Housewives Unite," *NYT,* July 15, 1946; "Consumers Fight Price Rise but Not in 'Buyers' Strikes,' " *NYT,* July 21, 1946; "Rallies Will Open Strike of Buyers," *NYT,* July 23, 1946; "Today Is THE Day for Consumers to Strike," *PM,* July 23, 1946; "Buyers' Protests Held in Downpour," *NYT,* July 24, 1946; "BUYERS' STRIKE: Housewives and Price Tags," *Newsweek,* July 29, 1946, pp. 15–17.

124. Nelson Lichtenstein, *The Most Dangerous Man in Detroit: Walter Reuther and the Fate of American Labor* (New York: Basic Books, 1995), p. 257. Meg Jacobs has interpreted the Republican victory in November 1946 as a sign of popular disenchantment with price controls. Although it is clear that support for them declined as they became absent or unenforceable after June 1946, I think voters were repudiating the Truman administration and congressional leadership for their mismanagement of the entire business. Ten million Democrats who had voted in 1944, many of them urban and working class, chose to register their disenchantment with the status quo by staying home on election day 1946. In the 1948 election, as prices continued to rise, the Democrats recaptured congressional control, suggesting that voters again used their votes to punish incumbents whom they held responsible for high prices. See James T. Patterson, *Great Expectations: The United States, 1945–1974* (New York: Oxford University Press, 1996), pp. 144–46 for elaboration. Jacobs, " 'How About Some Meat?' " pp. 937–41.

125. "OPA in City Confused; 1,500 Unsure of Fate," *New York Herald Tribune,* Oct. 16, 1946; "OPA Death Rattle," *NSL,* Nov. 2, 1946; "Price Control Board's City Office Closes Today After Five Years," *NSL,* Nov. 4, 1946; "OPA Dies Saturday, Files Here Closing," *NYT,* May 27, 1947. The Consumer Advisory Committee resigned as a body on December 17, 1946, with strong calls for the President to appoint a permanent national consumer committee to advise him and for rent control to survive intact: "OPA Consumer Unit Quits Advisory Job," *NYT,* Dec. 18, 1946; "OPA Advisers on Consumers' Problems Quit," *New York Herald Tribune,* Dec. 18, 1946.

126. Galbraith, *A Life in Our Times,* p. 170; Creighton, *Pretenders to the Throne,* p. 32; Campbell, *Consumer Interest,* p. 184.

127. Excerpt from *Kiplinger Letter,* June 30, 1945, p. 2, CR, General Files, Government

War Preparation, "Rationing as Social, Political and Economic Control Device, 1945–50"; Philip Roth establishes the left credentials of his fictional hero Ira Ringold through frequent reference to his championing of price controls in the late 1940s in *I Married a Communist*, pp. 43, 95.

128. From CR, General Files, Government War Preparation, "New Food Saving Program, 1947–1948"; *The Kiplinger Washington Letter*, Oct. 11, 1947; "Up Like a Rocket, Down Like the Stick," *Chicago Daily Tribune*, Oct. 13, 1947; "Truman Says His Food Plan Avoids Police-State Methods," *NYT*, Oct. 17, 1947; "Food Saving?: First Two Weeks of 'Eat Less' Campaign Shows Skimpy Results," *WSJ*, Oct. 20, 1947; "Food Campaign," *Tide*, Oct. 24, 1947; "Planners' Last Stand," *WSJ*, Oct. 27, 1947; " 'Who's the Father of Poultryless Thursday?' Buzz the Bureaucrats," *WSJ*, Nov. 5, 1947; "Mr. Luckman's Chickens Roost in the Treasury," *Chicago Daily Tribune*, Nov. 24, 1947; "The Consumer's Observation Post," *Consumers' Research Bulletin*, December 1947, pp. 4, 29.

129. Schwartz, "Tenant Power in the Liberal City, 1943–1971," pp. 134–208; "OPA Dies Saturday; Files Here Closing," *NYT*, May 27, 1947; David Lawrence, "On Right of Landlords to Strike," *New York Sun*, Feb. 10, 1949; "Very, Very Close," *Time*, Mar. 21, 1949.

130. Caroline F. Ware, "The Consumer Voice: Lobbying in the Consumer Interest," in Erma Angevine, ed., *Consumer Activists, They Made a Difference: A History of Consumer Action Related by Leaders in the Consumer Movement* (Mount Vernon, NY: Consumers Union Foundation, n.d.), p. 325, Angevine, Box 6, Folder E-4. On the veterans involvement, see "Shortage of Meat Grows Worse Here," *NYT*, June 28, 1946; "Senate Votes to Keep Meat, Poultry and Eggs Exempt in New Price Control Bill," *NYT*, July 10, 1946; "Consumer Charges of 'Gouging' Denied by Retail Grocers Here," *New York Herald Tribune*, July 10, 1946; " 'Buyers Strike' Pickets Fail to Reduce Store Sales Here," *Times-Herald of Washington, D.C.*, July 12, 1946.

131. Form letter soliciting "Founders" of the National Association of Consumers, n.d. but c. January 1947, and Charter of National Association of Consumers, NAC, Box 1, Folder 2, "Correspondence 1947–April 1948"; press release, Jan. 17, 1947, NAC, Box 5, folder "Press Releases and Clippings, 1937, 1947–52, 1958." In some states, like New Jersey, the state-level OPA Consumer Advisory Committee became a permanent consumer organization when the OPA ended; "Consumers' Group Votes to Continue," *NYT*, Dec. 19, 1946. Delegates from Louisiana women's clubs embracing about 100,000 members organized the United Women to Combat Inflation in December 1946: *NYT*, Dec. 22, 1946.

132. Schwartz, "Tenant Power in the Liberal City, 1943–1971," p. 142; "Court of Public Opinion of the City of New York, County of New York, Borough of Manhattan, 'The People of the State of New York Against High Prices,' " June 10, 1947, Campbell, Series II, Box 1, Folder 10; "The Squeeze on Meat Consumers," *U.S. News & World Report*, July 23, 1948, pp. 30–31; " 'Phone War' Started on High Meat Costs," *NYT*, July 30, 1948; "Rebellion at High Prices of Meat Spreads as Men and Dealers Join Women," *Easton Express*, Aug. 4, 1948; "Highway Robbery!" *Daily Worker*, Aug. 10, 1948; "Buyer Resistance Cuts Meat Sales Throughout Nation," *NYT*, Aug. 15, 1948; "Meat Boycott Spreads Across the Nation," *Food Field Reporter*, Aug. 16, 1948; "The Revolt of the Housewives," *Newsweek*, Aug. 16, 1948, p. 15; "Meat Price Strike Throughout Nation Pushed by Women," *Easton Express*, Aug. 17, 1948; "They're All Hollering," *Time*, Aug. 23, 1948, p. 18; "The Housewives' Strikes," *The New Republic*, Aug. 30, 1948, pp. 9–10. Also see Kathleen Michelle Newman, "Critical Mass: Advertising, Audiences and Consumer Activism in the Age of Radio" (Ph.D. diss., Yale University, 1997), pp. 225–28; Sarah Heath, " 'Petticoat Rebels': The Consumer Conference of Cincinnati and the National Meat Boycotts of 1948," May 31, 1994, paper in possession of author, pp. 15–22.

133. "CARNIVAL" by Dick Turner, *Easton Express*, Sept. 20, 1948.

134. From NAACP, II, A 485, file "Price Control, 1946–48": press release, "NAACP Supports Price Control Legislation"; "A Statement on High Prices for Consumers' Goods in Chicago, Illinois, Particularly as Such Prices Obtain and Relate to Negro Families," prepared by Chicago Branch of NAACP for presentation before the Sub-Committee of the Congressional Joint Committee of the Economic Report, Oct. 2, 1947; "Statement of Mrs. Ruth Thomas before the Joint Committee on the Economic Report for the NAACP, September 23, 1947, New York City"; press release, "NAACP Branches Ask for Price Controls," Sept. 12, 1947; statement of Leslie S. Perry, NAACP, Before Senate Banking and Currency Committee for Support of Price Control Legislation, Sept. 23, 1948.

135. French, *U.S. Economic History Since 1945*, p. 93; Nelson Lichtenstein, "Labor in the Truman Era: Origins of the 'Private Welfare State,'" in Lacey, ed., *Truman Presidency*, p. 129. For Reuther quote see Jacobs, "'How About Some Meat?'" p. 937. For claims that "organized labor now speaks with the voice of consumers," see "Inflation! Now What?" *Economic Outlook* 7 (July 1946): 8. On growing CIO identification with consumer protection during wartime, see "Report by Philip Murray," *Final Proceedings of the Sixth Constitutional Convention of the CIO,* Nov. 1, 1943, pp. 55–56.

136. On consumer work of CIO and AFL women's auxiliaries during wartime, see remarks by President Faye Stephenson, chairman of the Women's Auxiliary of the CIO, *Final Proceedings of the Eighth Constitutional Convention of the Congress of Industrial Organizations,* Nov. 18, 1946, pp. 32–33; "Price Control and Rationing," *Report of Proceedings of the 1943 AFL Convention,* p. 554.

137. Nelson Lichtenstein, *Labor's War at Home: The CIO in World War II* (Cambridge, Eng.: Cambridge University Press, 1982), pp. 224–32; Steven Fraser, *Labor Will Rule: Sidney Hillman and the Rise of American Labor* (New York: Free Press, 1991), pp. 565–67.

138. United Steelworkers of America, *The Braddock Steelworker* (Pittsburgh: USWA, 1945), p. 6.

139. Roosevelt delivered this "Second Bill of Rights" in his annual State of the Union address, Jan. 11, 1944. See David M. Kennedy, *Freedom from Fear: The American People in Depression and War, 1929–1945* (New York: Oxford University Press, 1999), p. 784.

140. John Khanlian (former assistant regional price board executive, Region 2, OPA), letter to the *New York Herald Tribune,* Nov. 12, 1947; Department of Information, OPA, "People's Program . . . Wartime Rationing, Price and Rent Control" (Washington, DC: OPA, 1945), CR, General Files, Government War Preparation, Role of Consumers, "OPA, 1945–46."

CHAPTER 3. RECONVERSION: THE EMERGENCE OF THE CONSUMERS' REPUBLIC

1. "Family Status Must Improve," *Life,* May 5, 1947, pp. 32–33; for an insightful reading of the photographs in this photo-essay, see Wendy Kozol, *Life's America* (Philadelphia: Temple University Press, 1994), pp. 87–89.

2. "USA, 1950–1960," supplement to *Electrical Merchandising,* May 1, 1947, prepared by Department of Economics, McGraw-Hill, 1947.

3. "Cagey Consumers," *BW,* Oct. 20, 1945; in *WSJ:* "Christmas Shopping: Record Sales Forecast; Buyers Must Take What They Get—and Like It," Nov. 10, 1945; "Their Business Booms as West Coast Firms Try to Measure Markets," Nov. 24, 1945; "The Consumer Grows Wary," June 5, 1946; "Deflation Fear: U.S. Economists See Trouble in Year or Less, Inflation Scare Over," June 18, 1946; "Pre-Christmas Sales: Big City Stores Slash Many Prices; Beat Gun with Clearances Now," Dec. 19, 1946. William B. Dutton, author of *Adventures in Big Business,* looked back on the war's end from the vantage of 1958: "Americans had to be 'sold' new habits, new ways of viewing life, new ambitions"; quoted in Marty Jezer, *The Dark Ages: Life in the United States 1945–1960* (Boston: South End, 1982), p. 27.

4. Robert Griffith, "Forging America's Postwar Order: Domestic Politics and Political Economy in the Age of Truman," in Michael J. Lacey, *The Truman Presidency* (Washington, DC: Woodrow Wilson International Center for Scholars; New York: Cambridge University Press, 1991), pp. 57–88; Michael French, *U.S. Economic History Since 1945* (Manchester, Eng.: Manchester University Press, 1997), pp. 42–44; Elizabeth A. Fones-Wolf, *Selling Free Enterprise: The Business Assault on Labor and Liberalism, 1945–60* (Urbana: University of Illinois Press, 1994), pp. 22–25, on the diversity of business perspectives; and Harold G. Vatter and John F. Walker, "Why Has the United States Operated Below Potential Since World War II?" in Vatter and Walker, eds., *History of the U.S. Economy Since World War II* (Armonk, NY: Sharpe, 1996), pp. 481–92, on the importance of demand to investment and economic growth. NAM's and the Chamber of Commerce's anti-statist commitment was not just articulated in corporate boardrooms and stockholder meeting halls, but also led to an expensive and all-out campaign to "sell free enterprise" to the American people, launched with an expenditure of $37 million. By the early 1950s, American businesses were spending more than $100 million a year to reorient the nation away from New Deal statism toward a new corporate-led order: Griffith, "Forging America's Postwar Order," pp. 84–85.

Robert Collins argues powerfully in his study of the postwar growth economy that the consumer culture "would so color American life for the remainder of the twentieth century that most Americans simply assumed that the consumer culture *was* America and vice versa. As growthmanship came increasingly to be discussed in explicitly Keynesian terms, with an emphasis on boosting aggregate demand (which came to be translated as: consumption, more consumption), the convergence between the postwar political economy and the voracious postwar culture of consumption became ever more complete." Collins also identifies a broad consensus supporting this economy: *More: The Politics of Economic Growth in Postwar America* (New York: Oxford University Press, 2000), pp. 16, 38–39.

5. Robert R. Nathan, *Mobilizing for Abundance* (New York: McGraw-Hill, 1944), pp. 98, 228; Chester Bowles, *Tomorrow Without Fear* (New York: Simon & Schuster, 1946), p. 49; Chester Bowles, "Why OPA Will Stand Pat on Price Control," *PI*, Oct. 12, 1945, p. 149; Griffith, "Forging America's Postwar Order," pp. 66–67, 70. An outstanding example of the liberal capitalist position on reconversion is Seymour E. Harris, ed., *Saving American Capitalism: A Liberal Economic Program* (New York: Knopf, 1948); also see Jesse J. Friedman, "That Key Man, the Consumer," *NYT Magazine*, Mar. 16, 1947, pp. 20, 53–54, 56, for a quintessential statement of how "the consumer plays the strategic role in the economic system"; Byrd L. Jones, "The Role of Keynesians in Wartime Policy and Postwar Planning, 1940–1946," *American Economic Review* 62 (May 1972): 130–32. John Morton Blum offers a useful analysis of the moderates and liberals in *V Was for Victory: Politics and American Culture During World War II* (New York: Harcourt Brace Jovanovich, 1976), pp. 323–32, as does Nelson Lichtenstein in "From Corporatism to Collective Bargaining: Organized Labor and the Eclipse of Social Democracy in the Postwar Era," in Steve Fraser and Gary Gerstle, eds., *The Rise and Fall of the New Deal Order, 1930–1980* (Princeton: Princeton University Press, 1989), pp. 129–31. The Twentieth Century Fund, sponsor of the report cited in *Life* in May 1947, was itself a major voice for the liberal capitalist wing. Founded by retailer Edward Filene, it was long committed to the importance of public-private partnership in the economy to produce a stable, democratic nation.

6. "Unemployment and Social Security," *Economic Outlook* 5 (November 1944): 6; "Wage Freeze Is Assailed," *American Federationist* 51 (December 1944): 6–7; "Reuther Challenges 'Our Fear of Abundance,'" *NYT Magazine*, Sept. 16, 1945, pp. 8, 32–33, 35. On the drive for full employment, with its link to a "high-consumption economy" that

engaged liberals and labor, see Alan Brinkley, *The End of Reform: New Deal Liberalism in Recession and War* (New York: Knopf, 1995), pp. 231–35. For a later articulation of this position by labor and its liberal allies, see Conference on Economic Progress, *Consumption, Key to Full Prosperity: Toward Rising Living Standards* (Washington, DC: Conference on Economic Progress, May 1957), which attributes the slowdown in economic growth during the recession of 1953–54 to "an even greater slowdown in consumption growth."

7. In the *Economic Report of the President to the Congress, January 8, 1947* (Washington, DC: USGPO, 1947), pp. 1–2, President Truman cited purchasing power as the driving force in the economy: "The Congress, by setting maximum purchasing power as an objective of National policy in the Employment Act, pointed to the importance of purchasing power in keeping our economy fully employed and fully productive. When people stop buying, business stops producing and employment drops. It is therefore of the utmost importance that at all times we be concerned as to the volume of purchasing power of the Nation and its relation to the volume of production of goods and services."

8. French, *U.S. Economic History Since 1945*, pp. 26–27, 138–39; Harold G. Vatter, *The U.S. Economy in World War II* (New York: Columbia University Press, 1985), pp. 150–52; Thomas Hine, *Populuxe* (New York: Knopf, 1987), pp. 128–29. For a typical *Wall Street Journal* editorial of the era arguing for the interconnectedness of the civilian and military economies, see "Civilian Economy," Jan. 28, 1949.

9. *Public Papers of the Presidents of the United States: Harry S. Truman, Containing the Public Messages, Speeches, and Statements of the Presidents, January 1 to December 31, 1949* (Washington, DC: USGPO, 1964), pp. 356, 374; Conference on Economic Progress, *Consumption, Key to Full Prosperity*, p. 2; *Economic Report of the President, Transmitted to the Congress January 20, 1959* (Washington, DC: USGPO, 1959), p. 16.

10. "Special Message to the Congress: The President's First Economic Report," Jan. 8, 1947, *Public Papers of the Presidents of the United States: Harry S. Truman, 1947* (Washington, DC: USGPO, 1963), p. 15; address in Pendleton, Oregon, May 10, 1950, *Public Papers of the Presidents of the United States: Harry S. Truman, 1950* (Washington, DC: USGPO, 1965), p. 358; "The President's News Conference of March 5, 1958," *Public Papers of the Presidents of the United States: Dwight D. Eisenhower, 1958* (Washington, DC: USGPO, 1959), p. 199; also see pp. 218–19.

For a cogent analysis of the economy of the postwar boom and the ways it has declined since the mid-1970s, see Robert Kuttner, *Everything for Sale: The Virtues and Limits of Markets* (New York: Knopf, 1997), particularly pp. 29–38. For a defense of the "mixed economy" in the period, see Merle Fainsod, "Government and Business in a Mixed Economy," and Seymour E. Harris, "Introduction" to "Part Five: Stabilization of Demand" in Harris, ed., *Saving American Capitalism*, pp. 175–82, 211–17. On the importance of government spending to a successful demand economy, see Vatter and Walker, "Why Has the United States Operated Below Potential Since World War II?" pp. 481–92.

11. George Katona and Eva Mueller, *Consumer Expectations, 1953–1956* (Ann Arbor: Survey Research Center, Institute for Social Research, University of Michigan, 1957), p. 30; "Consumers Regard Government as Guard Against Depression," *AFL-CIO News*, Mar. 26, 1960, p. 8.

12. *Bride's* magazine handbook quote from Brett Harvey, *The Fifties: A Women's Oral History* (New York: HarperCollins, 1993), p. 110; Scrooge McDuck mentioned in William S. Graebner, *The Age of Doubt: American Thought and Culture in the 1940s* (Boston: Twayne, 1991), p. 12; William H. Whyte quote from *Fortune*, May 1956, in George Katona, *The Powerful Consumer: Psychological Studies of the American Economy* (New York: McGraw-Hill, 1960), pp. 97–98. Alan Roy Berolzheimer has arrived at a conclusion similar to mine about the way Americans' "own particular strivings for an improved

standard of living embodied the public good, the national interest" in his dissertation, "A Nation of Consumers: Mass Consumption, Middle Class Standards of Living, and American National Identity, 1910–1950" (Ph.D. diss., University of Virginia, 1996), pp. 485–87. Relatedly, Alan Brinkley ends his study of the New Deal with the postwar consensus among liberals in favor of a consumer-oriented rather than producer-oriented liberal state and fiscal policies, as well as a redefinition of "citizenship to de-emphasize the role of men and women as producers and to elevate their roles as consumers": Brinkley, *End of Reform*, pp. 268–69. President Truman's papers are filled with warnings about inflation, particularly in the midst of the Korean War. See, for example, "Radio and Television Report to the American People on the Need for Extending Inflation Controls," June 14, 1951, *Papers of the President of the United States: Harry S. Truman, 1951* (Washington, DC: USGPO, 1965), pp. 333–38.

After I drafted this book, I stumbled upon Alan Wolfe's *America's Impasse: The Rise and Fall of the Politics of Growth* (New York: Pantheon, 1981) and discovered that he makes an argument not unlike my own. Wolfe builds a compelling case that liberals and centrists alike embraced a politics of economic growth in the postwar era, where "growth politics" substituted for more genuinely liberal commitments to economic equality and social justice.

13. Research Division of the Newark Community Committee, Committee for Economic Development, Newark, N.J., "Newark Will Have Money to Spend!" September 1944, "Q" Files, NPL. Not long after this report was published, the Newark Committee for Economic Development and other local groups, including the New Jersey League of Women Shoppers, sponsored a one-day forum, "Jobs to Win the War and Keep the Peace." Summaries of the sessions reveal a similar emphasis on the importance of consumption for ensuring stable, well-paid employment: Program, "The Newark Committee for Economic Development and Participating Groups Invite You to Attend a Community Forum of Great Importance to Newark: Jobs to Win the War and Keep the Peace," Apr. 15, 1945; James E. Bryan, "Summary of Afternoon Session"; Robert Widdop, "Summary of Evening Session," "Q" Files, NPL.

14. "Recovery? Not in Your Paycheck," *NYT,* Jan. 8, 1995; Eric Foner, *The Story of American Freedom* (New York: Norton, 1998), p. 264; Conference on Economic Progress, *Consumption, Key to Full Prosperity,* pp. 1–5; Private Consumption Expenditure as a Percentage of GNP, calculated from United Nations, Statistics Office, *Statistical Yearbooks* (New York: United Nations Printing Office, 1960, 1970, and 1980); data here make possible international comparisons.

15. Sheldon Danziger and Peter Gottschalk, *America Unequal* (New York: Russell Sage Foundation; Cambridge, MA: Harvard University Press, 1995), pp. 40–41. Whenever recession threatened, the *Economic Report of the President* urged greater consumer spending (and often reduced saving) as a surefire remedy; see for 1955 (pp. 18–21), for 1958 (pp. 16–17, 39), for 1959 (pp. 16–17, 40), for 1961 (pp. 42–43, which focused in particular on efforts to stimulate home building).

On the growth of the service sector and its interconnections with mass consumption, see "Marketing in the '60s: The Coming Battle for Discretionary Dollars," *PI,* Sept. 11, 1959, which quoted economist Lionel Edie as saying, "No shift has been more persistent and extensive than the growing importance of services in the consumer budget," p. 30. Lynne E. Browne, "Taking in Each Other's Laundry—The Service Economy," argues that "new and superior products" fueled new kinds of services, and "the growth of services in turn stimulates the growth of related manufacturing"; excerpted from *New England Economic Review* (Federal Reserve Bank of Boston, July–August 1986), pp. 20–31, reprinted in Vatter and Walker, eds., *History of the U.S. Economy,* p. 76. Also see Louis Galambos,

"Myth and Reality in the Study of America's Consumer Culture," in Karen R. Merrill, ed., *The Modern Worlds of Business and Industry: Cultures, Technology, Labor* (Davis Center, Princeton University, and Turnhout, Belgium: Brepols, 1998).

16. *Kansas City Star* quoted in "The Boom," *Fortune,* June 1946, p. 99; "The Great Housing Shortage," *Life,* Dec. 17, 1945; "Radio Report to the American People on the Status of the Reconversion Program," Jan. 3, 1946, *Public Papers of the Presidents of the United States: Harry S. Truman, 1946* (Washington, DC: USGPO, 1962), p. 7; Foner, *Story of American Freedom,* p. 264; Kozol, *Life's America,* p. 80; U.S. Bureau of Labor Statistics, Department of Labor, *How American Buying Habits Change* (Washington, DC: USGPO, 1959), pp. 74–75. For excellent treatment of the political battles over government funding of housing, see Rosalyn Baxandall and Elizabeth Ewen, *Picture Windows: How the Suburbs Happened* (New York: Basic Books, 2000), pp. 87–116. Congress did authorize some public housing in the postwar period, first through the Federal Emergency Housing Program, providing subsidized low- and moderate-cost dwelling units to families including many veterans, and then through the Wagner-Ellender-Taft (WET) Act of 1949, authorizing the construction of between 135,000 and 200,000 public housing units a year and adding to the public housing supply built under the Wagner-Steagall Act of 1937, which had created the United States Housing Authority to extend long-term long-interest loans to local housing agencies to construct low-rent housing. The Federal Emergency Housing Program was a stopgap emergency measure that made little long-term impact, and WET never lived up to its promise. By 1962 only about 30 percent of those units called for in the law had been built, contributing substantially to the harsh reality that only about 10 percent of the housing units needed between 1939 and 1960 were actually constructed. Educational Testing Service, *Final Report on Educational Assistance to Veterans: A Comparative Study of Three G.I. Bills, Submitted to the Committee on Veterans' Affairs, United States Senate* (Washington, DC: USGPO, 1973), p. 128; Michael J. Bennett, *When Dreams Came True: The GI Bill and the Making of Modern America* (Washington, DC: Brassey's, 1996), pp. 284–85; Mark I. Gelfand, *A Nation of Cities: The Federal Government and Urban America, 1933–1965* (New York: Oxford University Press, 1975), pp. 62–65, 144–56, 168–69, 199–205; Leon H. Keyserling, "Homes for All—and How," reprinted from *Survey Graphic,* February 1946, in NAACP, II, A 657, "Veterans Housing, 1945–55"; "Victory in Housing," *American Federationist,* July 1949, p. 10.

17. The implications of this shift from urban and rural to suburban housing will be analyzed in Chapters 5 and 6. For expenditures on residential construction, see *Economic Report of the President, Transmitted to the Congress January 18, 1961* (Washington, DC: USGPO, 1961), pp. 48–49. On the housing boom more broadly, see Bowles, *Tomorrow Without Fear,* p. 61; Pearce C. Kelley, *Consumer Economics* (Homewood, IL: Irwin, 1953), pp. 464–67; Harold Vatter, "The Inheritance of the Preceding Decades," in Vatter and Walker, eds., *History of the U.S. Economy;* Department of Commerce, "We the Americans . . . Our Homes"; and President's Committee on Urban Housing, "A Decent Home," pp. 21–23, 235–37, 358–62; David M. Kennedy, Lizabeth Cohen, and Thomas A. Bailey, *The American Pageant,* 12th ed. (Boston: Houghton Mifflin, 2002), p. 908; Bureau of the Census, Department of Commerce, *Census of Housing: General Housing Characteristics,* Part 1: United States Summary (Washington, DC: Department of Commerce, 1983), Figure 11; Kathryn Murphy, *New Housing and Its Materials, 1940–56,* Bulletin No. 1231 (Washington, DC: U.S. Department of Labor, Bureau of Labor Statistics, 1958), p. 2; James Grant, *Money of the Mind: Borrowing and Lending in America from the Civil War to Michael Milkin* (New York: Noonday/Farrar, Straus and Giroux, 1992), pp. 350–54. Although the overwhelming bulk of new housing units were intended for private ownership, some were built for public ownership and then rented by local housing authorities

at subsidized rates to low-income families. Between 1936 and 1956, however, only 4 percent of total home construction was publicly owned; Housing and Home Finance Agency, *Housing in the United States . . . a Graphic Presentation* (Washington, DC: Housing and Home Finance Agency, 1956), p. 34.

Secretary of Commerce, and then President, Hoover had had a similar faith in the potential of private home construction to boost the economy when he established the Better Homes in America initiative during the 1920s. What became a nationwide housing competition of model homes gave broad exposure to the ideal, but it was not until the postwar era that mass home ownership became anywhere near a reality; see Gail Radford, *Modern Housing for America* (Chicago: University of Chicago Press, 1996), pp. 51–53.

18. U.S. Department of Commerce, Bureau of the Census, *Construction Reports—Housing Starts*, C-20 Supplement, 1972, p. 68. Prior to 1959, housing starts were estimated on a monthly basis and calculated on an annual basis by the Bureau of Labor Statistics, suggesting that the interest then was as much in employment opportunities as in construction activity.

19. Stanley Lebergott, *Pursuing Happiness: American Consumers in the Twentieth Century* (Princeton: Princeton University Press, 1993), p. 113; F. Thomas Juster, *Consumer Expectations, Plans, and Purchases: A Progress Report*, Occasional Paper 70 (New York: National Bureau of Economic Research, 1959), p. xi. The swift integration of the television into American households was remarkable. In 1949 only 3 million television sets were produced; seven years later, in 1956, three-quarters of American homes had at least one: U.S. Bureau of Labor Statistics, *How American Buying Habits Change*, p. 208.

20. Lebergott, *Pursuing Happiness*, p. 130; French, *U.S. Economic History Since 1945*, p. 189; William H. Chafe, "Postwar American Society: Dissent and Social Reform," in Lacey, *Truman Presidency*, p. 158; Barry Bluestone and Bennett Harrison, *The Deindustrialization of America: Plant Closings, Community Abandonment, and the Dismantling of Basic Industry* (New York: Basic Books, 1982), pp. 114–15; Murphy, *New Housing and Its Materials*, p. iii. Another measure of the quick rise in automobile purchases after the war was the 75 percent jump in auto registrations as early as 1946–54; Gelfand, *Nation of Cities*, p. 231.

21. Philip A. Klein, *The Cyclical Timing of Consumer Credit, 1920–67*, Occasional Paper 113 (New York: National Bureau of Economic Research, 1971), passim, and particularly pp. 4–5, 75–76, 89–90, 91–92; French, *U.S. Economic History Since 1945*, pp. 4, 189; "As Instalment Debt Hits New Peak and the Boom Rolls On, a Hard Look at Consumer Credit," *Life*, Nov. 21, 1955, pp. 33–38; "Soft Spots: Amid Business Boom, Some Economists See Danger Signals Flying" and "The Outlook," *WSJ*, Mar. 14, 1955; Lewis Mandell, *The Credit Card Industry: A History* (Boston: Twayne, 1990), pp. xii–xv, 1–32; *I'll Buy That! 50 Small Wonders and Big Deals That Revolutionized the Lives of Consumers: A 50-Year Retrospective by the Editors of Consumer Reports* (Mount Vernon, NY: Consumers Union, 1986), "Credit Card." The 1920s is also often viewed as a period of great growth in credit, but the scale was much more modest than in the postwar era. Total private debt increased 21 percent between 1925 and 1930, while it grew nearly three times as fast, 62 percent, between 1949 and 1954: Grant, *Money of the Mind*, pp. 265, 267. While acknowledging that installment credit had mushroomed in 1955, President Eisenhower decided in 1957 not to request legislation giving the president standby authority to regulate consumer installment credit, as some urged. Rather, he expressed satisfaction that "a greater proportion of middle-income families" were "using this type of credit": "White House Statement on Regulation of Consumer Instalment Credit," May 25, 1957, *Public Papers of the Presidents of the United States: Dwight D. Eisenhower, Containing the Public Messages, Speeches, and Statements of the President, 1957* (Washington, DC: USGPO, 1958), pp. 413–15.

22. Grant, *Money of the Mind*, p. 260; U.S. Bureau of Labor Statistics, *How American Buying Habits Change*, pp. 32, 189–91; Katona, *Powerful Consumer*, pp. 12–13, 100. For the early history of consumer credit, see Lendol Calder, *Financing the American Dream: A Cultural History of Consumer Credit* (Princeton: Princeton University Press, 1999). The *Economic Report of the President, Transmitted to the Congress January 20, 1955*, p. 23, noted that "perhaps at no time in the past has the desire for material improvement played so large a role in the economy as it does today," and acknowledged that "people are no longer timid about borrowing."

23. Encyclopaedia Britannica Films, *Despotism*, 1946, 10 minutes, 35 mm, from Rick Prelinger, ed., *Our Secret Century: Archival Films from the Darker Side of the American Dream*, vol. 10, *Make Mine Freedom*, Voyager CD, 1996. On sponsored films in general, see William Bird, "Enterprise and Meaning: Sponsored Film, 1939–1949," *History Today* 39 (December 1989): 24–30.

24. From *House Beautiful*, 1953, quoted in Hine, *Populuxe*, p. 147; "About Our $1,300,000,000,000 Economy," *Life*, Jan. 5, 1953, p. 7.

25. U.S. Bureau of Labor Statistics, *How American Buying Habits Change*, p. 196; "Annual Message to the Congress on the State of the Union," Jan. 4, 1950, *Public Papers of Harry S. Truman, 1950*, p. 6; "Address in Detroit at the National Automobile Show Industry Dinner," Oct. 17, 1960, *Public Papers of the Presidents of the United States: Dwight D. Eisenhower, 1960–61* (Washington, DC: USGPO, 1961), p. 769.

26. American Economic Foundation and Wilding Picture Productions, *How to Lose What We Have*, Part 3 of "In Our Hands" Series, 1950, 12 minutes, 35 mm, from Prelinger, *Our Secret Century*, vol. 10.

27. On Nixon and Khrushchev's "kitchen debate," see Karal Ann Marling, *As Seen on TV: The Visual Culture of Everyday Life in the 1950s* (Cambridge, MA: Harvard University Press, 1994), pp. 243–83; Hine, *Populuxe*, pp. 129–31; Foner, *Story of American Freedom*, pp. 262–73. For the edited transcription of the "kitchen debate" that appeared the next day in the *New York Times*, see http://www.cnn.com/SPECIALS/cold.war/episodes/14/documents/debate.

28. David E. Lilienthal, *Big Business: A New Era* (New York: Harper, 1953), cited in Foner, *Story of American Freedom*, p. 264; Bowles, *Tomorrow Without Fear*.

29. American Petroleum Institute and John Sutherland, *Destination Earth*, 1954, 14 minutes, 35 mm, from Prelinger, *Our Secret Century*, vol. 10.

30. "Address at Republican National Committee Dinner in Honor of the Republican Members of Congress," May 6, 1958, *Papers of Dwight D. Eisenhower, 1958*, p. 383; "Address in Detroit at the National Automobile Show Industry Dinner," Oct. 17, 1960, *Papers of Dwight D. Eisenhower, 1960*, p. 774; John F. Kennedy, "Address Before the White House Conference on Exports," Sept. 17, 1963, *Public Papers of the Presidents of the United States: John F. Kennedy, 1963* (Washington, DC: USGPO, 1964), p. 685.

David Riesman wrote a hilarious parody of the American use of consumer commodities to win the Cold War against the Soviets in his essay "The Nylon War," in *Individualism Reconsidered and Other Essays* (Glencoe, IL: Free Press, 1954), pp. 426–34. "All-out bombing of the Soviet Union with consumers' goods" in 1951 was premised on the confidence "that if allowed to sample the riches of America, the Russian people would not long tolerate masters who gave them tanks and spies instead of vacuum cleaners and beauty parlors." One might argue that that is exactly what happened some forty years later.

31. W. W. Rostow, *Stages of Economic Growth: A Non-Communist Manifesto* (Cambridge, Eng.: Cambridge University Press, 1960).

32. "Address in Pendleton, Oregon," May 10, 1950, *Public Papers of Harry S. Truman, 1950*, p. 362; John Kenneth Galbraith, *The Affluent Society* (Boston: Houghton Mifflin,

1958), pp. 94–97. David Plotke notes some divergence between progressive Democrats and Republicans in the late 1940s, but he stresses the common commitment of both to achieving redistribution through economic growth rather than social and political reforms: *Building a Democratic Political Order: Reshaping American Liberalism in the 1930s and 1940s* (Cambridge, Eng.: Cambridge University Press, 1996), pp. 294–96.

33. My discussion on the decline of the consumer movement after the war is based on Plotke, *Building a Democratic Political Order*, pp. 271–79; Lucy Black Creighton, *Pretenders to the Throne: The Consumer Movement in the United States* (Lexington, MA: Lexington Books/Heath, 1976), pp. 31–32; Mark V. Nadel, *The Politics of Consumer Protection* (Indianapolis: Bobbs-Merrill, 1971), p. 31; Kelley, *Consumer Economics*, p. 147; Erma Angevine and Dr. Caroline F. Ware, *Effective Consumer Participation: Consumer Participation in Federal Decision Making* (Washington, DC: National Consumers' League, 1981), in Angevine, Box 6, pp. 11–12; Caroline F. Ware, *The Consumer Goes to War: A Guide to Victory on the Homefront* (New York: Funk & Wagnalls, 1942), pp. 218–22; for a similar statement to Ware's, only later, see "History of Consumer Advisory Committee, Office of Price Stabilization," n.d. but c. 1953, NAC, Box 4, folder "Government Activities, Consumer Advisory Committee, History and Minutes." Persia Campbell, *Bringing the Consumer Point of View into Government* (Greeley, CO: Council on Consumer Information, 1958), pp. 7–8, 20, points to some constructive action during the 1950s in New York State under the recently elected Governor Averell Harriman, who appointed the author, a longtime consumer activist, to the cabinet-rank position of consumer counsel. Massachusetts and California soon followed New York's example.

34. On advertising and business efforts to usurp the consumer movement, see in *PI:* Harold E. Green, "7 Good Elements in a Company Program of Public Service," Mar. 30, 1945, pp. 19–20, 108, 110; Rosanne Amberson, "School Texts for Tomorrow's Buyers: Business and Education Cooperate on New Consumer Study Units," Jan. 11, 1946, pp. 46, 48, 53–54; Green, "How Advertisers Are Helping Consumers in Their Buying," Feb. 15, 1946, pp. 21–22, 94, 96, 99; Green, "Advertisers Have Big Good-will Opportunity as Consumers Mobilize," Feb. 22, 1946, pp. 49, 52, 54, 56; Kenneth Dameron, "The Consumer in the Coming Decade," Oct. 29, 1948, pp. 83–84, 89, 92.

35. On red-baiting of consumer activists and organizations in the postwar era, see Annelise Orleck, " 'We Are That Mythical Thing Called the Public': Militant Housewives During the Great Depression," *Feminist Studies* 19 (Spring 1993): 165–66; Colston E. Warne, "Wither Consumerism?" Apr. 19, 1977, Angevine, Box 2, Folder D-3, p. 2; material on the disbanding of the League of Women Shoppers in CR, General Files, Political Front Organizations, 1935–70, "L"—League of Women Shoppers.

36. The revival of consumer organizing in the 1960s and 1970s will be discussed in Chapter 8. Cambell, *Bringing the Consumer Point of View into Government*, p. 8; Congressional Quarterly Service, *Congress and the Nation, 1945–1964: A Review of Government and Politics in the Postwar Years*, vol. 1 (Washington, DC: Congressional Quarterly Service, 1964), pp. 1159–85; Erma Angevine, ed., *Consumer Activists, They Made a Difference: A History of Consumer Action Related by Leaders in the Consumer Movement* (Mount Vernon, NY: Consumers Union Foundation, n.d.), pp. 325–26, 332–33, Angevine, Box 6, Folder E-4.

37. Kathleen Michelle Newman, "Critical Mass: Advertising, Audiences and Consumer Activism in the Age of Radio" (Ph.D. diss., Yale University, 1997), pp. 176–80; "Bread and Butter: Consumers and the 81st Congress," *Consumer Reports,* January 1949, pp. 38–41; Editors of Consumer Reports Books with Monte Florman, *Testing: Behind the Scenes at Consumer Reports, 1936–1986* (Mount Vernon, NY: Consumers Union, 1986).

38. The Consumers Union Archives has a very rich collection of the papers of the

National Association of Consumers. When combined with related material in the papers of consumer activist and economist Persia Campbell in the same archive, a full picture of the activities of the NAC emerges. For additional background on the NAC, see Newman, "Critical Mass," pp. 141, 164–70, and Angevine, ed., *Consumer Activists*, p. 325. Civil rights leader Ella Baker remained committed to cooperatives and consumer organizing well into the 1960s: Joanne Grant, *Ella Baker: Freedom Bound* (New York: Wiley, 1998), pp. 93–96.

39. Persia Campbell, *The Consumer Interest: A Study in Consumer Economics* (New York: Harper & Bros., 1949), pp. 634–35.

40. Friedman, "That Key Man, the Consumer," *NYT Magazine*, p. 54; from *POQ*: Angus Campbell and George Katona, "A National Survey of Wartime Savings" 10 (Fall 1946): 373–81; "Living Research" 13 (Summer 1949): 325–28; Louis Harris and Elmo Roper, "Two Years of the *Fortune* Consumer Outlook" 13 (Fall 1949): 415–22; George Katona, "Public Opinion and Economic Research" 21 (Spring 1957): 117–28; Juster, *Consumer Expectations, Plans, and Purchases: A Progress Report; Survey of Consumer Finances: Part I, Expenditures for Durable Goods and Investments* (Washington, DC: Board of Governors of the Federal Reserve System, 1947); George Katona and Eva Mueller, *Consumer Attitudes and Demand, 1950–52* (Ann Arbor: Survey Research Center, Institute for Social Research, University of Michigan, 1953); Katona and Mueller, *Consumer Expectations, 1953–1956*; Katona, *Powerful Consumer*; "Three Decades of Dwindling Hope for Prosperity," *NYT*, May 9, 1993. For background on Katona, see Daniel Horowitz, "The Emigré as Celebrant of American Consumer Culture: George Katona and Ernest Dichter," in Susan Strasser, Charles McGovern, and Matthias Judt, eds., *Getting and Spending: European and American Consumer Societies in the Twentieth Century* (Washington, DC: German Historical Institute; New York: Cambridge University Press, 1998), pp. 149–66.

41. Katona and Mueller, *Consumer Expectations, 1953–1956*, p. 6; quote from business leader in *NYT*, cited in ibid., p. 44; "Address at Economic Mobilization Conference of the American Management Association," May 20, 1958, *Public Papers of Dwight D. Eisenhower, 1958*, p. 417. During the recessions of 1954 and 1958, Eisenhower acted on his recognition of the importance of consumer attitudes by enlisting the services of the Advertising Council in mounting a massive advertising campaign promoting "Confidence in a Growing America." See Robert Griffith, "Dwight D. Eisenhower and the Corporate Commonwealth," *AHR* 87 (February 1982): 104.

42. Don B. Wilmeth and Tice L. Miller, eds., *The Cambridge Guide to American Theatre* (Cambridge, Eng.: Cambridge University Press, 1993), p. 123.

43. Frank A. Pearson and Don Parlberg, "OPA, Economics and Politics," New York State College of Agriculture at Cornell University, May 10, 1946, CR, General Files, Government War Preparation, Role of Consumer, "OPA, 1946"; "Statement by the President Commending the Office of Price Administration," May 1, 1945, *Public Papers of the Presidents of the United States: Harry S. Truman, 1945* (Washington, DC: USGPO, 1961), p. 28; "Radio Report to the Nation Announcing the Lifting of Major Price Controls," Oct. 14, 1946, *Public Papers of Harry S. Truman, 1946*, p. 451; Frederick C. Othman, "Decontrol Y'self," *New York World Telegram*, Aug. 13, 1946.

44. Plotke, *Building a Democratic Political Order*, pp. 273–74. Robert G. Moeller in *Protecting Motherhood: Women and the Family in the Politics of Postwar West Germany* (Berkeley: University of California Press, 1993) probes the centrality of gender definitions, particularly "women's place," in the reconstruction of a democratic West Germany after World War II. Although Germany's reconstruction was more total than ours, new gender prescriptions were no less significant here.

45. Many historians discuss women's loss of manufacturing jobs at the war's end. See, for example, Sherna Berger Gluck, *Rosie the Riveter Revisited: Women, the War, and Social Change* (New York: New American Library, 1987); Karen Anderson, *Wartime Women: Sex Roles, Family Relations, and the Status of Women During World War II* (Westport, CT: Greenwood, 1981), chap. 5; Ruth Milkman, *Gender at Work: The Dynamics of Job Segregation by Sex During World War II* (Urbana: University of Illinois Press, 1987), chap. 7; Nancy F. Gabin, *Feminism in the Labor Movement: Women and the United Auto Workers, 1935–1975* (Ithaca, NY: Cornell University Press, 1990), chap. 3; Susan M. Hartmann, *American Women in the 1940s: The Home Front and Beyond* (Boston: Twayne, 1982), pp. 23–25.

Historians have also made much of the way women were encouraged, at times compelled, to return to traditional roles with demobilization, though their arguments often rest on the influence of government, business, and labor propaganda and the familial demands of the high postwar birthrate, and not on the larger political struggle with which I am concerned. See, for example, Elaine Tyler May, *Homeward Bound: American Families in the Cold War Era* (New York: Basic Books, 1988); Chafe, "Postwar American Society," in Lacey, ed., *Truman Presidency,* pp. 168–70. An exception is David Plotke's *Building a Democratic Political Order,* which probes how and why the Democratic Party's policies of the late 1940s failed to build on women's social and political activism as consumers in the 1930s and World War II.

46. Annual Programs of the Consumer Conference of Greater Cincinnati, 1946–1955, NAC, Box 5, "Publications—Local Chapters, Cincinnati Consumer Conference Flyers and Programs, 1946–1955"; Helen Hall, "Consumer Protection," January 1949, NAC, Box 5, "Writings and Speeches, Hall, 1947–1950," pp. 2–3.

47. "Remarks at the Opening Session of the Women's Bureau Conference," Feb. 17, 1948, *Public Papers of the Presidents of the United States: Harry S. Truman, 1948* (Washington, DC: USGPO, 1964), p. 142. Truman frequently identified consumers narrowly as housewives who bought goods to feed and clothe their families; see in the same volume "Statement by the President Upon Signing Resolution 'To Aid in Protecting the Nation's Economy Against Inflationary Pressures,'" Aug. 16, 1948, and "Labor Day Address in Cadillac Square, Detroit," Sept. 6, 1948, pp. 450, 478; "Rear Platform Speech at Troy, Ohio," Oct. 31, 1952, and "Special Message to the Congress on the Nation's Land and Water Resources," Jan. 19, 1953, *Public Papers of the Presidents of the United States: Harry S. Truman, Containing the Public Messages, Speeches and Statements of the President, 1952–53* (Washington, DC: USGPO, 1966), pp. 1017–18, 1210.

48. Mrs. Raymond Sayre, "The Homemaker as Citizen," *Journal of Home Economics* 39 (September 1947): 391–95; see also Frances Maule, "Accent Is on Political Action," *Independent Woman,* August 1947, pp. 210–14, 239. On women's political activity during the 1950s, see the essays in Joanne Meyerowitz, ed., *Not June Cleaver: Women and Gender in Postwar America, 1945–1960* (Philadelphia: Temple University Press, 1994); interview with Carol Freeman in Harvey, *The Fifties,* pp. 126–27, describing her involvement with the League of Women Voters and political campaigns.

49. Kozol, *Life's America,* p. 89.

50. "The Act That Changed America," *The American Legion Magazine,* June 1984, p. 26; Bennett, *When Dreams Came True;* James A. Michener, "After the War: The Victories at Home," *Newsweek,* Jan. 11, 1993, pp. 26–27.

51. The Veterans Administration and congressional inquiries have created a rich bank of documentation evaluating the workings of the GI Bill for veterans of World War II, the Korean War, and Vietnam War. Some of those studies have been published and are available in libraries; others were shared with me by Paul Nehrenberg, Mike Wells, and Diane

Hartmann in the Washington headquarters of the Department of Veterans Affairs, and Joe Thompson in the New York Regional Office, to all of whom I am grateful. The following studies, listed in chronological order, have been particularly helpful and contributed to the discussion which follows: Special Issue on World War II Veterans, *AAAPSS* 238 (March 1945); Reports and Statistics Service, Office of Controller, Veterans Administration, "VA Benefits to World War II Veterans, 1945–1950: A Study of Participation by World War II Veterans in the Major Veterans Administration Programs During the Five Years After VJ-Day," n.d. but c. 1950; President's Commission on Veterans' Pensions [Bradley Commission], *A Report on Benefits in the United States,* printed for the Use of the House Committee on Veterans' Affairs, 84th Cong., 2nd Sess. (Washington, DC: USGPO, 1956), multiple volumes of staff reports; Educational Testing Service, *Final Report on Educational Assistance to Veterans: A Comparative Study of Three G.I. Bills,* submitted to the Committee on Veterans' Affairs, United States Senate, 93rd Cong., 1st Sess., Sept. 20, 1973; National Academy of Public Administration Foundation, *GI Course Approvals: A Report Prepared for the Veterans Administration,* submitted to the Committee on Veterans' Affairs, United States Senate, October 1979; Richard Hammond, project director, "1979 National Survey of Veterans, Summary Report, Reports and Statistics Service, Office of the Controller, 1979; Louis Harris and Associates, "Survey of Aging Veterans: A Study of the Means, Resources, and Future Expectations of Veterans Aged 55 and Over," conducted for the Veterans Administration, December 1983; Veterans Administration, "Historical Data on the Usage of Educational Benefits, 1944–1983," Office of Information Management and Statistics, April 1984; U.S. Bureau of the Census, "1987 National Survey of Veterans," conducted for the Department of Veterans' Affairs, July 1989; "Phase I: Summary of Reports, Independent Commissions and Other Published Analyses on Veterans' Benefits and Their Administration," prepared for the Chief Benefits Direction [Department of Veterans' Affairs] by the Office of the Assistant Secretary for Policy and Planning, November 1991; Federal Research Division, Library of Congress, "The Veterans Benefits Administration and Its Predecessors: An Organizational History, 1776–1993," revised July 12, 1993; Department of Veterans' Affairs, "History of the GI Bill, 1944–1994, 50th Anniversary," 1994.

Useful secondary sources on the GI Bill include Davis R. B. Ross, *Preparing for Ulysses: Politics and Veterans During World War II* (New York: Columbia University Press, 1969), and Bennett, *When Dreams Came True.* For an update on VA mortgages, see "For Veterans, a Higher Limit on No-Down-Payment Loans, *BG,* Jan. 5, 2002.

52. Anne Bosanko Green, *One Woman's War: Letters Home from the Women's Army Corps, 1944–1946* (St. Paul: Minnesota Historical Society Press, 1989), p. 304.

53. June A. Wilentz, *Women Veterans: America's Forgotten Heroines* (New York: Continuum, 1983), pp. 163–96. More details on benefit discrimination against female veterans are described here than I have space to explore. After researching this question myself, I learned of several other scholars pursuing similar investigations into the gender and class ramifications of the GI Bill, although the only work of theirs I have seen is as yet unpublished: Melissa Murray (Yale Law School), Gretchen Ritter (University of Texas, Austin), and Suzanne Mettler (Syracuse University).

54. "State Commission Seeks to Equalize Role and Benefits for Women Vets," *NSL,* May 30, 1988; "Women Veterans May Be Eligible for Benefits," *NSL,* July 23, 1989; "Jersey Women Veterans to Get Day in the Sun," *NSL,* Nov. 3, 1985; "The Open Door to Belleville," Belleville Foundation, prepared in July 1944, NPL, clipping file, "N.J. Veterans," p. 26.

55. In addition to general sources cited on the GI Bill, see on education David M. Kennedy, *Freedom from Fear: The American People in Depression and War, 1929–1945*

(New York: Oxford University Press, 1999), p. 787; Bennett, *When Dreams Came True*, p. 19.

56. For women on college and university campuses after the war, see Harvey, *The Fifties*, pp. 48, 52; Anderson, *Wartime Women*, p. 176; Green, *One Woman's War*, p. 5.

57. Karen Brodkin Sacks, "How Did Jews Become White Folks?" in Steven Gregory and Roger Sanjek, eds., *Race* (New Brunswick, NJ: Rutgers University Press, 1994), p. 89.

58. In addition to the sources on the GI Bill already listed, see for California mortgage statistics Ronald Tobey, Charles Wetherell, and Jay Brigham, "Moving Out and Settling In: Residential Mobility, Home Owning, and the Public Enframing of Citizenship, 1921–1950," *AHR* 95 (December 1990): 1414.

59. *Census of Housing: 1950 (taken as part of the Seventeenth Decennial Census of the United States)*, vol. 4, *Residential Financing, Morgaged Nonfarm Properties*, Part 2: "Large Standard Metropolitan Areas" (Washington, DC: USGPO, 1952), p. 565.

60. George Amick, "The View from Here: N.J. Veterans' Bonus: Endless, Unfair," *Trenton Evening Times*, Dec. 5, 1967.

61. James Elton McMillan, Jr., "Ernest W. McFarland: Southwestern Progressive, The United States Senate Years, 1940–52" (Ph.D. diss., Arizona State University, 1990), pp. 139–41.

62. Joseph C. Goulden, *The Best Years, 1945–1950* (New York: Atheneum, 1976), p. 60.

63. New Jersey Division of Veterans' Services, "Loan Section," *New Jersey Veteran*, February 1953, pp. 28–29.

64. President's Commission on Veterans' Pensions, *Report on Veterans' Benefits in the United States* (Staff Report No. 1, May 9, 1956), p. 161. For more on the Bradley Commission, see the other volumes of the report and the Congressional Quarterly Service, *Congress and the Nation, 1945–1964: A Review of Government and Politics in the Postwar Years*, Veterans' Benefits, 1945–64, p. 1338; Wilentz, *Women Veterans*, p. 167; *Phase 1: Summary of Reports*, November 1991, "Bradley Commission Recommendations," pp. 21–38.

65. Wilentz, *Women Veterans*, pp. 194–95.

66. William L. O'Neill, *A Democracy at War: America's Fight at Home and Abroad in World War II* (New York: Free Press, 1993), p. 329; Michael C. C. Adams, *The Best War Ever: America and World War II* (Baltimore: Johns Hopkins University Press, 1994), p. 145; Allan Bérubé, *Coming Out Under Fire: The History of Gay Men and Women in World War II* (New York: Free Press, 1990).

67. My discussion of the World War II– and reconversion-era income tax is based on the following, unless other sources are cited: Alice Kessler-Harris, " 'A Principle of Law but Not of Justice': Men, Women and Income Taxes in the United States, 1913–1948," *Southern California Review of Law and Women's Studies* 6 (Spring 1997): 331–60, though much of this discussion now appears in her book *In Pursuit of Equity: Women, Men, and the Quest for Economic Citizenship in 20th-Century America* (New York: Oxford University Press, 2001), pp. 170–202; Carolyn C. Jones, "Class Tax to Mass Tax: The Role of Propaganda in the Expansion of the Income Tax During World War II," *Buffalo Law Review* 37 (1988–89): 685–737; Carolyn C. Jones, "Split Income and Separate Spheres: Tax Law and Gender Roles in the 1940s," *Law and History Review* 6 (Fall 1988): 259–310; Edward J. McCaffery, *Taxing Women, With a New Preface* (Chicago: University of Chicago Press, 1999); John F. Witte, *The Politics and Development of the Federal Income Tax* (Madison: University of Wisconsin Press, 1985), particularly pp. 110–54; O'Neill, *Democracy at War*, pp. 92–96; Harvard Sitkoff, "The American Home Front," in Barbara McLean Ward, ed., *Produce and Conserve, Share and Play Square: The Grocer and the Consumer on the Home-Front During World War II* (Portsmouth, NH: Stawbery Banke Museum, 1994), pp. 44–45; John N. Hart, "Taxation and the War," in Kenneth Dameron, ed., *Consumer Problems in Wartime* (New York: McGraw-Hill, 1944), pp. 122–44.

68. Bartholomew H. Sparrow, *From the Outside In: World War II and the American State* (Princeton: Princeton University Press, 1996), p. 298, Table 7.5.

69. Tobey, Wetherell, and Brigham, "Moving Out and Settling In," p. 1415; "Annual Message Transmitting the Economic Report to the Congress," Jan. 28, 1954, *Public Papers of the Presidents of the United States: Dwight D. Eisenhower, 1954* (Washington, DC: USGPO, 1955), p. 217.

70. Joy Terr, "Handling Your Money," *BR, Weekend Magazine Section,* Jan. 25, 1958; Bruce Bartlett, "Tax Spending, Not Savings," *NYT,* July 6, 1997.

71. Kessler-Harris, " 'A Principle of Law but Not of Justice,' " p. 333, including *n*.3; Dennis Joseph Ventry, Jr., "The Treatment of Marriage Under the U.S. Federal Income Tax, 1913–2000" (Ph.D. diss., University of California, Santa Barbara, 2001).

72. Stanley S. Surrey, "Federal Taxation of the Family—The Revenue Act of 1948," *Harvard Law Review* 61 (1948): 1111.

73. Lawrence H. Seltzer, *The Personal Exemptions in the Income Tax* (New York: Columbia University Press, 1968), pp. 120–22.

74. Tobey, Wetherell, and Brigham, "Moving Out and Settling In," p. 1415*n*.46; "The Divine Write-Off: Republicans Tiptoe Around the Mortgage Deduction," *NYT,* Jan. 12, 1996; Henry Aaron, "Income Taxes and Housing," *American Economic Review* 60 (December 1970): 789–806; Kenneth T. Jackson, *Crabgrass Frontier: The Suburbanization of the United States* (New York: Oxford University Press, 1985), pp. 293–94, 379*n*.15.

75. McCaffery, *Taxing Women,* pp. ix–xv, 268–69; McCaffery, "Women and Taxes," National Center for Policy Analysis, February 2002, http://www.womenintheeconomy .org/publications/taxes/women&taxes2pdf; Richard W. Stevenson, "For Marriage Tax, a Messy Divorce," *NYT,* June 7, 1998; "Marriage-Penalty Proposal Could Ease Way to Tax Cut," *NYT,* Jan. 28, 2000; "House Plan Cuts Marriage Tax, Doubles Child Credit," *BG,* Mar. 30, 2001; Ann Crittenden, "Overtaxed Mothers Need Relief," *NYT,* Mar. 24, 2001, which argues that the Bush tax cut of 2001, with its modest reduction in the marriage penalty, did very little to give married women more of an incentive to work. The exception to this general pattern is the small proportion of families where the wife earns considerably more than her male spouse.

76. Margaret J. Gates, "Credit Discrimination Against Women: Causes and Solutions," *Vanderbilt Law Review* 27 (April 1974): 409–41; "Where Credit Is Due: An Update," Women's Equity Action League, *WEAL Washington Report* 7 (June 1978): 1, 6, in Cynthia Harrison Papers, Schlesinger, Carton 1, Folder 3; Oregon Student Public Interest Research Group, "No Credit for Women: Sexual Discrimination in the Marketplace of Consumer Credit," February 1973; "U.S. Seeks to End Mortgage Barriers Facing Women," *NYT,* Mar. 10, 1979; Geoffrey H. Moore and Philip A. Klein, *The Quality of Consumer Installment Credit* (New York: Columbia University Press, 1967), p. 87; Kansas Advisory Committee to the U.S. Commission on Civil Rights, *The Availability of Credit to Kansas Women,* October 1975. For a wealth of materials on discrimination on the basis of race, color, religion, national origin, age, sex, and marital status in the granting of credit, see *Hearings Before the Subcommittee on Consumer Affairs of the Committee on Banking and Currency, House of Representatives, 93rd Congress, 2nd Session on H.R. 14856 and H.R. 14908,* June 20–21, 1974, Parts 1–3.

Women's legal status improved gradually. In 1968 the IRS rules changed to let widowed, single, or divorced women declare head-of-household status and deductions. In 1973 the Federal Home Loan Bank prohibited sex discrimination by savings and loan institutions. Although the Equal Credit Opportunity Act of 1974 ended sex discrimination in individual lending, it would take fourteen more years for Congress to pass the Women's Business Ownership Act of 1988, giving women the same rights and protections when applying for commercial credit: Debra Michals, "Checks & Balances," *Smith Alumnae Quarterly*, Winter 1999–2000, p. 22.

77. Harry Sharp and Paul Mott, "Consumer Decisions in the Metropolitan Family," *JM* 21 (October 1956): 149–56; Elizabeth H. Wolgast, "Do Husbands or Wives Make the Purchasing Decisions?" *JM* 23 (October 1958): 151–58; "Bait for the Male Shopper," *BW*, Apr. 5, 1952, pp. 36, 38, 40, including A & P ad campaign, which is also discussed in Frank Stafford, "Appealing to Men Customers," *Playthings*, June 1947, p. 135; U.S. Bureau of Labor Statistics, *How American Buying Habits Change*, p. 106; Thomas S. Robertson, *Consumer Behavior* (Glenview, IL: Scott, Foresman, 1970), p. 75; Mirra Komarovsky, *Blue-Collar Marriage* (1962; reprint, New York: Random House, 1962; Vintage, 1967), pp. 222–25; Lee Rainwater, Richard D. Coleman, and Gerard Handel, *Workingman's Wife* (1959; reprint, New York: Arno, 1979), pp. 83–84, for quote on men as architects and their wives as purchasing agents; Isabella C. M. Cunningham and Robert T. Green, "Marketing Notes and Communications: Purchasing Roles in the U.S. Family, 1955 and 1973," *JM* 38 (October 1974): 61–81. Advertisements often assumed a male provider and female dependent. See, for example, an ad for the John Hancock Insurance Company, "If Jane had to support our family," that assumed the husband's total responsibility for income, both now and in the case of his death: *Life*, Mar. 11, 1957. Barbara Ehrenreich has argued that by the 1950s and 1960s, psychiatry was insisting that marriage—and within that, the breadwinner role—was the only normal state for the adult male, viewing any efforts to stray from this ideal as evidence of psychological disorder: *The Hearts of Men: American Dreams and the Flight from Commitment* (New York: Anchor, 1983), p. 15.

78. Friedman, "That Key Man, the Consumer," *NYT Magazine*, Mar. 16, 1947, pp. 20, 56; Special Issue, "The American and His Economy," *Life*, Jan. 5, 1953.

79. Miscellaneous television advertisements and programs from 1950s and 1960s, including episodes of *The Adventures of Ozzie and Harriet*, Museum of Broadcast Communications at River City, Chicago; programs of *Queen for a Day, The Price Is Right*, and *Let's Make a Deal*, Museum of Television and Radio, New York City; "The Freezer," from *I Love Lucy*, Apr. 28, 1952, CBS Video, 1998; "Classic TV Commercials: Best of 50's and 60's," Alpha Video, 1997; Mary Beth Haralovich, "Sit-coms and Suburbs: Positioning the 1950s Homemaker," in Lynn Spigel and Denise Mann, eds., *Private Screenings: Television and the Female Consumer* (Minneapolis: University of Minnesota Press, 1992), pp. 111–41; for *The Donna Reed Show* episode, see Mary Ann Watson, *Defining Visions: Television and the American Experience Since 1945* (Fort Worth, TX: Harcourt Brace, 1998), pp. 59–61.

80. "Telephone Broadcast to the AFL-CIO Merger Meeting in New York City," Dec. 5, 1955, *Public Papers of the Presidents of the United States: Dwight D. Eisenhower, 1955* (Washington, DC: USGPO, 1956), pp. 852–53.

81. Samuel P. Hays, "The Welfare State and Democratic Practice in the United States Since the Second World War," in George Reid Andrews and Herrick Chapman, eds., *The Social Construction of Democracy, 1870–1990* (New York: New York University Press, 1995), p. 269.

82. The historical literature on the Taft-Hartley Act is vast. Some of the most useful sources I found include John T. Dunlap, "A National Labor Policy," in Harris, *Saving American Capitalism*, pp. 295–308; Robert H. Zieger, *The CIO, 1935–1955* (Chapel Hill: University of North Carolina Press, 1995), pp. 246–52; Nelson Lichtenstein, "Taft-Hartley: A Slave-Labor Law?" in "Taft-Hartley Symposium: The First Fifty Years," *Catholic University Law Review* 47 (Spring 1998): 763–89; Nelson Lichtenstein, *Labor's War at Home: The CIO in World War II* (New York: Cambridge University Press, 1982), pp. 238–41; Nelson Lichtenstein, *The Most Dangerous Man in Detroit: Walter Reuther and the Fate of American Labor* (New York: Basic Books, 1995), pp. 261–70; and Melvyn

Dubofsky, *The State and Labor in Modern America* (Chapel Hill: University of North Carolina Press, 1994), pp. 202–208. Works that shed useful light on corporate efforts to contain organized labor include Howell John Harris, *The Right to Manage: Industrial Relations Policies of American Business in the 1940s* (Madison: University of Wisconsin Press, 1982); Fones-Wolf, *Selling Free Enterprise;* and Kim McQuaid, *Uneasy Partners: Big Business in American Politics, 1945–1990* (Baltimore: Johns Hopkins University Press, 1994), pp. 18–35.

83. The sources documenting labor's endorsement of a demand economy where workers enjoyed influential buying power are endless; a few particularly good examples are "Challenge to Mr. Roosevelt," *The Progressive,* Jan. 1, 1945, p. 5; "Don't Cut Production—Build Purchasing Power," *Economic Outlook,* April 1949, pp. 1–8; "Report by Walter P. Reuther," *1955 CIO Convention Proceedings,* pp. 117–21; address by George Meany upon his election as President, *1st Constitutional Convention, AFL-CIO, Proceedings,* Dec. 5–8, 1955, p. 27; Conference on Economic Progress, *Consumption, Key to Full Prosperity;* "High Wages Make for Prosperity," *AFL-CIO American Federationist,* March 1956, p. 10; "Wider Coverage Is Needed," *AFL-CIO American Federationist,* June 1956, p. 4; "Purchasing Power Increase Vital to Prosperity, AFL-CIO Declares," *AFL-CIO News,* Aug. 25, 1956, p. 2; "President Meany's Labor Day Message," *AFL-CIO American Federationist,* September 1957, pp. 15–16; "Higher Worker Buying Power Seen 'Essential' to Recovery," *AFL-CIO News,* Dec. 17, 1960, p. 2.

For discussion of COLAs and AIFs, see Lichtenstein, *The Most Dangerous Man in Detroit,* pp. 277–78. The work of Lawrence Glickman reveals that workers had endorsed a high-wage/low-price strategy to reward workers as consumers as early as the late nineteenth century; see his *A Living Wage: American Workers and the Making of Consumer Society* (Ithaca, NY: Cornell University Press, 1997).

84. "Credit Unions Save You Money," *AFL-CIO American Federationist,* September 1957, pp. 19–20; "Consumer Counselling," *Proceedings of the 2nd Constitutional Convention of the AFL-CIO,* vol. 1, Dec. 10, 1957, p. 257; "AFL-CIO to Help Workers as Buyers," *AFL-CIO News,* Dec. 27, 1958, p. 2; "Safeguarding Labor's Dollar," *AFL-CIO American Federationist,* January 1959, pp. 3–4; "Consumer Counselling," *Proceedings of the 4th Constitutional Convention of the AFL-CIO,* vol. 1, Dec. 13, 1961, p. 586.

85. "Economic Policies in the Crisis," *American Federationist,* September 1950, pp. 10–11; "Economic Trends," *Report of Proceedings of the 70th Convention of the AFL,* Sept. 17, 1951, pp. 201–206; "Report by Philip Murray: Price and Rent Control," *Proceedings of the 13th Constitutional Convention of the CIO, 1951,* pp. 86–87; "Report by Philip Murray: Suspension of Controls," *Proceedings of the 14th Constitutional Convention of the CIO, 1952,* pp. 41–43; and United Labor Conference, "United Labor's Program for Action" and "United Labor's Declaration of Principles," Mar. 21, 1951, IUE, RG1, Research and Education, Box 25, File "United Labor Policy Committee"; James B. Carey to David Lasser RE: Liberalizing Consumer Credit Regulation, Apr. 7, 1952, IUE, RG 1, Box 28, Folder 18.

Calls for tax cuts to give more purchasing power to working-class consumers include "Resolution No. 6, Tax Policy," *Final Proceedings of the 8th Constitutional Convention of the CIO,* Nov. 19, 1946, pp. 128–29; "Essential Features of a Sound Tax Program," *Economic Outlook,* April 1947, pp. 3–8; "Tax Bill Unfair," *Proceedings of the 13th Constitutional Convention of the CIO, 1951,* pp. 70–73; "Taxation," *Report of Proceedings of the 70th Convention of the AFL,* Sept. 24, 1951, p. 445. Demands for more, better, and cheaper housing were constant in the labor press and during annual meetings. See the AFL, CIO, and AFL-CIO convention proceedings, the *American Federationist,* the CIO's *Economic Outlook, AFL-CIO American Federationist,* passim, for example, "The Housing Fiasco," *Economic Outlook,* May 1951.

86. United Steelworkers of America, *The Braddock Steelworker,* 1945, p. 31; also see "A Woman's Place Is—Where?" *Talk It Over,* 1946, p. 10.

87. Testimony of New Jersey State CIO Industrial Union Council by Carl Holderman, President, at Subcommittee Hearing of the Joint Congressional Committee on the Economic Report, Trenton, New Jersey, Oct. 3, 1947, "Q" Files, NPL, p. 5.

88. The shift away from consumer-oriented activities by CIO auxiliaries can be traced in the annual Proceedings of the Constitutional Conventions of the CIO. The union label and related involvements of the AFL auxiliaries appear in the annual Reports of the Proceedings of the Conventions of the AFL and in the *American Federationist.* After the merger in 1955, auxiliary activities appeared in the Proceedings of the Constitutional Conventions of the AFL-CIO. Interestingly, the more tradition-bound AFL gave women more authority as consumers than the CIO, which had been founded only in the 1930s and was quicker to incorporate consumer issues into its mainstream agenda.

89. Cartoon, "He Could Buy More If They'd Remove the Ball from His Leg," *Economic Outlook,* April 1947, p. 3; "Can Mr. Consumer Hold His Own?" *Economic Outlook,* October 1948, p. 3; Opening Remarks by President Philip Murray, *Proceedings of the 13th Constitutional Convention of the CIO, 1951,* p. 17; illustrations in "Danger Ahead in '53 and '54," *Economic Outlook,* June 1952, pp. 41–44; speech by Walter Reuther, *Proceedings of the 8th Constitutional Convention of the CIO, 1946,* p. 243.

90. Department of Labor, *How American Buying Habits Change,* pp. 6, 196; "Worker Loses His Class Identity," *BW,* July 11, 1959, p. 90; "*Fortune* Magazine Applauds the U.S. Labor Movement, 1951," in Eileen Boris and Nelson Lichtenstein, eds., *Major Problems in the History of American Workers* (Lexington, MA: Heath, 1991), p. 507.

91. Nelson Lichtenstein has written extensively on the Treaty of Detroit. See his *The Most Dangerous Man in Detroit,* chap. 13, and a conference paper in my possession, "The Treaty of Detroit: Old Before Its Time," delivered at the American Historical Association, January 1995. Also see Kevin Boyle, *The UAW and the Heyday of American Liberalism, 1945–1968* (Ithaca, NY: Cornell University Press, 1995), pp. 1–9. Observers of labor's trade-off at the time include Roger Davenport, *USA: The Permanent Revolution* (New York: Time-Life, 1951), and Richard Lester, *As Unions Mature: An Analysis of the Evolution of American Unionism* (Princeton: Princeton University Press, 1958). An important model of this paradigm of "embourgeoisement" and the "affluent worker" was developed by British social scientists J. H. Goldthorpe, D. Lockwood, F. Bechhofer, and J. Platt in *The Affluent Worker,* 3 vols. (London: Cambridge University Press, 1968).

92. Assertions that the GI Bill created a mass middle class are ubiquitous, both in the publications of the Veterans Administration and in the discourse of the larger society. Most are unsubstantiated. For example, Federal Research Division, Library of Congress, "The Veterans Benefits Administration and Its Predecessors: An Organizational History, 1776–1993," claims that the GI Bill "served as a more general vehicle for upward mobility. Millions of veterans who had been blue-collar workers before the war were able to acquire much-improved housing and move into the middle class. . . . Large numbers of veterans who before the war had been restricted to low-paid, unskilled occupations were able to move into the professions. In short, the GI Bill served as a great equalizer in U.S. society" (pp. 69–70).

93. Keith Olson, *The G.I. Bill, the Veterans, and the Colleges* (Lexington: University Press of Kentucky, 1974), p. 47.

94. The Veterans Administration made a concerted effort in the Vietnam era to reverse its past record and offer more programs for "the educationally disadvantaged": Veterans Administration, "Historical Data on the Usage of Educational Benefits, 1944–1983," Table 1; President's Commission on Veterans' Pensions (Bradley Commission), *Readjustment Benefits: Education and Training, And Employment and Unemployment,* Staff Report

No. 9, Part B, pp. 109–10; "GI Bill's Birthday Tomorrow, Millions of Veterans Aided Over 20-Year Period," *NN,* June 21, 1964; Louis Harris and Associates, "Survey of Aging Veterans," pp. 16, 33; Richard Hammond, "1979 National Survey of Veterans, Summary Report," pp. 60–61; Educational Testing Service, *Final Report on Educational Assistance to Veterans,* pp. x, 59, 62, 98, 142–43.

95. "History & Origin of the 3 GI Bills," Part I, *The Stars and Stripes—The National Tribune,* June 10, 1976; Committee on Veterans Affairs, "The Provision of Federal Benefits for Veterans: An Historical Analysis of Major Veterans' Legislation, 1862–1954," Dec. 28, 1955, pp. 209–11; speech by Kermit Eby, director, Department of Research and Education, National CIO, "Conference on Labor and the Veteran, Sponsored by the New Jersey State Industrial Council, March 3–4, 1945," "Q" Files, "NJ State CIO Industrial Council," NPL, pp. 34–35. Eby went so far as to suggest that this aspect of the GI Bill had been written by representatives of institutions of higher learning. His charge of elitism had a long history in the drafting of the GI Bill; the original recommendation of the Osborn Committee Report to the President in 1943 had favored veterans judged to be superior in intelligence and educational preparation: National Academy of Public Administration Foundation, *GI Course Approvals,* p. 2. Also see the President's Commission on Veterans' Pensions (Bradley Commission), *Readjustment Benefits,* Staff Report No. 9, Part B, pp. 24, 41.

96. "S.R.O.," *Time,* Mar. 18, 1946, p. 75; Educational Testing Service, *Final Report on Educational Assistance to Veterans,* pp. viii, 158.

97. Testimony of New Jersey State CIO Industrial Union Council before the Subcommittee Hearing on the Joint Congressional Committee on the Economic Report, Oct. 3, 1947, pp. 13–14.

98. Remarks of Discussant Buckley and Discussant Roller, "Conference on Labor and the Veteran, Sponsored by the New Jersey State Industrial Union Council," pp. 67, 84; E. W. Wollmuth (chairman, Administrative Committee, Newark War Veterans Service Bureau) to Hon. John A. Brady (director, Department of Public Affairs, Newark), Dec. 31, 1946, Newark Document File, NPL, pp. 4–5; "Newark-Operated Veterans Bureau Hasn't Completed Single Case," *Call,* Mar. 31, 1946; "Former Sailor Aids Veterans in Getting Loans for Business," *Newark Times,* Jan. 13, 1946.

99. Boris Shishkin, "Organized Labor and the Veteran," *AAAPSS* 238 (March 1945): 156; "Altered GI Measure Would Rob Vets," *CIO News,* Dec. 17, 1945; Reports and Statistics Service, Office of Controller, Veterans Administration, "VA Benefits to World War II Veterans, 1945–1950," pp. 33–34; Goulden, *The Best Years, 1945–1950,* pp. 58, 135; from Document File "New Jersey Vets Programs," NPL: "Loan Section," *New Jersey Veteran,* February 1953, p. 28, and State of New Jersey, Division of Veterans' Services, "Veterans' Guaranteed Loan Section," p. 20; The President's Commission on Veterans' Pensions (Bradley Commission), *Readjustment Benefits: General Survey and Appraisal,* Staff Report No. 9, Part A, p. 81.

100. Robert J. Havighurst et al., *The American Veteran Back Home: A Study of Veteran Readjustment* (New York: Longmans, Green, 1951), pp. 110–11, 120–22, 143–49, 192–95.

101. Counseling Branch, Fort George G. Meade, Study by Separation Center, 1945, Anthony, Box 1, File 2.

102. Lichtenstein, *The Most Dangerous Man in Detroit,* pp. 288, 294–95; Gus Tyler, "White Workers/Blue Mood," in Irving Howe, ed., *The World of the Blue-Collar Worker* (New York: Quadrangle, 1972), p. 203; "The U.A.W.'s Fight for an Annual Wage," *Life,* June 13, 1955; Concerned Employees for Responsible Business to "Sir" [at Consumers' Research], Apr. 21, 1974, CR, General Files, Consumerism, Consumer Boycotts–General, 1967–1979, p. 1.

103. Pierre Martineau, "Social Classes and Spending Behavior," *JM* 23 (October 1958): 121–30; Lee Rainwater, Richard P. Coleman, and Gerald Handel, *Workingman's Wife*

(1959; reprint, New York: Arno, 1979), p. xii; Gerald Handel and Lee Rainwater, "Persistence and Change in Working-Class Life Style," in Arthur B. Shostak and William Gomberg, eds., *Blue-Collar World: Studies of the American Worker* (Englewood Cliffs, NJ: Prentice-Hall, 1964), pp. 36–41.

104. Ely Chinoy, *Automobile Workers and the American Dream* (1955; reprint, Boston: Beacon, 1965), p. 126; Bennett M. Berger, *Working-Class Suburb: A Study of Auto Workers in Suburbia* (1960; reprint, Berkeley: University of California Press, 1968); Lee Rainwater and Gerald Handel, "Status of the Working Class in Changing American Society," prepared for Macfadden Publications by Social Research, 1961, Manuscript Report, p. 42. For a conclusion similar to that of Berger, Rainwater, and Handel, see Milton M. Gordon and Charles H. Anderson, "The Blue-Collar Worker at Leisure," in Shostak and Gomberg, eds., *Blue-Collar World*, p. 415.

105. Daniel Bell, *The End of Ideology: On the Exhaustion of Political Ideas in the Fifties* (1962; reprint, Cambridge, MA: Harvard University Press, 1988), p. 254.

106. "Action Bulletin," Mar. 21, 1961; "Dear Brother ———," Apr. 3, 1961; Kay Rabinowitz (Rec. Sec'y) and George Moffatt to Ralph W. Burger (Chairman, The Great A & P Company), Apr. 21, 1961; Rabinowitz to C. A. Conklin (Lamp Sales Dept., Westinghouse Electric), May 4, 1961; Rabinowitz to Charles Erb (Manager, Lamp Sales Dept., Westinghouse, Bloomfield), May 4, 1961; Richard A. Lynch to David Yunich (President, Bamberger's), May 3, 1962; Lynch to Local 410 Steward and Executive Board Members, June 5, 1962; all in IUE, Box 20.

107. A valuable collection of Local 410 IUE's mimeographed newsletter, *The Torch*, has survived in the IUE Papers, stretching from 1946 through 1971. See passim for how the local endorsed the importance of workers' purchasing for their own well-being as well as Bloomfield's, Westinghouse's, and the nation's, and for their other concerns: Local 410 Materials, IUE.

108. Robert Asher, "The 1949 Speed Up Strike and the Post War Social Compact, 1946–1961," pp. 148–49; Garth L. Mangum, "Taming Wildcat Strikes," *HBR* 38 (1960): 88, cited in Lichtenstein, *Labor's War at Home*, p. 243; on wildcat striking, also see Lichtenstein, *The Most Dangerous Man in Detroit*, pp. 287–92, and Zieger, *The CIO, 1935–1955*, pp. 326–27. For graphs that show record-breaking levels of work stoppages between 1950 and 1960, see Boris and Lichtenstein, eds., *Major Problems in the History of American Workers*, Appendix, p. ii.

109. "Organization of White Collars' Calls for New Approaches," *AFL-CIO News*, Dec. 27, 1958, p. 4; polls on class identity from Nicholas Lemann, "Mysteries of the Middle Class," *New York Review of Books*, Feb. 3, 1994, p. 9.

CHAPTER 4. REBELLION: FORCING OPEN THE DOORS OF PUBLIC ACCOMMODATIONS

1. This discussion of racial discrimination toward black veterans is drawn from Charles G. Bolte and Louis Harris, *Our Negro Veterans*, Public Affairs Pamphlet No. 128 (New York: Public Affairs Committee, 1947), pp. 4, 8–15, 20–22, 25, 28–30; Neil A. Wynn, *The Afro-American and the Second World War* (New York: Holmes & Meier, 1975), pp. 114–16; Sar A. Levitan and Karen A. Cleary, *Old Wars Remain Unfinished: The Veteran Benefits System* (Baltimore: Johns Hopkins University Press, 1973), p. 4; "Negro Unit Accuses South's Postmasters," *NYT*, June 1, 1947; "Negro GI's in South Seen Shorn of Rights," *NYT*, June 2, 1947; interview with Howard "Stretch" Johnson in Peter Jennings and Todd Brewster, *The Century* (New York: Doubleday, 1998), pp. 286–87; "Conference on Labor and the Veteran, sponsored by The New Jersey State Industrial Union Council," Mar. 3–4, 1945, Newark, NJ, "Q" Files, NPL, "New Jersey State CIO Industrial Union

Council," p. 54; Howard University Medical School statistics in Michael J. Bennett, *When Dreams Came True: The GI Bill and the Making of Modern America* (Washington, DC: Brassey's, 1996), p. 268.

VA counselors in the South often treated black veterans who had received "general" or "blue" discharges (as they were commonly known) as if they were dishonorable discharges, as the army had issued them disproportionately to black "troublemakers" who protested against discriminatory treatment: David H. Onkst, " 'First a Negro . . . Incidentally a Veteran' : Black World War Two Veterans and the G.I. Bill of Rights in the Deep South, 1944–1948," *Journal of Social History* 31 (Spring 1998): 520; see more generally for excellent discussion of poor treatment of black veterans in the South.

2. On veterans' organizations, see Bolte and Harris, *Our Negro Veterans,* pp. 27–28; St. Clair Drake, *The Negro Veteran and the Church* (Washington, DC: United Negro and Allied Veterans of America, n.d. but c. 1946); "Groups Called Disloyal," *NYT,* Dec. 5, 1947; "Denies Communist Link," *NYT,* Dec. 8, 1947; "UNAVA Insists Red Charge 'Lie,' " *New York Amsterdam News,* June 24, 1947; Jane F. Levey, " 'I Went into the Army a Nigger; I'm Comin' Out a Man': Citizenship, Civil Rights, and African-American Veterans After World War II," seminar paper, Yale University, October 1995, in possession of author; Educational Testing Service, *Final Report on Educational Assistance to Veterans: A Comparative Study of Three G.I. Bills, Submitted to the Committee on Veterans' Affairs, United States Senate* (Washington DC: USGPO, 1973), pp. 14, 117–20.

3. VA survey cited in *Afro-American,* May 10, 1947, in Onkst, " 'First a Negro,' " p. 532.

4. Quoted in "Red, White, Blue—and Black," *Talk It Over* (1947), in Anthony, Box 2, p. 3.

5. Bolte and Harris, *Our Negro Veterans,* pp. 16–18; Karen Brodkin Sacks, "How Did Jews Become White Folks?" in Steven Gregory and Roger Sanjek, eds., *Race* (New Brunswick, NJ: Rutgers University Press, 1994), pp. 93–94; housing overcrowding statistics in Robert C. Weaver, *The Negro Ghetto* (New York: Russell & Russell, 1948), pp. 130–34, 264–66; E. A. Crawford to Doctor H. Boyd Hall (NAACP, Corpus Christi Branch), June 13, 1946, NAACP, II, G 11, "GI Benefits, 1945–June 1946"; *Ebony* survey in "GI Loans: Colored Vets Who Borrow Cash Prove Sound Business Investments," *Ebony* 2 (August 1947), cited in Onkst, " 'First a Negro,' " p. 522; complaints about exclusion from Veterans' Emergency Housing Program, NAACP, II, A 657, "Veterans' Housing, 1945–55"; Harry Oliver Moore (East Paterson Chamber of Commerce) to Gloster B. Current (NAACP, Paterson Branch), Oct. 23, 1950, and flyer, "Comments on Housing for Negro GIs by Harry Oliver Moore," NAACP, II, B 78, "Housing, NJ, General, 1949–50"; G. L. Holland (assistant to the administrator, VA) to Madison S. Jones (NAACP), Aug. 10, 1955, NAACP, II, A 657, "Veterans Housing, 1945–55"; also see other correspondence in NAACP, II, G 11, "GI Benefits, 1945–June 1946," and "GI Benefits, July 1946–1949."

For mortgages held by non-whites, see Table 8, "New York–Northeastern New Jersey Metropolitan Area, Owner-Occupied Properties with One Dwelling Unit: Property and Owner Characteristics, by Government Insurance Status of First Mortgage, 1950," in Bureau of the Census, U.S. Department of Commerce, *Census of Housing: 1950,* vol. 4, *Residential Financing, Mortgaged Nonfarm Properties,* Part 2, "Large Standard Metropolitan Areas," p. 517.

6. John Modell, Marc Goulden, and Sigurdur Magnusson, "World War II in the Lives of Black Americans: Some Findings and an Interpretation," *JAH* 76 (December 1989): 838–48.

7. Bennett, *When Dreams Came True,* pp. 269–71. For further testimony from blacks discriminated against as they tried to use their GI Bill education benefits, see Maggi M. Morehouse, *Fighting in the Jim Crow Army: Black Men and Women Remember World War II* (Lanham, MD: Rowman & Littlefield, 2000), pp. 203–206.

8. Interview with Lowell Steward in Studs Terkel, "*The Good War*": *An Oral History of World War Two* (New York: Pantheon, 1984), pp. 348–49.

9. Lorraine Hansberry, *A Raisin in the Sun and The Sign in Sidney Brustein's Window* (New York: Vintage, 1995), pp. 93, 148. Hansberry also recognized that satisfying their families' consumption needs bolstered men's confidence in their masculinity; her character Walter Younger measured his future manly success by the car he fantasized himself driving and the pearls his wife would wear around her neck. Judith Stein notes the same distinction between blacks' interest in ending discrimination or obtaining equality and liberal whites' obsession with integration in "History of an Idea," *The Nation*, Dec. 14, 1998, p. 13.

10. Weaver, *The Negro Ghetto*, pp. 266, 268. On Hansberry's class status and political perspective, see Ben Keppel, *The Work of Democracy: Ralph Bunche, Kenneth B. Clark, Lorraine Hansberry, and the Cultural Politics of Race* (Cambridge, MA: Harvard University Press, 1995), pp. 21–26, 177–229.

11. "Latest Thing in Klannishness: The Legion of Death in Jersey," *PM*, Mar. 26, 1941; "Full Citizenship in New Jersey," *Crisis*, October 1949; "North Jersey, Once Scene of Klan and Bund Activities, Now a Leading Center in Fight on Racial Intolerance," *NSL*, Nov. 17, 1946; Emil Frankel, "Social Work Among Negroes in New Jersey" (read before the meeting of the New Jersey Conference of Social Work, December 1929), *Hospital Social Service* 21 (1930): 339–46; Clement Alexander Price, ed., *Freedom Not Far Distant: A Documentary History of Afro-Americans in New Jersey* (Newark: New Jersey: Historical Society, 1980), pp. 194–201, 241, 312; Price, "The Strange Career of Race Relations in New Jersey History," *The Black Experience in Southern New Jersey, Papers Presented at a Symposium at the Camden County Historical Society, February 11–12, 1984* (Camden: Camden County Historical Society, 1985), pp. 10–17; Mamie Elaine Francis, "New Jersey: Those Inimitable Individualists," *The Messenger* 7 (August 1925), reprinted in Tom Lutz and Susanna Ashton, eds., *These "Colored" United States: African American Essays from the 1920s* (New Brunswick, NJ: Rutgers University Press, 1996), p. 191.

12. On school segregation in New Jersey, see in NAACP, II, A 624: Joseph L. Bustard, "The New Jersey Story, Concerning the Development of Racially Integrated Public Schools, Presented at a Conference on the Courts and Racial Integration in Education," Howard University, Apr. 16–18, 1952, pp. 3–4, and "Plague Spots in New Jersey," *Bulletin I*, November 1937, attached to E. Frederic Morrow to Branch Officer, Nov. 4, 1937; *Report of the New Jersey State Temporary Commission on the Condition of the Urban Colored Population to the Legislature of the State of New Jersey, 1939*, NPL, pp. 38–44; *Annual Report of the Urban Colored Population Commission, State of New Jersey, Year Ending December 31, 1943*, NPL, for discussion of Trenton case of successful protest against segregated New Lincoln Junior High School; Price, ed., *Freedom Not Far Distant*, p. 248; Document 79: "Away from the Democratic Ideal: Segregation in the Schools (1941)," in Howard L. Green, ed., *Words That Make New Jersey History* (New Brunswick, NJ: Rutgers University Press, 1995), pp. 236–37.

13. *The Negro in New Jersey, Report of a Survey by the Interracial Committee of the New Jersey Conference of Social Work in Cooperation with the State Department of Institutions and Agencies*, December 1932, pp. 19, 65–67.

14. For a very rich file on the struggle to integrate Atlantic City's movie theaters, see NAACP, I, G 115, "New Jersey Conference (Atlantic City Theatre Discrimination Case 1937–38)."

15. Barbara J. Kukla, *Swing City: Newark Nightlife, 1925–50* (Philadelphia: Temple University Press, 1991), pp. 3–8, 147; for "nigger heaven," see "William M. Ashby—A Tireless Leader," *New Community Clarion*, Ashby Papers, NPL. Price's *Freedom Not Far Distant* is invaluable for insight into conditions for blacks in the city and state during the

1930s and 1940s; also see Price, "The Beleaguered City as Promised Land: Blacks in Newark, 1917–1947," in Maxine N. Lurie, ed., *A New Jersey Anthology* (Newark: New Jersey Historical Society, 1994), pp. 436–61.

16. *Report of the NJ Temporary Commission on the Condition of the Urban Colored Population, 1939,* pp. 37–38.

17. John T. Cunningham, *Newark,* rev. ed. (Newark: New Jersey Historical Society, 1988), p. 282; *Report of the NJ Temporary Commission on the Condition of the Urban Colored Population, 1939,* pp. 5–6.

18. "Summary of the Activities of the Newark Interracial Council in Endeavor to Open Newark City and Other Hospitals, to Negro Professionals," "Q" Files, NPL, "Interracial Council"; *Report of the NJ Temporary Commission on the Condition of the Urban Colored Population, 1939,* pp. 31–35; interview with Harold Lett, Jan. 4 and Feb. 20, 1974, in Price, ed., *Freedom Not Far Distant,* pp. 229–30.

19. Memo to Miss Crump from F. D. Reeves, Aug. 22, 1941, also see E. Frederic Morrow to Intercity Bus Transportation Company, June 9, 1942, NAACP, II, B 187, "Transportation, General, 1940–42"; "Report of the Executive Director, New Jersey Negro Welfare Commission, July 23–September 11, 1942," NPL, p. 3; *Annual Report of the Urban Colored Population Commission, 1943;* "No J.C. Air Raid Shelters in N.J.," *NJAA,* Oct. 10, 1942. For more on blacks' experience in New Jersey during the war, see Helen Jackson Lee's memoir, *Nigger in the Window* (Garden City, NY: Doubleday, 1978), and New Jersey cases in NAACP, II, B 61, "Discrimination: Bars, Hotels, Restaurants, 1940–42."

20. For blacks' experience on Newark's home front, see memorandum to Mr. Warren Banner from H. A. Lett, Feb. 9, 1943, "Observations on Problems in the Newark Area," National Urban League Papers, Library of Congress, Series 6, D 63, folder "Newark, NJ, Misc. Correspondence and Notes, 1942–43," which charts some improvement in blacks' prospects after the dismal 1930s, particularly in employment; Kukla, *Swing City,* pp. 9–10; Kenneth T. Jackson, "Gentleman's Agreement: Race, Poverty, and Suburban Discrimination in Metropolitan America," Twentieth Century Fund Report, "Chapter 4: Industrial Workhouse and Bucolic Suburbs, 1910–1960," n.p. For the ongoing discrimination against blacks as clerks in department stores, see National Urban League, "Integration of Negroes in Department Stores: Practical Approaches for the Integration of Negroes in Department Store Personnel," July 1946, NAACP, II, A 333, and "Department Store Discrimination, 1945–49," particularly pp. 4, 6 on Newark; also see other related material in same file. The OPA statistics are from State of New Jersey Urban Colored Population Commission, *New Jersey Negro in World War II,* 1945, NPL, p. 6; an OPA report to the NAACP calculates the totals as of April 30, 1945, somewhat differently, but reveals equally poor representation of blacks; Frances Williams (OPA) to Walter White, Aug. 31, 1945, NAACP, II, A 462, "OPA 1945," Table 5.

21. "Jim Crow in Chinese Cafe," *NJAA,* Nov. 7, 1942; "White Cab Driver Loses License for Refusing Fare," *NJAA,* Dec. 18, 1943; "Theatre's J.C. Policy Draws Dual Attack," *NJAA,* Oct. 10, 1942; "Opposes Separate Negro USO Center," *NN,* Oct. 23, 1943; "Jim-Crow USO Plan Defeated," *NJAA,* Nov. 20, 1943; "Historical Summary: The Interracial Movement in Newark," c. 1946, "Q" Files, NPL, "Interracial Council," pp. 5–6 for protests against the Red Cross and p. 9 on the riot; "ABC Board Aids Racial Trade Ban," *NJAA,* July 5, 1941; "Tavern Owner Sued for Overcharging," *NJAA,* Aug. 29, 1942; "Both Races Picket Newark Tavern," *NJAA,* Sept. 19, 1942; Robert A. Hill, ed., *The FBI's RACON: Racial Conditions in the United States During World War II* (Boston: Northeastern University Press, 1995), p. 168; Clement A. Price, "The Struggle to Desegregate Newark: Black Middle Class Militancy in New Jersey, 1932–1947," *New Jersey History* 99 (1981): 215–28; NAACP, II, B 61, folder "Civil Rights, New Jersey, 1941–48."

22. Curtis Lucas, *Third Ward Newark* (Chicago: Ziff Davis, 1946), pp. 38, 40, 69–70,

73. The FBI's informants reported "no foreign-inspired agitation" but still noted "frequent voicings of dissatisfaction and unrest"; Hill, ed., *The FBI's RACON*, pp. 166–68.

23. William M. Ashby, *Tales Without Hate* (Newark: Newark Preservation and Landmarks Committee, 1996), passim and p. 188.

24. Harry Hazelwood, Jr. (Newark Branch, NAACP), to Mr. Current (Director of Branches), Feb. 18, 1948, NAACP, II, C 110, "Newark, New Jersey, 1940–42"; see NAACP, II, B 61, "Discrimination, 1946," passim, for a range of protests; "Skating Rink Race Trouble Called All Negroes' Fault," *BR*, Jan. 15, 1947; Housing Authority of the City of Newark, *Public Housing in Newark*, November 1944, NPL; "Housing Survey, Third Ward, Newark, NJ," January 1938, NPL; "Medical Board President," *NJAA*, Jan. 31, 1942; Cunningham, *Newark*, p. 301; Price, "The Struggle to Desegregate Newark," p. 224.

25. Urban Colored Population Commission, State of New Jersey, *Fourth Annual Report: Discrimination in Public Places and the Civil Rights Laws of New Jersey*, 1946, NPL, pp. 45, 52–54, 76–77.

26. An excellent summary of New Jersey's efforts to protect civil rights, and particularly of the state's Division Against Discrimination, can be found in John P. Milligan, "Perspective on: Civil Rights in New Jersey," reprint from *NJEA Review*, March 1956, NPL, "NJ Law and Public Safety Dept., Civil Rights Division." Also see "Civil Rights in New Jersey," 1961, and "Report to John P. Milligan," June 4, 1958, Lett, Box 1, and Barbara Williams Prabhu, ed., *Spotlight on New Jersey Government*, 6th ed. (New Brunswick: League of Women Voters of New Jersey Education Fund and Rutgers University Press, 1992), p. 200.

27. On the new state constitution, see Marion Thompson Wright, "Extending Civil Rights in New Jersey through the Division Against Discrimination," reprint of an article appearing in the *Journal of Negro History*, January 1953 (Washington, DC: Association for the Study of Negro Life and History, 1953), NPL, "N.J. Civil Rights," pp. 100–102; Prabhu, *Spotlight on New Jersey Government*, pp. 3–4; Price, *Freedom Not Far Distant*, pp. 248–49, 260–69; Cunningham, *Newark*, p. 300; John T. Cunningham, *New Jersey: America's Main Road* (Garden City, NY: Doubleday, 1966), pp. 301–302. On the successes and failures of integrating New Jersey's schools, see Wright, "Extending Civil Rights in New Jersey," pp. 102–103.

28. *Civil Liberties in New Jersey, A Report Submitted to The Honorable Alfred E. Driscoll, Governor of New Jersey by the Committee on Civil Liberties*, Apr. 22, 1948, NPL, p. 17; also see State of New Jersey, Governor's Committee on Civil Liberties, "Memorandum on Behalf of Joint Council for Civil Rights in Support of a Proposed Comprehensive Civil Rights Act for New Jersey," 1948, NAACP, II, B 8, "Civil Rights, New Jersey 1941–48."

29. On the Freeman Civil Rights Act, see "Civil Rights Bill Advanced," *NN*, Mar. 15, 1949; Clifford R. Moore, "Full Citizenship in New Jersey," *The Crisis* 56 (October 1949): 272–73; "Rights Bill Passed by Jersey Senate," *NYT*, Mar. 15, 1949; "Jersey Bans Bias in Hotels, Bars, Theatres, on Beaches, Boardwalks," *NYT*, Mar. 17, 1949; "Civil Rights in Jersey," *New York Herald Tribune*, Mar. 20, 1949; "Civil Rights Bill Signed in Jersey," *NYT*, Apr. 6, 1949. On the lobbying effort behind the bill's success, see NAACP, II, B 61 (Legal Files, 1940–55), "Civil Rights, New Jersey, 1941–48": Shad Polier to Roy Wilkins, May 4, 1948, with memo to Shad Polier from Leo Pfeffer, May 4, 1948, and State of New Jersey, Governor's Committee on Civil Liberties, "Memorandum on Behalf of Joint Council for Civil Rights in Support of a Proposed Comprehensive Civil Rights Act for New Jersey," Feb. 17, 1948; and "Report of Legislative Committee, New Jersey State Conference of NAACP Branches," Mar. 26, 1949, NAACP, II, B 8, "Civil Rights NJ, 1949." For extension of the state's anti-discrimination law to cover employment in the military in 1951, public housing in 1954, and house purchases guaranteed by FHA, VA, and other government

loans in 1957, see "N.J. Marks Civil Rights Progress," *NN,* Nov. 5, 1959. For efforts to publicize protections under New Jersey's anti-discrimination laws to the public, see New Jersey Department of Education, "A Primer for the Public on the New Jersey 'Law Against Discrimination,' " c. 1951, NPL, "New Jersey Law and Public Safety Civil Rights Division"; Essex County Intergroup Council, "What Are Your Rights?" c. 1955, Anthony.

30. Chester Rapkin and Eunice and George Grier, "Group Relations in Newark—1957: Problems, Prospects, and a Program for Research," report of Newark Interracial Council, 1957, NPL, pp. 59–60, on how things had changed for the better.

31. Division Against Discrimination, State of New Jersey, *Renting Policies and Practices of Motels to Non-Whites in New Jersey,* June 1955, NPL; for a listing of New Jersey accommodations willing to accept blacks, see *Travelguide: Vacation & Recreation Without Humiliation,* 1949, Schomburg, "Resorts," pp. 45–49; Milligan, "Perspective on: Civil Rights in New Jersey."

32. "The Negro in Essex Series," *NN:* "The Negro in Essex: No Bed of Roses, His Position Here Is Better—But," Apr. 23, 1956; "No Fiery Crosses, but Housing Is His Big Problem," Apr. 24, 1956; "Dissatisfied Pupil, Sees Segregation in County's Schools," Apr. 25, 1956; "Good Jobs Aplenty," Apr. 26, 1956; "Money and the Vote: In These He Is Equal with Whites," Apr. 27, 1956. Enforcement of New Jersey's laws against discrimination in public accommodations improved with the eventual move of the DAD into the Department of Law and Public Safety. For an overview of the "Unfinished Business" as of 1961, including employment, education, housing, and public accommodations, see "Civil Rights in New Jersey," 1961, Lett, Box 1. For more on the lack of progress in other sectors of civil rights, see the *Newark News* series cited and the sources listed below.

For barriers to employment opportunity, see in NPL: Law and Public Safety, Civil Rights Division, Division Again Discrimination, State of New Jersey, "Report of a Preliminary Study of Employment Practices Involving Minority Workers, Union County, New Jersey, February, 1948," p. 12, and Division Against Discrimination, State of New Jersey, "Follow-up Survey of Selected Satisfactorily Adjusted Employment Complaints," July 1960; National Urban League, "Integration of Negroes in Department Stores, Practical Approaches for the Integration of Negroes in Department Store Personnel," July 1946, NAACP, II, A 333; "Department Store Discrimination, 1945–49," pp. 4, 6 for Newark. In 1962, Adolph Holmes of the Essex County Urban League testified to the U.S. Civil Rights Commission that in the banking industry in Essex County, only 150 of 4000 employees were black, and all except three or so tellers were in custodial, messenger, or other menial jobs: *Hearings Before the U.S. Commission on Civil Rights,* Newark, NJ, Sept. 11–12, 1962, p. 12. By the end of 1962, 71 percent of the complaints filed with the DAD since its inception were for employment discrimination: Division of Civil Rights, State of New Jersey, "Complaint Report, November & December 1962," NPL, "Law and Public Safety Dept., Civil Rights Division."

On the continuing segregation of New Jersey's schools, see "Report of the Newark Branch, NAACP, vol. 1, no. 1 (September 1951) in NAACP, II, C 110, "Newark, NJ, 1951–52"; in NAACP, II, A 624, "Supreme Court—School Cases—New Jersey, 1952–55," see Bustard, "The New Jersey Story, Concerning the Development of Racially Integrated Schools," pp. 6–10; Norma Jensen, "A Survey of the Public School Systems in the State of New Jersey, Made Under the Direction of the New Jersey State Conference of NAACP Branches," 1947; material on Englewood school segregation case, 1954–55. Also, Price, *Freedom Not Far Distant,* pp. 251, 253, on Englewood, and Jack Washington, *The Quest for Equality: Trenton's Black Community: 1890–1965* (Trenton: Africa World Press, 1993), pp. 104–13, on Trenton.

Other relevant material on continued segregation include for housing, Division

Against Discrimination, State of New Jersey, "Policies and Practices of New Jersey Housing Authorities with Respect to Minority Groups," August 1956, NPL, "Law and Public Safety Dept., Civil Rights Division," p. 4; for hospitals, Division Against Discrimination, State of New Jersey, "Report on a Survey of Eighty-five General Hospitals in New Jersey," November 1949, NPL, "Law and Public Safety Department, Civil Rights Division"; for unfairness of judicial system, see discussion of the "Trenton Six" cause célèbre, in Price, *Freedom Not Far Distant,* pp. 251–52, 277–82, and Washington, *Quest for Equality,* pp. 113–20.

For quotation, Jack Greenberg, *Race Relations and American Law* (New York: Columbia University Press, 1959), p. 113.

33. On the struggle over defining facilities as public or private, see Jack Greenberg's very helpful *Race Relations and American Law,* Chapter 3, "Public Accommodations and Services," pp. 79–114. The Committee on Civil Liberties complained that "the discrimination practiced in bowling alleys is strengthened and excused by the local proprietor because of a rule of the American Bowling Congress that it will not list the record of any team which is Negro or has a Negro player on it," in "Civil Liberties in New Jersey," p. 17. Also on bowling discrimination, Harold A. Lett to the Editor, n.d., Lett, Box 1. For cases involving skating rinks, see NAACP, II, A 238, "Discrimination: Skating Rinks," and "Organizations Map Fight on Skating Rink's Color Bars," *NJAA,* Aug. 16, 1947. On the Palisades Amusement Park pool case, see Milligan, "Perspective on: Civil Rights in New Jersey," n.p.; material in NAACP, II, B 63, folder "Discrimination, General, 1948 (June–July)"; "New Jersey Pool Race Policy Challenged," *ACLU Press Service,* Aug. 11, 1947, clippings file, 1925–1974, "Civil Rights New Jersey," Schomburg; "Palisades Park Protests Result in 19 New Arrests," *NJAA,* Sept. 6, 1947; and August Meier and Elliott Rudwick, *CORE: A Study in the Civil Rights Movement, 1942–1968* (Urbana: University of Illinois Press, 1975), pp. 57–58. On the exemption of barbershops and beauty parlors, see "Memorandum, Harold A. Lett to John P. Milligan, May 22, 1956, Subject: Discrimination in Barber Shops," Lett, Box 1. On the continued segregation of private pools and swimming clubs, see "The Negro in Essex: No Bed of Roses," *NN,* Apr. 23, 1956; Division Against Discrimination, State of New Jersey, "Policies and Practices of Admission of Certain Inland Swimming Facilities in New Jersey," November 1959, NPL, "Law and Public Safety Department, Civil Rights Division"; "Jersey Beach Club Is Accused of Bias" (no newspaper title available), Aug. 3, 1958, Schomburg; "Swim Club in Hot Water Over Bias," *NJAA,* Oct. 3, 1964.

34. On the involvement of Jews in the civil rights struggle in New Jersey, and the link they identified between discrimination against them and against blacks, see "New Jersey Civil-Rights Bill, Extension of Remarks of Hon. Hugh J. Addonizio of New Jersey, House of Representatives," *Congressional Record,* Mar. 24, 1949; Charles Abrams, " '. . . Only the Very Best Christian Clientele': Discrimination in Hotels and Resorts: U.S.A., 1955," *Commentary,* January 1955, pp. 10–17; Price, "Strange Career of Race Relations," p. 14.

35. New Jersey Recreation Commission, "Report to the Legislature," February 1950, NPL. The effort to open up beaches to the public reached beyond New Jersey and into the 1960s. "NAACP to Fight Curbs at Beaches," *NYT,* May 8, 1960, describes a campaign targeting the thousands of miles of beaches and public parks maintained with tax funds "from Cape May, New Jersey, to Brownsville, Texas."

36. Marian Wynn Perry to Miss Hilda Vaughn, Sept. 4, 1946, NAACP, II, B 67, "Discrimination in Theaters, General 1945–49"; Abrams, " '. . . Only the Very Best Christian Clientele,' " *Commentary,* p. 10.

37. For a recent overview of civil rights efforts in the 1940s and 1950s, see Steven F. Lawson and Charles Payne, *Debating the Civil Rights Movement, 1945–1968* (Lanham, MD: Rowman & Littlefield, 1998). On President Truman's efforts in the late 1940s, see *To*

Secure These Rights: The Report of the President's Committee on Civil Rights (Washington, DC: USGPO, 1947); Peter J. Kellogg, "Civil Rights Consciousness in the 1940s," *The Historian* 42 (November 1979): 18–41. For a case study of one CORE chapter's struggle to gain equal access to public accommodations by a participant, see Mary Kimbrough and Margaret W. Dagen, *Victory Without Violence: The First Ten Years of the St. Louis Committee of Racial Equality (CORE), 1947–1957* (Columbia: University of Missouri Press, 2000), particularly pp. 41–92.

38. On challenges to segregated commercial spaces in Birmingham from the 1940s to 1960s, see the pathbreaking work of Robin Kelley, " 'We Are Not What We Seem': Rethinking Black Working-Class Opposition in the Jim Crow South," *JAH* 80 (June 1993): 75–112; and Louise Maxwell, "Remaking Jim Crow: The Battle over Segregation in Birmingham, Alabama, 1938–1963" (Ph.D. diss., New York University, 1999). Also, Papers of William O. Reichert, 1958–60, WHS, on civil rights activism around sites of consumption in Lexington, Kentucky.

39. David J. Garrow, ed., *The Montgomery Bus Boycott and the Women Who Started It: The Memoir of Jo Ann Gibson Robinson* (Nashville: University of Tennessee Press, 1987), particularly pp. 97, 165; Aldon D. Morris, *The Origins of the Civil Rights Movement: Black Communities Organizing for Change* (New York: Free Press, 1984), pp. 48–76; Miles Wolff, *Lunch at the 5 & 10*, rev. ed. (Chicago: Dee, 1990), pp. 173–74; Merrill Proudfoot, *Diary of a Sit-in* (Chapel Hill: University of North Carolina Press, 1962), p. 185; Howell Raines, *My Soul Is Rested: The Story of the Civil Rights Movement in the Deep South* (New York: Penguin, 1983), pp. 27–34, 38–59, 83–105, 151, 437–44; Cynthia Griggs Fleming, *Soon We Will Not Cry: The Liberation of Ruby Doris Smith Robinson* (Lanham, MD: Rowman & Littlefield, 1998), pp. 54–58; Fleming, "White Lunch Counters and Black Consciousness: The Story of the Knoxville Sit-ins," *Tennessee Historical Quarterly* 49 (Spring 1990): 40–52; Andrea Oppenheimer Dean, "Savannah's Law," *Historic Preservation*, January–February 1995, p. 33; Ted Ownby, *American Dreams in Mississippi: Consumers, Poverty & Culture, 1830–1998* (Chapel Hill: University of North Carolina Press, 1999), pp. 149–58; Juan Williams, *Eyes on the Prize: America's Civil Rights Years, 1954–1965* (New York: Penguin, 1987), pp. 126–35. For particularly rich material on the Jackson, Mississippi, boycott, see Papers of John R. Salter, Jr., WHS, Box 1, Files 14, 15, and 17. Salter defended the boycott at the heart of the "Jackson Movement" in his notes: "Boycott entrenched as a 'permanent institution'—continued. Weakened the businessmen who eventually did make concessions; drove wedge between Jackson businessmen on the one hand, and CC [Citizens Council] on the other. Businessmen tired of suffering economically because of dictates of CC—Weakened Jackson complied with CR [Civil Rights] Act of '64." "Notes by JRS re Jackson Movement," Box 1, Folder 14. The Jackson boycott and sit-ins were vividly described by a participant, Anne Moody, in her memoir, *Coming of Age in Mississippi* (New York: Dell, 1968), pp. 263–76, 364.

40. Southern Regional CORE Papers, National CORE Papers (1941–67), and Mississippi CORE Papers, latter on microfilm, WHS, for material on national Variety Store Boycott Project, Freedom Rides, and Freedom Highways Project, and local selective buying campaigns and public accommodations testing. For Chicago CORE Chapter's support for these efforts, see CORE Papers, CHS; and also Meier and Rudwick, *CORE*.

41. For history of sites of consumption as contested space in the South back to the late nineteenth century, see Grace Elizabeth Hale, *Making Whiteness: The Culture of Segregation in the South, 1890–1940* (New York: Pantheon, 1998), pp. 121–97; Ownby, *American Dreams in Mississippi*; Gerald David Jaynes and Robin M. Williams, Jr., eds., *A Common Destiny: Blacks and American Society* (Washington, DC: National Academy Press, 1989), pp. 221–23. On whites' use of boycotts, see interview with Virginia Durr in Williams, *Eyes*

on the Prize, p. 82; Ownby, *American Dreams in Mississippi*, pp. 156–57; "Conflict in Dixie: Whites Boycott Whites Thought to Support Integration of Schools," *WSJ*, Mar. 9, 1956; "All-Out Segregationists Vow No Retreat Despite New Negro Militancy," *WSJ*, May 23, 1963.

42. As quoted in Clarence Mitchell, "The Civil Rights Scene, 1954–1969," *The Crisis*, November 1980, p. 355, also pp. 356–57; for discussion of the limitations in federal protections in public accommodations, see Robert D. Loevy, *To End All Segregation: The Politics of the Passage of the Civil Rights Act of 1964* (New York: United Press of America, 1990), pp. 29–31, 38, 45–46, 74–75, 89, 95–97, 100, 111, 183, 286; *Civil Rights Act of 1964: What It Means to . . . Employers, Businessmen, Unions, Employees, Minority Groups: Text, Analysis, Legislative History* (Washington, DC: BNA, 1964), p. 81; Joseph William Singer, "No Right to Exclude: Public Accommodations and Private Property," *Northwestern Law Review* 90 (Summer 1996): 1288–90, 1296–97, 1300–1301; Charles Whalen and Barbara Whalen, *The Longest Debate: A Legislative History of the 1964 Civil Rights Act* (Washington, DC: Seven Locks, 1985), pp. 34–35, 47.

43. E. Franklin Frazier, *Black Bourgeoisie: The Rise of a New Middle Class in the United States* (1957; reprint, New York: Collier Books, 1962).

44. Barbara Dianne Savage makes a similar point about much of black radio broadcasting through the 1940s and 1950s, which she argues embraced "the politics of inclusion, a strategy grounded in making claims for themselves based on their Americanness. This approach of arguing for inclusion as opposed to a more nationalist strategy of embracing exclusion characterized this period," which she suggests stretched into the 1950s and early 1960s. Although this "dominant black discourse of the postwar era [which] called for full American rights and full access to the nation's institutions and privileges" could be viewed as conservative on its face, Savage adds, achieving its goals "would require an aggressive and unified claim for freedom by African Americans and a willingness to engage in the struggle necessary to attain it": *Broadcasting Freedom: Radio, War, and the Politics of Race, 1938–1948* (Chapel Hill: University of North Carolina Press, 1999), pp. 45, 243.

45. John Lewis quoted in Williams, *Eyes on the Prize*, p. 139; Baldwin quoted in Louis E. Lomax, *The Negro Revolt* (New York: New American Library, 1963), p. 88. For a similar testimonial by a civil rights activist who linked the denial of his rights as a consumer to his larger politicization, see interview with Hosea Williams in Raines, *My Soul Is Rested*, pp. 437–44.

46. Waldo E. Martin, Jr., *Brown v. Board of Education: A Brief History with Documents* (Boston: Bedford/St. Martin's, 1998), pp. 11–12.

47. Quoted in Williams, *Eyes on the Prize*, p. 136. Philip Roth captures the appeal of the public accommodations struggle to people on the left more generally when he has his Communist protagonist Ira Ringold declare in Newark of 1948, "A Negro has the right to eat any damn place he feels like paying the check!": Roth, *I Married a Communist* (Boston: Houghton Mifflin, 1998), p. 91.

48. Ella Baker, "Bigger Than a Hamburger," *Southern Patriot*, June 1960, quoted in Williams, *Eyes on the Prize*, p. 137. For more on Baker and her involvement with the consumer movement, see my Chapters 1 and 2.

49. "The Negro in Essex: Money and the Vote, In These He Is Equal with Whites," *NN*, Apr. 27, 1956.

CHAPTER 5. RESIDENCE: INEQUALITY IN MASS SUBURBIA

1. On Film, Inc. for *Redbook* magazine, *In the Suburbs*, 1957, 19:30 minutes, 35 mm, from Rick Prelinger, ed., *Our Secret Century: Archival Films from the Darker Side of the*

American Dream, vol. 6, *The Uncharted Landscape,* Voyager CD, 1996. On *Redbook,* see Nancy A. Walker, ed., *Women's Magazines, 1940–1960: Gender Roles and the Popular Press* (Boston: Bedford/St. Martin's, 1998), p. 4.

2. New York World's Fair Corporation, *Your World of Tomorrow,* informational brochure on "Democracity" (New York, 1939), cited in A. Joan Saab, "Painting the Town Red (and White and Blue): Art and Politics in 1930s New York" (Ph.D. diss., New York University, 1999), pp. 297–312.

3. Editors of *Fortune, The Changing American Market* (Garden City, NY: Hanover House, 1955), p. 76; "The Lush New Suburban Market," *Fortune,* November 1953, pp. 128–31; "Suburban Customers—Sometimes Strange, Indeed . . . but They Promise Prosperity," *Newsweek,* Apr. 1, 1957, pp. 40–41 (note *Newsweek's* identification of the typical suburban homeowner as "he," consistent with my discussion in Chapter 3); also see the rest of this special issue on "The New America," and "The Boom in Suburban Recreation," *Playthings,* January 1959, pp. 108–109. For 1950–60 population shift in metropolitan areas, see Jon C. Teaford, *The Twentieth-Century American City: Problem, Promise, and Reality* (Baltimore: Johns Hopkins University Press, 1986), p. 98. On growth in consumer spending on automobiles and housing, see U.S. Bureau of the Census, *The Statistical History of the United States* (New York: Basic Books, 1976), cited in Richard L. Florida and Marshall M. A. Feldman, "Housing in US Fordism," *International Journal of Urban and Regional Research* 12 (June 1988): 198; Elaine Tyler May, *Homeward Bound: American Families in the Cold War Era* (New York: Basic Books, 1988), pp. 165–66. On the rise in homeownership rates, see Table 2.

4. On the home as a setting for developing middle-class identity, see Richard Bushman, *The Refinement of America: Persons, Houses, Cities* (New York: Vintage, 1993), and Stuart Blumin, *The Emergence of the Middle Class: Social Experience in the American City, 1760–1900* (New York: Cambridge University Press, 1989). On earlier eras of suburbanization, see Margaret Marsh, *Suburban Lives* (New Brunswick, NJ: Rutgers University Press, 1990); Robert Fishman, *Bourgeois Utopias: The Rise and Fall of Suburbia* (New York: Basic Books, 1987); Kenneth Jackson, *Crabgrass Frontier: The Suburbanization of the United States* (New York: Oxford University Press, 1985); Michael H. Ebner, *Creating Chicago's North Shore: A Suburban History* (Chicago: University of Chicago Press, 1988); Mary Sies, "Paradise Retained: An Analysis of Persistence in Planned, Exclusive Suburbs, 1880–1980," *Planning Perspectives* 12 (1997): 165–91.

Home building in the 1920s tended to take place within city limits more than it did in the postwar era. For example, 74 percent of home building in Chicago in 1927 took place within the boundaries of the central city; in 1954 the figures were reversed, with only 28 percent inside and 72 percent outside: Mark I. Gelfand, *A Nation of Cities: The Federal Government and Urban America, 1933–1965* (New York: Oxford University Press, 1975), p. 218. The Great Depression brought the outward migration of the 1920s to an abrupt halt, while the shortages of labor, construction supplies, and tires and gasoline during the war kept a lid on how fast home building could resume: "The Lush New Suburban Market," *Fortune,* p. 129; Homer Hoyt, "The Structure of American Cities in the Post-War Era," *AJS* 48 (January 1943): 480. By 1949 only 4 percent of all builders and developers were constructing 45 percent of new dwelling units in the U.S., a dramatic shift in scale from the previous decades: Marc A. Weiss, *The Rise of the Community Builders* (New York: Columbia University Press, 1987), p. 161; for the sharp rise in housing starts, see Teaford, *Twentieth Century American City,* p. 100. For New Jersey's early suburban history, see Susanne Hand, "Making the Suburban State: Teenagers, Design, and Communities in New Jersey," in Kathryn Grover, ed., *Teenage New Jersey, 1941–1975* (Newark: New Jersey Historical Society, 1997), pp. 14–15.

5. John T. Cunningham, *New Jersey: America's Main Road* (Garden City, NY: Doubleday, 1966), pp. 302–303; Division of State and Regional Planning, Department of Community Affairs, State of New Jersey, "The Housing Crisis in New Jersey, 1970," NPL, pp. 9–13; Rutgers—State University Bureau of Economic Research in contract to State of New Jersey Department of Conservation and Economic Development Division of State and Regional Planning for the Meadowlands Regional Development Agency and the State of New Jersey, *Technical Report No. 1H: Patterns of Urban Growth and Decline, A Study of the Socio-Economic and Housing Characteristics of the Core Area of the Nine-County Northeastern–New Jersey Region*, November 1966, Erber, Box A, Folder 7, p. 1H-38; Robert W. Lake, *The New Suburbanites: Race and Housing in the Suburbs* (New Brunswick, NJ: Center for Urban Policy Research, Rutgers, 1981), p. 48.

Kenneth Jackson points out that Newark, one of the nation's leading industrial centers in the nineteenth century, began to lose its upper-class residents to a first ring of suburbs as early as the 1920s: Jackson, *Crabgrass Frontier*, pp. 322–23. But generally, the population losses in established urban centers reached unprecedented levels after World War II. Of the twenty-five largest cities in 1950, eighteen lost a substantial share of population by 1990: for example, Baltimore lost 22 percent, Philadelphia 23 percent, Chicago 25 percent, Boston 28 percent, Detroit 44 percent, and Cleveland 45 percent: Jackson, "America's Rush to Suburbia," *NYT*, June 9, 1996.

6. Interview with Cele Roberts in Brett Harvey, *The Fifties: A Women's Oral History* (New York: HarperCollins, 1993), p. 113. Many factors influenced whether or not individuals or social groups left urban neighborhoods; for one case study, see Gerald Gamm, *Urban Exodus: Why the Jews Left Boston and the Catholics Stayed* (Cambridge, MA: Harvard University Press, 1999).

7. Ernest Erber, "New Jersey: Issues and Action," *Regional Plan News*, no. 83 (April 1967): 12, 15; for details of New Jersey's highway construction, see New Jersey State Highway Department, *Highways: A Review of the New Jersey State Highway Department, 1954–1962*, 1962. National highway legislation in 1944, 1956, and 1958 went beyond New Deal efforts and helped make possible the construction of more than 350,000 miles of federally aided highways between 1950 and 1960: Florida and Feldman, "Housing in US Fordism," p. 197.

8. "Why Does Business Move to New Jersey?" *BR*, May 31, 1968; Mark A. Stuart, *Bergen County, New Jersey: History and Heritage*, vol. 7, *Our Era, 1960–Present* (Hackensack: Bergen County Board of Chosen Freeholders, 1983), pp. 25–29; "Annual Trans-Hudson Passengers," c. 1980, Erber, Box B, loose papers; Erber, "New Jersey: Issues and Action," p. 14. New Deal agencies also helped prepare the way for postwar suburbanization, through funding such projects as the Lincoln Tunnel under the Hudson River and the electrification of the Pennsylvania Railroad's New Jersey Division; see Joel Schwartz and Daniel Prosser, eds., *Cities of the Garden State: Essays in the Urban and Suburban History of New Jersey* (Dubuque, IA: Kendall/Hunt, 1977), p. x. By 1970 about 78 percent of residents in the New York suburbs also worked in the suburbs: Jackson, *Crabgrass Frontier*, pp. 266–69. In Bergen County, New Jersey—filled with classic bedroom suburbs—the breakdown was similar in 1970, with only one-quarter commuting to New York City: League of Women Voters of Bergen County, *Where Can I Live in Bergen County? Factors Affecting Housing Supply* (Closter, NJ: League of Women Voters of New Jersey, 1972), p. 5. In New Jersey, the process of residences and jobs moving farther out continued through the 1990s. Hundreds of new housing developments constructed on what was recently farmland and meadows in six outer suburban counties have been responsible for most of the population growth in the northern part of the state since 1990, while these counties have also dramatically outpaced the four inner suburban counties of Bergen, Essex, Hud-

son, and Passaic in terms of new jobs: "A New Kind of Suburbia Arises Out of the New Jersey Farmlands," *NYT,* July 3, 1995.

9. Untitled handwritten notes, with heading "The Region's Housing Stock," n.d. but c. early 1960s, Erber, Box B, loose papers; for national figures, see David M. Kennedy, Lizabeth Cohen, and Thomas A. Bailey, *The American Pageant,* 12th ed. (Boston: Houghton Mifflin, 2002), p. 908; statistics on single-family houses from New Jersey Department of Conservation and Economic Development, Bureau of Commerce, *Census of Housing, 1960,* Research Report #140 (Trenton, NJ, 1965), quoted in Hand, "Making the Suburban State," p. 16.

10. Hand, "Making the Suburban State," p. 13.

11. For an analysis of the New Jersey Supreme Court's activist tradition, see John B. Wefing, "The New Jersey Supreme Court 1948–1998: Fifty Years of Independence and Activism," *Rutgers Law Journal* 29 (Summer 1998): 701–31.

12. William M. Dobriner, "Social Change in Levittown," in Dobriner, *Class in Suburbia* (Englewood Cliffs, NJ: Prentice-Hall, 1963), pp. 85–126; Donald Katz, *Home Fires: An Intimate Portrait of One Middle-Class Family in Postwar America* (New York: HarperCollins, 1992).

13. Also see Harry Henderson, "The Mass Produced Suburbs, I. How People Live in America's Newest Towns," *Harper's Magazine,* November 1953, pp. 25–32; he found that in a community where he had interviewed twelve families on one block, three years later eight had moved, nearly all due to increased incomes which permitted more expensive homes. Although the median home value in Levittown by 1980 was $42,000 rather than $14,000, as in 1960, the community remained lower-middle- and working-class, prompting one long-term resident to remark, "When people move out of Levittown, they usually move up." A new resident, Theresa DeFalco, twenty-four, in 1987 had just bought a six-room ranch home with her husband Joseph, thirty-two, who commuted to his accounting job in Manhattan. Harboring middle-class aspirations, DeFalco confirmed both Levittown's current lower-middle-class status as well as its forty-year tradition of serving as a vehicle to upward mobility for some residents when she said, "We bought this house as a beginning. We had to start somewhere to get into home ownership. We look at this as a first step. Our duration here would be a maximum of five years. Then we'd move to a place that was a little more middle-class": "Levittown: An American Dream," *BG,* Nov. 8, 1987. Also see Michael Pollan, "The Triumph of Burbopolis," *NYT Magazine,* Apr. 2, 2000, p. 52.

14. "Statement by Ernest Erber, Director of Research, National Committee, to the Select Committee on Educational Opportunities, U.S. Senate, "August 16, 1970," Erber, Box B, Folder 12, p. 20.

15. "Living Atop a Civic Mushroom" and "Transient America—Case in Point," *Newsweek,* Apr. 1, 1957, pp. 36–37; William H. Whyte, Jr., "The Wives of Management," *Fortune,* October 1951, p. 88. In her memoir of growing up in Rockville Centre, Long Island, Doris Kearns Goodwin describes how neighbors moved to bigger homes in more affluent towns like Merrick and Baldwin as their businesses prospered: Goodwin, *Wait Till Next Year: A Memoir* (New York: Simon & Schuster, 1997), p. 216. Levitt and Sons responded to the changing socioeconomics of postwar suburbia between building its first and second Levittowns. Levittown, Pennsylvania, constructed between 1952 and 1958, tried to meet growing consumer interest in market differentiation by offering five house models, each targeted to a different consumer market by size and price. The Middletown Section, for example, contained the "Country Clubber" houses, aimed at executives and priced at $17,500, in stark contrast to the low-end houses that sold for less than half that, around $8000. "By putting the lower priced homes all in one section and on up

the scale," one early Levittown resident explained, "he built a caste system." In catering to the growing interest in making class distinctions through suburban housing within one 17,000-house community rather than through different communities, the Levitts indicated how much had changed since they planned the Long Island Levittown in 1946–47 with basically two styles—the Cape Cod and the ranch: Etan S. Diamond, "A House, a Yard, and the Right Kind of Neighbors: Levittown, Pennsylvania, as Suburban Archetype" (Senior honors thesis, University of Pennsylvania, Apr. 5, 1990), p. 33, in possession of the author.

16. Notes "The Region's Housing Stock," Erber, item 11; League of Women Voters of Bergen County, *Where Can I Live in Bergen County?*, p. 7.

17. New Jersey Committee, Regional Plan Association, "Economic Growth and Employment Location," Third Northern New Jersey Regional Conference, Apr. 13, 1966, "Q" Files, NPL, p. 6. Quote on Franklin Lakes from National Committee Against Discrimination in Housing, *Jobs and Housing: A Study of Employment and Housing Opportunities for Racial Minorities in Suburban Areas of the New York Metropolitan Region* (New York: March 1970), p. 116; League of Women Voters of Bergen County, *Where Can I Live in Bergen County?*, p. 7. On the Ford Motor Company plant in Mahwah, the largest auto assembly unit in the world when it opened in 1955, see Catherine M. Fogarty, John E. O'Connor, and Charles F. Cumming, *Bergen County: A Pictorial History* (Norfolk, VA: Donning, 1985), pp. 162, 194; on high absentee and turnover rates at this Ford plant, see National Committee, *Jobs and Housing*, pp. 20–21. For Local 410, IUE-CIO, mailing list of officers and stewards, see IUE, Box 9; for the AFL-CIO's concern about suburbanization, see *Proceedings of the 7th Constitutional Convention of the AFL-CIO*, vol. 2, Report of the Executive Council, Dec. 7, 1967, pp. 253–54. The worry that suburbanization would lessen union loyalty prompted the Institute of Management and Labor Relations of Rutgers University in the late 1950s to compare attitudes of United Automobile Workers, AFL-CIO, in two Newark-area plants living in suburban versus urban communities: William Spinrad, "Blue-Collar Workers as City and Suburban Residents—Effects on Union Membership," in Arthur B. Shostak and William Gomberg, eds. *Blue-Collar World: Studies of the American Worker* (Englewood Cliffs, NJ: Prentice-Hall, 1964), pp. 215–25.

The "cops and firemen" suburban real estate market is discussed in Schwartz and Prosser, *Cities of the Garden State*, p. xi. A marketing study of working-class female consumers sponsored by Macfadden Publications asserted in 1959 that "they usually live in neighborhoods populated mainly by other wage earning blue-collar families," where their housing goal "can be summarized in these words: a modern, comfortable, safe, soundly-built, inexpensive, unostentatious, cozy home." The "workingman's wife" seeks "a good neighborhood—by which she means an ordinary, friendly neighborhood where she and her family can feel socially comfortable, and not be 'outclassed' "; Lee Rainwater, Richard P. Coleman, and Gerald Handel, *Workingman's Wife* (1959; reprint, New York: Arno, 1979), pp. 16, 175, followed by Rainwater and Handel, "Status of the Working Class in Changing American Society," Manuscript Report, Social Research, February 1961. Bennett M. Berger's study of Milpitas, California, *Working-Class Suburb: A Study of Auto Workers in Suburbia* (Berkeley: University of California Press, 1968), p. 89, argued similarly that although these Ford workers felt "middle class in a certain sense," in that they were homeowners and better off than their parents, "the suburb in which they live probably constitutes a fairly good sample of their range of possibility—from unskilled labor, to foremen and very small businessmen, with a few lower white-collar workers (postmen, bank tellers, supermarket checkers, and the like) thrown in." See my Chapter 3 for more discussion of these studies.

Working-class Americans sought to own their own homes in the urban areas near the jobs, of course, long before they started moving to suburbs in large numbers, which was reflected in their relatively high home ownership rates (see Table 2). In precociously sub-urbanized California, the suburb of South Gate near Los Angeles was mixed class until 1940, when it became more uniformly working class: Becky M. Nicolaides, *My Blue Heaven: Life and Politics in the Working-Class Suburbs of Los Angeles, 1920–1965* (Chicago: University of Chicago Press, 2002).

18. "Economic Growth and Employment Location," p. 7, and "The Future of Our Cities and Older Suburbs" (background papers for discussion at conference workshops), Third Northern New Jersey Regional Conference, Apr. 13, 1966, "Q" Files, NPL; "Labor Force and Employment Characteristics in 10 Major Job Centers," 1960 statistics, Erber, Box B, Folder 6; Housing Authority of the City of Newark, *City Alive! Newark 1666–1966* (Newark: Housing Authority of Newark, 1966), p. 6.

19. Kenneth T. Jackson, "Federal Subsidy and the Suburban Dream: The First Quarter-Century of Government Intervention in the Housing Market," in *Records of the Columbia Historical Society of Washington, D.C.* 50 (Charlottesville: University Press of Virginia, 1980), pp. 425–42; U.S. Department of Housing and Urban Development, "Redlining: A Bibliography," 3rd ed., September 1977.

20. League of Women Voters of Bergen County, *Where Can I Live in Bergen County?*, pp. 9–10; "Statement of Ernest Erber to Senate Select Committee," Aug. 26, 1970, p. 22; Fred G. Stickel, "New Approach of New Jersey Courts to Zoning and Planning as Evi-denced by Recent Cases," *Proceedings of the New Jersey State Conference on Planning and Development*, Apr. 18, 1951, NPL, NJ Documents, pp. 66–69; "Group I-Planning," Erber, Box B, Folder 10; Charles M. Haar, "Zoning for Minimum Standards: The Wayne Town-ship Case," *Harvard Law Review* 66 (April 1953): 1051–63. For a useful general discussion of zoning, see Paul Davidoff and Mary E. Brooks, "Zoning Out the Poor," in Philip C. Dolce, ed., *Suburbia: The American Dream and Dilemma* (Garden City, NY: Anchor, 1976), pp. 135–36. Richard Briffault offers an excellent analysis of the evolution of subur-ban zoning in "Our Localism: Part II—Localism and Legal Theory," *Columbia Law Review* 90 (March 1990): 346–454. In an amusing effort to convince New Jersey citizens that inexpensive garden apartments would be a good solution to the growing wartime housing crisis, the New Jersey League of Women Voters devoted a show on its radio pro-gram *Leaguesboro* to a dispute in an imaginary town over whether or not to build them; doing so is portrayed as the democratic choice, resisting them as accommodating the real estate interests: New Jersey League of Women Voters, *Leaguesboro*, 1942, LWV-NJ, Box 21, Folder 17. After decades of suburban New Jersey towns resisting apartments, by the 1970s they would again become more common, particularly in what were now older suburbs, due to the growing scarcity and price of land combined with the increasing age and declining size of households.

21. Haar, "Zoning for Minimum Standards," p. 1062; Michael J. Birkner, *A Country Place No More: The Transformation of Bergenfield, New Jersey, 1894–1994* (Rutherford, NJ: Fairleigh Dickinson University Press, 1994), pp. 202, 330n.50. For more on use of exclu-sionary zoning by New Jersey's suburban municipalities, see National Committee, *Jobs and Housing*, pp. 53–58.

22. "Chart 19: Characteristics of New Homes in 1955," in Housing and Home Finance Agency, *Housing in the United States . . . a Graphic Presentation* (Washington, DC: Hous-ing and Home Finance Agency, 1956), pp. 38–39; U.S. Department of Labor, *New Hous-ing and Its Materials, 1940–56*, Bulletin No. 1231 (Washington, DC: USGPO, 1958), pp. 3–4. Statistics from the National Association of Home Builders over the postwar period document both increasing size and amenities in new homes as well as persistent variation in the number of bathrooms, bedrooms, garages, and the like: "Home Improvement," *House & Garden*, January 1998, p. 24. For more on the design of suburban homes, see

Thomas Hine, *Populuxe* (New York: Knopf, 1987), pp. 37–58; Clifford Edward Clark, Jr., *The American Family Home, 1800–1960* (Chapel Hill: University of North Carolina Press, 1986), pp. 193–236; and David Smiley, "Making the Modified Modern," *Perspecta 32, The Yale Architectural Journal: Resurfacing Modernism* (Cambridge, MA: MIT Press, 2001), pp. 38–51.

23. Ralph Bodek, *How and Why People Buy Houses: A Study of Subconscious Home Buying Motives* (Philadelphia: Municipal Publications, 1958), pp. 31–36, 43. A pioneer in the field of market segmentation, Pierre Martineau, reported that surveys of the tastes of working-class Chicagoans revealed that they rejected modern ranch homes and two-story colonials, along with functional modern furniture: *Motivation in Advertising* (New York: McGraw-Hill, 1957), p. 168.

24. "An Angry Housewife Speaks on Housing," *Life,* June 4, 1956, and "Housewife's House," *Life,* Dec. 24, 1956; Bodek, *How and Why People Buy Houses,* pp. 24–25.

25. Rainwater et al., *Workingman's Wife,* pp. 171, 175–77; "Houses Planned for Families That Are Going to Get Bigger," *Good Housekeeping,* August 1953, p. 83; also "The House with 50 Ideas," *Good Housekeeping,* March 1952, p. 87; Bodek, *How and Why People Buy Houses,* p. 49, also stresses the importance of privacy to middle-class homeowners, labeling the desire to isolate bedrooms as "the roosting instinct."

26. Daniel Horowitz, ed., *American Social Classes in the 1950s: Selections from Vance Packard's The Status Seekers* (Boston: Bedford/St. Martin's, 1995), p. 69. A similar observation was made by Robert C. Wood in the late 1950s in his *Suburbia: Its People and Their Politics* (Boston: Houghton Mifflin, 1958), pp. 106, 143, when he noted that settlers of suburban towns "literally choose their own fellow citizens"; in class and ethnic terms, "The suburban exodus appears to have renewed the old patterns of discrimination. Around New York City there are suburban districts which have become as heavily Jewish or Italian or Irish in family ancestry as were the ghettos of 'little Italies' or 'New Erins' of the Lower East Side twenty-five years ago."

27. George Sternlieb, *The Future of the Downtown Department Store* (Boston: Harvard Graduate School of Business Administration, 1961), p. 10; for comparable figures for New York City and its suburbs in Nassau, Suffolk, Westchester, and Rockland Counties, see Leonard Wallock, "The Myth of the Master Builder: Robert Moses, New York, and the Dynamics of Metropolitan Development Since World War II," *JUH* 17 (August 1991): 349–51.

28. Daniel S. Anthony, "Some Psychological Implications of Integration," Brookings Institution Committee on Problems of the American Community, Newark, New Jersey, Feb. 23, 1962, Anthony, Box 3, pp. 9, 12. For an enlightened effort to refute misconceptions about the impact of black Americans on property values and to expose the role played by homeowners, the real estate industry, and the government, see Algernon D. Black, *Who's My Neighbor? Public Affairs Pamphlet No. 273* (New York: Public Affairs Committee, 1958); Black was the chairman of the National Committee Against Discrimination in Housing. For a recent national history of residential segregation, see Stephen Grant Meyer, *As Long as They Don't Move Next Door: Segregation and Racial Conflict in American Neighborhoods* (Lanham, MD: Rowman & Littlefield, 2000).

29. Lake, *The New Suburbanites,* pp. 47–105; *Annual Report of the Urban Colored Population Commission, State of New Jersey for July 1943–December 1944,* NPL, concluded, "It is this Commission's opinion that there is not one urban center in New Jersey where residential segregation is not practiced against its Negro population. The denser the concentration of the Negro population . . . the more pronounced the pattern of segregation."

30. Michael N. Danielson and Jameson W. Doig, *New York: The Politics of Urban Regional Development* (Berkeley: University of California Press, 1982), p. 105.

31. "Statement of Ernest Erber to Senate Select Committee," Aug. 26, 1970, Erber, pp. 10, 12.

32. Newark's Commission on Group Relations, "Newark, a City in Transition," vol. 2, "Residents' Views on Inter-Group Relations and Statistical Tables," March 1959, NPL, pp. 80–82.

33. Charles Abrams, *Forbidden Neighbors: A Study of Prejudice in Housing* (New York: Harper, 1955), p. 229, cited in Karen Brodkin Sacks, "How Did Jews Become White Folks?" in Stephen Gregory and Roger Sanjek, eds., *Race* (New Brunswick, NJ: Rutgers University Press, 1994), pp. 94, also 96–97; *Building the American City, Report of the National Commission on Urban Problems to the Congress and to the President of the United States* (Washington, DC: USGPO, 1968), pp. 100–104; "State of New Jersey, Governor's Housing Conference," Apr. 5, 1955, Trenton, NJ, NPL, NJ Documents, pp. 30–32, 63–64, 67. Jackson's *Crabgrass Frontier* provides the most thorough discussion of the damage done by racist federal mortgage policies in his chapter "Federal Subsidy and the Suburban Dream: How Washington Changed the American Housing Market," pp. 190–218.

34. "Statement by Ernest Erber to Senate Select Committee," Aug. 26, 1970, Erber, Box B, Folder 12, p. 3.

35. In NAACP, II, B 78, "Housing—New Jersey—East Orange, 1945–47": Marian Wynn Perry (NAACP) to Mrs. Catherine Bauer Wurster, Feb. 18, 1946; Catherine Bauer to Mrs. Perry, Mar. 18, 1946; Perry to Mrs. Catherine Bauer Wurster, Mar. 20, 1946; Perry to Mr. Lester Granger (National Urban League), Mar. 19, 1946; Perry to Mrs. Octavia W. Catlett (Montclair NAACP), Apr. 9, 1946; Perry to Shirley Adelson, Esq. (American Jewish Congress), Apr. 13, 1946; form letter sent to branches in communities where Harland, Bartholomew & Associates worked from Perry, May 15, 1946. Also, in NAACP, II, B 78, "Housing, New Jersey, General, 1941–47": Scott Bagby to Mr. Walter White (NAACP), Dec. 4, 1946; memorandum to Mr. Current from Perry, Dec. 18, 1946; Perry to Mr. Flavel Shurtleff, Dec. 20, 1946; memorandum to Mr. White from Perry, Feb. 14, 1947; Bagby to Mr. Charles R. Lawrence, Jr. (Fisk University), Feb. 27, 1947; "Statement of Principles with Respect to Redevelopment," Jan. 27, 1947. Also "New Preiser Housing Bill," *NN*, Mar. 5, 1946. Andrew Wiese describes the same process of "slum" clearance under way on suburban Long Island in "Racial Cleansing in the Suburbs: Suburban Government, Urban Renewal, and Segregation on Long Island, New York, 1945–1960," in Marc L. Silver and Martin Melkonian, eds., *Contested Terrain: Power, Politics, and Participation in Suburbia* (Westport, CT: Greenwood, 1995), pp. 61–69.

36. Joseph M. Conforti, "Newark: Ghetto or City?" *Society* 9 (May 1972): 25.

37. Sacks, "How Did Jews Become White Folks?" p. 95; Diamond, "A House, a Yard, and the Right Kind of Neighbors," pp. 29–30, 35–48; "Integration Troubles Beset Northern Town," *Life*, Sept. 2, 1957, pp. 43–46; "Ordeal in Levittown," *Look*, Aug. 19, 1958; clippings "Housing-NJ, 002,324-1," Schomburg; File on Levittown, NJ case in Lett, Box 1; Herbert J. Gans, *The Levittowners: Ways of Life and Politics in a New Suburban Community* (New York: Columbia University Press, 1967), pp. 371–84; "New Jersey Conference on Fair Housing, Sponsored by New Jersey Committee Against Discrimination in Housing," Feb. 9, 1963, Erber, Box D, Folder 8; "The Myers' Case: An Instance of Successful Racial Invasion," *Social Problems* 8 (Fall 1960): 126–43; Levittown statistics in Harry Henderson, "Rugged American Collectivism: The Mass Produced Suburbs, Part II," *Harper's Magazine*, December 1953, p. 85, and "Levittown: An American Dream," *BG*, Nov. 8, 1987.

38. Sacks, "How Did Jews Become White Folks?" p. 95; website www.eichler network.com.

39. The Commission on Race and Housing interviewed some two hundred builders in various sections of the country and concluded that they overwhelmingly maintained a

strict policy of racial segregation out of concern for profits. A successful housing tract operation required a rapid rate of sales with a complete sellout; a development that sold slowly or not completely meant a commercial failure. Most builders were unwilling to risk a nondiscriminatory policy: *Where Shall We Live? Report of the Commission on Race and Housing* (Berkeley: University of California Press, 1958), pp. 26–28.

40. "Our Segregated Communities: 2, The Negro Meets the Neighbors—and the Realtor and 'Covenant,' " *Bernardsville News,* Jan. 23, 1964 (in four-part series); National Association of Real Estate Boards quoted in Gregory D. Squires, "The Indelible Color Line," *American Prospect,* January–February 1999, p. 67, and "The Negro in Essex: No Fiery Crosses, but Housing Is His Big Problem," *NN,* Apr. 24, 1956; "The Montclair Community Audit," as Reported at Montclair Forum, Dec. 11, 1947, Schomburg, "Housing"; Herbert Mitgang, "Created Equal?" *NYT Magazine,* June 13, 1948, pp. 54–55; Memorandum to Mayor Hugh J. Addonizio from Alexander Mark and Daniel S. Anthony, July 15, 1962, Anthony, Box 3, File 10, p. 2; "Speech given by Dr. Harold A. Lett for Workshop, Modern Trends in Intergroup Relations, Rutgers University, July 1959," Lett, Box 1, pp. 18–19. For a range of realtor reactions to black house seekers, see James H. Kirk and Elaine D. Johnson, "The Color Line in Northern Suburbia," in Alan F. Westin, ed., *Freedom Now!: The Civil Rights Struggle in America* (New York: Basic Books, 1964), pp. 175–82. For some fascinating tales of blockbusting attempts, and successful efforts to foil them, in New Jersey communities, see flyer from Law and Public Safety Department, Civil Rights Division, "Interracial Neighborhoods in New Jersey Communities," n.d. but c. 1960, NPL. For a study of the many subtle and not-so-subtle tactics used by realtors to discriminate, see National Committee, *Jobs and Housing,* pp. 65–82.

See the important work of Thomas Sugrue on the racial struggle within Detroit's working-class neighborhoods: "Crabgrass-Roots Politics: Race, Rights, and the Reaction Against Liberalism in the Urban North, 1940–1964," *JAH* 82 (September 1995): 551–78. For a fascinating case study of one block on Detroit's West Side undergoing "white flight" in the early 1950s, see "Broken Detroit: Death of a City Block, Life of the Street Mirrors City's Fall," *Detroit News and Free Press,* June 17, 2000.

41. "The Negro Meets the Neighbors—and the Realtor and 'Covenant,' " *Bernardsville News,* Jan. 23, 1964.

42. Luigi Laurenti, *Property Values and Race: Studies in Seven Cities,* Special Research Report to the Commission on Race and Housing (Berkeley: University of California Press, 1960); Gerald David Jaynes and Robin M. Williams, Jr., eds., *A Common Destiny: Blacks and American Society* (Washington, DC: National Academy Press, 1989), pp. 140–44.

43. "The Negro in Essex: No Fiery Crosses, but Housing Is His Big Problem," *NN,* Apr. 24, 1956; George Sternlieb, *The Tenement Landlord,* cited in *A Decent Home: The Report of the President's Committee on Urban Housing* (Washington, DC: USGPO, 1968), pp. 96–97. The Planning Board of the Township of Livingston confirmed to the NAACP in 1944 that, as revealed in a series of articles in the *Newark Evening News,* recent housing subdivisions had been approved with agreements between the town and developer providing for the "restriction of use or occupancy of dwellings by people of certain races." The township attorney having now decided that such racial restrictions were unconstitutional, the planning board assumed the clause would be omitted from future agreements: Dorothea Ochs, Secretary, Planning Board, to Mr. Milton Konvitz, Mar. 20, 1944, NAACP Papers on Microfilm, Part 5, Reel 21, Frame 382-3. The very white town of Nutley tried to put the same kind of restrictive covenant in its agreements with developers, but was stopped by opponents including the Committee on Discrimination of the New Jersey State Industrial Union Council (CIO): New Jersey State Industrial Union Council, *Tenth Anniversary Yearbook,* 1947, NPL, "Q" Files and "Nutley Race Restriction," *NN,* Feb. 18, 1944; NAACP Papers on Microfilm, Part 5, Reel 21, Frame 354.

For general documentation of redlining on racial grounds, in chronological order, see National Community Relations Advisory Council, *Equality of Opportunity in Housing: A Handbook of Facts,* June 1952; Department of Housing Activities, National Urban League, "Mortgage Financing for Properties Available to Negro Occupancy," 1954; Fred E. Case and James H. Kirk, "The Housing Status of Minority Families, Los Angeles, 1956," UCLA Real Estate Program in cooperation with the Los Angeles Urban League, pp. 55–58; Davis McEntire, *Residence and Race, Final and Comprehensive Report to the Commission on Race and Housing* (Berkeley: University of California Press, 1960), pp. 218–37, 299–311; *Housing in Washington: Hearings Before the United States Commission on Civil Rights,* Apr. 12–13, 1962; Rose Helper, *Racial Policies and Practices of Real Estate Brokers* (Minneapolis: University of Minnesota Press, 1969), pp. 166–72; Melvin L. Oliver and Thomas M. Shapiro, *Black Wealth/White Wealth: A New Perspective on Racial Inequality* (New York: Routledge, 1995), pp. 136–47.

44. Mortgage Reinvestment Campaign of New Jersey Citizen Action Alliance, "Home Mortgage Lending, Essex County, NJ: An Analysis," n.d. but c. late 1970s, "Q" Files, NPL; this report may have been inspired by the more thorough Richard J. Devine, with Winston O. Rennie and N. Brenda Sims, *Where the Lender Looks First: A Case Study of Mortgage Disinvestment in Bronx County, 1960–1970* (New York: National Urban League, 1973). See discussion of legislation prohibiting discrimination and evidence of its persistence nonetheless in Squires, "The Indelible Color Line," pp. 67–70; also, "Wide Racial Disparities Found in Costs of Mortgages," *NYT,* May 1, 2002. Estimates of the percentage of blacks who live in suburbia vary; by one measure, it rose from 23 percent in 1970 to 32 percent in 1990, when some 40 percent of all minorities were suburbanites, though many of them lived in older, deteriorating first-ring suburbs apart from whites: "Suburbia Outgrows Its Image in the Arts," *NYT,* Feb. 28, 1999; "Persistent Racial Segregation Mars Suburbs' Green Dream," *NYT,* Mar. 17, 1994; "Most Segregated US Cities Line the Great Lakes Basin," *CSM,* Apr. 11, 1994.

There is an impressive scholarly literature documenting the contemporary reality of segregation; see, for example, Reynolds Farely, "The Changing Distribution of Negroes Within Metropolitan Areas: The Emergence of Black Suburbs," *AJS* 75 (January 1970): 512–27; Kathryn P. Nelson, "Recent Suburbanization of Blacks: How Much, Who, and Where," U.S. Department of Housing and Urban Development, 1979; Lake, *The New Suburbanites,* which has case studies from New Jersey; John R. Logan and Mark Schneider, "Racial Segregation and Racial Change in American Suburbs, 1970–1980," *AJS* 89 (January 1984): 874–88; Douglas S. Massey and Nancy A. Denton, *American Apartheid: Segregation and the Making of the Underclass* (Cambridge, MA: Harvard University Press, 1993); W. Dennis Keating, *The Suburban Racial Dilemma: Housing and Neighborhoods* (Philadelphia: Temple University Press, 1994); Robert D. Bullard, J. Eugene Gribsby III, and Charles Lee, eds., *Residential Apartheid: An American Legacy* (Berkeley: University of California Press, 1994).

On the phenomenon of separate black suburbs, see Andrew Wiese, "Places of Our Own: Suburban Black Towns Before 1960," *JUH* 19 (May 1993): 30–54; Wiese, "The Other Suburbanites: African American Suburbanization in the North Before 1950," *JAH* 85 (March 1999): 1495–1524; David J. Dent, "The New Black Suburbs," *NYT Magazine,* June 14, 1992; "Blacks Rise as Power in Washington Suburb," *NYT,* July 1, 2000.

45. "The Ghosts of Roth, An Interview by Alan Finkielkraut," *Esquire,* September 1981, p. 95.

46. Philip Roth, *Goodbye, Columbus and Five Short Stories* (New York: Vintage, 1959), pp. 8–9.

47. Roth, *Goodbye, Columbus,* p. 90; Roth, *I Married a Communist* (Boston: Houghton Mifflin, 1998), p. 99.

48. "Newark Boyhood Fiction Material," *NN*, Nov. 30, 1958; for more on how Newark figures in Roth's work, see Henry Weil, "Philip Roth: Still Waiting for His Masterpiece," *Saturday Review of Literature*, June 1981, pp. 26–31; Philip Roth, *The Facts: A Novelist's Autobiography* (New York: Farrar, Straus and Giroux, 1988); Philip Roth, *Patrimony: A True Story* (New York: Simon & Schuster, 1991); "To Newark, with Love. Philip Roth," *NYT*, Mar. 29, 1991; Peter L. Cooper, "Philip Roth, 1933– ," in Lea Baechler and A. Walton Litz, eds., *American Writers: A Collection of Literary Biographies*, Supplement 3, Part 2 (New York: Scribner's, 1974), pp. 401–29; George J. Searles, ed., *Conversations with Philip Roth* (Jackson: University Press of Mississippi, 1992).

49. Roth, *Patrimony*, p. 39; Philip Roth, *American Pastoral* (New York: Vintage, 1997).

50. Imamu Amiri Baraka, *The Autobiography of LeRoi Jones/Amiri Baraka* (New York: Freundlich, 1984), p. 32; for more on Baraka's life, see Theodore R. Hudson, *From LeRoi Jones to Amiri Baraka: The Literary Works* (Durham, NC: Duke University Press, 1973); LeRoi Jones, *Tales* (New York: Grove, 1967); "Amiri Baraka, 1934– ," in Valerie Smith, Lea Baechler, and A. Walton Litz, eds., *African American Writers* (New York: Scribner's, 1991), pp. 15–29.

51. Baraka's poem "Black People!" was published in *Evergreen* 11 (December 1967); 49, between his arrest and his trial, when he was out on bail; see Chapter 8 for more discussion of the poem.

52. "Baraka Debates Haney on Blacks in Business," *NSL*, Feb. 2, 1972; Saul Gottlieb, "They Think You're an Airplane and You're Really a Bird," in Charles Reilly, ed., *Conversations with Amiri Baraka* (Jackson: University Press of Mississippi, 1994), p. 33; Imamu Amiri Baraka, "Newark—Before Black Men Conquered," in *Raise, Rage, Rays, Raze: Essays Since 1965* (New York: Random House, 1971), p. 65; Stewart Alsop, "The American Sickness," *Saturday Evening Post*, July 13, 1968, p. 6.

53. "Goodbye, Nathan Zuckerman," *Time*, Nov. 7, 1983.

54. "Speech given by Dr. Harold A. Lett," July 1959, Lett, pp. 2–3; working- and middle-class attitudes toward residential integration discussed in Clark, *The American Family Home*, pp. 232–33, and Michael N. Danielson, *The Politics of Exclusion* (New York: Columbia University Press, 1976), pp. 24–26; segregation indices from Jaynes and Williams, *A Common Destiny*, pp. 144–45. Oliver and Shapiro make a convincing argument that the artificially depressed values of black homes in segregated communities have greatly contributed to inequality in home equity accumulation and, in turn, a general deficit in black wealth: *Black Wealth/White Wealth*, pp. 18, 22–23, 147–51; also see Dalton Conley, *Being Black, Living in the Red: Race, Wealth, and Social Policy in America* (Berkeley: University of California Press, 1999). When residential areas with the same household incomes but different racial profiles were compared in racially polarized Washington, D.C., for a five-year period ending in June 1989, housing prices rose only 8 percent in the predominantly black Brookland/Catholic University area (actually a 10 percent drop after adjusting for inflation), while owners in white Dupont Circle saw their home prices rise by 99 percent: Walter L. Updegrave, "Race and Money," *Money*, December 1989, p. 159.

55. Marion Thompson Wright, "Extending Civil Rights in New Jersey Through the Division Against Discrimination," reprint from *Journal of Negro History*, January 1953, published by Association for Study of Negro Life and History, Washington, DC, p. 106.

56. *RPA News*, April 1967, cited in "New Jersey's 'Moment of Truth'—State Confronts Consequences of Decades of Pennypinching," August 1968, Erber, Box B, Folder 4, p. 51.

57. Hand, "Making the Suburban State," in Grover, ed., *Teenage New Jersey*, pp. 15, 33n.6; Wood, *Suburbia: Its People and Their Politics*, pp. 77–78; Jackson, *Crabgrass Frontier*, pp. 276–77; Danielson and Doig, *New York*, p. 77; Richard Briffault, "Our Localism: Part I—The Structure of Local Government Law," *Columbia Law Journal* 90 (January

1990): 77–81. The argument that the healthy survival of American cities depends on their ability to annex and participate in metropolitan area government is made persuasively by David Rusk in *Cities Without Suburbs* (Washington, DC: Woodrow Wilson Center, 1993) and *Inside Game/Outside Game: Winning Strategies for Saving Urban America* (Washington, DC: Brookings, 1999). When Rusk constructed a table of "elasticity" for the 145 central cities with over 100,000 population in 1990, New Jersey's four that qualified—Newark, Paterson, Jersey City, and Elizabeth—all showed up in the "Zero Elasticity" column (meaning the least amount of involvement in metropolitan-wide governance): *Cities Without Suburbs*, pp. 132–33. In contrast, Houston increased its area threefold from 1920 to 1950 and by another 50 percent between 1963 and 1978, thus qualifying it for "Hyper Elasticity": David R. Goldfield, *Cotton Fields and Skyscrapers: Southern City and Region, 1607–1980* (Baton Rouge: Louisiana State University Press, 1982), pp. 152–53.

58. Wood, *Suburbia*, pp. 12, 102, 104, 106; on the long history of local control in suburbs, see Sies, "Paradise Retained: An Analysis of Persistence in Planned, Exclusive Suburbs, 1880–1980." For a more recent example of a suburb invoking "home rule" and resisting regional planning, see "Affluent Town Seeks to Limit Development Outside Its Borders," *NYT*, Mar. 11, 2000.

59. "Planner Says Chambers Must Help Solve Traffic Congestion," *BR*, Nov. 26, 1957.

60. Robert C. Wood, with Vladimir V. Almendinger, *1400 Governments: The Political Economy of the New York Region* (Cambridge, MA: Harvard University Press, 1961); also see summary volume of the study, Raymond Vernon, *Metropolis 1985* (Cambridge, MA: Harvard University Press, 1960); "Metropolitan Apathy," *NYT*, July 17, 1961; "Our Metropolis Has Cancer," editorial in *New York Herald Tribune*, July 18, 1961, reprinted by Regional Plan Association, Erber, file "NJ Committee, Misc."; Wood, *Suburbia*, p. 106. For exploration of the problem nationally, see Michael N. Danielson, Alan M. Hershey, and John M. Bayne, *One Nation, So Many Governments: A Report to the Ford Foundation* (Lexington, MA: Lexington Books/Heath, 1977), and Gregory R. Weiher, *The Fractured Metropolis: Political Fragmentation and Metropolitan Segregation* (Albany: State University of New York Press, 1991).

61. "New Jersey's Future: The Issues," prepared for Forum on the Future of New Jersey, Bicentennial Celebration, Rutgers, sponsored by the Urban Studies Centers, Dec. 8–9, 1967; "Upsala Parley Airs State's Ills," clipping dated Jan. 30, 1969, in Erber, Box D, Folder 14. As Wood had pointed out, suburbs were multitudinous and small throughout the New York region. More than half of the 775 suburban jurisdictions in 1970 were less than 5 square miles; while the average suburb had 14,000 residents, 10 percent had fewer than 1000 inhabitants: Danielson and Doig, *New York*, p. 69. A similarly powerful statement of this postwar phenomenon of the creation of "new units of local government . . . by the thousands," making every metropolitan area "look as if it had been 'non-planned' by a mad man" is *Building the American City: Report of the National Commission on Urban Problems to the Congress and to the President of the United States* (Washington, DC: USGPO, 1968), particularly pp. 7–8.

62. Clement A. Price, "The Struggle to Desegregate Newark: Black Middle-Class Militancy in New Jersey, 1932–1947," *New Jersey History* 99 (Fall/Winter 1981): 223; Robert Curvin, "Black Ghetto Politics in Newark After World War II," in Schwartz and Prosser, *Cities of the Garden State*, pp. 148–50; Richard J. Krickus, "Organizing Neighborhoods: Gary and Newark," and Thomas R. Brooks, "Breakdown in Newark," in Irving Howe, ed., *The World of the Blue-Collar Worker* (New York: Quadrangle, 1972).

63. "Statement by Ernest Erber, Director of Research, National Committee Against Discrimination in Housing to the Select Committee on Educational Opportunities, U.S. Senate," Aug. 26, 1970, Erber, Box B, Folder 12, p. 15. Robert Wood made a similar point

in his *Suburbia* of 1959, pp. 289–302, arguing that contrary to common perception, urban government was more democratic than suburban, as the "personalized government, big city style" of neighborhood political bosses "is always government by a minority, not a majority," with opposition never more than a neighborhood away.

64. Ernest Erber, "Zoning Against People, Rejoinder Comments," New Jersey Federation of Planning Officials, Nov. 21–22, 1968, Erber, Box B, Folder 12, p. 2; Regional Plan Association, *The Future of Bergen and Passaic Counties: A Supplement to the Second Regional Plan, A Draft for Discussion,* May 1969, "Q" Files, NPL, pp. 19–20; see tables of growth in lot size of subdivisions, 1950–60, in *Spread City: Projections of Development Trends and the Issues They Pose: The Tri-State New York Metropolitan Region, 1960–1985,* Regional Plan Association Bulletin 100 (September 1962): 40–44; C. Perin, *Everything in Its Place: Social Order and Land Use in America* (1977), p. 181, cited in Briffault, "Our Localism: Part I," p. 41. Danielson and Doig have an excellent discussion of "upzoning" and related "fiscal zoning" in *New York,* pp. 81–98.

65. "To Move New Jersey Forward," *Regional Plan News,* no. 88 (October 1968): 9; Council of Social Agencies, "The Case for the Council of Social Agencies and Members' Concern with the Adequacy of Tax Support for Publicly Financed Health, Education, Welfare and Recreation Services in New Jersey: A Suggested Three Pronged Approach," Feb. 15, 1965, Erber, Box B, Folder 6, p. 4. The same dynamic sometimes played out within suburbia itself, where blacks in towns with substantial black populations and dropping property values paid higher taxes than whites in mostly white towns. On suburban Long Island, for example, black residents of Suffolk County in the mid-1990s paid 17.6 percent higher property taxes than whites on homes of comparable market value, while in Nassau County they paid 5.6 percent more, and both figures probably underestimated the difference by comparing homes bought in the 1980s and ignoring the lower property taxes paid by longtime, usually white, homeowners. Given the infrequency of tax reassessment, whites paid lower taxes than the market values of their houses, while blacks paid higher: "Persistent Racial Segregation Mars Suburbs' Green Dream," *NYT,* Mar. 17, 1994.

66. *Regional Plan News,* April 1967, quoted in Ernest Erber, "New Jersey's 'Moment of Truth,'—State Confronts Consequences of Decades of Pennypinching," August 1968, Erber, Box B, Folder 4, p. 51.

67. "To Beat the Bond: or Oh, State, Poor State, You're Hung Up on Finances and It May Be Too Late," October 1963, LWV-NJ, Box 21, Folder 45.

68. Chamber of Commerce of the City of Newark, NJ, "Make It . . . Market It . . . in Newark," 1953, "Q" Files, NPL, "Newark Chamber of Commerce"; 80 percent tax figure for 1957 from Chester Rapkin and Eunice and George Grier, "Group Relations in Newark—1957: Problems, Prospects, and a Program for Research," July 1957, NPL, "Newark, Essex County Document File," p. 17.

69. "New Jersey's 'Moment of Truth,' " Erber, pp. 4–5; Office of Economic Development, City of Newark, "Recommendations to Resolve Newark's Tax Crisis, Proposed by Mayor Hugh J. Addonizio, Based on a Study of Newark's Tax Problems by P. Bernard Nortman," January 1968, NPL, Newark Document File, "Newark, Economic Development Office"; "Driscoll and Meyner Agree on Need for Broad Base Tax," *NN,* May 12, 1968. Even as Governor Richard Hughes made a powerful moral case for a graduated personal income tax in his special message to the state legislature on April 25, 1968, "A Moral Recommitment for New Jersey," he felt compelled to stress its minimal cost to citizens, particularly in comparison to other states: Erber, Box D, Folder 10, pp. 48–50. New Jersey was the third state to adopt a lottery, after New Hampshire and New York, and its system quickly became a national model of sophisticated marketing: Charles T. Clotfelter

and Philip J. Cook, *Selling Hope: State Lotteries in America* (Cambridge, MA: Harvard University Press, 1989), pp. 4–6, 28, 52–53, 144, 190, 196.

70. On New Jersey's tax history more generally, see from the *NYT*: "Jersey Confused by 2% Sales Tax," July 2, 1935; "Jersey in Revolt over Its Sales Tax," July 3, 1935; "Jersey Sales Tax Again Is Flouted," Aug. 11, 1935; "Jersey's Sales Tax Causes Wide Rift," Sept. 1, 1935; "Jersey Sales Tax Begins Today; Yield of $160 Million Is Seen," July 1, 1966. Also Barbara G. Salmore and Stephen A. Salmore, *New Jersey Politics and Government: Suburban Politics Comes of Age* (Lincoln: University of Nebraska Press, 1993), pp. 244–58; Erber, "Zoning Against People, Rejoinder Comments," Erber, p. 2; New Jersey State CIO [Industrial Union] Council, "A Comprehensive Tax Program for New Jersey," 1949, "Q" Files, NPL; Rutgers Scholars Under Direction of Salomon J. Flink, Department of Economics, Rutgers University, *The Economy of New Jersey: A Report Prepared for the Department of Conservation and Economic Development of the State of New Jersey* (New Brunswick, NJ: Rutgers University Press, 1958), pp. 574–99.

71. On revenues from casino gambling, see "With Cash Rolling In, Atlantic City Raises Stakes," *NYT*, June 24, 1996, and "Gambling: Married to the Action, for Better or Worse," *NYT*, Nov. 8, 1998. On the exploitative nature of lottery playing, see Clotfelter and Cook, *Selling Hope*, pp. 98, 187–88, 190; Verna V. Gehring, "The American State Lottery: Sale or Swindle?" *Philosophy & Public Policy* 20 (Winter/Spring 2000): 12–17; Michael Nelson, "The Lottery Gamble," *American Prospect*, June 4, 2001, pp. 19–21; "Not an Extra for Schools," *NYT*, Mar. 29, 1997; "Meeting the Lotteries' Perfect Pitch," *NYT*, July 14, 1996.

On New Jersey's continued dependence on the property tax, see Salmore and Salmore, *New Jersey Politics and Government*, p. 244; "Panel Unveils Suggestions for Cutting Property Tax," *NYT*, Sept. 16, 1998. New Jersey's ongoing dependence on the property tax has created some absurd ironies. In 1998 the city of Newark argued in court against a state attorney general's order that it comply with state law that property taxes be based on 100 percent of a property's true value and undertake a major reassessment of property within the city for the first time in over forty years, its last full revaluation of property having been in 1961 (the longest any U.S. city has gone). Although recognizing that such a reassessment would correct outrageous inequities on the current tax rolls and perhaps bring the city more revenue, city officials also predicted that such a reassessment would shift 25 percent of the tax burden from commercial to residential owners and devastate many of the middle-class homeowners that the city so desperately needed to keep. So in the interest of survival, the city found itself arguing to preserve tax inequity. The situation is further complicated by the fact that by the late 1990s, almost 70 percent of property in Newark was property tax–exempt, belonging to the federal or state government, to an agency like the Port Authority of New York and New Jersey, or to schools, hospitals, or religious groups: "Newark's Painful Challenge: Property Taxes Out of Kilter," *NYT*, July 20, 1998. In a poll commissioned by the New Jersey School Boards Association and conducted by the Eagleton Institute of Politics at Rutgers University, apparently 57 percent of those surveyed said they would rather pay more state income tax in return for lower property taxes, which was heartening news to the School Boards Association even if not favored by Governor Christie Whitman and state legislators; Eagleton Institute, "New Jerseyans' Opinions on School Revenue Proposals," October 1999, summarized in "Income Tax Favored over Property Tax," *NYT*, Oct. 8, 1999.

72. *Guaclides* v. *Borough of Englewood Cliffs* (1951, upheld rezoning of all multi-family to single-family), *Lionshead Lake, Inc.* v. *Township of Wayne* (1952, allowed minimum floor space requirements), *Fischer* v. *Township of Bedminster* (1952, found a five-acre minimum not excessive), *Fanale* v. *Borough of Hasbrouck Heights* (1958, permitted exclusion of apartment houses), *Vickers* v. *Township Committee of Gloucester Township* (1962,

validated a ban on trailer parks); Briffault, "Our Localism: Part I," p. 39*n*.146, for national cases see p. 40*n*.151.

73. Regional Plan Association, *Future of Bergen and Passaic Counties,* p. 19; also National Committee, *Jobs and Housing,* p. 45.

74. Division of State and Regional Planning, Department of Community Affairs, State of New Jersey, "The Housing Crisis in New Jersey," 1970, p. 83; also see "Housing Six Million More Residents," prepared for Regional Plan Association Conference, "The Spreading Metropolis: A Burden to Business?" Feb. 11–14, 1962, Erber, Box B, Folder 8, p. 72. In 1968 planner Ernest Erber regretted the contribution he himself had made over his career to a suburban planning process that had become "an unspoken conspiracy against people—specifically those earning less than the median for the suburb in question, largely the non-white, and the unborn of all races." With the "devices to exclude the stranger from our midst, [we] also deprive our children and grandchildren of living space in this state. We are zoning the unborn generations into the Atlantic Ocean": Erber, "Zoning Against People," pp. 1–2.

75. My treatment of the *Mount Laurel* cases is based on a rich secondary literature, including David L. Kirp, John P. Dwyer, and Larry A. Rosenthal, *Our Town: Race, Housing, and the Soul of Suburbia* (New Brunswick, NJ: Rutgers University Press, 1995); Charles M. Haar, *Suburbs Under Siege: Race, Space, and Audacious Judges* (Princeton: Princeton University Press, 1996); Briffault, "Our Localism: Part I," pp. 48–57; Peter Wolf, *Land in America: Its Value, Use, and Control* (New York: Pantheon, 1981), pp. 156–58; Davidoff and Brooks, "Zoning Out the Poor," in Dolce, *Suburbia,* pp. 156–61; Keating, *The Suburban Racial Dilemma,* pp. 38–41.

76. Briffault, "Our Localism: Part I," p. 53.

77. "Slouching Toward Mount Laurel," *NYT,* Mar. 31, 1996; Gerard Fergerson, "Red Lines, White Zones," *The Nation,* Mar. 31, 1997, p. 33; "To Meet Goal for Housing, Suburb Seeks to Pay City," *NYT,* Aug. 4, 1998; "Affordable Housing for Low and Moderate Income Households in Princeton, New Jersey, 2001," prepared by Kinsey & Hand, revised June 2001, courtesy of Susanne Hand.

78. Jackson, "Federal Subsidy and the Suburban Dream," p. 447; *The Future of Bergen and Passaic Counties, 1969,* p. 19; Briffault, "Our Localism: Part II," p. 373*n*.122.

79. "As Taxes Rise, Suburbs Work to Keep Elderly," *NYT,* Feb. 27, 2001; Salmore and Salmore, *New Jersey Politics and Government,* p. 298; "Battling Sprawl, States Buy Land for Open Space," *NYT,* June 9, 1998; "The 1998 Campaign: Tax Proposals," *NYT,* Nov. 2, 1998; "New Jersey's Housing Law Works Too Well, Some Say," *NYT,* Mar. 3, 2001; Rikard Treiber, "Painting the Town Green: Anti-Growth Planning and Unaffordable Housing," graduate seminar paper, New York University, January 1997, in possession of author. On the link between suburbanization and a rising environmental consciousness, see Adam Rome, *The Bulldozer in the Countryside* (Cambridge, Eng.: Cambridge University Press, 2001).

80. "Slouching Toward Mount Laurel," *NYT;* Kirp et al., *Our Town,* p. 159; "New Jersey's Housing Law Works Too Well, Some Say," *NYT.*

81. "Low-Income Houses and a Suburb's Fears," *NYT,* Apr. 5, 1997; "A Suburb Votes to Build Homes for Poor," *NYT,* Apr. 12, 1997; phone conversations with Planning Department, Mount Laurel Township and Fair Share Housing Development, Cherry Hill, NJ, Aug. 4, 1999; "Mount Laurel Homes Open After 30 Years of Legal Battles and Delays," *Associated Press,* Mar. 24, 2001. For conflicting opinions about whether Mount Laurel has succeeded in creating much more affordable housing in New Jersey, see "New Jersey's Housing Law Works Too Well, Some Say," *NYT.*

82. Briffault, "Our Localism: Part I," pp. 42–48, 106–108; Jay Walljasper, "A Fair Share

in Suburbia," *The Nation,* Jan. 25, 1999, pp. 15–21; Keating, *Suburban Racial Dilemma;* Paul K. Stockman, "Anti-Snob Zoning in Massachusetts: Assessing One Attempt at Opening the Suburbs to Affordable Housing," *Virginia Law Review* 78 (1992): 535–80; "Affordable Housing Fight Looms," *BG,* Mar. 4, 2001; "Affordable Housing: The Debate Goes On," *BG,* Jan. 20, 2002; "Zoning Rule Seen Key to Solving a Housing Crisis," *BG,* Jan. 1, 2002; on affordable housing in California, "People Want a Place of Their Own," *The Economist,* Aug. 7, 1999, pp. 22–24.

83. Oliver and Shapiro, *Black Wealth/White Wealth,* pp. 81–82, Tables A4.3, A5.2, A5.3 in Appendix A; Maurice Isserman and Michael Kazin, *America Divided: The Civil War of the 1960s* (New York: Oxford University Press, 2000), p. 16.

84. For a description of how bad schools can get without adequate funding, see Jonathan Kozol on the schools of urban Camden, East Orange, Jersey City, Irvington, and Paterson compared to those in the affluent suburban districts of Cherry Hill, Millburn, Princeton, and Wayne in *Savage Inequalities: Children in America's Schools* (New York: Crown, 1991), chap. 4. He makes a powerful case that money matters significantly in determining the quality of education delivered. For a useful effort to assess the impact of differential school spending and school reform on education in New Jersey's districts, see William A. Firestone, Margaret E. Goertz, and Gary Natriello, *From Cashbox to Classroom: The Struggle for Fiscal Reform and Educational Change in New Jersey* (New York: Teachers College Press, 1997). For a comparison between high schools in all-black Roosevelt and almost all-white Plainview–Bethpage on Long Island, see "Persistent Racial Segregation Mars Suburbs' Green Dream," *NYT,* Mar. 17, 1994, and "Killing the Future in Roosevelt, L.I.," editorial, *NYT,* Nov. 30, 2001. The alternative argument, that more money does not make for better schools, has been made by some economists; see, for example, Eric A. Hanushek, "Have Times Changed?: The Relation Between School Resources and Student Performance," in Gary Burtless, ed., *Does Money Matter?: The Effect of School Resources on Student Achievement and Adult Success* (Washington, DC: Brookings, 1996). In Vermont, equalizing school spending across districts led to significant improvements in test results in poor towns over a three-year period: "Vermont Spending Plan Seems to Help Schools," *NYT,* Jan. 31, 2001.

85. For an analysis of the "school problem" plaguing many suburbs in the 1950s with the population boom—overcrowded buildings, teacher shortages, and mounting school taxes—see Benjamin Fine, "Educational Problems in the Suburbs," *NYT,* Jan. 30, 1957, reprinted in Dobriner, *Suburban Community,* pp. 317–25. Today, "report cards" on the results of standardized testing, by community and even by school, can have a significant impact on property values. The president of the Massachusetts Association of Realtors argued that the results from the Massachusetts Comprehensive Assessment System (MCAS) were quickly "translated by the consumers in the marketplace," as prospective house buyers "shop communities": "School Ratings Another Tool for Buyers," *BG,* Oct. 3, 1999. Also see "In Real Estate, It's Location, Location . . . and Test Scores," *NYT,* June 3, 2000. On the socioeconomic makeup of a community predicting test scores, see "A Pledge of Allegiance to Public Schools," *NYT,* Mar. 15, 2000.

86. Raymond M. Ralph, *Farmland to Suburbia, 1920–1960,* vol. 6 of *Bergen County, New Jersey: History and Heritage* (Hackensack: Bergen County Board of Chosen Freeholders, 1983), pp. 87–89; "After Whittling Taxes, Whitman Turns to a More Popular Cut," *NYT,* Jan. 17, 1999; "New Jersey School Board Asks for State Help Funding All-Day Kindergarten," *Associated Press,* May 19, 2001; Salmore and Salmore, *New Jersey Politics and Government,* p. 263; "School Colors," *NYT,* June 11, 1995, "Island in a Sea of White Resistance, Englewood's Neighbors Oppose All Regional School Plans," *NYT,* Dec. 21, 1995, and "New Jersey Will Not Force High School's Desegregation," *NYT,* Feb. 7, 1997,

all of which describe the resistance of Tenafly, Englewood Cliffs, and Leonia to joining Englewood, with its 96 percent black school enrollment, in a proposed regional school district. In 1996 one of the state's few regional school districts even voted to disband: "Questions Rise in Vote to Split School District," *NYT*, May 16, 1996. See also "Can Our Schools Be Merged? The Regional Approach: Some Say It Can Work. Some Say It Must Work. Others Aren't So Sure," *NYT*, June 2, 1996.

87. Briffault, "Our Localism: Part I," pp. 18*n*.58, 23.

88. Salmore and Salmore, *New Jersey Politics and Government*, pp. 263–78; Briffault, "Our Localism: Part I," pp. 31–35.

89. Salmore and Salmore, *New Jersey Politics and Government*, pp. 259–60. When the state legislature rejected many of Governor Hughes's state aid proposals after the civil disorders of 1967, the new state formula for aiding public schools had limited revenues to work with, and by structure awarded aid according to population, not by need: "The 1968 State Urban Aid Program," Oct. 2, 1968, Erber, Box D, Folder 10; "New Jersey Guts Its Cities," editorial, *NYT*, Sept. 16, 1968; "Bars Fast Decision on School Aid Plan," *NN*, Dec. 20, 1968.

90. For documentation of the continued inadequacy of state aid to reduce disparities between wealthy and poor districts, both urban and suburban, see reports to the New Jersey Education Reform Project, "Q" Files, NPL, "Greater Newark Urban Coalition": Joel S. Berke and Judy G. Sinkin, "Paying for New Jersey's Schools, Problems and Proposals," February 1974; Larry Rubin, "An Evaluation of the Fiscal Impact of New Jersey's Public School Education Act of 1975 on the State's Low Wealth and Urban School Districts," June 1978; Earl Preston Thomas, "Paterson, New Jersey: A Fiscal and Educational Profile," March 1979. Enormous increases in disparity between wealthy and poor districts between 1975 and 1980, both as a result of higher levels of state support with the Public School Act of 1975 and a growing gap in property values, were presented to the superior court in 1984; see Decision 195 N.J. Super. 59, 477 A.2d 1278, pp. 47–50.

91. Data on Camden from U.S. Department of Commerce, Bureau of the Census, *County and City Data Book, 1983*, pp. 740, 744, 746.

92. For discussion of *Abbott* v. *Burke* and the conditions leading up to it, see New Jersey Education Reform Project, "Newark School Finance Profile, 1977–1978," March 1978, "Q" Files, NPL, "Greater Newark Urban Coalition"; League of Women Voters of New Jersey, *Spotlight on New Jersey Government*, pp. 78–81; "Class of Abbott vs. Burke Takes Stock, 20 Pupils from 1981: Where Are They Now?" *NSL*, June 8, 1997. School funding figures for 1988–89 in Kozol, *Savage Inequalities*, p. 236.

93. Educational reformers began making the case soon after the *Robinson* v. *Cahill* suit that equalizing spending was not enough to ensure equality of opportunity, that children in poor districts had "special needs" that cost more to address. For an early statement of this perspective, see Alan Gurwitz, "Urban Schools and Equality of Educational Opportunity in New Jersey: A Report of the New Jersey Education Reform Project," "Q" Files, NPL, "Greater Newark Urban Coalition."

94. On Florio's difficulties, see Salmore and Salmore, *New Jersey Politics and Government*, pp. 253–58, 273–78; "Statewide School Tax Is Proposed," *NYT*, Dec. 6, 1993.

95. Whitman cut the income tax 30 percent in two rather than a projected three years, and then had to figure out how to make ends meet. The first tax increase of her administration doubled the state's cigarette tax to 80 cents a package to raise $205 million to help pay for hospital care for the uninsured and for school construction: "Whitman Approves Higher Cigarette Tax," *NYT*, Dec. 20, 1997. She also experimented with selling off state-owned facilities like marinas: Bob Herbert, "Marina Madness in New Jersey," *NYT*, Feb. 8, 1995. For her continued attention to tax cutting, see "Tax Rebates in New Jersey," editor-

ial, *NYT,* Jan. 23, 1999; "Whitman Presents Budget with Property Tax Rebates," *NYT,* Jan. 26, 1999.

96. For a good summary of the twenty-eight-year history of the New Jersey Supreme Court's involvement with school spending equity suits, see *Abbott by Abbott* v. *Burke,* 153 N.J. 480, 710, A.2d 450, 126 Ed. Law Rep. 258 (N.J. May 21, 1998); also, for recent history, "Whitman Asks for Time to Solve School Aid Gap," *NYT,* May 25, 1994; "Top Jersey Court Orders New Plan for School Funds," "Court's Decision Gives a Grateful Whitman Some Breathing Space," "At Issue: What Is Adequate for the Poor," "Excerpts of Court Ruling Requiring Parity in New Jersey's School Spending," all in *NYT,* July 13, 1994; "New Jersey Faces Suit Over Schools," *NYT,* Apr. 21, 1996; "Whitman Offers Fiscal Plan for Parity in Schools," *NYT,* May 16, 1996; "Told They Spend Too Much, Wealthier Districts Protest," *NYT,* Aug. 12, 1996; "School Funding Plan Hits Raw Nerve," *NSL,* Dec. 5, 1996; "Court Weighs Whitman Plan for Schools," *NYT,* Mar. 5, 1997; "New Jersey's School Financing Is Again Held Unconstitutional," *NYT,* May 15, 1997; "Whitman Stands on Record, but Newer Issues Stir Voters," *NYT,* Nov. 1, 1997; "Court Clears Plan for Poor Schools," *NSL,* May 22, 1998; "Bold Decisions in New Jersey," editorial, *NYT,* May 23, 1998; "School Solution?" *NSL,* May 24, 1998; "School Equity in New Jersey," editorial, *NYT,* May 27, 1998; "Legal War Brews over School Funding," *Times of Trenton,* June 4, 1998; "School Reform Stumbles, Programs Sought by Court Won't Be Ready in September," *NSL,* July 12, 1998; "State Wants Extra $2.7M for Elementary Schools," *BR,* Aug. 7, 1998; "Klagholz Directive Sets Off a New Fight with Superintendents," *NSL,* Aug. 18, 1998; "Racing to Be Ready for New Preschoolers," *NYT,* Sept. 2, 1998.

For new suits brought, see "Mid-Income Districts File Suit for Tax Relief," *NSL,* Apr. 21, 1998; "School-Taxes Suit Has Familiar Ring," *Times of Trenton,* Apr. 23, 1998; "Other Schools Line Up for Bigger Share of State Aid," *NSL,* May 24, 1998; "School-funding Suits Alive After Ruling, Middle-Income, Rural Schools Petition Courts," *Times of Trenton,* May 27, 1998; "New Jersey to Provide Full-Day Preschool in Its 28 Poorest Districts," *NYT,* Jan. 7, 1999; "Justices Fault Pace of Preschool Program," *NYT,* Oct. 14, 1999; "12 Billion for Schools in New Jersey," *NYT,* July 14, 2000; "Preschool Programs Still Substandard, Poor Districts Say," *NYT,* July 27, 2000; "Report Says Few Poor Children Receive Adequate Preschool Education in New Jersey," *NYT,* June 1, 2001; "Passaic Joins Suit to Bring Help for Preschool Programs," *NYT,* June 26, 2001. On Governor McGreevey's announcement, "A Truce in New Jersey's School War," editorial, *NYT,* Feb. 9, 2002, and on New Jersey's deficit, "Round One in New Jersey's Budget," editorial, *NYT,* Feb. 19, 2001.

97. "Low-Income Houses and a Suburb's Fears," *NYT,* Apr. 5, 1997.

98. Briffault, "Our Localism: Part I," p. 24.

99. For cases elsewhere in the nation, see Briffault, "Our Localism: Part I," pp. 24–39; Stan Karp, "Equity Suits Clog the Courts," *Funding for Justice: Money, Equity, and the Future of Public Education* (Milwaukee: Rethinking Schools, 1997), pp. 4–9, and other articles here as well, including a state-by-state overview as of 1997; "An Evaluation of the Fiscal Impact of New Jersey's Public School Education Act of 1975 on the State's Low Wealth and Urban School Districts," June 1978, pp. 6–9; "The National Context: Rulings on Other School Systems," *NYT,* July 13, 1994; "Pulse: School Financing," *NYT,* Nov. 27, 1995; "In the 'Live Free or Die' State, an Unpalatable Tax Decision," *NYT,* June 29, 1998; "With Ruling, New York Joins States Revamping School Financing," *NYT,* Jan. 13, 2001; "A Visionary School Plan in Maryland," *NYT,* Apr. 30, 2002. "Testimony Prepared for Delivery Before Senate Finance Committee on September 11, 1968 by Dr. Herbert J. G. Bab," Erber, Box B, Folder 1, is an excellent contemporary analysis of how overdependence on property taxes for school finance aggravated inequity in California, a charge that culminated in the California Supreme Court's landmark *Serrano* v. *Priest* decision of

1971, mandating on the basis of the constitution's equal protection clause equitable per pupil expenditures among school districts, regardless of discrepancies in property tax bases. Voter anger about the decision contributed to passage of the 1978 ballot initiative, Proposition 13, which capped property taxes and drastically cut revenues, ensuring disinvestment in the public schools more broadly. Supreme court decisions in Kentucky and Texas were noteworthy for mandating improvements in the quality of education, not just equal funding, in the poorest districts: Briffault, "Our Localism: Part II," pp. 442*n*.332, 449*n*.429.

100. On state contributions to school funding, see Jon Shure, "Tax Reform Takes More Than Baby Steps," reprint from *BR* by *New Jersey Policy Perspective,* http://www.mjpp .org/baby.html; "New Jersey's Fiscal Plight Inspires Hopes for Change," *NYT,* Apr. 8, 2002; Briffault, "Our Localism: Part I," p. 59 and *n*.257; "In the 'Live Free or Die' State, an Unpalatable Tax Decision," *NYT,* June 29, 1998; Harvard Project on School Desegregation, cited in "Slouching Toward Mount Laurel," *NYT,* Mar. 31, 1996; "After Whittling Income Taxes, Whitman Turns to a More Popular Cut," *NYT,* Jan. 17, 1999; Gary Orfield, "Schools More Separate: Consequences of a Decade of Resegregation" (Cambridge, MA: Harvard Civil Rights Project, July 2001); Orfield and John T. Yun, "Resegregation in American Schools" (Cambridge, MA: Harvard Civil Rights Project, June 1999); Orfield, *Public School Desegregation in the United States, 1968–1980* (Washington, DC: Joint Center for Policy Studies, 1983); Orfield, Susan E. Eaton, and the Harvard Project on School Desegregation, *Dismantling Desegregation: The Quiet Reversal of Brown v. Board of Education* (New York: New Press, 1996); "After 45 Years, Resegregation Emerges in Schools, Study Finds," *NYT,* June 13, 1999; "Court Says Denver Can End Forced Busing," *NYT,* Sept. 17, 1995; Jaynes and William, *A Common Destiny,* pp. 225–27; Waldo E. Martin, Jr., *Brown v. Board of Education: A Brief History with Documents* (Boston: Bedford/St. Martin's, 1998), pp. 230–37.

The influx of Latino students into states like New Jersey since 1970, a 208 percent enrollment rise by 1998, complicated but sharpened the racial divide.

101. Ira Katznelson and Margaret Weir, *Schooling for All: Class, Race, and the Decline of the Democratic Ideal* (New York: Basic Books, 1985); also see Harvey Kantor and Barbara Brenzel, "Urban Education and the Truly Disadvantaged: The Historical Roots of the Contemporary Crisis, 1945–1990," in Michael B. Katz, *The Underclass Debate: Views from History* (Princeton: Princeton University Press, 1993).

102. Bert Hunter, "Who Pays for Public Assistance in New Jersey?" Council of Social Agencies, United Community Fund and Council of Essex and West Hudson, February 1967, Lilley, Box 3, pp. 14–18.

103. Erber, "New Jersey's 'Moment of Truth,' " August 1968, Erber, Box B, Folder 4, pp. 29–30; Council of Social Agencies, Newark, "The Case for the Council of Social Agencies and Members' Concerns with the Adequacy of Tax Support for Publicly Financed Health, Education, Welfare and Recreation Services in New Jersey: A Suggested Three Pronged Approach," Feb. 15, 1965, Erber, Box B, Folder 6.

104. From NAACP, A 624, "Supreme Court—School Cases—New Jersey, 1952–55": NAACP, "A Survey of the Public School Systems in the State of New Jersey, Made Under the Direction of the New Jersey State Conference of N.A.A.C.P. Branches," 1947; Joseph L. Bustard, "The New Jersey Story Concerning the Development of Racially Integrated Public Schools," Presented at a Conference on the Courts and Racial Integration in Education," Apr. 16–18, 1952; Wright, "Extending Civil Rights in New Jersey through the Division Against Discrimination," pp. 95–96; memo to CRC Offices, ADL (Anti-Defamation League) Regional Offices, AJC (American Jewish Committee) Area Offices from Sol Rabkin and Ted Leskes, June 8, 1955, Subject: Decision of the Commissioner of

Education in New Jersey in the Englewood School Segregation Cases, Schomburg, 004,099-1; "School Attendance Figures," flyer "What Price Segregation?" press release "New Jersey Presses Discriminatory Charges Against Englewood School Board, February 4, 1955." From the microform NAACP Papers, Part 3, Series D, Central Office Records 1956–1965: Statement from the Montclair Public Schools, Sept. 12, 1961 (Reel 5, Frames 816–17); press release, "Negroes Win N.J. School Victory," Oct. 21, 1961 (Reel 5, Frames 824–25); NAACP, "Attacking Segregated Schools in New Jersey," quarterly meeting, New Jersey State Conference of Branches, Sept. 30, 1961 (Reel 6, Frames 114–17); memo to Roy Wilkins from June Shagaloff RE: Elementary Schools, Orange, New Jersey (Reel 6, Frames 152–55); Dan W. Dodson, "Racial Issues in Public Education in Orange, New Jersey, November 12, 1962" (Reel 6, Frames 211–25). Also see "Racial Policies in New Jersey School Districts, 1953–54" and "Schools Attended by Negroes, 1953–54," Lett, Box 1; Paul Hope, "Englewood, New Jersey—A Case Study in De Facto Segregation," in Westin, *Freedom Now!*, pp. 140–45; Louis E. Lomax, *The Negro Revolt* (New York: Harper & Row, 1962), pp. 156–57; "Pickets Boycott School in Jersey, Montclair Parents Ask Its End—New Rochelle Quiet," *NYT*, Sept. 8, 1961; "Montclair Hears Integration Plan," *NYT*, Apr. 12, 1962; "Teaneck Schools Shift Racial Plan," *NYT*, May 10, 1963; "400 Black Students Stage Sit-in at Montclair High," *NN*, Jan. 31, 1970.

105. Gelfand, *Nation of Cities*, p. 352; Briffault, "Our Localism: Part II," p. 348*n*.21.

106. Gretchen Sullivan Sorin, "'Respectable People': Growing Up Black in the New Jersey Suburbs," in Kathryn Grover, *Teenage New Jersey, 1941–1975*, pp. 37–49.

107. "Boom in Housing Keeps on Rolling, Surprising Many," *NYT*, May 27, 1999; "During a Bear Market, There's Really No Place Like Home," *NYT*, Aug. 15, 2001.

108. Wood, *Suburbia*, quoted in Barbara Norfleet, *When We Like Ike: Looking for Postwar America* (New York: Norton, 2001), p. 54.

109. State of New Jersey, Department of Community Affairs, Division of State and Regional Planning, "The Housing Crisis in New Jersey, 1970," p. 92; Erber, "Zoning Against People," 1968, p. 3.

110. One possible way of reconciling this apparent contradiction between a commitment to capitalist development through suburbanization and a strategy of exclusion that ultimately restrained economic expansion is provided by geographer David Harvey's theoretical insight that suburbanization as it unfolded demonstrated the irrationalities of postwar capitalism. As residential dispersal fueled socially differentiated submarkets built around "status, position, and prestige," he argues, the combined imperatives of individual status ambition and local community empowerment created obstacles to further capital accumulation, the supposed goal of "the suburban solution" in the first place. As elites used the powers available to them, particularly small-scale but influential zoning regulations, to protect their own status and privileges rather than to fuel the larger society's economic growth, they reproduced in the evolving suburban landscape the alienating social relations of capitalist society while inhibiting the more democratic inclinations of the expansion of the capitalist order: David Harvey, *The Urban Experience* (Baltimore: Johns Hopkins University Press, 1989), pp. 40–41, 120–24.

111. First quote by Rune Johansson, former minister of industry, from Roland Huntford, *The New Totalitarians* (New York: Stein and Day, 1972), p. 254, quoted in Bruce Headey, *Housing Policy in the Developed Economy: The United Kingdom, Sweden and the United States* (London: Croom Helm, 1978), p. 46; second quote from Huntford, *New Totalitarians*, p. 234; also see Peter Hall, *Cities in Civilization: Culture, Innovation, and Urban Order* (London: Weidenfeld & Nicolson, 1998).

112. *NYT* survey, Nov. 14, 1978, cited in Teaford, *Twentieth-Century American City*, p. 154.

113. "Housing Six Million More Residents," prepared for Regional Plan Association Conference, February 11–14, 1962, p. 71. Also see Briffault, "Our Localism: Part I," p. 1 and "Our Localism: Part II," pp. 282, 284, for related discussion of the privatization of suburbia.

114. "Houses, Homes and How Women Have Moved On," review of Jane Davison and Lesley Davison, *To Make a House a Home: Four Generations of American Women and the Houses They Lived In* (New York: Random House, 1994), *NYT,* May 25, 1994.

115. Janet L. Wolff, *What Makes Women Buy: A Guide to Understanding and Influencing the New Woman of Today* (New York: McGraw-Hill, 1958), p. 217.

CHAPTER 6. COMMERCE: RECONFIGURING COMMUNITY MARKETPLACES

1. Robert C. Wood, *Suburbia: Its People and Their Politics* (Boston: Houghton Mifflin, 1959), p. 63; 1961 statistic from Bert Randolph Sugar, "Suburbia: A Nice Place to Live, but I Wouldn't Want to Define It There," *Media/Scope* 11 (February 1967): 50; for further analysis, see James D. Tarver, "Suburbanization of Retail Trade in the Standard Metropolitan Areas of the United States, 1948–54," in William M. Dobriner, ed., *The Suburban Community* (New York: Putnam's, 1958), pp. 195–205. Estimates of the number of shopping centers before the International Council of Shopping Centers was founded in 1957 vary; Janet L. Wolff, author of *What Makes Women Buy: A Guide to Understanding and Influencing the New Woman of Today* (New York: McGraw-Hill, 1958), p. 223, claims that in 1952 "there were only about 100 organized shopping centers." Historians of suburbanization have paid far less attention to the restructuring of commercial life in the postwar period than to the transformation of residential experience.

2. Ann Durkin Keating and Ruth Eckdish Knack, "Shopping in the Planned Community: Evolution of the Park Forest Town Center," unpublished paper in possession of author; Howard Gillette, Jr., "The Evolution of the Planned Shopping Center in Suburb and City," *American Planning Association Journal* 51 (Autumn 1985): 449–60; Daniel Prosser, "The New Downtowns: Commercial Architecture in Suburban New Jersey, 1920–1970," in Joel Schwartz and Prosser, eds., *Cities of the Garden State: Essays in the Urban and Suburban History of New Jersey* (Dubuque, IA: Kendall/Hunt, 1977), pp. 113–15; "Park Forest Moves into '52," *House and Home: The Magazine of Building* 1 (March 1952): 115–16; William S. Worley, *J. C. Nichols and the Shaping of Kansas City: Innovation in Planned Residential Communities* (Columbia: University of Missouri Press, 1990); Richard Longstreth, "J. C. Nichols, the Country Club Plaza, and Notions of Modernity," *Harvard Architecture Review,* vol. 5, *Precedent and Invention* (New York: Rizzoli, 1986), pp. 121–32; William H. Whyte, Jr., "The Outgoing Life," *Fortune,* July 1953, p. 85; Michael Birkner, *A Country Place No More: The Transformation of Bergenfield, New Jersey, 1894–1994* (Rutherford, NJ: Fairleigh Dickinson University Press, 1994), pp. 174–77; Special Foster Village Edition, *BR,* Aug. 10, 1949.

3. Statistics compiled by the International Council of Shopping Centers, in advertising supplement to the *NYT,* "Shopping Centers Come of Age: International Council of Shopping Centers Observes 20th Anniversary," 1977, GSD, p. 7.

4. Richard Longstreth, "The Mixed Blessings of Success: The Hecht Company and Department Store Branch Development After World War II," Occasional Paper No. 14, January 1995, Center for Washington Area Studies, George Washington University.

5. Kenneth T. Jackson, *Crabgrass Frontier: The Suburbanization of the United States* (New York: Oxford University Press, 1985), pp. 255–61. On precedents in the pre–World War II period, see Richard Longstreth, "Silver Spring: Georgia Avenue, Colesville Road, and the Creation of an Alternative 'Downtown' for Metropolitan Washington," in Zeynep Celik, Diane Favro, and Richard Ingersoll, eds., *Streets: Critical Perspectives on Public*

Space (Berkeley: University of California Press, 1994), pp. 247–57; Longstreth, "The Neighborhood Shopping Center in Washington, D.C., 1930–1941," *Journal of the Society of Architectural Historians* 51 (March 1992): 5–33; Longstreth, "The Perils of a Parkless Town," in Martin Wachs and Margaret Crawford, eds., *The Car and the City: The Automobile, the Built Environment, and Daily Urban Life* (Ann Arbor: University of Michigan Press, 1992), pp. 141–53.

6. Samuel Feinberg, "Story of Shopping Centers," *What Makes Shopping Centers Tick,* reprinted from *Women's Wear Daily* (New York: Fairchild, 1960), p. 1. For background on the development of regional shopping centers, see William Severini Kowinski, *The Malling of America: An Inside Look at the Great Consumer Paradise* (New York: Morrow, 1985); Neil Harris, *Cultural Excursions: Marketing Appetites and Cultural Tastes in Modern America* (Chicago: University of Chicago Press, 1990), pp. 7, 76–77, 278–88; Margaret Crawford, "The World in a Shopping Mall," in Michael Sorkin, ed., *Variations on a Theme Park: The New American City and the End of Public Space* (New York: Noonday Press/Hill & Wang, 1992), pp. 3–30; Gillette, "Evolution of the Planned Shopping Center." For a useful case study of the development of suburban shopping centers in the Philadelphia region, see Stephanie Dyer, "Markets in the Meadows: Department Stores and Shopping Centers in the Decentralization of Philadelphia, 1920–1980" (Ph.D. diss., University of Pennsylvania, 2000).

7. On the postwar growth of Paramus and Bergen County, New Jersey, see Raymond M. Ralph, *Bergen County, New Jersey History and Heritage,* vol. 6, *Farmland to Suburbia, 1920–1960* (Hackensack, NJ: Bergen County Board of Chosen Freeholders, 1983), pp. 62–71, 76–90; Catherine M. Fogarty, John E. O'Connor, and Charles F. Cummings, *Bergen County: A Pictorial History* (Norfolk, VA: Donning, 1985), pp. 182–93; *Beautiful Bergen: The Story of Bergen County, New Jersey* (Ridgewood, NJ: s.n., 1962); Patricia M. Ryle, *An Economic Profile of Bergen County, New Jersey* (Trenton, NJ: Office of Economic Research, Division of Planning and Research, New Jersey Department of Labor and Industry, March 1980); League of Women Voters of Bergen County, *Where Can I Live in Bergen County?: Factors Affecting Housing Supply* (Closter, NJ: League of Women Voters, 1972).

8. Feinberg, *What Makes Shopping Centers Tick,* pp. 2, 94–102; Ralph, *Farmland to Suburbia,* pp. 70–71, 84–85; Mark A. Stuart, *Bergen County, New Jersey History and Heritage,* vol. 7; *Our Era, 1960–Present* (Hackensack, NJ: Bergen County Board of Chosen Freeholders, 1983), pp. 19–22; Prosser, "New Downtowns," pp. 119–20; Edward T. Thompson, "The Suburb That Macy's Built," *Fortune,* February 1960, pp. 195–200; "Garden State Plaza Merchant's Manual," May 1, 1957, and certain pages revised in 1959, 1960, 1962, 1963, 1965, 1969, GSP.

9. "The Economy: The Great Shopping Spree," *Time,* Jan. 8, 1965, pp. 58–62 and cover.

10. C. B. Plamer, "The Shopping Center Goes to the Shopper," *NYT Magazine,* Nov. 29, 1953, p. 40.

11. On the financing of shopping centers, and the great profits involved, see Jerry Jacobs, *The Mall: An Attempted Escape from Everyday Life* (Prospect Heights, IL: Waveland, 1984), p. 52.

12. ICSC, "Shopping Centers Come of Age," p. 2.

13. Victor Gruen, "Introverted Architecture," *Progressive Architecture* 38 (1957): 204–208; Gruen and Larry Smith, *Shopping Towns USA: The Planning of Shopping Centers* (New York: Reinhold, 1960), pp. 22–24; both quoted in Gillette, "Evolution of the Planned Shopping Center." For more on Gruen, see Kowinski, *Malling of America,* pp. 118–20, 210–14; "Exhibit of Shopping Centers," *NYT,* Oct. 19, 1954. For profile of Martin Bucksbaum, another shopping-center builder, see Paul Goldberger, "Selling the Suburban Frontier," *NYT Magazine,* Dec. 31, 1995, pp. 34–35.

14. ICSC, "Shopping Centers Come of Age," pp. 1, 39. One Florida architect whose firm built several shopping centers referred to making the department store the focal point of a center as the "Main Street Plan": Clinton Gamble, "Shopping Centers! A Modern Miracle," *Miami Herald*, Oct. 23, 1955. In a talk to the Urban History Seminar of the Chicago Historical Society, February 17, 1994, Robert Bruegmann made the same point about the way the earliest design of suburban shopping centers resembled downtown shopping streets.

15. Quoted in Feinberg, *What Makes Shopping Centers Tick*, p. 101. In addition to sources already cited on the control possible in a shopping center versus a downtown, see "Shopping Centers Get Personality," *NYT*, June 29, 1958. For a notion of shopping centers as an "integrated organism," see Howard T. Fisher, "The Impact of New Shopping Centers Upon Established Business Districts," talk at National Citizens' Conference on Planning for City, State and Nation, May 15, 1950, GSD, pp. 3–4. Chains were also favored over independents in shopping centers because they more easily reaped the big bonuses for depreciation of new store upfitting, while small independents had little surplus income to shelter and less specialized tax accounting expertise: e-mail correspondence with Thomas W. Hanchett, Nov. 20, 1996.

Insurance companies made no secret of why they were attracted to investing in shopping centers. John D. W. Wadhams, senior vice president of Aetna, explained that insurance companies saw buying a center "as a way of saying to policy holders that their company is aggressively seeking those equities which will have ever-increasing rates of return and can some day be sold at a good profit, increasing overall yield": ICSC, "Shopping Centers Come of Age," p. 54. Teachers Insurance and Annuity Association–College Retirement Equities Fund (TIAA-CREF) explained why it favored chain stores in centers: "TIAA normally requires a certain proportion of national tenants in the shopping centers it finances. This means that if a particular center does not turn out well, the leases held by its major tenants will be supported by other stores in that system around the country": William C. Greenough, *It's My Retirement Money, Take Good Care of It: The TIAA-CREF Story* (Homewood, IL: Irwin, 1990), p. 175. In a 1971 publication, TIAA boasted that with shopping center loans accounting for 43 percent of its total conventional mortgage loans, "today [it] is recognized as being one of the leaders among the institutions that finance shopping centers": *TIAA Investment Report for 1971*, pp. 8–9. A year later TIAA would claim investments in 133 shopping centers in 30 states: *The Participant* (Policyholder Newsletter), November 1972, p. 4.

16. Ernest Erber, "Notes on the 'City of Urban,'" Erber, Box B; Dean K. Boorman, "Shopping Centers: Their Planning and Control, Federation Planning Information Report," vol. 2, no. 4 (New Jersey Federation of Planning Officials, September 1967), p. 6, GSD; "Paramus Booms as a Store Center," *NYT*, Feb. 5, 1962; "The Mall the Merrier, or Is It?" *NYT*, Nov. 21, 1976. For details on particular stores and activities at Bergen Mall and Garden State Plaza, see Feinberg, *What Makes Shopping Centers Tick*, pp. 97–100; Fogarty et al., *Bergen County*, p. 189; Prosser, "New Downtowns," p. 119. Almost every issue of the *BR* beginning in 1957 yields valuable material (in articles and advertisements) on mall stores, services, and activities. The discussion here is based particularly on issues from Nov. 8, 13, 19, 1957, Jan. 8, 1958, June 10, 1959, and Mar. 2, 1960. Also see "Shoppers! Mass Today on Level 1," *NYT*, June 14, 1994; press release on Garden State Plaza's opening in GSP, folder "GSP History"; "It Won't Be Long Now . . . Bamberger's, New Jersey's Greatest Store, Comes to Paramus Soon," promotional leaflet, stamped Aug. 22, 1956, file "Bergen County Shopping Centers," Hackensack; "The Shopping Center," *NYT*, Feb. 1, 1976.

For data on the allocation of shopping center space in ten regional shopping centers in 1957, see William Applebaum and S. O. Kaylin, *Case Studies in Shopping Center*

Development and Operation (New York: ICSC, 1974), p. 101. For evidence of the community orientation of shopping centers nationwide, see Arthur Herzog, "Shops, Culture, Centers—and More," *NYT Magazine*, Nov. 18, 1962, pp. 34–35, 109–10, 112–14; in the *NYT*: "A Shopping Mall in Suffolk Offering More Than Goods," June 22, 1970; "Supermarkets Hub of Suburbs," Feb. 7, 1971; "Busy Day in a Busy Mall," Apr. 12, 1972. On the community relations efforts of branch stores, see Clinton L. Oaks, *Managing Suburban Branches of Department Stores*, Business Research Series No. 10 (Stanford, CA: Graduate School of Business, Stanford University, 1957), pp. 81–83.

17. George Sternlieb, *The Future of the Downtown Department Store* (Cambridge: Joint Center for Urban Studies of the Massachusetts Institute of Technology and Harvard University, 1962), p. 10.

18. Arthur L. Manchee, "Retailing," excepts from statement during a panel discussion on "Industrial Growth in New Jersey in the Next Decade," *New Jersey Economic Review* 6 (May–June 1964): 5; Victor Gruen Associates, *Shopping Centers of Tomorrow: An Architectural Exhibition*, circulated by the American Federation of Arts, n.d. but c. 1954, p. 16.

19. R. H. Macy & Co., *Annual Report for 1955; The Times-Advocate*, Mar. 14, 1976, argues that Bamberger's, Macy's store at the Garden State Plaza, was at the forefront of the chain's appeal to the middle- to upper-income shopper. On market segmentation of shopping centers, also see William H. Whyte, Jr., *The Organization Man* (New York: Simon & Schuster, 1956), pp. 316–17; Jacobs, *The Mall*, pp. 5, 12; and Albert Bills and Lois Pratt, "Personality Differences Among Shopping Centers," *Fairleigh Dickinson University Business Review* 1 (Winter 1961), which had already begun making finer socioeconomic distinctions among the middle-class customers of the Bergen Mall and Garden State Plaza. Crawford's "The World in a Shopping Mall" discusses the sophisticated strategies that market researchers used to analyze trade areas and pitch stores to different kinds of customers; pp. 8–9.

20. Pierre Martineau, "Social Classes and Spending Behavior," *JM* 23 (October 1958): 126–27; also see Manchee, "Retailing," p. 5, on "middle income" customers.

21. George Sternlieb, "The Future of Retailing in the Downtown Core," *AIP Journal* 24 (May 1963), as reprinted in Howard A. Schretter, *Downtown Revitalization* (Athens: Institute of Community and Area Development, University of Georgia, 1967), p. 95. Before the shopping centers were built and the Baltimore area's white shoppers had few options besides downtown stores, African Americans accused these stores of discriminating; see, for example, a letter to Clarence Mitchell, director of the Washington, D.C., Bureau of the NAACP, reporting a complaint that "the Baltimore Lane Bryant store would not serve Negroes": NAACP, II, B 64, "Discrimination, General, 1950–55."

22. First Federal Savings and Loan Association of Chicago newsletter, "Savings and Homeownership," August 1951, pp. 2–3, GSD; Samuel Feinberg, "Metropolis in the Making," *Women's Wear Daily*, Mar. 1, 1960; also see Wood, *Suburbia*, p. 211; and in *NYT*: "The Incredible Expanding Mall," Aug. 11, 1996, and "Suburban Comforts Thwart Atlanta's Plans to Limit Sprawl," Nov. 21, 1999.

23. For example, James A. Brunner and John L. Mason, "The Influence of Driving Time Upon Shopping Center Preference," *JM* 32 (April 1968): 57–61; William E. Cox, Jr., and Ernest F. Cooke, "Other Dimensions Involved in Shopping Center Preference," *JM* 34 (October 1970): 12–17; Pierre D. Martineau, "Customers' Shopping Center Habits Change Retailing: Secondary Areas and Scatter Zones Important with Mobility," *Editor and Publisher*, Oct. 26, 1963, p. 16.

24. U.S. Department of Labor, Bureau of Labor Statistics, "Consumer Expenditures and Income, Northern New Jersey, 1960–61," BLS Report No. 237-63, December 1963, Schomburg, clipping file "Consumer Expenses & Income—NJ."

25. "The Wonder on Routes 4 and 17: Garden State Plaza," brochure, file "Bergen County Shopping Centers," Hackensack; "Notes on Discussion Dealing with Regional (Intermunicipal) Planning Program for Passaic Valley Area (Lower Portion of Passaic Co. and South Bergen," n.d., Erber, Box A, Folder 3; "Memorandum to DAJ and WBS from EE," Nov. 22, 1966, Erber, Box B; National Center for Telephone Research (a division of Louis Harris and Associates), "A Study of Shoppers' Attitudes Toward the Proposed Shopping Mall in the Hudson County Meadowlands Area," conducted for Hartz Mountain Industries, February 1979, Rutgers.

On African-American dependence on public transportation, see Greater Newark Chamber of Commerce, "Survey of Jobs and Unemployment," May 1973, "Q" Files, NPL, "Greater Newark Chamber of Commerce," p. III-2; Donald E. Sexton, "Black Buyer Behavior," *JM* 36 (October 1972): 37. In another New York suburban area, Long Island, highway builder Robert Moses made sure that buses carrying poor and black city residents were unable to reach beaches, parks, and other sites of consumption and recreation by constructing overpasses too low to allow buses underneath: Robert A. Caro, *The Power Broker: Robert Moses and the Fall of New York* (New York: Vintage, 1975), pp. 318–19, 546, 951–52. As recently as 1995, a black teenager was killed crossing a seven-lane highway which had no light or crosswalk because the suburban mall where she worked would not allow her bus from inner-city Buffalo to enter mall property and drop off passengers: "Mall Accused of Racism in a Wrongful Death Trial in Buffalo," *NYT*, Nov. 15, 1999; "Galleria Oks City Bus Access," *Buffalo News*, Jan. 30, 1996; "Mall Bus Policy Called Anti-City," *Buffalo News*, Jan. 28, 1996; I am grateful to Katie Barry for alerting me to this case.

26. Stuart, *Our Era*, p. 20; Lois Pratt, "The Impact of Regional Shopping Centers in Bergen County," unpublished conference paper delivered April 23, 1960, in possession of the author. A survey of shopping habits in suburban Montclair, New Jersey, in 1945—before any shopping centers were built—revealed that Newark drew the biggest share of non-Montclair shoppers, with New York second: "Montclair Studies the Shopping Experiences of Its Residents," *JM* 10 (October 1945): 165–70.

27. Samuel Pratt and Lois Pratt, "The Impact of Some Regional Shopping Centers," *JM* 25 (October 1960): 44–50; S. Pratt, "The Challenge to Retailing," address to the 1957 annual meeting of the Passaic Valley Citizens Planning Association, Apr. 24, 1957, in possession of the author; L. Pratt, "Impact of Regional Shopping Centers in Bergen County"; S. Pratt and James Moran, "How the Regional Shopping Centers May Affect Shopping Habits in Rochelle Park (Preliminary)," *Business Research Bulletin* 1, Bureau of Business Research, Fairleigh Dickinson University, 1956; New York University study cited in Thompson, "Suburb That Macy's Built," pp. 196, 200; Regional Plan Association, Committee on the Second Regional Plan, "Work Book for Workshops," Princeton, NJ, May 25–26, 1966, Erber, Box D, pp. V, 7, 9; Stuart U. Rich, *Shopping Behavior of Department Store Customers: A Study of Store Policies and Customer Demand, with Particular Reference to Delivery Service and Telephone Ordering* (Boston: Division of Research, Graduate School of Business Administration, Harvard University, 1963), particularly pp. 133–56, 228; Plan One Research Corporation, New York City, for the Bergen Evening Record Corporation, *The Mighty Market* (Hackensack, NJ: The Record, 1971). For national statistics on the decline of retail sales in central business districts while they mushroomed in metropolitan areas between 1958 and 1963, see Jon C. Teaford, *The Rough Road to Renaissance: Urban Revitalization in America, 1940–1985* (Baltimore: Johns Hopkins University Press, 1990), pp. 129–31.

28. S. Pratt and Moran, "How the Regional Shopping Centers May Affect Shopping Habits in Rochelle Park"; S. Pratt, "Challenge to Retailing," pp. 13–15. For surveys of consumers outside of the New York area, see C. T. Jonassen, *Downtown Versus Suburban*

Shopping, Ohio Marketing Studies, Ohio State University Special Bulletin Number X-58 (Columbus: Bureau of Business Research, Ohio State University, 1953); Sternlieb, *Future of the Downtown Department Store,* pp. 33, 131–33; Rich, *Shopping Behavior of Department Store Customers;* and several important studies described in S. Pratt, "Challenge to Retailing," pp. 15–19.

29. See all the Pratts' studies listed in note 27, as well as "Hackensack Faces Year of Decision," *BR,* Jan. 10, 1958.

30. Herzog, "Shops, Culture, Centers—and More," p. 110, also quote p. 114.

31. "The Shopping Centers," *NYT,* Feb. 1, 1976; *U.S. News & World Report* study cited in ICSC, "Shopping Centers Come of Age," p. 39.

32. The discussion in the two previous paragraphs on the response of local businessmen to shopping center development is based on "From Now On—Until When?" *BR,* Dec. 6, 1957; "Bergen Shoppers Shun New York," *BR,* Dec. 19, 1957; "Main Street Making Comeback in Duel with Shopping Centers," *NYT,* May 31, 1962; "Malls Threaten Downtown Suburbia," *NYT,* Dec. 20, 1972; Samuel Pratt and Lois Pratt, *Suburban Downtown in Transition: A Problem in Business Change in Bergen County, New Jersey* (Rutherford, NJ: Institute of Research, Fairleigh Dickinson University, 1958); L. Pratt, "Impact of Regional Shopping Centers in Bergen County."

Articles on Hackensack merchants' struggle to compete include in *BR,* "A City with Faith: Hackensack Grows," Oct. 29, 1957; "Alma [Anderson-Linden Merchants Association] Continues to Work to Better Shopping Area," Dec. 2, 1957; "The Way of Alma," Dec. 7, 1957; "Life Line to a City's Future: Hackensack Must Plan, Promote," Jan. 10, 1958; "How to Stimulate Business," Jan. 10, 1958; "What's Ahead for Hackensack Business in '58," Jan. 10, 1958; "So the Fight Is Worth Making," Jan. 10, 1958; "Work Together to Build Business, Chamber Told," Jan. 30, 1958; "Gooding Introduced to City Merchants: First Paid Executive Secretary Will Plan Promotion for Stores," Jan. 30, 1958; "Main Street Is After Money," Mar. 21, 1968.

On other towns in northern New Jersey, see in *BR,* "O'Neil Proposes Park Garage as Boon to Englewood Stores," Oct. 18, 1957; "Village Preparing Spaces for Parking of 90 Cars" [Ridgewood], Nov. 6, 1957; "Chamber to Try Charge-It Plan" [Ramsey], Nov. 18, 1957; "Ridgewood Storekeepers Act to Attract Holiday Shoppers," Nov. 12, 1957; "Chamber President Finds Shopping Off" [Bergenfield], Dec. 27, 1957; "Drop of 5–10% Reported in Christmas Business" [Dumont], Dec. 31, 1957; "Shop at Local Stores, Kiwanis Members Told" [New Milford], Mar. 2, 1960.

For an excellent case study of Lancaster, Pennsylvania's struggle with suburban retail competition and central city decline, see David Schuyler, "Prologue to Urban Renewal: The Problem of Downtown Lancaster, 1945–1960," *Pennsylvania History* 61 (January 1994): 75–101. Strategies employed by merchants in the Cheviot business center to cope with the opening of the Cincinnati–Western Hills Plaza in 1954 included the distribution of trading stamps and the running of promotional contests and campaigns: "Effect of a Planned Shopping Center on an Older Center Serving the Same Area," *JM* 21 (July 1956): 71–73.

33. "Bergen Wary of Shoppers on Sundays," *NYT,* Sept. 7, 1993. This quote is from a later effort to uphold the Sunday closing ban, but it expresses a sentiment that long existed among independent retailers.

34. Thompson, "Suburb That Macy's Built," p. 200; Feinberg, *What Makes Shopping Centers Tick,* p. 101. The political and legal struggle over establishing blue laws in Paramus and Bergen County can be traced in the *BR,* beginning in 1957. The battle continued into recent times, with another Bergen County referendum in November 1993, which upheld the Sunday closing ban. Bergen County is among a very few places in New Jersey that still

has blue laws on the books. A new challenge to the closing law, to allow municipalities in Bergen County to make their own policies, surfaced just before this book went into production in Winter 2002. On the most recent conflicts, see "On Sundays, Bergen Shoppers Rest," *NYT,* Dec. 7, 1992; "Bergen Stores Try to Repeal 'Blue Laws,' " *NYT,* Aug. 27, 1993; "Bergen Wary of Shopping on Sundays," *NYT,* Sept. 7, 1993; "Malls Wrestle with the Blues," *NYT,* Sept. 26, 1993; "Both Sides of the Aisle Converge over Blue Laws," *BR,* Oct. 13, 1993; "Bergen Stores to Stay Closed on Sundays," *NSL,* Nov. 3, 1993; "Toys 'R' Us Sues to Halt Borough's 'Blue Law,' " *NYT,* May 13, 2001; "Towns Seek Right to Ditch Blue Laws, Don't Want to Be Tied by County Rule," *BR,* Nov. 22, 2001; "Teaneck Presses State for Right to Sunday Shopping," *BR,* Nov. 29, 2001; "Seeking a Chance to Shop Sundays, Fort Lee Favors End to Blue Laws," *BR,* Dec. 15, 2001.

On the struggle over blue laws nationwide, including New Jersey, during the late 1950s and 1960s, see Gerald Gunther, *Cases and Materials on Individual Rights in Constitutional Law,* 3rd ed. (Mineola, NY: Foundation Press, 1981), pp. 1183–84; E. B. Weiss, "*Never* on Sunday? A Study on Sunday Retailing" (New York: Doyle Dane Bernbach, 1962), mimeograph, esp. pp. 11, 36–43, 59, 63, 79, 83–84. My thanks to Alexis McCrossen for bringing this last document to my attention.

35. "Main Street Making Comeback in Duel with Shopping Centers," *NYT,* May 31, 1962; "Supermarkets Hub of Suburbs," Feb. 7, 1971; Feinberg, *What Makes Shopping Centers Tick,* pp. 100–102; Gillette, "Evolution of the Planned Shopping Center," pp. 454–56; "A New Hackensack Sky Line Looms on Drawing Boards," *BR,* Dec. 26, 1957; James B. Kenyon, *Industrial Localization and Metropolitan Growth: The Paterson-Passaic District,* Department of Geography, Research Paper No. 67 (Chicago: University of Chicago Press, 1960), pp. 209–10; Paterson Planning Board and Boorman and Dorram, Consultants, "Traffic and Transportation Survey, Paterson Master Plan, Report 3, August 1964"; Rutgers University Bureau of Economic Research in contract to New Jersey Department of Conservation and Economic Development for the Meadowlands Regional Development Agency and the State of New Jersey, "Technical Report No. 1H: Patterns of Urban Growth and Decline," November 1966, Erber, Box A, Folder 7, pp. IH-38, 64.

36. Sternlieb, *Future of the Downtown Department Store,* pp. 33–36; Rich, *Shopping Center Behavior of Department Store Customers,* pp. 52–54; Editors of *Fortune, The Changing American Market* (Garden City, NY: Hanover House, 1995), pp. 85–86; John Wallis Johnston, *The Department-Store Buyer: A View from Inside the Parent-Branch Complexes,* Studies in Marketing No. 12 (Austin: Bureau of Business Research, University of Texas at Austin, 1969), p. 25; Jay Scher, *Financial and Operating Results of Department and Specialty Stores of 1976* (New York: National Retail Merchants Association, 1977), cited in Teaford, *Rough Road to Renaissance,* p. 208; ICSC, *Shopping Centers Come of Age,* p. 11; E. H. Gault, "Suburban Branches: A New Trend in Retailing," *Michigan Business Review* 4 (November 1952): 9–13.

37. Shopping centers retreated from promoting themselves as central squares and street corners not only because of the free speech issue, but also to limit the loitering of young people. From *NYT:* "Supermarkets Hub of Suburbs," Feb. 7, 1971; "Coping with Shopping-Center Crises, Dilemma: How Tough to Get If Young Are Unruly," Mar. 7, 1971; "Shopping Centers Change and Grow," May 23, 1971.

38. For a useful summary of the relevant court cases and legal issues involved, see Curtis J. Berger, "*PruneYard* Revisited: Political Activity on Private Lands," *New York University Law Review* 66 (June 1991): 633–94; also "Shopping Centers Change and Grow," *NYT,* May 23, 1971. The corporate shopping center's antagonism to free political expression and social action is discussed in Herbert I. Schiller, *Culture, Inc.: The Corporate Takeover of Public Expression* (New York: Oxford University Press, 1989), pp. 98–101.

39. On *Amalgamated* v. *Logan Valley Plaza*, see "Property Rights vs. Free Speech," *NYT,* July 9, 1972; *Amalgamated Food Employees Union Local 590* v. *Logan Valley Plaza,* 88 S.Ct. 1601 (1968), *Supreme Court Reporter,* pp. 1601–20; 391 U.S. 308, U.S. Supreme Court Recording Briefs 1967, No. 478, microfiche; "Free Speech: Peaceful Picketing on Quasi-Public Property," *Minnesota Law Review* 53 (March 1969): 873–82. On *Marsh* v. *State of Alabama,* see 66 S.Ct. 276, *Supreme Court Reporter,* pp. 276–84.

Other relevant cases between *Marsh* v. *Alabama* and *Amalgamated* v. *Logan Valley Plaza* are *Nahas* v. *Local 905, Retail Clerks International Assoc.* (1956), *Amalgamated Clothing Workers of America* v. *Wonderland Shopping Center, Inc.* (1963), *Schwartz-Torrance Investment Corp* v. *Bakery and Confectionary Workers' Union, Local No. 31* (1964); with each case the Warren Court was moving closer to a recognition that the shopping center was becoming a new kind of public forum.

40. "4 Nixon Appointees End Court's School Unanimity, Shopping Centers' Right to Ban Pamphleteering Is Upheld, 5 to 4," *NYT,* June 23, 1972; "Shopping-Center Industry Hails Court," *NYT,* July 2, 1972; *Lloyd Corporation, Ltd.* v. *Donald M. Tanner* (1972), 92 S.Ct. 2219 (1972), *Supreme Court Reporter,* pp. 2219–37. The American Civil Liberties Union brief went to great lengths to document the extent to which shopping centers have replaced traditional business districts; see "Brief for Respondents," U.S. Supreme Court Record, microfiche, pp. 20–29. Also, People's Lobby Brief, U.S. Supreme Court Record, microfiche, p. 5.

The Supreme Court majority wanted to make it clear that in finding in favor of the Lloyd Center, it was not reversing the *Logan Valley* decision, arguing for a distinction based on the fact that anti-war leafletting was "unrelated" to the shopping center, while the labor union was picketing an employer. The four dissenting justices, however, were less sure that the distinction was valid and that the *Logan Valley* decision was not seriously weakened by *Lloyd.*

The important court cases between *Amalgamated* v. *Logan Valley Plaza* and *Lloyd* v. *Tanner* included *Blue Ridge Shopping Center* v. *Schleininger* (1968), *Sutherland* v. *Southcenter Shopping Center* (1971), and *Diamond* v. *Bland* (1970, 1974).

41. Berger, "*PruneYard* Revisited"; Kowinski, *The Malling of America,* pp. 196–202, 355–59; "Shopping Malls Protest Intrusion by Protesters," *NYT,* July 19, 1983; "Opening of Malls Fought," *NYT,* May 13, 1984; *Michael Robins* v. *PruneYard Shopping Center* (1979), 592 P.2nd 341, *Pacific Reporter,* pp. 341–51; *PruneYard Shopping Center* v. *Michael Robins,* 100 S.Ct. 2035 (1980), *Supreme Court Reporter,* pp. 2035–51; U.S. Supreme Court Record, *PruneYard Shopping Center* v. *Robins* (1980), microfiche.

The most important Supreme Court case between *Lloyd* v. *Tanner* and *PruneYard* was *Scott Hudgens* v. *National Labor Relations Board* (1976), where the majority decision backed further away from *Logan Valley Plaza* and refused to see the mall as the functional equivalent of downtown: *Scott Hudgens* v. *National Labor Relations Board,* 96 S.Ct. 1029 (1976), *Supreme Court Reporter,* pp. 1029–47.

During the Amalgamated Clothing and Textile Workers' boycott of J. P. Stevens in the late 1970s, union organizers in New Jersey tried to persuade Gimbel's and other stores at the Garden State Plaza not to carry Stevens's products. Fearful of eliciting injunctions and lawsuits for picketing inside or outside the mall, activists took their protest to linen departments inside the stores, wearing T-shirts emblazoned with "Boycott J. P. Stevens" slogans and staging guerrilla theater actions to dramatize their opposition. They argued that although they were not allowed to picket, they had every right as consumers to enter stores and voice their complaints. When the police were summoned to charge them with trespassing, they would leave. By avoiding the argument that the mall was as much public space as the street and instead justifying their actions as rights due consumers, these organizers managed to continue public protests despite the courts' decisions. They even concluded that their innovative activities within the stores were more effective than traditional picketing outside the stores would have been: e-mail to author from Bob Bussel, Nov. 15, 1996.

42. "Court Protects Speech in Malls," *NYT,* Dec. 21, 1994; "Big Malls Ordered to Allow Leafletting," *NSL,* Dec. 21, 1994; "Now, Public Rights in Private Domains," *NYT,* Dec. 25, 1994; "Free Speech in the Mall," *NYT,* Dec. 26, 1994; Frank Askin, "Shopping for Free Speech at the Malls," 1995, unpublished manuscript in possession of the author.

43. "Mall's Limits on Leafletting Struck Down," *NYT,* June 14, 2000; "Staying the Course; Justices Won't 'Mall' Free Speech," *New Jersey Lawyer,* June 19, 2000, p. 3; Michael Booth, "Court Sharpens Fine Print on Malls' Regulation of Leafletters," and *"Green Party of New Jersey et al.* v. *Hartz Mountain Industries, Inc.,* A-59 September Term," *New Jersey Law Journal,* June 19, 2000; "New Jersey Delineates Limits on Leafleting Restrictions at Malls," *State Constitutional Law Bulletin,* July 2000; John D. Cromie and James F. Jacobus, "The N.J. Supreme Court Adopts a Test to Balance Property Rights with Free-Speech Rights in Mall Leafleting Cases, but Fails to Give Guidance as to Which Restrictions Are Permissible," *New Jersey Law Journal,* Oct. 2, 2000.

44. Marshall dissent, *Lloyd* v. *Tanner,* 92 S.Ct 2219 (1972), *Supreme Court Reporter* (1972), p. 2237.

45. From *NYT:* "Business Districts Grow at Price of Accountability," Nov. 20, 1994; "Now, Public Rights in Private Domains," Dec. 25, 1994; " 'Goon Squads' Prey on the Homeless, Advocates Say," Apr. 14, 1995; "City Council Orders Review of 33 Business Improvement Districts," Apr. 19, 1995; "When Neighborhoods Are Privatized," Nov. 30, 1995; Bruce J. Schulman, *The Seventies* (New York: Free Press, 2001), pp. 249, 314–15; Lawrence O. Houstoun, Jr., *BIDS: Business Improvement Districts* (Washington, DC: Urban Land Institute and the International Downtown Association, 1997).

46. Jonassen, *Downtown Versus Suburban Shopping,* p. 15; Alan Voorhees, *Shopping Habits and Travel Patterns,* Technical Bulletin No. 24 (Washington, DC: Urban Land Institute, 1955), p. 6; Rich, *Shopping Behavior of Department Store Customers,* pp. 61–64; Jon Goss, "The 'Magic of the Mall': An Analysis of Form, Function, and Meaning in the Contemporary Retail Built Environment," *Annals of the Association of American Geographers* 83 (March 1993): 19. On the long history of women as shoppers, see Steven Lubar, "Men, Women, Production, and Consumption," in Roger Horowitz and Arwen Mohun, eds., *His and Hers: Gender, Consumption, and Technology* (Charlottesville: University Press of Virginia, 1998), pp. 7–37. The increasingly sophisticated field of market research addressed itself to motivating the female consumer. An excellent example is Wolff, *What Makes Women Buy.* See my Chapter 7 for more discussion.

47. My thanks to William Becker and Richard Longstreth, both of George Washington University, for their suggestions on comparing the gendered character of the downtown street to the shopping center. Also see Gunther Barth, *City People: The Rise of Modern City Culture in Nineteenth-Century America* (New York: Oxford University Press, 1980); Elaine Abelson, *When Ladies Go A-Thieving: Middle-Class Shoplifters in the Victorian Department Store* (New York: Oxford University Press, 1989); William Leach, "Transformations in a Culture of Consumption: Women and Department Stores, 1890–1925," *JAH* 71 (September 1984): 319–42.

48. On women driving, and specifically using a car for shopping, see Rich, *Shopping Behavior of Department Store Customers,* pp. 84–85, 137–38; L. Pratt, "Impact of Regional Shopping Centers in Bergen County"; Voorhees, *Shopping Habits and Travel Patterns,* p. 17.

49. Herzog, "Shops, Culture, Centers—and More," *NYT Magazine,* p. 35; "Busy Day in

Busy Willowbrook Mall," *NYT,* Apr. 2, 1972; Harris, *Cultural Excursions,* p. 281; Wolff, *What Makes Women Buy,* pp. 220–25.

50. On Film, Inc., for *Redbook* magazine, *In the Suburbs,* 1957, 19:30 minutes, 35 mm, from Rick Prelinger, ed., *Our Secret Century: Archival Films from the Darker Side of the American Dream,* vol. 6, *The Unchartered Landscape,* Voyager CD, 1996; Rich, *Shopping Behavior of Department Store Customers,* pp. 64, 71–74; Sternlieb, *Future of the Downtown Department Store,* pp. 27–28, 184; Wolff, *What Makes Women Buy,* p. 226; L. Pratt, "Impact of Regional Shopping Centers in Bergen County."

51. Martineau, "Customers' Shopping Center Habits Change Retailing," p. 16; Feinberg, *What Makes Shopping Centers Tick,* p. 97; Oaks, *Managing Suburban Branches of Department Stores,* p. 72; Irving Roberts, "Toy Selling Techniques in a Shopping Center," *Playthings,* July 1953, p. 112; also see "Lenox Toy & Hobby Selects Good Location in Atlanta Shopping Center—1,200 Sales a Week," *Playthings,* May 1961, p. 99.

52. JCPenney, "An American Legacy, A 90th Anniversary History," brochure (1992), pp. 22, 25, JCPenney Archives, Plano, TX; Mary Elizabeth Curry, *Creating an American Institution: The Merchandising Genius of J.C. Penney* (New York: Garland, 1993), pp. 311–13; William M. Batten, *The Penney Idea: Foundation for the Continuing Growth of the J.C. Penney Company* (New York: Newcomen Society in North America, 1967), p. 17. The opening of the JCPenney store in Garden State Plaza in 1958 is featured in a film, *The Past Is a Prologue* (1961), which is one of several fascinating movies made by the company that has been collected on a video, *Penney Premieres,* available through the JCPenney Archives. Also see *Penney News* 24 (November–December 1958): 1, 7 on the new Paramus store; JCPenney Archives. On activities for family members, see R. H. Macy & Company, *Annual Report for 1957,* p. 26; "Bait for the Male Shopper, *BW,* Apr. 5, 1952, p. 40; "300,000 Prospects Ten Minutes Away," *Playthings,* February 1955, p. 308; Samuel Feinberg, "The Spirit of Garden State Plaza," *Women's Wear Daily,* Feb. 29, 1960.

53. Barry Bluestone et al., *The Retail Revolution: Market Transformation, Investment, and Labor in the Modern Department Store* (Boston: Auburn House, 1981), pp. 46–47; Rich, *Shopping Behavior of Department Store Customers,* pp. 100–101; "Suburbia vs. Downtown . . . Two Different Worlds," *Playthings,* p. 59.

54. " 'It Won't Be Long Now . . .': Bamberger's, New Jersey's Greatest Store, Comes to Paramus Soon," stamped Aug. 22, 1956, Hackensack, file "Bergen County Shopping Centers"; press release, "The Garden State Plaza Opens Wednesday, May 1st at the Junction of Routes 4 and 17, Paramus," GSP; JCPenney, "An American Legacy," pp. 21–22; Curry, *Creating an American Institution,* pp. 305–307.

On the expansion of credit buying in the postwar period, see my discussion in Chapter 3 and Marie de Vroet Kobrak, "Consumer Installment Credit and Factors Associated with It" (M.A. thesis, University of Chicago, 1958); Lewis Mandell, *The Credit Card Industry: A History* (Boston: Twayne, 1990); Hillel Black, *Buy Now, Pay Later* (New York: Morrow, 1961); Wolff, *What Makes Women Buy,* pp. 236–37; on Sears, "What's the Best Way to Borrow?" n.d., Margolius, Box 5, "Credit," p. 1.

For a 1971 study documenting the possession of bank cards and store charge cards in the counties of Bergen, Passaic (New Jersey), and Rockland (New York) and when they were last used, see Plan One Research Corporation, *The Mighty Market,* pp. 382–85.

55. Women and Credit Study Group, *No Credit for Women: Sexual Discrimination in the Marketplace of Consumer Credit* (Portland: Oregon Student Public Interest Research Group, February 1973); Cynthia Harrison, "New Jersey: Action on Credit," August 1973, Cynthia Harrison Papers, Box 2, Folder 25, p. 1, Schlesinger; see the excellent treatment of domestic money handling before World War II in Viviana A. Zelizer, *The Social Meaning of Money* (New York: Basic Books, 1994), pp. 36–70.

56. Oaks, *Managing Suburban Branches of Department Stores,* p. 73; "Sales Personnel Ready to Work," *BR,* Nov. 13, 1957; "Paramus Booms as a Store Center," *NYT,* Feb. 5, 1962.

57. Rich, *Shopping Behavior of Department Store Customers,* p. 20; Sternlieb, *Future of the Downtown Department Store,* p. 27; R. H. Macy & Co., *Annual Report for 1955,* p. 29; JCPenney, *An American Legacy,* p. 25; Stuart, *Our Era,* p. 20.

58. My understanding of labor conditions and organizing in the New York area, and in the Paramus malls specifically, comes from two invaluable manuscript collections at the Robert F. Wagner Labor Archives, New York University: the papers of Local 1-S, Department Store Workers' Union (RWDSU) and District 65, now of the UAW, then of the RWDSU. I have based my analysis on the clippings, meeting minutes, and legal files in those collections, which I have not cited individually unless I quoted from them. Michelson quote from "NLRB Ruling Spurs New York Area Union: Target—50 Stores," District 65, Box 4, Folder 36; similar statement with two-thirds figure from "Report to General Council Meeting, Department Store Section, by William Michelson, January 12, 1965," District 65, Box 5, Folder 4. On department store efforts with part-timers, "Part-Timer: New Big Timer," *Women's Wear Daily,* Jan. 8, 1964, Local 1-S, Box 4, Folder 35; also see the records of a fascinating case that Local 1-S brought before the NLRB concerning the firing of a young woman employee who had shown interest in the union: Local 1-S, Box 9, Folder 21.

On industrial relations in department stores nationally, with a case study of the Boston metropolitan area, see Bluestone et al., *Retail Revolution,* pp. 70, 80–119, 148–49, which provides an excellent analysis of the restructuring of the labor market in the retail trade. Also see Jacobs, *The Mall,* p. 49.

59. Bamberger's Paramus, "Welcome to New Friends and a New Career," Employee Handbook, 1957, Local 1-S, Box 7, Folder 16, pp. 4, 9–12.

60. "Amtrak Is Ordered Not to Eject the Homeless from Penn Station," *NYT,* Feb. 22, 1995; "Chicago Expresses Annoyance but Understanding Over Decision on Loitering," *NYT,* June 12, 1999.

61. See Chapter 4 for discussion of the Freeman Bill and blacks' struggle to win access to public accommodations in New Jersey during the 1940s and 1950s.

62. From NAACP, II, A 333, "Department Store Discrimination in New York and Connecticut, 1945–49": Marian Wynn Perry to Charles A. Shorter, June 10, 1946; National Urban League, "Integration of Negroes in Department Stores: Practical Approaches for the Integration of Negroes in Department Store Personnel," July 1946; Madison S. Jones, Jr., to Norma Jensen, Mar. 4, 1948; Inter-racial Commission, State of Connecticut, "Newsletter No. 6: Customer Reactions to the Integration of Negro Sales Personnel," Jan. 20, 1949.

63. National Committee Against Discrimination in Housing, *Jobs and Housing: A Study of Employment and Housing Opportunities for Racial Minorities in Suburban Areas of the New York Metropolitan Region,* March 1970, pp. 13, 15, 219–23. By the late 1970s and 1980s, as white women began working full-time in higher-level jobs and the pay in retail remained low, stores in shopping centers increasingly looked to blacks and Latinos to work as salesclerks. The continued inaccessibility of suburban shopping centers to urban blacks made it hard to fill these jobs and led in at least one case, described in note 25, to a tragic death.

64. "Department Stores Redefine Their Role," *BW,* Dec. 13, 1976; from the *NYT:* "On Long Island, the Mall as History Book," Dec. 21, 1997; "Shopping the Madison Avenue of Manhasset (Don't Say Mall)," July 25, 2000; "Bergen Mall Journal: Almost like a Death in the Family," Feb. 11, 2001.

65. On Newark and other declining cities, see for Raymond Mungin quotation, "Two Guys Will Be Missed," *NSL*, Nov. 23, 1981; also "Last-Minute Bargain Hunters Abound as Chase Closes Up," *NN*, Feb. 12, 1967; "Newark: City Founded in Dissidence," *NYT*, July 15, 1967; "Ohrbach's Will Close Store in Newark, Cites Drop in Sales and Lack of Lease," *NYT*, Dec. 7, 1973; "S. Klein to Shut Last State Stores Sometime in June," *NSL*, May 9, 1975; "Sears to Shut Newark Store," *NSL*, June 13, 1978; "Closing of 'Last' Department Store Stirs Debate on Downtown Trenton," *NSL*, June 5, 1983; "Urban Areas Crave Return of Big Markets," *NSL*, July 17, 1984; "Hahne's Bids a Farewell to Newark," *NSL*, June 18, 1986; "Elizabeth Clothier Mourns Demise of Century-Old Customized Service," *NSL*, Jan. 10, 1988; "Macy's to Shut Stores in Newark, Plainfield," May 21, 1992; "Newmark & Lewis Is Closing 11 Stores," *NSL*, Oct. 15, 1993; "President's Report to the Annual Meeting, Passaic Valley Citizens Planning Association," Erber, Box A, Folder 3; *NYT*, Dec. 7, 1973; Greater Newark Chamber of Commerce, "Survey of Jobs and Unemployment," May 1973, "Q" Files, NPL; Greater Newark Chamber of Commerce, "Metro New Jersey Market Report," [1991], "Q" Files, NPL; Files; Brian D. Babo, *Regional Perspectives: Department Store Sales*, Regional Studies Section, Central Research and Statistics Division, Planning and Development Department, Port of New York Authority, April 1969, p. 7, cited in National Committee, *Jobs and Housing*, p. 203; Daniel Earl Georges, "Arson: The Ecology of Urban Unrest in an American City: Newark, New Jersey, A Case Study in Collective Violence" (Ph.D. diss., Syracuse University, 1974), p. 89. See Chapter 8 for more on the impact of Newark's racial disturbances on consumption patterns.

66. "Amtrak Is Ordered Not to Eject the Homeless from Penn Station," *NYT*, Feb. 22, 1995; "Can Amtrak Be a Censor?" *Washington Post*, Feb. 23, 1995; "Amtrak Can Be Sued on Poster, Court Rules," *NYT*, Feb. 22, 1995; "Judge Strikes Down Rule Limiting Protesters on City Hall Steps in New York," *NYT*, Apr. 7, 2000.

For more on how urban governments and developers have sought to re-create the suburban mall within the city, see City Planning Commission, Tacoma, Washington, *The Broadway Mall*, 1961; Goss, "The 'Magic of the Mall,' " pp. 23–25, including excellent quotes from downtown mall builders on the virtues of bringing the suburban retail solution to Main Street; "When Shoppers Walk Away from Pedestrian Malls," *NYT*, Nov. 5, 1996; "The State of the Cities: Downtown Is Up," *The Economist*, Aug. 22, 1998; Carole Rifkind, *A Field Guide to Contemporary American Architecture* (New York: Plume, 2001), pp. 331–51.

67. Jürgen Habermas, *The Structural Transformation of the Public Sphere: An Inquiry into a Category of Bourgeois Society*, trans. Thomas Burger with the assistance of Frederick Lawrence (Cambridge, MA: MIT Press, 1989); Geoff Eley, "Nations, Publics, and Political Cultures: Placing Habermas in the Nineteenth Century," in Nicholas B. Dirks, Geoff Eley, and Sherry B. Ortner, eds., *Culture/Power/History: A Reader in Contemporary Social Theory* (Princeton: Princeton University Press, 1994), pp. 297–335; Thomas Bender, "The New Metropolitanism and the Pluralized Public," *Harvard Design Magazine* 13 (Winter/Spring 2001): 73–74. Msgr. Linder quote from "In Riots' Shadow, a City Stumbles On," *NYT*, July 14, 1997.

CHAPTER 7. CULTURE: SEGMENTING THE MASS

1. Vernon Pope, "What They Know About You: Maybe Pollsters Never Talked to You, but They Know Just What You Are Thinking! Here's How," *New York Herald Tribune This Week*, Jan. 21, 1945, pp. 6–7.

2. Quote from Professor H. Gordon Hayes in *Harper's Magazine*, 1947, cited in Frederick Lewis Allen, *The Big Change: America Transforms Itself, 1900–1950* (New York: Harper & Bros., 1952), p. 193.

3. Thomas Hine, *Populuxe* (New York: Knopf, 1987), pp. 3–5.

4. "Marketing in the '60s: The Coming Battle for Discretionary Dollars," *PI*, Sept. 11, 1959, pp. 26, 28.

5. Wendell R. Smith, "Product Differentiation and Market Segmentation as Alternative Marketing Strategies," *JM* 21 (July 1956): 7.

6. "Marketing in the '60s," *PI*, Sept. 11, 1959, p. 28; Hine, *Populuxe,* pp. 19–21, 66, 90, 94, 98; Pluckett quote from *Time,* July 3, 1950, p. 72, cited in Douglas T. Miller and Marion Nowak, *The Fifties: The Way We Really Were* (Garden City, NY: Doubleday, 1977), p. 120; "Survey Shows How American Women Buy," *PI,* Oct. 2, 1959, p. 27. On the limited success of planned obsolescence, see Shelley Kaplan Nickles, "Object Lessons: Household Appliance Design and the American Middle Class, 1920–1960" (Ph.D. diss., University of Virginia, 1999), pp. 329–75.

7. Wall label, exhibition "The Work of Charles and Ray Eames: A Legacy of Invention," Cooper-Hewitt National Museum of Design, Smithsonian Institution, New York, 1999, and James Billington, "Foreword," *The Work of Charles and Ray Eames: A Legacy of Invention* (New York: Abrams, in Association with the Library of Congress and the Vitra Design Museum, 1997), p. 6. On industrial design more generally, see Neil Harris, "The Drama of Consumer Desire," in *Cultural Excursions: Marketing Appetites and Cultural Tastes in Modern America* (Chicago: University of Chicago Press, 1990), pp. 186–88; Hine, *Populuxe,* pp. 68–70, 83–106, with George Walker quote on p. 99; General Motors' Harley Earl quote from *Industrial Design,* October 1955, reprinted in exhibition brochure, "Packaging the New: Design and the American Consumer, 1925–1975," Cooper-Hewitt National Museum of Design, Feb. 8–Aug. 14, 1994.

8. D. F. Blankertz, "Shopping Habits and Income: A Philadelphia Department Store Study," *JM* 14 (January 1950): 573; *JR,* 1945–1960, passim; also see Olivier Zunz, *Why the American Century?* (Chicago: University of Chicago Press, 1998), which describes efforts to target the middle class during the 1920s and 1930s. The difference here, however, was that in this earlier effort, middle-class consumers were sought out as the most promising, while those who differed—because they were too poor or African American, for example—were bypassed. In the postwar period, "middle class" was assumed to encompass a wider swath of the population, though Zunz points out that even then it was an abstract conceptualization by social scientists (p. 69).

9. Smith, "Product Differentiation and Market Segmentation," p. 7.

10. Pierre Martineau, "Social Classes and Spending Behavior," *JM* 23 (October 1958): 121–30, quote from pp. 122–23; other important work by Martineau includes "The Personality of the Retail Store," *HBR* 46 (January–February 1958): 47–55, and *Motivation in Advertising: Motives That Make People Buy* (New York: McGraw-Hill, 1957). The first Martineau article and Wendell Smith's 1956 market segmentation article both won the *Journal of Marketing*'s award for most outstanding article in their respective years. For another example of a sociologist/marketer arguing for distinctiveness of buying by social class, see Richard P. Coleman, "The Significance of Social Stratification in Selling," in Martin L. Bell, ed., *Proceedings of the 43rd National Conference of the American Marketing Association,* Dec. 18–20, 1960 (Chicago: American Marketing Association, 1961), pp. 171–84. On the *Chicago Tribune*'s early leadership in market research, see Leo Bogart, "Opinion Research and Marketing," *POQ* 21 (Spring 1957): 133.

11. For an excellent rendering of the GM campaign, see Richard S. Tedlow, *New and Improved: The Story of Mass Marketing in America* (New York: Basic Books, 1990), pp. 112–81; also Nickles, "Object Lessons," pp. 70–75. Tedlow develops a three-stage model of market development where timing of implementation varied by industry: Phase I, market fragmentation, mostly geographic, due to lack of national transportation and com-

munication infrastructures; Phase II, market unification around mass markets, with large volumes, scale economies, low prices, and dominance of national brands; and Phase III—almost always a postwar phenomenon—market segmentation of specialized outputs that cater to demographic and psychographic consumer segments. An almost identical model, with a similar chronology breaking the "mass market" and the "fragmented market" in the first half of the 1960s, appeared at the time in Steven C. Brandt, "Dissecting the Segmentation Syndrome," *JM* 30 (October 1966): 22–27.

Early pioneers of the theory of market segmentation in the 1930s were Joan Robinson and Edward Chamberlain, who argued that the homogeneity of supply and demand typical of the early stages of American business was being replaced by increasing heterogeneity; cited in James F. Engel, Henry F. Fiorillo, and Murray A. Cayley, *Market Segmentation: Concepts and Applications* (New York: Holt, Rinehart and Winston, 1972), p. 21. Historian Regina Blaszczyk has argued that makers of pottery and glass began to think in terms of class markets by the 1920s and 1930s: *Imagining Consumers: Design and Innovation from Wedgwood to Corning* (Baltimore: Johns Hopkins University Press, 2000).

12. Sally Clarke has done important work on the way firms' understandings of consumers affected product design and marketing. She has focused in particular on GM. I thank her in particular for sharing the following document with me: H. G. Weaver to Mr. Charles F. Kettering, Jan. 15, 1941, with Customer Research Staff, General Motors, "How 10,000 Prospective Buyers Feel About Hydra-Matic," December 1940, CFK File 87-11.4–17, Box 110, Charles F. Kettering Archives, Kettering/GMI Alumni Foundation's Collection of Industrial History, Kettering University, Flint, MI. Also see Clarke, "Managing Design: The Art and Colour Section at General Motors, 1927–1941," *Journal of Design History* 12 (1999): 65–79, and Clarke, "Consumer Statistics," paper presented at American Historical Association, Jan. 8, 1999, in possession of author.

13. Thomas S. Robertson, *Consumer Behavior* (Glencoe, IL: Scott, Foresman, 1970), p. 115. Inspired by pioneering articles on market segmentation in the *Journal of Marketing* and the *Harvard Business Review,* the more practically oriented *Journal of Retailing* exploded with articles on segmenting the market between 1960 and 1962.

14. Richard T. Hise, "Have Manufacturing Firms Adopted the Marketing Concept?" *JM* 29 (July 1965): 9–12; on Estée Lauder, see Nancy F. Koehn, *Brand New: How Entrepreneurs Earned Consumers' Trust from Wedgwood to Dell* (Boston: Harvard Business School Press, 2001); Robert E. Weems, Jr., "Consumerism and the Construction of Black Female Identity in Twentieth-Century America," in Jennifer Scanlon, ed., *The Gender and Consumer Culture Reader* (New York: New York University Press, 2000), p. 175; "Department Stores Redefine Their Role," *BW,* Dec. 13, 1976, pp. 47–48; Martineau, "The Personality of the Retail Store," *HBR;* "Selling to the Hottest Market Ever," *BW,* Oct. 17, 1970, p. 124.

15. James F. Engel provides a useful definition of market segmentation in Engel, Fiorillo, and Cayley, *Market Segmentation,* pp. 1–2; also see Mack Hanan, *Market Segmentation: The Basis for New Product Innovation and New Product Renovation,* American Marketing Association Management Bulletin, No. 109, 1968; Ronald E. Frank, William F. Massy, and Yoram Wind, *Market Segmentation* (Englewood Cliffs, NJ: Prentice-Hall, 1972); Ronald D. Michman, Myron Gable, and Walter Gross, *Market Segmentation: A Selected and Annotated Bibliography* (Chicago: American Marketing Association Bibliography Series #28, 1977).

16. Vance Packard, *The Hidden Persuaders* (New York: McKay, 1957). For more about Packard, see the fascinating biography by Daniel Horowitz, *Vance Packard and American Social Criticism* (Chapel Hill: University of North Carolina Press, 1994).

17. For a discussion of Katona and Dichter, see Daniel Horowitz, "The Emigré as Cel-

ebrant of American Consumer Culture: George Katona and Ernest Dichter," in Susan Strasser, Charles McGovern, and Matthias Judt, *Getting and Spending: European and American Consumer Societies in the Twentieth Century* (Washington, DC: German Historical Institute; New York: Cambridge University Press, 1998), pp. 149–66. Katona's research is easily accessible through his periodic volumes published by the Survey Research Center, Institute for Social Research, University of Michigan, such as (with Eva Mueller): *Consumer Attitudes and Demand, 1950–52,* and *Consumer Expectations, 1953–1956;* his candid comments on the diversity of consumers' decisions appear in "Summary Minutes of First Conference—1952," in Lincoln H. Clark, ed., *Consumer Behavior: The Dynamics of Consumer Reaction* (New York: New York University Press, 1955), p. 100. On Dichter, see "Psychologist Dichter Tells Admen: You Either Offer Security or Fail," *BW,* June 23, 1951, pp. 68, 70, 72, 74, 76; Ernest Dichter, *The Strategy of Desire* (Garden City, NY: Doubleday, 1960), and *Handbook of Consumer Motivations: The Psychology of the World of Objects* (New York: McGraw-Hill, 1964). On Herzog, see Malcolm Gladwell, "True Colors: Hair Dye and the Hidden History of Postwar America," *The New Yorker,* Mar. 22, 1999, pp. 77–81.

Psychologists had been involved with advertising in a more limited way during the interwar period, the most notable case being the behaviorist John B. Watson, who moved from an academic position to the J. Walter Thompson Advertising Agency in 1920: Zunz, *Why the American Century?,* pp. 58–59.

18. A sampling of writing bringing the insights of psychology to marketing includes Robert N. McMurray, "Psychology in Selling," *JM* 9 (October 1944): 114–18; "Ernest Dichter, "A Psychological View of Advertising Effectiveness," *JM* 14 (July 1949): 61–66; Fred T. Schrier and Albert J. Wood, "Motivation Analysis in Market Research," *JM* 13 (October 1948): 172–82; Steuart Henderson Britt, "The Strategy of Consumer Motivation," *JM* 14 (April 1950): 666–74; Warren J. Bilkey, "A Psychological Approach to Consumer Behavior Analysis," *JM* 18 (July 1953): 18–23; "A New Language for Madison Avenue," *BW,* Sept. 5, 1953, pp. 40, 42, 44; "Behavior Research to Get Answers, Ask the People," *BW,* Aug. 21, 1954, pp. 140, 142–43; Norman Heller, "An Application of Psychological Learning Theory to Advertising," *JM* 20 (January 1955): 248–54. Packard described psychiatric research techniques in *Hidden Persuaders* on pp. 38–45, and gave the freezer example on p. 73 and the car example on p. 79.

19. Daniel Yankelovich, "New Criteria for Market Segmentation," *HBR* 42 (March–April 1964): 83–90. Yankelovich wrote, "Demography is not the only or best way to segment markets. Even more crucial to marketing objectives are differences in buyer attitudes, motivations, values, patterns of usage, aesthetic preferences and degree of susceptibility." The many studies that took off from Yankelovich in bringing psychological and motivational concerns to definitions of market segments include James F. Engel, David T. Kollat, and Roger D. Blackwell, "Personality Measures and Market Segmentation: Evidence Favors Interaction View," *Business Horizons* 12 (June 1969): 61–70, and William D. Wells, ed., *Life Style and Psychographics* (Chicago: American Marketing Association, 1974).

20. Henry A. Johnson, "Computer Technology Is Key to Segmentation and Service," *Direct Marketing,* June 1985, quoted in Erik Larson, *The Naked Consumer: How Our Private Lives Become Public Commodities* (New York: Holt, 1992), p. 13; Debra Jones Ringold, "Social Criticism of Target Marketing: Process or Product?" in Ronald Paul Hill, ed., *Marketing and Consumer Research in the Public Interest* (Thousand Oaks, CA: Sage, 1996), pp. 89–108; "That's Not a Skim Latte. It's a Way of Life," *NYT,* Mar. 21, 1999; "They've Got Your Number: Psychodemography, Give Marketers Your ZIP and They'll Sell You the World, from Fast Food to Fast Cars," *NYT,* Mar. 30, 1997, New Jersey Section;

"AmEx to Sell Information About Consumers," *USA Today,* May 13, 1998; "On-line Profiling of Users," National Public Radio, Nov. 10, 1999; "Buyers Choice Survey of America," March 1997, form in possession of author; "To Settle a Case, Chase Vows No More Customer Data to Marketers," *NYT,* Jan. 26, 2000.

Joseph Turow discusses at some length marketers' increasingly sophisticated research tools that allowed them to pinpoint clusters of relationships among demographic, attitudinal, behavioral, and geographical factors; they made use of everything from credit card records indicating what people bought to extensive questionnaires and phone interviews: *Breaking Up America* (Chicago: University of Chicago Press, 1997), pp. 43–47, 125–56, 172–83. The pioneer of direct marketing tells the story of its evolution in Lester Wunderman, *Being Direct: Making Advertising Pay* (New York: Random House, 1996). Also see two books by Michael J. Weiss, *The Clustering of America* (New York: Harper & Row, 1988) and *The Clustered World: How We Live, What We Buy, and What It All Means About Who We Are* (Boston: Little, Brown, 2000). The Internet has not only facilitated the collection of precise data on consumer preferences, as users and shoppers leave a web trail that can be easily tracked, but in at least the case of Amazon.com, information on virtual market segments—called "purchase circles"—is becoming available to the general public: "Navigating the Amazon Circle," *NYT Book Review,* May 21, 2000.

21. Charles Y. Glock and Francesco M. Nicosia, "Uses of Sociology in Studying 'Consumption Behavior,' " *JM* 28 (July 1964): 51–54; Tamotsu Shibutani, "Reference Groups as Perspectives," *AJS* 60 (May 1955): 562–69; Maneck S. Wadia, "The Concept of Culture," *JR* 41 (Spring 1965): 21–29, 55; Steuart Henderson Britt, ed., *Consumer Behavior and the Behavioral Sciences: Theories and Applications* (New York: Wiley, 1966). The concept of "subculture" emerged in the late 1940s and flourished in sociological literature during the 1950s and 1960s; see Ken Gelder and Sarah Thornton, eds., *The Subcultures Reader* (London: Routledge, 1997). On Lazarsfeld and Warner, see Zunz, *Why the American Century?,* pp. 99–105.

22. Wells, ed., *Life Style and Psychographics,* p. 4. An article in *Business Week* in 1964 proclaimed the computer "the market researcher's latest toy": "Special Report: Scouting the Trail for Marketers," Apr. 18, 1964. By 1970, *Business Week* claimed that "the computer is rapidly replacing seat-of-the-pants judgment in market analysis and strategy planning": "Selling to the Hottest Market Ever," Oct. 17, 1970, p. 124.

23. Britt, ed., *Consumer Behavior.* One analyst attributed the closer ties between social scientists and market researchers to the growing disparity between academic and business salary scales, providing an incentive for scholars to shift affiliation; a decline in social science's links to social reform and related skepticism about the prevailing economic system; social scientists' greater interest in the problems of business, and more appreciation for research on the part of businessmen: Bogart, "Opinion Research and Marketing," *POQ,* pp. 135–37. Also see Marty Jezer, *The Dark Ages: Life in the United States, 1945–1960* (Boston: South End, 1982), pp. 127–29.

24. "Marketing in the '60s," *PI,* Sept. 11, 1959, pp. 26–30, which measured the increase in another way as well: while GNP rose 109 percent between 1946 and 1958, advertising expenditures rose 206 percent: Miller and Nowak, *The Fifties,* p. 118. On the growth of suburban-based firms, see "Advertising Agencies Parallel Growth in Bergen Area," *BR,* Jan. 10, 1958. For an excellent survey of the expanding advertising field during the 1950s, see Stephen Fox, *The Mirror Makers: A History of American Advertising and Its Creators* (New York: Vintage, 1985), chap. 5: "The Second Boom." Another historian of advertising, Daniel Pope, has observed that as advertising agencies increasingly embraced market segmentation, the industry itself became more specialized and differentiated: *The Making of Modern Advertising* (New York: Basic Books, 1983), pp. 265–67.

25. John Kenneth Galbraith, *The Affluent Society* (Boston: Houghton Mifflin, 1958), pp. 155–60.

26. Smith, "Product Differentiation and Market Segmentation," *JM*, p. 6. In recent years, however, advertising revenues have declined even as market segmentation has expanded, as retailers have figured out new ways, such as the technology of bar-code scanners, to gain information about consumer preferences to feed back to manufacturers, who they then pressure to shift spending out of national advertising and into efforts that more directly benefit retailers, such as discounting, promotions, "slotting allowances" (fees to a store to stock a product), and in-store advertising. Meanwhile, retailers and manufacturers both have moved dollars away from traditional advertising budgets, much of it aimed at getting media exposure, to direct mail: "Change in Consumer Markets Hurting Advertising Industry," *NYT*, Oct. 3, 1989.

27. Quote from NBC, "Strangers into Customers," 1953, excerpted in The History Channel, "David Halberstam's *The Fifties*, vol. 2, *Selling the American Way*, 50 minutes, A & E Home Video, 1997; William Leuchtenburg, *A Troubled Feast: American Society Since 1945* (Boston: Little, Brown, 1973), p. 67; Lynn Spigel, *Make Room for TV: Television and the Family Ideal in Postwar America* (Chicago: University of Chicago Press, 1992), p. 1; Editors of Time-Life Books, *This Fabulous Century: 1950–60* (Alexandria, VA: Time-Life Books, 1970), p. 250.

28. Fox, *Mirror Makers*, pp. 210–11. The NBC Archives at WHS document well the network's efforts to demonstrate that advertising on television was more effective than through other media; see "Research and Planning": the Papers of Marvin Baiman, 1952–56, and Thomas E. Coffin, 1948–52; Markets and Media Files, 1947–57; Reports and Studies, 1948–67, in particular "Television Survey: A Study of Effectiveness, Report of a Survey by Alan C. Russell Marketing Research for the National Broadcasting Company," Aug. 1, 1955, Box 195.

29. My view is shared by Neil Gabler, who has argued that television, like radio, was conceived with diverse fragmented audiences in mind, in contrast to the more mass-oriented media of the movies. In his view, cable television, with its heightened capability for narrowcasting, was the logical extension, not the antithesis, of network television: Gabler, "A Merger or an Evolution?" *NYT*, Sept. 9, 1999. For a helpful analysis of narrowcasting on the radio during the 1940s and 1950s, as documented in *Sponsor*, the trade journal of broadcast advertisers, see Kathleen Michelle Newman, "Attention for Sale: The Broadcast Industry and Consumer Activism in Postwar America," February 1996, paper in my possession, and for an elaboration of the argument, see her dissertation, "Critical Mass: Advertising, Audiences and Consumer Activism in the Age of Radio" (Ph.D. diss., Yale University, 1997). A powerful statement of the increasing segmentation of the television audience can be found in Turow, *Breaking Up America*. For the conventional view of television as a mass media, see Michael Kammen, *American Culture, American Tastes: Social Change and the 20th Century* (New York: Knopf, 1999), pp. 86–88.

30. From the Daniel Starch and Staff Papers, WHS, Box 1, Folder 5-14: "Characteristics and Possessions of Households, September 1954"; "Recent Purchases of Rapid Turnover Products, February 1955"; "Characteristics and Personal Habits of Audiences," 1955–57; "Viewing Habits of Female Heads of Households," 1955–56. From NBC Papers, WHS, Box 194: "Children's Television Survey, A Study of the Howdy Doody Shows, Phase 1-A1, Report of a Survey by Alan C. Russell Marketing Research for the National Broadcasting Company," Dec. 1, 1955, Folder 45; "DAYTIME RENDEZVOUS . . . with the Women Who Buy," November 1959, Folder 36; and "Profile of Color Set Owners," 1958, Folder 1, which established an upper-class, or "luxury," market. Lynn Spigel recounts in wonderful detail how networks undertook daytime programming aimed at housewives

in *Make Room for TV,* pp. 76–86, while Steven Stark and Mary Ann Watson discuss early television for children in, respectively, *Glued to the Set: The 60 Television Shows and Events That Made Us Who We Are Today* (New York: Free Press, 1997), pp. 14–19, and *Defining Visions: Television and the American Experience Since 1945* (Fort Worth: Harcourt Brace, 1998), pp. 12–15, 166–72.

31. My discussion of television and advertising is based on Leo Bogart, *The Age of Television: A Study of Viewing Habits and the Impact of Television on American Life* (New York: Ungar, 1956), pp. 174–207; James L. Baughman, *The Republic of Mass Culture: Journalism, Filmmaking, and Broadcasting in America Since 1941* (Baltimore: Johns Hopkins University Press, 1992); Fox, *Mirror Makers,* pp. 210–16; James B. Twitchell, *Lead Us into Temptation: The Triumph of American Materialism* (New York: Columbia University Press, 1999), pp. 108, 115; Watson, *Defining Visions,* pp. 159–79; Miller and Nowak, *The Fifties,* pp. 348, 360–61. I also viewed television commercials and programs with commercials from the 1950s and 1960s at the Museum of Broadcast Communications, Chicago, see ID#2444.4 for the *Ozzie and Harriet Show;* at the Museum of Television & Radio, New York, including the integration of ads with programs on *Queen for the Day* (Dash detergent) and *The Price Is Right* (RCA); and on video, *Classic TV Commercials: Best of '50s and '60s,* Alpha Video Distributors, 1993.

Convincing advertisers and agencies to abandon program production and share program sponsorship was not easy, as many felt they would lose the "gratitude factor" of audiences linking an entertainer to a single product, such as Fred Allen to the laxative Sal Hepatica or Dinah Shore to Chevrolet. Comedian Art Carney comically captured advertisers' worries about breaking the link between sponsor and program when he referred to a skit on *Your Show of Shows* as "an original repeat of a drama presented by our alternate sponsor, who brings you next week's show on an every-other-week basis, and who is this week's co-sponsor but in three weeks will be the regular alternate sponsor": "Pat Weaver on Yesterday, 'Today' and 'Tonight,' " *NYT,* Jan. 24, 1994. For a thorough discussion of the struggle between networks and advertisers over program production, see William Boddy, *Fifties Television: The Industry and Its Critics* (Urbana: University of Illinois Press, 1990), pp. 93–100, 244–54.

32. Alan A. Roberts, "Applying the Strategy of Market Segmentation," *Business Horizons* 4 (Fall 1961): 67.

33. "What's a 'Market' to a Media Planner," *Media/Scope* 10 (June 1966): 66–72.

34. On the emergence and evolution of cable television see Turow, *Breaking Up America,* p. 33; Jeffrey B. Abramson, F. Christopher Arterton, and Gary R. Orren, *The Electronic Commonwealth: The Impact of New Media Technologies on Democratic Politics* (New York: Basic Books, 1988), pp. 288–90; Erik Barnouw, *Tube of Plenty: The Evolution of American Television,* 2nd ed. (New York: Oxford University Press, 1990), pp. 350–53, 493–96, 508, 512–13; Michele Hilmes, *Hollywood and Broadcasting: From Radio to Cable* (Urbana: University of Illinois Press, 1990), pp. 171–203; J. Fred MacDonald, *One Nation Under Television: The Rise and Decline of Network TV* (New York: Pantheon, 1990), pp. 223–30, 252–63, 268–70, 276–77; Wilson Dizard, Jr., *Old Media/New Media: Mass Communications in the Information Age* (New York: Longman, 1994), pp. 8–10, 81–127. For how the shift to cable affected an executive in network television, see Winifred White Neisser, "Searching for the Audience," *Radcliffe Quarterly* 85 (Winter 2000): 9. Today, cable advertising is often sold as a way of targeting high spenders: *SRDS TV & Cable Source* 83 (Spring 2001): A42.

35. "Shrinking Network TV Audiences Set Off Alarm and Reassessment," *NYT,* Sept. 22, 1998; "Losing Viewers to Cable, Again," *NYT,* May 22, 1997; "The Networks and Advertisers Try to Recapture Our Attention," *NYT,* Oct. 20, 1985; networks are now seeking through

deregulation to end limitations on the proportion of television stations they can own; "Networks' New Life: Ownership Ruling Is Latest Gain to Industry Once Seen as Doomed," *NYT*, Feb. 21, 2002. Also MacDonald, *One Nation Under Television*, p. 228; James G. Webster and Patricia F. Phalen, *The Mass Audience: Rediscovering the Dominant Model* (Mahwah, NJ: Erlbaum, 1997), pp. 99–114; Stark, *Glued to the Set*, pp. 59–62; Tom Shales, "TV's Sinking Net Worth," *Washington Post*, July 31, 1991, quoted in Dizard, *Old Media/New Media*, p. 102. NBC executive Alan Wurtzel has pointed out that "the multiset family" is only brought together on rare occasions, such as the Super Bowl, the Oscars, or a special event like the final episode of *Survivor:* "When It Comes to TV, Coveted Adolescents Prove to Be Unpredictable," *NYT*, Mar. 13, 2001.

36. Frank, Massy, and Wind, *Market Segmentation*, pp. 4–5; Pope, *Making of Modern Advertising*, pp. 259–65.

37. Smith, "Product Differentiation and Market Segmentation," p. 6.

38. Packard, *Hidden Persuaders*, pp. 115–18; David Riesman, *The Lonely Crowd: A Study of the Changing American Character* (1950; reprint, New Haven: Yale University Press, 1989); C. Wright Mills, *White Collar: The American Middle Classes* (New York: Oxford University Press, 1951); Sloan Wilson, *The Man in the Gray Flannel Suit* (New York: Simon & Schuster, 1955); William H. Whyte, Jr., *The Organization Man* (New York: Simon & Schuster, 1956). In his prefaces to the 1961 and 1969 editions, Riesman argued that his contrast between inner-directedness and other-directedness had been misinterpreted, and that he intended more ambivalence about both, including attributing better qualities to the other-directed social personality than critics had understood. But the fact remains that much of his analysis dwelled on the impact on the individual of the pressure to conform to a peer group in the prosperous metropolitan America of the post–World War II era.

39. "Anatomy of the Family Budget," *BW*, Sept. 28, 1957, pp. 73, 76, 78, 80; Richard H. Ostheimer, "Who Buys What? *Life*'s Study of Consumer Expenditures," *JM* 22 (January 1958): 270. Wendy Kozol has pointed out that the survey did not include race as a category, suggesting that while *Life*'s marketers were taking note of many variations in their readers, they still imagined them as white: *Life's America: Family and Nation in Postwar Photojournalism* (Philadelphia: Temple University Press, 1994), p. 38.

40. Wendell Smith quoted in "Marketing in the '60s," *PI*, Sept. 11, 1959, p. 26.

41. Russell I. Haley, "Benefit Segmentation: A Decision-Oriented Research Tool," *JM* 32 (July 1968): 30, 34; Rom J. Markin, *The Psychology of Consumer Behavior* (Englewood Cliffs: Prentice-Hall, 1969), p. 227.

42. "Marketing Observer," *BW*, July 25, 1977, p. 141.

43. My thinking about the way market segmentation affected subcultures was influenced by David Steigerwald's grant proposal to the Charles Warren Center for Studies in American History, Harvard University, "One World and None: Premature Reports of the Death of Mass Society and the Rise of the Subjective Ideal of Culture," Dec. 15, 1998; Turow, *Breaking Up America;* and Yiannis Gabriel and Tim Lang, *The Unmanageable Consumer: Contemporary Consumption and Its Fragmentations* (London: Sage, 1995). For Tom Wolfe's analysis of how Detroit made use of working-class youth cultures, see *The Kandy-Kolored Tangerine-Flake Streamline Baby* (New York: Farrar, Straus and Giroux, 1965), pp. xiii, 97–171. Also see Thomas Frank, *The Conquest of Cool: Business Culture, Counterculture, and the Rise of Hip Consumerism* (Chicago: University of Chicago Press, 1997); I disagree with Frank that the counterculture of the 1960s was the creation of advertisers seeking a new hip market, but I concur that, as it appeared on the cultural horizon, Madison Avenue pursued it relentlessly, producing ad campaigns that trafficked in alienation and rebellion.

44. My emphasis on the role that consumers have played in developing market segmentation does not necessarily contradict the insight that Antonio Gramsci offered in his notion of "hegemony" in capitalist societies, that a capitalist ruling class manages not through coercion but more indirectly through "total social authority" to win the consent of subordinate classes, thereby legitimizing its own rule. By responding to the demands of social rebels in the capitalist marketplace, manufacturers, advertisers, and retailers did ultimately ensure their own survival, but social groups nonetheless helped shape the contours of that commercial culture and influence its impact: Antonio Gramsci, *Selections from the Prison Notebooks* (New York: Lawrence and Wishart, 1971); John Clarke et al., "Subcultures, Cultures and Class [1975]," in Gelder and Thornton, *Subcultures Reader,* pp. 100–111.

45. Thorstein Veblen, *The Theory of the Leisure Class: An Economic Study of Institutions* (New York: Macmillan, 1899).

46. Daniel Horowitz, *The Morality of Spending: Attitudes Toward the Consumer Society in America, 1875–1940* (Baltimore: Johns Hopkins University Press, 1985).

47. Zunz, *Why the American Century?,* pp. 94–97.

48. Martineau, *Motivation in Advertising,* pp. 164, 166–67; Richard P. Coleman, "The Significance of Social Stratification in Selling," in Louis E. Boone, ed., *Classics in Consumer Behavior* (Tulsa: Petroleum Publishing, 1977), pp. 288–302; also see Frank, Massy, and Wind, *Market Segmentation,* pp. 42–50. Class patterns emerged not only in what consumers bought, but also how they bought; see H. Lee Mathews and John W. Slocum, Jr., "Social Class and Commercial Bank Credit Card Usage," *JM* 33 (January 1969): 71–78.

49. "COLORTOWN: A Profile of Color Set Owners," 1958, conducted for BBDO (Batten Barton Durstine and Osborn)-NBC by Advertest Research, Box 194, Folder 1, NBC Papers, WHS.

50. Martineau, *Motivation in Advertising,* pp. 163–64, 172. Elsewhere, particularly in his *Yankee City* study of Newburyport, Massachusetts, Warner elaborated a six-class structure by dividing the upper class into upper-upper and lower-upper; see Frank et al.'s discussion in *Market Segmentation,* pp. 45–48. In 1975, Richard Coleman of Social Research, Inc. argued that Warner's six-class view had become dated and proposed instead a scheme of three main classes—Upper Americans, Middle Americans, and Lower Americans—each subdivided into three or four lifestyle groupings, suggesting the growing centrality of lifestyle to class categorization: Coleman, "The Significance of Social Stratification in Selling," pp. 300–302.

51. Lee Rainwater, Richard P. Coleman, and Gerald Handel, *Workingman's Wife: Her Personality, World and Life Style* (1959; reprint, New York: Arno, 1979), and the following manuscript reports prepared by Social Research, Inc. (SRI) for Macfadden Publications, some of which served as the research base for *Workingman's Wife:* "The FBG Housewife Market," December 1957; "Meaning and Use of Personal Products in the Family Behavior Group Reader Market," 1958; "Motivations and Behaviors of Family Behavior Group Housewife-Readers in Consumption of Appliances," 1958; "Motivations and Behaviors of FBG Housewife-Readers in Consumption of Appliances and Automobiles," April 1958; "The FBG Reader as Family Food Manager," April 1958; "A Memorandum on the Role of Children in the FBG Market," July 1958; "The Meaning to FBG Housewife-Readers of Advertising in Four Types of Media: A Pilot Report," February 1959; "The Meaning of Magazine and Television Advertising to the FBG Housewife-Reader," July 1959; "The Motivational Basis for Demand in the Working Class, Outline of Findings from a Pilot Study," June 3, 1960; "Status of the Working Class in Changing American Society," February 1961. I am grateful to Daniel Horowitz for sharing these reports with me.

Other studies of working-class consumption patterns include Arthur B. Shostak and

William Gomberg, eds., *Blue-Collar World: Studies of the American Worker* (Englewood Cliffs, NJ: Prentice-Hall, 1964), pp. 36–41, 76–80, 110–20: Gerald Handel and Lee Rainwater, "Persistence and Change in Working-Class Life Style"; James M. Patterson, "Marketing and the Working-Class Family"; David Caplovitz, "The Problems of Blue-Collar Consumers." For the way class segmentation of the postwar market affected designers, see Nickles, "Object Lessons," pp. 279–328. For background on SRI, see John Easton, "Consuming Interests," *University of Chicago Magazine,* August 2001, pp. 16–22; my thanks to George Chauncey for bringing this article to my attention.

52. First quotation from SRI for Macfadden Publications, "The Motivational Basis for Demand in the Working Class," 1960, pp. 4, 7; second two quotations from "Status of the Working Class in Changing American Society," pp. 41, 107.

53. On expansion of the "upscale" market in the 1980s, see Turow, *Breaking Up America,* pp. 57–60, 82, including quote on p. 59 from Susan Spillman, "CAB: Advertisers Must Recognize Two-TV Universe," *AA,* Apr. 11, 1983, p. 1. On origins of the consumer category of "Yuppie," see Bruce J. Schulman, *The Seventies* (New York: Free Press, 2001), pp. 242–43.

54. James H. Myers and Jonathan Gutman, "Life Style: The Essence of Social Class," in Wells, ed., *Life Style and Psychographics,* pp. 235–56; "The Rich Are Different," *Transaction* 1 (September–October 1964): 21–24, reprinted in Britt, ed., *Consumer Behavior,* pp. 266–67. Zunz makes a similar point in *Why the American Century?* when he convincingly argues that the way social scientists and marketers like Lloyd Warner and Pierre Martineau brought consumption into their conceptualization of social class deradicalized it; pp. 102, 108–109. Kathleen Newman has a fascinating discussion of the marketing of hillbilly/country music to working-class consumers in "Critical Mass," pp. 252–70.

55. *PI,* Nov. 7, 1929, p. 133, quoted in Roland Marchand, *Advertising the American Dream: Making Way for Modernity, 1920–1940* (Berkeley: University of California Press, 1985), p. 66; on extent of female control over consumption, see pp. 162, 251, 278n.43.

56. "Head of Spending Unit" from "A National Survey of Liquid Assets," *Federal Reserve Bulletin* 32 (June 1946): 579, quoted in Horowitz, "Emigré as Celebrant of American Consumer Culture," p. 162; survey in Lori Rotskoff, "Power of the Purse: The Gendering of Consumption During the 1940s and 50s," Dec. 26, 1992, paper for American Studies 787a, Yale University, in possession of author, p. 34, Graphs 1–3; "Appealing to Men Customers," *Playthings,* June 1947, p. 135; Betty Friedan, *The Feminine Mystique* (1963; reprint, New York: Dell, 1984), pp. 219–20; *Advertising and Selling,* October 1954, back cover ad "Just who *does* wear the pants in the family, these days?" cited in Rotskoff, "Power of the Purse," p. 35; on the same theme, see "Bait for the Male Shopper," *BW,* Apr. 5, 1992, p. 40. Kenon Breazeale traces the displacement of the female consumer and legitimation of the male back to the promotion of consumption as a remedy to the Great Depression of the 1930s in her essay "In Spite of Women: *Esquire* Magazine and the Construction of the Male Consumer," *Signs* 20 (Autumn 1994): 1–22; see my discussion in Chapter 1.

57. Janet L. Wolff, *What Makes Women Buy: A Guide to Understanding and Influencing the New Woman of Today* (New York: McGraw-Hill, 1958), pp. 60–120; Avrom Fleishman, "M/R: Part 2," *Industrial Design* 3 (February 1958): 37, cited in Mary Beth Haralovich, "Sit-coms and Suburbs: Positioning the 1950s Homemaker," in Lynn Spigel and Denise Mann, eds., *Private Screenings: Television and the Female Consumer* (Minneapolis: University of Minnesota Press, 1992), p. 126; also see "Advertising Should Help Modern Woman Find Herself, Weiss Says," *AA,* Oct. 4, 1965.

58. Frank et al., *Market Segmentation,* pp. 30–32, which cites P. Boomer, "Male Market: Big, Rich, and Tough," *PI* 280 (July 20, 1962): 21–25. On later investigation of the male

market, see "There's a Male in Your Market," *AA*, May 28, 1973; "Once Supermarket Dilettantes, Men Shop Seriously Now," *NYT*, June 5, 1974; Patrick Reilly, "Magazines Beckon 'New Man,'" *AA*, Apr. 17, 1989, p. 3; B. G. Yovovich, "Pinning Down the Elusive Man of Men's Magazines," *AA*, Oct. 19, 1991, p. S26; and "Men's Magazines Take On TV: Publishers Battle for Bigger Share of Ad Dollars," *NYT*, May 29, 2000. Also see Turow, *Breaking Up America*, pp. 60–62. The emergence of men's magazines such as *Playboy* (1953) and *Sports Illustrated* (1954) in the postwar era provided an important vehicle for male-oriented advertising.

59. *Printers' Ink* heralded the release of a landmark and comprehensive survey by Street & Street Publications (a division of Condé Nast), "The American Woman," in 1959, which analyzed more than 5000 questionnaires to document the purchasing patterns of women across the nation: "Survey Shows How American Women Buy," *PI*, Oct. 2, 1959, pp. 23–30. Also see "Who Decides: Man or Wife?" *BW*, Sept. 14, 1957, pp. 46–50; Packard, *Hidden Persuaders*, pp. 81–83, on life insurance; David Halberstam, *The Fifties* (New York: Villard, 1993), pp. 504–505, for history of Marlboro campaign in mid to late 1950s; "DAYTIME RENDEZVOUS . . . with the Women Who Buy," November 1959, NBC Papers, WHS; "What Do Women Want? A Network Has an Idea," *NYT*, Jan. 23, 2000; "Nike Trying New Strategies for Women," *NYT*, June 19, 2001. For discussion of how the Internet is being marketed to women consumers, see Francine Prose, "A Wasteland of One's Own," *NYT Magazine*, Feb. 13, 2000.

60. Martineau, *Motivation in Advertising*, pp. 165–66; Frank et al., *Market Segmentation*, pp. 45–47; Jim Auchmutey, "Graphic Changes Charted in the Middle Class," *AA*, Sept. 12, 1985, p. 15, cited in Turow, *Breaking Up America*, p. 64, also see pp. 65–68; "How They Look to Other Women," *BW*, Jan. 28, 1961. See also from special issue of *JM* 41 (July 1977): William Lazer and John E. Smallwood, "The Changing Demographics of Women": 14–22; Rena Bartos, "The Moving Target: The Impact of Women's Employment on Consumer Behavior": 31–37; Suzanne H. McCall, "Meet the 'Workwife'": 55–65.

61. From *AA:* "'Journal' Hit for Lack of Ladies in Sales," Mar. 23, 1970; "Militant Femmes Shake Up CBS' Annual Meeting," Apr. 27, 1970; "Women's Libs Fume at 'Insulting' Ads; Ad Gals Are Unruffled," July 27, 1970; "The Picture of Women You Have in Your Mind Is All Wrong," Dec. 7, 1970; "Women's Lib 'Dialog' Tells Adfolk: Mend Ad Implications," Jan. 25, 1971; "O&M [Ogilvy & Mather] and NOW Rap About Ads That Lib Group Finds 'Demeaning,'" July 10, 1972; "Women's Rights Drive Gets Off the Ground," Sept. 25, 1972.

62. Susan J. Douglas, *Where the Girls Are: Growing Up Female with the Mass Media* (New York: Times Books, 1994), pp. 152, 202–203, and Douglas, "Narcissism as Liberation," in Scanlon, ed., *Gender and Consumer Culture Reader*, pp. 267–82; "U.S. Seeks to End Mortgage Barriers Facing Women," *NYT*, Mar. 10, 1979; the same discovery of the female banking market is recorded in "Giving Credit to Women," *AA*, Apr. 2, 1973; "Women Win More Credit," *BW*, Jan. 12, 1974, pp. 76–78, and "Where Credit Is Due," *WEAL Washington Report* 7 (June 1978): 1; "Advertising and Women: A Report on Advertising Portraying or Directed to Women, Prepared by a Consultative Panel of the National Advertising Review Board," March 1975; "Female Executives Become a Target for Ads," *BW*, Aug. 22, 1977, p. 66. Also see from special issue of *JM* 41 (July 1977): Fred D. Reynolds, Melvin R. Crask, and William D. Wells, "The Modern Feminine Life Style," pp. 38–45, and William J. Lundstrom and Donald Sciglimpaglia, "Sex Role Portrayals in Advertising," pp. 72–79. From *AA:* "Admen Must Reinvent Woman; Old Fictions Flop, Says Adwoman," Jan. 17, 1970; "New Magazines (and Ads) Show New Attitude Toward Women," Mar. 13, 1972; "Today's Woman Explodes Yesterday's Ad Dream World," Mar.

18, 1974; "Honda Adds Campaign to Woo Women Car Buyers," Aug. 26, 1974. Also Rena Bartos, "What Every Marketer Should Know About Women," *HBR* 56 (May–June 1978): 73–85; Rena Bartos, *The Moving Target: What Every Marketer Should Know About Women* (New York: Free Press, 1982); Mary Thom, *Inside Ms.: 25 Years of the Magazine and the Feminist Movement* (New York: Holt, 1997). An article, "Shifting Female Market Will Kill Some Products," in *AA*, Aug. 16, 1971, suggested that the rise of feminism fueled the segmentation of the female market: "Except for the very rich and the very poor, marketing men have tended to lump women together as one mass market. This seeming simplification worked well enough as long as women had little choice. . . . Free, complex and highly mobile, women's pursuit of an ever widening spectrum of individual interests is breaking the mass market into segments that criss-cross each other and change with mercurial speed."

63. W. D. Wells and G. Gubar, "Life Cycle Concept in Marketing Research," *JMR* 3 (November 1966): 355–63, cited in Frank et al., *Market Segmentation*, p. 36, also see pp. 32–37; "Marketing in the '60s: The Coming Battle for Discretionary Dollars," *PI*, Sept. 11, 1959, pp. 24–25. For a discussion of developments in age segmentation in the 1980s and 1990s, including the age-based subdivision of "Generation X," see Turow, *Breaking Up America*, pp. 68–79.

64. "Special Copy Pays Off," in Daniel Starch and Staff, "Tested Copy: Highlights from the Starch Advertisement Readership Service," no. 51, July 1949, Starch Papers, WHS, Box 1, Folder 3; Grace Palladino, *Teenagers: An American History* (New York: Basic Books, 1996), particularly pp. xv–xx, 97–115. On youth culture in the 1920s, see Paula Fass, *The Damned and the Beautiful: American Youth in the 1920s* (New York: Oxford University Press, 1977). On Eugene Gilbert and the emergence of the teenage market after World War II, see Eugene Gilbert, "The Youth Market," *JM* 13 (July 1948): 79–80; James Gilbert, *A Cycle of Outrage: America's Reaction to the Juvenile Delinquent in the 1950s* (New York: Oxford University Press, 1986), pp. 204–11, 213–15, which quotes (pp. 207, 209) from Eugene Gilbert's statement about "Why Today's Teen-agers Seem So Different," *Harper's Magazine* 219 (November 1959): 77–79. On the "Pepsi Generation" campaign, see Tedlow, *New and Improved*, pp. 101, 109–11, 371–72, and Thomas Frank, *The Conquest of Cool: Business Culture, Counterculture, and the Rise of Hip Consumerism* (Chicago: University of Chicago Press, 1997), pp. 23–24, 169–83.

Also see William Graebner, *Coming of Age in Buffalo: Youth and Authority in the Postwar Era* (Philadelphia: Temple University Press, 1990); Ellen M. Snyder-Grenier, "Bobby Soxers and Youth Run Wild: Looking for the 'Real' New Jersey Teenager," in Kathryn Glover, ed., *Teenage New Jersey, 1941–1975* (Newark: New Jersey Historical Society, 1997), pp. 99–123; and from *BW*: "Who Are Tomorrow's Customers?" Dec. 8, 1951, pp. 146–52; "Ford Soups Up Its Youth Drive," Jan. 4, 1964, pp. 32–34; "Young, Single Spenders Pour It on the Market," Jan. 1, 1966, pp. 62–63; "Getting Across to the Young," Oct. 18, 1969, pp. 89–90. In addition, "The Dreamy Teen-Age Market: 'It's Neat to Spend,'" *Newsweek*, Sept. 16, 1957; "Your Teenager Is Big Business," *American Mercury* 87 (July 1958): 94–96; "A New, $10-Billion Power: The U.S. Teen-age Consumer," *Life*, Aug. 31, 1959, pp. 78–85; a special issue on the teenage market of *Media/Scope* 11 (December 1967); Sidney Margolius, "Teen Agers Are Avid Spenders, Need Information on Budgeting," *AFL-CIO News*, Oct. 19, 1963; "Touting the Teen-agers," *Time*, Feb. 2, 1968, p. 68. A thoughtful review of much of the market segmentation literature on youth is Stanley C. Hollander and Richard Germain, *Was There a Pepsi Generation Before Pepsi Discovered It? Youth-Based Segmentation in Marketing* (Chicago: NTC Business Books, 1992). *Frontline*, "The Merchants of Cool," 60 minutes, broadcast on WGBH-TV, Feb. 27, 2001, investigates the "cool hunters" who seek out teen trends for market exploitation, indicating the continued influence of the grass roots on merchandising.

65. Watson, *Defining Visions*, pp. 16–72; Gary Cross, *Kids' Stuff: Toys and the Changing World of American Childhood* (Cambridge, MA: Harvard University Press, 1997), pp. 157–77; Stephen Kline, "Toys, Socialization, and the Commodification of Play," in Strasser et al., *Getting and Spending*, pp. 39–58; M. G. Lord, *Forever Barbie: The Unauthorized Biography of the Real Doll* (New York: Morrow, 1994); "Big Business Goes Tiny: Toys Help Promote Trade Names," *Life*, November 1953, pp. 97–102; "Tiny Toys Aiding Big Products," *NYT*, Dec. 19, 1956; "Advertising: Toys Pushing Brand Names," *NYT*, Aug. 3, 1960; Amsco quote in "Over Three Million Amsco-Pond's Tie-In Miniatures Marketed," *Playthings* 61 (September 1963): 129, and evidence for brand-name recognition by children in Florence Brumbaugh, "What Effect Does TV Advertising Have on Children?" *Education Digest* 19 (April 1954): 32–33, and Lester Guest, "Brand Loyalty Revisited: A Twenty-Year Report," *Journal of Applied Psychology* 48 (April 1964): 93–97; description of "Acme Checkout Game" and other similar ones from catalogue sheets of the Strong Museum, Rochester, NY; Bogart, *The Age of Television*, pp. 231–45; Stark, *Glued to the Set*, pp. 14–19; Maurice E. Shelby, Jr., "Children's Programming Trends on Network Television," *Journal of Broadcasting* 8 (Summer 1964): 247–56, and Cy Schneider, *Children's Television* (Chicago: NTC Business Books, 1989), on early children's television; Bob Max, "How TV Character Merchandising Works to Sell Toys," *Playthings*, May 1957, pp. 74–75; Twitchell, *Lead Us into Temptation*, pp. 115–16, on "kidvids"; "Shoppers! Deciding? Just Ask Your Child," *NYT*, Jan. 8, 1995. The dispute over the morality of selling to children continues; see "Marketwatch: Consuming Kids," *The American Prospect*, Jan. 31, 2000, p. 13.

66. Sidney Goldstein, "The Aged Segment of the Market, 1950 and 1960," *JM* 32 (April 1968): 62–68; "Discovering the Over-50 Set," *BW*, Nov. 19, 1979, pp. 194–95; "The Power of the Aging in the Marketplace," *BW*, Nov. 20, 1971, pp. 52–58; Hollander and Germain, *Pepsi Generation*, pp. 110–13.

67. "Radio Listens Closely to Mature Market," *AA*, Oct. 19, 1987, p. 52, quoted in Turow, *Breaking Up America*, p. 75; Watson, *Defining Visions*, pp. 218–21; "Sixty Something," *Chain Store Age Executive*, July 1991, pp. 30–32. Seniors' growing preference for spending has contributed significantly to a drop in the nation's savings rate: "Older Americans Cited in Studies of National Savings Rate Slump," *NYT*, Feb. 21, 1995. For a recent advocacy action by the AARP on behalf of senior consumers, see "AARP Wants Bigger Role in Prescription Drug Cases, Group's Goal Is Lower Prices for Medicines," *NYT*, Apr. 23, 2002.

68. Edgar A. Steele, Research Company of America, "Some Aspects of the Negro Market," *JM* 11 (April 1947): 399–401. In addition to the many sources below, note two secondary works in particular: Jannette L. Dates, "Advertising," in Dates and William Barlow, eds., *Split Image: African Americans in the Mass Media* (Washington, DC: Howard University Press, 1990), pp. 429–53, and Robert E. Weems, Jr., *Desegregating the Dollar: African American Consumerism in the Twentieth Century* (New York: New York University Press, 1998).

69. "Pepsi-Cola's Campaign to the Negro Market," *PI*, Sept. 9, 1949, pp. 38–39, including Canada quote; "The Negro Market: How to Tap $15 Million in Sales," *Time*, July 5, 1954. Pepsi experimented with some ads that included blacks, such as the "Leaders in His/Her Field" advertising campaign of 1949, which tried to associate prominent blacks with Pepsi. By the early 1950s marketers specializing in the "Negro Market" had founded their own organization, the National Association of Market Developers: Weems, *Desegregating the Dollar*, pp. 52–53.

For other examples of black media efforts to promote the "Negro Market," which began in the 1930s, see Paul K. Edwards, *The Southern Urban Negro as a Consumer* (New York: Prentice-Hall, 1932); in Barnett: *The Negro Market: Published in the Interest of the Negro Press* (Chicago: Ziff, 1932), Box 131, Folder 5; David J. Sullivan, Negro Market Organization, "America's Negro Market Is Growing!" 1945, Box 131, Folder 2; "The

Negro Market Today," n.d., but c. 1949, Box 132, Folder 7; reprint of article from *AA* by *Pittsburgh Courier*, Dec. 26, 1949, "Advertisers Step Up Negro Market Drives," Box 131, Folder 2; Associated Publishers, *A Cross Section of the American Market Worthy of Direct Cultivation, a Market Not Penetrated by 'General Media'* (New York: Associated, 1950), Box 132, Folder 7. Also see "Newark: A Market for Better Income Families Ideal for Partial–New York Test," in *A Practical Guide to Basic Selling in 21 Key Urban Negro Markets* (New York: Associated, 1959); "'Ebony' Survey Reveals Negro Buying Habits," *AA*, Aug. 28, 1950; Joseph Johnson, "Selling the Negro Market: A Manual for Salesmen" (Chicago: Ebony pamphlet, n.d. but c. 1950); Fath Davis Ruffins, "Ethnic Imagery in the Landscape of Commerce," in Strasser et al., eds., *Getting and Spending*, pp. 393–97. On racist stereotyping in advertising, see William M. O'Barr, *Culture and the Ad: Exploring Otherness in the World of Advertising* (Boulder, CO: Westview, 1994), pp. 107–56, and Grace Elizabeth Hale, *Making Whiteness: The Culture of Segregation in the South, 1890–1940* (New York: Pantheon, 1998).

An early pioneer of market segmentation was "Negro-Appeal radio," which got off the ground in 1949 and by 1952 could boast two hundred radio stations throughout the country programming partially or entirely to the Negro radio listener. One could argue, however, that the black radio station was more like the old media organs of segregated America, the black newspaper and magazine, than a mass market vehicle: "The Forgotten $15,000,000 . . . Three Years Later," *Sponsor Magazine* 6 (July 28, 1952): 29–49.

70. "Nation Within a Nation," *Premium Practice*, May 1957, pp. 25–47; Henry Allen Bullock, "Consumer Motivations in Black and White," *HBR* 39 (May–June 1961): 89–104; D. Parke Gibson/Associates, "The Negro Market—Recommended Reading 1961–62" and "Confidential Report on the Negro Market," October 1962, in Barnett, Box 131, Folder 2; Seymour Banks, "Dimensions of the Negro Market," Leo Burnett Company office memorandum, Apr. 8, 1964, reprinted in Britt, ed., *Consumer Behavior*, pp. 254–55; D. Parke Gibson, "Promoting to a Special Market: The Negro," *Advertising and Sales Promotion* 12 (July 1964): 26–33; Raymond A. Bauer, Scott M. Cunningham, and Lawrence H. Wortzel, "The Marketing Dilemma of Negroes," *JM* 29 (July 1965): 1–6; "Why the Negro Market Counts," *BW*, Sept. 2, 1967, p. 64; Raymond Bauer and Scott M. Cunningham, "The Negro Market," *JAR* 10 (April 1970): 3–13; Dennis H. Gensch and Richard Staelin, "The Appeal of Buying Black," *JMR* 9 (May 1972): 141–48; Donald E. Sexton, "Black Buyer Behavior," *JM* 36 (October 1972): 36–39.

The African-American media continued to undertake surveys of black American buying behavior. In 1993 the Essence/Simmons African-American National Survey interviewed 10,000 respondents in urban, suburban, and rural areas to enable advertisers "to position, market and sell their products more cost effectively," according to the director of corporate marketing research at Essence Communications, publisher of the magazine of the same name: "New Survey Planned of Black Americans," *NYT*, Aug. 23, 1993.

71. "Toys That Build Pride," *Ebony*, November 1975, p. 137; on *Alma John Show*, see excerpt from *National Bottlers' Gazette*, February 1963, in Moss H. Kendrix Papers, Black History Resource Center, Alexandria, Virginia.

72. Regina Austin, "'A Nation of Thieves': Securing Black People's Right to Shop and Sell in White America," *Utah Law Review* 1994, no. 1: 147–77; in addition to Weems's book cited earlier, see his article "The Revolution Will Be Marketed: American Corporations and Black Consumers During the 1960s," *Radical History Review* 59 (Spring 1994): 94–107.

73. "The Negro's Force in Marketplace," *BW*, May 26, 1962, p. 76; also "Why the Negro Market Counts," *BW*, Sept. 2, 1967, p. 64; D. Parke Gibson, *The $30 Billion Negro* (New York: Macmillan, 1969), pp. 12, 196, 200, 263; "Marketing to Negro Isn't Segregation in

Reverse: Gibson," *AA,* Sept. 27, 1965; "Negro Market Will Be Controlling Factor in Profit Margins of Big U.S. Companies in 15 Years: Johnson," *AA,* Sept. 21, 1964; also see "Uncle Tom Magazine Removes the Kid Gloves," *BW,* Mar. 23, 1968, for more views of John Johnson. For black militance aimed at advertisers and marketers, see "WRG Discriminates in Employment, Media Policies, Stockholder Charges," *AA,* Mar. 5, 1973, p. 2. On social-class segmenting within the black market, see Kelvin Wall, "Positioning Your Brand in the Black Market," *AA,* June 18, 1973; Kevin Wall, "New Market: Among Blacks, the Haves Are Now Overtaking the Have-nots," Feb. 11, 1974; James Cicarelli, "On Income, Race, and Consumer Behavior," *American Journal of Economics and Sociology* 33 (July 1974): 243–47.

74. "We Think White Is Beautiful, Too," *Ebony* ad, *AA,* Mar. 10, 1969; also see "Mixing Black Power, Peace and Packaging," *AA,* Apr. 14, 1969; "Buying Black: Mainstream Companies Are Cashing In on African-American Consumers," *Time,* Aug. 31, 1992, pp. 52–53. For another protest against advertisers' targeting black consumers to their detriment, see "Data on Tobacco Show a Strategy Aimed at Blacks," *NYT,* Feb. 6, 1998. For continued attention to racialized markets, see "Consumed by Race: White and Black Buying Habits, by the Number," *NYT Magazine,* July 16, 2000.

75. Mary Tannen, "Makeup Goes Multicultural," *NYT Magazine,* Feb. 23, 1997, pp. 48–51; Salim Muwakkil, "Need for Make-over in Black Business," *In These Times,* Dec. 24, 1986–Jan. 14, 1987, p. 5; Weems, "Consumerism and the Construction of Black Female Identity in Twentieth-Century America," pp. 166–78; Russ Rymer, "Integration's Casualties," *NYT Magazine,* Nov. 1, 1998, pp. 48–50. For slightly different figures on black firms' share of black consumer spending, but a similar conclusion, see Gerald David Jaynes and Robin M. Williams, Jr., eds., *A Common Destiny: Blacks and American Society* (Washington, DC: National Academy Press, 1989), pp. 180–83; 1992 figures from "Black Entrepreneurs: Have Capital, Will Flourish," *The Economist,* Feb. 27, 1993. For a compelling exploration of the decline of the segregated black business district of Tulsa, Oklahoma, see the documentary "Goin' Back to T'Town," *The American Experience,* WGBH-TV, Mar. 1, 1993, Show #512; on Savannah, GA, "Back to Business," *BG,* Sept. 16, 1997.

76. "Advertising: Negro Market Plays Big Role," *NYT,* Sept. 24, 1961; James D. Culley and Rex Bennett, "Equality in Advertising: Selling Women, Selling Blacks," *Journal of Communications* 26 (Autumn 1976): 168–73; James E. Stafford, Al E. Birdwell, and Charles E. Van Tassel, "Integrated Advertising—White Backlash?" *JAR* 10 (April 1970): 15–20; James W. Cagley and Richard N. Cardoza, "White Response to Integrated Advertising," *JAR* 10 (April 1970): 35–39. The hypocrisy involved in targeting black consumers but not integrating the white media was well illustrated by the Xerox Corporation's sponsorship of a television series called *Black America* and refusal to run commercials during the series showing blacks using Xerox products: " 'Black America' TV Series Is Short of Negroes," *AA,* May 27, 1968. Celebrity Bill Cosby led the way in integrating mainstream television commercials for such products as Coca-Cola and Jell-O: Donald Bogle, *Primetime Blues: African Americans on Network Television* (New York: Farrar, Straus and Giroux, 2001).

Advertising Age was filled with articles during the 1960s and 1970s about black organizations pressuring advertising agencies to hire more black employees. See, for example, "Affirmative Effort to Hire Minority People Urged on Four A's by Elliott," Apr. 29, 1968; "Positive Hiring Policy Emerged as Result of Negro Boycott, Says B&B," July 22, 1968; "Gains in Hiring Minority People Seen Minimal," Jan. 13, 1969.

77. "Airline Deal: The Novice; Trying to Transfer Niche Marketing from the Cable TV Industry to the Skies," *NYT,* May 25, 2000; on recent demands by black consumers that corporations prove their worthiness, see "McDonald's Promotes Image Among Blacks,"

NYT, July 19, 1993; "Denny's Gets a Bill for the Side Orders of Bigotry," *NYT,* May 29, 1994; "Flex Your Financial Muscles," "Supermarket Blackout," "The Madison Avenue Initiative," and "Doing Well by Doing Good," in *Black Enterprise,* July 1999. Also see "The N.A.A.C.P. Means Business," *NYT,* Aug. 31, 1993.

78. "Black TV Audience Picking Its Own Top 10," *Chicago Tribune,* Apr. 4, 1992; "TV Viewing and Selling, by Race," *NYT,* Apr. 5, 1993. For a similar recognition much earlier, see "Negroes' Favorite Brands Differ from Whites in Half of Categories, RKO Finds," *AA,* Feb. 10, 1969.

79. Marilyn Halter, *Shopping for Identity: The Marketing of Ethnicity* (New York: Schocken, 2000); " 'American Indian Horizon' Aims to Serve Original Group of Consumers," *AA,* Mar. 11, 1963; "Ethnic Marketing Is Profitable but Tricky, Article Says," *AA,* Apr. 4, 1966; Frank et al., *Market Segmentation,* pp. 39–40; "Audience Research Units Have 'Deficiencies' in Ethnic Coverage: Y&R [Young & Rubicam]," *AA,* Nov. 5, 1973; "Businesses That Ride a Rebirth of Ethnic Pride," *BW,* Oct. 22, 1979, pp. 152–56; "Catering to Consumers' Ethnic Needs," *NYT,* Jan. 23, 1992. Also see Viviana A. Zelizer, "Multiple Markets, Multiple Cultures," in Neil Smelser and Jeffrey Alexander, eds., *Diversity and Its Discontents* (Princeton: Princeton University Press, 1999), pp. 193–212. The marketing literature is filled with handbooks instructing the trade in how to market more successfully to ethnic communities through segmentation; see, for example, Alfred L. Schreiber with Barry Lenson, *Multicultural Marketing, Selling to the New America: Position Your Company Today for Optimal Success in the Diverse America of Tomorrow* (Chicago: NTC Business Books, 2001), and Marye C. Tharp, *Marketing Consumer Identity in Multicultural America* (Thousand Oaks, CA: Sage, 2001).

80. Richard P. Jones, "Spanish-Language Market in U.S. Now 8 Million," *Media/Scope* 11 (July 1967): 85–92; "America's Latinos: The Keenest Recruits to the Dream," *The Economist,* Apr. 25, 1998, pp. 25–27; Turow, *Breaking Up America,* pp. 84–89; "TV Advertising Drives Fight Over Size of Spanish Audience," *NYT,* July 17, 2000; "Asian-Americans' Tastes Are Surveyed by Marketer," *NYT,* Jan. 14, 1991; "Complaints to Spanish TV: Where Are the Americans?" *NYT,* Aug. 21, 2000; Arlene Davila, *Latinos, Inc.: The Marketing of a People* (Berkeley: University of California Press, 2001), for the impact of becoming a market segment on Latinos; Charles R. Tayler, Ju Yung Lee, and Barbara B. Stern, "Portrayals of African, Hispanic, and Asian Americans in Magazine Advertising," in Ronald Paul Hill, *Marketing and Consumer Research in the Public Interest* (Thousand Oaks, CA: Sage, 1996), pp. 133–50; Tannen, "Makeup Goes Multicultural."

81. Advertisers have been slower to appeal to lesbians than male homosexuals: Karen Stabiner, "Tapping the Homosexual Market," *NYT Magazine,* May 2, 1982; Denae Clark, "Commodity Lesbianism," in Scanlon, ed., *Gender and Consumer Culture Reader,* pp. 372–87; "MTV and Showtime Plan Cable Channel for Gay Viewers," *NYT,* Jan. 10, 2002; see sample ad for Mitchell Gold Furniture, "A kid deserves to feel at home," with child surrounded by two paternal males in a living room, *House & Garden,* October 2000, near p. 129.

82. Paul Lazarsfeld, Bernard Berelson, and Hazel Gaudet, *The People's Choice* (New York: Columbia University Press, 1948); Bernard R. Berelson, Paul F. Lazarsfeld, and William N. McPhee, *Voting: A Study of Opinion Formation in a Presidential Campaign* (Chicago: University of Chicago Press, 1954); Packard, *Hidden Persuaders,* pp. 181, 193; on Reeves, see Fox, *Mirror Makers,* pp. 187–94.

83. Richard Jensen, "American Election Campaigns: A Theoretical and Historical Typology," paper presented at the meeting of the Midwest Political Science Association, Bloomington, IN, 1968, cited in Dan Nimmo, "Images and Voters' Decision-Making Processes," *Advances in Consumer Research* 1 (1974): 771. For a wonderful overview of the

shift from military-style political campaigns to merchandising ones, see Robert B. Westbrook, "Politics as Consumption: Managing the Modern American Election," in Richard Wightman Fox and T. J. Jackson Lears, eds., *The Culture of Consumption: Critical Essays in American History, 1880–1980* (New York: Pantheon, 1983), pp. 145–73. Another source that ranges helpfully over the entire period discussed below is Kathleen Hall Jamieson's extremely thorough *Packaging the Presidency: A History and Criticism of Presidential Campaign Advertising,* 3rd ed. (New York: Oxford University Press, 1996).

84. Stanley Kelley, Jr., *Professional Public Relations and Political Power* (Baltimore: Johns Hopkins Press, 1956), pp. 9–14; Liette Patricia Gidlow, "Getting Out the Vote: Gender and Citizenship in an Age of Consumer Culture" (Ph.D diss., Cornell University, 1997), particularly pp. 331–437.

85. Kelley, *Professional Public Relations,* pp. 14–17, 16–38; Westbrook, "Politics as Consumption," p. 161–62; Daniel J. Robinson, *The Measure of Democracy: Polling, Market Research, and Public Life, 1930–1945* (Toronto: University of Toronto Press, 1999), pp. 7, 16–17, 39–63. Importantly, market research and opinion research remained closely connected, seeking mutual benefit; see Leo Bogart, "Opinion Research and Marketing," *POQ* 21 (Spring 1957): 129–40; Larry J. Sabato, *The Rise of Political Consultants: New Ways of Winning Elections* (New York: Basic Books, 1981), p. 69.

86. Kelley, *Professional Public Relations,* quote on crudeness of political propaganda on p. 27, on Campaigns, Inc., pp. 39–66. For more on Campaigns, Inc., see Sabato, *Rise of Political Consultants,* p. 11; Edwin Diamond and Stephen Bates, *The Spot: The Rise of Political Advertising on Television,* rev. ed. (Cambridge, MA: MIT Press, 1988), p. 42.

87. On the 1952 and 1956 presidential campaigns, see Packard, *Hidden Persuaders,* pp. 182–200; Kelley, *Professional Public Relations,* pp. 150–69; Stephen C. Wood, "Television's First Political Spot Ad Campaign: Eisenhower Answers America," *Presidential Studies Quarterly* 20 (Spring 1990): 265–83; Diamond and Bates, *The Spot,* pp. 45–92; "The 30 Second President" from series *A Walk Through the 20th Century with Bill Moyers,* Corporation for Entertainment and Learning, and Bill Moyers, 1984; Halberstam, *The Fifties,* pp. 224–42; Craig Allen, *Eisenhower and the Mass Media: Peace, Prosperity and Prime-Time TV* (Chapel Hill: University of North Carolina Press, 1993); Fox, *Mirror Makers,* pp. 309–11.

88. John G. Schneider, *The Golden Kazoo* (New York: Rinehart, 1956); also review by W. H. Lawrence, "A Political Producer to Market," *NYT Book Review,* Jan. 22, 1956.

89. Easton, "Consuming Interests," p. 21.

90. Lawrence R. Jacobs and Robert Y. Shapiro, "Issues, Candidate Images, and Priming: The Use of Private Polls in Kennedy's 1960 Presidential Campaign," *American Political Science Review* 88 (September 1994): 527–40; "Scouting the Trail for Marketers," *BW,* Apr. 18, 1964, p. 110; Maureen Dowd, "Playing the Jesus Card," *NYT,* Dec. 15, 1999; Theodore H. White, *The Making of the President, 1960* (New York: Atheneum, 1965), pp. 239–43; Stanley Kelley, Jr., "The Presidential Campaign," in *The Presidential Election and Transition, 1960–1961* (Washington, DC: Brookings Institute, 1961), pp. 57–87; Sabato, *Rise of Political Consultants,* pp. 69–70; Daniel M. Ogden, Jr., and Arthur L. Peterson, *Electing the President: 1964* (San Francisco: Chandler, 1964), pp. 124–43; Diamond and Bates, *The Spot,* pp. 93–112.

91. The Johnson campaign pulled the daisy commercial off the air because of its sensationalism, but then it was shown over and over again on the news: Diamond and Bates, *The Spot,* pp. 15–47.

92. Richard Viguerie, *The New Right: We're Ready to Lead* (Falls Church, VA: Viguerie, 1981); on the Nixon-Lodge campaign's use of direct mail in 1960, see Ogden and Peterson, *Electing the President: 1964,* pp. 138–41; "Buchanan Inc.: How Pat and Bay Built an

Empire on Our Money," *The Nation,* Nov. 22, 1999, pp. 11–16; Reagan mail solicitation cited in Nicholas O'Shaughnessy and Gillian Peele, "Money, Mail and Markets: Reflections on Direct Mail in American Politics," *Electoral Studies* 4 (August 1985): 118, and see rest of article as well; Sabato, *Rise of Political Consultants,* pp. 220–63; Brian A. Haggarty, "Direct-Mail Political Fund-Raising," *Public Relations Journal* 34 (March 1979): 10–12; James D. Snyder, "Playing Politics by Mail," *Sales & Marketing Journal* 129 (July 5, 1982): 44, 46; "Politics by Mail: A New Platform," *The Wharton Magazine* 7 (Fall 1982): 16–19; Irwin B. Arieff, "Computers and Direct Mail Are Being Married on the Hill to Keep Incumbents in Office," *Congressional Quarterly Weekly Report,* July 21, 1979, pp. 1445–52. On the development of the direct marketing strategy in advertising, before it was picked up by campaigners, see Wundeman, *Being Direct.*

93. On Nixon's campaign in 1968, see Joe McGinniss's classic *The Selling of the President* (New York: Trident, 1969), pp. 120–25; Neil Gabler, *Life the Movie: How Entertainment Conquered Reality* (New York: Knopf, 1999), pp. 102–104. The Nixon campaign's "Man in the Arena" hour-long television programs, featuring Nixon answering citizens' questions, were also broadcast by regional grouping of stations, not nationally, to facilitate the tailoring of shows: Diamond and Bates, *The Spot,* p. 170 and more generally pp. 153–84.

94. "New Battle Over 'Compulsory' Unionism,'" *U.S. News & World Report,* Oct. 30, 1978, p. 81; Larson, *The Naked Consumer,* pp. 222–23; "'Right-to-Work' Fight: High Stakes, Little Logic," *Washington Post,* Oct. 31, 1978; and from *St. Louis Post-Dispatch:* "Right-to-Work," Oct. 8, 1978; "Catholics Form Group for 'Right to Work,'" Oct. 24, 1978; "'Right-to-Work' Campaigns Intensified," Nov. 6, 1978; "Right-to-Work Soundly Defeated," Nov. 8, 1978.

95. Sabato, *Rise of Political Consultants,* p. 232; "The Power of the Aging in the Marketplace," *BW,* Nov. 20, 1971, pp. 5, 57.

96. My assessment of the impact of political marketing techniques on the American political system has benefited from John Judis, "The Pressure Elite: Inside the Narrow World of Advocacy Group Politics," *The American Prospect,* Spring 1992, pp. 15–29; Robert V. Friedenberg, *Communication Consultants in Political Campaigns: Ballot Box Warriors* (Westport, CT: Praeger, 1997), particularly pp. 95–126, with the Miami case described on p. 100; James Davison Hunter, *Culture Wars: The Struggle to Define America* (New York: Basic Books, 1991), pp. 163–70; Gillian Peele, "Campaign Consultants," *Electoral Studies* 1 (1982): 358; Sabato, *Rise of Political Consultants,* pp. 231, 241; Diamond and Bates, *The Spot,* pp. 151–52, 373–95; Michael T. Hayes, "Interest Groups: Pluralism or Mass Society?" in Allan J. Cigle and Burdett A. Loomis, eds., *Interest Group Politics* (Washington, DC: CQ Press, 1983), pp. 11–25; Larsen, *Naked Consumer,* pp. 215–24; Westbrook, "Politics as Consumption," passim, and p. 164 on the "law of minimal effects." What he calls "new-style campaigning" and its larger political consequences are straightforwardly laid out for practitioners in Daniel Shea's electioneering manual, *Campaign Craft: The Strategies, Tactics, and Art of Political Campaign Management* (Westport, CT: Praeger, 1996). For evidence that identifying and catering to electoral market niches remains a thriving business, see James Bennet, "The Guru of Small Things," *NYT Magazine,* June 18, 2000, pp. 60–65, on pollster Mark Penn, whose "data helped transform the Clinton presidency into a service provider for various niche voters. Now he's thinly slicing New Yorkers to get Hillary to the Senate." For an analysis of the shift from voter "mobilization" to "activation" (by electoral niches), see Steven E. Schier, *By Invitation Only: The Rise of Exclusive Politics in the United States* (Pittsburgh: University of Pittsburgh Press, 2000).

Whether or not political party identification has declined among Americans is a subject of recent debate among political scientists. The prevailing view is that it has ebbed substantially since the 1950s. A few scholars, however, have begun to argue for its rebound since the 1980s, particularly among elites and the declining portion of Americans who vote: Stephen C. Craig, "Polity Forum: 'Do Political Parties Really Matter?' " *Polity* 20 (Summer 1988): 705–13; Martin P. Wattenberg, *The Decline of American Political Parties: 1952–1994* (Cambridge, MA: Harvard University Press, 1996); Larry M. Bartels, "Partisanship and Voting Behavior, 1952–1996," *American Journal of Political Science* 44 (January 2000): 35–50; Marc J. Hetherington, "Resurgent Mass Partisanship: The Role of Elite Polarization," *American Political Science Review* 95 (September 2001): 619–31.

97. Lizabeth Cohen, *Making a New Deal: Industrial Workers in Chicago, 1919–1939* (New York: Cambridge University Press, 1990).

CHAPTER 8. POLITICS: PURCHASERS POLITICIZED

1. "President to Ask Tighter Control Over New Drugs, Special Message Next Week Will Also Request Added Safeguards for Food," *NYT,* Mar. 4, 1962; "Kennedy Submits a Broad Program to Aid Consumer" and "Text of Kennedy's Message to Congress on Protections for Consumers," *NYT,* Mar. 16, 1962.

2. Quoted in Esther Peterson with Winifred Conkling, *Restless: The Memoirs of Labor and Consumer Activist Esther Peterson* (Washington, DC: Caring, 1995), p. 119. Note Kennedy's identification of the consumer as a "man," a gendering discussed in Chapter 3.

3. "Special Message to the Congress on Consumer Interests," Feb. 5, 1964, *Public Papers of the Presidents of the United States: Lyndon B. Johnson, 1963–64, Book I* (Washington, DC: USGPO, 1965), pp. 263–68; "Annual Message to the Congress on the State of the Union," Feb. 17, 1968, *Public Papers of the Presidents of the United States: Lyndon B. Johnson, 1968–69* (Washington, DC: USGPO, 1970), pp. 25–32.

4. "Nixon Proposes a 'Bill of Rights' for Consumers," *NYT,* Oct. 31, 1969. On Carter's commitment to consumer issues, see Peterson, *Restless,* pp. 159–69.

5. Lucy Black Creighton, *Pretenders to the Throne: The Consumer Movement in the United States* (Lexington, MA: Lexington Books, 1976), p. 35.

6. Mark V. Nadel, *The Politics of Consumer Protection* (Indianapolis: Bobbs-Merrill, 1971), p. 35.

7. "Consumerism" was a label originally coined by industry to associate the emerging consumer movement with other dangerous "isms," such as communism and socialism. Consumer activists like Betty Furness and Erma Angevine recognized the derogatory origin of the label, but continued to use it nonetheless to represent their new campaign against bureaucratic neglect and corporate disregard of consumers: testimony by Furness and Angevine in William T. Kelley, ed., *New Consumerism: Selected Readings* (Columbus, OH: Grid, 1973), p. vi.

8. David Halberstam, *The Fifties* (New York: Villard, 1993), p. 504.

9. Ralph Nader, "The *Safe* Car You Can't Buy," *The Nation,* Apr. 11, 1959, reprinted in *The Ralph Nader Reader* (New York: Seven Stories, 2000), p. 270; Douglas T. Miller and Marion Nowak, *The Fifties: The Way We Really Were* (Garden City, NY: Doubleday, 1977), p. 141.

10. Persia Campbell, *Bringing the Consumer Point of View into Government* (Greeley, CO: Council on Consumer Information, 1958), pp. 20–21.

11. Michael Pertschuk, *Revolt Against Regulation: The Rise and Pause of the Consumer Movement* (Berkeley: University of California Press, 1982), p. 20; *Congress and the Nation, 1945–1964: A Review of Government and Politics in the Postwar Years,* (Washington, DC: Congressional Quarterly Service, 1964), 1:1159–85; Nadel, *Politics of Consumer Protection,* pp. 31–34.

12. Pearce C. Kelley, *Consumer Economics* (Homewood, IL: Irwin, 1953), p. 147.

13. Quoted in paper by Commissioner Mary Gardiner Jones, Federal Trade Commission, delivered before the Sixth Biennial World Conference of the International Organization of Consumer Unions, June 29, 1970, Angevine, Box 2, D-3, pp. 20–21. Another business voice also attributed the rise of consumerism to a wide range of factors, including the success of a mass consumption economy: Philip Kotler, "What Consumerism Means for Marketers," *HBR* (May–June 1972), pp. 48–57.

14. Pertschuk, *Revolt Against Regulation*, pp. 18–19; "Remarks of Senator Philip A. Hart (D. Michigan) Before the International Organization of Consumers Unions, July 1, 1968," in Angevine, Box 2, D-3, p. 1.

15. Furness quoted in Laurence P. Feldman, "Consumer Protection: Problems and Prospects," excerpted from Feldman, ed., *Consumer Protection: Problems and Prospects* (St. Paul, MN: West, 1980), in Harold G. Vatter and John F. Walker, eds., *History of the U.S. Economy Since World War II* (Armonk, NY: Sharpe, 1996), p. 323; Halberstam, *The Fifties*, pp. 497–500; also see "Betty Furness, 78, TV Reporter and Consumer Advocate, Dies," *NYT*, Apr. 4, 1994. Economist David Hamilton linked the consumer movement to postwar affluence in a speech: "But today's consumer movement is largely characterized by the outlook of the 'affluent society' and the 'mass-consumption' society. Anyone need check only the monthly publications of the two United States consumer testing organizations between the 1930s and today to perceive the general difference in outlook—from one of scarcity and the need for thrift to one of acceptance of abundance. Today's consumer movement reflects the problem of a consumer overwhelmed with problem of selection—or, as George Katona has put it, with the problems of the consumer with discretionary income": David Hamilton, "Technology and Consumption: The Theoretical Implications," n.d. but 1960s, Angevine, Box 2, D-3, pp. 4–5.

16. Feldman, "Consumer Protection," p. 321.

17. Gary Cross, *An All-Consuming Century: Why Commercialism Won in Modern America* (New York: Columbia University Press, 2000), pp. 156–57; Albert J. Zanger, "What Was the Impact of the Choate Study on the Cereal Market?" in Kelley, *New Consumerism*, pp. 285–300, 547–61; Pertschuk, *Revolt Against Regulation*, pp. 69–71, 101–105, 130; "Citizens Group Opens Chicago Parley," *NYT*, Mar. 26, 1973; in a similar vein, see the discussion of the Senior Citizens Council of Union County, New Jersey, in "Business Bureau Alters Consumer Questionnaire," *NYT*, May 7, 1973. Also, proceedings of "New Jersey Consumers Conference 1967," Mar. 14, 1967, in New Jersey Consumers' League Papers, NPL, Box 1, folder "Conferences," pp. 10–11; "Special Concerns Session on the Elderly Consumer," in 1971 White House Conference on Aging, *Recommended for Action: Protective and Social Support*, Angevine, Box 1, Folder D-4, pp. 17–24. A more recent analysis of elderly consumer activism is Ruth Belk Smith and George T. Baker, "The Elderly Consumer: A Perspective on Present and Potential Sources of Consumerism Activity," in Paul N. Bloom and Ruth Belk Smith, eds., *The Future of Consumerism* (Lexington, MA: Lexington Books, 1986), pp. 99–112. For consideration of African-American and male consumer activism, see, respectively, in *NYT*: "Ebony Surveys Black Attitudes," May 31, 1973, and "Once Supermarket Dilettantes, Men Shop Seriously Now," June 5, 1974.

18. Sidney Margolius, "What Consumers Need in Government Protection," address to Council on Consumer Information Annual Conference, Mar. 22, 1963, Department of Health, Education and Welfare, Washington, DC, in Angevine, Box 2, D-3, p. 3: "The truth of the matter is, that today consumer exploitation to a large extent has replaced labor exploitation as the real shame of our times, and the potential political fuse." Also see Cross, *All-Consuming Century*, p. 147, for insight into the shift from labor exploita-

tion to consumer exploitation. Nader quote from Lucia Mouat, "The Consumer Fights Back," *CSM*, Jan. 24–26, 1970.

There is a vast literature on interest group politics; see in particular Allan J. Cigler and Burdett A. Loomis, eds., *Interest Group Politics* (Washington, DC: CQ Press, 1983), particularly "Introduction: The Changing Nature of Interest Group Politics," pp. 1–30; Ronald J. Hrebenar and Ruth K. Scott, *Interest Group Politics in America* (Englewood Cliffs, NJ: Prentice-Hall, 1982); and two classic works, Theodore Lowi, *The End of Liberalism: Ideology, Policy, and the Crisis of Public Authority* (New York: Norton, 1969), and Mancor Olson, *The Logic of Collective Action* (Cambridge, MA: Harvard University Press, 1971).

19. There were differences of opinion over the nature of the tax cut. The AFL-CIO, for example, while insistent on the need for an immediate cut "to provide the economy with the maximum thrust of high-velocity buying power," favored a more redistributive proposal, one that concentrated its benefits among low- and middle-income taxpayers, and gave no reduction to corporations; "Report of the Economic Policy Committee to the Executive Council on Immediate Tax Cut to Get America Back to Work," St. Louis, Missouri, May 15, 1963," IUE, RG 2, Box, 52, folder "AFL-CIO Exec. Comm.—St. Louis, May 14/63." Also see Robert M. Collins, "Growth Liberalism in the Sixties: Great Societies at Home and Grand Designs Abroad," in David Farber, ed., *The Sixties: From Memory to History* (Chapel Hill: University of North Carolina Press, 1994), p. 18, and Collins, *More: The Politics of Economic Growth in Postwar America* (New York: Oxford University Press, 2000), p. 39; *Economic Report of the President, Transmitted to the Congress January 1962, Together with the Annual Report of the Council of Economic Advisers* (Washington, DC: USGPO, 1962), pp. 17–18; *Economic Report of the President, Transmitted to the Congress January 1965, Together with the Annual Report of the Council of Economic Advisers* (Washington, DC: USGPO, 1965), pp. 5, 80. *Economic Reports of the President* between those two made the same points. On the Kennedy/Johnson tax cut, also see Judith Stein, *Running Steel, Running America: Race, Economic Policy, and the Decline of Liberalism* (Chapel Hill: University of North Carolina Press, 1998), p. 34; Julian E. Zelizer, *Taxing America: Wilbur D. Mills, Congress, and the State, 1945–1975* (New York: Cambridge University Press, 1998), pp. 209–11; Zelizer, "Learning the Ways and Means: Wilbur Mills and a Fiscal Community, 1954–1964," in W. Elliot Brownlee, ed., *Funding the Modern American State, 1941–1995: The Rise and Fall of the Era of Easy Finance* (Washington, DC: Woodrow Wilson Center Press; New York: Cambridge University Press, 1996), pp. 289–352.

20. "Text of Kennedy's Message to Congress on Protections for Consumers," *NYT*, Mar. 16, 1962. Eisenhower's Keynesianism angered the emerging right within the Republican Party. In 1957, Barry Goldwater blasted Ike's Keynesian budget in the Senate: "[It] not only shocks me, but weakens my faith"; quoted in Sam Tanenhaus, "The GOP, or Goldwater's Old Party—Why W. Is No Surprise," *The New Republic*, June 11, 2001.

21. Pertschuk, *Revolt Against Regulation*, pp. 9–36. Pertschuk borrowed the concept of "entrepreneurial politics" from political scientist James Q. Wilson, as developed in Wilson, ed., *The Politics of Regulation* (New York: Basic Books, 1980). Pertschuk elaborated on many of the points in interviews with me, Nov. 10, 2000, Boston, and Nov. 13, 2001, Cambridge, MA.

22. Quote from *AFL-CIO American Federationist* (November 1973), p. 27, in Creighton, *Pretenders to the Throne*, p. 73; also see the President's Committee on Consumer Interests, "A Summary of Activities, 1964–1967," March 1967, Margolius, Box 4, p. 33. Evidence of the labor movement's support for the consumerist agenda is extensive in labor publications through the 1960s and early 1970s; see, for example, *AFL-CIO American Federationist*, *AFL-CIO News*, and *Proceedings of the Constitutional Conventions of the*

AFL-CIO, passim. On labor's consumer education efforts, see Sandra L. Willett, "Consent and Future Purposes and Objectives of Consumer Education, Condensed and Edited Version," Aug. 31, 1980, prepared for the Office of Consumers' Education, Department of Education, pp. 21–22, Angevine, Box 5, D-2; "Organizing a Consumer Education Program," *AFL-CIO Education News and Views* 6 (January–February 1961): 14–15, Margolius, Box 4; "Betty Furness Lauds IUE Consumer Program," *IUE Convention 1968,* p. 1, IUE.

Labor unions often aided consumer boycotts by making phones, printing presses, and staff time available. See, for example, discussion of the involvement of District Council 37 of the State, County and Municipal Employees Union of New York City in the meat boycotts of 1973; from *NYT:* "Consumers Scoff at Ceiling and Step Up Boycott Plans," Mar. 31, 1973, and "Behind the Metropolitan Boycott, a Militant Union," Apr. 6, 1973.

23. The material on Ralph Nader is extensive. A handy compendium of Nader's own writings is *The Ralph Nader Reader.* I have found particularly useful Pertschuk, *Revolt Against Regulation,* pp. 30–33, 40–41; Robert D. Holsworth, *Public Interest Liberalism and the Crisis of Affluence: Reflections on Nader, Environmentalism, and the Politics of a Sustainable Society* (Cambridge, MA: Hall, 1980); Jonathan Rowe, "Ralph Nader Reconsidered," *Washington Monthly,* March 1985, pp. 12–21; David Ignatius, "Stages of Nader," *NYT Magazine,* Jan. 18, 1976, p. 9; Ken Auletta, "Ralph Nader, Public Eye," *Esquire,* December 1983; Julius Dusha, "Stop! In the Public Interest!" *NYT Magazine,* Mar. 21, 1971; "The U.S.'s Toughest Customer," *Time,* Dec. 12, 1969, in Kelley, *New Consumerism,* pp. 51–64; Creighton, *Pretenders to the Throne,* pp. 51–68; Nadel, *Politics of Consumer Protection,* pp. 176–86, 207–11; Hrebenar and Scott, *Interest Group Politics in America,* pp. 212–27. The theory of "regulatory capture" was developed by social scientist Marver Bernstein in *Regulating Business by Independent Commission* (Princeton: Princeton University Press, 1955).

24. George S. Day and David A. Aaker, "A Guide to Consumerism," *JM* 34 (July 1970): 16.

25. James Baldwin, *Nobody Knows My Name: More Notes of a Native Son,* in *James Baldwin: Collected Essays* (New York: Library of America, 1998), pp. 173–74; David Caplovitz, *The Poor Pay More* (New York: Free Press, 1963); Paul Rand Dixon, chairman of the Federal Trade Commission, "High Credit Costs and Deception—The Misinformed Consumer's Burden," speech at Conference on Consumer Affairs, Vanderbilt University Law School, May 25, 1968, Margolius, Box 5, "Credit Abuses"; Donald E. Sexton, Jr., "Comparing the Cost of Food to Blacks and to Whites—A Survey," *JM* 35 (July 1971): 40–46; and from *NYT:* "Democrats Score A.& P. Over Prices," July 18, 1963; "Gray Reports Improvements in Slums," Aug. 11, 1964; editorial, "Gouging the Poor," Aug. 13, 1966; "Poor in West Virginia Town, Worried About the High Price of Food, Open Own Grocery Store," Dec. 16, 1966; "Price Rises Tied by Poor to Timing of Food Stamps," Aug. 23, 1967; "Overpricing of Food in Slums Alleged at House Hearing," Oct. 13, 1967; "City Charges 12 Stores in Spanish Harlem with Price Violations," Oct. 27, 1967; "Legislators, Shopping in Harlem, Confirm Consumers' Complaints," Nov. 25, 1967; "A College Opens Consumer Center, Bronx Community Institute Serves Poverty Area," Oct. 8, 1972; "City Charges A.&P. to Ignore Promises on Sales," Mar. 20, 1973; Praise for Harlem 'People's Advocate' Marks Opening of 2d Consumer Office," July 16, 1974.

26. Quoted in Feldman, ed., "Consumer Protection," p. 326. Peterson discusses her efforts on behalf of low-income consumers when she was Johnson's special assistant for consumer affairs in her memoir, *Restless,* pp. 125–26.

27. Statistics from Manuel Castells, *The City and the Grassroots: A Cross-Cultural Theory of Urban Social Movements* (Berkeley: University of California Press, 1983), p. 50.

Kerner Commission quote from "Exploitation of Disadvantaged Consumers by Retail Merchants," *Report of the National Advisory Commission on Civil Disorders* (New York: Bantam, 1968), pp. 274–77. Also see memo to Esther Peterson from Ted Rowse, Dec. 15, 1965, "Re: Consumer Aspects of Race Riots," Peterson, Series 3, Folder 1309; memo from Attorney General Arthur J. Sills to Governor Richard J. Hughes, Sept. 1, 1967, including "Food Price Comparison Study—August, 1967," Lilley, Box 3; and from the Papers of President Lyndon Baines Johnson on microfilm: "Violence in the City—An End or a Beginning? A Report by the Governor's Commission on the Los Angeles Riots, December 2, 1965," Reel # 2:0362, pp. 62–65; memo from James A. Johnson to Richard P. Nathan, Subject: Consumer Protection for the Poor, Nov. 1, 1967, Reel #16:0456-0476; official transcript of Proceedings Before the National Advisory Commission on Civil Disorders, Washington, DC, Nov. 3, 1967, Reel #5:0847-0924, pp. 3632–3708, testimony of David Caplovitz, Earl Johnson, Jr., and Clarence G. Adamy.

Also see Frederick D. Sturdivant, ed., *The Ghetto Marketplace* (New York: Free Press, 1969); Carolyn Shaw Bell, "Consumers and Markets," in *The Economics of the Ghetto* (New York: Pegasus, 1970), pp. 126–47; U.S. Commission on Civil Rights, "Mortgage Money: Who Gets It? A Case Study in Mortgage Lending Discrimination in Hartford, Connecticut," U.S. Commission on Civil Rights Clearinghouse Publication No. 46 (June 1974), submitted as evidence at Hearings before the Subcommittee on Consumer Affairs of the Committee on Banking and Currency, House of Representatives, 93rd Congress, Second Session on H.R. 14856 (a bill to prohibit discrimination on the basis of race, color, religion, national origin, age, sex, or marital status in the granting of credit); "Consumer Problems of the Poor, One of a Series for Expanded Programs in Consumer Education," University of the State of New York, State Education Department, Bureau of Secondary Curriculum Development, 1972, Angevine, Box 6, Folder E-4.

"Wage garnishment" involved the holding back of a specified sum from a worker's wages to satisfy a creditor.

28. "The Low-Income Consumer," in the President's Committee on Consumer Interests, "A Summary of Activities, 1964–1967," March 1967, Angevine, Box 3, pp. 17–20; President's Committee on Consumer Interests, "The Most for Their Money: A Report of the Panel on Consumer Education for Persons with Limited Incomes," 1965. The commission investigating the civil disorders in New Jersey during the summer of 1967, in particular the five-day rebellion in Newark, questioned intensely the state's commissioner of banking and insurance on all the problems encountered by the ghetto consumer: Testimony of Charles Howell, Oct. 10, 1967, Lilley, Box 6, pp. 58–79.

29. Minutes of New Jersey Council on Social Issues meeting, Jan. 24, 1969, Erber, Box D, Folder 11. From NPL, Newark Document File, "Newark Mayor's Policy Development Office": "Newark Consumer Program: Evaluation and Recommendations," January 1975; "Evaluation Report, Consumer Action Program," April 1975; Newark Office of Consumer Action, "Annual Report, 1974–1975," "Annual Report, 1976–1977," "Annual Report, 1977–1978," "Annual Report, 1978–1979," "Annual Report, 1979–1980." Also "The First Annual Report, Greater Newark Urban Coalition, 1969," "Q" Files, NPL, "Greater Newark Urban Coalition"; "3 Negro Groups Seek Control of Community's Radio Station," *NYT*, Sept. 8, 1971. Also see "Flash-o-gram, Rid Newark of Gyp Artists & Swindlers by Operation-Consumer Fraud," Erber, Box D, Folder 12; "A Consumer Study of Supermarket Chains by the Newark N.A.A.C.P.," December 1968, "Q" Files, NPL, "Newark NAACP"; and Gledhill Cameron, "Shopping Plight of the Poor" *Trenton Evening Times*, Jan. 9, 1968, reprinted in Kelley, *New Consumerism*, pp. 177–79.

30. There are several calculations on the numbers of consumer-oriented laws passed, as analysts include different laws in their counts. For twenty-five figure, see David Vogel,

"Business Finds a Winning Combination on Capital Hill," *San Jose Mercury,* Dec. 23, 1979, cited in Pertschuk, *Revolt Against Regulation,* p. 53. Also see Robert Kuttner, *Everything for Sale: The Virtues and Limits of Markets* (New York: Knopf, 1997), p. 232. Day and Aaker, in "A Guide to Consumerism," p. 18, estimate that at the end of 1969, 400 consumer bills were pending in congressional committees. Statistics on economic and social regulation are cited in Robert Miles and Kim S. Cameron, *Coffin Nails and Corporate Strategies* (Englewood Cliffs, NJ: Prentice-Hall, 1982), pp. 23–24.

On the interconnectedness and overall compatibility of the consumer and environmental movements, see Robert Cameron Mitchell, "Consumerism and Environmentalism in the 1980s: Competitive or Companionable Social Movements?" in Bloom and Smith, *Future of Consumerism,* pp. 23–36. For another useful discussion of the links see Cross, *All-Consuming Century,* pp. 148–52. The two movements had organizational and ideological affiliations. One obvious connection was that because environmental problems arose out of the character of energy and resource use, consumer choices were critical.

31. FDR quote from Pertschuk, *Revolt Against Regulation,* p. 126.

32. David Angevine, "Two Routes to Consumer Sovereignty," speech to Michigan Credit Union League, Apr. 20, 1963, Angevine, Box 2, D-3, p. 9.

33. On the nationwide grape boycotts orchestrated by Cesar Chavez's United Farm Workers of America, see John Gregory Dunne, *Delano: The Story of the California Grape Strike* (New York: Farrar, Straus and Giroux, 1967); Barbara L. Baer and Glenna Matthews, "The Women of the Boycott," *The Nation,* Feb. 23, 1974; Frank Barnacke, "Cesar's Ghost," *The Nation,* July 26–Aug. 2, 1993; minutes of board meeting, Consumer Federation of America, Jan. 31, 1969, resolution in support of grape boycott, pp. 5–6, Angevine; and "'La Huelga' Becomes 'La Causa,'" *NYT Magazine,* Nov. 17, 1968.

For other national boycotts in support of union drives, see on the J. P. Stevens boycott, in *NYT:* Albert Shanker, "Where We Stand: Boycott Launched for Economic Justice," Feb. 27, 1977, and "Murray H. Finley, Labor Leader for Textile Workers, Dies at 73," Aug. 3, 1995; on the Farah Manufacturing Company boycott, "Clothing Union Reports Farah Boycott," *NYT,* Dec. 18, 1972, and "A Texas Pants Maker Loses to a Boycott," *BW,* Mar. 2, 1974; and on the Coors Beer boycott, Milt Moskowitz, "A Political Fight Over Beer," *San Francisco Chronicle,* Apr. 18, 1976. On other boycotts with political agendas, see "War-tainted Products Listed to Guide Consumer Boycott," *Daily World,* June 23, 1970, which describes the nationwide consumer boycotts organized by the National Boycott for Peace; and much documentation of the use of boycotts in the civil rights struggle, for example: "Negroes Step Up Use of Boycotts to Back Drives for Better Jobs," *WSJ,* Jan. 8, 1963; "What a Negro Boycott Did to a Store," *U.S. News & World Report,* May 13, 1963; "The Negro Drive for Jobs: Picketing and Boycotts Make Up a National Phenomenon of a Sort That U.S. Businessmen Have Rarely Had to Face," *BW,* Aug. 17, 1963; "Boycott in Capital Will Be Expanded" [of merchants who oppose home rule], *NYT,* Apr. 1, 1966; "White Merchants in South Sue Civil Rights Activists in Effort to End Shopping Boycotts," *NYT,* Apr. 15, 1974; "N.A.A.C.P. Loses $1.2 Million Lawsuit for 1966 Boycott in Mississippi Town," *NYT,* Aug. 12, 1976.

34. Holsworth, *Public Interest Liberalism and the Crisis of Affluence,* on the left critique; Creighton, *Pretenders to the Throne,* pp. 64–66, on the right.

35. George L. Priest, "The Invention of Enterprise Liability: A Critical History of the Intellectual Foundations of Modern Tort Law," *Journal of Legal Studies* 14 (December 1985): 461–528; G. Edward White, *Tort Law in America: An Intellectual History* (New York: Oxford University Press, 1980); Peter Schuck, *Agent Orange on Trial: Mass Toxic Disasters in the Courts* (Cambridge, MA: Harvard University Press, 1986), p. 32.

36. "Things to Fight About Besides Food Prices," *NYT,* Aug. 25, 1973. The FTC did

establish more authority and gain more respect from consumer groups; see from *NYT*: "Court Upholds F.T.C.'s Right to Rule on Deceptive Practices," July 3, 1973; "Food Companies Scored on Prices," Dec. 11, 1973. Also Richard A. Shaffer, "More Customers Press Lawsuits Against Firms Selling Faulty Products," *WSJ*, Nov. 3, 1972, and Richard D. Silverstein, "The Consumer Class Action Debate," both in Kelley, *New Consumerism*, pp. 383–85, 405–24. On the limitations of the CPSC, see E. Marla Felcher, "The U.S. Product Safety Commission: The Paper Tiger of American Product Safety," http://www.understandinggovt.org/Felcher/html.

37. Senator Guy M. Gillette of Iowa, with twenty-three co-sponsors, unsuccessfully sought to establish a select committee on consumer interests as early as 1952 to investigate the consumer implications of all proposed legislation and government policies; he continued to agitate for a similar standing committee in the House, and when those efforts failed, for subcommittees on consumer affairs in all the major committees. That last proposal, as well as Senator Maurine Neuberger's 1962 bill to create a Senate committee on consumer interests, languished until the mid-1960s; Campbell, *Bringing the Consumer Point of View into Government*, pp. 25–26, and Caroline F. Ware, "The Consumer Voice: Lobbying in the Consumer Interest," in Erma Angevine, ed., *Consumer Activists: They Made a Difference, A History of Consumer Action Related by Leaders in the Consumer Movement* (Mount Vernon, NY: National Consumers Committee for Research and Education, Consumers Union Foundation, n.d. but early 1980s), p. 326; Lucia Mouat, "Consumers Want a Loud, Permanent Voice," *CSM*, Mar. 5, 1970; press release of Sidney Margolius, "Lady Senator Gives Candid Comments on Saving Money, Protecting Consumers," Feb. 19, 1962, *The Machinist*, Margolius, Box 4, p. 4. I am grateful to Mike Pertschuk for sharing Magnuson's quote with me; interview, Nov. 13, 2001. Over the years, the title of the proposed agency varied.

38. On efforts to lobby for a permanent consumer protection agency or department, see Hrebenar and Scott, *Interest Group Politics in America*, pp. 222–23; Peterson, *Restless*, pp. 159–63; "Newsletter of National Coalition for the Consumer Protection Agency," July 8, 1977, and a National Coalition reprint from the *Washington Post*, February 1978, "House Votes Down Measure to Create Consumer Agency," Angevine, Box 2, Folder "National Coalition for the CPA"; "Consumer Aid Bill Losing Corporate Support," *Washington Post*, Aug. 2, 1977; "11th Hour Effort Under Way to Pass Consumer Unit Bill," *Washington Star*, Oct. 15, 1977; "Eight-Year Effort for Consumer Bill Ends in Defeat," *Washington Star*, Feb. 9, 1978; and in *NYT*: "Congress Studies 2 Consumer Bills," Apr. 28, 1971; "Consumer Agency Balked in Senate as Closure Fails," Oct. 6, 1972; "Miss Furness Warns Business of Possible Consumer Revolt," Oct. 9, 1974; "Senate Debates Consumer Bill; Agency Supporters Optimistic," May 8, 1975.

When the independent agency was defeated in 1978, Carter signed Executive Order 12160 establishing consumer programs within individual executive branch departments and agencies and a Consumer Affairs Council to coordinate these consumer programs; see "Consumer Offices in the Agencies—The Best the Activists Can Expect?" *National Journal*, Sept. 5, 1980; Erma Angevine and Dr. Caroline F. Ware, "Effective Consumer Participation" (Washington, DC: National Consumers' League, 1981), pp. 19–24, Angevine, Box 6, Folder E-4; and National Consumers' League, "Effective Consumer Participation: A Look at the Current Consumer Activist Movement: 1981," Angevine, Box 5, D-3, p. 73*n*.8.

39. Rosenthal quote from "Enemies Endanger Consumer Agency," *Washington Star*, June 19, 1977. For an overview of consumer representation in the White House, see Esther Peterson, "Consumer Representation in the White House," in Angevine, ed., *Consumer Activists*, pp. 198–212.

40. Ralph Nader, "The Great American Gyp," originally published in the *New York Review of Books,* Nov. 21, 1968, reprinted in Nader, *The Ralph Nader Reader,* p. 235; also see Peterson, *Restless,* p. 131.

41. E. B. Weiss, "Does Consumerism Show Signs of Giving Up the Ghost? Not Quite," *AA,* Apr. 30, 1973, p. 52.

42. "Consumerism Here to Stay, Study Shows," *National Consumers' League Bulletin* 103 (May–June 1977): 1, Angevine, Box 5, A-8; *Consumerism at The Crossroads: A National Opinion Research Survey of Public, Activist, Business and Regulatory Attitudes Toward the Consumer Movement,* conducted for Sentry Insurance by Marketing Sciences Institute and Louis Harris and Associates, 1977, Angevine, Box 6, E-4.

43. "Scouts: Survival in Supermarket," *NYT,* Nov. 24, 1975. The association of consumerism with motherhood was made by a New York State government official, who also commented that consumerism was "a handy bouquet for courting voters": "Is a So-Called 'Seal of Approval' What Consumers Think It Is?" *NYT,* Mar. 22, 1969.

44. Mayer, *Consumer Movement,* pp. 43–52; Nadel, *Politics of Consumer Protection,* pp. 158–59; Creighton, *Pretenders to the Throne,* p. 70; from Angevine: "The President's Committee on Consumer Interests: A Summary of Activities, 1964–1967," March 1967, Box 3, pp. 31–36; "Memo to Distribution from Roy Kiesling, Jr., Subject: The American Consumer Movement," Apr. 25, 1972, Box 2, D-3; "What Is CFA?" Jan. 27, 1971, Box 1, A-5; "What Is Consumer Federation of America—a fact sheet," Jan. 7, 1972, Box 1, A-1; National Consumers' League, "Effective Consumer Participation, A Look at the Current Activist Movement: 1981," Box 5, D-3.

The Consumer Federation grew out of an extremely successful three-day "Consumer Assembly" conference in Washington, DC, in April 1966, organized by thirty-three national, not-for-profit organizations representing nearly fifty million people.

45. NCL's Executive Director to NCL's Executive Committee, "Recommendations for 1977 NCL Program," Jan. 31, 1977, Angevine, Box 5, A-6; also see other items in Angevine, Box 5, concerning her tenure as president of the NCL. The league's gradual reorientation from labor standards to consumer issues can be tracked in policy statements over the 1960s and 1970s; see, for example, in Box 5, "Make Your Voice Heard," 1963 (B-2); "Policy Statement of the National Consumers' League," 1969 (A-2); and "Statement of Priorities," 1980 (A-2), which states plainly: "The National Consumers' League is a national consumer advocacy organization primarily dedicated to achieving effective representation of the consumer interest in both private and public decision-making" (p. 1). On the occasion of its 75th anniversary in 1975, the Consumers' League of New Jersey said it was "more convinced than ever of the need for grass-roots activity to protect consumer interests": "Byrne Action on Unit Pricing Awaited," *NYT,* Mar. 31, 1975. Interestingly, progressive New Deal economist Robert Nathan, one of the framers of the Consumers' Republic in the 1940s, resurfaced as the new chairman of the board of the NCL in 1977, just as this reorientation was taking place. For a review of his career, see "Robert R. Nathan, 92, Dies; Set Factory Goals in War," *NYT,* Sept. 10, 2001.

46. From Margolius, Box 4, "Consumer Counsel" file: President's Committee on Consumer Interests, "Forming Consumer Organizations," January 1969, pp. 64–65; Department of Health, Education and Welfare, Office of the Secretary, Office of Consumer Affairs, State and Local Programs Division, "Directory Federal, State, County and City Government Consumer Offices," Jan. 1, 1976, pp. 17–20; *Directory of Consumer Organizations, A Selected Listing of Nongovernmental Organizations at Local, State and National Levels* (Washington, DC: Department of Health, Education and Welfare, Office of Consumer Affairs, 1976), p. 16; "In New Jersey, a Watchdog for Consumers Is Eliminated," *NYT,* Nov. 9, 1994; League of Women Voters of New Jersey Education Fund, Karen A.

West, ed., *New Jersey: Spotlight on Government,* 5th ed. (New Brunswick, NJ: Rutgers University Press, 1985), pp. 255–63; "State May Alter Policy on Complaints," *NYT,* Nov. 25, 1974; "State Consumer Parley Stirs Mixed Reactions," *NYT,* May 21, 1973. Also see a regular column in the New Jersey Living section of *NYT,* "Jersey Consumer Notes," 1973–75, passim. The New Jersey Supreme Court's landmark tort decision was *Hennigsen* v. *Bloomfield Motors* (1960); John B. Wefing, "The New Jersey Supreme Court 1948–1998: Fifty Years of Independence and Activism," *Rutgers Law Journal* 29 (Summer 1998): 704.

On state and local organizations in general, see Colston E. Warne, "Consumer Protective Movements on the State and Local Levels—1964," revised May 1964, and "Recent Developments in the Consumer Movement, Remarks of Colston E. Warne," Aug. 8, 1968, Angevine, Box 2, D-3.

New York City in particular was ablaze with consumer activity in the late 1960s and 1970s, boasting a Consumer Affairs Department (under successive Commissioners Bess Myerson, Betty Furness, and Elinor Guggenheimer); a Consumers Protection Corps under the Commissioner of Markets; neighborhood consumer complaint offices and organizations, such as the Harlem Consumer Education Council; much consumer legislation and regulation; and frequent conferences and other initiatives. See as a sampling of articles from *NYT:* "Consumers Corps Will Check Stores," Feb. 7, 1968; "Stern Is Selected as Consumer Aide," June 30, 1969; "Housewives Here Receive Hints on Problems Facing Consumers," July 13, 1969; "Consumer Complaint Office Dedicated in Forest Hills," Mar. 20, 1971; "Caveat Vendor—or, a Tale of 3 Cities," Jan. 7, 1973; "Betty Furness Appointed to Bess Myerson's Post," Mar. 31, 1973; "Consumer Agency to Shift Emphasis," Mar. 24, 1974; "City Unit Focuses on Overcharging," May 17, 1974; "Farmer and Consumer: Getting Them Together," Apr. 2, 1975.

47. Cigler and Loomis, *Interest Group Politics,* p. 28; Robert Lampman, "The New Frontier and the Consumer Interest," prepared for delivery at Council on Consumer Information, Mar. 22, 1963, Washington, DC, Margolius, Box 4, folder "Consumer Counsel—Federal," p. 9.

48. Creighton, *Pretenders to the Throne,* p. 55; Marylin Bender, "Capitalism Lives—Even in Naderland," *NYT,* Jan. 7, 1973, in Kelley, *New Consumerism,* p. 68.

49. Robert D. Putnam laments the loss of what he considers valuable "social capital" with this decline: *Bowling Alone: The Collapse and Revival of American Community* (New York: Simon & Schuster, 2000), pp. 48–64. Other scholars of civic engagement, such as Theda Skocpol, note the same shift but assess its impact differently: Skocpol and Morris P. Fiorina, eds., *Civic Engagement in American Democracy* (Washington, DC: Brookings Institution; New York: Russell Sage Foundation, 1999), particularly Jeffrey M. Berry, "The Rise of Citizen Groups," pp. 367–93.

50. Sandra L. Willett, "Elements of an Effective Corporate Consumer Affairs Program: An Overview of Selected Consumer Programs in Large Service-Oriented Companies," prepared for Aetna Life and Casualty by the National Consumers' League, July 30, 1982, Angevine, Box 5, D-4, p. 1; Moss quoted in "Part I: Crusade for the '70s: The Consumer Revolution: An Angry Public Strikes Back," *The Express,* Jan. 9, 1970. The more mainstream management guru Peter Drucker, criticizing the plethora of low-quality, over-priced, and hazardous goods on the market, recognized the same grassroots revolt: "We have been a very patient people by and large. Now people are fed up, and I do not blame them"; quoted in "The U.S.'s Toughest Customer," *Time,* Dec. 12, 1969, p. 92.

51. Peterson interview with *NYT* reporter in "Housewives' Friend: Esther Eggertsen Peterson," *NYT,* Nov. 5, 1966; also see "Boycotts Backed by Johnson Aide," *NYT,* Oct. 28, 1966. Photograph of Peterson hugging Denver boycotter in "FOOD: Behind the Boycotts, Why Prices Are High," *Time,* Nov. 4, 1966. The documentation for the so-called

housewives' protests of 1966–67 is extensive in the contemporary press; among the most helpful articles are "Margolius Tells It as It Is: How Business Backlash Toppled Esther Peterson," *Co-op Highlights,* April 1967, pp. 1–2; Consumer Federation of America, *Consumer Action* 1 (July 1, 1967): 4–5; Rita Lang Kleinfelder, *When We Were Young: A Baby-Boomer Yearbook* (New York: Prentice-Hall, 1993), p. 420; and from *NYT:* "Food Price Rises Stir Resentment, Cost-Conscious Consumers Rebelling with Boycotts and Selective Selling" and "Market Gives In, Will Cut Prices," Oct. 16, 1966; "Denver Housewives Boycott Markets," Oct. 18, 1966; "Housewives' Revolt Against Rising Food Prices Spreads Across the Nation," Oct. 23, 1966; "Food-Price Rises Laid to Retailers and Processors," Oct. 26, 1966; "Food Chain Executives Pledge to Join Housewives in Fight on High Prices," Oct. 27, 1966; "U.S. Studies Price Impact of Food Store Promotions," Oct. 29, 1966; "Supermarket Price Protest Spreads to 21 States," Oct. 30, 1966; "G.O.P. Fears Food Boycott Weakens Its Inflation Issue," Nov. 2, 1966; "The Housewife vs. the Supermarket," Nov. 6, 1966; "The Merchant's View, Retailers Wonder If Food-Price Revolt Is Spreading," Nov. 20, 1966; "Housewives Look Back on Boycotts," Mar. 5, 1967. And from *WSJ:* "Several Food Store Chains Slash Prices in Midwest to Woo Complaining Shopper," Oct. 12, 1966; "Bring Home No Bacon: Housewives' Boycotts of Food Chains Grow," Oct. 20, 1966; "Housewives' Rebellion Spreads; More Chains Reduce Food Prices," Oct. 26, 1966; "Housewives' Price Protests Proliferate, Evoking Few Cuts but Much Commotion," Oct. 31, 1966; "Pleasing the Ladies: Supermarkets Attempt to Placate Housewives as Higher Prices Loom," June 26, 1967.

That the Johnson White House's interest in consumers was an effort to appeal politically to suburban white women comes through very clearly in Peterson, Series III—U.S. Government, 1961–69, and in Margolius, Box 4, folder "Consumer Counsel—Federal."

52. From the *NYT:* "Boycott of Meat Begins with Leaders Optimistic," Apr. 2, 1973; "Consumers Scoff at Ceiling and Step Up Boycott Plans," Mar. 31, 1973; "Consumers, in Protest, Mailing Tapes from Supermarket Registers to Nixon," Apr. 30, 1973.

53. On the 1973 boycott, see "Meat Boycotting Begins to Make Headlines—Again," *National Observer,* Feb. 27, 1973; "Consumer Activists Urge Meat Boycott for April 1–7," *NYT,* Mar. 17, 1973; "Consumer Mobilizing for a War on Food Prices," *NYT,* Mar. 18, 1973; "Consumer Resistance Starting to Affect Price of Food Here," *NYT,* Mar. 24, 1973; "If Consumer Leagues Spring Up, Boycotts' Results Are Hard to Predict" and "The Roast Beef Rebellion," *NYT,* Mar. 25, 1973; "Consumers Rally for Meat Boycotts," *NYT,* Mar. 30, 1973; "The Revolt of the Masses," *NYT,* Apr. 1, 1973; "Meat Sales Drop 80% in Places as the Boycott Begins" and "Valid Boycott," *NYT,* Apr. 3, 1973; "Meat Group to Shoppers: 'Please, Buy Something,'" *NYT,* Apr. 5, 1973; "Meat Retailers Say Boycott Slashed Sales but Prices Remain Tied to Wholesale Costs," *WSJ,* Apr. 9, 1973; "Shoppers Cut Meat Purchases to Protest Static Prices Here," *NYT,* Apr. 30, 1973; "Remember Last Year's Irate Boycotters? They're Still Irate," *National Observer,* Feb. 23, 1974.

On the creation of the National Consumers Congress, see "Boycott Leaders Plan a Protest; Urge 2 Meatless Days a Week," *NYT,* Apr. 12, 1973, and "Consumer: Going to the Grassroots," *Washington Star-News,* Sept. 9, 1973; "Coke and Pepsi Boycott Called by Consumer Unit," *NYT,* June 11, 1973; Feldman, "Consumer Protection," p. 325.

54. I am grateful to Debra Michals for sharing material on the NOW campaign for the Equal Credit Opportunity Act that she gathered in two collections at the Schlesinger Library, both of which contain extensive letters from ordinary women: the Papers of Cynthia Harrison, chair of NOW's Women's Credit Task Force, and the Papers of NOW. In addition, see Commercial Credit Corporation, "A Survey of Women and Credit: How They Use It and What They Think," August–September 1978, Margolius, Box 5, folder

"Credit"; "U.S. Seeks to End Mortgage Barriers Facing Women," *NYT,* Mar. 10, 1979; Lisa Cronin Wohl, "Equal Credit Opportunity Act: Some Good News, Some Not So Good," *Ms.,* March 1977, pp. 95–98.

55. "The U.S.'s Toughest Customer," *Time,* Dec. 12, 1969, pp. 94, 96; "Consumers' Guardian: Virginia Harrington Wright Knauer," *NYT,* Apr. 10, 1969; "Consumer Drive at a Critical Stage," *NYT,* Oct. 5, 1970.

56. "Big motherism" from a speech by the Chamber of Commerce's Carl Madden, quoted in "Consumerism: Uphill Struggle," *NYT,* Jan. 6, 1974; "Price 'Girlcott' Is Starting Here," *NYT,* Oct. 28, 1966. The one-time FBI agent turned private detective who was hired by GM to investigate Nader instructed his agents to "check Nader's life and current activities, to determine what makes him tick . . . his marital status, his friends, his women, boys, etc." In reprinting this excerpt, *Time* noted, "They questioned why a 32-year-old man with adequate means should still be unmarried." Although no trace of homosexuality ever surfaced, suspicion long dogged Nader: "Investigations," *Time,* Apr. 1, 1966; also see "The U.S.'s Toughest Customer," *Time,* Dec. 12, 1969. Gloria Steinem and Robin Morgan both recalled how the meat boycott of 1973 was tarred and feathered as "feminist": "At Home with Gloria Steinem: Decades as Icon; Now, Freedom," *NYT,* Feb. 9, 1995; Robin Morgan, "Rights of Passage," *Ms.,* November 1975, reprinted in William H. Chafe and Harvard Sitkoff, eds., *A History of Our Time: Readings on Postwar America,* 3rd ed. (New York: Oxford University Press, 1991), p. 247.

57. There is a great deal of documentation of blacks' using consumer pressure against discriminating employers during the 1960s. For example, see Howell Raines, *My Soul Is Rested: The Story of the Civil Rights Movement in the Deep South* (New York: Penguin, 1983), p. 229; "Yule Boycott Is Threatened in Negroes' Drive for Jobs," *NN,* Nov. 1, 1963; and in *NYT:* "28 White Castles Will Be Picketed," July 21, 1963; "Chicago Negroes Invade a Market," July 26, 1968; "Pickets Demand Negro Manager at Harlem A. & P.," Aug. 21, 1968.

58. *The Autobiography of Malcolm X,* with the assistance of Alex Haley (New York: Grove, 1965), p. 313.

59. From *NYT:* "Negro Concern Sets Supermarket Chain," Feb. 8, 1967; "Interracial Council Starts Fund to Aid Negro Businesses Here" and "Co-op Store for Harlem," Dec. 21, 1967; "Group Bids Blacks Avoid the A. & P.," Dec. 10, 1970; "22 Sit in at A. & P.'s Offices to Seek Help for Blacks," Jan. 28, 1971; "A Black Coalition Planned at A. & P.," Feb. 18, 1971; "69 Are Arrested in A. & P. Protests," Apr. 10, 1971. Later in the 1970s, Jackson's Operation PUSH (People United to Save Humanity) similarly addressed consumer issues; *Advertising Age* ran an ad for a PUSH-sponsored "Black Consumer Behavioral Symposium," May 6, 1974.

60. "It Takes Only 10 to Start: Housewives United: A Merchant's Nightmare," *Detroit News,* Jan. 18, 1970; "Voluntary Action Gets Results," *CSM,* Feb. 24, 1970; "Consumer Rift Widens," *Detroit News,* Jan. 29, 1971; and *Consumers' Voice,* CEPA's newspaper, Angevine, Box 1, B-2; "22 Sit In at A. & P.'s Offices to Seek Help for Blacks," *NYT,* Jan. 28, 1971. The Harlem Consumer Education Council's boycott is discussed in "Price 'Girlcott' Is Starting Here," *NYT,* Oct. 28, 1966; for more on the council, see materials from its Sixth Annual Conference in 1968 in the SEDFRE, Box 51, Folder 19.

61. Peter Goldman, *The Death and Life of Malcolm X,* 2nd ed. (Urbana: University of Illinois Press, 1979), p. 51.

62. Television study cited in *Report of the National Advisory Commission,* p. 274; statement of Berkeley Burrell, president, National Business League, before the National Advisory Commission on Civil Disorders, Washington, DC, Oct. 23, 1967, Official Transcript of Proceedings, Johnson, Reel #5:0002-0007, p. 2832; looter quoted in Jim F. Heath, *Decade of Disillusionment: The Kennedy-Johnson Years* (Bloomington: Indiana University

Press, 1975), pp. 250–51, cited in Robert Weisbrot, *Freedom Bound: A History of America's Civil Rights Movement* (New York: Penguin, 1991), p. 160; Detroit participant quoted in *Report of the National Advisory Commission,* p. 133.

Martin Luther King, Jr., had recognized how television fed consumer desires as early as his historic "Letter from a Birmingham Jail," written in spring 1963 in defense of the massive demonstrations to desegregate Birmingham. King listed among what he called the most "stinging darts of segregation" "when you suddenly find your tongue twisted and your speech stammering as you seek to explain to your six-year-old daughter why she can't go to the public amusement park that has just been advertised on television, and see tears welling up in her eyes when she is told that Funtown is closed to colored children"; reprinted in Chafe and Sitkoff, eds., *History of Our Time,* p. 188.

There have been extensive debates among social scientists and historians about the identities of the ghetto rebels and their motives. A recently published, sound review of that literature and the available evidence by Jack M. Bloom concludes that the rioters were fairly representative of the black urban population and not a violent, hard-core ghetto underclass; "Ghetto Revolts, Black Power, and the Limits of the Civil Rights Coalition," in Raymond D'Angelo, *The American Civil Rights Movement: Readings and Interpretations* (New York: McGraw-Hill/Dushkin, 2001), pp. 383–408. Also see Kenneth L. Kusmer, ed., *The Ghetto Crisis of the 1960s: Causes and Consequences,* vol. 7 of *Black Communities and Urban Development in America, 1720–1990* (New York: Garland, 1991).

63. My treatment of the Newark rebellion of 1967 is based on *Report of the National Advisory Commission,* pp. 56–69; Governor's Select Commission on Civil Disorder, State of New Jersey, *Report for Action* (Trenton: State of New Jersey, 1968), known as the Lilley Commission after its chair, Robert D. Lilley; in Lilley: Timeline of Newark Events from January–August 1967, Box 2; Committee on Education and Labor, U.S. House of Representatives, "Staff Report of Investigation, Involvement of Anti-Poverty Personnel in Newark, New Jersey, Racial Disturbances, 1967," Sept. 7, 1967, Box 3; "Special Report, July 1967 Riot, Completed 10-24-1967," Box 3, including arrest records; "Memorandum for the File, From: Sanford M. Jaffe and Robert B. Goldmann, Subject: Meeting with Mr. Russell Sackett, Reporter on *Life* Magazine," Dec. 15, 1967, Box 3; from *NYT:* "Newark Violence Breaks Out Again," July 14, 1967; "Hughes Observes Looting of Stores," July 15, 1967; "In Riots' Shadow, a City Stumbles On," July 14, 1997. Also, from the *NN:* "Riots, Mobs Loot, Start Fires," July 14, 1967; "Curfew Remains" and "Patrol Is Like WWII's, Guardsmen, Troopers with Guns at Ready," July 16, 1967; "Tally on Rioting," July 22, 1967; "Guard Troopers Called to Newark," *NSL,* July 14, 1967; "Residents Claim State Police Hit Colored Shops" and "Orgy of Destruction Ravaged Newark; Sniper Fire Deadly," *NJAA,* July 22, 1967; "In a Grim City, a Secret Meeting with the Snipers," *Life,* July 28, 1967, pp. 27–28; Clement Alexander Price, ed., *Freedom Not Far Distant: A Documentary History of Afro-Americans in New Jersey* (Newark: New Jersey Historical Society, 1980), pp. 255–57, 288–90; Daniel Earl Georges, "Arson: The Ecology of Urban Unrest in an American City—Newark, New Jersey, a Case Study in Collective Violence" (Ph.D. diss., Syracuse University, 1974), pp. 112–16; Thomas A. Johnson, "Newark's Summer '67," *The Crisis* 74 (August–September 1967); 371–79; Joseph M. Conforti, "Newark: Ghetto or City?" *Society* 9 (May 1972): 20–32.

64. Quoted in "Home-Grown Ills Cited by Negroes," *NYT,* July 16, 1967; "Shoppers and Carpenters Crowd Newark's Springfield Avenue, but the Angry Discontent Remains," *NYT,* July 27, 1967.

65. "Black People!" in "Three Poems by LeRoi Jones," *Evergreen* 11 (December 1967); 49. See discussion of Baraka's involvement in the Newark rebellion in Theodore R. Hudson, *From LeRoi Jones to Amiri Baraka: The Literary Works* (Durham, NC: Duke Univer-

sity Press, 1973), pp. 26–31; Imamu Amiri Baraka, *The Autobiography of LeRoi Jones/Amiri Baraka* (New York: Freundlich, 1984), pp. 258–61, 269–72; Charlie Reilly, "An Interview with Amiri Baraka," in Reilly, ed., *Conversations with Amiri Baraka* (Jackson: University of Mississippi Press, 1994), pp. 252–54.

66. LeRoi Jones's testimony to the Lilley Commission, Nov. 27, 1967, Lilley, Box 7, pp. 83–84; *Autobiography of LeRoi Jones,* p. 260. For Philip Roth, the Jewish native Newark writer also discussed in Chapter 5, the 1967 rebellion represented final taps for the Jewish presence in Newark. In Roth's novel *American Pastoral,* his Jewish protagonist, Swede Levov, remembers sitting alone in his family's glove factory, surrounded by "looting crowds crazed in the street, kids carrying off radios and lamps and television sets, men toting armfuls of clothing, women pushing baby carriages heavily loaded with cartons of liquor and cases of beer, people pushing pieces of new furniture right down the center of the street, stealing sofas, cribs, kitchen tables, stealing washers and dryers and ovens— stealing not in the shadows but out in the open. Their strength is tremendous, their team-work is flawless. The shattering of the glass windows is thrilling. The not paying for things is intoxicating. The American appetite for ownership is dazzling to behold." Although Swede refuses to abandon his factory, the business "entrusted to him by his father," he rec-ognizes how unusual he is: "And then they left, everyone, fled the smoldering rubble— manufacturers, retailers, the banks, the shop owners, the corporations, the department stores; in the South Ward, on the residential blocks, there are two moving vans per day on every street throughout the next year, homeowners fleeing, deserting the modest houses they treasure for whatever they can get"; Roth, *American Pastoral* (New York: Vintage, 1997), pp. 268–70.

67. Quote in St. Clair Drake and Horace A. Cayton, *Black Metropolis: A Study of Negro Life in a Northern City,* rev. ed. (Chicago: University of Chicago Press, 1993), "Postscript 1969," p. 832; Audrey Olsen Faulkner et al., *When I Was Comin' Up: An Oral History of Aged Blacks* (Hamden, CT: Archon, 1982), pp. 18, 58; Fred J. Cook, "Mayor Kenneth Gib-son says—'Wherever the Central Cities Are Going, Newark Is Going to Get There First,'" *NYT Magazine,* July 25, 1971; Thomas R. Brooks, "Newark," *Atlantic,* August 1969, pp. 2–10; "Insurance Adjusters Assess Damage from Riots," *NYT,* July 18, 1967; "Unrest in Newark Doomed Motel Plan," *NN,* Apr. 13, 1969; "Urban Areas Crave Return of Big Mar-kets," *NSL,* July 17, 1984; "Where the Markets Are Never Super," *NYT,* June 6, 1992; "A Market Scores a Success in Newark," *NYT,* Apr. 30, 1995. Harlem, with its 500,000 resi-dents, had to wait until 1999 to get its first major supermarket in fifty years, a Pathmark store on 125th Street; "Harlem on the Cusp," *NYT,* Aug. 26, 2001.

The recent building of a new performing arts center in downtown Newark has spurred some economic revitalization, but debate still rages over the extent to which recovery has reached into the city's neighborhoods. The tense battle for mayor between incumbent Sharpe James and challenger Cory Booker in May 2002 revolved around this dispute. See "Newark's Competing Visions of Itself: Reborn or Struggling? Each View Is Reflected by a Mayoral Candidate," *NYT,* May 10, 2002, and Argelio R. Dumenigo, "Renewing Newark," *Princeton Alumni Weekly,* Apr. 10, 2002.

68. Although I had made the connection between the politics of consumption and the NWRO before I learned of her dissertation-in-progress, I am grateful to the pathbreak-ing work of Felicia Ann Kornbluh in developing this analysis in greater depth; see her "The Goals of the National Welfare Rights Movement: Why We Need Them Thirty Years Later," *Feminist Studies* 24 (Spring 1998): 65–78; "To Fulfill Their 'Rightly Needs': Con-sumerism and the National Welfare Rights Movement," *Radical History Review* 69 (Fall 1997): 76–113; and her dissertation, "A Right to Welfare? Poor Women, Professionals, and Poverty Programs, 1935–1975" (Ph.D. diss., Princeton University, 2000). Other useful

sources include the very rich materials documenting the Welfare Rights Project in Newark, 1967–68, SEDFRE, Box 12, Folder 3; also on welfare rights organizing in Newark, memo to Sanford Jaffe (executive director, Governor's Commission on Civil Disorder), from Julia Miller, Oct. 23, 1967, Lilley, Box 3; and Guida West, *The National Welfare Rights Movement: The Social Protest of Poor Women* (New York: Praeger, 1981), p. 218. On welfare rights organizing more generally, see Jackie Pope, "Women in the Welfare Rights Struggle: The Brooklyn Welfare Action Council," in West and Rhoda Lois Blumberg, eds., *Women and Social Protest* (New York: Oxford University Press, 1990), pp. 57–74; Milwaukee County Welfare Rights Organization, *Welfare Mothers Speak Out: We Ain't Gonna Shuffle Anymore* (New York: Norton, 1972); Thomas Byrne Edsall with Mary D. Edsall, *Chain Reaction: The Impact of Race, Rights, and Taxes on American Politics* (New York: Norton, 1992), pp. 67–69.

69. George Wiley, "Testimony for the National Welfare Rights Organization Before the Fiscal Policies Sub-Committee of the Joint Economic Committee of the U.S. Congress," June 12, 1968, Box 22, Folder 4, Papers of George Wiley, WHS, quoted in Kornbluh, "Goals of the National Welfare Rights Movement," p. 68.

70. James T. Patterson, *America's Struggle Against Poverty, 1900–1994* (Cambridge, MA: Harvard University Press, 1994), pp. 179, 197; Steve M. Teles, *Whose Welfare? AFDC and Elite Politics* (Lawrence: University Press of Kansas, 1996), p. 20; both cited in Schudson, *The Good Citizen,* p. 263; City of New York, Department of Welfare, Reports June, July, August 1963–68, cited in Pope, "Women in the Welfare Rights Struggle."

71. Letter from Delores Hassell to Carl Rachlin, Apr. 26, 1967, in case of Delores Hassell, Box 47, Folder 149, SEDFRE, quoted in Kornbluh, "A Right to Welfare?" p. 340.

72. The nationwide credit campaigns of NWRO are well discussed in Kornbluh's "To Fulfill Their 'Rightly Needs.' "

73. Juliet Greenlaw, "Statement of National Welfare Rights Organization to the Democratic Platform Hearing," Aug. 16, 1968, Box 2101, file "Demo Platform Aug. 19, 1968," NWRO Papers, Moorland-Spingarn Research Center, Howard University, quoted in Kornbluh, "Goals of the National Welfare Rights Movement," p. 72; "Johnnie Tillmon Blackston, Welfare Reformer, Dies at 69," *NYT,* Nov. 27, 1995. Debate over how much consumer choice to give the poor—whether to offer cash relief or to control spending more closely—has a long history in welfare circles; see Viviana A. Zelizer, *The Social Meaning of Money* (New York: Basic Books, 1994), pp. 143–216.

74. Mrs. Cassie B. Downer, "Guaranteed Adequate Income Now," in Milwaukee County Welfare Rights Organization, *Welfare Mothers Speak Out,* p. 135.

75. On Nader's support among young people, and the growth of student-funded PIRGs, see Nadel, *Politics of Consumer Protection,* pp. 184–85; "The U.S.'s Toughest Customer"; Consumer Federation of America, *Consumer Newsletter,* Nov. 25, 1970, p. 2, on the Villanova meeting; Ignatius, "Stages of Nader," *NYT Sunday Magazine,* Jan. 18, 1976, p. 52; "Fighting for a Group to Fight for Consumers," *Newsday,* n.d., Margolius, Box 4, Folder "Consumer Counsel"; and from *NYT:* "350,000 Students in Research Groups Reported by Nader," Nov. 24, 1972; "Public Interest Research Groups on 138 Campuses Set to Fight Local Problems," Sept. 5, 1973; "College Based Consumer Advocates Keep Busy," Aug. 18, 1974. On New Jersey PIRG activity, see "Middlesex Stores' Prices and Ad Policies Studied," *NYT,* July 2, 1973, and "College-Based Consumer Advocates Keep Busy," *NYT,* Aug. 18, 1974; and from the "Q" Files, NPL: "NJPIRG, The First Five Years, 1972–1977," New Jersey Public Interest Research Group, *Citizen Action '76: One Year in Review* (1976); *New Jersey Public Interest Research Group Annual Report, 1977–1978.* Also "Part I: Crusade for the '70s, The Consumer Revolution: An Angry Public Strikes Back," *The Express,* Jan. 9, 1970; "Consumerism Is His Career: Bruce Charles Ratner," *NYT,* Jan. 23, 1978.

76. *Kiplinger Washington Letter* quoted in Consumer Federation of America, *Consumer Action* 1 (October 1967): 11; "New Look," *National Business Woman*, February 1967; "Advertising: The Senator Asks Some Whys," *NYT*, Feb. 4, 1970. Also see from *NYT*: "Retail Meeting Warned on Consumer," Jan. 11, 1972; "Consumers Spur Industry Response," Jan. 7, 1973; and "Consumer Activists Get Backing," May 18, 1974.

77. "A Proclamation for National Consumer Education Week [of Oct. 5, 1980] by President Jimmy Carter," Angevine, Box 7, Scrapbook; National Consumers' League, "Effective Consumer Participation: A Look at the Current Consumer Activist Movement: 1981," Angevine, Box 5, D-3; *Report of the National Advisory Commission*, p. 133; letter from Eugene May, president, Pike County Citizens Association, to Manager, Sears, Roebuck & Company, June 15, 1969, NWRO Papers, Howard, Box 2038, File "Local WRO Sears Material," quoted in Kornbluh, "To Fulfill Their 'Rightly Needs,' " p. 90.

78. The citizen consumer ideal, that the consumer was "the symbol of the common interest," persisted throughout third-wave consumerism, even as the reality of consumer politics may have changed. This quote was from a luncheon address to the California Retailers Association and the Central City Association in Los Angeles by a progressive businessman, Charles Y. Lazarus, president of the American Retail Federation and vice president of Federated Department Stores: "Let the Consumer Decide," Mar. 11, 1969, Angevine, Box 1, B-2, pp. 6–7.

79. On the economic crisis of this era, see Cross, *All-Consuming Century*, p. 173; Michael A. Bernstein, "Understanding American Economic Decline: The Contours of the Late-Twentieth-Century Experience," in Bernstein and David E. Adler, eds., *Understanding American Economic Decline* (New York: Cambridge University Press, 1994), for an excellent overall analysis, including GNP figures on p. 17, and in the same volume, Jane Knodell, "Financial Institutions and Contemporary Economic Performance," pp. 132–37, on inflation rates; and from *NYT*: "Excerpts from Reagan TV Address on the Economy," Oct. 25, 1980; "Three Decades of Dwindling Hopes for Prosperity," May 9, 1993; "Feeling Poor in a Rich Economy," Jan. 10, 1995; "That Was Then and This Is the 90's," June 18, 1997.

80. Memorandum from Richard A. Lynch, former executive vice president, New Jersey State AFL-CIO, n.d., cited in Barry Bluestone and Bennett Harrison, *The Deindustrialization of America: Plant Closings, Community Abandonment, and the Dismantling of Basic Industry* (New York: Basic Books, 1982), p. 68; also see book on deindustrialization more generally.

81. Unemployment figures in Bernstein, "Understanding American Economic Decline," p. 17. Real weekly earnings of nonagricultural private sector employees are cited in Robert A. Blecker, "The New Economic Stagnation and the Contradictions of Economic Policy Making," in Bernstein and Adler, eds., *Understanding American Economic Decline*, pp. 286–87.

82. Two clippings in Margolius, Box 3: "Carter Tells Consumers He Hopes to Rival Nader," Aug. 10, 1976, and "Esther Peterson Sees Consumer 'Input' at the White House If Carter Triumphs," Oct. 18, 1976; "Malaise Speech," 1978, in Senator Robert Torricelli and Andrew Carroll, *In Our Own Words: Extraordinary Speeches of the American Century* (New York: Kodansha International, 1999), pp. 336–37. For an astute analysis of Carter's economic policies, see Bruce J. Schulman, "Slouching Toward the Supply Side: Jimmy Carter and the New American Political Economy," in Gary M. Fink and Hugh Davis Graham, eds., *The Carter Presidency: Policy Choices in the Post–New Deal Era* (Lawrence: University Press of Kansas, 1998), pp. 51–71.

83. Pertschuk, *Revolt Against Regulation*, pp. 56–66; Cross, *All-Consuming Century*, pp. 158–60.

84. Michael deCourcy Hinds, "Laissez-Faire Consumerism," *NYT,* Aug. 21, 1982; U.S. Congress, House of Representatives, *Congressional Record, 96th Congress,* Nov. 14, 1979: 10, 757–58.

President Gerald Ford articulated the ethos of deregulation during his short presidency, even if he made little headway with its implementation. See "Remarks at the White House Conference on Domestic and Economic Affairs in Concord, New Hampshire," Apr. 18, 1975, and "The Trucking Industry," Nov. 14, 1975, in *The Public Papers of the Presidents: Gerald R. Ford, 1975* (Washington, DC: USGPO, 1976), pp. 518, 1870; "Agenda for Government Reform Act," "Aviation Act of 1975," "Motor Carrier Reform Act," "Financial Institutions Act," and "New Natural Gas Deregulation," July 22, 1976, *The Public Papers of the Presidents: Gerald R. Ford, 1976* (Washington, DC: USGPO, 1977), pp. 1870, 2064–65.

85. National Consumers' League, "The Economy: A Consumer Perspective," flyer enclosed with "Teach-Ins on Inflation, Energy, and the Economy," and full-page ad for The COIN Campaign, *Bulletin,* 116 (July–August 1979): 1–2, Angevine, Box 5, A-8. President Carter welcomed COIN's efforts after he met with leaders of the organization on December 19, 1978; see "Consumers Opposed to Inflation in the Necessities, Carter Statement Following a Meeting with the Organization," Dec. 20, 1978, in *Public Papers of the Presidents of the United States: Jimmy Carter, Book 2—July 1, 1978–December 31, 1978* (Washington, DC: USGPO, 1979), p. 2279. On tax revolts of the late 1970s, see Bruce J. Schulman, *The Seventies: The Great Shift in American Culture, Society, and Politics* (New York: Free Press, 2001), pp. 205–15; Alan Brinkley, "Reagan's Revenge, as Invented by Howard Jarvis," *NYT Magazine,* June 19, 1994, pp. 36–37; Robert Kuttner, *Revolt of the Haves: Tax Rebellions and Hard Times* (New York: Simon & Schuster, 1980).

86. "The FTC as National Nanny," *Washington Post,* quoted in Pertschuk, *Revolt Against Regulation,* p. 69; see p. 116 for discussion of congressional attack on "overzealous regulators"; Robert Kuttner, *Everything for Sale: The Virtues and Limits of Markets* (New York: Knopf, 1997), pp. 232–36, 255–57. Quote from Deborah Leff from correspondence with author, Feb. 19, 2002. Congress passed, and Carter signed, the Airline Deregulation Act in the fall of 1978, which was the first major step in the deregulation process, following hearings held by Senator Kennedy in 1975: *Senate Subcommittee on Administrative Practices and Procedures of the Judiciary Committee, 94th Cong. 1st Sess., Civil Aeronautics Board Practices and Procedures,* 1976. For an overview of the deregulation process, see Martha Derthick and Paul J. Quirk, *The Politics of Deregulation* (Washington, DC: Brookings Institution, 1985); for a defense of deregulation, see B. Robert Okun, "Let Markets Be Markets: How Deregulation Has Strengthened the American Economy," *Heritage Foundation Policy Review,* no. 35 (Winter 1986): 63. On the rise in business's influence in Washington, particularly in Congress, see Loree Bykerk and Ardith Maney, "Where Have All the Consumers Gone?" *Political Science Quarterly* 106 (Winter 1991): 677–93. On the role of the economics profession, see John Cassidy, "The Decline of Economics," *The New Yorker,* Dec. 2, 1966, pp. 50–60, and Michael A. Bernstein, *A Perilous Progress: Economists and Public Purpose in Twentieth-Century America* (Princeton: Princeton University Press, 2001), pp. 156–73, which is also useful for discussions of deregulation and privatization, pp. 173–84.

On the muzzling of the FTC, see "Mike Pertschuk and the Federal Trade Commission," Kennedy School of Government Case, 1981, Harvard University; "Clipped Wings: FTC's Mike Pertschuk Tilts Against Congress to Keep Agency Power," clipping from *WSJ* in Angevine, Box 6, D-10, "Coalition to Save the FTC, 1979–80." See other materials related to the defense of the FTC in this file as well. On the evisceration of the CPSC beginning in the late 1970s, see Felcher, "The U.S. Product Safety Commission."

87. Press release from Consumer Federation of America, "Reaganomics Still Harmful to Consumers, Second-Year Report Warns: Leaders Announce Consumer Agenda for '83," Jan. 21, 1983, Angevine, Box 5, C-2.

88. *President's Private Sector Survey on Cost Control: A Report to the President* [*J. Peter Grace, Chairman*], submitted to the Full Executive Committee for Consideration at Its Meeting, Jan. 15, 1984, p. VI-2.

89. "Remarks at the Essex County Democratic Gala Dinner," Oct. 29, 1980, in *The Public Papers of the Presidents: Jimmy Carter, 1980* (Washington, DC: USGPO, 1981), p. 2532; for more on Carter's commitment to deregulation see Schulman, *The Seventies,* pp. 124–25; "What the Platforms Say About Consumer Issues," *NCL Bulletin* 46 (September 1984): 1; "Knauer's Theme—the Satisfied Customer," *NYT,* Sept. 14, 1984; "Radio Address to the Nation on Proposed Natural Gas Deregulation Legislation," Feb. 26, 1983, in *The Public Papers of the Presidents: Ronald Reagan, 1983* (Washington, DC: USGPO, 1984), pp. 308–309; Michael deCourcy Hinds, "The Rational Consumer May Be Just a Deregulator's Dream," *NYT,* Nov. 1, 1981; Hinds, "The Consumer Movement: Whatever Happened?" *NYT,* Jan. 21, 1983.

Presidents Ford, Carter, and Reagan's programs of deregulation and justifications for them can be beautifully tracked in the annual *Economic Report of the President,* delivered every January to Congress. Beginning with Ford's report of January 1976, deregulation appears every year as a substantial topic of discussion.

90. "Proclamation 5162—National Energy Education Day, 1984," Mar. 17, 1984, in *The Public Papers of the Presidents: Ronald Reagan, 1984* (Washington, DC: USGPO, 1985), p. 364; Reagan claimed his natural gas deregulation proposal offered "protection, real protection, for the consumer" in "Reagan Criticizes Banks Over Rates," *NYT,* Feb. 24, 1983; "Reagan's Drive to Cut Rules: Impact Depends on Industry," *NYT,* Jan. 22, 1982; "U.S. Expects Deregulation to Save Over $150 Billion," *NYT,* Aug. 12, 1983; Felcher, "The U.S. Consumer Product Safety Commission."

91. Reagan made it clear that he was referring to consumption when he added, "Is it easier for you to go and buy things in stores than it was four years ago?" in his 1980 presidential debate with Carter: *NYT,* Oct. 29, 1980, quoted in Schulman, "Slouching Toward the Supply Side," p. 51; *Public Papers of Ronald Reagan 1984,* pp. 1282, 1627.

92. Bernstein, "Understanding American Economic Decline," pp. 26–28; Blecker, "The New Economic Stagnation," pp. 278–94; Collins, *More,* pp. 193–97.

93. U.S. Census Bureau, "Historical Tables—Families," Table F-2, "Share of Aggregate Income Received by Each Fifth and Top 5 Percent of Families (All Races): 1947 to 2000," http://www.census.gov/bhes/income/histinc/f02.html; Chuck Collins and Felice Yeskel, *Economic Apartheid in America: A Primer on Economic Inequality and Insecurity* (New York: New Press, 2000), reprinted on TomPaine.com, p. 3; Robert Kuttner, "A Living Wage Without Inflation," *BG,* Sept. 19, 1999; ". . . and Tax Breaks for All," *Belmont Citizen-Herald,* Sept. 16, 1999; "Income Gap Widens Between Rich and Poor in 5 States and Narrows in 1," *NYT,* Apr. 24, 2002.

94. On Clinton's supply-side orientation, see Robert Kuttner, "2002: A Haste Odyssey," *The New Yorker,* June 5, 1995, pp. 7–8, and "How Both Sides Joined the Supply Side," *NYT,* Aug. 25, 1996. Reagan's statements in "Message to the Congress on 'A Quest for Excellence,'" Jan. 27, 1987, *The Public Papers of the Presidents: Ronald Reagan, 1987* (Washington, DC: USGPO, 1988), p. 69; "Address Before a Joint Session of the Congress on the State of the Union," Feb. 6, 1985, *The Public Papers of the Presidents: Ronald Reagan, 1985* (Washington, DC: USGPO, 1986), p. 132. For a recent study of privatization efforts and their effects since the 1970s, see Elliott D. Sclar, *You Don't Always Get What You Pay For: The Economics of Privatization* (Ithaca, NY: Cornell University Press, 2000).

95. *From Red Tape to Results: Creating a Government That Works Better and Costs Less* (Washington, DC: USGPO, 1993), p. 6; Al Gore, *Common Sense Government: Works Better and Costs Less* (Interim Report of the National Performance Review) (New York: Random House, 1995), p. 139, in Kuttner, *Everything for Sale,* p. 358. On Clinton's redefinition of the federal government, see Jacob Weisberg, "The Governor-President, Bill Clinton," *NYT Magazine,* Jan. 17, 1999, p. 30. On New Jersey, Iver Peterson, "The Price of Privatization: Will Labor Get Its Due?" and "Privatization: Leaner Government, or Just Another Fad?" *NYT,* May 28, 1995; Montclair Township Council, "One Montclair: A Plan for Action," July 9, 1996.

96. From *NYT:* "Aiding Consumers Is Now the Thrust of Antitrust Push," Mar. 22, 1998, including quote from Charles Koob of Simpson Thatcher & Bartlett; "In Managed Care, 'Consumer' Laws Benefit Doctors," Jan. 16, 1998; "House Acts to Ease 30's Banking Curbs by One-Vote Margin," May 14, 1998. The anti-trust cases referred to were proposed mergers of drug companies and office supply retailers (Staples and Office Depot), all of which were rejected, and the government suit against Microsoft for denying consumers choices through its monopoly practices.

EPILOGUE

1. On consumer confidence and spending, "Consumers' Faith Wavers," *BG,* Jan. 31, 2001; "Honey, Can We Afford It?" *Fortune,* Sept. 3, 2001, pp. 129–32; "The Bright Side: Spending Still Strong," *BG,* Apr. 21, 2001; "Consumers Help Give Surprise Jolt to U.S. Economy," *Los Angeles Times,* Apr. 28, 2001; and in *NYT:* "How Long Can Consumers Keep Spending?" Sept. 2, 2001; "Back-to-School Retailer Blues, Consumers Now Seem to Be in Belt-Tightening Mode," Aug. 25, 2001; "Belt Tightening Is Called Threat to the Economy," July 15, 2001; "Consumers Still Spending with Gusto," May 12, 2001; "March Survey of Consumers Is Brighter," Mar. 28, 2001; "Consumer Confidence Is Wild Card in the Nation's Economy," Feb. 17, 2001; "The Mystery of Economic Recessions, Confidence, not the Fed, Determines Our Ups and Downs," Feb. 4, 2001; "Shopping Perks Up, Defying Worries of a Slowing Economy," Jan. 24, 2001; "Drop in Spending by U.S. Consumers Signals Slowdown," Dec. 3, 2000; "Consumer Confidence Plunges, Especially Among the Affluent," Dec. 23, 2000; "The Consumer Will Prevail," Oct. 2, 1998.

On the continued importance of housing starts and home purchases to the economy, see "Home Building Surges, Boosting U.S. Recovery," *Los Angeles Times,* Mar. 21, 2002; Joint Center for Housing Studies, "The State of the Nation's Housing: 2001," Cambridge, MA, 2001; from *NYT:* "Fed Is Trying to Determine How Assets Affect Spending," Sept. 1, 2001; "New-Home Sales Rose in July, Cushioning Industrial Slump," Aug. 25, 2001; "Housing May Rescue Economy from Wilting Wealth Effect," Aug. 15, 2001; "Casinos Redefine 'Up the River' in Boom City," June 19, 2001; full-page ad for Freddie Mac, "In America, homeownership is a dream. Overseas, it's more of a rude awakening," Oct. 18, 2000. Also, "Dip in Home Production Forecast," *BG,* May 27, 2000.

2. President Bush's and Congress's expectation that a consumer tax cut would jump-start a slowing economy was extensively documented in the press; see, for example, from *NYT:* "Bush Tax Plan: The Debate Takes Shape," Aug. 26, 2000; "Tuesday's Big Test: How Deep in the Heart of Taxes," Jan. 30, 2000; "Excerpts from Bush Speech Promoting His Tax Cuts," Mar. 28, 2001; "Bush Says Tax Cut Is the Quickest Way to Help Consumers with Energy Costs," May 12, 2001; "The Zero-Sum Tax Cut," June 1, 2001. On the response to the September 11 attacks, see "Already, Grim Statistics for New York Consumer Sales," *NYT,* Sept. 22, 2001; "Patriotic Purchasing," *BG,* Sept. 28, 2001; "Bush Wants More Tax Cuts in Effort to Help Economy" and "A Flawed Stimulus Plan," *NYT,* Oct. 6, 2001; "Recession? What Recession?" *The Economist,* Feb. 2, 2002. Changes in rules governing the granting of credit in

recent years have allowed borrowers, who previously would have been forced to stop spending, to keep buying with only the penalty of higher interest rates: "Economists Simply Shrug as Savings Rate Declines," *NYT,* Dec. 21, 1998. Americans have sustained consumer spending by accumulating debt, which is now at its highest level since 1946: "The Mystery of Economic Recessions," *NYT,* Feb. 4, 2001; Economic Policy Institute, "Consumption and Economic Growth," *Economic Snapshots,* www.epinet.org/webfeatures/snapshots.html.

3. Masako Notoji, "Comment on Lizabeth Cohen, 'Mass Consumption and American Political Culture in the Twentieth Century,' " Ritsumeikan University American Studies Seminar, Kyoto, Japan, July 31, 1998, in possession of the author; see in particular her discussion of the "Sanshu-no-Jingi," or "Three Sacred Regalia," introduced in 1956 (washing machine, refrigerator, and television set) and the "3Cs" of 1966 (car, cooler, and color TV), p. 4; and from the *NYT:* "Parasites in Prêt-à-Porter," *NYT Magazine,* July 1, 2001; "To Revive a Sick Economy, Japan Hands Out Coupons," Mar. 14, 1999; "Japan Is Torn Between Efficiency and Egalitarian Values," Oct. 26, 1998; "Shopping for Recovery," May 29, 1998; "Ruffled, Japan Advises U.S.: Mind Your Own Business," Apr. 9, 1998.

4. The Lewis Mumford Center for Comparative Urban and Regional Research at the State University of New York at Albany has done extensive analysis of the 2000 census, documenting how most major metropolitan areas have become more racially and ethnically diverse overall, but at the same time more segregated community by community; see http://www.albany.edu/mumford/census. As the center's director, John Logan, told a *New York Times* reporter: "What we see is that where groups are growing, they are most likely to experience increasing segregation. It's counterintuitive. How can we be more diverse if we're separating at the same time? Well, that's what we do": "Behind the Big Numbers, a Million Little Stories," *NYT,* Mar. 26, 2001. The New Jersey and New York metropolitan areas, often the focus of my study, are classic examples: "Jersey's New Blend Isn't Block by Block," *Star-Ledger,* Mar. 11, 2001, and "Races Mostly Live Apart in New York, Census Shows," *NYT,* Mar. 23, 2001. Also see "Ethnic Diversity Grows, but Not Integration," *CSM,* Mar. 14, 2001; "Chicago Clinging to Color Lines," *Chicago Sun-Times,* Mar. 18, 2001; and from *NYT:* "Whites in Minority in Largest Cities, the Census Shows," Apr. 30, 2001; "Segregation Growing Among U.S. Children," May 6, 2001; "Rethinking Segregation Beyond Black and White," July 29, 2001; "Failed Disney Vision: Integrated City, Community Is Part of U.S. Trend Toward Suburban Segregation," Sept. 23, 2001. Also see Gary Orfield, "Schools More Separate: Consequences of a Decade of Resegregation," Civil Rights Project, Harvard University, July 2001.

5. On New Jersey: Geoff Mulvihill, "Mount Laurel Homes Open After 30 Years of Legal Battles and Delays," *Associated Press State & Local Wire,* Mar. 24, 2001; from *NYT:* "New Jersey's Housing Law Works Too Well, Some Say," Mar. 3, 2001; "In the Region/New Jersey; A New Type of Project for Affluent Saddle River," June 24, 2001; "Development: In South Orange, the Pressure Is On," Mar. 11, 2001; "To Meet Goal for Housing, Suburb Seeks to Pay City," Aug. 4, 1998. Concerning struggles for affordable housing elsewhere, see "Are Prison Cells 'Affordable Housing'?" *Belmont Citizen Herald,* May 21, 2001; "Affordable Housing: The Debate Goes On," *BG,* Jan. 20, 2002.

On recent battles over equalizing—or ensuring the adequacy of, as it is more commonly expressed nowadays—school spending, see for New Jersey: Education Law Center, "The Abbott Children—Once Again, Challenge NJ DOE's Implementation of Preschool," *The Abbott Bulletin* 3 (Jan. 12, 2001); in *NYT:* "Report Says Few Poor Children Receive Adequate Preschool Education in New Jersey," June 1, 2001; "$12 Billion for Schools in New Jersey," July 14, 2001; "A Truce in New Jersey's School War," Feb. 9, 2002. On elsewhere, "The Times Change—Sometimes Decisive Action Is One Missing Element in the State's School Funding Debate," *New Hampshire Sunday News,* July 29, 2001; in

NYT: "Ohio Justices Say School System Is Legal but Must End Disparities," Sept. 7, 2001; "Vermont Spending Plan Seems to Help Schools," Jan. 31, 2001; "The Courts Try to Get City Schools Their Fair Share," Jan. 14, 2001; "With Ruling, New York Joins States Revamping School Financing," Jan. 13, 2001.

6. "Sneaker-Clad Army Wins Battle of the Mall," *NYT,* Aug. 28, 2001; "Staying the Course, Justices Won't 'Mall' Free Speech," *New Jersey Lawyer,* June 19, 2000; New Jersey Court's 1st Woman Justice Retiring," *NYT,* Dec. 23, 1999; "Fur Protest Not Protected by Minnesota Constitution," *National Law Journal,* Apr. 5, 1999; "Mall Dispute Stirs Free-Speech Debate, Protesters Arrested While Handing Out Pamphlets in the Mall of New Hampshire, Say Malls Should Be Considered a Public Space," *Providence Journal-Bulletin,* Sept. 27, 1998; "Shopping Centers May Impose Restrictions on Picketing of Their Tenants," *California Employment Law Monitor,* Aug. 18, 1997; "KKK Cancels Mall Recruiting Drive," *Newsday,* July 19, 1997; "Free Speech vs. Property Rights," NPR, *Morning Edition,* July 14, 1997, transcript pp. 4–5.

7. Tables No. 1285, "Online Retail Sales, Penetration of Total Market, and Growth Rate by Kind of Business: 1998–2000"; No. 1286, "Online Consumer Spending Forecast by Kind of Businesses: 1998–2000"; No. 1287, "U.S. Online Retail and Business to Business E-Commerce Projections: 1999 to 2000"; No. 1288, "Retail E-Commerce Sales, Number of Orders, and Average Purchase Amount in Key Categories: 1998 to 1999"; No. 1289, "U.S. Mail Order Sales by Kind of Business: 1997 and 1998"; No. 1290, "Catalog Sales—Method Used and Characteristic of Purchaser: 1997"; No. 1291, "Merchandise or Services Ordered by Mail or Phone in Last 12 Months by Characteristics of Purchaser: 1997"; No. 1292, "Population Ordering by Catalog by Type of Product and Characteristic of Purchaser: 1997," in U.S. Census Bureau, *Statistical Abstract of the United States 2000: The National Data Book,* 120th ed. (Washington, DC: USGPO, 2000), pp. 763–64; Lester C. Thurow, "5,000 More Years of Shopping: Internet's Altering Retail, but We Still Crave Human Contact," *BG,* Feb. 22, 2000.

8. On Starbucks's entry into the public library of Stamford, Connecticut, Tracy Challenger, "Agora Coalition, Network Member Update," Feb. 8, 2000. On public telephone booths disappearing, recent estimates claim that more than 40 percent of the U.S. population uses wireless telephones: "Cellphone Users: Options Abroad," *NYT,* Oct. 14, 2001; "Pay Phones to Cost 50 Cents as Use Falls," *BG,* Sept. 8, 2001. On the growth of self-taxing districts, "Council Reports Abuses in Improvement Districts," *NYT,* Nov. 8, 1995; "Mayor's Rules Aim to Rein In City Districts for Businesses," *NYT,* Apr. 2, 1998. On the explosion of private residential associations, "The Growth of Private Communities: America's New Utopias," *The Economist,* Sept. 1, 2001; "The Gated Menace of 'Private Cities,'" *Harvard Magazine,* July–August 2000; Evan McKenzie, *Privatopia* (New Haven: Yale University Press, 1994). On apartments in shopping centers, "Five Rooms, Gucci View," *NYT,* Feb. 21, 2002.

For other controversies over whether space is public or private, see from *NYT:* "Greenwich Cities Fear of 'Jerseyfication' in Beach Dispute," Nov. 11, 2000; "Small Towns in Connecticut Begin Allowing Beach Access," Aug. 28, 2001; "Greenwich Sets Beach Fees for Nonresidents," Feb. 15, 2002; "National Briefing Rockies, Utah: Restrictions on Church-Owned Property Appealed," June 5, 2001.

9. "As Big PC Brother Watches, Users Encounter Frustration" and "The Browser as a Cookie-Control Key," *NYT,* Sept. 5, 2001; "The U.S. Consumer's Friend," *NYT,* Sept. 21, 2000; "The End of the Mass Market, How a New Television Technology Could Destroy Advertising as We Know It," *NYT Magazine,* Aug. 13, 2000; "Don't People Want to Control Their TV's?" *NYT,* Aug. 24, 2000. Also, "Doubted as Business, Valued as Asset, Network News Will Be Hard to Displace," *NYT,* Mar. 18, 2002.

10. The election of 2000 offered an opportunity to observe political market segmentation at work; see "The League of Web Voters," *BW,* Oct. 23, 2000; "Calculating One Kind of Middle Class," *NYT,* Oct. 29, 2000; James Fallows, "Internet Illusions," *The New York Review of Books,* Nov. 16, 2000; Andrew Levison, "Who Lost the Working Class?" *The Nation,* May 14, 2001; "Gore Tries Pitching Himself as Drug Industry Opponent," *NYT,* July 1, 2000; "Campaigns Set a Brisk, Focused TV Pace," *NYT,* Oct. 17, 2000, which explicitly analyzes the tactical selectivity of the Bush and Gore advertising campaigns, concluding that campaigns were regional rather than national; virtually no presidential spots ran in more than thirty-two of the top seventy-five markets. On the increasing expenditures on television, making political spots 8.2 percent of total station billings and 15 percent of network affiliate billings in 1999 (up from 3.2 percent of total billings in only 1992), see "A Political Nightmare: Not Enough Airtime," *BW,* Oct. 23, 2000. For a newly emergent political segment, see "O, to Be Single and Have a Politician Pay Attention," *NYT,* Aug. 27, 2000.

11. The current state of the consumer movement ranges from continued retrenchment from consumerist legislation and regulation, on the one hand, and effective, if somewhat infrequent grassroots boycotts, along with strategic lobbying by issue-oriented consumer organizations, on the other. On the retrenchment, see "Novel Antipollution Tool Is Being Upset by Courts," *NYT,* June 5, 1999; "Explosive Meat Survey," *The Nation,* Oct. 2, 2000; and the ongoing struggle, at the state and federal level, over "tort reform" (limiting the negligence and liability of companies), which is documented frequently in the press. The activities of those still existing consumer organizations are best gauged from their newsletters and other publications; see, for example, material from the various state Public Interest Research Groups, the National Consumers' League, the Consumer Federation of America, and Consumers Union. Ralph Nader, of course, brought renewed attention to consumer/citizen politics through his Green Party candidacy for president in the 2000 election.

Typical boycotts and other grassroots consumer actions are discussed in N. Craig Smith, "Changes in Corporate Practices in Response to Public Interest Advocacy and Actions: The Role of Consumer Boycotts and Socially Responsible Consumption in Promoting Corporate Social Responsibility," in Paul N. Bloom and Gregory T. Gundlach, eds., *Handbook of Marketing and Society* (Thousand Oaks, CA: Sage, 2001), pp. 140–61; "Actors Take P&G Product Boycott to Web, e-mail," *USA Today,* Oct. 20, 2000; "Boycotts Will Be Boycotts," *American Prospect,* July 31, 2000; "Growing Up and Getting Practical Since Seattle," *NYT,* Sept. 24, 2000.

"Final MTA Appeal of Bus Accord Fails," *Los Angeles Times,* Mar. 19, 2002; "A Los Angeles Commuter Group Sees Discrimination in Transit Policies," *NYT,* Sept. 16, 2001; photograph, "Bus Riders' Union Demonstrators, Los Angeles, Fall 2000," *Harvard Design Magazine,* Winter/Spring 2001, p. 71, which shows a hand-painted placard reading "No A La Privatizacion."

12. See Regina Austin, "'A Nation of Thieves': Securing Black People's Right to Shop and to Sell in White America," *Utah Law Review,* 1994, pp. 147–77; Joe R. Feagin, "The Continuing Significance of Race: Antiblack Discrimination in Public Places," in Raymond D'Angelo, *The American Civil Rights Movement: Readings and Interpretations* (New York: McGraw-Hill/Dushkin, 2001), pp. 546–56; from the *NYT:* "Into the World of Banking Comes a Hip-Hop Credit Union," Apr. 25, 1993; "'Buying Black' Approach Paying Off in Los Angeles," May 23, 1993; "African-Americans Asked to Boycott Shopping Areas," Mar. 20, 1999; "The Boycott Returns," Mar. 26, 2000; "Long Before Recent Unrest, Cincinnati Simmered," May 1, 2001.

13. University of Michigan Business School, "American Customer Satisfaction Index: Federal Agencies Government-wide Customer Satisfaction Report for the General Ser-

vices Administration," December 1999. On continued efforts to privatize and deregulate, see from *American Prospect*, Sept. 10, 2001: Robert Dreyfuss, "Bush's House of Cards" and "Bill of Wrongs"; Brooke Harrington, "Investor Beware"; Judith Greene, "Bailing Out Private Jails." From *NYT*: Paul Krugman, "Paying the Price," Sept. 16, 2001; "Feeling Powerless in a World of Greater Choice, Consumers Grow More Anxious as They Are Cut Loose in Electricity's New Free Market," Aug. 27, 2000. "The Governor-President Bill Clinton invented a new way to use the Oval Office, and not just for tawdry sex. Like Andrew Jackson and Franklin Roosevelt, he has changed the very nature of the American Presidency; they enlarged it, necessarily. He has shrunk it, necessarily—and made a legacy for himself that could supersede the Monica mess": *NYT Magazine*, Jan. 17, 1999. Also "A Government Agency Becomes a Company," *WSJ*, May 14, 1998; Elliot D. Sclar, *You Don't Always Get What You Pay For: The Economics of Privatization* (Ithaca, NY: Cornell University Press, 2000). For discussion of the more general anti-government mood of the country, see "Government of, by, and for the Comfortable," *NYT Magazine*, Nov. 1, 1998; "A Question of Values," *Washington Post National Weekly Section*, Jan. 11, 1999; "A Nation Loosening Its Bonds," *NYT*, Aug. 26, 1999; Susan J. Pharr and Robert D. Putnam, "Why Is Democracy More Popular Than Democracies?" *Chronicle of Higher Education*, May 26, 2000.

14. "Does Inequality Matter?" *The Economist*, June 16, 2001, p. 9.

15. Despite major efforts to facilitate voter registration, with access on-line and at Departments of Motor Vehicles, registration for the 2000 presidential election fell 2 percentage points, to 65 percent of eligible voters. When it came to actual voting, voter turnout as a portion of those eligible inched up 2.2 percentage points from 1996, to 51.2 percent of the eligible electorate. Still, however, half of eligible Americans decided not to vote, and the Committee for the Study of the American Electorate saw no evidence that increases in voter registration and turnout would persist. "We are still at levels 25 percent below what turnout was in the 1960s, and each succeeding generation of young potential citizens is voting at an ever lower rate," the committee's director somberly concluded: "Voter Turnout Rose in 2000, but No Lasting Impact Is Seen," *NYT*, Aug. 31, 2001. Also see Alexander Keyssar, *The Right to Vote* (New York: Basic Books, 2000), pp. 314–15; Frances Fox Piven and Richard A. Cloward, *Why Americans Still Don't Vote and Why Politicians Want It That Way* (Boston: Beacon, 2000); and "The Mystery of Nonvoters and Whether They Matter," *NYT*, Aug. 27, 2000.

16. On the link between citizenship and independent earning, see Judith N. Shklar, *American Citizenship: The Quest for Inclusion* (Cambridge, MA: Harvard University Press, 1991), pp. 63–101.

17. T. H. Marshall and Tom Bottomore, *Citizenship and Social Class* (1950; reprint, London: Pluto, 1992), p. 28.

18. Christopher Lasch, *The True and Only Heaven: Progress and Its Critics* (New York: Norton, 1991); Michael J. Sandel, *Democracy's Discontent: America in Search of a Public Philosophy* (Cambridge, MA: Harvard University Press, 1996).

19. On anti-privatization and anti-deregulation sentiment and efforts, and a new confidence in "big government," see, for example, "Jersey City Librarians Protest Plan for Private Contractor," *NYT*, June 29, 1998; "Capitalism Is Giddy with Triumph; Is It Possible to Overdo It? The Privatization of America, from Roads to Uranium, Begins to Stir a Backlash," *WSJ*, May 14, 1998; "Governor Pledges to Save California from Power Crisis, Deregulation a 'Failure,'" *NYT*, Jan. 9, 2001; "Population Shifts in the Southeast Realign Politics in the Suburbs," *NYT*, June 3, 2000, which suggests that some southern suburbanites are retreating from a conservative agenda favoring lower taxes, the dismantling of welfare, and anti-crime measures and supporting government spending around quality-of-life issues like education, the environment, parkland, and public transportation.

20. "White House Battles Plan on Airports," *NYT*, Oct. 13, 2001; Richard Just, "Cut-Rate Security: How the Airlines Privatized the Nation's Safety," *American Prospect*, Oct. 22, 2001; Nicholas Lemann, "Letter from Washington: The Hillary Perspective, Government Suddenly Looks Good Again," *The New Yorker*, Oct. 8, 2001; John D. Donahue, "Is Government the Good Guy?" *NYT*, Dec. 13, 2001.

Acknowledgments

If I ever hoped I could disguise the fact that I have been working on this book for a decade, the list of friends, colleagues, research assistants, archivists, editors, and audiences who have contributed to its creation would give me away. It is a cliché to assert that in the course of writing a book one has incurred many debts, but anyone reading this list will know how particularly true it is in my case. As I compiled these acknowledgments, I was struck by how well they reflected my intellectual itinerary over the last ten years—lectures given, conferences attended, colleagues interacted with, and students taught, who have also taught me. Despite assumptions to the contrary, historians' books do not emerge solely from weeks alone in archives and libraries, and months alone in front of the computer. They also take shape as we talk, argue, defend ourselves, and shift ground, acts usually performed in the company of various kinds of audiences—our families and students, other historians, and the larger public.

I will begin by thanking the extensive infrastructure that has supported me as I have written this book. The first public talk I ever gave about this project, in April 1992, was part of the President's Distinguished Lecture Series at Carnegie Mellon University, where I was an assistant professor of history. It was there that this book began to take shape, and when I moved to New York University the following fall as an associate professor, I incorporated the metropolitan New York area as a research setting into my conception of the book. In the fall of 1997, I moved to Harvard University, where I finally finished this book. At all of these institutions, history departments and colleagues in and outside of history have generously offered intellectual sustenance. Along the way I also enjoyed critical financial support from foundations and grantors: the American Council of Learned Societies; the National Endowment for the Humanities; the John Simon Guggenheim Foundation; the Dean's Research Fund at NYU; the Clark Fund, the Faculty Aide Program, and Dean Jeremy Knowles's research support at Harvard; and the Radcliffe Institute, where I have had the good fortune to be a fellow as I completed this book. The Radcliffe Institute has given Virginia Woolf's "room of one's own" new meaning, bestowing upon me for the first time a writing room set apart from the distractions of both home and office. Having a space dedicated solely to finishing this book has been a true gift, and I thank Drew Faust, Judy Vichniac, their wonderful staff, and the other Radcliffe fellows for knowing when to offer community support and when simply to leave me alone.

My next debt is to the large number of people who have read and commented on parts of this book, and, in some cases, the entire manuscript. Nine people took precious time from their own work to read all of mine, often volunteering their help, and for their generosity and trenchant insights I am deeply indebted. To Sven Beckert, Herrick Chapman, Sally Clarke, Gary Gerstle, Mike Kazin, Alice Kessler-Harris, Debby Leff, Susan Ware, and Viviana Zelizer, simple thanks seem inadequate. Many others have read overviews or one or more chapters at different moments in their evolution, offering me the benefit of their expertise, for which I am also extremely grateful: Caitlin Anderson, Tony Badger, Michael Birkner, Richard Butsch, Sue Cobble, Michael Ebner, Walter Friedman, Louis Galambos, Alan Gluck, Suzanne Hand, JuNelle Harris, Jennifer Hochschild, Roger Horowitz, Alan Hyde, Ken Jackson, Mickey Keller, Gerd Korman, Richard

Longstreth, Jim Patterson, Mike Pertschuk, Judith Plaskow, Tricia Rose, Chris Schmidt, David Schuyler, Sylvie Schweitzer, Phil Scranton, Kim Sims, Judith Smith, Tom Sugrue, Joseph Tolhill, Jon Wiener, and Rebecca Zurier. With so much good advice, it is inevitable that I have spurned some of it, perhaps to my own detriment. Only I am responsible for what now appears in this book.

I could never have written *A Consumers' Republic* without the help of another group of individuals, the undergraduate and graduate students who have served as dogged and resourceful research assistants over the years. Aware as I am of how significantly their efforts have contributed to the book, I only wish I had more space to detail them. For their persistence as researchers, perceptiveness as historians-in-training, and companionship as colleagues, I would like to express my deep appreciation to Caitlin Anderson, Katie Barry, Kirsten Fermaglich, JuNelle Harris, Isa Helfgott, Cree LeFavour, David Quigley, Robbie Silverman, Kim Sims, Deb Steinbach, Liz Thornberry, Rebekah Welch, and Liz Zuckerman. Two students were not employed by me but contributed valuable material nonetheless. Debra Michals always had my interests in mind as she did her own dissertation research on women entrepreneurs, and Susan Spaet, introduced to me through our mutual high school mentor, Eric Rothschild, spent many, many hours voluntarily helping. Three of these assistants—Caitlin Anderson, JuNelle Harris, and Kim Sims—also helped with the herculean task of assembling the illustrations for this book, and like it or not learned, along with me, how to pick their way through the minefield of permissions and licensing. For so energetically embracing my problems as their own, I am extremely grateful.

Over the years I have also tried out arguments and shared parts of chapters with numerous audiences at lectures and conferences. They have improved my work far more than they likely realized. For both challenging me and putting up with me when I dug in my heels, I would like to thank audiences at the American Studies Association back in 1992; the Australian and New Zealand American Studies Association Biennial Meeting in 2000; the Berkshire Conference in 1993; Brown University's Replogle Lecture Forum on Consumer Culture and National Identity; the University of California–Irvine's Annual History Conference in 2000; the Chicago Historical Society's Urban History Seminar; Churchill College at Cambridge University's Conference on "Material Politics: State, Consumers, and Political Cultures"; the Cleveland-area Consortium of Historians; Columbia University's Twentieth-Century Politics and Society Seminar and special conference on "Gender and Modernity in the Era of Rationalization"; the University of Connecticut's History Department; the University of Delaware's Seminar in American Art, History, and Material Culture; George Washington University's History Department; the German Historical Institute and Smithsonian Institution's joint conference "The Development of Twentieth-Century Consumer Society"; the Ghent Urban Studies Team's "Post Ex Sub Dis: Fragmentations of the City" Conference; the Hagley Library's Research Seminar in its Center for the History of Business, Technology and Society; Harvard University's History Department and monthly librarians' meeting; Harvard Business School's Business History Seminar; the Kyoto American Studies Summer Seminar; the Massachusetts Historical Society's Boston Seminar in Immigration and Urban History; the University of New Hampshire's Dunfey Conference on "Making Sense of the Twentieth Century: Historical Perspectives on Modern America"; the New Jersey Historical Commission's Annual Conference for 2000; the New School for Social Research's Seminar in Social Change; New York University's conference on "Consumerism, Domesticity, and Middle-Class Identity"; the University of Pennsylvania's Economic History Seminar; the Radcliffe Institute's Colloquium Series; the University of Rochester's Vernon L. Moore Lecture in History; Rutgers University's Center for Historical Change and its library's annual Louis Faugeres Bishop III Lecture in 1996; Vassar College's A. C. Mildred Thompson Lecture; the University of Washington's Interdisciplinary American Studies Conference "U.S. Cultures: New Conversations"; Wesleyan University's Center for the Humanities; the University of Wisconsin's Labor History Conference and Mellon Graduate History Seminar; and York University's History Department's visiting scholar program. Obviously, I have done a lot of talking about this book for over a decade. One might reasonably wonder to whom I have not spoken! I am completely truthful when I say, however, that even now I can vividly recall every one of these events and can point to at least one idea—usually more—that I took away with me.

Historians depend on libraries and archives to do their work. The libraries in all the universities where I have taught have provided me with precious sources, either from their own collections or through interlibrary loan. In summers, I have been blessed to live near the Wellfleet Public Library, whose librarians have always managed, with the help of interlibrary loan, seemingly to pluck needed books out of the air. In addition, archivists at Consumers Union, the Library of Congress, the New Jersey Historical Society, Vassar College, and the Wisconsin Historical Society have made my visits there as efficient as possible. I spent a great deal of time doing research at two places, where librarians were more than helpful: I want to extend particular thanks to Ron Becker and his staff at the Special Collections of Rutgers University–New Brunswick and Charles Cummings and his staff in the New Jersey Information Center of the Newark Public Library. In my search for illustrations, I received help from archivists and staff members too numerous to name, but if any of them ever see this book, I hope they will know how much they are appreciated.

Several parts of this book have already made their way into print, and I am grateful for permission to incorporate them into this larger work. A part of Chapter 1 appeared as "The New Deal State and Citizen Consumers," in Susan Strasser, Charles McGovern, and Matthias Judt, eds., *Getting and Spending: American and European Consumption in the Twentieth Century* (Washington, DC: German Historical Institute; New York: Cambridge University Press, 1998). An earlier version of Chapter 6 appeared as "From Town Center to Shopping Center: The Reconfiguration of Community Marketplaces in Postwar America," *American Historical Review* 101 (October 1996). I am gratified that this latter article has received recognition from the Urban History Association, winning its prize for best journal article in urban history in 1998, and from the Organization of American Historians, which in 1999 gave it the ABC-CLIO, *America: History and Life* Award for the journal article that most advances new perspectives on accepted interpretations or previously unconsidered topics. I would also like to acknowledge permission to quote from three poems: "Speaking of Food," by Langston Hughes from *The Collected Poems of Langston Hughes*. Copyright © 1994 by The Estate of Langston Hughes. Reprinted by permission of Alfred A. Knopf, a division of Random House, Inc. "Is There Democracy?" by Roland Fallin from the Afro-American Newspapers Archives and Research Center. Reprinted by permission of the Afro-American Archives. "Black People!" reprinted by permission of Sterling Lord Literistic, Inc., copyright by Amiri Baraka.

In conclusion, I wish to thank some additional individuals whose support for me has helped make this book a shared enterprise. During the three years I lived in Montclair, New Jersey, not only did I inhabit a wonderful town, but I learned an enormous amount about the complexities surrounding local and state taxation, school funding, affordable housing policies, and suburban settlement patterns. Many friends there became my tutors and comrades in arms, but I want in particular to thank Lucy O'Brien for helping me analyze New Jersey's postwar evolution, as we lived very personally with its legacy. Another Montclair friend, Rutgers Law School professor Jim Pope, showed early enthusiasm for this project and introduced me to two helpful colleagues, Paul Trachtenberg and Frank Askin, who, respectively, litigated key school funding and free speech cases in New Jersey courts. When this book was barely a twinkle in my eye, Steve Fraser expressed great enthusiasm for it, and signed on to be my editor at Basic Books. Though circumstances intervened to prevent us from continuing to work together, Steve's early confidence propelled me forward. The book was later adopted by Jane Garrett at Alfred A. Knopf, and a more supportive and caring adoptive parent is hardly imaginable. No question or problem has proved too minor for Jane's attention, and be assured I have tested her well. Others at Knopf have also given generously of their time and talents: Sophie Fels superbly facilitated communication; Ellen Feldman supervised the book's production with an editor's care and a scholar's commitment; Avery Fluck ably saw it into print; Charlotte Gross brought a razor-sharp eye to the copyediting; Bette Graber was endlessly resourceful in securing permissions; Steven Amsterdam distinguished himself as a jacket designer who "got it"; Barbara Balch and Virginia Tan created a beautiful interior design; and as the book goes to press, Jill Morrison, Katy Barrett, and Christine Casaccio are already proving themselves promotional pros.

At Harvard, Laura Johnson, Cory Paulsen, and Janet Hatch have assisted me with tasks large and small with utmost good cheer. Others whose contributions along the way I would like to acknowledge include Dan Horowitz, for generously sharing valuable primary sources that were critical to Chapter 7; Michael Pertschuk, for not only reading my renderings of his own past history with great care, but also assenting to be interviewed twice; Lois and Samuel Pratt, for providing me with unpublished studies from the 1950s on the Paramus shopping centers; Paul Nehrenberg, Mike Wells, Diane Hartmann, Jim Jensen, and Joe Thompson from the Veterans Administration, for making rich material on the GI Bill available to me; David Cohen, for information on Newark in the 1920s; and Judith Rew, for her beautiful graphics.

At last, I want to thank those closest to me who may be the only people more eager than I am to have this book out of the house. My parents, Paul Cohen and Dorothy Roberts, have provided all kinds of support over the years, including, in my father's case, reading the daily papers—scissors in hand—with my book in mind, and mining the recesses of his memory for recollections that might be of help. I cannot even express in words all that my husband, Herrick Chapman, has contributed to me and this book. When I have wanted it, he has been cook, babysitter, colleague, editor, confidant, husband, and friend, often putting my needs before his own. I could have no more loving or generous partner in life. Finally, my two daughters, Julia and Natalie, are probably the happiest of all to see this book between two covers. It has been the third sibling to rival, the one who always demanded my attention, the one who too often made sure that imagined family pleasures remained just that. I promise you we will celebrate together now. Although it may be small recompense, this book is for you.

Lizabeth Cohen
2002

Index

Page numbers in *italics* refer to illustrations and tables.

A NOTE ABOUT THE AUTHOR

Lizabeth Cohen received her A.B. at Princeton University and her M.A. and Ph.D. at the University of California, Berkeley. She has taught at the University of California, Berkeley; Stanford University; Carnegie Mellon University; New York University; and is now Howard Mumford Jones Professor of American Studies in the Department of History at Harvard University. In 2001 she was president of the Urban History Association. She is the author of *Making a New Deal: Industrial Workers in Chicago, 1919–1939* (1990), which won the Bancroft Prize and the Philip Taft Labor History Award and was a finalist for the Pulitzer Prize; *The American Pageant* (with David Kennedy, 1998, 2002); and numerous articles and essays. She lives in Belmont, Massachusetts, with her husband and two daughters.

A NOTE ABOUT THE TYPE

This book was set in Minion, a typeface produced by the Adobe Corporation specifically for the Macintosh personal computer, and released in 1990. Designed by Robert Slimbach, Minion combines the classic characteristics of old style faces with the full complement of weights required for modern typesetting.

Composed by North Market Street Graphics
Lancaster, Pennsylvania
Printed and bound by Berryville Graphics, Berryville, Virginia
Designed by Barbara Balch